Handbook of Interventions that Work with Children and Adolescents

Prevention and Treatment

Handbook of Interventions that Work with Children and Adolescents

Prevention and Treatment

Edited by

Paula M. Barrett
Griffith University, Australia

and

Thomas H. Ollendick
Virginia Polytechnic Institute and State University, USA

WILEY

Other Wiley Editorial Offices

John Wiley & Sons Inc., 111 River Street, Hoboken, NJ 07030, USA

Jossey-Bass, 989 Market Street, San Francisco, CA 94103-1741, USA

Wiley-VCH Verlag GmbH, Boschstr. 12, D-69469 Weinheim, Germany

John Wiley & Sons Australia Ltd, 33 Park Road, Milton, Queensland 4064, Australia

John Wiley & Sons (Asia) Pte Ltd, 2 Clementi Loop #02-01, Jin Xing Distripark, Singapore 129809

John Wiley & Sons Canada Ltd, 22 Worcester Road, Etobicoke, Ontario, Canada M9W 1L1

Wiley also publishes its books in a variety of electronic formats. Some content that appears in print
may not be available in electronic books.

Library of Congress Cataloging-in-Publication Data
Handbook of interventions that work with children and adolescents : prevention and
treatment / edited by Paula M. Barrett and Thomas H. Ollendick.
     p.   cm.
  ISBN 0-470-84453-1
  1. Child psychiatry—Handbooks, manuals, etc.   2. Adolescent psychiatry—Handbooks,
manuals, etc.   I. Barrett, Paula M.   II. Ollendick, Thomas H.
  RJ499.3.H363 2004
  618.92′89—dc21

                                                                              2003008386

British Library Cataloguing in Publication Data
A catalogue record for this book is available from the British Library

ISBN 0-470-84453-1

Typeset in 10/12pt Times by SNP Best-set Typesetter Ltd., Hong Kong
Printed and bound in Great Britain by Antony Rowe Ltd, Chippenham, Wiltshire
This book is printed on acid-free paper responsibly manufactured from sustainable forestry in which
at least two trees are planted for each one used for paper production.

Contents

About the Editors

Paula M. Barrett, **PhD**, Dr Paula Barrett is a prolific publisher in the field of clinical child psychology. She is currently employed as a Senior Lecturer with the Postgraduate Clinical Program at Griffith University, and together with colleagues, has recently started the exciting new clinical research centre Pathways, in Brisbane, Australia. She has successfully supervised 20 honours, 14 Masters, and 8 PhD students to completion of their postgraduate degrees, and each one of them, in turn, is making an important contribution to the well-being of families and to research advances in the field of clinical child psychology. Dr Barrett possesses international respect and acclaim for her work in the field of childhood/adolescent anxiety. She published the world's first family treatment control trial for childhood anxiety in 1995, and her 1996 paper on the treatment of anxiety disorders in children and adolescents is highly cited and is in the foreground of empirically supported or evidence-based practices. Together with Dr Robi Sonderegger, she has also made significant advances in mapping the psychological adjustment of young non-English-speaking migrants and refugees to Australia; receiving grants totalling close to $0.5 million for the development and validation of culturally sensitive adjustment resources for Chinese and former-Yugoslavian families. Besides treatment-oriented research, she has also contributed to the field theoretically looking at the processes by which these treatments work. Since 1996, Dr Barrett has been the prime investigator or associate investigator for university research grants worth over $1.5 million and continues to head a highly productive research group as well as coordinating and liaising with the many ongoing research and clinical trials now underway with the program in Australia, Europe and the USA. Dr Barrett's research group have published more controlled trials for childhood anxiety than any other group in the world. Collectively, this body of literature has had a significant global impact not only for the treatment of childhood anxiety, but in research and public policy arenas as well. She authored and evaluated the well-known Coping Koala treatment protocol during her doctorate in 1993, and as senior author published the FRIENDS program in 1999 (recognized world wide as best practice for the treatment of anxiety and depression in children and adolescents). The latest edition of FRIENDS is now used as both a treatment protocol and a school-based prevention intervention for the development of anxiety and depression. In addition to her research being published in numerous prestigious international peer-reviewed journals, she has written numerous book chapters and presented keynote addresses at national and international conferences on the topic. She was the recipient of the National Australian Association for Cognitive and Behaviour Therapy Early Career Award for her research and clinical innovation in the field of clinical psychology in

1998, and the National Australian Psychological Society Award for outstanding scholarship in the discipline of psychology in 1999.

Thomas H. Ollendick, PhD, is University Distinguished Professor in Clinical Psychology and Director of the Child Study Center at Virginia Polytechnic Institute and State University, Blacksburg, Virginia, USA. He is the author of over 200 research publications, 51 book chapters, and 23 books. His books include *Clinical Behavior Therapy with Children, Child Behavioral Assessment: Principles and Procedures, Handbook of Child Psychopathology*, and *Children's Phobias: A Behavioural Perspective*. Dr Ollendick is the immediate past Editor of the *Journal of Clinical Child Psychology* (1996–2001) and founding Co-Editor of *Clinical Child and Family Psychology Review*. He serves on the editorial boards of 16 other journals, including *Journal of Consulting and Clinical Psychology, Clinical Psychology: Science and Practice, Behavior Therapy, Journal of Anxiety Disorders*, and *Child and Family Behavior Therapy*. In addition, he is Past-President of the Association for the Advancement of Behavior Therapy (1995) and the Society of Clinical Psychology (1999), a division of the American Psychological Association. He served as Scientific Program Chair of the 2001 World Congress on Cognitive and Behavior Therapies in Vancouver, Canada, and is the current President of the Society of Clinical Child and Adolescent Psychology, a division of the American Psychological Association. The recipient of several NIH grants, his clinical and research interests range from the study of diverse forms of child psychopathology to the assessment and treatment of these child behaviour disorders from a social learning/social cognitive theory perspective.

List of Contributors

J. Stuart Ablon, *Department of Psychiatry, Harvard Medical School & CPS Institute, Massachusetts General Hospital, 313 Washington Street, Suite 402, Newton MA 02458, USA*

Paula M. Barrett, *Griffith University, Mt Gravatt Campus, School of Applied Psychology, Mt Gravatt, QLD 4111, Australia*

Thompson E. Davis III, *Child Study Center, Virginia Polytechnic Institute and State University, Department of Psychology, Blacksburg, Virginia 24061-0436, USA*

Jean E. Dumas, *Department of Psychology, The Pennsylvania State University, University Park, PA 16802, USA*

Cecilia A. Essau, *Westfälische Wilhelms-Universität Münster, Psychologisches Institut I, Fliednerstr. 21, 48149 Münster, Germany*

Vanessa Fazio, *Department of Psychology, Suffolk University of Chicago, Donahue Bldg 6th Floor, 41 Temple Street, Boston, MA 02114, USA*

Elizabeth A. Franks, *Department of Psychology, Loyola University Chicago, 6562 N. Sheridan Road, Chicago, IL 60626, USA*

Jennifer C. Goring, *Department of Psychology, Virginia Tech., Blackburg, VA 24061, USA*

Amanda B. Goza, *Northern Virginia Mental Health Institute, 3302 Gallows Road, Falls Church, Virginia 22042, USA*

Rachel Neff Greenley, *Department of Psychology, Loyola University Chicago, 6562 N. Sheridan Road, Chicago, IL 60626, USA*

Ross W. Greene, *Collaborative Problem Solving Institute, Department of Psychiatry, Massachusetts General Hospital, 313 Washington Street, Suite 402, Newton MA 02458, USA*

Lara Healy-Farrell, *Griffith University, Mt Gravatt Campus, School of Applied Psychology, Mt Gravatt, QLD 4111, Australia*

David Heyne, *Faculty of Social and Behavioural Sciences, Department of Developmental and Educational Psychology, P.O. Box 9555, 2300 RB Leiden, The Netherlands*

Grayson N. Holmbeck, *Department of Psychology, Loyola University Chicago, 6525 N. Sheridan Road,Chicago, IL 60626-5385, USA*

Jennifer L. Hudson, *Department of Psychology, Macquarie University, Sydney, NSW 2109, Australia*

Alicia A. Hughes, *Child and Adolescent Anxiety Disorders Clinic (CAADC), Clinical Psychology, Temple University, 1701 North 13th Street, Philadelphia, PA 19122 6085, USA*

Philip C. Kendall, *Division of Clinical Psycholog, Temple University, 1701 North 13th Street, Philadelphia, PA 19122-6085, USA*

Sheryl Kern-Jones, *ORI Center for Family & Adolescent Research, 2700 Yale SE, Suite 200 Albuquerque, NM 87106, USA*

Neville J. King, *Faculty of Education, Monash University, Claytona, VIC 3168, Australia*

Julie S. Kotler, *Department of Psychology, University of Washington, Box 351525, Seattle, WA 98195-1525, USA*

John March, *Department of Psychiatry and Behavioral Sciences, Duke Child and Family Study Center, 718 Rutherford Street, Durham, NC 27705, USA*

Carol Markie-Dadds, *Strategic Directions Policy and Research, Education Queensland, Level 20 Education House, 30 Mary Street, Brisbane 4000, Australia*

Sara G. Mattis, *Boston University, The Center for Anxiety and Related Disorders at Boston University, 648 Beacon St., 6th Floor, Boston, MA 02215-2015, USA*

Robert J. McMahon, *Department of Psychology, University of Washington, Box 351525, Seattle, WA 98195-1525, USA*

Tracy L. Morris, *West Virginia University, Department of Psychology, Morgantown, WV 26506-6040, USA*

Lauren R. Morse, *CPS Institute, Department of Psychiatry, Massachusetts General Hospital, 313 Washington Street, Suite 402, Newton MA 02458, USA*

Peter Muris, *Department of Medical, Clinical, and Experimental Psychology, Maastricht University, P O Box 616, 6200 MD Maastricht, The Netherlands*

Thomas H. Ollendick, *Child Study Center, Virginia Polytechnic Institute and State University, Department of Psychology, Blacksburg Virginia 24061-0436, USA*

Donald P. Oswald, *Institution Department, Department of Psychiatry, Virginia Commonwealth University, P.O. Box 980489, Richmond, VA 23298-0489, USA*

Sean Perrin, *Department of Clinical Psychology, Institute of Psychiatry, King's College London, De Crespigny Park, Denmark Hill, London SE5 8AF, UK*

John Piacentini, *UCLA Child OCD, Anxiety, and Tic Disorders Program, UCLA-NPI, Room 68-251, 760 Westwood Plaza, Los Angeles, CA 90024, USA*

Donna B. Pincus, *Boston University, The Center for Anxiety and Related Disorders at Boston University, 648 Beacon St., 6th Floor, Boston, MA 02215-2015, USA*

Ronald J. Prinz, *Department of Psychology, University of South Carolina, Barnwell Bldg., Rm. 430 (Pendleton & Bull Streets), Columbia, SC 29208-0182, USA*

Alan Ralph, *Parenting and Family Support Centre, The University of Queensland, School of Psychology, Brisbane 4072, Australia*

Lissette M. Saavedra, *Child and Family Psychosocial Research Center, Department of Psychology, Florida International University, University Park, Miami, FL 33199, USA*

Matthew R. Sanders, *Director, Parenting and Family Support Centre, The University of Queensland, School of Psychology, Brisbane 4072, Australia*

Laura D. Seligman, *Department of Psychology, University of Toledo, Toledo, OH 43606, USA*

Wendy K. Silverman, *Child and Family Psychosocial Research Center, Department of Psychology, Florida International University, University Park, Miami, FL 33199, USA*

Nirbhay N. Singh, *Professor of Psychiatry, Paediatrics and Clinical Psychology, Department of Psychiatry, Virginia Commonwealth University, P.O. Box 980489, Richmond, VA 23298-0489, USA*

Patrick Smith, *Department of Clinical Psychology, Institute of Psychiatry, King's College London, De Crespigny Park, Denmark Hill, London SE5 8AF, UK*

Robi Sonderegger, *Griffith University, Mt Gravatt Campus, School of Applied Psychology, Mt Gravatt, QLD 4111, Australia*

Cynthia M. Turner, *Griffith University, Mt Gravatt Campus, School of Applied Psychology, Mt Gravatt QLD 4111, Australia*

Karen M.T. Turner, *Parenting and Family Support Centre, The University of Queensland, School of Psychology, Brisbane 4072, Australia*

Holly Barrett Waldron, *Oregon Research Institute, 1715 Franklin Blvd., Eugene, Oregon 974 03, USA*

Karen C. Wells, *P. O. Box 3320, Duke University Medical Center, 718 Rutherford St., Durham NC 277105, USA*

William Yule, *Department of Clinical Psychology, Institute of Psychiatry, De Crespigny Park, Denmark Hill, London SE5 8AF, UK*

Preface

This is an exciting time in the field of child and adolescent treatment research and practice. Whether referred to as empirically validated treatments, empirically supported treatments, evidence-based treatments, evidence-based practice, or simply "treatments that work", much has been accomplished in recent years and equally exciting developments loom on the horizon. Such has not always been the case. For years, child and adolescent psychotherapy outcome research lagged behind that in the adult area and could truly be described as its "ugly step-sister". Moreover, effective prevention programs were largely nonexistent. For much too long, our discipline relied upon anecdotal evidence and unproven interventions to stake our claim to being able to help children and adolescents. Such practices, we assert, do not have a home in the twenty-first century. Although much remains to be learned, as we demonstrate in this volume, concerted progress has been made in both the prevention and treatment of diverse behaviour problems in children and adolescents.

While this volume is written specifically for researchers and clinicians, readers from diverse professional backgrounds involved in the welfare of children and adolescents (from education providers to policy makers) are carefully presented with advanced theoretical foundations for unique therapeutic strategies, techniques, and intervention programs currently being developed and employed. This volume endeavours to offer a glimpse of these developments and a look into the future state of child and adolescent psychotherapy and prevention outcome research. In doing so, both the potential value and limitations of specific approaches for children and adolescents experiencing a wide range of pathology are illustrated.

To facilitate these objectives, only the very best contributors in the world were recruited to provide us an overview of their intervention and prevention efforts. Contributors recruited from the United States of America, the United Kingdom, Australia, The Netherlands, and Germany, are widely published in their fields. Many of these contributors have conducted leading randomized clinical control trials about the efficacy of their interventions. We are fortunate to draw upon their collective experiences and expertise.

The volume is presented in three major parts. In Part I, the foundations of "treatments that work" with children and adolescents are laid out. Specifically, chapters on what constitutes evidence-based treatments, developmental principles that underlie these treatments, cross-cultural issues that typify much of this work, and strategies for how to assess and diagnose behaviour problems in childhood and adolescence are presented. Moreover, Part I includes a chapter on how to evaluate treatment outcomes in a developmentally and culturally sensitive but rigorous and exacting way.

In Part II, the evidence base for the treatment of a host of behaviour problems is offered. Leading authorities in the field address disorders such as generalized anxiety disorder, separation anxiety disorder, social anxiety disorder, obsessive-compulsive disorder, specific phobia, major depressive disorder, eating disorders, substance abuse disorder, attention deficit hyperactivity disorder, oppositional defiant disorder, and conduct disorder. In each of these chapters, after briefly describing the various disorders, the contributors provide in-depth coverage of both the assessment and treatment of these disorders. Careful attention is afforded assessment strategies that possess empirical support for their use and that are developmentally and culturally sensitive. In addition, considerable detail is offered about "how" to conduct the treatments and, in some cases, portions of actual treatment manuals are presented. We hope the readers will find this section to be of particular clinical utility.

Part III addresses prevention programs that attempt to intervene with several child and adolescent problems *before* they become disorders. In particular, prevention programs for internalizing problems that lead to anxiety and depression and for externalizing problems that lead to oppositional, conduct, and substance abuse disorders are highlighted. These prevention efforts are truly exciting. As is evident, we are beginning to obtain considerable evidence that many common disorders can be prevented, and at little cost to society.

We present encouraging evidence in this volume that we can intervene successfully at the psychosocial level with children and adolescents who already have major psychiatric disorders and, as importantly, that we can even prevent some of these disorders from occurring in the first place. We hope our readers concur with this appraisal of our field and that the contents of this volume will help them to provide such interventions in their own settings and contexts. To ensure maximum utility of content made available in this volume, many tables and figure provide readers with ready access to important summaries of conceptual data, empirical research endeavours, and most relevant assessment tools and intervention strategies. Together, the sections and chapters in this volume provide a leading summation of the developmental issues, aetiology, epidemiology, assessment, treatment, and prevention of childhood and adolescent psychopathology in its most contemporary form.

Paula M. Barrett
Griffith University, Mt Gravatt Campus
Brisbane, QLD, Australia

and

Thomas H. Ollendick
Virginia Polytechnic Institute and State University
Blacksburg, VA, USA

Acknowledgments

First and foremost I (Dr. Paula Barrett) want to thank my two beautiful children Ana and Thomas who have brought so much hope, support, and happiness in my life. Thank you to Mark Dadds for modeling empowerment of families in child clinical work. Also, thank you to all the children and families I have worked with for the past 15 years—they have taught me so much.

And, I (Prof. Thomas Ollendick) wish to give special thanks to my family as well. Mary, my spouse and friend, has been a source of support and love over the many years we have been together. She has been an integral part of my (our) journey. Our daughters, Laurie Kristine and Kathleen Marie, have also been a source of much joy and happiness. They are now young women with mates of their own (David Perryman and Brian Smith, respectively) and are pursuing their own paths to vitality and happiness. Our grandchildren, Braden Thomas Perryman and Ethan Ray Perryman, are also to be thanked as they keep us young and in touch with many of the new societal developments. We are anticipating that future grandchildren will keep us young and in touch over the years ahead! Finally, a special thank you is extended to the many children, adolescents and families whom I have had the great pleasure of working with over the past 30+ years. They have taught me much.

Many persons are to be thanked in a venture such as this. First and foremost, we wish to thank all the children and adolescents who have so richly informed us throughout our developments as clinicians and researchers. They have helped us to grow as mental health professionals and taught us much more than they probably realize. We also wish to thank our many contributors—without whom this volume would have been only a dream or vision on our part. Their collective expertise and wisdom make this volume what it is. In addition, we wish to thank Vivien Ward, Editor, and the entire production staff at Wiley for their invaluable support in bringing this project to fruition. Thanks also to my (Dr Paula Barrett's) family in Portugal for all their unconditional support over the years, despite us living so far apart—my mum Albertina, my dad Manuel, and my brother Vasco. Portugal is and will always be in my heart and, more than anything else, has given me strength over time. Finally, it has been an interesting journey for us to pull this project together from different continents and, in particular, different time zones and seasons of the year. Without the capable day-to-day prompts, assistance, and consequences of Dr Robi Sonderegger at Griffith University, it would not have been possible. We thank you Robi and all the others mentioned above for your invaluable assistance and dedication to this project.

PART I

Contemporary Issues Related to Competent Clinical and Research Practice

Empirically Supported Treatments for Children and Adolescents: Advances Toward Evidence-Based Practice

Thomas H. Ollendick

Virginia Polytechnic Institute and State University, USA

and

Neville J. King

Monash University, Australia

INTRODUCTION

About 50 years ago, Eysenck (1952) published his now (in)famous review of the effects of adult psychotherapy. Boldly, he concluded that psychotherapy practices in vogue at that time were no more effective than the simple passage of time. Subsequently, Levitt (1957, 1963) reviewed the child psychotherapy literature and arrived at a similar conclusion. These reviews were both contentious and provocative, leading many to question the continued viability of the psychotherapy enterprise for both adults and children.[1]

Fortunately, as noted by Kazdin (2000), these reviews also served as a wake-up call and led to a host of developments including advances in child psychopathology, psychiatric diagnostic nomenclature, assessment and treatment practices, and experimental designs for the study of treatment process and outcome. These

Correspondence to Thomas H. Ollendick, Virginia Polytechnic Institute and State University, Blacksburg, Virginia 24061-0436; email: tho@vt.edu

[1] The term *children* is used throughout to refer to both children and adolescents, unless otherwise specified.

Handbook of Interventions that Work with Children and Adolescents: Prevention and Treatment.
Edited by P.M. Barrett and T.H. Ollendick. © 2004 John Wiley & Sons, Ltd. ISBN 0-470-84453-1.

developments, in turn, resulted in well over 1500 studies (Durlak et al., 1995; Kazdin, 2000) and four major meta-analyses examining the effects of child psychotherapy (Casey & Berman, 1985; Kazdin et al., 1990; Weisz et al., 1987, 1995). As noted recently by Weersing and Weisz (2002), there is now little doubt that at present child psychotherapy results in beneficial impacts on the lives of children and their families. Consistently, these reviews demonstrate that therapy for children outperforms waiting list and attention-placebo conditions; moreover, in several studies, it is becoming **clear** that some forms of therapy work better than others. As a result, much progress has been made and we can conclude that the field of clinical child psychology has moved beyond the simple question, "Does psychotherapy work for children?" to identify the efficacy of *specific* treatments for children who present with *specific* behavioural, emotional, and social problems. Basically, then, the field has moved from the generic question of whether psychotherapy "works" at all for children to a more specific one that seeks to determine the evidence base for these various treatments and the conditions under which they are effective. This is an exciting time in the field of child psychotherapy research, and the various chapters in this volume attest to what we know and what we do not know in treating various childhood problems and disorders.

This chapter[2] describes some of the early work undertaken to identify empirically supported psychosocial treatments for children and raises some critical issues attendant to this movement. First, it should be acknowledged that this movement is part of a larger zeitgeist labelled "evidence-based medicine" (Sackett et al., 1997, 2000), which we refer to here as "evidence-based practice". Evidence-based practice is at its core an approach to knowledge and a strategy for improving performance outcomes (Alvarez & Ollendick, 2003). It is not wedded to any one theoretical position or orientation. It holds that treatments of whatever theoretical persuasion need to be based on objective and scientifically credible evidence—evidence that is obtained from randomized clinical trials (RCTs), whenever possible. In a RCT, children with a specific presenting problem are randomly assigned to one treatment or another or to some control condition, such as a waiting list or attention-placebo condition. Although such a design is not failsafe, it appears to be the best strategy for ruling out biases and expectations (on the part of both the child and the therapist) that can result in misleading research findings. By its nature, evidence-based practice values information or opinions obtained from observational studies, logical intuition, personal experiences, and the testimony of experts less highly. Such evidence is not necessarily "bad" or "undesired", it is just less credible and acceptable from a scientific, evidentiary-based standpoint. And, it simply occupies a lower rung on the evidentiary ladder of evidence.

The movement to develop, identify, disseminate, and use empirically supported psychosocial treatments (initially referred to as empirically "validated" treatments; see Chambless, 1996, and Chambless & Hollon, 1998) has been controversial. On the surface, it hardly seemed possible that anyone could or would object to the initial report issued by the Society of Clinical Psychology (Division 12) of the American

---

[2] Portions of this chapter are based on Ollendick, T.H., & King, N.J. (2000). Empirically supported treatments for children and adolescents. In P.C. Kendall (Ed.), *Child and adolescent therapy: Cognitive-behavioural procedures* (2nd edn; pp. 386–425). New York: Guilford Publications.

Psychological Association in 1995 or that the movement associated with it would become so controversial. Surely, identifying, developing, and disseminating treatments that have empirical support should be encouraged, not discouraged, especially for a profession that is committed to the welfare of those whom it serves.

Sensible as this may seem, the task force report was not only controversial, but it also, unfortunately, served to divide the profession of clinical psychology and related mental health disciplines (Ollendick & King, 2000). In this chapter, we first define empirically supported treatments and then briefly examine the current status of such treatments. In doing so, we illustrate the potential value of these treatments. Other chapters in this volume provide in-depth detail on the efficacy of these treatments for specific problems and disorders. Next, we illustrate and discuss some of the contentious issues associated with these treatments and their development and promulgation. We conclude our discourse by offering recommendations for future research and practice.

ON THE NATURE OF EMPIRICALLY SUPPORTED TREATMENTS

In 1995, as noted earlier, the Society of Clinical Psychology Task Force on Promotion and Dissemination of Psychological Procedures published its report on empirically validated psychological treatments. The task force was constituted of members who represented a number of theoretical perspectives, including psychodynamic, interpersonal, and cognitive-behavioural points of view. This diversity in membership was an intentional step taken by the committee to emphasize a commitment to identifying and promulgating *all* psychotherapies of proven worth, not just those emanating from one particular school of thought. Defining empirically validated treatments proved to be a difficult task, however. Of course, from a scientific standpoint no treatment is ever fully validated and, as noted in the task force report, there are always more questions to ask about any treatment, including questions about the essential components of treatments, client characteristics that predict treatment outcome, and the mechanisms or processes associated with behaviour change. In recognition of this state of affairs, the term *empirically supported* was adopted subsequently to describe treatments of scientific value—a term that many agreed was more felicitous than *empirically validated*.

Three categories of treatment efficacy were proposed in the 1995 report: (1) *well-established treatments*, (2) *probably efficacious treatments*, and (3) *experimental treatments* (see Table 1.1). The primary distinction between *well-established* and *probably efficacious* treatments was that a well-established treatment should have been shown to be superior to a psychological placebo, pill, or another treatment whereas a probably efficacious treatment should be shown to be superior to a waiting list or no treatment control only. In addition, effects supporting a well-established treatment should be demonstrated by at least two different investigatory teams, whereas the effects of a probably efficacious treatment need not be (the effects might be demonstrated in two studies from the same investigator, for example). For both types of empirically supported treatments, characteristics of the clients should be clearly specified (e.g., age, sex, ethnicity, diagnosis) and the

Table 1.1 Criteria for empirically validated treatments

I. *Well-established treatments*
    A. At least two good between-group design experiments demonstrating efficacy in one or more of the following ways:
        1. Superior to pill or psychological placebo or to another treatment
        2. Equivalent to an already established treatment in experiments with adequate statistical power (about 30 per group)
    or
    B. A large series of single case design experiments ($n > 9$) demonstrating efficacy. These experiments must have:
        1. Used good experimental designs, and
        2. Compared the intervention to another treatment as in A.1.

    Further criteria for both A. and B.:
    C. Experiments must be conducted with treatment manuals.
    D. Characteristics of the client samples must be clearly specified.
    E. Effects must have been demonstrated by at least two different investigators or investigatory teams.

II. *Probably efficacious treatments*
    A. Two experiments showing the treatment is more effective than a waiting-list control group
    or
    B. One or more experiments meeting the well-established treatment criteria A, C, D, but not E
    or
    C. A small series of single case design experiments ($n > 3$) otherwise meeting well-established treatment criteria B, C, and D.

clinical trials should be conducted with treatment manuals. Furthermore, it was required that these outcomes be demonstrated in "good" group design studies or a series of controlled single case design studies. "Good" designs were those in which it was reasonable to conclude that the benefits observed were due to the effects of treatment and not due to chance or confounding factors such as passage of time, the effects of psychological assessment, or the presence of different types of clients in the various treatment conditions (Chambless & Hollon, 1998; also see Kazdin, 1998, and Kendall, Flannery-Schroeder, & Ford, 1999, for a fuller discussion of research design issues). Ideally, and as noted earlier, treatment efficacy should be demonstrated in randomized clinical trials (RCTs)—group designs in which patients would be assigned randomly to the treatment of interest or one or more comparison conditions—or carefully controlled single case experiments and their group analogues. Finally, *experimental* treatments were those treatments not yet shown to be at least probably efficacious. This category was intended to capture long-standing or traditional treatments that had not yet been fully evaluated or newly developed ones not yet put to the test of scientific scrutiny. The development of new treatments was particularly encouraged. It was also noted that treatments could "move" from one category to another dependent on the empirical support available for that treatment *over time*. That is, an experimental procedure might move into probably efficacious or well-established status as new findings became available. The categorical system was intended to be fluid, not static.

EMPIRICALLY SUPPORTED PSYCHOSOCIAL TREATMENTS FOR CHILD BEHAVIOUR PROBLEMS AND DISORDERS

The 1995 Task Force Report on Promotion and Dissemination of Psychological Procedures identified 18 well-established treatments and 7 probably efficacious treatments, using the criteria described above and presented in Table 1.1. Of these 25 efficacious treatments, only *three* well-established treatments for children (behaviour modification for developmentally disabled individuals, behaviour modification for enuresis and encopresis, and parent training programs for children with oppositional behaviour) and *one* probably efficacious treatment for children (habit reversal and control techniques for children with tics and related disorders) were identified. As noted in that report, the list of empirically supported treatments was intended to be representative of efficacious treatments, not exhaustive. In recognition of the need to identify additional psychosocial treatments that were effective with children, concurrent task forces were set up by the Society of Clinical Psychology and its offspring, the Society of Clinical Child and Adolescent Psychology (Division 53 of the American Psychological Association). The two independent task forces joined efforts and in 1998 published their collective reviews in the *Journal of Clinical Child Psychology*. Reviews of empirically supported treatments for children with autism, anxiety disorders, attention deficit hyperactivity disorder (ADHD), depression, and oppositional and conduct problem disorders were included in the special issue. As noted by Lonigan, Elbert, and Johnson (1998), the goal was not to generate an exhaustive list of treatments that met criteria for empirically supported treatments; rather, the goal was to focus on a number of high-frequency problems encountered in clinical and other settings serving children with mental health problems. As such, a number of problem areas were not reviewed (e.g., eating disorders, childhood schizophrenia), and the identification of empirically supported treatments for these other problem areas remains to be accomplished, even to this day. Overall, the goal was to identify effective psychosocial treatments for a limited number of frequently occurring disorders in childhood.

In a recent review of empirically supported psychological interventions for adults *and* children published in the *Annual Review of Psychology*, Chambless and Ollendick (2001) noted that other ventures have also been instrumental in identifying empirically supported treatments for children and adults. Namely, edited books by Roth et al. (1996, *What works for Whom?*) and Nathan and Gorman (1998, *A Guide to Treatments that Work*) have identified other treatments and evaluated many of the same ones identified by the Society of Clinical Psychology and the Society of Clinical Child and Adolescent Psychology. In general, the criteria used by the various groups have been similar, although some relatively minor differences are evident (see Chambless & Ollendick, 2001, for details). In Table 1.2, we present a summary of interventions for children with various problems and disorders found to be empirically supported by at least one of these four review groups. In many, if not most, instances the same treatments were identified as effective by two or more of these groups.

As shown in Table 1.2, it is evident that many well-established and probably efficacious treatments have been identified. Yet, we must be somewhat modest, inasmuch as no well-established treatments have been identified for the treatment of

Table 1.2 Well-established and probably efficacious psychosocial treatments for children (adapted from Chambless & Ollendick, 2001, and Ollendick & King, 2000)

Problem/ Disorder	Treatments	
	Well-established	Probably efficacious
ADHD	Behavioural parent training Behaviour modification in classroom	Cognitive-behaviour therapy
Anxiety	None	Cognitive-behaviour therapy Cognitive-behaviour therapy + family anxiety management
Autism	None	Contingency management
Depression	None	Behavioural self-control therapy Cognitive-behavioural coping skills
Enuresis	Behaviour modification	
Encopresis	Behaviour modification	
OCD	None	Exposure/response prevention
ODD/CD	Behavioural parent training Functional family therapy Multisystemic therapy Videotape modelling	Anger control training with stress inoculation Anger coping therapy Assertiveness training Cognitive-behaviour therapy Delinquency prevention program Parent–child interaction therapy Problem-solving skills training Rational-emotive therapy Time out plus signal seat treatment
Phobias	Graduated exposure Participant modelling Reinforced practice	Imaginal desensitization *In vivo* Desensitization Live modelling Filmed modelling Cognitive-behaviour therapy

Note: Anxiety = Generalized Anxiety Disorder, Separation Anxiety Disorder, Social Phobia; OCD = Obsessive-Compulsive Disorder; ODD = Oppositional Defiant Disorder; CD = Conduct Disorder

such common problems as autism, childhood depression, or childhood anxiety. Although a host of interventions appear promising and can be described as probably efficacious, it is evident that support for them is relatively meagre. Rarely did any one treatment have more than the two requisite studies to support its well-established or probably efficacious status (with the exception of parenting programs for oppositional and conduct problem children and for children with ADHD). It should also be evident that *all* of these probably efficacious and well-established treatments are based on behavioural and cognitive-behavioural principles. As a result, using these criteria, we do not really know whether frequently practiced treatments from other orientations work or not (e.g., play therapy, interpersonal psychotherapy); in many instances, they simply have not been evaluated sufficiently. Still, the value of identifying and promulgating treatments that do have support for their use is apparent. Demonstration of the efficacy of treatments in well-controlled randomized trials may point the way to determining the effectiveness of the treatments in real-life clinical settings (see Chorpita et al., 2002).

ON EMPIRICALLY SUPPORTED TREATMENTS: ISSUES OF CONCERN

As noted in our opening comments, the movement to identify, develop, disseminate, and use empirically supported psychosocial treatments has been contentious. As noted by Ollendick (1999), three major concerns about this movement have been raised: (a) some treatments have been shown to be more effective than others and, as a result, the "Dodo Bird" effect (i.e., no one treatment is superior to another) that has long characterized the state of psychosocial treatment interventions can no longer be asserted; (b) use of treatment manuals might lead to mechanical, inflexible interventions and that such "manually driven" treatments might stifle creativity and innovation in the therapy process; and (c) treatments shown to be effective in randomized clinical trials and based largely in university-based settings might not be generalizable or applicable to "real-life" clinical practice setting. What is the status of these concerns for empirically supported treatments for children and how might they be addressed? In the sections that follow, we address these concerns in some detail.

Differential Effectiveness of Psychosocial Treatments

Regarding the first issue, our previous reviews of the literature (Ollendick & King, 1998, 2000) as well as the present one reveals a rather startling finding. It is obvious that interventions other than behavioural or cognitive-behavioural ones have not been examined adequately in controlled treatment outcome literature and therefore cannot be said to be well established or probably efficacious. For example, across such frequently occurring problem areas of autism, depression, phobias, anxiety, ADHD, oppositional behaviours, and conduct problems, *no* randomized-controlled trials using "good" experimental designs were found for psychodynamic psychotherapies or family systems therapies (with the exception of research in the area of oppositional behaviour wherein psychodynamic and family systems interventions were shown to be *less* efficacious than behavioural parenting programs; see Brestan & Eyberg, 1998). In addition, only two studies were found to examine the efficacy of interpersonal psychotherapy (Mufson et al., 1994, 1999), and they were limited to the treatment of depression in adolescents. Inasmuch as these treatments have not been evaluated systematically, we simply do not know whether or not they are effective. They could be; but, we must determine whether that is or is not based on evidentiary support, and not on the absence of well-controlled studies.

Although behavioural and cognitive-behavioural treatment procedures fare better than other interventions (a conclusion identical to that arrived at in meta-analytic studies of treatment outcomes with children; see Weisz et al., 1987 and 1995, for reviews that indicate the superiority of behavioural over "non-behavioural" treatments), we were able to identify only two well-established psychosocial treatments for specific phobias in children (participant modelling, reinforced practice), two well-established treatments for ADHD (behavioural parent training, operant classroom management), and two well-established treatments for oppositional and conduct problems (Webster-Stratton's videotape modelling parent training, and Patterson's social learning parent training program). Thus, even support for behavioural and cognitive-behavioural interventions is modest, at best.

What should we do in our clinical practices in the absence of firmer support for our interventions? Unfortunately for the children and families we serve, we probably need to continue "treatment as usual" until such support is available; however, it seems to us that these alternative treatments, as well as many behavioural and cognitive-behavioural ones, urgently need to be submitted to systematic enquiry in RCTs before their routine use can be endorsed. We simply do not have sufficient evidence at this time for the efficacy of psychosocial treatments for many child behaviour problems (excepting perhaps specific phobias, ADHD and oppositional/conduct problems, where we also have a number of probably efficacious treatments). Although the desirability and utility of RCTs for obtaining "reasonable evidence" has been the focus of much debate (see Persons & Silberschatz, 1998), there is little doubt in our minds that such trials are well suited for establishing the *initial* efficacy of various treatments. Of course, the transportability of such treatments to practice settings and their efficacy in such settings (i.e., their effectiveness) must also be established (see below).

Given the state of empirically supported psychosocial treatments and the need to rely on current clinical practices until support for additional treatments is garnered, we pose the obvious question: "What is the current status of 'treatment as usual' in clinical practice settings? And, how effective is it?" Weisz, Huey, and Weersing (1998) examined this question in a re-analysis of their 1995 meta-analytic study. They searched for studies that involved treatment of clinic-referred children who were treated in service-oriented clinics or clinical agencies and who were treated by practicing clinicians. Nine candidate studies, spanning a period of 50 years, were identified that compared "treatment as usual" in a clinical setting to a control group who received no treatment or a placebo condition. Effect sizes associated with these nine studies were computed: they ranged from −0.40 to +0.29, with a mean effect size of 0.01, falling well below the average effect size (+0.70) obtained in their overall meta-analyses of "research" and "clinic" based treatments. The effect size of 0.01 indicates that, after treatment, the treated children were no better off than the untreated children. Clearly, based on these analyses, outcomes associated with "treatment as usual" are most disquieting.

Bickman and his colleagues reported similar outcomes in their examination of a comprehensive mental health services program for children (Bickman, 1996; Bickman et al., 1995). Popularly known as the Fort Bragg Project, the United States Army spent over $80 million to provide an organized continuum of mental health care (organized and coordinated by a case manager) to children and their families and to test its cost-effectiveness relative to a more conventional and less comprehensive intervention (treatment as usual) in a matched comparison site. Although there was good evidence that the program produced better access to treatment and higher levels of client satisfaction, the program cost significantly more and, most importantly for our purposes, failed to demonstrate clinical and functional outcomes superior to those in the comparison site. In brief, the Fort Bragg children and their families received more interventions at a higher cost, but their outcomes were not improved by the increased intensity of treatment and cost.

Finally, in a recent study conducted by Weiss et al. (1999), a RCT was used to ascertain the effectiveness of child psychotherapy as typically delivered ("treatment as usual") in a school setting. A total of 160 children who presented with problems of anxiety, depression, aggression, and attention were randomly assigned to treatment and control conditions. Children were enrolled in normal elementary and middle schools and their mean age was 10.3. Treatment was provided by mental health professionals hired through regular clinic practices (six were Masters' level clinicians and one was a doctoral level clinical psychologist); therapists reported favouring cognitive and psychodynamic-humanistic approaches over behavioural ones. Treatment itself was open-ended (i.e., not guided by manuals) and delivered over an extended two-year period on an individual basis. Overall, results of the trial provided little support for the effectiveness of "treatment as usual" in this setting. In fact, treatment produced an overall effect size of −0.08, indicating that the treatment was no better than the control condition in which children simply received academic tutoring. Even so, parents of children who received treatment reported higher levels of satisfaction with the services than parents of children in the academic tutoring condition. These results, along with those of Bickman and colleagues, in addition to those reported by Weisz, Huey, and Weersing (1998) in their meta-analytic review, argue for the importance of developing, validating, and transporting effective treatments to clinical settings. Apparently, "treatment as usual" is not effective treatment—such "treatments" have little support for their ongoing use and remind us of the conclusions derived by Levitt (1957, 1963); namely, "treatment as usual" is no more effective than the mere passage of time. In fact, these findings suggest that, for some children, it may be detrimental to their ongoing functioning.

One final comment should be offered about the ethics of continuing to provide treatments that have not been shown to be helpful to children and their families and, in fact, in some instances have been shown to be harmful (recall that the effect sizes for the nine clinic-based studies reviewed by Weisz et al. ranged from −0.40 to +0.29 and that the effect size reported by Weiss et al. was −0.08). As psychologists, the identification, promulgation, and use of empirically supported treatments is certainly in accord with ethical standards asserting that psychologists "should rely on scientifically and professional derived knowledge when making scientific or professional judgments" (Canter et al., 1994, p. 36). Yet, as noted in a lively debate on this issue (Eiffert et al., 1998; Persons, 1998; Zvolensky & Eiffert, 1998, 1999), the identification and use of empirically supported treatments represent a two-edged sword. On the one hand, it might seem unethical to use a treatment that has not been empirically supported; on the other hand, inasmuch as few empirically supported treatments have been developed, it might be unethical to delimit or restrict practice to those problem areas and disorders for which treatment efficacy has been established (Ollendick & King, 2000). What, after all, should we do in instances in which children and their families present with problems for which empirically supported treatments have not yet been developed? Quite obviously, there are no easy solutions; nor, can we address them in sufficient depth in this chapter. However, we are supportive of the conclusions reached by Kinscherff (1999) in an article entitled "Empirically supported treatments: What to do until the data arrive (or now that they have)?". He suggests:

> Generally, clinicians should develop a formulation of the case and select the best approaches for helping a client from among the procedures in which the clinician is competent. Clinicians should remain informed about advances in treatment, including empirically supported treatments, and maintain their own clinical skills by learning new procedures and strengthening their skills in areas in which they are already accomplished. Because there are limitations to how many treatments any one clinician can master, a key professional competence is knowing when to refer for a treatment approach that may be more effective for the client. This, in turn, requires at least a basic ongoing familiarity with the evolution of psychotherapeutic treatments and scientific basis for them in clinical populations. (p. 4)

We concur.

Manualization of Psychosocial Treatments

The recommendation that well-established and probably efficacious treatments should use a treatment manual was the second major source of controversy identified by Ollendick (1999). As noted by Chambless et al. (1996), there were two reasons for this requirement. First, inclusion of a treatment manual leads to the standardization of treatment. In experimental design terms, the manual provides an operational definition of the treatment. That is, a treatment manual provides a description of the treatment that makes it possible to determine whether the treatment, as intended, was actually delivered (i.e., the treatment possesses "integrity"). Second, use of a manual allows other mental health professionals and researchers to know what the treatment actually consisted of and therefore exactly what procedures were supported in the efficacy trial. Manualization (as it has come to be called) is especially important to clarify the many types or variants of therapy. For example, there are many types of cognitive-behavioural therapy or psychodynamic therapy. To say that cognitive-behaviour therapy or psychodynamic therapy is efficacious is largely meaningless. What type of psychodynamic therapy was used in this study? What form of cognitive-behavioural therapy was used in that study? There are many interventions and there are many variations of those interventions that fall under any one type of psychotherapy. As Chambless et al. (1996, p. 6) noted, "the brand names are not the critical identifiers. The manuals are."

A flood of commentaries—some commendatory, others derogatory—filled the pages of several major journals, including the *American Psychologist, Australian Psychologist, Journal of Clinical Psychology, Journal of Consulting and Clinical Psychology, Clinical Psychology: Science and Practice, Clinical Psychology Review,* and *Psychotherapy.* Some authors viewed manuals as "promoting a cookbook mentality" (Smith, 1995), "paint by numbers" (Silverman, 1996), "more of a straitjacket than a set of guidelines" (Goldfried & Wolfe, 1996), "somewhat analogous to cookie cutters" (Strupp & Anderson, 1997), and a "hangman of life" (Lambert, 1998). Others viewed them in more positive terms (e.g., Chambless & Hollon, 1998; Craighead & Craighead, 1998; Heimberg, 1998; Kendall, 1998; King & Ollendick, 1998; Ollendick, 1995, 1999; Strosahl, 1998; Wilson, 1996a, 1996b, 1998). Wilson (1998, p. 363), for example, suggested "the use of standardized, manual-based treatments in clinical practice represents a new and evolving development with far-reaching implications for the field of psychotherapy".

In its simplest form, a treatment manual can be defined as a set of guidelines that instruct or inform the user as to "how to do" a certain treatment (Ollendick, 1999). They specify and, at the same time, standardize treatment. Although many opponents of manual-based treatment support efforts for greater accountability with respect to the effects of psychotherapy, they are concerned that treatments evaluated in research settings will not be generalizable to "real-life" clinical settings and that manual-based treatments will need to be implemented in a lockstep fashion with little opportunity for flexibility or clinical judgement in implementation of the treatment procedures. Seligman (1995, p. 967), for example, indicated that unlike the manual-based treatment of controlled, laboratory research—in which "a small number of techniques, all within one modality" are delivered in fixed order for a fixed duration, clinical practice "is self-correcting. If one technique is not working, another technique—or even modality—is usually tried." As noted by Wilson (1998), this characterization or depiction of a manual-based treatment is simply wrong. A variety of treatments have been "manualized", including those embedded in psychodynamic (e.g., Strupp & Binder, 1984), interpersonal (e.g., Klerman et al., 1984), and behavioural (Patterson & Gullion, 1968) or cognitive-behavioural theory (e.g., Beck et al., 1979); moreover, these manuals allow for flexible use and, for the most part, are responsive to progress or regress in treatment.

One final comment about manuals should be offered. The movement to manualization of treatment practices existed long before the Task Force issued its report in 1995. Almost 30 years earlier, Patterson and Gullion (1968) published their now-classic book *Living with Children: New Methods for Parents and Teachers*, a "how to" parent and teacher manual that has served as the foundation for many behavioural treatments of oppositional, defiant, and conduct problem children. Not surprisingly, treatment based on this "manual" was one of the first treatments designated as "evidence based". Over a decade prior to the issue of the Task Force Report, Luborsky and DuRubeis (1984) commented upon the potential use of treatment manuals in a paper entitled "The use of psychotherapy treatment manuals: A small revolution in psychotherapy research style". Similarly, Lambert and Ogles (1988) indicated that manuals were not new; rather, they noted, manuals have been used to train therapists and define treatments since the 1960s. It seems to us that the 1995 Task Force Report simply reaffirmed a movement that had been present for some years and had become the unofficial, if not official, policy of the National Institute of Mental Health for funding research studies exploring the efficacy of various psychotherapies. On the other hand, and this is where its actions became contentious, the Task Force Report asserted that psychotherapies described and operationalized by manuals should not only be identified but should also be disseminated to clinical training programs, practicing mental health professionals, the public, and to third party payers (i.e., insurance companies, health maintenance organizations). Many authors were concerned that such actions were premature and that they would prohibit or, in the least, constrain the practice of those psychotherapies that had not yet been manualized or not yet shown to be efficacious. They also were concerned that the development of new psychotherapies would be curtailed, if not stifled totally. Although these are possible outcomes of the movement to manualize and evaluate psychotherapies, they need not be the inevitable outcome. In fact, some have argued that these developments can serve to stimulate additional treatments by systematically examining the parameters of effective treatments as well as the therapeutic mechanisms of change (see Kendall, 1998, and Wilson, 1998, for examples), a position in which we are in full accord.

What is the current status of this movement toward manualization in the treatment of children? First, it should be clear that the studies summarized in our review of empirically supported treatments for children either used manuals or the procedures were described in sufficient detail as to not require manuals (as originally suggested by the Task Force Report [1995] and by Chambless et al. [1996]). As we noted earlier, manuals are simply guidelines that describe treatment procedures and therapeutic strategies and, in some instances, provide an underlying theory of change on which the procedures or techniques are based. Kendall and his colleagues (Kendall, 1998; Kendall & Chu, in press; Kendall et al., 1998) have addressed some of the issues surrounding the use of treatment manuals and have recommended that we undertake systematic research of the issues identified. They identified six (mis)perceptions that plague manual-based treatments: How flexible are they? Do they replace clinical judgment? Do manuals detract from the creative process of therapy? Does a treatment manual reify therapy in a fixed and stagnant fashion, and thereby stifle improvement and change? Are manual-based treatments effective with patients who present with multiple diagnoses or clinical problems? Are manuals primarily designed for use in research programs, with little or no use or application in service-providing clinics? Although answers to each of these penetrating questions are not yet available, Kendall and his colleagues submit that careful research is needed to explore each of these perceptions. In addition, they provide evidence from their own work with children who have anxiety disorders that at least some of these issues or questions may be pseudo ones, or at least not particularly esoteric. For example, flexibility of treatment implementation is an issue that many critics have raised; accordingly, it should be investigated empirically to determine if the degree to which a manual is implemented flexibly affects treatment outcome. Does it really make a difference? In a recent study by Kendall and Chu (in press) such a study was conducted.

Flexibility can be defined in a variety of ways; in their research, it was defined as a construct that measures the therapist's adaptive stance to the *specific* situation at hand while adhering *generally* to the instructions and suggestions in the manual. Ratings on the degree to which the manual was implemented in a flexible manner were obtained from 18 different therapists who had implemented their cognitive-behavioural, manual-based treatment for anxious children (Kendall et al., 1992). Flexibility ratings were obtained retrospectively on a 13-item questionnaire, with each item rated on 1- to 7-point scale as to the extent of flexibility used in implementing treatment (e.g., "The manual suggests that clinicians spend 40–45 minutes of the session teaching the outlined skills to the child and 10–15 minutes of the session playing games. How flexible with this were you?" And, "During therapy sessions, how flexible were you in discussing issues not related to anxiety or directly related to the child's primary diagnoses?"). Firstly, results revealed that therapists reported being flexible in their implementation of the treatment plan (both in general and with specific strategies). Secondly, and perhaps unexpectedly, the indices of flexibility were *not* related to whether the children were comorbid with other disorders *or* treatment outcome. The important point here is that flexibility, however defined, is amenable to careful and systematic inquiry. Kendall (1998) asserts that other issues raised by the manualization of treatment are also amenable to empirical investigation and need not remain in the area of "heated" speculation.

One additional example may help to illustrate how issues such as flexibility might be addressed empirically. In these studies, primarily conducted with adults, manual-based treatments have been "individualized" in a flexible manner by matching certain characteristics or profiles of the individuals being treated to specific elements or components of previously established effective treatments. These efforts have been labelled "prescriptive matching" by Acierno et al. (1994). At the core of this approach is the assumption that an idiographic approach to treatment is more effective in producing positive treatment outcomes than a nomothetic approach (e.g., not all patients who receive the same diagnosis or who present with similar behaviour problems are *really* the same—the homogeneity myth put forth some years ago by Kiesler, 1966). For example, in one of these studies, Jacobson et al. (1989) designed individually tailored marital therapy treatment plans, where the number of sessions and the specific modules selected in each case were determined by the couple's specific needs and presenting problems. Individualized treatments were compared to a standard cognitive-behavioural treatment program. Each was manualized. At post-treatment, couples treated with individually tailored protocols could not be distinguished from those receiving standardized protocols. However, at six-month follow-up, a greater proportion of couples receiving standardized treatment showed decrements in marital satisfaction whereas a majority of those in the individually tailored program maintained their treatment gains, suggesting that individually tailored programs may help to reduce relapses.

Similar beneficial findings have been obtained in the treatment of adults with depression (Nelson-Gray et al., 1990). In this study, Nelson-Gray et al. assigned adult depressed patients to treatment protocols (e.g., cognitive treatment, social skills treatment) that were either matched or mismatched to presenting problems (e.g., irrational cognitions, social skills problems). Those in the matched conditions fared better than those in the mismatched condition upon completion of treatment. Similarly, Ost, Jerremalm, and Johansson (1981) examined the efficacy of social skills training and applied relaxation in the treatment of adults with social phobia who were categorized as either "behavioural" or "physiological" responders. Physiological responders benefited most clearly from the applied relaxation training whereas behavioural responders showed the most benefit from the social skills program. Not all studies with individualized treatments have produced such positive results, however. For example, Schulte and colleagues (1992) found that standardized treatment, contrary to expectations, proved more successful than either matched or mismatched treatments in an investigation of adults with agoraphobia or specific phobias. Mersch and coworkers (1989) also failed to demonstrate the value of categorizing adults with social phobia into those with primarily cognitive or behavioural deficiencies and assigning them to matched or mismatched treatments. Matched treatments were not found to be superior to mismatched treatments.

In the child arena, Eisen and Silverman (1993, 1998) have provided preliminary support for the value of prescriptive matching in the treatment of fearful and anxious children. In the first study, the efficacy of cognitive therapy, relaxation training, and their combination was examined with four overanxious children, 6 to 15 years of age, using a multiple baseline design across subjects. The children received both relaxation training and cognitive therapy (counterbalanced), followed by a combined treatment that incorporated elements of both treatments. Results suggested that interventions were most effective when they matched the specific problems of the children. That is, children with primary symptoms of worry responded more favourably to cognitive therapy whereas children with primary symptoms of somatic complaints responded best to relaxation treatment. Similar findings were obtained in the second study (Eisen & Silverman, 1998) with four children between 8 and 12 years of age who were diagnosed with overanxious disorder. The interventions that were prescribed on the basis of a match between the treatment and the response class (cognitive therapy for cognitive symptoms, relaxation therapy for somatic symptoms) produced the greatest changes and resulted in enhanced treatment effectiveness. These findings must be considered preliminary because of limitations associated with the single case designs used to evaluate their efficacy; to our knowledge, no controlled group design studies have been conducted examining these issues. Nonetheless, these studies and those conducted with adults show yet another possible way of individualizing treatment and exploring flexibility in the use of empirically supported treatment manuals.

In sum, issues with the manualization of treatment are many. However, as noted by Kendall (1998), most of these issues are open to experimental scrutiny. It seems to us that we could continue to debate the value of manualized treatments for a very long time, and such debate would likely be stimulating and fruitful; however, for the benefit of children and the families we serve, it seems to us that it would be more beneficial to get on with the business of developing manualized treatments for those problems and disorders for which we do not currently have empirically supported treatments, and carefully refining those manuals that we do have to make them more clinician-friendly, determining how they can be used in a clinically sensitive and flexible manner (Ollendick & King, 2000).

Issues with Efficacy and Effectiveness:
The Transportability of Treatments

Still, a third major concern about the empirically supported or evidence-based treatment movement is evident in differences between what have come to be called *efficacy* studies versus *effectiveness* studies (Hibbs, 1998; Hoagwood et al., 1995; Ollendick, 1999). Basically, efficacy studies demonstrate that the benefits obtained from a given treatment administered in a fairly standard way (with a treatment manual) are due to the treatment and not to chance factors or to a variety of other factors that threaten the internal validity of the demonstration of efficacy. Typically, as noted by Seligman (1995), these studies are conducted in laboratory or university settings under tightly controlled conditions. Most consist of RCTs and provide clear specification of sample characteristics, features reflective of "good" experimental designs. Appropriate concern has been raised about the exportability of these "laboratory-based" treatments to the real world—the world of clinical practice. Arguments have been mustered that the "subjects" in randomized clinical trials do not represent real-life "clients" or that the "experimenter" therapists in these trials do not represent "clinical" therapists in applied practice settings. Moreover, or so it is argued, the settings themselves are significantly different—ranging from tightly controlled laboratory conditions to ill-defined and highly variable conditions in practice settings. Weisz et al. (1995) refer to practice settings as the "real test" or the "proving ground" of interventions. To many of us, this distinction raises the ever-present concern about the need to build a strong bridge between science and practice—a bridge recommended over 50 years ago and embodied in the Boulder model of clinical training. Building this bridge is admittedly not easy, and a gap between efficacy and effectiveness studies remains.[3]

Nonetheless, it is evident that effectiveness studies that demonstrate the external validity of psychotherapies are very important; moreover, they need to be conducted in a way that will allow us to conclude that the treatments are responsible for the changes observed in our clients—not chance or other extraneous factors. Demonstration of both internal and external validity is important, and one should not be viewed as more important than the other (Ollendick & King, 2000). Of course, not all treatments shown to be efficacious in clinical trials research will necessarily be shown to be effective in clinical settings. Such failures may be associated with a host of difficulties, including problems in implementing the treatment procedures in less-controlled clinical settings and the "acceptability" of the efficacious treatments to clients and therapists alike. In the final analysis, whether the effects found in randomized clinical trials and conducted in research-based settings generalize to "real-world" clinical settings is an empirical question that awaits additional research (see Kendall & Southam-Gerow, 1995, and Persons & Silberschatz, 1998, for further discussion of these issues).

The issues surrounding transportability and efficacy versus effectiveness studies are numerous and well beyond the scope of this chapter (e.g., training of therapists, supervision of therapists, homogeneous/heterogeneous samples, development of manuals, adherence to manuals, competence in executing manual-based treatment, and the acceptability of manual-based treatments to clinicians and clients, among others). Weisz, Huey and Weersing (1998) have examined these issues in some detail and have identified a set of characteristics frequently associated with child psychotherapy outcome research that distinguishes efficacy from effectiveness research. They are reproduced in Table 1.3 under the headings of "research therapy" and "clinic therapy". As evident in Table 1.3, Weisz et al. characterize "research" therapy as serving a relatively homogeneous group of children who exhibit less severe forms of child psychopathology and who present with single-focus problems.

---

[3] Although the gap is being closed, as will be illustrated later in this chapter.

Table 1.3   Some characteristics frequently associated with child psychotherapy in outcome research (research therapy) and in clinics (clinic therapy)

Research therapy	Recruited cases (less severe, study volunteers)
	Homogeneous groups
	Narrow or single-problem focus
	Treatment in lab, school settings
	Researcher as therapist
	Very small caseloads
	Heavy pre-therapy preparation
	Pre-planned, highly structured treatment (manualized)
	Monitoring of therapist behaviour
	Behavioural methods
Clinic therapy	Clinic-referred cases (more severe, some coerced into treatment)
	Heterogeneous groups
	Broad, multi-problem focus
	Treatment in clinic, hospital settings
	Professional career therapists
	Very large caseloads
	Little/light pre-therapy preparation
	Flexible, adjustable treatment (no treatment manual)
	Little monitoring of therapist behaviour
	Non-behavioural methods

Moreover, they suggest that such studies are conducted in research laboratories or school settings with clinicians who are "really" researchers, are carefully trained and supervised, and have "light" client loads. Finally, such studies typically use manualized treatments of a behavioural or cognitive-behavioural nature. In contrast, "clinic" therapy is characterized by heterogeneous groups of children who are frequently referred for treatment and have a large and diverse range of clinical problems. Treatment in such settings is, of course, delivered in a clinic, school, or hospital setting by "real" therapists who have "heavy" caseloads, little pre-therapy training, and are not carefully supervised or monitored. Finally, treatment manuals are rarely used and the primary form of treatment is non-behavioural.

Clearly, a number of differences are evident. Although such distinctions are important to make, in our opinion they tend to be broad generalizations that may or may not be true for various studies conducted in laboratory *or* clinical settings. Moreover, they may serve to accentuate differences in types of studies rather than to define areas of rapprochement and, inadvertently, create a chasm, rather than a bridge, between laboratory and clinic research. We shall illustrate how these distinctions become blurred by describing three studies: (a) a "research" therapy study conducted by Kendall et al. (1997); (b) a "clinic" therapy study conducted by Weiss et al. (1999); and (c) a study examining the transportability of effective treatment into a practice setting (Tynan, Schuman, & Lampert, 1999).

In the Kendall et al. (1997) study, the efficacy of cognitive-behavioural treatment for anxious children was compared to a wait-list condition. Efficacy of treatment was determined at post-treatment and at one-year follow-up. A RCT was undertaken, detailed but flexible manuals were used, and the therapists were well-trained and supervised graduate clinicians who carried "light" clinical loads. Treatment was conducted in a university-based clinic. Ninety-four children (aged 9–13 years) and their parents, referred from multiple community sources (not volunteers or normal children in school settings), participated. All received primary anxiety disorder diagnoses (attesting to the relative severity of their problems), and the majority was comorbid with other disorders (affirming multiple problems in these children, including other anxiety disorders, affective disorders, and disruptive behaviour disorders). In short, a relatively heterogeneous group of children with an anxiety disorder was treated. Treatment was found to be highly effective both at post-treatment and one-year follow-up. In reference to Table 1.3, it is evident that some of the characteristics associated with "research" therapy obtained and that in at least some respects "clinic" therapy was enacted.

In the Weiss et al. (1999) study previously described, treatment as routinely practiced in an outpatient setting (a school setting) was evaluated by comparing it to an attention control placebo (academic tutoring). The seven therapists were hired through standard clinic practices (six were Masters' level clinicians and one was a doctoral level clinical psychologist) and were allowed to select and use whatever interventions they believed were necessary (most selected and used psychodynamic-humanistic or cognitive strategies). No manuals were used. They received no additional clinical training as part of the clinical trial and were provided with a minimal amount of supervision. One hundred and sixty children participated and were randomly assigned to one of the two "experimental" conditions. Children were identified in the school setting and presented with problems of anxiety, depression, aggression, and inattention. Diagnostic data were not obtained; however, the identified children were thought to represent a heterogeneous sample of children with multiple and serious problems. As noted earlier, traditional therapy, as implemented in this study, was determined to be largely ineffective. In reference to Table 1.3, it is evident that only some of the characteristics of "clinic" therapy obtained and that at least in some respects "research" therapy was examined.

Finally, in the study undertaken by Tynan, Schuman, and Lampert (1999), the transportability of a well-established treatment for oppositional defiant disorder and ADHD in children between 5 and 11 years of age (behavioural parent management training and child social skills training) was examined in a "real-life" clinical setting (a child psychiatry outpatient clinic). Therapy was conducted in a group format. All children who were referred for ADHD or oppositional defiant disorder were assigned to the groups as the first line of treatment. Parents and children were treated in separate groups. Diagnostic interviews were conducted and the children all met diagnostic criteria for disruptive behaviour disorders and a majority was comorbid with other disorders. Problems were judged by the clinicians to be serious. Treatment was manualized and therapists in this clinical setting were carefully trained and supervised by the primary author. No control group was used and no follow-up data were reported. Nonetheless, the treatment was shown to be highly efficacious at post-treatment (effect size of 0.89 from pre-treatment to post-treatment). Although several methodological problems exist with this "uncontrolled" clinical trial, it nicely illustrates the potential to extend findings from laboratory settings to clinical settings. This study also illustrates characteristics of "research" therapy and "clinic" therapy. To which is it more similar?

These three studies illustrate that demarcations between efficacy and effectiveness studies are not always easy or true to form. Perhaps more importantly, they illustrate the types of studies that need to be conducted that will bridge the gap between research and clinic settings. Recently, Chorpita and his colleagues (2002) have embarked upon a major effectiveness study in the State of Hawaii that also illustrates this rapprochement. In 1994, the State of Hawaii settled a class action lawsuit brought before federal court on behalf of children with special needs. The Feliz Consent Decree (named for the index plaintiff) ensured that the state would provide all services deemed necessary in order for children with significant mental health problems to be able to benefit maximally from their education provided in the school settings. Basically, the state agreed to develop a coordinated and comprehensive system of care for students aged 0 to 20 with mental health needs. As noted by Chorpita et al., the number of children identified and receiving mental health services as part of this decree increased from 1400 to over 11 000 over a six-year period. In 1999, the Child and Adolescent Mental Health Division of the State of Hawaii established the Empirical Basis to Services Task Force whose charge was to evaluate the evidence base for treatment of the common disorders of childhood and adolescence and to train and disseminate such practices. Although this initiative is still in its early stages, it represents the exact kind of work that is needed and awaits us in the years ahead. Through such efforts a "bridge" might actually be built between clinical research and practice and the transportability of treatments developed in research settings might be able to be more fully evaluated.

Summary of Issues Attendant to Empirically Supported Treatments

Although other concerns about empirically supported treatments undoubtedly exist, these three major concerns (some treatments are more effective than others, use of treatment manuals and the independence of the therapist, and the transportability of treatments from the research setting to the clinical setting) seem central to most arguments in support or against this movement. For many of us, the movement toward determining the empirical status of our treatments holds considerable promise; for others, however, it signifies a major pitfall, full of lurking and unspecified dangers (Ollendick, 1999). Continued dialogue between clinicians and researchers on these issues is of utmost importance.

CONCLUSIONS

In this chapter we have identified salient issues associated with empirically supported treatments and determined their significance for psychosocial treatments with children and adolescents. We have concluded that some treatments are more effective than others, that manualization need not be a stumbling block to providing effective psychotherapies in both research and clinic settings, and that the transportability of treatments from the laboratory setting to the practice setting is feasible (although still being tested). We have also noted that tensions remain about each of these issues, and we have illustrated various avenues of possible rapprochement.

Somewhat unexpectedly, however, our present overview of empirically supported psychosocial treatments for children reveals that our armamentarium is relatively "light" and that more work remains to be done. We really do not have very many psychosocial treatments that possess well-established status in research settings let alone clinical settings. Still, we assert that this is an exciting time and that we have the tools to close the oft-lamented gap between laboratory and clinic studies and that rapprochement is on its way (see Chorpita et al., 2002). Children and their families presenting at our clinics deserve our concerted attention to further the true synthesis of these approaches and to transform our laboratory findings into rich and clinically sensitive practices (Ollendick & King, 2000).

REFERENCES

Acierno, R., Hersen, M., Van Hasselt, V.B., & Ammerman, R.T. (1994). Remedying the Achilles heel of behaviour research and therapy: Prescriptive matching of intervention and psychopathology. *Journal of Behaviour Therapy and Experimental Psychiatry*, **25**, 179–188.

Alvarez, H.K., & Ollendick, T.H. (2003). Evidence based treatment. In T.H. Ollendick and C. Schroeder (Eds.), *Encyclopedia of clinical child and pediatric psychology*. New York: Kluwer Academic/Plenum Publishers.

Beck, A.T., Rush, A.T., Shaw, B.F., & Emery, G. (1979). *Cognitive therapy of depression*. New York: Guilford Press.

Bickman, L. (1996). A continuum of care: More is not always better. *American Psychologist*, **51**, 689–701.

Bickman, L., Guthrie, P.R., Foster, E.M., Lambert, E.W., Summerfelt, W.T., Breda, C.S., & Heflinger, C.A. (1995). *Evaluating managed mental health services: The Fort Bragg experiment*. New York: Plenum Press.

Brent, D.A., Kolko, D.J., Birmaher, B., Baugher, M., & Bridge, J. (1999). A clinical trial for adolescent depression: Predictors of additional treatment in the acute and follow-up phases of the trial. *Journal of the American Academy of Child and Adolescent Psychiatry*, **38**, 263–270.

Brestan, E.V., & Eyberg, S.M. (1998). Effective psychosocial treatments of conduct-disordered children and adolescents: 29 years, 82 studies, and 5272 kids. *Journal of Clinical Child Psychology*, **27**, 179–188.

Canter, M.B., Bennett, B.E., Jones, S.E., & Nagy, T.F. (1994). *Ethics for psychologists: A commentary on the APA ethics code*. Washington, DC: American Psychological Association.

Casey, R.J., & Berman, J.S. (1985). The outcome of psychotherapy with children. *Psychological Bulletin*, **98**, 388–400.

Chambless, D.L. (1996). In defense of dissemination of empirically supported psychological interventions. *Clinical Psychology: Science and Practice*, **3**, 230–235.

Chambless, D.L., & Hollon, S.D. (1998). Defining empirically supported therapies. *Journal of Consulting and Clinical Psychology*, **66**, 7–18.

Chambless, D.L., & Ollendick, T.H. (2001). Empirically supported psychological interventions: Controversies and evidence. *Annual Review of Psychology*, **52**, 685–716.

Chambless, D.L., Sanderson, W.C., Shoham, V., Bennett Johnson, S., Pope, K.S., Crits-Cristoph, P., Baker, M., Johnson, B., Woody, S.R., Sue, S., Beutler, L., Williams, D.A., & McCurry, S. (1996). An update on empirically validated therapies. *The Clinical Psychologist*, **49**, 5–18.

Chorpita, B.F., Yim, L.M., Donkervoet, J.C., Arensdorf, A., Amundsen, M.J., McGee, C., Serrano, A., Yates, A., Burns, J.A., & Morelli, P. (2002). Toward large-scale implementation of empirically supported treatments for children: A review and observations by the Hawaii Empirical Basis to Services Task Force. *Clinical Psychology: Science and Practice*, **9**, 165–190.

Craighead, W.E., & Craighead, L.W. (1998). Manual-based treatments: Suggestions for improving their clinical utility and acceptability. *Clinical Psychology: Science and Practice*, **5**, 403–407.

Durlak, J.A., Wells, A.M., Cotton, J.K., & Johnson, S. (1995). Analysis of selected methodological issues in child psychotherapy research. *Journal of Clinical Child Psychology*, **24**, 141–148.

Eiffert, G.H., Schulte, D., Zvolensky, M.J., Lejuez, C.W., & Lau, A.W. (1998). Manualized behaviour therapy: Merits and challenges. *Behaviour Therapy*, **28**, 499–509.

Eisen, A.R., & Silverman, W.K. (1993). Should I relax or change my thoughts? A preliminary examination of cognitive therapy, relaxation training, and their combination with overanxious children. *Journal of Cognitive Psychotherapy: An International Quarterly*, **7**, 265–279.

Eisen, A.R., & Silverman, W.K. (1998). Prescriptive treatment for generalized anxiety disorder in children. *Behaviour Therapy*, **29**, 105–121.

Eysenck, H.J. (1952). The effects of psychotherapy: An evaluation. *Journal of Consulting Psychology*, **16**, 319–324.

Fonagy, P., & Target, M. (1994). The efficacy of psychoanalysis for children with disruptive disorders. *Journal of the American Academy of Child and Adolescent Psychiatry*, **33**, 45–55.

Goldfried, M.R., & Wolfe, B.E. (1996). Psychotherapy practice and research: Repairing a strained alliance. *American Psychologist*, **51**, 1007–1016.

Heimberg, R.G. (1998). Manual-based treatment: An essential ingredient of clinical practice in the 21st century. *Clinical Psychology: Science and Practice*, **5**, 387–390.

Hibbs, E.D. (1998). Improving methodologies for the treatment of child and adolescent disorders: Introduction. *Journal of Abnormal Child Psychology*, **26**, 1–6.

Hoagwood, K., Hibbs, E., Brent, D., & Jensen, P. (1995). Introduction to the special section: Efficacy and effectiveness in studies of child and adolescent psychotherapy. *Journal of Consulting and Clinical Psychology*, **63**, 683–687.

Jacobson, N.S., Schmaling, K.B., Holtzworth-Munroe, A., Katt, J.L., Wood, L.F., & Follette, V.M. (1989). Research-structured vs clinically flexible versions of social learning-based marital therapy. *Behaviour Research and Therapy*, **27**, 173–180.

Kazdin, A.E. (1998). *Research design in clinical psychology* (3rd edn). Boston: Allyn & Bacon.

Kazdin, A.E. (2000). Developing a research agenda for child and adolescent psychotherapy. *Archives of General Psychiatry*, **57**, 829–836.

Kazdin, A.E., Bass, D., Ayers, W.A., & Rodgers, A. (1990). Empirical and clinical focus of child and adolescent psychotherapy research. *Journal of Consulting and Clinical Psychology*, **58**, 729–740.

Kendall, P.C. (1998). Directing misperceptions: Researching the issues facing manual-based treatments. *Clinical Psychology: Science and Practice*, **5**, 396–399.

Kendall, P.C., & Chu, B.C. (in press). Retrospective self-reports of therapist flexibility in a manual-based treatment for youths with anxiety disorders. *Journal of Clinical Child Psychology*.

Kendall, P.C., & Southam-Gerow, M.A. (1995). Issues in the transportability of treatment: The case of anxiety disorders in youth. *Journal of Consulting and Clinical Psychology*, **63**, 702–708.

Kendall, P.C., Flannery-Schroeder, E., & Ford, J.D. (1999). Therapy outcome research methods. In P.C. Kendall, J.N. Butcher, & G.N. Holmbeck (Eds), *Handbook of research methods in clinical psychology* (2nd edn; pp. 330–363). New York: John Wiley & Sons, Inc.

Kendall, P.C., Chansky, T.E., Kane, M.T., Kim, R.S., Kortlander, E., Ronan, K.R., Sessa, F.M., & Siqueland, L. (1992). *Anxiety disorders in youth: Cognitive-behavioural interventions*. Needham Heights, MA: Allyn & Bacon.

Kendall, P.C., Chu, B., Gifford, A., Hayes, C., & Nauta, M. (1998). Breathing life into a manual: Flexibility and creativity with manual-based treatments. *Cognitive and Behavioural Practice*, **5**, 177–198.

Kendall, P.C., Flannery-Schroeder, E., Panichelli-Mindel, S., Southam-Gerow, M., Henin, A., & Warman, M. (1997). Therapy for youths with anxiety disorders: A second randomized clinical trial. *Journal of Consulting and Clinical Psychology*, **65**, 366–380.

Kiesler, D.J. (1966). Some myths of psychotherapy research and the search for a paradigm. *Psychological Bulletin*, **65**, 110–136.

King, N.J., & Ollendick, T.H. (1998). Empirically validated treatments in clinical psychology. *Australian Psychologist*, **33**, 89–95.

Kinscherff, R. (1999). Empirically supported treatments: What to do until the data arrive (or now that they have)? *Clinical Child Psychology Newsletter*, **14**, 4–6.

Klerman, G.L., Weissman, M.M., Rounsaville, B.J., & Chevron, E.S. (1984). *Interpersonal psychotherapy for depression*. New York: Basic Books.

Lambert, M.J. (1998). Manual-based treatment and clinical practice: Hangman of life or promising development? *Clinical Psychology: Science and Practice*, **5**, 391–395.

Lambert, M.J., & Ogles, B.M. (1988). Treatment manuals: Problems and promise. *Journal of Integrative and Eclectic Psychotherapy*, **7**, 187–204.

Levitt, E.E. (1957). The results of psychotherapy with children: An evaluation. *Journal of Consulting and Clinical Psychology*, **21**, 189–196.

Levitt, E.E. (1963). Psychotherapy with children: A further evaluation. *Behaviour Research and Therapy*, **60**, 326–329.

Lonigan, C.J., Elbert, J.C., & Johnson, S.B. (1998). Empirically supported psychosocial interventions for children: An overview. *Journal of Clinical Child Psychology*, **27**, 138–145.

Luborsky, L., & DuRubeis, R. (1984). The use of psychotherapy treatment manuals: A small revolution in psychotherapy research style. *Clinical Psychology Review*, **4**, 5–14.

Mersch, P.P.A., Emmelkamp, P.M.G., Bogels, S.M., & van der Sleen, J. (1989). Social phobia: Individual response patterns and the effects of behavioural and cognitive interventions. *Behaviour Research and Therapy*, **27**, 421–434.

Mufson, L., Moreau, D., Weissman, M.M., Wickramaratne, P., Martin, J., & Samoilov, A. (1994). Modification of interpersonal psychotherapy with depressed adolescents (IPT-A): Phase I and II studies. *Journal of the American Academy of Child and Adolescent Psychiatry*, **33**, 695–705.

Mufson, L. Weissman, M.M., Moreau, D., & Garfinkel, R. (1999). Efficacy of interpersonal psychotherapy for depressed adolescents. *Archives of General Psychiatry*, **56**, 573–579.

Nathan, P., & Gorman, J.M. (1998). *A guide to treatments that work*. New York: Oxford University Press.

Nelson-Gray, R.O., Herbert, J.D., Herbert, D.L., Sigmon, S.T., & Brannon, S.E. (1990). Effectiveness of matched, mismatched, and package treatments of depression. *Journal of Behaviour Therapy and Experimental Psychiatry*, **20**, 281–294.

Ollendick, T.H. (1995). AABT and empirically validated treatments. *Behaviour Therapist*, **18**, 81–82.

Ollendick, T.H. (1999). Empirically supported treatments: Promises and pitfalls. *Clinical Psychologist*, **52**, 1–3.

Ollendick, T.H., & King, N.J. (1998). Empirically supported treatments for children with phobic and anxiety disorders: Current status. *Journal of Clinical Child Psychology*, **27**, 156–167.

Ollendick, T.H., & King, N.J. (2000). Empirically supported treatments for children and adolescents. In P.C. Kendall (Ed.), *Child and adolescent therapy: Cognitive behavioural procedures* (2nd edn; pp. 386–425). New York: Guilford Publications.

Ost, L.G., Jerremalm, A., & Johansson, J. (1981). Individual response patterns and the effects of different behavioural methods in the treatment of claustrophobia. *Behaviour Research and Therapy*, **20**, 445–560.

Patterson, G.R., & Gullion, M.E. (1968). *Living with children: New methods for parents and teachers*. Champaign, IL: Research Press.

Persons, J.B. (1998). Paean to data. *Behaviour Therapist*, **21**, 123.

Persons, J.B., & Silberschatz, G. (1998). Are results of randomised controlled trials useful to psychotherapists? *Journal of Consulting and Clinical Psychology*, **66**, 126–135.

Pisterman, S., Firestone, P., McGrath, P., Goodman, J.T., Webster, I., Mallory, R., & Goffin, B. (1992). The effects of parent training on parenting stress and sense of competence. *Canadian Journal of Behavioural Science*, **24**, 41–58.

Pisterman, S., McGrath, P., Firestone, P., Goodman, J.T., Webster, I., & Mallory, R. (1989). Outcome of parent-mediated treatment of preschoolers with ADD with hyperactivity. *Journal of Consulting and Clinical Psychology*, **57**, 628–635.

Roth, A., Fonagy, P., Parry, G., & Target, M. (1996). *What works for whom? A critical review of psychotherapy research*. New York: Guilford Press.

Sackett, D., Richardson, W., Rosenberg, W., & Haynes, B. (1997). *Evidence-based medicine*. London: Churchill Livingston.

Sackett, D., Richardson, W., Rosenberg, W., & Haynes, B. (2000). *Evidence-based medicine* (2nd edn). London: Churchill Livingston.

Schulte, D., Kunzel, R., Pepping, G., & Schulte-Bahrenberg, T. (1992). Tailor-made versus standardized therapy of phobic patients. *Advances in Behaviour Research and Therapy*, **14**, 67–92.

Seligman, M.E.P. (1995). The effectiveness of psychotherapy. *American Psychologist*, **50**, 965–974.

Silverman, W.H. (1996). Cookbooks, manuals, and paint-by-numbers: Psychotherapy in the 90's. *Psychotherapy*, **33**, 207–215.

Smith, E.W.L. (1995). A passionate, rational response to the "manualization" of psychotherapy. *Psychotherapy Bulletin*, **33** (2), 36–40.

Strosahl, K. (1998). The dissemination of manual-based psychotherapies in managed care: Promises, problems, and prospects. *Clinical Psychology: Science and Practice*, **5**, 382–386.

Strupp, H.H., & Anderson, T. (1997). On the limitations of therapy manuals. *Clinical Psychology: Science and Practice*, **4**, 76–82.

Strupp, H.H., & Binder, J.L. (1984). *Psychotherapy in a new key: A guide to time-limited dynamic psychotherapy*. New York: Basic Books.

Task Force on Promotion and Dissemination (1995). Training in and disseminaiton of empirically validated treatments: Report and recommendations. *The Clinical Psychologist*, **48**, 3–23.

Tynan, W.D., Schuman, W., & Lampert, N. (1999). Concurrent parent and child therapy groups for externalising disorders: From the laboratory to the world of managed care. *Cognitive and Behavioural Practice*, **6**, 3–9.

Weersing, V.R., & Weisz, J.R. (2002). Mechanisms of action in youth psychotherapy. *Journal of Child Psychology and Psychiatry*, **43**, 3–29.

Weiss, B., Catron, T., Harris, V., & Phung, T.M. (1999). The effectiveness of traditional child psychotherapy. *Journal of Consulting and Clinical Psychology*, **67**, 82–94.

Weisz, J.R., Huey, S.J., & Weersing, V.R. (1998). Psychotherapy outcome research with children and adolescents: The state of the art. In T.H. Ollendick & R.J. Prinz (Eds), *Advances in clinical child psychology* (vol. 20; pp. 49–91). New York: Plenum Publishing.

Weisz, J.R., Donenberg, G.R., Han, S.S., & Weiss, B. (1995). Bridging the gap between laboratory and clinic in child and adolescent psychotherapy. *Journal of Consulting and Clinical Psychology*, **63**, 688–701.

Weisz, J.R., Weiss, B., Alicke, M.D., & Klotz, M.L. (1987). Effectiveness of psychotherapy with children and adolescents: A meta-analysis for clinicians. *Journal of Consulting and Clinical Psychology*, **55**, 542–549.

Weisz, J.R., Weiss, B., Han, S.S., Granger, D.G., & Morton, T. (1995). Effects of psychotherapy with children and adolescents revisited: A meta-analysis of treatment outcome studies. *Psychological Bulletin*, **117**, 450–468.

Wilson, G.T. (1996a). Manual-based treatments: The clinical application of research findings. *Behaviour Research and Therapy*, **34**, 295–314.

Wilson, G.T. (1996b). Empirically validated treatments: Reality and resistance. *Clinical Psychology: Science and Practice*, **3**, 241–244.

Wilson, G.T. (1998). The clinical utility of randomized controlled trials. *International Journal of Eating Disorders*, **24**, 13–30.

Zvolensky, M.J., & Eiffert, G.H. (1998). Standardized treatments: Potential ethical issues for behaviour therapists? *Behaviour Therapist*, **21**, 1–3.

Zvolensky, M.J., & Eiffert, G.H. (1999). Potential ethical issues revisited: A reply to Persons. *Behaviour Therapist*, **22**, 40.

CHAPTER 2

Developmental Issues in Evidence-Based Practice

Grayson N. Holmbeck

Rachel Neff Greenley

and

Elizabeth A. Franks

Loyola University Chicago, USA

INTRODUCTION

Suppose that a 5-year-old and a 15-year-old are referred for problematic levels of aggressive behaviour. Although the presenting symptoms for the two children are similar, it is unlikely that identical treatments could be provided with equivalent effectiveness to both children. Multiple developmental differences between young children and adolescents would likely necessitate the use of different treatment strategies for children of different ages. Unfortunately, however, we know little about how or when a given treatment should be modified for use with children functioning at different developmental levels. That is, the proposition that treatment outcomes for children and adolescents will be enhanced if clinicians attend to developmental issues is largely an untested assumption. On the other hand, it is our contention that the effectiveness of child and adolescent treatments will be improved if treatment is tailored to the developmental level of the target child, although we acknowledge that more research is needed on this issue (Holmbeck et al., 2000; Holmbeck & Updegrove, 1995; Kendall, Lerner, & Craighead, 1984; Ollendick, Grills, & King, 2001; Shirk, 1988, 1999, 2001; Silverman & Ollendick, 1999; Weisz, 1997; Weisz & Hawley, 2002). The goal of this chapter is to provide recommendations to clinicians and researchers for ways that developmental issues can be incorporated into child treatment as well as treatment outcome research. Before providing such recommendations, we will discuss what is meant by a

Correspondence to Grayson N. Holmbeck, Loyola University Chicago, Department of Psychology, 6525 N. Sheridan Road, Chicago, IL 60626; email: gholmbe@luc.edu

Handbook of Interventions that Work with Children and Adolescents: Prevention and Treatment.
Edited by P.M. Barrett and T.H. Ollendick. © 2004 John Wiley & Sons, Ltd. ISBN 0-470-84453-1.

developmentally oriented treatment. We will also examine the degree to which existing treatments are, in fact, developmentally oriented.

WHAT MAKES A TREATMENT DEVELOPMENTALLY ORIENTED?

Prior to answering this question, we will explain what we mean by developmental level. A child's developmental level can be conceptualized as a snapshot at one point in time of the accumulation of predictable age-related changes that occur in an individual's biological, cognitive, emotional, and social functioning (Feldman, 2001). Although developmental level comprises all of these domains of functioning, researchers in the area of child treatment have largely focused on the cognitive domain, since many treatments designed for children and adolescents are predicated on the assumption that altering one's thinking is an important precursor to more adaptive functioning in emotional, behavioural, or social domains (Shirk, 2001). More generally, the course of developmental change varies across individuals, such that two children who are the same age may differ dramatically with respect to cognitive, emotional, physical, and social functioning (Eyberg, Schuhmann, & Rey, 1998). Moreover, there are developmental and age variations in the nature and frequency of child symptomatology, with the same behaviours that are developmentally normative at younger ages becoming developmentally atypical at later ages (e.g., temper tantrums; Kazdin, 1993). We also know that the same underlying psychopathology may be expressed differently at different stages of development (i.e., heterotypic continuity) and that two children who exhibit the same level of psychopathology may have reached that level of pathology along very different pathways (i.e., equifinality; Cicchetti & Rogosch, 2002; Ollendick, Grills, & King, 2001).

A developmentally-oriented treatment takes into account the critical developmental tasks and milestones relevant to a particular child's or adolescent's presenting problems (e.g., development of age-appropriate same-sex friendships, self-control, and emotion regulation in early and middle childhood; pubertal development and development of behavioural autonomy and social perspective-taking during adolescence). Such a treatment would also be flexible enough that therapists could choose which presenting symptoms to prioritize, depending on the degree to which each of the symptoms is developmentally atypical (Weisz & Hawley, 2002). For example, an adolescent might present with inappropriately low levels of behavioural self-control (e.g., poor anger management, high levels of risk-taking) as well as moderate levels of parent–adolescent conflict. The therapist might determine that the former is more developmentally atypical and problematic than the latter, thus necessitating a focus on self-control difficulties in treatment. A developmentally-sensitive treatment would also be tailored to take into account the developmental level of the child or adolescent (Forehand & Wierson, 1993); in fact, different versions of the same treatment may be needed to serve children over a wide age range. For example, it may be that a less complex version of a treatment is provided for children at lower cognitive developmental levels, with a more sophisticated version being provided for those at higher levels (Shirk, 2001). Indeed, many cognitive-behavioural treatments require that children be able to evaluate and change their own thought processes as well as consider links between their own thinking and their subsequent emotional states—skills that require more advanced cognitive abilities (Shirk, 2001). Finally, a treatment that is developmentally-oriented would take a child's current social context into account (Forehand & Wierson, 1993). Thus, in early childhood, parents may be incorporated into the treatment, whereas during adolescence, relations with peers are more likely to be considered.

Given this examination of factors that make treatments developmentally-sensitive, we now examine the degree to which current treatments and treatment outcome studies are sensitive to developmental issues.

ARE CURRENT CHILD AND ADOLESCENT TREATMENTS DEVELOPMENTALLY-ORIENTED?

In general, the answer to this question is "no" (Holmbeck et al., 2000; Weisz & Hawley, 2002). For example, Holmbeck and colleagues (2000) conducted a review of recent treatment outcome studies employing cognitive-behavioural treatments (CBT) with adolescents. Of the 34 studies reviewed, only 26% (9 of 34) considered developmental issues when discussing the design or evaluation of the treatment. Of these nine studies, only one examined a developmental variable (i.e., age) as a moderator of treatment effects. Some of these developmentally-oriented studies considered various adolescent developmental issues in the design of the treatments (e.g., the advantages and disadvantages of parental involvement in treatment, the use of outcome measures developed specifically for adolescents) whereas others included developmentally-oriented interpretations of treatment outcome findings. Authors of book chapters, literature reviews, and meta-analyses were more likely than authors of empirical papers to consider developmental issues when discussing the literature on CBT (43%; 20 of 46 review articles; see Holmbeck et al., 2000). Although many authors suggest possible adaptations of treatment manuals to make them more developmentally sensitive, few provide methods for doing so (Weisz & Hawley, 2002). Several authors recommend that the therapist assess an adolescent's cognitive developmental level; again, little advice has been forthcoming for how to do this (although, see Bierman, 1988, and Ollendick & Vasey, 1999, for exceptions). Finally, almost half of the authors of literature reviews and book chapters discuss developmental variability in relation to the course of psychopathology (e.g., child and adolescent depression); unfortunately, little guidance is provided for how this information can be taken into account when designing treatments. In summary, most of those who study outcomes of CBT for adolescent clients do not mention developmental issues. Of those who do, there is little information regarding how such issues could be incorporated into the treatment process.

In their comprehensive review of the literature on the treatment of adolescents, Weisz and Hawley (2002) examined 25 empirically supported psychotherapies that have been used with children and adolescents. According to these authors, 14 of the 25 therapies have been shown to be effective with adolescents. Interestingly, seven are downward adaptations of treatments originally designed for adults and six are upward adaptations of treatments originally designed for children, leaving only one that was developed specifically for adolescents (Henggeler et al., 1998). In other words, few of the 14 empirically supported treatments that have been used with adolescents take into account the primary developmental tasks of adolescence. Thus, at least in the literature on adolescents, little attention has been paid to developmental issues in the design, implementation, or evaluation of treatments.

Meta-analyses

Meta-analyses have focused on the age of children or adolescents (a proxy for cognitive developmental level) as a potential moderator of the effectiveness of cognitive-behaviour therapy (CBT; e.g., Durlak, Fuhrman, & Lampman, 1991; Dush, Hirt, & Schroeder, 1989; also see Weisz et al., 1995). In general, the techniques of CBT emphasize self-reflection and metacognition (thinking about one's thinking), consequential thinking (reflecting on the outcome of a particular pattern of thinking), and consideration of future possibilities (thinking about how changes in one's thinking might affect one's life in the future). As such, proponents of cognitive and cognitive-behavioural theories maintain that interventions will be more effective for those functioning at more advanced levels of cognitive development (e.g., Shirk, 2001). Results of meta-analyses focusing on CBT are consistent with this contention (Durlak et al., 1991; Dush et al., 1989); effect sizes for adolescents (presumably those in the formal operational stage of Piagetian development) are nearly twice the magnitude of effect sizes for younger children (those in the pre-operational or concrete operational stages of development; although see Keating, 1990, and Moshman, 1998, for critiques of Piaget's stage theory). Of course, there are disadvantages in using age as a proxy for cognitive-developmental level (Durlak, Fuhrman, & Lampman, 1991; Kazdin, 1993; Weisz & Hawley, 2002). For example, it is possible that developmental variables other than cognitive-developmental level (which differ across age) could account for these findings. Moreover, age is likely to be a weak proxy for cognitive-developmental level given the vast heterogeneity in cognitive development, even within adolescents the same age (Keating, 1990). But, given that few researchers who evaluate outcomes of CBT actually include measures of cognitive-developmental level in their research protocols, meta-analysts have not had access to data on more sophisticated measures of developmental level and have, therefore, chosen to rely on age as an approximation.

Examples of Treatment Outcome Studies: Taking Development into Account

In addition to the meta-analyses, researchers have attempted to assess the impact of developmental level on treatment outcome. In general, this body of developmentally-sensitive research has focused on the effectiveness of cognitive, behavioural, or cognitive-behavioural interventions across different domains of child and adolescent adjustment. Rather than attempting to provide an exhaustive review of this literature, a few programs of research will be highlighted.

For example, researchers have considered the impact of developmental factors on the effectiveness of parent-training programs in reducing disruptive behaviour disorders (Dishion & Patterson, 1992; Forehand & Wierson, 1993; Ruma, Burke, & Thompson, 1996). Developmental theory suggests that the effectiveness of parent training may differ across early childhood, middle childhood, and adolescence for several reasons (Forehand & Wierson, 1993). First, as children progress through middle childhood and adolescence, the peer group takes on an increasingly significant role (Holmbeck et al., 2000). Indeed, a large body of literature has documented the salience of the peer group as both a motivator and reinforcer of behaviour during adolescence. Moreover, comparatively less time is spent with parents during this period. Second, the period of adolescence is characterized by an increased desire for autonomy as children traverse the early adolescent developmental period (i.e., increases in emotional and behavioural autonomy; Holmbeck et al., 2000). Based on such developmental changes, it might be anticipated that traditional parent-training programs would be less effective for older children and adolescents. Guided by the above theoretical predictions, Dishion and Patterson (1992) focused on two groups of children with behavioural problems, those in early childhood (ages 2 years, 6 months to 6 years, 6 months) and those in middle childhood (ages 6 years, 6 months to 12 years, 5 months). Results of their investigation suggested that, although the effectiveness of the parent training did not vary as a function of the child's age, younger children demonstrated more clinically significant change than did older children, even after eliminating subjects who were in the subclinical range prior to treatment. Moreover, early termination from treatment was more common in the older group.

Extending these findings, Ruma, Burke, and Thompson (1996) examined the impact of parent-training on three groups of children with disruptive behaviour disorders: those in early childhood (2 to 5 years), those in middle childhood (6 to 11 years), and those in adolescence (12 to 16 years). Results of their investigation supported Dishion and Patterson's (1992) previous work such that more young children fell in the subclinical range following intervention, although adolescents evidenced the most severe problems relative to the other groups at pre-treatment.

A separate line of research conducted by Schleser and colleagues has focused on measures of cognitive developmental level as moderators of CBT effectiveness (Borden et al., 1987; Schleser et al., 1984; Schleser, Meyers, & Cohen, 1981). These researchers argued that the impact of their self-instructional training program should be greater in children functioning at higher levels of cognitive development because more cognitively sophisticated children would be better able to systematically apply problem-solving strategies and employ recursive thought processes (Forehand & Wierson, 1993; Ollendick & Cerny, 1981). Schleser and associates (1981, 1984) found support for their central thesis in samples of pre-operational and concrete operational normal children. Specifically, both groups of children benefited from training and made gains in terms of their problem-solving skills, but children who had more advanced levels of cognitive development evidenced significantly better performance on perceptual perspective-taking tasks and were better able to generalize their learning to different perspective-taking tasks after being coached in appropriate self-instructions.

Finally, Fantuzzo and colleagues (1996) considered a critical social developmental milestone by targeting children's peer play in the treatment of socially withdrawn, maltreated pre-school children. Play activities were the focus of this program because peer play is the primary means by which pre-schoolers learn rules for social behaviour; such learning may be less well developed in withdrawn children. For this treatment, socially withdrawn children were paired with peers who exhibited well-developed adaptive play skills. Findings suggested that, relative to controls, children in the treatment condition (regardless of maltreatment status) evidenced gains in their prosocial behaviours and self-concept, as well as decreases in their antisocial behaviour.

Unfortunately, examples such as these are rare; most clinicians and investigators do not consider developmental issues when designing, conducting, or evaluating a treatment. Given the potential utility of considering developmental issues in both clinical and empirical work and given the lack of attention to such issues in past work, we now provide recommendations to both clinicians and researchers for ways that developmental issues can be incorporated into treatments and treatment outcome research.

RECOMMENDATIONS FOR CLINICIANS

Recommendation 1: Read Developmentally-Oriented Journals

It is recommended that therapists subscribe to journals such as *Development and Psychopathology*, *Child Development*, *Developmental Psychology*, and the *Journal of Research on Adolescence*. All of these journals regularly publish papers that examine clinical issues within a developmental context. Also, outlets such as the *Journal of Consulting and Clinical Psychology*, the *Journal of Clinical Child and Adolescent Psychology*, the *Journal of Child Psychology and Psychiatry*, and *Clinical Child and Family Psychology Review* often publish papers that integrate developmental and clinical issues and the American Psychological Association publishes abstracts from developmental and clinical journals as part of their PsycSCAN series (PsycSCAN: Developmental Psychology and PsycSCAN: Clinical Psychology). Therapists are more likely to stay current with the developmental literature if training programs integrate their clinical-child programming with offerings from a developmental program. Finally, clinicians should be attentive to the growing literature on empirically supported treatments (see Chapter 1).

Recommendation 2: Acquire Knowledge of Developmental Level, Norms, Tasks, and Milestones

In Table 2.1 we review important developmental stages and milestones that are relevant at different ages and developmental periods (based on Arnett, 2000; Feldman, 2001; Forehand & Wierson, 1993; Holmbeck et al., 2000). One implication of this list of milestones is that therapists who work with children and adolescents may not only need to address a client's presenting symptoms (e.g., ADHD and aggressiveness) but also the normative skills (e.g., self-control, emotion regulation) that the child failed to develop as a consequence of having a severe behaviour problem (Shirk, 1999). It is also clear that the context and targets of treatment change dramatically as one

Table 2.1 Developmental stages and milestones

Infancy (0–2 years)	• Infants explore world via direct sensory/motor contact • Emergence of emotions • Object permanence and separation anxiety develop • Critical attachment period: secure parent–infant bond promotes trust and healthy growth of infant; insecure bonds create distrust and distress for infant • Initial use of sounds and words to communicate • Piaget's Sensorimotor stage
Toddler/pre-school years (2–6 years)	• Use of multiple words and symbols to communicate • Learns self-care skills • Mainly characterized by egocentricity, but pre-schoolers appreciate differences in perspectives of others • Use of imagination, engagement in "pretend" play • Increasing sense of autonomy and control of environment • Develops school readiness skills • Piaget's Pre-operational stage
Middle childhood (6–10 years)	• Develops social, physical, and academic skills • Logical thinking and reasoning develops • Increased interaction with peers • Increasing self-control and emotion regulation • Piaget's Concrete Operational stage
Adolescence (10–18 years)	• Pubertal development; sexual development • Development of metacognition (i.e., use of higher-order strategizing in learning; thinking about one's own thinking) • Higher cognitive skills develop, including abstraction, consequential thinking, hypothetical reasoning, and perspective-taking • Transformations in parent–child relationships; increase in family conflicts • Peer relationships increasingly important and intimate • Making transition from childhood to adulthood • Developing sense of identity and autonomous functioning • Piaget's Formal Operations stage
Emerging adulthood (18–25 years)	• Establishment of meaningful and enduring interpersonal relationships • Identity explorations in areas of love, work, and worldviews • Peak of certain risk behaviours • Obtaining education and training for long-term adult occupation

Source: Reproduced by permission of the Guilford Press, New York, from Kazdin, A.E. & Weisz, J.R. (2003) *Evidence-Based Psychotherapies for Children and Adolescents*

moves across the first two decades of life. For example, whereas cognitive factors and peer relationships are less relevant when applying parent-training in families of pre-school children, such factors become highly salient in the treatment of those in middle childhood and adolescence (Forehand & Wierson, 1993).

As noted by Henggeler and Cohen (1984), when discussing treatment options for children and adolescents who have experienced trauma (e.g., sexual abuse), consideration of developmental stage is critical when selecting an appropriate treatment. For example, when working with an adolescent who has experienced a traumatic event, it is important that the therapist distinguish between recent traumatic events *versus* events that occurred during childhood which are now being revisited anew during adolescence. With a previously experienced event, an adolescent may view the event from a new perspective (e.g., he or she can comprehend the injustice of the events). Such a new perspective on an "old" event may necessitate additional therapeutic attention. Indeed, treatment for a given trauma (e.g., early child abuse, marital disruption) may need to be administered *intermittently* at different critical periods as the original trauma is re-experienced at new developmental stages. For example, if an adolescent was sexually abused as a child, new issues may arise for the adolescent as he or she develops physically and begins developing opposite-sex friendships.

Knowledge of developmental norms serves as a basis for making sound diagnostic judgments (and avoiding overdiagnosis and underdiagnosis). Unfortunately, the DSM system tends to ignore developmental issues when providing diagnostic criteria, despite evidence that symptoms of most child psychopathologies vary with age. For example, although young children often display obsessive-compulsive symptoms and separation anxiety as part of normal development (March & Mulle, 1998), such behaviours are not typical of adolescents. Knowledge of normative behaviour also has implications for decisions about treatment necessity and selecting the appropriate treatment. For example, strategies that focus on self-control may be more useful with older adolescents than behavioural programs where parents may be involved in the intervention.

With respect to developmental level, Weisz and Weersing (1999) detailed ways in which cognitive-developmental level affects the process of therapy and the types of treatments that are selected. A child's cognitive-developmental level may limit (or enhance) the degree to which the child understands the purpose and process of therapy. Similarly, the degree to which a child is able to employ abstract reasoning or perspective-taking skills may determine, in part, whether certain cognitive or insight-oriented techniques as well as strategies that require hypothetical thinking (e.g., role-playing exercises) can be implemented (Weisz, 1997). If a child does not have such skills, other therapeutic techniques may be necessary (e.g., therapists may need to demonstrate how to identify maladaptive thoughts by talking aloud during role plays; Piacentini & Bergman, 2001). Finally, knowledge of developmental level may guide the stages of treatment. When teaching a child increasingly complex levels of social interaction as part of social skills training, for example, the therapist can follow the developmental sequencing and stages of social play and social relationships (Selman, 1981). In other words, "development" can be the target of treatment. In this way, knowledge of developmental stages can guide decisions about termination because a child who is on track in accomplishing certain developmental tasks may be ready for termination.

Weisz and Hawley (2002) have argued that developmental research may not always be useful in guiding the treatment of individuals, since group trends that emerge in developmental research may not apply to a specific case. On the other hand, these authors provide some useful suggestions for ways to incorporate knowledge of developmental tasks into one's clinical work. First, they suggest that knowledge of developmental findings can *alert* the therapist to specific domains of functioning that are likely salient at a given age. In this way, the knowledgeable therapist is aware of what developmental issues to assess in an individual child client. Second, findings from developmental research can aid therapists in *prioritizing* certain presenting complaints over others, depending on which are most developmentally atypical or pathological. Finally, developmental research data can help the therapist in *selecting* treatment strategies or modules (from a more comprehensive set of treatments) that may be developmentally appropriate for a given individual.

Recommendation 3: Acquire Knowledge of Developmental Psychopathology

With such knowledge (as well as knowledge of norms and milestones; see above), one is in a better position to answer questions such as: In the absence of treatment, is it likely that this child's disturbance will change, abate, or stay the same over time? Is the observed disturbance typical of the problems that are usually seen for a child of this age? Without answers to these questions, the therapist may misdiagnose, be prone to apply inappropriate treatments, or be overly concerned about the presence of certain symptoms.

Developmental psychopathology is an extension of developmental psychology insofar as the former is concerned with variations in the course of normal development (Rutter & Garmezy, 1983). Research based on a developmental psychopathology perspective has informed us about the developmental precursors and future outcomes of child and adolescent psychopathology. Moreover, the field of developmental psychopathology has provided us with a vocabulary with which to explain phenomena that are relevant to therapists and researchers (e.g., risk and protective processes, cumulative risk factors, equifinality, multifinality, heterotypic continuity, resilience, developmental trajectories, distinctions between factors that produce symptom onset versus those that serve to maintain or exacerbate existing symptoms; Cicchetti & Rogosch, 2002; Olin, 2001). Developmental psychopathologists have also informed us about boundaries between normal and abnormal and how such distinctions are often blurred at certain stages of development for certain symptoms (e.g., substance abuse versus normative experimentation with substances; Cicchetti & Rogosch, 2002). In fact, some symptoms may even be reflections of children's attempts to negotiate normative developmental tasks (Siegel & Scoville, 2000).

Research indicates that the frequency and nature of most disorders vary as a function of age. Regarding changes in frequencies, Loeber and colleagues (1998) have documented age shifts in the prevalence of certain disorders (e.g., delinquency, substance use, sexual behaviours, etc.). Loeber and his colleagues have also documented important differences between children and adolescents with early onset problem behaviour (i.e., life-course persistent delinquency; Moffitt, 1993) versus those with later onset problem behaviours (i.e., adolescent-limited delinquency). Rutter (1980) reviewed changes that occur in behaviour disorders from childhood to adolescence and concluded that roughly half of all adolescent disorders are continuations of those seen in childhood. Those that emerge during adolescence (e.g., anorexia) tend to be quite different from those that began during childhood (e.g., ADHD), with the symptomatology of most child and adolescent disorders being manifestations of particular stages of development (e.g., for anorexia: pubertal and body image concerns during adolescence; for ADHD: self-regulation concerns during early childhood). The field of developmental psychopathology also addresses issues of continuity/discontinuity. Antisocial behaviour tends toward continuity insofar as antisocial adults have almost always been antisocial children (Loeber et al., 1998), but many depressed adults tend not to have been depressed children (Rutter, 1980). Similarly, schizophrenia is often not preceded by psychotic disorders during childhood (Rutter, 1980).

A clinician's knowledge of developmental psychopathology has a number of implications for the treatment of children and adolescents, as illustrated by the following examples. First, if we know, based on longitudinal studies, that a specific set of behavioural deficits in early childhood (e.g., externalizing behaviour symptoms; oppositional defiant disorder) tends to be associated with more serious pathology later in the individual's life (e.g., delinquency; conduct disorder), we can then treat the less severe antecedent disturbance before having to deal with the more serious subsequent disturbance. Early intervention is critical, since children with behavioural difficulties often "choose" environments that exacerbate psychopathology. Second, some children with certain developmental trajectories (e.g., girls who experience early pubertal development) may be at risk for subsequent behavioural symptoms (e.g., early sexual risk behaviours) and these individuals could be the targets of intervention. Third, the literature on peer relationships and later personal adjustment suggests that poor peer relationships early in childhood (e.g., peer rejection, aggressiveness, shyness, social withdrawal) place children at risk for developing later adjustment difficulties.

Although individuals such as those just described are often the focus of both universal and targeted *group* prevention efforts, the risk status of a given individual is also relevant within the context of *individual* treatment. In addition to focusing on behaviours that are most likely to place the individual at risk for future psychopathology, therapists can also identify opportunities for "protection" in the child's life (e.g., the availability of supportive non-parental adults) that can buffer the at-risk child from developing later adaptational difficulties.

The terms *equifinality*, *multifinality*, and *heterotypic continuity* are also likely to be useful to the clinician who works with children and adolescents. Interestingly, it appears that equifinality and multifinality are more the rule than the exception (Cicchetti & Rogosch, 2002; Ollendick, Grills, & King, 2001). Specifically, equifinality is the process by which a single disorder is produced via different developmental pathways ("children may share the same diagnosis but not the same pathogenic process"; Shirk, 1999, p. 65). For example, it is likely that two depressed adolescents will have very different aetiological factors present in their backgrounds. Shirk, Talmi, and Olds (2000) have suggested that treatment should not be guided exclusively by diagnostic status. Indeed, treatments may be unsuccessful for some children because the developmental precursors for their symptoms differ from the precursors of symptoms for children exhibiting successful treatment outcomes. Put another way, if equifinality proves to be an adequate explanatory model for most child psychopathologies, then treatments that are based on single causal/mediational models will likely not be effective for sizable proportions of affected children (Cicchetti & Rogosch, 2002). Some researchers have isolated developmentally-oriented typologies for certain psychopathologies that will be useful in matching treatment with pathology subtype (e.g., substance abuse, delinquency; Cicchetti & Rogosch, 2002).

Multifinality involves the notion that the same developmental events may lead to different adjustment outcomes (some adaptive, some maladaptive). For example, two young children who are sexually abused at the same level of severity may exhibit very different developmental trajectories over time. Given past research support for the concepts of equifinality and multifinality (Cicchetti & Rogosch, 2002), it appears that therapists are best served by gathering as much developmental and historical information as possible about a given child (in addition to what the therapist already knows about the aetiology of the disorder in question). Finally, heterotypic continuity involves the notion that a given pathological process will be exhibited differently with continued development. For example, behavioural expression of an underlying conduct disorder may change over time even though the underlying disorder and "meaning" of the behaviours remain relatively unchanged (Cicchetti & Rogosch, 2002).

Recommendation 4: Use Developmentally-Sensitive Treatment Techniques

Researchers who conduct interventions with young children (ages 4–8) often have success using techniques such as videotape modelling strategies or life-sized puppets rather than strict cognitive approaches (Eyberg, Schuhmann, & Rey, 1998). Most young children are unable to distinguish between different types of emotions; thus, drawings and pictures from media publications may be useful. The degree to which children are motivated by the possibility of acquiring future benefits of treatment also varies as a function of age and should be considered when addressing motivational issues (Ollendick, Grills, & King, 2001; Piacentini & Bergman, 2001).

Recommendation 5: Think Multisystemically

When working with older children and adolescents, consider the child's context (Forehand & Wierson, 1993; Henggeler et al., 1998; Kazdin, 1997; Reid, 1993). Working with adolescents, Henggeler and colleagues (1998) have documented the importance of attending to the multiple systems (family, peer, school) in which a child interacts. Similarly, if a family-oriented CBT approach is deemed optimal, the adjustment of parents and the quality of parenting should be assessed prior to including the parents as part of the intervention (Shirk, 1999). Incorporating peers and/or teachers as "therapists" may be a particularly useful strategy (Holmbeck et al., 2000), if age-appropriate.

Recommendation 6: Help Parents and Teachers to Become Developmentally Sensitive and Anticipate Future Developmental Tasks and Milestones

Adults will likely benefit from training in appropriate developmental expectations. Moreover, parents are likely to manage their children differently if they know, for example, that increases in parent–child conflict over certain issues are normative during the transition to adolescence than if they did not have this knowledge. Finally, parents can be guided to recognize signs that additional treatment is needed as their children move into new developmental periods (Forehand & Wierson, 1993). For example, therapists can discuss the normative tasks of adolescence with a family seeking treatment for a pre-adolescent. Discussing how such future tasks may affect a particular child with certain vulnerabilities may be helpful.

Recommendation 7: Consider Alternative Models of Treatment Delivery

Kazdin (1997) has provided a useful discussion of how different types of psychopathology may require different types of treatment delivery. Indeed, it is likely that most children will not derive maximum benefits from traditional time-limited treatment. Kazdin (1997) describes six such models of treatment delivery, which vary with respect to dosage, the number of systems targeted, and the degree to which the treatment is continuous or intermittent. He draws parallels between treatment for psychological symptoms and treatments for various medical conditions. Some psychopathologies may require continued care, much like ongoing treatment for diabetes. Treatment is modified over time but is never discontinued. Other psychopathologies may be best treated within a "dental" model. With this approach, ongoing psychological treatment is discontinued, but the child is monitored at regular intervals (particularly during important developmental transition points). Such treatment delivery models differ from the more standard notion of booster sessions. Booster sessions are typically used to reinforce treatment already provided; the types of care Kazdin (1997) is advocating are entirely different from treatment-as-usual.

Recommendation 8: Fill your Therapeutic "Toolbox" with Empirically Supported Treatment Modules

An analogy can be drawn between neuropsychological assessment strategies and the treatment of children and adolescents. In the area of neuropsychological assessment, both fixed battery and flexible assessment strategies have been advocated, with the latter becoming increasingly popular (Sattler, 2002). If an individual presents with a specific neuropsychological difficulty and a fixed battery approach is used, it is likely that many of the tests administered will be irrelevant to the presenting symptoms. Moreover, because of the time required to administer a complete battery, certain areas of functioning that are relevant to the presenting problems may be under-assessed. Advocates of the module/toolbox approach view treatment of children in a similar manner. Rather than using a more rigidly defined set of therapeutic techniques, it may make more sense to have a set of empirically supported techniques that can be used (or not used) as indicated (see Weisz & Hawley, 2002, for an example involving youth depression; also see Shirk, Talmi, & Olds, 2000).

RECOMMENDATIONS FOR RESEARCHERS

Recommendation 1: Generate a Developmentally-Oriented Conceptualization of the Disorder of Interest

Prior to developing or evaluating a treatment, it is critical that an investigator conceptualize the disorder in question from a developmental perspective. In this way, the investigator comes to understand developmental antecedents in relation to the onset, maintenance, and escalation of the disorder, the developmental course of the symptoms, and any subtypes (Kazdin, 1997; see Conduct Problems Prevention Research Group, 1992; and Weisz et al., 1992, for examples). Such an analysis will provide initial hypotheses concerning types of treatments that may be effective as well as mediational mechanisms that may account for significant treatment effects.

Recommendation 2: Include Measures of Developmental Level in Treatment Outcome Studies and Use Them to Evaluate *Moderational* Effects

If evaluations of age differences in treatment outcome were to become the norm, this would be progress for the field. But it would be even better if researchers included measures of developmental level, so that the moderational effects of these variables could be assessed.

A moderator is a variable that specifies conditions under which a given predictor is or is not related to an outcome (see top of Figure 2.1; Baron & Kenny, 1986; Holmbeck, 1997, 2002; Kraemer et al., 2001). For example, it may be that the impact of a given intervention on a given outcome varies as a function of some moderator (e.g., developmental level, age, gender, social class, etc.). In this way, the treatment may be more effective at one level of the moderator than at another level. By examining *moderators* of treatment effectiveness, we are interested in isolating conditions that determine when a treatment is particularly effective or ineffective.

A relevant moderator that we highlighted above is the cognitive-developmental level. Some of the examples discussed earlier focused on differences between children with pre-operational and concrete operational abilities. With regard to older children, Piaget (1972) identified adolescence as the period in which formal operational thinking typically emerges; adolescents who have achieved such abilities are able to think more complexly, abstractly, and hypothetically and are able to take the perspective of others and employ future-oriented thinking. Although, there is

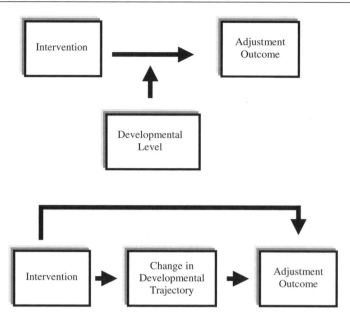

Figure 2.1 Moderational (top) and mediational (bottom) models of treatment outcome: The role of developmental level. Reproduced by permission of the Guilford Press, New York, from Kazdin, A.E. & Weisz, J.R. (2003). *Evidence-Based Psychotherapies for Children and Adolescents*

general agreement that a shift in thinking occurs during the transition from childhood to adolescence, critics of the Piagetian approach have suggested alternatives (Moshman, 1998). Proponents of the information-processing perspective, for example, have sought to isolate specific changes in cognitive activity that may account for advances in thinking. They maintain that there are significant advances in processing capacity or efficiency, knowledge base, and cognitive self-regulation (Keating, 1990). A third approach to cognitive development during adolescence is the contextualist perspective. Vygotsky (1978) suggested that psychological processes have a social basis. Of interest here are the child's socially-relevant cognitions such as one's understanding of significant others and their behaviours. The development of role-taking and empathy skills, the role of affect in understanding people, attributional processes in social situations, and prosocial behavior are a few of the social cognitive-developmental tasks that may influence progress in therapy (Nelson & Crick, 1999).

Given this list of cognitive changes during childhood and adolescence, it seems reasonable to propose that the degree to which a child has developed these skills will enhance or limit the potential effectiveness of a given psychotherapeutic intervention (Bierman, 1988; Downey, 1995; Forehand & Wierson, 1993; Ollendick & Vasey, 1999; Ollendick, Grills, & King, 2001; Wasserman, 1984; Weisz et al., 1992). It is even possible that more advanced cognitive abilities may exacerbate some types of psychopathology (e.g., depressogenic cognitions; Eyberg, Schuhmann, & Rey, 1998). Research on cognitive-developmental moderator variables can be of use to those who develop new cognitively-oriented treatments or those who wish to provide alternative versions of existing treatments.

How might therapists assess the cognitive-developmental level of their adolescent clients? Unfortunately, a straightforward, user-friendly method of assessing level of cognitive development across different cognitive subdomains is not available. On the other hand, researchers in the area of cognitive development have been successful in developing several measures, some of which may be relevant within the therapeutic context. Some examples include: (1) Fischhoff's measure of perceived consequences of risky behaviours (Beyth-Marom et al., 1993); (2) the Youth Decision-Making Questionnaire that assesses social decision-making in various peer and parent approval conditions (Ford et al., 1989); (3) the Selection Task (Chapell & Overton, 1998) which requires evaluation of 10 conditional "if . . . then" propositions that assess deductive reasoning abilities; (4) the Similarities subtest of the WISC-III (Wechsler, 1991), which assesses abstract reasoning abilities; and (5) Dodge's measures of social information processing (Dodge et al., 2002; also see Nelson & Crick, 1999, for other similar measures). Other more complex measures are also available, but these may be more useful to researchers than to clinicians (e.g., Flavell's and Selman's measures of role-taking, perspective-taking, and friendship development; Flavell, 1968; Selman, 1981).

Despite this list of measures, user-friendly measures of cognitive-developmental constructs are sorely needed. For example, a measure of metacognition would be useful to clinicians attempting to select the best fitting cognitive-behavioural therapeutic strategies. Clinician-friendly measures of social perspective-taking, empathy skills, self-control, future-oriented thinking, and decision-making would also have considerable utility, although it is important to note that paper-and-pencil measures may provide somewhat limited and less ecologically valid assessments of cognitive skills than would observations of real-life encounters (e.g., self-reports of decision-making strategies vs decision-making in an actual peer relationship situation).

Of course, cognitive-developmental variables are not the only developmentally-oriented variables that can serve as moderators of treatment impact. Weisz and Hawley (2002; also see Shirk, 2001) highlight one such psychological moderator: motivation. Here the focus is on the motivation to engage in treatment and the motivation for therapeutic change. This variable is "developmental" insofar as children of different ages may exhibit differing levels of motivation. As noted by Weisz and Hawley (2002), motivation may be lower in adolescence and particularly for those who are more peer-oriented (versus adult/parent-oriented). On the other hand, therapists who work with adolescents may be more successful in using "future benefits" as a motivator than those who work with children (Piacentini & Bergman, 2001). Regarding biological development, interventions focusing on early sexual risk behaviours may prove to be more effective with adolescents who have begun to experience the changes of puberty because such interventions may be viewed as more salient by this subset of adolescents (although we know that there are certain preventive benefits to providing such interventions in *pre*-pubertal children).

Examples of non-cognitive variables that could be included in studies of moderational effects are as follows (names of measures that could be used are included with references): pubertal development (Pubertal Development Scale; Petersen et al., 1988), social skills and friendship quality (Social Skills Rating Scale; Gresham

& Elliott, 1990; see Bierman, 1988, for methods of assessing conceptions of social relationships), emotion regulation and self-control (Child Affect Questionnaire; Garber, Braafladt, & Weiss, 1995; also see Greenberg et al., 1995, for other measures of emotion regulation), autonomy development (Decision-Making Questionnaire; Steinberg, 1987), and change in parent–child relationships (Issues Checklist; a measure of parent–child conflict; Robin & Foster, 1989). Of course, the types of variables included would vary depending on the treatment under investigation.

Recommendation 3: Examine *Mediators* of Treatment Effects

A significant mediator is a variable that specifies a mechanism by which a predictor has an impact on an outcome (see bottom of Figure 2.1; Baron & Kenny, 1986; Holmbeck, 1997, 2002; Kraemer et al., 2001). With mediation, the predictor (e.g., treatment condition) is associated with the mediator (e.g., change in developmental level) that is, in turn, associated with the outcome (e.g., adjustment). The mediator accounts for a significant portion of the relationship between predictor and outcome. If one has already established that a given treatment affects a given outcome, one is likely to pose questions regarding possible mechanisms by which the treatment affects the outcome of interest (Kazdin, 1997). From this perspective, a mediator is assumed to account for at least a portion of the treatment effect. Also, the mediator is viewed as causally antecedent to the outcome, such that change in the mediator is expected to be associated with subsequent changes in the outcome.

Interestingly, some may prefer to focus on the mediator (rather than the adjustment outcome) as the preferred target of treatment because of some known causal connection between the mediator and the outcome. For example, Treadwell and Kendall (1996) found that negative self-statements (or more accurately, change in self-statements) mediated the effect of treatment on anxiety severity. In this way, self-statements accounted for a portion of the treatment effect. Moreover, self-statements were not only a target of the treatment, but were also viewed as causally antecedent to anxiety severity. Perhaps more relevant to our discussion regarding developmental mediators, Guerra and Slaby (1990) found that change in problem-solving ability was associated with positive outcomes in delinquent behaviour. Arbuthnot and Gordon (1986) have found similar results with moral reasoning as a mediator. Finally, changes in parenting skills (Forgatch & DeGarmo, 1999; Martinez & Forgatch, 2001), family relations (Eddy & Chamberlain, 2000; Huey et al., 2000), and deviant peer affiliation (Eddy & Chamberlain, 2000; Huey et al., 2000) have been examined as mediators of treatment/adjustment effects.

Examining mediator models in the context of treatment outcome studies is a particularly useful research strategy because of the experimental (i.e., random assignment) aspects of the design. As noted by Collins and coworkers (2000), if the manipulated variable (i.e., treatment) is associated with change in the mediator which is, in turn, associated with change in the outcome, there is significant support for the hypothesis that the mediator is a causal mechanism. To further support this hypothesis, it would be important to demonstrate (via the research design) that changes in the mediator precede changes in the treatment outcome (Kraemer et al., 2001).

An important corollary of these findings and speculations is that developmental level can be the *focus* of treatment (Table 2.1; Eyberg, Schuhmann, & Rey, 1998; Shirk, 1999). That is, if research suggests that children who have failed to master certain developmental tasks or successfully navigate certain developmental milestones are more likely to exhibit certain symptoms, the developmental level of the child could be the target of the intervention. Returning to our example involving cognitive-developmental changes, adolescents may benefit from treatment that initially focuses on changing or accelerating cognitive-developmental processes (Shirk, 1999; Temple, 1997), particularly if lack of development in this domain has been linked with subsequent increases in symptoms. For example, treatment that affects children's perspective-taking abilities or their development of social-cognitive hostile attribution biases may ultimately produce a decrease in a child's level of aggression (Aber et al., 1998). Aiding adolescents in developing more intimate relationships with their same-age peers may affect his or her level of social anxiety (Ollendick & Hirshfeld-Becker, 2002). In the area of substance use, treatments that focus on an adolescent's level of future-oriented thinking or decision-making autonomy may facilitate his or her ability to make decisions that reduce health risks. Finally, for externalizing symptoms and ADHD, level of impulse control and self-regulation may be developmentally-oriented mediators of treatment impact (Mezzacappa, Kindlon, & Earls, 1999).

Moderated mediation is also possible. For example, it may be that increased perspective taking is a significant mediator of treatment effectiveness for aggression, *but* only for adolescent-aged participants. In this way, the mediational model is moderated by age. What are the implications of such a finding? Perhaps a different treatment is needed for younger children or it may be that this treatment works for younger children but the mechanism by which the treatment has an effect differs across age. Or, it may be that both are true; different treatments may be needed at different ages because the mediational mechanisms vary with age. For example, if we are attempting to treat externalizing symptoms in younger and older children, we may find that parent training works well with younger children and that change in parenting quality is a significant mediating mechanism. With older children, however, we may find that use of a cognitively-oriented approach works well and that a cognitive-developmental mediator (e.g., self-regulation) is a significant intervening causal mechanism. Despite the plausibility of these speculations, it is important to note that time-limited child treatments may not have dramatic effects on "development" (although see Keating, 1990, for an alternative perspective). If this were the case, the mediational role of developmental level would need to be reconsidered.

In models that include moderated mediation, the mediator could be non-developmental and the moderator could be developmental. For example, as noted earlier, Treadwell and Kendall (1996) found that negative self-statements mediated the impact of treatment on outcome (see Weersing & Weisz, 2002, for an extended discussion of non-developmental mediators of treatment effects). It could be that this mediational model is moderated by a cognitive-developmental variable such as metacognitive ability (i.e., thinking about one's own thinking). That is, it may be that the most favourable outcomes are found for those who possess more well-developed metacognitive skills, since such skills would likely enhance children's ability to identify their own negative self-statements (S. Shirk, personal communication, April, 2002).

Recommendation 4: Begin to Examine the Efficacy and Effectiveness of Alternative Modes of Treatment

As noted by Kazdin (1997), most studies of treatment outcome examine time-limited interventions. As reviewed earlier, there are other ways that we could conduct our treatments (e.g., continued care, intervention followed by regular monitoring). The effectiveness of these strategies should be compared with traditional treatments.

Recommendation 5: Build "Development" into Treatment Strategies

When discussing mediational effects, it was noted that developmental outcomes could be the target of treatment efforts. An example of this strategy is the Promoting Alternative Thinking Strategies (PATHS) program developed by Greenberg and colleagues (1995). The focus of their work is on increasing a child's ability to express and understand emotions in both low- and high-risk samples.

SUMMARY AND CONCLUSIONS

In this chapter, we have articulated the importance of tailoring psychological treatments to the developmental level of a child or adolescent, as well as the importance of considering developmental issues in designing and evaluating treatment approaches. Indeed, there is great potential for the integration of developmental research with clinical practice—but more research is sorely needed in this area. For this reason, we have provided recommendations for both clinicians and researchers who wish to integrate developmental principles into their work, including ways in which "development" can moderate and/or mediate the effects of treatment on outcome.

ACKNOWLEDGMENT

Completion of this manuscript was supported in part by research grants from the March of Dimes Birth Defects Foundation (12-FY01-0098) and the National Institute of Mental Health (R01-MH50423). The authors wish to thank Stephen Shirk and Joseph Durlak for comments on an earlier version of this chapter.

REFERENCES

Aber, J.L., Jones, S.M., Brown, J.L., Chaudry, N., & Samples, F. (1998). Resolving conflict creatively: Evaluating the developmental effects of a school-based violence prevention program in neighborhood and classroom context. *Development and Psychopathology*, **10**, 187–213.

Arbuthnot, J., & Gordon, D.A. (1986). Behavioural and cognitive effects of a moral reasoning development intervention for high-risk behavior-disordered adolescents. *Journal of Consulting and Clinical Psychology*, **54**, 208–216.

Arnett, J.J. (2000). Emerging adulthood: A theory of development from the late teens through the twenties. *American Psychologist*, **55**, 469–480.

Baron, R.M., & Kenny, D.A. (1986). The moderator-mediator variable distinction in social psychological research: Conceptual, strategic, and statistical considerations. *Journal of Personality and Social Psychology*, **51**, 1173–1182.

Beyth-Marom, R., Austin, L., Fischhoff, B., Palmgren, C., & Jacobs-Quadrel, M. (1993). Perceived consequences of risky behaviors: Adults and adolescents. *Developmental Psychology*, **29**, 549–563.

Bierman, K.L. (1988). The clinical implications of children's conceptions of social relationships. In S.R. Shirk (Ed.), *Cognitive development and child psychotherapy* (pp. 247–272). New York: Plenum.

Borden, K.A., Brown, R.T., Wynne, M.E., & Schleser, R. (1987). Piagetian conservation and response to cognitive therapy in attention deficit disordered children. *Journal of Child Psychology & Psychiatry & Allied Disciplines*, **28**, 755–764.

Chapell, M.S., & Overton, W.F. (1998). Development of logical reasoning in the context of parental style and test anxiety. *Merrill-Palmer Quarterly*, **44**, 141–156.

Cicchetti, D., & Rogosch, F.A. (2002). A developmental psychopathology perspective on adolescence. *Journal of Consulting and Clinical Psychology*, **70**, 6–20.

Collins, W.A., Maccoby, E.E., Steinberg, L., Hetherington, E.M., & Bornstein, M.H. (2000). Contemporary research on parenting: The case for nature and nurture. *American Psychologist*, **55**, 218–232.

Conduct Problems Prevention Research Group (1992). A developmental and clinical model for the prevention of conduct disorder: The FAST Track Program. *Development and Psychopathology*, **4**, 509–527.

Dishion, T.J., & Patterson, G.R. (1992). Age effects in parent training outcome. *Behavior Therapy*, **23**, 719–729.

Dodge, K.A., Laird, R., Lochman, J.E., Zelli, A., & Conduct Disorders Prevention Research Group (2002). Multidimensional latent-construct analysis of children's social information processing patterns: Correlations with aggressive behavior problems. *Psychological Assessment*, **14**, 60–73.

Downey, J. (1995). Psychological counseling of children and young people. In R. Woolge & W. Dryden (Eds), *The handbook of counseling psychology* (pp. 308–333). Thousand Oaks, CA: Sage.

Durlak, J.A., Fuhrman, T., & Lampman, C. (1991). Effectiveness of cognitive-behavior therapy for maladapting children: A meta-analysis. *Psychological Bulletin*, **110**, 204–214.

Dush, D.M., Hirt, M.L., & Schroeder, H.E. (1989). Self-statement modification in the treatment of child behavior disorders: A meta-analysis. *Psychological Bulletin*, **106**, 97–106.

Eddy, J.M., & Chamberlain, P. (2000). Family management and deviant peer association as mediators of the impact of treatment condition on youth antisocial behavior. *Journal of Consulting and Clinical Psychology*, **68**, 857–863.

Eyberg, S., Schuhmann, E., & Rey, J. (1998). Psychosocial treatment research with children and adolescents: Developmental issues. *Journal of Abnormal Child Psychology*, **26**, 71–81.

Fantuzzo, J.W., Sutton-Smith, B., Atkins, M., Meyers, R., Stevenson, H., Collahan, K., Weiss, A., & Manz, P. (1996). Community-based resilient peer treatment of withdrawn maltreated preschool children. *Journal of Consulting and Clinical Psychology*, **64**, 1377–1386.

Feldman, R.S. (2001). *Child development* (2nd edn.). Upper Saddle River, NJ: Prentice-Hall.

Flavell, J.H. (1968). *The development of role-taking and communication skills in children*. New York: Wiley.

Ford, M.E., Wentzel, K.R., Wood, D., Stevens, E., & Siesfeld, G.A. (1989). Processes associated with integrative social competence: Emotional and contextual influences on adolescent social responsibility. *Journal of Adolescent Research*, **4**, 405–425.

Forehand, R., & Wierson, M. (1993). The role of developmental factors in planning behavioral interventions for children: Disruptive behavior as an example. *Behavior Therapy*, **24**, 117–141.

Forgatch, M.S., & DeGarmo, D.S. (1999). Parenting through change: An effective prevention program for single mothers. *Journal of Consulting and Clinical Psychology*, **67**, 711–724.

Garber, J., Braafladt, N., & Weiss, B. (1995). Affect regulation in depressed and nondepressed children and young adolescents. *Development and Psychopathology*, **7**, 93–115.

Greenberg, M.T., Kusche, C.A., Cook, E.T., & Quamma, J.P. (1995). Promoting emotional competence in school-aged children: The effects of the PATHS curriculum. *Development and Psychopathology*, **7**, 117–136.

Gresham, F.M., & Elliott, S.N. (1990). *Social skills rating system: Manual*. Circle Pines, MN: American Guidance Service.

Guerra, N.G., & Slaby, R.G. (1990). Cognitive mediators of aggression in adolescent offenders: II. Intervention. *Developmental Psychology*, **26**, 269–277.

Henggeler, S.W., & Cohen, R. (1984). The role of cognitive development in the family-ecological systems approach to childhood psychopathology. In B. Gholson & T.L. Rosenthal (Eds), *Applications of cognitive-developmental theory* (pp. 173–189). New York: Academic.

Henggeler, S.W., Schoenwald, S.K., Borduin, C.M., Rowland, M.D., & Cunningham, P.B. (1998). *Multisystemic treatment of antisocial behavior in children and adolescents*. New York: Guilford.

Holmbeck, G.N. (1997). Toward terminological, conceptual, and statistical clarity in the study of mediators and moderators: Examples from the child-clinical and pediatric psychology literatures. *Journal of Consulting and Clinical Psychology*, **65**, 599–610.

Holmbeck, G.N. (2002). Post-hoc probing of significant moderational and mediational effects in studies of pediatric populations. *Journal of Pediatric Psychology*, **27**, 87–96.

Holmbeck, G.N., & Updegrove, A.L. (1995). Clinical-developmental interface: Implications of developmental research for adolescent psychotherapy. *Psychotherapy*, **32**, 16–33.

Holmbeck, G.N., Colder, C., Shapera, W., Westhoven, V., Kenealy, L., & Updegrove, A. (2000). Working with adolescents: Guides from developmental psychology. In P.C. Kendall (Ed.), *Child and adolescent therapy: Cognitive-behavioral procedure* (pp. 334–385). New York: Guilford Press.

Huey, S.J., Henggeler, S.W., Brondino, M.J., & Pickrel, S.G. (2000). Mechanisms of change in multisystemic therapy: Reducing delinquent behavior through therapist adherence and improved family and peer functioning. *Journal of Consulting and Clinical Psychology*, **68**, 451–467.

Kazdin, A.E. (1993). Psychotherapy for children and adolescents: Current progress and future research directions. *American Psychologist*, **48**, 644–657.

Kazdin, A.E. (1997). A model for developing effective treatments: Progression and interplay of theory, research, and practice. *Journal of Clinical Child Psychology*, **26**, 114–129.

Kazdin, A.E., & Weisz, J.R. (2003). *Evidence-Based Psychotherapies for Children and Adolescents*. New York: Guilford Press.

Keating, D.P. (1990). Adolescent thinking. In S.S. Feldman & G.R. Elliott (Eds), *At the threshold: The developing adolescent* (pp. 54–89). Cambridge, MA: Harvard University Press.

Kendall, P.C., Lerner, R.M., & Craighead, W.E. (1984). Human development and intervention in childhood psychopathology. *Child Development*, **55**, 71–82.

Kraemer, H.C., Stice, E., Kazdin, A., Offord, D., & Kupfer, D. (2001). How do risk factors work together? Mediators, moderators, and independent, overlapping, and proxy risk factors. *American Journal of Psychiatry*, **158**, 848–856.

Loeber, R., Farrington, D.P., Stouthamer-Loeber, M., & Van Kammen, W.B. (1998). *Antisocial behavior and mental health problems: Explanatory factors in childhood and adolescence*. Mahwah, NJ: Erlbaum.

March, J.S., & Mulle, K. (1998). *OCD in children and adolescents: A cognitive-behavioural treatment manual*. New York: Guilford Press.

Martinez, C.R., & Forgatch, M.S. (2001). Preventing problems with boys' noncompliance: Effects of a parent training intervention for divorcing mothers. *Journal of Consulting and Clinical Psychology*, **69**, 416–428.

Mezzacappa, E., Kindlon, D., & Earls, F. (1999). Relations of age to cognitive and motivational elements of impulse control in boys with and without externalizing behavior problems. *Journal of Abnormal Child Psychology*, **27**, 473–483.

Moffitt, T.E. (1993). Adolescent-limited and life-course-persistent antisocial behavior: A developmental taxonomy. *Psychological Review*, **100**, 674–701.

Moshman, D. (1998). Cognitive development beyond childhood. In D. Kuhn & R.S. Siegler (Eds), *Handbook of child psychology*. Vol. 2: *Cognition, perception, and language*, (pp. 957–978). New York: John Wiley & Sons.

Nelson, D.A., & Crick, N.R. (1999). Rose-colored glasses: Examining the social information-processing of prosocial young adolescents. *Journal of Early Adolescence*, **19**, 17–38.

Ollendick, T.H., & Cerny, J.A. (1981). *Clinical behavior therapy with children*. New York: Plenum Press.

Ollendick, T.H., & Hirshfeld-Becker, D.R. (2002). The developmental psychopathology of social anxiety disorder. *Biological Psychiatry*, **51**, 44–58.

Ollendick, T.H., & Vasey, M.W. (1999). Developmental theory and the practice of clinical child psychology. *Journal of Clinical Child Psychology*, **28**, 457–466.

Ollendick, T.H., Grills, A.E., & King, N.J. (2001). Applying developmental theory to the assessment and treatment of childhood disorders: Does it make a difference? *Clinical Psychology and Psychotherapy*, **8**, 304–314.

Olin, S. (2001). Blueprint for change: Research on child and adolescent mental health. *The Child, Youth, and Family Services Advocate*, **24**, 1–5.

Petersen, A.C., Crockett, L., Richards, M., & Boxer, A. (1988). A self-report measure of pubertal status: Reliability, validity, and initial norms. *Journal of Youth and Adolescence*, **13**, 93–111.

Piacentini, J., & Bergman, R.L. (2001). Developmental issues in cognitive therapy for childhood anxiety disorders. *Journal of Cognitive Psychotherapy*, **15**, 165–182.

Piaget, J. (1972). Intellectual evolution from adolescence to adulthood. *Human Development*, **15**, 1–12.

Reid, J.B. (1993). Prevention of conduct disorder before and after school entry: Relating interventions to developmental findings. *Development and Psychopathology*, **5**, 243–262.

Robin, A.L., & Foster, S.L. (1989). *Negotiating parent–adolescent conflict: A behavioral-family systems approach*. New York: Guilford.

Ruma, P.R., Burke, R.V., & Thompson, R.W. (1996). Group parenting training: Is it effective for children of all ages? *Behavior Therapy*, **27**, 159–169.

Rutter, M. (1980). *Changing youth in a changing society: Patterns of adolescent development and disorder*. Cambridge, MA: Harvard University Press.

Rutter, M., & Garmezy, N. (1983). Developmental psychopathology. In P.H. Mussen (Ed.), *Handbook of child psychology* (Vol. IV; E.M. Hetherington, Volume editor; pp. 775–912). New York: John Wiley & Sons.

Sattler, J.M. (2002). *Assessment of children: Behavioural and clinical applications* (4th edn). San Diego, CA: Jerome M. Sattler, Publisher, Inc.

Schleser, R., Meyers, A.W., & Cohen, R. (1981). Generalization of self-instructions: Effects of general versus specific content, active rehearsal, and cognitive level. *Child Development*, **52**, 335–340.

Schleser, R., Cohen, R., Meyers, A., & Rodick, J.D. (1984). The effects of cognitive level and training procedures on the generalization of self-instructions. *Cognitive Therapy and Research*, **8**, 187–200.

Selman, R.L. (1981). The child as friendship philosopher. In S.R. Asher & J.M. Gottman (Eds), *The development of children's friendships* (pp. 242–272). Cambridge: Cambridge University Press.

Shirk, S.R. (Ed.) (1988). *Cognitive development and child psychotherapy*. New York: Plenum.

Shirk, S.R. (1999). Developmental therapy. In W.K. Silverman & T.H. Ollendick (Eds), *Developmental issues in the clinical treatment of children* (pp. 60–73). Boston, MA: Allyn & Bacon.

Shirk, S.R. (2001). Development and cognitive therapy. *Journal of Cognitive Psychotherapy*, **15**, 155–163.

Shirk, S., Talmi, A., & Olds, D. (2000). A developmental psychopathology perspective on child and adolescent treatment policy. *Development and Psychopathology*, **12**, 835–855.

Siegel, A.W., & Scoville, L.C. (2000). Problem behavior: The double symptom of adolescence. *Development and Psychopathology*, **12**, 763–793.

Silverman, W.K., & Ollendick, T.H. (Eds) (1999). *Developmental issues in the clinical treatment of children*. Boston, MA: Allyn & Bacon.

Steinberg, L. (1987). Impact of puberty on family relations: Effects of pubertal status and pubertal timing. *Developmental Psychology*, **23**, 451–460.

Temple, S. (1997). *Brief therapy for adolescent depression*. Sarasota, FL: Professional Resource Press.

Treadwell, K.R.H., & Kendall, P.C. (1996). Self-talk in youth with anxiety disorders: States of mind, content specificity, and treatment outcome. *Journal of Consulting and Clinical Psychology*, **64**, 941–950.

Vygotsky, L. (1978). *Mind in society: The development of higher psychological processes*. Cambridge, MA: Harvard University Press.

Wasserman, T.H. (1984). The effects of cognitive development on the use of cognitive behavioural techniques with children. *Child and Family Behavior Therapy*, **5**, 37–50.

Wechsler, D. (1991). *Wechsler Intelligence Scale for Children—Third Edition*. San Antonio: The Psychological Corporation.

Weersing, V.R., & Weisz, J.R. (2002). Mechanisms of action in youth psychotherapy. *Journal of Child Psychology and Psychiatry*, **43**, 3–29.

Weisz, J.R. (1997). Effects of interventions for child and adolescent psychological dysfunction: Relevance of context, developmental factors, and individual differences. In S.S. Luthar, J.A. Burack, D. Cicchetti, & J.R. Weisz (Eds), *Developmental psychopathology: Perspectives on adjustment, risk, and disorder* (pp. 3–22). Cambridge, UK: Cambridge University Press.

Weisz, J.R., & Hawley, K.M. (2002). Developmental factors in the treatment of adolescents. *Journal of Consulting and Clinical Psychology*, **70**, 21–43.

Weisz, J.R., & Weersing, V.R. (1999). Developmental outcome research. In W.K. Silverman, & T.H. Ollendick (Eds), *Developmental issues in the clinical treatment of children* (pp. 457–469). Boston, MA: Allyn & Bacon.

Weisz, J.R., Rudolph, K.D., Granger, D.A., & Sweeney, L. (1992). Cognition, competence, and coping in child and adolescent depression: Research findings, developmental concerns, therapeutic implications. *Development and Psychopathology*, **4**, 627–653.

Weisz, J.R., Weiss, B., Han, S.S., Granger, D.A., & Morton, T. (1995). Effects of psychotherapy with children and adolescents revisited: A meta-analysis of treatment outcome studies. *Psychological Bulletin*, **117**, 450–468.

CHAPTER 3

Assessment and Diagnosis in Evidence-Based Practice

Wendy K. Silverman

and

Lissette M. Saavedra

Florida International University, USA

INTRODUCTION

As the chapters in this volume attest, the clinical trials conducted largely during the decade of the 1990s on internalizing and externalizing problems of children and adolescents established a strong empirical knowledge base about treatments that are likely "to work" in reducing these types of problems in youth. Despite the considerable progress made, there remain critical gaps in knowledge. Most critical are gaps relating to "why do these treatments work?" (i.e., mediators of change) and "for whom do these treatments work (or not)?" (i.e., moderators of change). The authors of this chapter hope that the present volume serves to stimulate research on these critically important questions and thereby close the existing gaps in knowledge.

In the meantime, thanks to the strong empirical knowledge base that has been established from the clinical trials, practitioners have never been as well posed as currently in being able to effectively help children and adolescents who suffer from psychological/psychiatric disorders. More specifically, practitioners now have some clear starting points from which to proceed when working with youth who have internalizing and externalizing problems. From these starting points, further development, adaptation, and innovation of interventions may unfold (Chorpita & Donkervoet, 2001; Silverman & Treffers, in press).

Based on the current content and structure of the evidence-based treatment research literature, clinical researchers and practitioners might presume

Correspondence to Wendy K. Silverman, Child and Family Psychosocial Research Center, Child Anxiety and Phobia Program, Department of Psychology, University Park, Florida International University, Miami, FL 33199; email: Silverw@fiu.edu

Handbook of Interventions that Work with Children and Adolescents: Prevention and Treatment.
Edited by P.M. Barrett and T.H. Ollendick. © 2004 John Wiley & Sons, Ltd. ISBN 0-470-84453-1.

(erroneously) that the starting points in evidence-based practice lie within the particulars of an intervention, whether it be in the conceptualization of the intervention or its implementation. The authors are grateful that the editors of this volume included a chapter on assessment and diagnosis as *assessment and diagnosis are the starting points, the launching pads, the lynch pins, of evidence-based practice.* Assessment and diagnosis are the starting points of evidence-based practice because in the absence of assessment and diagnosis, it is not possible to identify and select the evidence-based treatment that should be used and/or adapted. This is because the evidence-based treatments were developed and evaluated for children whose problems have been carefully identified and selected (e.g., anxiety disorders, attention deficit hyperactivity disorder). Thus, existing evidence-based treatments are successful in reducing youth's internalizing and externalizing disorders to the extent that the appropriate (evidence-based) treatment has been selected for use in reducing a given disorder or set of disorders. To ascertain which disorder or set of disorders should be targeted in treatment can be accomplished only through the use of evidence-based assessment and diagnostic procedures.

The present chapter focuses on providing evaluative summaries of the assessment and diagnostic procedures used in the randomized clinical trials for child and adolescent internalizing and externalizing problems as from these trials suggestions can be made regarding "evidence-based practice." The chapter also discusses issues involved in the use of these procedures. The chapter begins with a brief discussion about the classification of children's and adolescent's internalizing and externalizing behaviour problems and how classification impacts on methods of assessment and diagnosis. This is followed by a brief discussion about the importance of considering development when assessing and diagnosing children's and adolescent's problems.

CLASSIFICATION OF INTERNALIZING AND EXTERNALIZING CHILD BEHAVIOUR PROBLEMS

Although early views were that the classification of child problems failed to meet consensual scientific standards (i.e., reliability, validity) and lacked clinical utility (i.e., classification was done mostly for administrative rather than therapeutic purposes) (e.g., Achenbach, 1980; Ross, 1980; Rutter & Shaffer, 1980), these views no longer have merit and can be put to rest. Classification schemes have evolved that better meet consensual scientific standards with respect to reliability and validity (e.g., Achenbach & Edelbrock, 1984; APA, 1980, 1987, 1994; see Saavedra & Silverman, 2002). The classification scheme used in *all* the randomized clinical trials is the *Diagnostic and Statistical Manual of Mental Disorders* (DSM), mainly the third (1980), third-revised (1987), and fourth (1994) editions. The DSM uses a *categorical approach* to classifying. In a categorical approach, diagnostic entities are qualitatively discrete, with distinct boundaries between them represented by dichotomous outcomes (meets criteria for disorder, does not meet criteria for disorder) (Silverman, 1992, 1993).

Given the ubiquitous use of DSM in all the clinical trials, it would seem critical that practitioners who wish to implement evidence-based treatments use the DSM and ensure that children are receiving reliable and accurate DSM diagnoses, prior to implementing treatment. The authors acknowledge, however, that strict reliance on DSM diagnoses in the evidence-based treatments has been a matter of concern mainly stemming from limitations of the DSM-categorical perspective. This point is elaborated on in our concluding comments.

Another approach to classifying children's internalizing and externalizing behaviour problems is to use a *dimensional approach*. A dimensional approach assumes that entities are quantitative and continuous. Each dimension is assumed to be relatively independent and to consist of a cluster of behaviours that tend to covary with one another. Rather than assuming that the entities to be classified are qualitative and discrete as in the categorical approach, a dimensional approach assumes that the entities are quantitative, continuous, and linear. Seminal reviews (Achenbach & Edelbrock, 1978; Quay, 1979) on dimensional classification have indicated that despite the diversity across factor- and cluster-analytic studies (with respect to assessment instruments, type of population, and type of respondent) two broadband behavioural dimensions can be reliably obtained: internalizing and externalizing. Internalizing refers to behaviours such as anxiety, inhibition, shyness, immaturity, sadness, and social withdrawal. Externalizing refers to behaviours such as aggression, coercive behaviour, and a tendency toward delinquency.

Strengths associated with the dimensional perspective include the conceptualization of the child's problem in terms of his or her position along different behavioural dimensions. This allows for quantifying the degree of change observed and for conducting statistical comparisons to determine whether the change is statistically significant (e.g., from pre- to post-treatment for children in the treatment condition versus children in the control condition). It also allows for comparing the child's behaviour to normative standards to determine whether the change is clinically significant relative to other children of the same age and gender (Kendall & Grove, 1988). Most of the evidence-based treatment studies included dimensional methods of assessment in conjunction with categorical methods (i.e., DSM) and conducted statistical and clinical/normative comparisons.

Despite the advantages in using dimensional approaches, from a practical perspective, third party payers usually require practitioners to report the results of their treatments using DSM diagnoses, not the child's position on dimensional measures. Consequently, there is little incentive in clinic settings to complement diagnostic measures with dimensional measures. It is the authors' hope that over time the situation will change, and both categorical and dimensional approaches will be viewed as important, complementary facets of the assessment process.

Developmental Considerations

There is increased recognition of the importance of conceptualizing behaviour problems in children and adolescents within a developmental context. This recognition stems from the tenets of developmental psychopathology (Sroufe & Rutter, 1984), which is concerned with the origins and course of a disorder, including its precursors and sequelae, with respect to developmental level (Sroufe & Rutter, 1984). Developmental psychopathology emphasizes the importance of understanding how behaviour in youth compares to a set of developmental norms as well as the bi-directional transactions between the youth's behaviours and his or her socio-cultural environment, particularly across varying contexts such as school, home, or with peers (Cicchetti, Rogosch, & Toth, 1994; Silverman & Ollendick, 1999).

In considering development when diagnosing and assessing disorders in youth, there is general consensus in clinical child psychology and psychiatry that when time and funds allow multiple methods (e.g., interviews, questionnaires, observations) and multiple sources (e.g., child, parent, teachers, peers) are preferable over a single source and method (e.g., Mash & Terdal, 1988). *Multi-method assessment* is common in evidence-based treatment studies as various child problems may be more or less evident across different types of response systems (e.g., some children may display their problems via obvious, overt behaviour such as avoidance in some anxiety disordered cases; other children may display their problems via less overt behaviour but more by how they think about a given situation such as harmful catastrophizing thoughts in some anxiety-disordered cases). The manner in which children display their problems may also be influenced by development in that, for very young children, it may be preferable to use observational procedures, though as children develop, increased reliance may be made on self-report procedures. Multi-method assessment thus captures the complexities in which children's internalizing and externalizing problems may manifest and vary with development, and further allows for the evaluation of therapeutic changes across the response systems.

Multi-source assessment also is common in evidence-based treatment studies because research findings generally show relatively low levels of agreement among different sources in their ratings of children's behaviour problems (e.g., Achenbach, McConaughy, & Howell, 1987). The reason for low levels of agreement is not necessarily because one source is "right" and one source is "wrong," but because children and adolescents may display different levels or intensities of a given set of behaviours across settings. To the extent that certain problem behaviours, such as those associated with attention deficit hyperactivity disorder, often are impairing "in two or more settings (e.g., at school and at home)" (APA, 1994, p. 84) then this might suggest the presence of the actual clinical syndrome of attention deficit hyper-activity disorder. If, however, the problem behaviours are reported as occurring only at home by the parents, then this may be more suggestive of problematic parent–child interactional patterns rather than the clinical syndrome of attention deficit hyperactivity disorder. These types of circumstances underscore the impor-tance of obtaining information from multiple sources who have the opportunity to observe the youth in diverse settings in order to obtain as full and accurate a diagnostic picture of the youth as possible.

Obtaining multiple sources' perspectives is also important because the issue of whether different sources vary in their reliability of children's problem behaviours, depending on the type of child problem or behaviour (internalizing versus exter-nalizing) and the child's age (young children versus adolescents), remains generally unresolved (see Grills & Ollendick, 2002). For example, when it comes to internal-izing problems, Edelbrock (1985), using the highly structured Diagnostic Interview Schedule for Children, found that parents of younger children (aged 6–9 years) gave more reliable reports of their child's internalizing symptoms than the child's self-report; older children (aged 10–13 and 14–18 years) were more reliable reporters of their own internalizing symptoms than their parents (Edelbrock, 1985). Other studies using different data-capturing methods (e.g., child self-rating scales, parent rating scales, semistructured interviews) have found young children to be as reliable as parents in reporting internalizing symptoms (Epkins & Meyers, 1994; Silverman & Eisen, 1992; Silverman, Saavedra, & Pina, 2001). Given that "who is the more reliable source", for assessing and diagnosing children's internalizing disorders and symptoms remains unresolved and appears to vary with the specific data-capturing method as well as other factors (e.g., presence/absence of parental psychopathology, parent–child gender combination) it would seem that the "best" strategy for evidence-based practice is to obtain both children's and parents' interview data.

Although the authors would make a similar recommendation that *both* children's and parents' interview data should be obtained when assessing and diagnosing children's externalizing disorders and symptoms, it is worth noting that the research evidence is more consistent (relative to the child internalizing area) in showing that parents are more reliable informants of younger and older children's externalizing symptoms in comparison to younger and older children's self-reports of their own externalizing symptoms (Angold & Costello, 1996; Edelbrock, 1985, 1994; Epkins & Meyers, 1994; Schwab-Stone et al., 1994). In light of this, although child and parent interview data are recommended for use in evidence-based practice for externalizing disorders, increased reliance on parents (and other sources) might be placed on children's externalizing behaviours; other methods might be used as well, such as rating scales.

Relatedly, when assessing externalizing problems in evidence-based practice, it is more common to rely on teachers, particularly to administer to teachers behaviour checklists or rating scales, than when assessing internalizing problems. This is because research shows that teachers are not as reliable informants as children and parents for internalizing symptoms (Edelbrock, 1994). Research further shows that teachers are as reliable as parents in their ratings of younger and older children's externalizing symptoms (Edelbrock, 1994; Epkins & Meyers, 1994; Pelham et al., 1993). In addition, whereas teacher ratings for internalizing problems have not been found to be sensitive for detecting therapeutic change (Kendall, 1994), teacher ratings are sensitive for detecting change in externalizing problems (e.g., Pelham et al., 1993; Webster-Stratton, 1984).

EVALUATIVE SUMMARIES OF ASSESSMENT METHODS IN EVIDENCE-BASED TREATMENTS

The evaluative summary sections that follow are organized in accordance with the main assessment methods used in evidence-based treatment studies. The main methods are (a) diagnostic interviews, (b) parent rating scales, (c) child self-rating scales, and (d) observation techniques.

Diagnostic Interview Schedules

As indicated above, it is the authors' view that practitioners who wish to implement evidence-based treatments need to use the DSM and ensure that children are receiving reliable and accurate DSM diagnoses, prior to implementing treatment. This is important to do given that the evidence-based treatments "work" to the extent that the appropriate groups of children are receiving the given treatment for carefully identified problems (e.g., an exposure-based cognitive-behavioural treatment for a child with a diagnosis of a phobic or anxiety disorder). Thus, for evidence-based practice, diagnostic information needs to be gathered with structured or semistructured interview schedules, not unstructured, clinical interviews. This is because structured or semistructured interview schedules yield more reliable and valid information as variance attributed to interviewers and/or usage in diagnostic criteria is significantly reduced relative to unstructured, clinical interviews. Moreover, given the high rates of comorbid (co-occurring) disorders in youth, it is not simple to determine and prioritize the various problems children display. Interview schedules facilitate in making such determination and prioritization, reliably and accurately, and thereby assist in the selection of specific diagnoses/problem behaviours to be targeted in treatment.

Despite the clear advantages and benefits to using a structured or semistructured interview for evidence-based practice, clinicians often are wary of such interviews. As noted elsewhere, it is useful to think of the interview schedules as templates that can guide clinicians' questioning (Silverman & Kurtines, 1996). When viewed in this way, the interviews serve mainly as a tool to ensure that accurate and complete questioning occurs for the various disorders, not as rigid, inflexible scripts.

Most interview schedules are appropriate for use with children across a wide age range (as young as 6–8 years of age and as old as 16–18 years of age). The interviews generally do not require children to have extensive verbal expressive skills, and the interview questions tend to be geared toward the language capabilities of young children. Most take 60 to 90 minutes to administer, have undergone revision or modification to improve content and diagnostic reliability, and have accompanying parent versions (see Silverman, 1994).

In light of the previous discussion that different informants are likely to provide different perspectives or views about a given behaviour or set of behaviours, how does one weigh the information given by a child during the child interview and the parent during the parent interview? Given that there is insufficient research evidence to support clear guidelines for viewing information from one source as superior to another source, less complex compilations of information from multiple sources should be employed (Piacentini, Cohen, & Cohen, 1992), including consideration of a symptom as present if either child or parent endorses the symptom. Such "simple" algorithms are psychometrically superior to more complex algorithms, given the existing empirical knowledge base. Most of the existing interview schedules have provided further guidelines regarding the combining of child and parent interview data (see e.g., Albano & Silverman, 1996).

Table 3.1 presents information about the diagnostic interview schedules recommended for use in evidence-based practice. More specifically, these were the schedules used in the clinical trials to diagnose the targeted disorder or set of disorders and diagnostic rates showed improvement in the trials. The ages listed in Table 3.1 represent the age range of the youth who participated in the diagnostic reliability study. Although the interview schedules listed in the table can be used to assess and diagnose *all* the various types of child internalizing and externalizing disorders, the interviews' varying content and structure render some of them particularly applicable for certain disorders.

Table 3.1 Main diagnostic interviews used for assessment of DSM-IV disorders in evidence-based practice

Disorder	Diagnostic interview	Ages	Informants	Psychometric properties:
Anxiety disorders	Anxiety Disorders Interview Schedule for DSM-IV: Child and Parent Versions (ADIS for DSM-IV: C/P; Silverman & Albano, 1996; Silverman et al., 2001)	7 to 16 years	Child and parent	Kappa coefficients for anxiety disorders range from 0.80 to 0.92. Kappa coefficients for mood disorders, ADHD, and ODD range from 0.62 to 1.00
Mood	Schedule for Affective Disorders and Schizophrenia for School-Age Children (K-SADS; Ambrosini, 2000)	6 to 18 years	Child and parent	Kappa coefficients range from 0.90 to 1.00 for mood disorders. Kappa coefficients range from 0.55 to 0.80 for specific anxiety disorders, ODD, and CD diagnoses
Attention deficit hyperactivity	NIMH Diagnostic Interview Schedule for Children Version IV (NIMH DISC-IV; Shaffer et al., 2000)	9 to 17 years	Child and parent	Kappa coefficient for ADHD was 0.62. Kappa coefficients for specific anxiety disorders, MDD, ADHD, ODD, and CD diagnoses range from 0.55 to 0.86
Conduct	NIMH Diagnostic Interview Schedule for Children Version IV (NIMH DISC-IV; Shaffer et al., 2000)	9 to 17 years	Child and parent	Kappa coeffient for CD was 0.55. Kappa coefficients for specific anxiety disorders, MDD, ADHD, and ODD range from 0.51 to 0.86

Note: ADHD = attention deficit hyperactivity disorder. ODD = oppositional defiant disorder. CD = conduct disorder. MDD = major depressive disorder. DSM-IV = *Diagnostic and Statistical Manual of Mental Disorders* (4th edition)

Anxiety Disorders Interview Schedule for DSM-IV: Child and Parent Versions (ADIS for DSM-IV; Silverman & Albano, 1996). The ADIS for DSM-IV: C/P, a semi-structured interview appropriate for children between the ages of 7 and 17 years, has been the interview used in *all* the evidence-based anxiety treatment outcome studies (e.g., Barrett, 1998; Barrett, Dadds, & Rapee, 1996; Beidel, Turner, & Morris, 2000; Cobham, Dadds, & Spence, 1998; Flannery-Schroeder & Kendall, 2000; Hayward et al., 2000; Kendall, 1994; Kendall et al., 1997; Silverman et al., 1999a, 1996b; Spence, Donovan, & Brechman-Toussaint, 2000). Trained clinicians or other mental health professionals can administer the ADIS for DSM-IV: C/P and parallel versions are available for children and parents. The ADIS for DSM-IV: C/P has been translated into various languages including Spanish and Dutch (Siebelink & Treffers, 2001). The interview assesses all of the DSM-IV disorders appropriate for childhood and adolescence (e.g., separation anxiety disorder, social phobia, specific phobia, obsessive-compulsive disorder, posttraumatic stress disorder, panic disorder and agoraphobia) and mood disorders (e.g., major depression, dysthymia), and the externalizing disorders such as oppositional defiant disorder, attention deficit hyperactivity disorder, and conduct disorder.

NIMH Diagnostic Interview Schedule for Children Version IV (NIMH DISC-IV; Shaffer et al., 2000). The NIMH DISC-IV is the latest version of the DISC, based on DSM-IV criteria. The NIMH DISC and previous versions of the DISC have been the primary diagnostic interview schedules used in many of the evidence-based treatments of ADHD (e.g., MTA Cooperative Group, 1999; Pelham et al., 1993). As with previous versions of the DISC, the NIMH DISC-IV is a highly structured interview appropriate for children between the ages of 6 and 17 years. The NIMH DISC-IV can be administered by lay interviewers. Parallel versions are available for children and parents in both English and Spanish languages. The NIMH DISC-IV contains under 3000 questions used to assess over 30 DSM-IV psychiatric diagnoses including anxiety disorders (e.g., social phobia, separation anxiety disorder, specific phobia, panic, agoraphobia, generalized anxiety disorder, selective mutism, obsessive-compulsive disorder, post-traumatic stress disorder), mood disorders (e.g., major depressive episode, dysthymia), manic/hypomanic episode, attention deficit hyperactivity disorder, oppositional defiant disorder, and conduct disorder, among other psychiatric disorders.

Schedule for Affective Disorders and Schizophrenia for School-Age Children (K-SADS 2000; Kaufman et al., 1997). Similar to the NIMH DISC-IV, the K-SADS was one of the first structured interviews for children and has undergone several revisions. The K-SADS is the interview most often used in evidence-based treatment for depression and other mood disorders in children (e.g., Brent et al., 1993; Butler et al., 1980; Clarke et al., 1993; Fine et al., 1991; Lewinsohn et al., 1990; Reynolds & Coats, 1986; Stark, Reynolds, & Kaslow, 1987; Weisz et al., 1997).

The latest version of this interview, K-SADS-P/L (Present and Lifetime disorders) is DSM-IV compatible (Kaufman et al., 1997). The K-SADS-P/L is a semistructured interview appropriate for children between the ages of 6 and 18 years. The K-SADS-P/L can be administered by trained clinicians or other mental health professionals. The K-SADS-P/L assesses the major DSM-III-R and DSM-IV disorders appropriate for childhood and adolescence, including the internalizing disorders such as most of the specific anxiety disorders (e.g., generalized anxiety disorder, separation anxiety disorder, specific and social phobia, obsessive-compulsive disorder, post-traumatic stress disorder, panic disorder and agoraphobia), the most prevalent mood disorders (e.g., major depression, dysthymia), and externalizing disorders such as oppositional defiant disorder, attention deficit hyperactivity disorder, and conduct disorder.

Parent Rating Scales

Table 3.2 presents information about the parent rating scales, also referred to as behaviour problem checklists, recommended for use in evidence-based practice. These were the rating scales used in the clinical trials to assess the children's symptoms and the ratings generally showed improvements in the trials. Parent rating scales assess children's internalizing and externalizing behaviour problems using a dimensional approach, thereby offering several advantages. As noted previously, a main advantage is that practitioners can evaluate clinical significance by comparing the child's dimensional score with normative scores based on children of the target child's age and gender (Barkley, 1988). Additional advantages of problem behaviour checklists for use in evidence-based practice include: (1) ease and low cost in administering; (2) an objective scoring procedure, thereby minimizing the role of clinical inference and interpretation in the assessment process; (3) utility for a wide range of populations and problems; and (4) utility for obtaining information from multiple informants, as several of the parent behaviour checklists have versions for use by other sources such as the youth and teacher (e.g., Achenbach, McConaughy, & Howell, 1987; Silverman & Rabian, 1999; Silverman & Serafini, 1998).

The parent rating scale the authors would most recommend for use in evidence-based practice is the Child Behavior Checklist (CBCL; Achenbach, 1991) as the CBCL has been used in most of the clinical trials, including the anxiety/phobic (e.g., Barrett, 1998; Barrett, Dadds, & Rapee, 1996; Beidel, Turner, & Morris, 2000; Cobham et al. 1998; Flannery-Schroeder & Kendall, 2000; Kendall, 1994; Kendall et al., 1997; Mendlowitz et al., 1999; Silverman et al., 1999a, 1999b; Spence et al., 2000), mood (e.g., Jaycox et al., 1994; Lewinsohn et al., 1990), attention deficit hyperactivity (e.g., Anastopoulos et al., 1993; Hinshaw et al., 1997; Horn et al., 1990, 1991; MTA Cooperative Group, 1999), and conduct disorders trials (e.g., Webster-Stratton, 1984, 1990, 1994). Because parent rating scales are particularly useful for assessing children's externalizing problems, several other scales are recommended for use in evidence-based practice for assessing these types of problems. These include the Conners Parent Rating Scale (CPRS-R; Goyette, Conners, & Ulrich, 1978—used, for example, in Hinshaw et al., 1997; MTA Cooperative Group, 1999; Pelham et al., 1993), and Eyberg Child Behaviour Inventory (ECBI; Eyberg, 1980; Eyberg & Robinson, 1983—used, for example, in Eyberg, Boggs, & Algina, 1995; Webster-Stratton, 1984, 1990, 1994).

Child Self-Rating Scales

Table 3.3 presents information about the child self-rating scales recommended for use in evidence-based practice. These were the rating scales used in the clinical trials to assess the children's symptoms and the ratings generally showed improvements

Table 3.2 Main parent rating scales used for assessment of child behaviour problems in evidence-based practice

Symptoms	Instrument	Ages	Brief description	Psychometric properties
Anxiety, mood, attention deficit hyperactivity, and conduct	Child Behavior Checklist (Achenbach, 1991)	4 to 18 years	118 items; assesses a broad range of child behaviour problems including positive child behaviours and behaviour problems. Behaviour problems are assessed broadly using the externalizing and internalizing subscales or narrowly using the narrow-band subscales, which assess: withdrawn, somatic complaints, anxious/depressed, social problems, thought problems, attention problems, delinquent behaviour, and aggressive behaviour	Internal consistency: alpha coefficients range from 0.54 to 0.96; test–retest reliability range from 0.86 to 0.89
Attention deficit hyperactivity and conduct	Behaviour Assessment System for Children (Reynolds & Kamphus, 1992)	4 to 18 years	130 items; assesses a broad range of problem domains. Behaviour problems assessed include hyperactive, aggression, conduct problems, anxiety, somatisation, depression, atypicality, withdrawal, attitude to school and attitude to teacher, locus of control, sensation seeking, sense of inadequacy, social stress adaptability, leadership, social skills, study skills, self-esteem, and self-reliance	Internal consistency: alpha coefficients range from 0.76 to 0.90; test–retest reliability >0.90
	Conners' Rating Scales (Conners, 1990)	3 to 17 years	48 items; assesses five factors: conduct problems, learning problem, psychosomatic, impulsive-hyperactive, and anxiety	Internal consistency: alpha coefficients >0.90; test–retest reliability >0.90
Conduct	Eyberg Child Behaviour Inventory (Eyberg & Ross, 1978)	2 to 12 years	36 items; assesses symptoms of conduct disorder and yields a Total Problem Score and a Total Intensity Score	Internal consistency: alpha coefficients = 0.98; test–retest reliability range from 0.86 to 0.88

Table 3.3 Main child self-rating scales used for assessment of child behaviour problems in evidence-based practice

Disorder	Instrument	Ages	Brief description	Psychometric properties
Anxiety and phobia	Revised Children's Manifest Anxiety Scale (RCMAS; Reynolds & Richmond, 1985)	6 to 17 years	37 items; assesses symptoms of anxiety and yields a total anxiety score and three factor scale scores (Physiological Anxiety, Worry/Oversensitivity, and Social Concerns/Concentration) and a Lie Scale Score	Internal consistency: alpha coefficients >0.80 for the total, and factor scales range from 0.64 to 0.76; test–retest reliability range from 0.64 to 0.76
Anxiety and phobia	State-Trait Anxiety Inventory for Children (STAIC; Spielberger, 1973)	6 to 18 years	Two 20-item scales—the A-Trait Scale and A-State Scales. The A-Trait scale assesses chronic cross-situational anxiety. The A-State scale assesses acute, transitory anxiety	Internal consistency: alpha coefficients range from 0.80 to 0.90 for A-State and ~0.80 for A-Trait scale; test–retest reliability range from 0.65 to 0.72
Anxiety and phobia	Fear Survey Schedule for Children-Revised (FSSC-R; Ollendick, 1983)	6 to 17 years	80 items; assesses subjective levels of fear and yields a total fear score and five factor scale scores (Fear of Failure and Criticism, Fear of the Unknown, Fear of Danger and Death, Medical Fears, and Small Animals)	Internal consistency: alpha coefficients range from 0.92 to 0.95; test–retest reliability 0.82 for the total score
Depression	Center for Epidemiological Studies—Depression (CESD; Weissman, Orvaschel, & Padian, 1980)	6 to 17 years	20 items; assesses depression symptoms from six components of depression (depressed mood, feelings of guilt and worthlessness, feelings of helplessness, psychomotor retardation, loss of appetite, and sleep disturbance)	Internal consistency: alpha coefficients >0.92; test–retest reliability range from 0.51 to 0.59
Depression	Children's Depression Inventory (Kovacs, 1985)	7 to 11 years	27 items; assesses affective, cognitive, and behavioural symptoms of depression	Internal consistency: alpha coefficients >0.80 for the total score; test–retest reliability range from 0.65 to 0.85
ADHD and conduct disorder	Youth Self Report (Achenbach & Edelbrock, 1987)	11 to 18 years	102 items; assesses a broad range of child behaviour problems including positive and negative child behaviours. Behaviour problems can be assessed broadly using the externalising and internalizing subscales, or narrowly using the narrow-band subscales which assess: withdrawn, somatic complaints, anxious/depressed, social problems, thought problems, attention problems, delinquent behaviour, and aggression	Internal consistency: alpha coefficients range from 0.64 to 0.92; test–retest reliability range from 0.78 to 0.85

in the trials. Child self-rating scales, similar to parent rating scales, are useful in evidence-based practice as they serve to identify and quantify specific symptoms and behaviours. From these scales, a summary score is assumed to be a quantitative index of the degree to which particular problems (e.g., anxiety, depression, aggression, inattention, hyperactivity, delinquency) are relevant to a child, or the probability that the child will emit a class of behaviours (e.g., worry/oversensitivity; disruptive behaviours) (Jensen & Haynes, 1986). Departures from the norm can usually be determined on the basis of standard deviation units that define a particular percentile of the sample (Silverman & Serafini, 1998).

In evidence-based practice it is useful to administer child self-rating scales prior to treatment, midway through treatment, and at the end of treatment. Improvements on the scales may be interpreted as a reduction of the particular set of symptoms or problem behaviour. Because some research shows fluctuations in these scores irrespective of treatment (e.g., Finch et al., 1987; Nelson & Politano, 1990), it has been recommended that the scales be administered at least twice prior to the actual intervention, such as once at the initial screening or assessment and again immediately prior to treatment. Similar to problem behaviour checklists, child self-rating scales can be easily administered with relatively low cost and they have objective scoring procedures (Silverman & Rabian, 1999; Silverman & Serafini, 1998). As mentioned previously, in evidence-based treatments studies, child self-ratings are particularly useful for assessing children's internalizing problems.

Observational Procedures

Several observational procedures were developed for use across the various clinical trials. Results obtained from these observational procedures reveal significant improvements in children's direct behaviours across the various trials, thereby suggesting possible clinical utility of observational procedures in evidence-based practice. Because practical constraints render it difficult to conduct direct observations in children's naturalistic settings, the authors would recommend that, if observational procedures are used, they be conducted in the clinic setting, i.e., an analogous situation be devised. The analogue should correspond as closely as possible to the situation that elicits the child's problem behaviour in the natural environment. To ensure close correspondence, it is important for the clinician to obtain detailed information from the child and parent about the specifics of the child's problem behaviours and use this information for devising the analogue. Brief descriptions of the observational procedures used to assess children's internalizing (i.e., fear/anxiety) and externalizing (i.e., conduct) behaviours are provided in the subsequent sections.

Assessing Internalizing Behaviours

Observational procedures have been used in several of the anxiety disorders clinical trials, and as noted, they have been found to be sensitive to detecting therapeutic change (i.e., improvements in the children's behaviours have been observed from pre- to post-treatment (Beidel, Turner, & Morris, 2000; Kendall, 1994). Following the procedures used in Kendall (1994), for example, children with anxiety disorders could be asked to talk about themselves in front of a small group of people. Alternatively, following the procedures used in Beidel, Turner, and Morris (2000), children could be asked to read aloud a story in front of a small group and/or, if possible, the practitioner should set up an interaction with a peer. These situations could last for 5 to 10 minutes. Although it is important that children be told that they can stop the task at any time, they also should be encouraged to "try as hard as they can".

The behaviour codes used in Kendall (1994) were adapted from the codes established by Glennon and Weisz (1978) and included behaviours such as: (a) gratuitous vocalizations (e.g., stating a physical complaint, desire to leave, dislike for the task); (b) gratuitous body movements (e.g., leg kicking or shaking, rocking body, biting lips); (c) trembling voice (e.g., shaking speech, stuttering, volume shifts); and (d) absence of eye contact. In Kendall (1994) observers rated on a 5-point rating scale the child's (a) overall level of anxiety/fear (1 = "no signs of anxiety", 5 = "subject appears to be in crisis"), (b) fearful facial expression (1 = "no tears, tension, or biting of lips", 5 = "tearful, facial tension, clenching of jaws"), and (c) problematic performance (1 = "composed, non-avoidant behaviour", 5 = "disjointed and difficult-to-understand"). In Beidel, Turner, and Morris (2000) observers rated how "effective" the child was in his or her performance on the task (i.e., peer interactions, reading out loud) on a 5-point scale where 1 = completely ineffective and 5 = very effective. In addition, children self-rated their anxiety also using a 5-point scale where 1 = very relaxed and 5 = very anxious or distressed. Interobserver agreement reported in both studies (Beidel, Turner, & Morris, 2000; Kendall, 1994) was in the good to excellent range (kappas from 0.79 to 0.93).

Other variations of analogues that are directly akin to the child's problems (e.g., asking children with phobic disorders to attempt to approach the phobic object or situations; Silverman et al., 1999a,b: asking children with separation anxiety disorder to attempt a separation from the parent while in the clinic setting) can be used to assess the child's behaviour directly in specific fear-provoking situations. Another observational procedure used in evidence-based treatment studies for anxiety disorders are parent–child interaction tasks. These tasks assess threat interpretation and response plans to ambiguous situations discussed by the parent and child (Barrett, Dadds, & Rapee, 1996) providing a rich picture of how parents and children interact to generate problem-solving solutions to hypothetical anxiety-provoking situations. In general, behavioural analogues all have the potential to provide a rich picture of children's behaviours in anxiety-provoking situations and might be selected as treatment targets in evidence-based practice. Further research is needed, however, particularly in the child depression area, in designing analogue tasks and evaluating their reliability, validity, and sensitivity in detecting therapeutic change.

Assessing Externalizing Behaviours

The Dyadic Parent–Interaction Coding System has been used in several of the conduct behaviour problem/disorder clinical trials, and they have been found to be sensitive to detecting therapeutic change (i.e., improvements in the children's behaviours have been observed from pre- to post-treatment (Webster-Stratton, 1984, 1990, 1994). The Dyadic Parent–Interaction Coding System (Robinson, Eyberg, & Ross, 1981) contains 22 parent and child behaviour categories in parent-directed and 19 categories in child-directed interaction. The behaviour codes mainly involve observing child–parent (usually the mother) interactions or specific target behaviours of the child. Observations consist of two 5-minute interactions (child-directed interaction and parent-directed interaction) with each child and parent in a structured observation playroom. In the child-directed interaction, parents are instructed to allow the child to choose an activity the child wanted and participate in this activity. For the parent-directed interaction, parents are instructed to select an activity and "make sure" that the child participates in this activity throughout the observation period. Observations are coded in terms of the total frequency of each target behaviour or sequence of target behaviours for each 5-minute observation.

The target behaviours observed for the parent include: direct command, indirect command, labelled praise, unlabelled praise, positive physical, negative physical, and critical statement. The target behaviours observed for the child include: ignores or responds to parent commands, complies, does not comply, or no opportunity. These behaviours are coded in terms of the total frequency of occurrence per interval. Interobserver reliability for child behaviours has been found to be 0.92 and 0.91 for parent behaviours (Robinson, Eyberg, & Ross, 1981). Although some parent–child observation tasks have been developed in the attention deficit hyperactivity area (Pfiffner et al., 1994) further research is needed, particularly in evaluating the sensitivity of the tasks in detecting treatment change.

CONCLUDING COMMENTS

Guided by the child clinical trials research literature, this chapter summarized the assessment and diagnostic procedures recommended for use in evidence-based practice. In addition to providing evaluative summaries, the chapter summarized issues involved in the use of these procedures. The chapter also discussed issues relating to the classification of children's and adolescent's internalizing and externalizing behaviour problems, how classification impacts on methods of assessment and diagnosis, and the importance of considering development.

As mentioned earlier, assessment and diagnosis are the starting points of evidence-based practice. Consequently, it is the authors' hope that when practitioners begin their work with children and parents, they will be begin by using one of the structured interview schedules summarized earlier. If the child's primary presenting set of problems appears to be related to anxiety, for example, the practitioner might consider using the ADIS for DSM-IV: C/P; if the presenting set of problems appears to be related to externalizing problems such as oppositional behaviours, the practitioner might consider using the DISC-IV. Relatedly, depending on the presenting problems, practitioners might select the specific parent and child rating scales that would appear to be most relevant to that case. Practitioners also might be open to using some type of observational procedures as summarized earlier.

The information yielded from a comprehensive multi-source, multi-method assessment procedure will probably result in practitioners' increased confidence regarding the child's main set of diagnoses, the various levels and types of symptoms/problem behaviours emitted by the child, and how these symptoms/problem behaviours may manifest themselves in the "real world" (via the analogue task). This should thereby improve practitioners' abilities in identifying and selecting an appropriate evidence-based intervention, summarized in the other chapters in this volume. The authors further hope that practitioners will make use of these assessment and diagnostic procedures not just at the onset, before treatment has begun, but also at some point midway in treatment, and also toward the end, when children, parents and therapists have agreed that termination is coming near.

Nevertheless, as the authors have said repeatedly in this chapter, they view the evidence-based assessment (and intervention) procedures as starting points and further development, adaptation, and innovation should occur on a case by case basis, as necessary, in practice. One area in which the authors believe further development is particularly urgent is with respect to moving beyond DSM diagnoses. More specifically, although the DSM was a good place to begin the development and evaluation of evidence-based treatments because DSM was/is the common language of researchers and practitioners and because managed care also "speaks" this language, there are concerns with this emphasis on DSM, mainly stemming from DSM-categorical approach. For example, because problems are viewed in a categorical approach as "present" versus "absent", the degree of change using only DSM diagnoses is limited. This is why it was recommended that dimensional approaches via the use of ratings scales be used, rather than relying solely on the diagnostic interviews.

Another concern relates to DSM's emphasis on disorder rather than functional impairment. This is a matter of concern given that most children and parents who present to general outpatient mental health clinics (e.g., community mental health centres, private practice), do so because the child is showing disturbing or severe deterioration/impairment in functioning in multiples areas, such as school, peers, family, and/or the child is showing increasing signs of distress about his or her functioning (or lack thereof) (Angold et al., 1999). It therefore is the authors' hope that increased use of and emphasis on assessing children's impairment be made in the future. This can only happen through increased efforts in developing instruments for assessing impairment and in evaluating these instruments' utility in detecting therapeutic change during the course of an intervention. Efforts in the development of instruments such as the *Child and Adolescent Social and Adaptive Functioning Scale* (Price et al., 2002) represent an important step in this direction.

Of related concern is that DSM's strict reliance on diagnoses fails to capture other goals of child therapy that usually occur in practice, beyond elimination of diagnosis (Persons & Silberschatz, 1998). In child therapy, these other goals might include improving the child's friendships, school grades, and/or family relationships. Extending the goals of treatment would require an extension in the assessment measures used (i.e., measures that do not focus exclusively on assessing diagnoses and symptoms). Although such measures are available, what is currently lacking is sufficient and adequate calibration of measures with inherent meaning. (This is also true for the symptom measures summarized earlier.) For example, statistical improvement on a measure following an evidence-based treatment—whether it be a depression symptom measure or a friendship measure—means *what* when it comes to real behaviours (e.g., more smiles, less crying) and real events (e.g., more friends calling; reduced teasing interactions from peers) in children's lives? To date, there are no answers to these critical and "real-world" questions (Secherest, McKnight, & McKnight, 1996).

The above are just a few of the many issues and challenges relating to assessment and diagnoses of child internalizing and externalizing problems in evidence-based practice. The authors hope this chapter serves to stimulate continued work and improvements in this very important starting point of evidence-based practice.

ACKNOWLEDGMENT

Preparation for this chapter was funded in part by NIMH grant #1R01MH063997.

REFERENCES

Achenbach, T.M. (1980). DSM-III in light of empirical research on the classification of child psychopathology. *Journal of the American Academy of Child Psychiatry*, **19**, 395–415.

Achenbach, T.M. (1991). *Manual for the Child Behavior Checklist 14–18 and 1991 profile*. Burlington, VT: University of Vermont, Department of Psychiatry.

Achenbach, T.M., & Edelbrock, C.S. (1978). The classification of child psychology: A review and analysis of empirical efforts. *Psychological Bulletin*, **85**, 1275–1301.

Achenbach, T.M., & Edelbrock, C.S. (1984). Psychopathology of childhood. *Annual Review of Psychology*, **35**, 227–256.

Achenbach, T.M., & Edelbrock, C.S. (1987). *Manual for the Youth Self-Report and profile*. Burlington: University of Vermont, Department of Psychiatry.

Achenbach, T.M., McConaughy, S.H., & Howell, C.T. (1987). Child/adolescent behavioural and emotional problems: Implications of cross-informant correlations for situational specificity. *Psychological Bulletin*, **101**, 213–232.

Albano, A.M., & Silverman, W.K. (1996). *Guide to the Anxiety Disorders Interview Schedule for Children-IV (Child and Parent Versions)*. San Antonio, TX: Psychological Corporation.

Ambrosini, P.J. (2000). Historical development and present status of the Schedule for Affective Disorders and Schizophrenia for School-Age Children (K-SADS). *Journal of the American Academy of Child and Adolescent Psychiatry*, **39**, 49–58.

American Psychiatric Association (1980). *Diagnostic and Statistical Manual of Mental Disorders* (3rd edn; DSM-III). Washington, DC: Author.

American Psychiatric Association (1987). *Diagnostic and Statistical Manual of Mental Disorders* (3rd edn, revised; DSM-III-R). Washington, DC: Author.

American Psychiatric Association (1994). *Diagnostic and Statistical Manual of Mental Disorders* (4th edn; DSM-IV). Washington, DC: Author.

Anastopoulos, A.D., Shelton, T.L., DuPaul, G.J., & Guevremont, D.C. (1993). Parent training for attention-deficit hyperactivity disorder: Its impact on parent functioning. *Journal of Abnormal Child Psychology*, **21**, 581–596.

Angold, A., & Costello, E.J. (1996). The relative diagnostic utility of child and parent reports of oppositional defiant behaviours. *International Journal of Methods in Psychiatric Research*, **6**, 253–259.

Angold, A., Costello, E.J., Farmer, E.M.Z., Burns, B.J., & Erkanli, A. (1999). Impaired but undiagnosed. *Journal of the American Academy of Child and Adolescent Psychiatry*, **38**, 129–137.

Barkley, R.A. (1988). *Hyperactive children: A handbook for diagnosis and treatment.* New York: Guilford Press.

Barrett, P.M. (1998). Evaluation of cognitive-behavioural group treatments for childhood anxiety disorders. *Journal of Clinical Child Psychology*, **27**, 459–468.

Barrett, P.M., Dadds, M.R., & Rapee, R.M. (1996). Family treatment of childhood anxiety: A controlled trial. *Journal of Consulting and Clinical Psychology*, **64**, 333–342.

Beidel, D.C., Turner, S.M., & Morris, T.L. (2000). Behavioural treatment of childhood social phobia. *Journal of Consulting and Clinical Psychology*, **68**, 1072–1080.

Brent, D.A., Holder, D., Kolko, D., Birmaher, B., & Baugher, M. (1993). A psychoeducational program for families of affectively ill children and adolescents. *Journal of the American Academy of Child and Adolescent Psychiatry*, **32**, 770–774.

Butler, L., Miezitis, S., Friedman, R., & Cole, E. (1980). The effect of two school-based intervention programs on depressive symptoms in preadolescents. *American Educational and Behavioural Disorders*, **2**, 247–253.

Chorpita, B.F., & Donkervoet, J.C. (2001). Special series: Pushing the envelope of empirically based treatments for children. Introduction. *Cognitive and Behavioural Practice*, **8**, 336–337.

Clarke, G.N., Hawkins, W., Murphy, M., & Sheeber, L.B. (1993). School-based primary prevention of depressive symptomology in adolescents: Findings from two studies. *Journal of Adolescent Research*, **8**, 183–204.

Cicchetti, D., Rogosch, F.A., & Toth, S.L. (1994). A developmental psychopathology perspective on depression in children and adolescents. In W.M. Reynolds & H.F. Johnston (Eds), *Handbook of depression in children and adolescents. Issues in clinical child psychology* (pp. 123–141). New York: Plenum Press.

Cobham, V.E., Dadds, M.R., & Spence, S.H. (1998). The role of parental anxiety in the treatment of childhood anxiety. *Journal of Consulting and Clinical Psychology*, **66**, 893–905.

Conners, C.K. (1990). *Manual for Conner's Rating Scales.* Toronto: Multi-Health Systems, Inc.

Edelbrock, C. (1985). Age differences in the reliability of the psychiatric interview of the child. *Child Development*, **56**, 265–275.

Edelbrock, C. (1994). Assessing child psychopathology in developmental follow-up studies. In S.L. Friedman & H.C. Haywood (Eds), *Developmental follow-up: Concepts, domains, and methods* (pp. 183–196). San Diego, CA: Academic Press.

Epkins, C.C., & Meyers, A.W. (1994). Assessment of childhood depression, anxiety, and aggression: Convergent and discriminant validity of self-, parent-, teacher- and peer-report measures. *Journal of Personality Assessment*, **62**, 364–381.

Eyberg, S.M. (1980). Eyberg Child Behaviour Inventory. *Journal of Clinical Child Psychology*, **9**, 22–29.

Eyberg, S.M., & Robinson, E.A. (1983). Conduct problem behaviour: Standardization of a behavioural rating scale with adolescents. *Journal of Clinical Child Psychology*, **12**, 347–354.

Eyberg, S.M., & Ross, A.W. (1978). Assessment of child behavior problems: The validation of a new inventory. *Journal of Clinical Child Psychology*, **7**, 113–116.

Eyberg, S.M., Boggs, S., & Algina, J. (1995). Parent–child interaction therapy: A psychosocial model for the treatment of young children with conduct problem behaviour and their families. *Psychopharmacology Bulletin*, **31**, 83–91.

Finch, A.J., Saylor, C.F., Edwards, G.L., & McIntosh, J.A. (1987). Children's Depression Inventory: Reliability over repeated administrations. *Journal of Clinical Child Psychology*, **16**, 339–341.

Fine, S., Forth, A., Gilbert, M., & Haley, G. (1991). Group therapy for adolescent depressive disorder. A comparison of social skills and therapeutic support. *Journal of the American Academy of Child and Adolescent Psychiatry*, **30**, 79–85.

Flannery-Schroeder, E.C., & Kendall, P.C. (2000). Group versus individual cognitive behavioural treatment for youth with anxiety disorders: A randomised clinical trial. *Cognitive Therapy and Research*, **24**, 251–278.

Glennon, B., & Weisz, J.R. (1978). An observational approach to the assessment of anxiety in young children. *Journal of Consulting and Clinical Psychology*, **46**, 1246–1257.

Glow, R.A., Glow, P.A., & Rump, E.E. (1982). The stability of child behaviour disorders: A one year test-retest study of Adelaide versions of the Conners Teacher and Parent Rating Scales. *Journal of Abnormal Child Psychology*, **10**, 33–60.

Goyette, C.H., Conners, C.K., & Ulrich, R.F. (1978). Normative data on revised Conner's Parent and Teacher Rating Scales. *Journal of Abnormal Child Psychology*, **6**, 221–236.

Grills, A.E., & Ollendick, T.H. (2002). Issues in parent–child agreement: The case of structured diagnostic interviews. *Clinical Child and Family Psychology Review*, **5**, 57–82.

Hamilton, D.I., & King, N.J. (1991). Reliability of a behavioural avoidance test for the assessment of dog phobic children. *Psychological Reports*, **69**, 18.

Hayward, C., Varardy, S., Albano, A.M., Thienemann, M., Henderson, L., & Schatzberg, A.F. (2000). Cognitive-behavioural group therapy for social phobia in female adolescents: Results of a pilot study. *Journal of the American Academy of Child and Adolescent Psychiatry*, **39**, 721–726.

Hinshaw, S.P., March, J.S., Abikoff, H., Arnold, L.E., Cantwell, D.P., Conners, C.K., et al. (1997). Comprehensive assessment of childhood attention-deficit hyperactivity disorder in the context of a multisite, multimodal clinical trial. *Journal of Attention Disorders*, **1**, 217–234.

Horn, W.F., Ialongo, N., Greenberg, G., Packard, T., & Smith-Winberry, C. (1990). Additive effects of behavioural and parent training and self-control therapy with ADHD children. *Journal of Clinical Child Psychology*, **19**, 98–110.

Horn, W.F., Ialongo, N., Pascoe, J.M., Greenberg, G., Packard, T., Lopez, T., et al. (1991). Additive effects of psychostimulants, parent training, and self-control therapy with ADHD children: A 9-month follow-up. *Journal of the American Academy of Child and Adolescent Psychiatry*, **32**, 182–189.

Jaycox, L.H., Reivich, K.L. Gillham, J., & Seligman, M.E.P. (1994). Prevention of depressive symptoms in school children. *Behaviour Research and Therapy*, **32**, 801–816.

Jensen, B.J., & Haynes, S.N. (1986). Self-report questionnaires and inventories. In A.R. Ciminero, K.S., Calhoun, & H.E. Adams (Eds), *Handbook of behavioural assessment* (pp. 150–175). New York: John Wiley & Sons.

Kaufman, J., Birmaher, B., Brent, D., & Rao, U. (1997). Schedule for Affective Disorders and Schizophrenia for School-Age Children—Present and Lifetime Version (K-SADS-PL): Initial reliability and validity data. *Journal of the American Academy of Child and Adolescent Psychiatry*, **36**, 980–988.

Kendall, P.C. (1994). Treating anxiety disorders in children: Results of a randomized clinical trial. *Journal of Consulting and Clinical Psychology*, **62**, 200–210.

Kendall, P.C., & Grove, W.M. (1988). Normative comparisons in therapy outcome. *Behavioural Assessment*, **10**, 147–158.

Kendall, P.C., Flannery-Schroder, E.C., Panichelli-Mindel, S.M., Southham-Gerow, M., Henin, A., & Warman, M. (1997). Therapy for youths with anxiety disorders: A second randomised clinical trial. *Journal of Consulting and Clinical Psychology*, **65**, 366–380.

Koot, H.M., & Verhulst, F.C. (1992). Prediction of children referred to mental health and special education services from earlier adjustment. *Journal of Child Psychology and Psychiatry*, **33**, 717–729.

Kovacs, M. (1985). The Children's Depression Inventory (CDI). *Psychopharmacology Bulletin*, **21**, 995–998.

Lewinsohn, P.M., Clarke, G.N., Hops, H., & Andrews, J. (1990). Cognitive-behavioural treatment for depressed adolescents. *Behaviour Therapy*, **21**, 385–401.

Mash, E.J., & Terdal, L.G. (Eds) (1988). *Behavioural assessment of child disorders* (2nd edn). New York: Guilford.

McClellan, J.M., & Werry, J.S. (2000). Introduction. *Journal of the American Academy of Child and Adolescent Psychiatry*, **39**, 19–27.

Mendlowitz, S.L., Manassis, K., Bradley, S., Scapillato, D., Miezitis, S., & Shaw, B.F. (1999). Cognitive-behavioural group treatments in childhood anxiety disorders: The role of parental involvement. *Journal of the American Academy of Child and Adolescent Psychiatry*, **38**, 1223–1229.

MTA Cooperative Group (1999). A 14-month randomised clinical trial of treatment strategies for Attention-Deficit Hyperactivity Disorder (ADHD). *Archives of General Psychiatry*, **56**, 1073–1086.

Nelson, W.M., III, & Politano, P.M. (1990). Children's Depression Inventory: Stability over repeated administrations in psychiatric inpatient children. *Journal of Clinical Child Psychology*, **19**, 254–256.

Ollendick, T.H. (1983). Reliability and validity of the Revised Fear Survey Schedule for Children (FSSC-R). *Behaviour Research and Therapy*, **21**, 395–399.

Persons, J.B., & Silberschatz, G. (1998). Are results of randomised controlled trials useful to psychotherapists? *Journal of Consulting and Clinical Psychology*, **66**, 126–135.

Pelham, W.E., Carlson, C., Sams, S.E., Vallano, G., Dixon, M.J., & Hoza, B. (1993). Separate and combined effects of methylphenidate and behaviour modification on boys with attention-deficit hyperactivity disorder in the classroom. *Journal of Consulting and Clinical Psychology*, **61**, 506–515.

Pfiffner, L., Hinshaw, S.P., Johnston, C., & Wells, K.C. (1994). *MTA Study Parent–Child Interaction Protocol*. Unpublished manuscript. University of California, Irvine.

Piacentini, J.C., Cohen, P., & Cohen, J. (1992). Combining discrepant information from multiple sources: Are complex algorithms better than simple ones? *Journal of Abnormal Child Psychology*, **20**, 51–63.

Price, C.A., Spence, S.H., Sheffield, J., & Donovan, C. (2002). The development and psychometric properties of a measure of social and adaptive functioning for children and adolescents. *Journal of Clinical Child and Adolescent Psychology*, **31**, 111–122.

Quay, H.C. (1979). Classification. In H.C. Quay & J.S. Werry (Eds), *Psychopathological disorders of childhood* (2nd edn; pp. 1–42). New York: John Wiley & Sons.

Reynolds, C.R., & Coats, K.I. (1986). A comparison of cognitive-behavioural therapy and relaxation training for the treatment of depression in adolescents. *Journal of Consulting and Clinical Psychology*, **54**, 653–660.

Reynolds, C.R., & Kamphus, R.W. (1992). *Behaviour Assessment Scale for Children*. Circle Pines, MN: American Guidance Services.

Reynolds, C.R., & Richmond, B.O. (1985). *Revised Children's Manifest Anxiety Scale: Manual*. Los Angeles: Western Psychological Services.

Robinson, E.A., Eyberg, S.M., & Ross, A.W. (1981). The standardization of an inventory of child conduct problem behaviours. *Journal of Clinical Child Psychology*, **9**, 22–28.

Ross, A.O. (1980). *Psychological disorders of children*. New York: McGraw-Hill.

Rutter, M., & Shaffer, D. (1980). DSM-III: A step forward or back in terms of the classification of child psychiatric disorders? *Journal of the American Academy of Child and Adolescent Psychiatry*, **19**, 371–393.

Saavedra, L.M., & Silverman, W.K. (2002). Classification of anxiety disorders in children: What a difference two decades make. *International Review of Psychiatry*, **14**, 87–101.

Schwab-Stone, M., Fallon, T., Briggs, M., & Crowther, B. (1994). Reliability of diagnostic reporting for children aged 6–11 years: A test–retest study of the Diagnostic Interview Schedule for Children—Revised. *American Journal of Psychiatry*, **151**, 1048–1054.

Sechrest, L., McKnight, P., & McKnight, K. (1996). Calibration of measures for psychotherapy outcome studies. *American Psychologist*, **51**, 1065–1071.

Shaffer, D., Fisher, P., Lucas, C., Dulcan, M.K., & Schwab-Stone, M.E. (2000). NIMH diagnostic interview schedule for children version IV (NIMH DISC-IV): Description, differences from previous versions, and reliability of some common diagnoses. *Journal of the American Academy of Child and Adolescent Psychiatry*, **39**, 28–38.

Siebelink, B.M., & Treffers, P.D.A. (2001). *Dutch adaptation of the ADIS for DSM-IV, child version by Silverman WK, Albano AM*. Lisse, Netherlands: Swets & Zeitlinger.

Silverman, W.K. (1992). Taxonomy of anxiety disorders in children. In G.D. Burrows, M. Roth, & R. Noyes (Eds), *Handbook of anxiety*. (vol. 5; pp. 281–307). Amsterdam: Elsevier.

Silverman, W.K. (1993). DSM and classification of anxiety disorders in children and adults. In C.G. Last (Ed.), *Anxiety across the lifespan: A developmental perspective* (pp. 7–35). New York: Springer.

Silverman, W.K. (1994). Structured diagnostic interviews. In T.H. Ollendick, N.J. King, & W. Yule (Eds), *International handbook of phobic and anxiety disorders in children and adolescents* (pp. 293–315). New York: Plenum Press.

Silverman, W.K., & Albano, A.M. (1996). *Anxiety Disorders Interview Schedule for Children for DSM-IV (Child and Parent Versions)*. San Antonio, TX: Psychological Corporation.

Silverman, W.K., & Eisen, A.R. (1992). Age differences in the reliability of parent and child reports of child anxious symptomatology using a structured interview. *Journal of the American Academy of Child and Adolescent Psychiatry*, **31**, 117–124.

Silverman, W.K., & Kurtines, W.M. (1996). *Anxiety and phobic disorders: A pragmatic approach*. New York: Plenum Press.

Silverman, W.K., & Ollendick, T.H. (Eds) (1999). *Developmental issues in the clinical treatment of children*. Needham Heights, MA: Allyn & Bacon.

Silverman, W.K., & Rabian, B. (1999). Rating scales for anxiety and mood disorders. In D. Shaffer & C.P. Lucas (Eds), *Diagnostic assessment in child and adolescent psychopathology* (pp. 127–166). New York: Guilford Press.

Silverman, W.K., & Serafini, L.T. (1998). Assessment of child behaviour problems: Internalising disorders. In A.S. Bellack & M. Hersen (Eds), *Behavioural assessment: A practical handbook* (4th edn; pp. 342–360). Boston: Allyn & Bacon.

Silverman, W.K., & Treffers, P.D.A. (in press). Bridging research and practice: the Miami, United States and Leiden, Netherlands experience. In T.H. Ollendick & J.S. March (Eds), *Phobic and anxiety disorders: A clinician's guide to effective psychosocial and pharmacological interventions*. New York: Oxford University Press.

Silverman, W.K., Saavedra, L.M., & Pina, A.A. (2001). Test–retest reliability of anxiety symptoms and diagnoses using the Anxiety Disorders Interview Schedule for DSM-IV: Child and Parent Versions (ADIS for DSM-IV: C/P). *Journal of the American Academy of Child and Adolescent Psychiatry*, **40**, 937–944.

Silverman, W.K., Kurtines, W.M., Ginsburg, G.S., Weems, C.F., Lumpkin, P.W., & Hicks-Carmichael, D. (1999a). Treating anxiety disorders in children with group cognitive behaviour therapy: A randomised clinical trial. *Journal of Consulting and Clinical Psychology*, **67**, 995–1003.

Silverman, W.K., Kurtines, W.M., Ginsburg, G.S., Weems, C.F., Rabian, B., & Serafini, L.T. (1999b). Contingency management, self-control, and education support in the treatment of childhood phobic disorders: A randomised clinical trial. *Journal of Consulting and Clinical Psychology*, **67**, 675–687.

Spence, S.H., Donovan, C., & Brechman-Toussaint, M. (2000). The treatment of childhood social phobia: The effectiveness of a social skills training-based, cognitive behavioural intervention, with and without parental involvement. *Journal of Child Psychology and Psychiatry and Allied Disciplines*, **41**, 713–726.

Spielberger, C.D. (1973). *Manual for the State-Trait Anxiety Inventory for Children*. Palo Alto, CA: Consulting Psychologists Press.

Sroufe, L.A., & Rutter, M. (1984). The domain of developmental psychopathology. *Child Development*, **55**, 17–29.

Stark, K.D., Reynolds, W.M., & Kaslow, N.J. (1987). A comparison of the relative efficacy of self-control therapy and a behavioural problem-solving therapy for depression in children. *Journal of Abnormal Child Psychology*, **15**, 91–113.

Webster-Stratton, C. (1984). Randomised trial of two parent-training programs for families with conduct-disordered children. *Journal of Consulting and Clinical Psychology*, **52**, 666–678.

Webster-Stratton, C. (1990). Enhancing the effectiveness of self-administered videotape parent training for families with conduct-problem children. *Journal of Abnormal Child Psychology*, **18**, 479–492.

Webster-Stratton, C. (1994). Advancing videotape parent training: A comparison study. *Journal of Consulting and Clinical Psychology*, **62**, 583–593.

Weissman, M.M., Orvaschel., H., & Padian, N. (1980). Children's symptom and social functioning self-report scales: Comparison of mothers' and children's reports. *Journal of Nervous and Mental Disease*, **168**, 736–740.

Weisz, J., Thurber, C., Sweeney, L., Proffit, V., & LeGagnoux, G. (1997). Brief treatment of mild to moderate depression usually primary and secondary control enhancement training. *Journal of Consulting and Clinical Psychology*, **65**, 703–707.

CHAPTER 4

Evaluation Issues in Evidence-Based Practice

Nirbhay N. Singh

ONE Research Institute, USA

and

Donald P. Oswald

Virginia Commonwealth University, USA

INTRODUCTION

The American Psychological Association's Society of Clinical Psychology Task Force on Promotion and Dissemination of Psychological Procedures published its report on empirically validated treatments with children and adolescents[1] in 1995 (Task Force on Promotion and Dissemination of Psychological Procedures, 1995), the same year that an evidence-based approach was first mentioned in the field of clinical psychiatry (Bilsker & Goldner, 1995). The Task Force Report identified empirically validated psychosocial treatments, and later task forces expanded on these efforts (Chambless et al., 1996, 1998; Chambless & Ollendick, 2001; Ollendick & King, see Chapter 1 this volume). Empirically validated treatments are, in fact, what has been more commonly known in medical practice as evidence-based medicine.

The term *evidence-based medicine* originated at McMaster University in Canada in 1981 when staff in the Department of Clinical Epidemiology and Biostatistics began publishing a series of papers designed to teach physicians how to critically review medical research literature (Guyatt & Rennie, 2002). This slowly developed into an approach to using research evidence in decision-making about routine patient care. Evidence-based medicine has been described as

---

Correspondence to Nirbhay N. Singh, ONE Research Institute, 7401 Sparkleberry Lane, Chesterfield, VA 23832-8000; email: nirbsingh52@aol.com
[1] The term *children* is used throughout to refer to both children and adolescents, unless otherwise specified.

Handbook of Interventions that Work with Children and Adolescents: Prevention and Treatment.
Edited by P.M. Barrett and T.H. Ollendick. © 2004 John Wiley & Sons, Ltd. ISBN 0-470-84453-1.

the conscientious, explicit, and judicious use of current best evidence in making decisions about the care of individual patients. The practice of evidence-based medicine means integrating individual clinical expertise with the best available external clinical evidence from systematic research. By individual clinical experience we mean the proficiency and judgment that individual clinicians acquire through clinical experience and clinical practice. (Sackett et al., 1996, p. 71)

When compared to standard clinical care based only on the knowledge and skills of an individual clinician, it is believed that an evidence-based approach leads to "more effective and efficient diagnosis and in the more thoughtful identification and compassionate use of individual patient's predicaments, rights, and preferences in making clinical decisions about their care" (Sackett et al., 1996, p. 71).

Evidence-based practice (EBP) is the informed use of empirically validated or more properly empirically supported treatments in individual patient care. This approach is grounded not only in the best that scientific research has to offer the clinician but also the best clinical expertise the clinician has to offer in terms of patient-centred care. It provides clinicians a methodology for deriving from the published and unpublished research evidence a sound, justifiable approach to the treatment of specific disorders and conditions in specific, individual patients. In this chapter, we discuss a broad range of issues related to evaluation and evidence-based practice. We consider how the research evidence is searched, evaluated, and applied to individual patients, with particular attention to how outcomes are evaluated.

EVALUATING EVIDENCE OF TREATMENTS THAT WORK: GENERAL METHODOLOGICAL ISSUES

The present era has been marked by an explosion of information on every conceivable topic. To keep abreast of the current literature in general medicine, it has been estimated that physicians would need to read 19 journal articles a day, 365 days per year (Davidoff et al., 1995). In the treatment of children's psychological and emotional problems alone, dozens of new print and electronic journal articles, treatment manuals, and books appear weekly. At a time when clinical psychology researchers must work hard to stay current in their chosen area, clearly, practicing clinicians cannot keep up with the literature on all possible interventions for their increasingly heterogeneous patient populations.

Indeed, even in academic medical centres, up to 40% of clinical decisions are without any research support (Greenhalgh, 2001), suggesting that clinicians tend to rely on their own experience with a limited number of patients or on the counsel of authentic or self-proclaimed experts rather than on systematic reviews of the current literature. Further, exposure to the scientific literature may not, of itself, serve the desired purpose; when personal beliefs and scientific evidence are at odds, clinicians almost invariably act on their personal beliefs (Garb, 1998).

Finally, even if clinicians had the time to read all the necessary research literature, many would have difficulty critically examining the research design, methodology, and results sections of research articles to determine which treatments would be the most appropriate for their specific patients. They may be confounded by research studies that report contradictory findings if they fail to appreciate that some of the contradictions may be due to false-positive and false-negative results in studies with small samples (Collins & MacMahon, 2001). They may rely unduly on review articles and overlook how reviewers' biases with regard to selecting the original set of studies for review and reconciling contradictory results can affect their conclusions. Until there is a simpler method for evaluating the research literature, clinicians are unlikely to apprehend and use empirically validated treatments.

Evaluation and Evidence-Based Practice

Evaluation is at the heart of evidence-based practice. The term itself implies that practicing clinicians evaluate the treatment choices available for a given patient and select the intervention that best matches their clinical formulation of the patient's problems and the findings obtained from the relevant scientific research literature. But this level of evaluation is only one of the ways in which the topic of evaluation enters into evidence-based practice. In this section, we provide an overview of the multiple levels of evaluation that must be considered to arrive at a successful implementation of evidence-based child mental health practice.

Evaluating Efficacy

Implicit in the term *evidence-based practice* is the assumption that there exist in the scientific literature a number of treatment approaches or intervention techniques that have substantial and demonstrated empirical support, according to some generally accepted set of criteria. This assumption rests on the principle that the efficacy of a treatment procedure can be judged by the extent, the methodological rigor, and the empirical outcomes of the research supporting it. (Although some might question even this principle, we propose to accept it for the purposes of the present work because a philosophical justification would take us too far afield.)

The specific criteria chosen to evaluate efficacy represent choices made by thoughtful scholars dedicated to the progress of the field; but they are, nonetheless, choices, lacking the authority of moral imperative or divine revelation or even a demonstrable empirical basis. Thus, we should not be surprised that the criteria that are employed vary somewhat across, and even within, disciplines.

The American Psychological Association Task Force on Psychological Intervention Guidelines (1995) took the position that treatment efficacy

> must be demonstrated in controlled research in which it is reasonable to conclude that benefits observed are due to the effects of the treatment and not to chance or confounding factors such as passage of time, the effects of psychological assessment, or the presence of different types of clients in the various treatment conditions. (Chambless & Hollon, 1998, p. 7)

In an extension of those guidelines, if a treatment approach has been found efficacious in at least two studies by independent research teams, in conditions that control for non-specific processes or that provide comparisons to another bona fide treatment, the procedure was designated "Efficacious and specific". If a treatment has been found efficacious in at least two studies by independent research teams, it was designated "Efficacious" while if the treatment has been found efficacious in only one study, or all of the research has been conducted by one team, it was labelled "Possibly Efficacious" (Chambless & Hollon, 1998).

The US Food and Drug Administration (FDA), by way of comparison, for approval of a new drug requires two published, independent, controlled studies demonstrating statistically significant findings when treatment is compared to inactive or placebo treatment (Beutler, 2000).

The American Psychiatric Association develops its Practice Guidelines (analogous to a designation of evidence-based practices for a particular disorder) by consensus panel (e.g., American Psychiatric Association, 1997) through an iterative process among experts (Frances, Docherty, & Kahn, 1996). The Guidelines must also be approved by a vote of the APA Assembly and Board of Trustees. Consensus panels clearly consider relevant literature but the specifics of their decisions about the value of that literature are generally not clearly stated. Consensus guidelines are typically not based on a thorough analysis and evaluation of the research literature and an explicit assumption of some practice guidelines is that the research literature often does not include critical information for treatment decisions that is of interest to clinicians (Frances et al., 1996).

Experts for consensus panels may be chosen because they represent the views of the sponsors of the panel. This bias is often reflected in the practice guidelines recommended by the consensus panels and their recommendations may diverge substantially from the research literature (Barlow, 1994; Beutler, Clarkin, & Bongar, 2000). However, clinicians generally value these guidelines because they provide information about practices for which limited or no experimental evidence may exist.

Thus, the designation of a treatment procedure as a member of a set of "approved" or evidence-based practice procedures is not as straightforward as it seems and clinicians would do well to keep in mind the specifics of the evaluation process to which the procedures were subjected. The above examples illustrate how several professional bodies have endeavoured to simplify the clinician's task by establishing a set of evaluation criteria and judging the scientific literature related to the efficacy of a treatment approach according to those criteria. While, no doubt, there exist isolated examples of treatment approaches that received their imprimatur by underhanded, self-serving, political, or otherwise nefarious means, in general the designations may be assumed to have been made with integrity and with the best information available to the designating body. While professional organizations have taken somewhat different approaches to the task, the practice of evidence-based practice is immeasurably simplified by these efforts to evaluate the efficacy of alternative treatment approaches.

Evaluating Effectiveness

Treatment efficacy is demonstrated under the rigorously controlled conditions of randomized clinical trials. Randomized-controlled trials (RCTs) are seen as one of the most important ways of generating new knowledge regarding effective treatments for a given disorder or condition. In the hierarchy typically used in EBM, RCTs are ranked as providing the best evidence for the potential impact of a specific treatment (Geddes, 1999; Phillips et al., 2002). Researchers use this approach as the method of choice for evaluating the differential effects of two (or more) treatments, or for evaluating a new treatment compared to a placebo control.

Randomized-controlled trials that compare the effects of a new treatment against a placebo or no-treatment condition maximize the chances of finding a treatment effect. The patients are often highly homogeneous in terms of their social demographics, and they typically have a single disorder that is targeted by the new treatment. Clinical efficacy is often measured using assessment instruments that are disorder-specific. RCTs that evaluate the efficacy of a treatment address the question: "Can it work?"

Increasingly, however, the field of child mental health has recognized that the availability of a set of efficacious treatment procedures falls short of the goal of evidence-based practice. Few RCTs are designed to answer a second question that deals with the effectiveness of a new treatment: "Does it work?" Studies that evaluate the *effectiveness* of a treatment generally include a more heterogeneous patient population and seek to more closely replicate the conditions under which the new treatment is likely to be routinely used.

The literature on the evaluation of effectiveness of treatment procedures is substantially less well developed, compared to the efficacy literature. Thus, it is not surprising that professional organizations seeking to provide guidelines for clinical decision-making with regard to selection of treatment procedures have largely ignored the question of effectiveness. The knowledge base is, at present, too limited to allow for a compendium of treatment procedures that demonstrate acceptable levels of both efficacy and effectiveness. However, the evaluation of effectiveness has been recognized as an essential goal to be pursued in the promulgation of evidence-based practice.

Evaluating Cost-Effectiveness

Evaluating efficacy and effectiveness are essential to the very nature of EBP. If, however, EBP is to exist in the real world of health care, clinicians considering a particular treatment approach are also required to seek the answer to a third question: "Is it worth it?" (Harrington, 2001). Thus, a third level of evaluation embedded within the construct of EBP is consideration of cost-effectiveness. The Institute of Medicine's Committee on Clinical Practice Guidelines has recommended that all clinical practice guidelines include cost-effectiveness data on alternative preventive, diagnostic, and treatment strategies (Field & Lohr, 1992). Such guidelines would provide clinicians with a more informed basis for selecting a specific treatment approach or strategy and would clarify the clinical and fiscal consequences that may result from their choice.

The majority of clinicians currently do not make treatment decisions in terms of cost-utility ratios, in part because of their basic mistrust of economic modelling by managed care for deriving cost-utility ratios (Drummond, Cooke, & Walley, 1997). Publishing cost-effectiveness data would allow clinicians and their patients to balance their judgment about the best treatment against the cost of providing that treatment. The realistic and pragmatic evaluation of cost-effectiveness is an important extension of the principle of evidence-based practice.

With a few notable exceptions (e.g., Byford et al., 1999), cost-effectiveness findings are rarely provided because of major methodological and practical challenges in costing the services including the lack of (a) accurate cost data for the majority of psychological and related clinical treatments and services, (b) a method to convert data on charges to data on the cost of the service, and (c) methods to gather and analyse data that are suited to different contexts (rural vs urban clinics, medical centre-based vs private clinics, group vs single practice, multi-site vs individual clinical trials).

Further, the calculation of cost-effectiveness assumes that the field has enough solid evidence regarding the benefits and harms that result from each kind of therapy to be able to characterize and quantify those effects. By all accounts, this is an exceedingly tenuous assumption; our knowledge of the benefits and harms of specific therapies is, at best, incomplete.

Given the problems associated with the assessment of costs and benefits of treatments, there is an urgent need to develop and refine methodologies for evaluating cost-effectiveness within the practice of EBP. Methodologies for comparing the benefits of alternative treatments on the basis of cost-effectiveness, cost per life year saved, or the cost per quality of life year saved are available in the field of economics (e.g., Rosser & Shafir, 1998), and mental health researchers would do well to include consideration of these factors in their clinical research trials. Failure to do so abandons the field to the business interests of managed care.

Evaluating Goodness-of-Fit

An under-appreciated aspect of the application of evidence-based procedures in clinical practice relates to how well the intervention fits the patient along a range of other factors in addition to diagnosis. Important questions in evaluating goodness-of-fit (Donald & Muthu, 2001, p. 36) include:

1. Is the treatment or technique available/affordable?
2. How large is the likely effect?
3. How uncertain are the study results?
4. What are the likely adverse effects of treatment? Are they reversible?
5. Are the patients included in the studies similar to the patient(s) I am dealing with? If not, are the differences great enough to render the evidence useless?
6. Was the study setting similar to my own setting?
7. Will my patient receive the same interventions that were used in the study? If not, will it matter?
8. How good was adherence (compliance) in the study? Is adherence likely to be similar in my own practice?
9. Are the outcomes examined in the studies important to me/my patients?
10. What are my patients' preferences regarding the treatment: its likely harms and its likely benefits?

11. If I apply the evidence inappropriately to my patient, how harmful is it likely to be? Will it be too late to change my mind if I have inappropriately applied the evidence?

Evaluating goodness-of-fit represents a systematic effort to address the question: "What is the most appropriate treatment approach for this specific problem in this particular patient at this present time?" While issues of efficacy, effectiveness, and cost-effectiveness are important aspects of goodness-of-fit, this approach also introduces, and places substantial value on, other more personal, patient-specific considerations.

Evaluating the Outcomes of Treatment

The evaluation of efficacy, effectiveness, and cost-effectiveness are central components of the development of EBP. The preceding discussion illustrates the fact that these components are still evolving. At the same time, the question of goodness-of-fit recognizes that there exists another set of evaluation issues that lies within those central components. Evaluating goodness-of-fit introduces some basic conceptual and methodological challenges, particularly in the area of the evaluation of the outcomes of treatment.

The evaluation of treatment outcomes in most child mental health research is inextricably tied to the choice of outcome measures selected and that choice is made on the basis of the researcher's goals for the study. In most clinical trials involving the mental health treatment of children, the primary purpose is to decrease or control the signs and symptoms of a given disorder or condition. Thus, the standardized measures chosen to demonstrate an improvement in the patient's condition are directly related to the signs and symptoms of the disorder or condition. However, these measures may not tap into the patient's (or the patient's parents') goals for seeking treatment. If the standardized measures do not assess the patients' major goals then the effectiveness of the treatment procedure may be judged by effects related to wrong, or at best partial, outcomes (Guyatt & Cook, 1994; Rothwell et al., 1997).

When clinical trials in child and adolescent mental health do include consideration of subjective outcomes (such as quality of life), researchers often employ generic measures that fail to tap into the reasons why each individual is seeking treatment. The evaluation of outcomes must be judged incomplete unless it addresses the patient's (or the patient's parents') individual, sometimes idiosyncratic, reasons for entering into treatment.

Many psychological treatments are directed at improving patients' presenting problems and complaints and, thus, subjective outcomes may be important outcome measures (Testa & Nackley, 1994; Testa & Simonson, 1996). Although randomized-controlled trials sometimes include standardized measures of quality of life as indices of change, there is little agreement on the quality-of-life construct itself. This lack of conceptual clarity has produced an important methodological issue; the absence of a sound, consensus-based definition of quality of life has yielded a wide range of quite divergent assessment instruments whose contents do not substantially overlap (Gill & Feinstein, 1994; Leplàge & Hunt, 1997). For example, when five standardized measures of health were used with the same group of patients, their health status and changes in health status over time varied substantially across the measures (Beaton, Bombardier, & Hogg-Johnson, 1996; Beaton, Hogg-Johnson, & Bombardier, 1997). Although the five measures each had good psychometric properties, they were essentially measuring different things. Thus, in a controlled trial to compare two different treatments, the magnitude of the quality-of-life effects would depend on which scale was used and on the nature of the outcome evidence resulting from the trial intervention.

An even more fundamental conceptual question, however, is whether standardized quality of life instruments actually measure variables of interest to patients in a research study. That is, do the quality-of-life instruments used in clinical outcomes research take into account the unique and individual, sometimes idiosyncratic, concerns of the patients? In many cases, these concerns are not reflected because the field lacks a methodology for quantifying each patient's concerns into the standard metric that is needed in a randomized-controlled trial. In mental health research, unfortunately, little effort has been devoted to developing standardized scales that document individual patient's concerns and priorities.

Clinicians, however, routinely elicit and respond to individual patient concerns because the resolution of those concerns defines the success of the therapy. If clinicians are going to rely on research evidence for their practice, it behoves researchers to begin including patient concerns as a standard part of their research efforts when assessing treatment outcomes. This approach requires the development of a methodology that is able to specify and quantify each patient's individual concerns when evaluating the effects of psychological or psychopharmacological interventions.

The idea that patient-specific measures should be included as a regular part of outcome measures in research studies is not new (Haynes, 1988) and, indeed, such measures are increasingly used in some areas, if not in child mental health research (Tugwell et al., 1990). For example, patient-specific outcome measures have been developed in various medical specialties, such as surgery (Wright & Young, 1997). In evaluating the outcomes of clinical interventions, children and their parents should be provided the opportunity to voice their specific concerns or goals of treatment and, after the intervention, to express their opinion regarding whether those concerns and goals were addressed.

At a minimum, such an approach requires the researcher to ask each patient to (a) specify his or her presenting complaints and goals of treatment, (b) rate the severity of those complaints, (c) prioritize the complaints and goals according to relative importance, and (d) periodically re-evaluate any complaints and goals as treatment progresses. Identifying patient-specific goals as potential outcomes provides a forum for discussing expectations for treatment (which may be unrealistic and can be redirected early in therapy) and enhances patient satisfaction with mental health care if the patient's and therapist's goals are in accord. There are a host of methodological issues associated with this approach that have yet to be resolved in applying it to child mental health research, but the necessity for doing so is apparent.

Evaluating Practice-Based Evidence

Margison et al. (2000) introduced the notion that an essential feature of evidence-based practice is the collection and thoughtful analysis of "practice-based evidence". This term captures the reality that clinical practice possesses tremendous potential for ongoing evaluation of the integrity and effectiveness of specific interventions. Margison and colleagues go well beyond traditional outcome assessment in describing seven domains for the evaluation of clinical practice: (a) component skills (i.e., specific therapist behaviours); (b) case formulation; (c) treatment integrity (i.e., adherence to prescribed procedures, competent delivery of intervention, differentiation from other interventions); (d) performance—synthesizing adherence, competence and skilfulness; (e) treatment definitions (i.e., use of treatment manuals); (f) therapeutic alliance; and (g) routine outcome measurement.

Evaluating the effectiveness of a treatment intervention in an applied clinical setting presents special difficulties. It is not the case, however, that in such a setting methodological considerations must be compromised. An extensive literature exists documenting the utility of single subject research designs in measuring treatment effects. Approaching clinical intervention as a research study with an N of 1 extends the principles of evidence-based practice into the daily work of the clinician. Resources designed for training the single-subject researcher (e.g., Barlow & Hersen, 1984; Kazdin, 1982; Ollendick & Hersen, 1983, 1984) are easily adapted to evaluate intervention effects in an applied clinical setting (Ottenbacher & Hinderer, 2001).

EVALUATING EVIDENCE OF TREATMENTS THAT WORK: A SPECIFIC METHODOLOGY

In spite of the efforts of professional organizations to identify empirically supported or "evidence-based" interventions, some portion of the burden for evaluating treatment approaches will always remain with individual practitioners. The flood of child mental health research reports appearing each year guarantees that any summary of evidence-based treatment is virtually obsolete by the time it appears in print. Further, a critical aspect of the evaluation of treatment approaches at the point of clinical application is selecting the appropriate intervention for a particular patient with a specific set of strengths, symptoms, and other psychological characteristics. Sackett and colleagues (2000) have developed a five-step process that clinicians can use to evaluate the research literature and determine what will work best for their patients. The process involves: (1) formulating the question, (2) searching for answers, (3) evaluating the research evidence, (4) applying the results, and (5) evaluating the outcomes.

Step 1: Formulating the Question

Step 1 involves formulating the evaluation question in a clear and succinct manner. Typically, the question specifies (a) target patients or problem, (b) target treatment or intervention, (c) presence of a no-treatment control or alternative treatment or intervention, and (d) target outcome. Examples of evaluation questions include: (1) "In adolescents with major depressive disorder, is interpersonal psychotherapy more effective than a wait-list control for reducing symptoms of depression and improving functioning?" and (2) "In children with specific phobias, are approaches based on modelling as effective as systematic desensitization in reducing anxiety and avoidance?"

Each type of question is associated with an experimental design that can best answer the question: for example, treatment efficacy questions usually involve randomized-controlled designs while questions about longer-term prognosis may require a cohort design (Geddes, 1999; Greenhalgh, 2001). However, for some evaluation questions the research literature may not include studies with optimal designs and, the clinician must decide what level of evidence is acceptable. The Agency for Healthcare Research and Quality (AHRQ) has proposed three levels for classifying the strength of the research evidence: A, good evidence from well-conducted clinical trials or cohort studies; B, evidence that is fair and based on other types of research studies; and C, recommendations based on expert opinion where evidence is lacking.

Another commonly used hierarchy of evidence (Geddes, 1999; Phillips et al., 2002) ranks evidence along a continuum from best to worst:

(1) systematic review of RCTs (best)
(2) single RCT, all or none case series
(3) systematic review of cohort studies
(4) single cohort study or RCT with <80% follow-up
(5) outcomes research and ecological studies
(6) systematic review of case-control studies
(7) single case-control study
(8) case series, and
(9) expert opinion (worst).

In practice, clinicians may begin their literature search at the best level of evidence and work their way down until the evidence is found. Put simply, working within the framework of a hierarchy of evidence provides a means for judging the quality of research and for determining the level of confidence that may be placed in the results.

Step 2: Searching for Answers

Searchable computerized databases of original research literature such as Psych-Info and Medline are powerful and comprehensive. However, depending on the question being asked and the availability of research evidence pertaining to the general topic involved, a search may yield thousands of research articles.

If the literature is extensive, Haynes' (2001) "4S" strategy may prove to be a more efficient way of undertaking a search. The 4S's are: systems (comprehensive resources), synopses (structured abstracts), syntheses (systematic reviews), and individual studies (original research papers). An efficient search strategy may begin with Systems resources, working down to Individual Studies only if needed. System sources provide frequently updated summaries of results of high-quality systematic reviews of original research studies. Clinical Evidence (*http:// www.clinicalevidence.org*) that appears in electronic and print versions (published semi-annually) is a good example of a System source in mental health.

If System sources fail to answer the target question, the search continues at the next level. Synopses are structured abstracts of high-quality systematic reviews. Evidence-Based Mental Health (*http://www.ebmh.bmjjournals.com*) that appears in electronic and print versions (quarterly) is a good example of a Synopsis source. If more information is needed to make a treatment decision, the clinician can proceed to the next level (Synthesis), examining high-quality systematic review papers. The Cochrane Library, for example (*http://www.update-software.com/abstracts/ mainindex.htm*) is a good source for such reviews.

Finally, original studies can be searched through a number of excellent databases, including PsychInfo (*http://www.psychinfo.com*) or PsychLit (a subset of PsychInfo) and PubMed (*http://www4.ncbi.nlm.nih.gov/entrez*). Given that the search is focused on original studies, there is a good chance that a large number of studies will turn up in a search. Services such as PubMed make the task somewhat easier by allowing a search to be narrowed by question type (aetiology, diagnosis, therapy, or prognosis).

Step 3: Evaluating the Research Evidence

Once the search is completed and copies are obtained, the quality of the research must be evaluated. Evaluation worksheets are available to make this step easier; examples can be found at the Centre for Evidence-Based Mental Health website (*http://cebmh.warne.ox.ac.uk*) and the Centre for Evidence-Based Medicine website (*http://www.library.utoronto.ca/medicine/ebm*). These worksheets are specific to the type of article (e.g., overviews, treatment, diagnosis, and prognosis) being evaluated. For example, for treatment articles, a clinician may concentrate on three critical evaluation questions: validity of the study, importance of the results, and applicability to individual patients.

Having evaluated the available evidence, a clinician can discuss with the patient, and the patient's family, one or more treatment interventions in terms of the strength of the evidence, the probable effects and side-effects of the treatment, cost, and benefit–harm equation, thus offering consumers an opportunity to participate in the selection of the treatment procedure.

If there is insufficient evidence to evaluate, but a treatment decision still needs to be made, the clinician may consider the following questions (Donald & Muthu, 2001, p. 36):

1. What is professional consensus on the matter?
2. What do my own knowledge and experience tell me?

3. What is the safest decision?
4. How harmful would the "wrong" decision be?
5. What are my patient's preferences?

The issue of patient preferences is a critical one in mental health. In the case of two equally effective treatments, it may be easy to leave the choice to the patient and the family. However, even when two treatments yield unequal treatment effects, patient preference is an essential consideration. Children or their parents may choose an intervention that is predicted to have a smaller direct effect in terms of treatment outcome because of other considerations. Treatment choice should reflect the goals of patients who want as normal a life as possible and one that is functional, productive, and satisfying (Mead & Copeland, 2000; Torrey & Wyzik, 2000). This means that treatment outcomes are evaluated not only in terms of efficacy with regard to the reduction of signs and symptoms, but also in terms of patients' independence, educational attainment, satisfying social relationships, and quality of life.

Step 4: Applying the Results

After a treatment approach has been chosen, and questions about the treatment answered, the clinician can then proceed to the application of the chosen treatment. Implementing the treatment with fidelity is essential to obtaining the expected results (e.g., Jerrel & Ridgely, 1999).

However, there are many challenges in implementing evidence-based treatment procedures. A clinician who is not familiar with the intervention, or who has not had the requisite training, may not be able to implement it as specified. Referral to a specialist clinician who can provide the treatment may not be an option in many mental health care markets. However, many of the empirically validated approaches in child mental health, especially those that have been tested in controlled trials, are manualized cognitive-behavioural treatments. While many clinicians do not like using manuals (Silverman, 1996) or may not prefer a cognitive-behavioural approach (Woody, 2000), treatment manuals extend the options available to practicing clinicians.

An issue virtually unmentioned in the treatment literature is the application of the empirically validated individual treatment interventions in groups consisting of several individuals that require similar therapy for a given disorder or problem (e.g., a group on anger management). The group leader will be called upon to individualize the therapy to some extent within the group and no randomized-controlled trial data are currently available on individualization in a group context.

Finally, the application of evidence-based treatment approaches may involve more than one mental health professional. In psychiatric hospitals, the unit responsible for a patient's treatment is often a treatment team. The practice of evidence-based treatment in such a setting requires the alteration of the treatment team's mode of operation in terms of prescribing treatments, a much greater challenge than changing the habits of a single therapist (Torrey et al., 2001). Given the diverse theoretical orientations often found on treatment teams, even when the team has made a commitment to the use of evidence-based interventions, there is likely to be some disagreement regarding the range of interventions to consider and the hierarchies of evidence for making treatment decisions.

Step 5: Evaluating the Outcomes

The evaluation of outcomes considers how the patient responded to the chosen treatment. Outcomes, both at the individual patient level and at various organizational levels, provide the basis for improving quality of patient care, increasing efficiency of the service system, and reducing overall costs of providing quality care. A variety of scientific and patient-specific measures are available to measure individual patient outcomes (see above).

At the organizational level, the practice of benchmarking provides a means for evaluating the effectiveness of EBP (Camp & Tweet, 1994). Benchmarking allows an organization to compare and measure its philosophy, policies, practices, and outcomes against other similar, high-performing organizations. Further, it includes the development, implementation, and evaluation of continuous quality improvement. Linking EBP with benchmarking enables a mental health service agency to continuously evaluate the quality of its services and to develop remedial action plans for enhancing its standards of care.

The evaluation of outcomes may also include the clinician's self-evaluation of the process of selecting an evidence-based treatment approach. As with any new skill, this process becomes easier and more efficient with practice, particularly if it concludes with a thoughtful, systematic review leading to the development of individually tailored methods matching the clinician's level of research training, access to materials, and time available for the task.

CONCLUSION

Much of the child and adolescent mental health services research literature reflects a belief that, once the efficacy of a therapeutic modality has been shown to be empirically supported, the treatment can be used to equal effect in any context (e.g., clinic, school, home, rural vs urban). This extrapolation goes beyond the current evaluation data and the question of fit between treatment procedure and context is an area that we know very little about. Current studies indicate that while strong efficacy of treatment may be evidenced in university or research-based clinics, the effectiveness of the intervention may be much weaker in routine clinical practice settings (Weisz, Weiss, & Donenberg, 1992), possibly because the treatment cannot be delivered under the same tightly controlled conditions in non-research settings. Thus, the demonstration of effectiveness requires either that the evidence for a treatment's efficacy must be obtained in non-research settings or the non-research settings must improve their capacity to implement evidence-based therapies as prescribed (Hoagwood et al., 2001).

Evidenced-based treatments also need to be evaluated in terms of their transportability (Schoenwald & Hoagwood, 2001). Factors that enable evidenced-based therapies to be implemented across multiple settings include: adaptability of treatments and treatment manuals, characteristics and training of therapists, case-loads of therapists and case managers, monitoring and maintenance of treatment fidelity, treatment of heterogeneous populations, age range of children treated, developmental issues and contexts, socioeconomic status of families and family contexts, dose and intensity of therapeutic services, cultural context of the therapists and families, culturally informed services, accessibility of services, treatment adherence, funding of services, follow-up services, and interagency issues (Hoagwood, Burns, & Weisz, 2002; Norquist, Lebowitz, & Hyman, 2000; Schoenwald & Hoagwood, 2001).

There has been little evaluation of EBP in routine mental health practice with children. In many practice settings, issues of philosophy of care, organizational infrastructure, commitment of administration and clinicians, resource development, and training have yet to be resolved before EBP becomes a reality. While EBP is beginning to impact clinical training, outcomes research, medical informatics, managed care, liability issues and public policy, evaluation at every stage of this development is imperative.

Evidence-based approaches are defined by the results of standardized, objective, scientific measurement systems. Such systems generally fail to take into account the subjective issues that may be of primary importance to the patient, i.e., the subjective, phenomenological experiences that give meaning and purpose to a person's life (Deegan, 1992; Pelka, 1998). Successful treatment is a value judgment, and the clinician and patient may not always agree on the definition of a successful outcome. Thus, clinicians need to find a way of combining evidence-based treatments with the patient's preferences and judgments of what constitutes success. Consideration of preferences may be more difficult when the patient is very disabled by mental illness but, as treatment progresses, the patient should be encouraged to exercise increasing autonomy in the therapeutic process.

Evidence-based practice is transforming the landscape of clinical practice with children. Clinicians are used to reading reviews of the literature about specific treatment modalities or disorders. EBP enables clinicians to ask very specific questions pertaining to the treatment of individual patients and to utilize a sophisticated methodology for searching, summarizing, and synthesizing the best available evidence to answer the questions. It can facilitate clinical decision-making, improve patient outcomes, and optimize benefit–cost of providing clinical services to children. Still, much remains to be realized before we can conclude that EBP has been or will be common clinical practice.

REFERENCES

American Psychological Association Task Force on Psychological Intervention Guidelines. (1995). *Template for developing guidelines: Interventions for mental disorders and psychological aspects of physical disorders*. Washington, DC: Author.

American Psychiatric Association (1997). *Practice guidelines for the treatment of patients with schizophrenia*. Washington, DC: Author.

Barlow, D.H. (1994). Psychological interventions in the era of managed competition. *Clinical Psychology: Science and Practice,* **1**, 109–122.

Barlow, D.H., & Hersen, M. (1984). *Single-case experimental designs: Strategies for studying behavior change* (2nd edn). New York: Pergamon Press.

Beaton, D.E., Bombardier, C., & Hogg-Johnson, S.A. (1996). Measuring health in injured workers: A cross-sectional comparison of five generic health instruments in workers with musculoskeletal injuries. *American Journal of Industrial Medicine, 29*, 618–631.

Beaton, D.E., Hogg-Johnson, S., & Bombardier, C. (1997). Evaluating changes in health status: Reliability and responsiveness of five generic health status measures in workers with musculoskeletal disorders. *Journal of Clinical Epidemiology, 50*, 79–93.

Beutler, L.E. (2000). David and Goliath: When empirical and clinical standards of practice meet. *American Psychologist, 55*, 997–1007.

Beutler, L.E., Clarkin, J.F., & Bongar, B. (2000). *Guidelines for systematically treating the depressed patient.* New York: Brunner/Mazel.

Bilsker, D., & Goldner, E.M. (1995). Evidenced-based psychiatry. *Canadian Journal of Psychiatry, 40*, 97–101.

Byford, S., Harrington, R.C., Torgerson, D., Kerfoot, M., Dyer, E., Harrington, V., Woodham, A., Gill, J., & McNiven, F. (1999). Cost-effectiveness analysis of a home-based social work intervention for children and adolescents who have deliberately poisoned themselves: The results of a randomized controlled trial. *British Journal of Psychiatry, 174*, 56–62.

Camp, R.C., & Tweet, A.G. (1994). Benchmarking applied to health care. *Joint Commission Journal of Quality Improvement, 20*, 229–238.

Chambless, D.L., Baker, M.J., Baucom, D.H., Beutler, L.E., Calhoun, K.S., Crits-Christoph, P., Daiuto, A., DeRubeis, R., Detweiler, J., Haaga, D.A.F., Johnson, S.B., McCurry, S., Mueser, K.T., Pope, K.S., Sanderson, W.C., Shoham, V., Stickle, T., Williams, D.A., & Woody, S.R. (1998). Update on empirically validated therapies, II. *The Clinical Psychologist, 51*, 3–16.

Chambless, D.L., & Hollon, S.D. (1998). Defining empirically supported therapies. *Journal of Consulting and Clinical Psychology, 66*, 7–18.

Chambless, D.L., & Ollendick, T.H. (2001). Empirically supported psychological interventions: Controversies and evidence. *Annual Review of Psychology, 52*, 685–716.

Chambless, D.L., Sanderson, W.C., Shoham, V., Johnson, S.B., Pope, K.S., Crits-Christoph, P., Baker, M.J., Johnson, B., Woody, S.R., Sue, S., Beutler, L.E., Williams, D.A., & McCurry, S. (1996). An update on empirically validated therapies. *The Clinical Psychologist, 49* (2), 5–14.

Collins, R., & MacMahon, S. (2001). Reliable assessment of the effects of treatment on mortality and major morbidity, I: Clinical trials. *Lancet, 357*, 373–380.

Davidoff, F., Haynes, B., Sackett, D., & Smith, R. (1995). Evidence based medicine: A new journal to help doctors identify the information they need. *British Medical Journal, 310*, 1085–1086.

Deegan, P.E. (1992). The independent living movement and people with psychiatric disabilities: Taking back control of our own lives. *Psychosocial Rehabilitation Journal, 15* (3), 3–19.

Donald, A., & Muthu, V. (2001). *BMJ clinical evidence: Evidence-based medicine introductory workshop.* London, UK: BMJ Publishing Group.

Drummond, M., Cooke, J., & Walley, T. (1997). Economic evaluation under managed competition: Evidence from the UK. *Social Science and Medicine, 45*, 583–595.

Field, M.J., & Lohr, K.N. (1992). *Guidelines for clinical practice: From development to use.* Washington, DC: National Academy Press.

Frances, A.J., Docherty, J., & Kahn, D.A. (1996). The expert consensus guideline series: Treatment of schizophrenia. *Journal of Clinical Psychiatry, 57* (Suppl. 12B), 1–58.

Frances, A.J., Kahn, D., Carpenter, D., Ross, R., & Docherty, J.P. (1996). The Expert Consensus Practice Guideline Project: A new method of establishing best practice. *Journal of Practicing Behavioural Health, 5*, 295–305.

Garb, H. (1998). *Studying the clinician.* Washington, DC: American Psychological Association.

Geddes, J. (1999). Asking structured and focused clinical questions: Essential first step of evidence-based practice. *Evidence-Based Mental Health, 2*, 35–36.

Gill, T.M., & Feinstein, A.R. (1994). A critical appraisal of the quality of quality-of-life measurements. *Journal of the American Medical Association, 272*, 619–626.

Greenhalgh, T. (2001). *How to read a paper: The basics of evidence-based medicine* (2nd edn). London: BMJ Books.

Guyatt, G.H., & Cook, E.J. (1994). Health status, quality of life, and the individual. *Journal of the American Medical Association, 272,* 619–626.

Guyatt, G., & Rennie, D. (2002). *Users' guides to the medical literature: A manual for evidence-based clinical practice.* Chicago: AMA Press.

Harrington, R. (2001). Commentary: Evidence-based child and adolescent mental health services. *Child Psychology and Psychiatry Reviews, 6,* 65.

Haynes R.B. (1988). Selected principles of the measurement and setting of priorities of death, disability, and suffering in clinical trials. *American Journal of Medical Sciences, 296,* 364–369.

Haynes, R.B. (2001). Of studies, summaries, synopses, and systems: The "4S" evolution of services for finding current best evidence. *Evidence-Based Mental Health, 4,* 37–39.

Hoagwood, K., Burns, B.J., Kiser, L., Ringeisen, H., & Schoenwald, S.K. (2001). Evidence-based practice in child and adolescent mental health services. *Psychiatric Services, 52,* 1179–1189.

Hoagwood, K., Burns, B.J., & Weisz, J.R. (2002). A profitable conjunction: From research to practice in children's mental health. In B.J. Burns & K. Hoagwood (Eds), *Community treatment for youth: Evidence-based interventions for severe emotional and behavioural disorders* (pp. 327–338). New York: Oxford University Press.

Jerrel, J.M., & Ridgely, M.S. (1999). Impact of robustness of program implementation on outcomes of clients in dual diagnosis programs. *Psychiatric Services, 50,* 109–112.

Kazdin, A.E. (1982). *Single-case research designs: Methods for clinical and applied settings.* New York: Oxford University Press.

Leplàge, A., & Hunt, S. (1997). The problem of quality of life in medicine. *Journal of the American Medical Association, 278,* 47–50.

Margison, F.R., Barkham, M., Evans, C., McGrath, G., Clark, J.M., Audin, K., & Connell, J. (2000). Measurement and psychotherapy: Evidence-based practice and practice-based evidence. *British Journal of Psychiatry, 177,* 123–130.

Mead, S., & Copeland, M.E. (2000). What recovery means to us: Consumers' perspectives. *Community Mental Health Journal, 36,* 315–328.

Norquist, G., Lebowitz, B., & Hyman, S. (2000). Expanding the frontier of treatment research. Available at http://journals.apa.org/prevention/volume2/pre0020001a.html.

Ollendick, T.H., & Hersen, M. (Eds) (1983). *Handbook of child and adolescent assessment.* Boston: Allyn & Bacon.

Ollendick, T.H., & Hersen, M. (Eds) (1984). *Child behavioural assessment: Principles and procedures.* New York: Pergamon Press.

Ollendick, T.H., & King, N.J. (2004). Empirically supported treatments for children and adolescents: Advances toward evidence-based practice. In P. Barrett & T.H. Ollendick (Eds), *Handbook of interventions that work with children and adolescents: From prevention to treatment* (pp. 3–26). Chichester: John Wiley & Sons.

Ottenbacher, K.L., & Hinderer, S.R. (2001). Evidence-based practice: Methods to evaluate individual patient improvement. *American Journal of Physical Medicine and Rehabilitation, 80,* 786–796.

Pelka, F. (1998). Shrink resistant. *Mainstream: Magazine of the Able-Disabled, 22* (9), 22–27.

Phillips, B., Ball, C., Sackett, D., Haynes, B., Straus, S., & McAlister, F. (March 2002). Levels of evidence and grades of recommendations [Evidence-Based On Call website]. Available at: http://www:eboncall.co.uk. Accessed 26 December 2002.

Rosser, W.W., & Shafir, M.S. (1998). *Evidence based family medicine.* Hamilton, Canada: B.C. Decker.

Rothwell, P.M., McDowell, D., Wong, C.K., & Dorman, P.J. (1997). Doctors and patients don't agree: Cross sectional study of patients' and doctors' perceptions and assessments of disability in multiple sclerosis. *British Medical Journal, 314,* 1580–1583.

Sackett, D.L., Rosenberg, W.M.C., Gray, J.A.M., Haynes, R.B., & Richardson, W.S. (1996). Evidence based medicine: What it is and what it isn't. *British Medical Journal, 312,* 71–72.

Sackett, D.L., Straus, S.E., Richardson, W.S., Rosenberg, W., & Haynes, R.S. (2000). *Evidence-based medicine: How to practice and teach EBM* (2nd edn). Edinburgh, UK: Churchill Livingstone.

Schoenwald, S.K., & Hoagwood, K. (2001). Effectiveness, transportability, and dissemination of interventions: What matters when? *Psychiatric Services, 52*, 1190–1197.

Silverman, W.H. (1996). Cookbooks, manuals, and paint-by-numbers: Psychotherapy in the 90s. *Psychotherapy, 33*, 207–215.

Task Force on Promotion and Dissemination of Psychological Procedures (1995). Training in and dissemination of empirically validated treatments: Report and recommendations. *The Clinical Psychologist, 48* (1), 3–23.

Testa, M.A., & Nackley, J.F. (1994). Methods for quality-of-life studies. *Annual Review of Public Health, 15*, 535–559.

Testa, M.A., & Simonson, D.C. (1996). Assessment of quality-of-life outcomes. *New England Journal of Medicine, 334*, 835–840.

Torrey, W.C., Drake, R.E., Dixon, L., Burns, B.J., Flynn, L., Rush, A.J., Clark, R.E., & Klatzker, D. (2001). Implementing evidence-based practices for persons with severe mental illnesses. *Psychiatric Services, 52*, 45–50.

Torrey, W.C., & Wyzik, P. (2000). The recovery vision as service improvement guide for community mental health center providers. *Community Mental Health Journal, 36*, 209–216.

Tugwell, P., Bombardier, C., Buchanan, W.W., Goldsmith, C., Grace, E., Bennett, K.J., Williams, H.J., Egger, M., Alarcon, G.S., & Guttadauria, M. (1990). Methotrexate in rheumatoid arthritis: Impact on quality of life assessed by traditional standard-item and individualized patient preference health status questionnaires. *Archives of Internal Medicine, 150*, 59–62.

Weisz, J.R., Weiss, B., & Donenberg, G.R. (1992). The lab versus the clinic: Effects of child and adolescent psychotherapy. *American Psychologist, 47*, 1578–1585.

Woody, S.R. (2000). On babies and bathwater: Commentary on Beutler (2000). Prevention and Treatment, 3, Article 30, posted 1 September. Available at: http://www.journals.apa.org/prevention/volume3/preoo30027a.html

Wright, J.G., & Young, N.L. (1997). The patient-specific index: Asking patients what they want. *Journal of Bone Joint Surgery, 79A*, 974–983.

CHAPTER 5

Assessment and Treatment of Ethnically Diverse Children and Adolescents

Robi Sonderegger

and

Paula M. Barrett

Griffith University, Australia

INTRODUCTION

At no point in modern history have so many people from culturally diverse backgrounds lived together in plural societies. With the continuing influx of migrants and refugees into many host countries around the world, there is a growing necessity for culturally appropriate research to identify the needs of expatriate families and better understand how cultural factors influence the development of psychological symptoms, cognitive processing, and behavioural expression. The concerns of uprooted children and adolescents (hereon referred to as youth) from dissimilar linguistic and racial backgrounds range from acculturation difficulties and identity confusion, to the manifestation of anxiety and dysfunctional coping responses (e.g., drug and alcohol misuse, school yard aggression, and suicide) (Ponterotto, Baluch, & Carielli, 1998; Roberts & Schnieder, 1999; Selvamanickam, Zgryza, & Gorman, 2001). Consequently, the provision of ethnically sensitive clinical services to diverse community members is of increasing importance. This chapter reviews a selection of contemporary cross-cultural research endeavours, and addresses a number of relevant issues concerning culturally competent assessment and treatment practice.

Much of the clinical focus within cross-cultural psychology examines the adjustment process of individuals who have been raised in a specific culture, defined by a

Correspondence to Robi Sonderegger, Griffith University, Mt Gravatt Campus, School of Applied Psychology, Mt Gravatt, QLD, 4111; email: r.sonderegger@griffith.edu.au

Handbook of Interventions that Work with Children and Adolescents: Prevention and Treatment.
Edited by P.M. Barrett and T.H. Ollendick. © 2004 John Wiley & Sons, Ltd. ISBN 0-470-84453-1.

unique identity, social traditions, community norms, and ethnic expression (Jones & Chao, 1997; McGoldrick, Pearce, & Giordano, 1982), and take up residence in a new cultural setting. The process by which relocated individuals assume the values and behavioural standards of the host culture is commonly referred to as *acculturation*. This cultural adjustment process is often fraught with personal difficulty at different levels. In addition to the absence or loss of extended family members and friends, and the perceived pressure to adopt new cultural traditions, practices, and basic norms, one's very own moral beliefs and attitudes particularly concerning independence, sex-roles, and intergenerational family dynamics are often impinged on (Storer, 1985). The alacrity to which family members embrace or resist elements of their new culture often serves as a platform for conflict between parents and youth, and may exacerbate peer prejudice in the school setting. With such complex and multilayered adjustment difficulties being paired with migration, it is not surprising that acculturative-stress is indicated in the development of internalizing problems among young migrants and refugees (Barrett, Sonderegger, & Sonderegger, in press; Barrett, Sonderegger, & Xenos, 2003; Berry, 1998).

Cultural Transition and Stress

The experience of cultural adjustment problems following transcultural migration has received considerable attention over recent years from numerous academic disciplines, including anthropology, education, psychology, and sociology (Sam, 2000). While each field has contributed to a broadly accepted understanding of acculturation and associated health responses, methodological and operational definition variance has plagued cultural adjustment research, resulting in a number of overlapping and poorly specified models (Arcia et al., 2001; Gutierrez, 1995). Despite the diversity of theoretical premise, increasing efforts (e.g., Berry & Kim, 1987; Berry et al., 1988; Nguyen, Messé, & Stollak, 1999; Rogler, 1994) are being made to systematize research outcomes for the benefit of scholarly consensus and investigative frameworks.

Of the many acculturation theories proposed, Nguyen, Messé, and Stollak (1999) report the emergence of two dominant perspectives that have formed the basis of current acculturation assessment inventories. The first perspective suggests that acculturation is defined by a single assimilation index—the acquisition of new values and behaviours represented by the host culture. The more sociocultural norms adopted in place of those affiliated with one's culture of origin, the greater the level of acculturation an individual will develop. In contrast, the second perspective supports cultural pluralism—inferring that the adoption of new values and behaviours can coexist with the social norms of one's original culture. In this regard, the adoption of new sociocultural norms can be seen as a selective process that does not necessarily replace existing behaviours. As individuals build confidence to engage in social situations with members of both the host culture, and ethnic enclaves that may exist within their community, acculturation becomes reflective of one's adjustment aptitude to a variety of social circumstance. One element central to both these perspectives of acculturation is that in order for successful adjustment to occur, individuals must first simultaneously maintain a level of cultural identity (whether one's original cultural identity, the development of a new identity reflective of the host culture, or an amalgamation of the two), and, second, participate in behaviours and social customs of the host culture (Sam, 2000).

Arcia et al. (2001) contend that the extent to which cultural practices are adopted or maintained by migrants is directly related to the cultural interactions they encounter. If initial interaction experiences are positive, they in turn become reinforcing. Unfortunately, the experience of cultural change is often fraught with stress, conflict, and a sense of loss that results in cultural identity confusion, low self-esteem, and internalizing problems. Inasmuch that young migrants are often faced with premature separation from extended family members, decreased parental support, communication and education difficulties, and peer rejection (Winter & Young, 1998), it is not surprising that young migrants are vulnerable to the development of psychopathology.

Despite broad recognition of the difficulties that ethnically diverse youth experience when making the transition to a new culture, few clinical research initiatives have sought to evaluate cultural risk and protective mechanisms among young migrants and refugees. The overwhelming majority of research into the emotional concerns of youth is disproportionately focused on Anglo populations in developed English-speaking nations. Without a clear understanding of the cultural, developmental, and situational variables that mediate both psychological dysfunction and well-being among non-English-speaking background (NESB) youth, mental health professionals are ill equipped to develop and administer culturally appropriate assessment and intervention resources.

Cultural Construct Difficulties

When appraising the risk and protective factors among culturally diverse youth, it is important to obtain a good understanding of culture itself. While there is no singular consensus on a definition of culture, this phenomenon that appears to shape every aspect of our lives from the time we are born has been described as representative of communal beliefs, languages, rules, values and knowledge (Rice & O'Donohue, 2002; Matthews, 1997). However, with vague concepts such as "beliefs", "values", and "knowledge" that warrant further delineation, the field of cross-cultural psychology is plagued by definitional variance. Moreover, Rice and Donohue contend that if communities differ in such important constructs, they may also vary in their foundational construct of "culture" itself. In this regard, the concept of culture may have little meaning other than what the Western world pontificates it to be. To further extrapolate the concept of culture, many researchers take the approach of differentiating community groups by other salient constructs such as race (physical/biological characteristics) and ethnicity (language/nationality). Regardless of its framework, culture must be viewed as a distinct ever-evolving trait, influenced by numerous variables at both a personal and a societal level. This is especially evident among young migrants and refugees who relocate countries with their families, and attempt to balance traditional family beliefs and practices while at the same time conforming to new behavioural and societal norms. Consequently, in attempting to assess different forms of psychopathology in different cultures, it is important to remember that psychometric measures are only capable of assessing aspects of an individual at one particular point in time.

While cross-cultural literature is besieged with calls for the development of culture-specific assessment inventories, forming constructs about specific cultures may incorrectly presume that culture does not change. Acknowledgment of salient cultural aspects of any given population may exist, however mental health professionals and researchers alike are further challenged to consider within-cultural group distinctions and variance. This is especially true when assessing diverse cultural cleavages within the context of a broader plural society. For example, Zvolensky et al. (2001) recently sought to compare levels of anxiety among American Indian, Alaskan Native and Anglo-American college students using the Anxiety Severity Index. Among the Native American participant population ($N = 282$), a total of 70 different tribes were represented, including Cherokee ($n = 20$), Choctaw ($n = 18$), Creek ($n = 14$) and Navajo ($n = 45$). The lack of internal heterogeneity among this group of participants who were all classified under the same banner of Native American, leads to questions regarding the accuracy of cultural representation. A lack of mutual exclusion would further complicate the matter, if for example, a number of participants were part Navajo and part Cherokee, and thus identified with one or both tribal group cultural norms. Moreover, if participants were part Navajo and part Anglo-American, they may dismiss or appeal to one heritage in favour of the other, making it difficult for researchers to draw accurate conclusions.

A similar study by Barrett, Sonderegger, and Sonderegger (in press) examined the cultural adjustment experiences of 158 children and adolescents from former-Yugoslavian ($n = 42$), Chinese ($n = 60$), and Anglo-Australian (n = 56) backgrounds. To ensure accurate cultural representation, all participants were born, and spent a number of years growing up in their culture of origin. However, migrant participants had been residing in Australia for different lengths of time (ranging from 2.5 months to 7.5 years), moved to Australia for different reasons (e.g., refugees versus free migrants), and came from different ports of origin. Chinese origin participants who had migrated to Australia came from the People's Republic of China, Hong Kong, Taiwan, and Singapore, whereas former-Yugoslavian participants came from Croatia, Bosnia, and Serbia. Moreover, while former-Yugoslavian language dialects are quite similar, Chinese origin participants comprised both Mandarin- and Cantonese-speaking backgrounds. Although Barrett et al. found greater between group cultural differences than within, with so many intragroup variables to control for, such cross-cultural research initiatives tend to become logistically awkward.

Given that culture is so unique at many different levels, cross-cultural mental health professionals and researchers alike must ask to what extent the internal heterogeneity of cultural groups should be measured. If we consider the intragroup cultural differences between individuals in urban and rural dwelling settings, sociopolitical differences, and generational influence on families within plural societies, accurate cultural appraisal becomes litigious, debatable, and controversial. At a time when cross-cultural research should be encouraged and not discouraged, the onus on researchers is to exercise wisdom in developing a culturally inclusive framework of cross-cultural distinction. Clearly, if the value of examining and comparing psychopathology in different cultures is to be truly upheld from an empirical stand-point, the study of cross-cultural psychology requires well-defined guidelines that are consistently maintained.

Despite obvious assessment limitations, according to Bird (1996), epidemiological studies that compared disorders among culturally diverse populations by using the Child Behaviour Checklist (CBCL; Achenbach & Edelbrock, 1981, 1983) have been most suitable. The CBCL has three parallel versions (parent, teacher, and self rating), and has been translated into more than 40 languages. Diagnostic studies around the world (including Germany, USA, New Zealand, The Netherlands, Canada, Puerto Rico, Ireland, and France) using the CBCL over the past two decades have revealed that although assessment methodologies have been com-patible, culturally mediated symtomological differences are evident (refer to Bird, 1996, for a complete review of trans-national major diagnosis-based epidemiological studies). Yet, despite observed cultural group differences in mean scores, the rank order of items were found to be similar between different nationalities. Although symptom expression or severity may vary between cultures, it may be sug-gested that rank order patterns indicate similar diagnostic patterns to be present in each culture. It should be noted however, that although methodologies employed were consistent and diagnostic patterns emerged, this should not be taken as con-firmation that the procedures employed or the diagnostic outcomes were culturally valid. Without a culturally valid investigative framework, cross-cultural psycho-pathology may be interpreted in a variety of different ways.

CROSS-CULTURAL PSYCHOPATHOLOGY

Western diagnostic classification systems are based upon the philosophies of Western medical science and universal theories of disease (Prince & Tcheng-Laroche, 1987). Although cross-cultural investigations into the presentation and prevalence of psychopathology as recognized by Western medicine are on the increase, cultural-specific forms of psychopathology are also gaining recognition. Consequently, there is debate as to whether the various psychopathological symp-toms evident across cultures are merely different expressions of the same or similar disorders, or whether psychopathology is a distinct phenomenon between culturally diverse groups. In recent years, two opposing theories have emerged; universalist and relativist approaches to cross-cultural psychopathology. In simple terms, the universalist approach assumes that the same disorders are evident in all cultures across humanity, while the relativist approach theorizes that each culture has its own unique disorders that are as diverse as the cultures themselves. Both of these orientations have been examined over recent years using different methods of investigation.

The universalist approach has used Western classifications to examine major psychiatric disorders across cultures. Some of the initial and most significant investigations have examined the universality of schizophrenia (e.g., Jablensky et al., 1992; World Health Organization, 1973, 1979) and depression (e.g., Jablensky et al., 1981; Thakker, Ward, & Strongman, 1999; Ulusahin, Basoglu, & Pakyel, 1994; World Health Organization, 1983) among diverse cultural groups. These and other studies highlight how culture can shape perceptions and responses to pathology.

The WHO's International Pilot Study of Schizophrenia (IPSS) and the follow-up Determinant Outcomes of Severe Mental Disorder (DOSMD) were conducted across nine and ten different countries respectively, each comprising in excess of 1000 participants. Not only was schizophrenia found to be present in different cultures, but also it was revealed that the disorder has a more favourable course in developing countries than in developed ones, suggesting that cultural perception plays a moderating role (Lopez, 2000). However, before conclusions can be made, we must question the role the different languages and cultural norms play in shaping an individual's perceptions of what is essentially a Western understanding of "core symptoms". Friedman, Paradis, and Hatch (1994) report that misdiagnosis frequently occurs due to language differences, and among African-American populations has led to the unnecessary prescription and use of antipsychotic drugs.

Iwata and Buka (2002) compared depressive symptoms among students in East Asia, North and South America using the Centre for Epidemiologic Studies Depression Scale (CES-D). The 20-item self-report CES-D which assesses the frequency of depressive symptoms during "the past week" is a widely used assessment tool, validated mainly with Anglo-Americans. Anglo-American scores and percentages were used as a reference for comparison. A total of 307 Japanese, 377 Anglo-American, 353 Native American, and 110 Argentinian undergraduate students took part. The researchers reasoned that undergraduate students presented a comparable group due to their similar ages and current life circumstances, thereby reducing the impact of extraneous variables. The mean age (18–24 years) was comparable across all groups except the Anglo-Americans, who on average were two years younger.

The outcomes of this study showed that Japanese participants report a significantly greater level of low positive affect than their Anglo-American or Argentinian counterparts, but no higher on negative symptoms. The authors suggest that this finding supports other studies (Iwata, Saito, & Roberts, 1994) that have found Japanese participants tend to inhibit the expression of positive affect. This finding may be understood as a product of cultural norms in Japanese society that value the welfare of the group over the individual and therefore promote the development of compliance, nurturance, and interdependency (Iwata & Buka, 2002). In this regard, it is argued that differences found between cultural groups are related to cultural norms and modes of expression rather than the actual experience of depression itself.

One of the most consistent cultural group distinctions that emerge when assessing depressive symptoms is the variation in somatization—the presentation or experience of physical symptoms perceived to be the cause of, or related to, mood change (Farooq et al., 1995; Thakker, Ward, & Strongman, 1999). In their comparison of depression between British and Turkish populations, Ulusahin, Basoglu, and Paykel (1994) found similar mood disorder prevalence. However, unlike those from Britain, Turkish participants typically presented somatic symptoms rather than psychological symptoms of depression. In contrast to Western populations who typically describe depressive symptoms in psychological terms, Weiss, Raguram, and Channabasavanna (1995) also report that Indian and Asian cultures describe negative affect in terms of more somatic symptoms. To determine whether these cultural differences were a function of experience or description, participant responses were closely examined. When probed, all participants reported being able to identify both psychological and physical symptoms; however, participants expressed clear preferences in describing their experience of depression.

One explanation posited by Thakker and Ward (1998) as to why depression is sometimes described in somatic terms among non-Western populations, relates to an overriding social disapproval of strong emotional expression in particular cultures. For example, Munakata (1989) reports that in Japanese culture, a psychiatric diagnosis is often greatly stigmatized and has negative social consequences not only for the individual, but also for associated family members. Consequently, an individual experiencing psychological problems may be more likely to describe his or her symptoms in the form of physical illness in order to avoid social reprisal. Moreover, because somatic presentation is even sometimes a cultural norm among non-Western populations, ethnically diverse minority groups may even lack the words to describe phenomenon like anxiety and depression in psychological terms (Farooq et al., 1995). Unfortunately, in a Western setting, physiological symptom descriptions of mental concerns may result in misdiagnosis and reduce the likelihood of an individual receiving adequate social and emotional support for his or her psychological concerns. Farooq et al. report that patients presenting with persistent somatic symptoms, yet have no pathological basis, pose a diagnostic and therapeutic dilemma. In this regard, mental health professionals working with non-Western immigrants may profit from giving special attention to the presentation of somatic symptoms.

In contrast to Universalism, the relativist approach has largely focused on cultural-specific forms of psychopathology in a quest to uncover the uniqueness of each culture's model of pathology. One such cultural-specific form of psychopathology, known as Neurasthenia, helps to shed light on the way psychopathology and culture correlate. Neurasthenia was initially a recognized psychological syndrome of the Western world, but in more recent years it has become a common concept in Eastern nations such as China and is no longer a widely understood phrase in the Western psychiatric realm. The *Diagnostic and Statistical Manual of Mental Disorders— Second Edition* (DSM-II; American Psychiatric Association, 1968) listed Neurasthenia as a condition characterized by weakness, fatigue, lack of stamina, and exhaustion. The word Neurasthenia literally means "weak nerves". However, Western concepts of pathology require black and white guidelines that denote cause and effect. It is the vagueness of the term Neurasthenia that is probably the reason it has not appeared in subsequent DSM publications. Yet Neurasthenia is now a common psychiatric diagnosis in China, and is commonly used among Chinese medicine practitioners to refer to a range of neurotic, psychosomatic, and psychotic disorders (Cheung, 1998). Consistent with Thakker and Ward (1998), Cheung contends that Neurasthenia is commonly diagnosed in China because, unlike other forms of psychological disorders, Neurasthenia is socially acceptable. Considering that the aetiology of Neurasthenia is perceived to be over work, irregular lifestyle, and extended intellectual abilities, it is not entirely perceived as a mental disorder.

The existence of other culture-specific syndromes that do not conform to current diagnostic-classification systems suggest cultural factors contribute differentially to aetiology, symptoms, individual interpretation, and sociocultural acceptance (Al-Issa & Oudji, 1998). For example, Taijinkyofusho—a Japanese obsessive phobic state associated with feelings of anxiety about publicly harming or humiliating others (Takahashi, 1989); Waswas, whispered promptings of the devil, concerning one's doubt about the validity of the ritual procedures during Islamic prayer rituals leading to obsessive ablution recommencement (Pfeiffer, 1982); and Brain fag, a cognitive and physiological response to and intense fear of academic failure reported in Nigeria, Uganda, and West Africa, brought on by ancestral guilt for betraying cultural traditions (Al-Issa & Oudji, 1998). Although causal interpretations may differ from Western concepts, components of these culture-specific syndromes do show some similarity diagnostic classifications, namely, agoraphobia, obsessive-compulsive disorder, and specific phobia. However, unlike typical Western responses, the experience of such syndromes often generates community respect for the sufferer due to their own cultural respect, devotedness, or consideration. Without this cultural framework with which to interpret "unusual" behaviours, when displaced in a new culture, sufferers of these conductions are likely to experience misunderstanding and ridicule. Consequently, the need to examine cross-cultural concepts of psychopathology in relation to cultural perceptions as well as symptom presentation is clear. Culture has the ability to influence how disorders are understood, related to, and can even determine specific diagnoses.

Communication and Interpersonal Styles

In order to identify and address the specific needs of ethnically diverse youth at risk for the development of psychopathology, cross-cultural researchers and mental health professionals are faced with a number of methodological challenges. In addition to working with distinct symptomological characteristics (e.g., experience, severity and expression differences), culture-specific coping mechanisms, beliefs, and attitudes, popular therapeutic foundations and clinical techniques (e.g., cognitive-behavioural applications) are further challenged by language diversity and communication/interpersonal styles.

Notwithstanding the obvious social barrier that language differences present for ethnically diverse youth, clear communication ability between therapist and client is essential for valid assessment and treatment procedures. Without an appreciation of diverse interpersonal communication styles, the culture-specific presentation of young ethnically diverse clients alone may be enough to misinterpret behaviour as suspicious, impolite, untrustworthy, or abnormal. For example, many non-Western cultures differ in their interpersonal and ideological demonstration of respect or defiance, as demonstrated by the use of direct eye contact, posture, expression of emotion, and direct question and answer conversation style (Parsons, 1990). Avoidance of direct eye contact in relation to authority figures is reportedly a sign of respect in many cultures (e.g., Pacific Islanders, West Africans). However, such well-intended posture may be interpreted by Western teachers and mental health professionals as being shy, inattentive, hostile, or even rude (Waxer, 1985).

A study by Chen, Rubin, and Sun (1992) investigated culturally normative behaviours of a Chinese culture that may be misinterpreted as deviant in a Western context. The study was conducted among Chinese migrant school children living in Canada. Results revealed that characteristics of shyness and sensitivity among Chinese children were positively correlated with peer acceptance and leadership. The same characteristics among Canadian children were negatively correlated with peer acceptance. This finding supports prior research (see Ho, 1986) which suggests that Chinese child socialization practices are consistent with being cautious, behaviourally inhibited, self-restrained, and sensitive early in life. Chen and colleagues also found that a good sense of humour among Chinese participants was believed to reflect aggressive and disruptive behaviour, while among Canadian participants, this characteristic was highly valued. These investigations illustrate the power of culture in shaping perceptions and interpretations of language and behaviour. According to Wyspianski and Fournier-Ruggles (1985), language difficulties contribute to feelings of inadequacy and inferiority among migrant children. In addition to young clients feeling misunderstood, victimized, and frustrated, the obvious consequences of communication discrepancy in the clinical setting include misdiagnosis and inappropriate therapeutic interventions.

Mental health professionals would do well to consider that despite actual levels of distress, youth from cultural backgrounds that discourage the open display of emotions may perform poorly in emotion recognition tests, or obtain low scores on symptom severity inventories (i.e., anxiety and depression). When administering assessment inventories, tools that have been validated and normed using Western participants may reflect an inaccurate psycho-emotional representation of culturally diverse clients. Conversely, individuals from more expressive societies (e.g., Latino and Hispanic cultures) may score especially high on both general and specific emotional experience ratings (Markham & Wang, 1996). According to Evans and Lee (1998), African-American children provide a clear example of how dialect moves beyond a particular form of expression and involve "fundamentally different styles of communicating" (p. 301). For example, the frequency and style of questions asked by African-American parents to their offspring have been shown to differ from Anglo-American children. African-American parents have been observed to ask fewer, yet more open-ended questions allowing for recital of knowledge or experiences through elaborate verbal responses. Anglo-American parents typically ask more direct questions, and enquire of their children more often. As a consequence, in the school or therapeutic setting, African-American children may display hesitation in providing brief factual answers for unfamiliar direct questions. In building client rapport and obtaining successful assessment and intervention outcomes, it would seem that even the most basic cultural linguistic sensitivity has the potential to make a dramatic difference.

The failure to understand language and expression differences and the culturally inappropriate use of assessment methodologies has been found to result in atypical diagnosis and inappropriate treatment regimes (see Williams & Chambless, 1990). Misdiagnosis is of special concern when it results in hospitalization and the harmful prescription and use of pharmaceutical medication (Friedman, Paradis, & Hatch, 1994). Although research and mental health professionals broadly acknowledge language accuracy to play a vital role in valid assessment and diagnostic procedures, few assessment inventories for NESB youth have been developed, culturally modified, or had statistical norms established for specific cultural groups.

Depending on the client's culture of origin and appropriateness, Western consultation methods may need to be substituted or culturally modified. The interpretation of assessment materials and implementation of appropriate treatment strategies may be greatly enhanced through extensive consultation with ethnic communities (including youth themselves), the inclusion of other family members or community/religious elders, and the use of trained bilingual interpreters.

ASSESSMENT ISSUES

The area of cross-cultural psychological assessment was one of the first issues to come under the microscope of cultural appropriate and ethical practice (Martinez, 1994). As the current literature reveals, cross-cultural psychopathology is more than just a matter of measuring cultural group differences on a general continuum. The appropriateness (validity and reliability) of assessment tools that have been developed for Western Anglo populations and yet administered to culturally diverse groups have been repeatedly called into question (Rice & O'Donohue, 2002). As summarized in Butcher, Nezami, and Exner (1998), variables such as language, ethnic group, motivational differences, definitions or perceptions of what is abnormal, and interpersonal expectations all impact upon assessment and diagnosis. A variety of procedural variables operate concurrently and include task and form appropriateness and psychological equivalence. The responses of participants must be understood in terms of cultural background. For example, as Butcher and his coworkers point out, people who are unfamiliar with paper and pencil tests may make their responses out of politeness or social desirability, and without true understanding and due consideration for the purpose of the assessment. Clinicians from Western cultures, where psychological, behavioural and performance testing are common, may incorrectly assume that people from different cultures are comfortable with "the standardized verbal, limited-opinion format of many Western measures" (p. 65). Limited literacy levels in developing countries may also pose a problem where tests are normed upon a minority subgroup of literate individuals. The risk of misdiagnosis warrants that it is of utmost importance to accurately assess individuals from diverse ethnic backgrounds using methods that are relevant to their cultural heritage.

According to Michaud, Blum, and Slap (2001), assessment, study designs and sampling methods, and clinical diagnosis are only valid when adequate representation of cultural and ethnic minorities have been accounted for, and differentiate factors related to race, ethnicity, culture, and socioeconomic status. Therefore culturally sensitive and accurate assessment, research, and diagnosis have become ethically mandatory (Rice & O'Donohue, 2002). *The Diagnostic and Statistical Manual of Mental Disorders—Fourth Edition* (DSM-IV; American Psychiatric Association, 1994) contains a cultural appendix that acts as a supplement to the five diagnostic axes. Five categories are outlined for consideration, aimed to assist the mental health professional to achieve a culturally sensitive assessment. These include: (1) the cultural identity of the individual; (2) cultural explanations of the individual's illness; (3) cultural factors related to psychosocial environment and level of functioning; (4) cultural elements of the relationship between the individual and the clinician; and (5) overall assessment for diagnosis and care (Kaiser, Katz, & Shaw, 1998).

Despite these guidelines, very few researchers have set out to develop culturally sensitive interview schedules or assessment tools, probably due to the vast array of methodological challenges that accompany each technique when used in a cross-cultural scenario. For example, although interpreters may accommodate linguistic difficulties, interviews allow the clinician or interpreter to unduly emphasize salient sociocultural issues and, moreover, the client may respond in a socially favourable way in order to "save face" in front of the interpreting cultural representative (Kaiser, Katz, & Shaw, 1998). Self-report measures, alternatively, may eliminate interpreter or clinician bias and over-representation of the culture, and quantitative measurement means may be difficult to gauge due to language, expression and interpretation difficulties, as well as norms that are usually based upon a Western sample population.

Current methods for cross-cultural assessment have come a long way in recent years. Butcher, Nezami, and Exner (1998) assert that most inventory translations and adaptations today follow standard procedures, including the translation of questions into the target language; use of key formats to verify linguistic and social appropriateness; independent back-translations into the original language for linguistic validity; and the pre-testing of the translations on a bilingual sample before use. However, this process does not take into account client reading and writing abilities, nor does it take into account culturally diverse pathogenesis. In this regard, linguistic translations alone are insufficient to ensure the cultural validity of self-report or clinically administered assessment tools. Recent cross-cultural work by Barrett and colleagues (2000, 2001a–c, in press) has seen the introduction of verbally interpreted assessment techniques administered in group settings, providing both an English and native cultural language interpretation of each question by trained bilingual mental health professionals. Although all participants were capable of speaking rudimentary English, and possessed basic literacy skills, to ensure that participants understood each question (controlling for differences in reading and writing ability), the participants were at no stage required to read questions for themselves, or provide written responses. Rather, participants were only required to tick the appropriate category (multiple choice, true/false, or yes/no) answer that best described them. Despite new initiatives, there is still a long way to go in the definitive assessment of culturally diverse groups, and contemporary techniques need to be tested for reliability and validity at each level.

TREATMENT ISSUES

Though often suggested as a necessary topic for "future research", few empirical studies have been conducted to validate existing treatment protocol with culturally diverse youth. Moreover, treatment programs developed specifically for NESB participants are relatively scarce. However, in recent years, a number of authors have made culturally sensitive recommendations for therapists working with NESB populations, and have outlined the necessity for research that develops and evaluates culturally relevant and sensitive treatment programs. A summary of culturally sensitive assessment and treatment recommendation resources published in the past five years is presented in Table 5.1.

It is broadly recognized that ethnic minority groups underutilize mental health services, and among those that do seek help, there are high attrition rates (Takeuchi, Sue, & Yeh, 1995). An Australian sample census of mental health service utilization among clients for whom English was not their first language (Stuart et al., 1996), revealed language difficulties to be paired with the underutilization of specialist outpatient services. Of the clients who consulted a mental health professional, those not fluent in English were less likely to receive psychotherapy than those with a firm grasp of the English language. Closser and Blow (1993) contend that it is the lack of emphasis on cultural dynamics in treatment programs that may "contribute to existing barriers to treatment, including lack of relevance, language, and treatment access problems" (p. 199). Based on a comprehensive review of the cross-cultural literature to examine the construct and role of cultural sensitively, Rice and O'Donohue (2002) highlight treatment issues and propose several key points relating to cultural sensitivity in the therapeutic setting (see Table 5.2).

Whether from a universalist or relativist perspective, the experience of some forms of psychopathology (e.g., depression) are observed among all cultural groups (Jenkins, Kleinman, & Good, 1991). The degree to which culture impacts upon the manifestation and experience of emotional problems, however, remains a source of controversy and debate. The DSM-IV identifies various cultural expressions of emotional distress, including: "complaints of nerves and headaches (in Latino and Mediterranean cultures), of weakness, tiredness, or imbalance (in Chinese or Asian cultures), of problems of the 'heart' (in Middle Eastern cultures) . . ." (American Psychiatric Association, 1994, p. 324). In order to adequately apply the above principles outlined by Rice and O'Donohue (2002), clinicians need to determine whether the reported differences in both manifestation and expression of emotional distress are due to social conditions, biological differences, or methodological flaws in the devices used to measure symptoms (Kaiser, Katz, & Shaw, 1998). Consequently, in order for treatment strategies to be successful with NESB clients, treatment planning, research, and consideration of unique client symptom-concerns is essential. Whatever the true underlying dynamics of emotional distress across different cultures, culturally different cognitive constructs warrant that successful treatment must accommodate aetiological, symptomological, and perceptual differences. Without such consideration, what may be deemed a successful treatment in one culture may not be appropriate or even relevant in another.

In an attempt to investigate how factors such as cultural norms, beliefs, practices and values affect the outcome of specific therapeutic interventions, Ma (2000) conducted a study into the treatment expectations and experiences of Chinese families who had taken part in family therapy programs. The rationale behind Ma's investigation was that the best way to assess the relevance and effectiveness of therapeutic interventions with different cultural groups, is simply to understand their perceptions of treatment. It is a common assumption that family therapy should be made culturally specific in order to be effective and Ma asserts that this can result in "overgeneralised cultural stereotyping" (p. 298). Considering the value societal

Table 5.1 A selection of contemporary resource manuals for working with culturally diverse populations, published in the past five years

Year	Publication title	Authors (Au.)/Editors (Ed.)	Publisher
2002	Assessment and culture: Psychological tests with minority populations	Gopaul-McNicol, Sharon A. (Au.); Armour-Thomas, Eleanor (Au.)	San Diego, CA, USA: Academic Press
2001	Handbook of multicultural assessment: Clinical, psychological, and educational applications (2nd edn)	Suzuki, Lisa A. (Ed.); Ponterotto, Joseph G. (Ed.)	San Francisco, CA, USA: Jossey-Bass, Inc.
2000	Play and literacy in early childhood: Research from multiple perspectives	Roskos, Kathleen A. (Ed.); Christie, James F. (Ed.)	Mahwah, NJ, USA: Lawrence Erlbaum Associates, Inc.
2000	Culturally diverse children and adolescents: Assessment, diagnosis, and treatment (2nd edn)	Canino, Ian A. (Au.); Spurlock, Jeanne (Au.)	New York, NY, USA: The Guilford Press
2000	Handbook of multicultural mental health	Cuellar, Israel (Ed.); Paniagua, Freddy A. (Ed.)	San Diego, CA, USA: Academic Press, Inc.
2000	Psychological intervention and cultural diversity (2nd edn)	Aponte, Joseph F. (Ed.); Wohl, Julian (Ed.)	Needham Heights, MA, USA: Allyn & Bacon
2000	Al-Junun: Mental illness in the Islamic world	Al-Issa, Ihsan (Ed.)	Madison, CT, USA: International Universities Press, Inc.
1999	Cross-cultural dialogue on psychotherapy in Africa	Madu, Sylvester N. (Ed.); Baguma, Peter K. (Ed.), et al.	Sovenga, South Africa: UNIN Press
1999	Culturally competent family therapy	Ariel, Shlomo (Au.)	London, UK: Greenwood Press
1998	Cross-cultural practice: Assessment, treatment, and training	Gopaul-McNicol, Sharon A. (Au.); Brice-Baker, Janet (Au.)	New York, NY, USA: John Wiley & Sons, Inc.
1998	Studying minority adolescents: Conceptual, methodological, and theoretical issues	McLoyd, Vonnie C. (Au.); Steinberg, Laurence (Au.)	Mahwah, NJ, USA: Lawrence Erlbaum Associates, Inc.
1998	Cultural clinical psychology: Theory, research, and practice	Kazarian, Shahe S. (Ed.); Evans, David R. (Ed.)	New York, NY, USA: Oxford University Press
1997	Culture and psychopathology: A guide to clinical assessment	Tseng, Wen S. (Ed.); Streltzer, Jon (Ed.)	Philadelphia, PA, USA: Brunner/Mazel, Inc.

Table 5.2   Cultural considerations in the therapeutic setting

1 Accurately identifying what culture(s) a person belongs to/identifies with

2 Accurately knowing factual regularities associated with the culture

3 Ability to accurately judge when these irregularities are relevant

4 Knowing when cultural practices should be judged by a higher moral standard and not simply accepted at face value

5 Implementation of treatment strategies that are culturally appropriate

6 Knowledge of the global perspective and how this culture fits within it

7 Awareness of own culture and how this can bias therapeutic outcomes

Note: data taken from Rice and O'Donohue, 2002

norms of Chinese families, such as controlled emotional expression, self-reliance, educational achievement, and family cohesiveness, family therapy may be tailored to accommodate these values. However, Ma's investigation calls these assumptions of cultural-specific therapy into question.

A total of 17 families seeking family therapy (comprising between 2 and 5 people) took part in Ma's (2000) investigation, experiencing a range of concerns involving children (41.2%), adolescents (35.3%; including school refusal, theft, anorexia nervosa, aggressive behaviour, and uncontrollable temper tantrums at school), marital difficulties (17.6%), and family distress (5.8%; due to terminal illness). Each of these families received family therapy, which encouraged members to interact with each other directly, rather than rely on the therapist to act as the go-between. Open-ended questions were used to examine issues such as (1) treatment expectations; (2) helpfulness of the treatment in resolving the current problems and in improving familiar relationships; (3) the function and roles of the therapist; (4) the therapeutic relationship between families and therapist; (5) issues to improve the service provided; (6) willingness of families to recommend referral to other families; and (7) ways of explaining the service to other families.

Responses from each of these categories were analysed separately to further investigate the specifics of the participants' beliefs, expectations and values. For example, in regard to treatment expectations, most families anticipated being taught by the therapist whom they regarded as the professional. Although this expectation was not met by the structure of family therapy, a significant majority of participants still found therapy to be effective, having helped in resolving their families' current difficulties, enhancing family relationships, and/or their connection to the educational system. Ma (2000) concludes that despite holding unrealistic expectations of family therapy, this Western-style approach is nevertheless helpful in achieving positive outcomes with Chinese families. Considering that factors such as place of origin, years of education, class, religion, and sociocultural background can all influence the dynamics of therapy and the final treatment outcomes, Ma states that instead of dismissing the use of Western treatment approaches with ethnically diverse families, therapists should instead increase their knowledge about the diversity of the lives of ethnic families. Recently, researchers using the widely recognized and validated program (FRIENDS), originally designed for the treatment of anxiety and depression among Western youth, have attempted to do just that.

The FRIENDS program has been developed through extensive research and clinical validation over the past 15 years, targeting the prevention of serious mental disorders, emotional distress, and impairment in social functioning (FRIENDS; Barrett, Lowry-Webster, & Turner, 2000c–2000d). In addition to learning important personal development skills (e.g., building self-esteem, problem-solving, self-expression of ideas and beliefs, and establishing positive relationships), FRIENDS teaches children (ages 7–11) and adolescents (ages 12–17) how to cope with and manage anxiety and depression. Given the high prevalence of psychological distress among refugee and migrant youth, which places great demand on transcultural mental health agencies, Barrett, Moore, and Sonderegger (2000) and Barrett, Sonderegger, and Sonderegger (2001a) trailed the FRIENDS program in Queensland, Australia, with former-Yugoslavian, Chinese, and mixed cultural background migrants and refugees in primary and high schools. Similar to Ma (2000), the results of these trials provided preliminary evidence that the Western-based FRIENDS program was helpful in reducing levels of stress and anxiety, promoting resilience, and enhancing coping skills in young NESB migrants and refugees.

Social validity ratings from 204 participants (Barrett, Sonderegger, & Sonderegger, 2001a) revealed that all cultural and school-age groups enjoyed the FRIENDS program and found it to be a valuable learning experience—developing new skills to solve problems and reduce levels of anxiety and stress. However, the study demonstrated that culturally diverse participants differed in their evaluation of those activities that were most useful. For example, unlike former-Yugoslavian youth, Chinese and mixed-ethnic participants, reported seldom using cognitive restructuring, graded exposure, step-problem-solving techniques. Barrett and coworkers contend that, due to sociocultural predispositions, some cultural groups may be able to relate to specific behaviour plans better than others. They conclude that FRIENDS may be able to adequately address the universal stressors associated with cultural change, however, the variables that moderate comprehension (e.g., ranging from familiarity with culture-specific problem-solving styles to FRIENDS presentation format and use of language) require further examination in order to modify activities for greater cultural sensitivity and to address culture-specific needs.

In their quantitative appraisal of FRIENDS, Barrett, Sonderegger, and Sonderegger (2001a) failed to account for demographic and cultural group difference due to statistical power limitations. While social validity and treatment integrity data were able to provide insight into cultural learning preferences, responsiveness, and topic interest profiles of participants, treatment results were only provisional at best. To address some of the methodological difficulties that commonly plague cross-cultural clinical trials, Barrett, Sonderegger, and Xenos (2003) conducted a national FRIENDS trial exclusively with 320 former-Yugoslavian and Chinese migrants and refugees to Australia. In an effort to enhance the generalizability of the FRIENDS' trial outcomes, this study incorporated more detailed analysis and cross-compared young culturally diverse migrants from different Australian States. More than half of the participants in this study were re-evaluated at six months follow-up so as to determine the longer-term efficacy and sustainability of the treatment components. Consistent with previous clinical (Barrett, Moore, & Sonderegger, 2000), and non-clinical (Barrett, Sonderegger, & Sonderegger, 2001a) trials, Barrett, Sonderegger, and Xenos found FRIENDS to be effective in building emotional resilience against cultural adjustment difficulties. A preliminary six-month follow-up analysis with culturally diverse elementary and high school age migrants also revealed improvements in emotional resiliency to be sustained over time. Among culturally diverse primary school children, marked improvements in self-esteem and expectations for the future, and a significant decrease in anxiety symptoms were observed from pre- to post-assessment. Similarly, high school students reported significantly reduced levels of anxiety, depression, anger, post-traumatic stress, and dissociation from pre- to post-assessment.

By administering the program to a large number of young migrants from diverse cultural backgrounds and developmental stages (elementary and high school) in different States of Australia at pre-, post-, and six-month follow-up assessment intervals, trial outcomes were more robust. However, interviews with group facilitators and participants revealed that not all FRIENDS activities were considered entirely practical NESB participants. Barrett, Sonderegger, and Sonderegger (2001a) report language and comprehension barriers caused delays (especially where writing is involved), rendering it difficult for NESB participants to complete all in-session and homework activities in the allocated timeframe. Consequently, some FRIENDS activities have now been culturally enhanced through the creation of primary and high school NESB sensitive program supplements (Barrett, Sonderegger, & Sonderegger, 2001b–2001c). Based on the feedback obtained from facilitators and participants, activities have been amended to incorporate music, art, and creative stories that are personally relevant to migrant youth. To cater for different interests and maturity levels among culturally diverse high school students, the NESB supplement includes flexible, open forums for group discussion on topics of cultural and personal relevance. A breakdown of amended components is presented in Table 5.3.

One additional outcome from the cross-cultural FRIENDS research conducted by Barrett and colleagues (2000, 2001a, in press) is a new stand-alone intervention program that has been specifically designed for new NESB migrant arrivals. The "Non-English Speaking Background Life Skills Program for New Arrivals" (Barrett & Sonderegger, 2001a, 2001b) was created to assist young migrants, at an appropriate developmental level, to learn important skills and techniques for coping with the adjustment difficulties that typically accompany cultural change. The term "Life Skills" is representative of the strategies employed to teach NESB students the importance of becoming friends with themselves and others, while respecting cultural differences. As with the FRIENDS program, this intervention has been designed for school and community settings, and comprises 10 separate one-hour group sessions (see Table 5.4). However, strategies and activities in the program may also be adopted for individual client therapy.

By developing acculturation skills that promote positive aspects of host and origin cultures, the program serves to promote self-confidence, self-esteem, and coping strategies to effectively manage emotional stress, and develop resilience against the more serious psychopathology that is frequently paired with cultural change (Ponterotto, Baluch, & Carielli, 1998; Roberts & Schnieder, 1999). The tridimensional premise underpinning the program's objectives are featured in

Table 5.3 Cultural considerations and amendments to select FRIENDS strategies

Focus on Self-Esteem	Introducing the idea of self-esteem (feeling good about ourselves). Self-esteem is often a difficult concept for NESB participants to understand, and therefore requires careful explanation. In some cultures (e.g., Pacific Islands) the concepts of self-esteem and self-love (recognizing the need to appreciate and value yourself) can be confusing, as love is often only associated with sexual intimacy. In explaining self-esteem in a way that is sensitive to participant's cultural background, the terms "liking" or "feeling good" about oneself, are replaced with being "cool", "fun", or a "nice person".
Focus on Inner Thoughts	Learning how thoughts can influence feelings and behaviour. NESB participants may have difficulty understanding the concept of inner thoughts and self-talk, and therefore it should be approached in a sensitive way. It is emphasized that everyone, regardless of culture, "thinks" and "talks" to him/herself constantly in their mind. Moreover, there are many different ways of thinking about the same situation. Some ways of thinking are not helpful, making us feel bad, while helpful thoughts help us to succeed and cope in difficult situations.
Focus on Problem-Solving	Learning to identify new problem-solving techniques to deal with difficult situations. Group Leaders are encouraged to be flexible in the discussion of issues that are relevant to each group. For example, issues such as sex and drugs may be more of a concern for older adolescents than younger adolescents. Similarly, different issues may be more relevant to certain ethnic groups and not so relevant to others. The fear or promotion of violence and conflict may be more relevant to refugees from war-torn countries. Non-refugee migrants may be more concerned with issues such as academic achievement, racism/prejudice, or the threat of failure.

Rather than written homework, practice and reminder handouts accompany sessions

Table 5.4 Outline of multicultural life skills program sessions

Session 1	Introduction
Session 2	Reason for changing countries
Session 3	Difficulties in changing countries: Effect on well being
Session 4	Cultural differences and the challenges they present
Session 5	Family changes and the individual's role
Session 6	Individual characteristics and coping
Session 7	Methods of coping with current life challenges
Session 8	Barriers to effective coping strategies
Session 9	Positive aspects of change: New culture
Session 10	Review and party

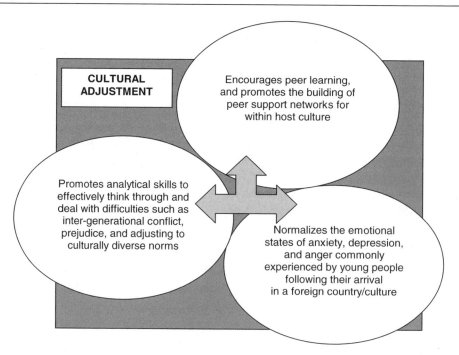

Figure 5.1   Social, cognitive, and acculturative premise for the multicultural life skills program

Figure 5.1. While NESB FRIENDS supplements and the Non-English Speaking Background Life Skills Program for New Arrivals are currently being used in Australia, the efficacy and generalizability of these programs await empirical validation.

SUMMARY AND FUTURE DIRECTIONS

Although limited by number and scope, the studies reviewed in this chapter indicate that cultural sensitivity in the therapeutic setting is a challenging process. Before culturally appropriate assessment instruments can be developed to discriminate between sociocultural factors of experience and expression among migrant families, influential variables across ethnic groups need to be delineated. More detailed examination into the complex interplay of cultural adjustment variables may help to reveal the pathways through which migrant children become resilient or vulnerable to the development emotional problems.

Young NESB youth who migrate with (and in some cases without) their families to a foreign host culture/country are subject to a plethora of risk factors (e.g., loss of loved ones, independence and role conflicts, intergenerational discord, acculturation stress, language and communication difficulties, prejudice). More detailed cross-cultural clinical studies into these factors are vital for the development of culturally sensitive assessment and treatment strategies appropriate for NESB youth. Although issues such as mutual exclusion and internal heterogeneity pose a problem for the accuracy of cross-cultural research, it is possible for future investigations to overcome such issues by evaluating cultural sub-groups at finite levels of commonality (e.g., demographic status, ethnic subgroups, reason for migration, duration in host culture). Limitations notwithstanding, clinical research initiatives to date indicate that the more risk factors to which youth are subjected, the greater propensity they have to develop more serious psychopathology.

In an effort to address the adjustment and psychological needs of NESB migrant youth who migrate to increasingly multicultural Western societies, preliminary trials of existing well-validated intervention programs (e.g., FRIENDS) have yielded positive outcomes. Over the years, family stress resilience and anxiety/depression prevention training with FRIENDS has revealed strategies by which parents can best support their children in times of distress. The FRIENDS program not only builds upon children's strengths and positive coping skills, but also enhances parental and coping skills, modelling behaviours, and networks of tangible support. However, Anglo parent training programs tend to focus on individual parent–child practice. Such a model excludes ethnic family values where parenting is commonly a community and extended family practice. Consequently, it is imperative that existing well-validated parent-training programs should also be tailored for global ethnic sensitivity, and build upon existing specific NESB parenting practice strengths. By respecting parents' cultural identity and validating their parenting practices through culturally sensitive parent-training resources, parents may feel more secure and confident to adopt positive-parenting techniques that have been demonstrated to enhance children's emotional resilience. Moreover, by participating in culture-specific family workshops, parents may gain access to affiliated NESB mental health resources and services by networking with NESB health professionals, English as a Second Language (ESL) school support teachers, and transcultural community agencies. Cross-cultural studies are currently underway in Australia, enhancing the cultural applicability of existing well-validated Anglo-parenting programs and developing new culturally sensitive NESB parenting programs and resources (Barrett, Sonderegger, & Sonderegger, 2003; Xenos, Hudson, & Gavidia-Payne, 1997; 1998; Xenos & Hudson, 1999).

While in recent years researchers and practitioners alike have become much more aware of the need to be culturally sensitive when working with ethnically diverse families, additional research is still required to further our understanding of the cultural adjustment process among different cultural groups. With access to such information, mental health professionals will be better equipped to tailor assessment and treatment strategies to specific cultural groups and enhance the current quality of service being offered to culturally diverse group members. Until such time, mental health professionals working with young ethnically diverse clientele are encouraged to consult existing culturally sensitive guidelines, for example those featured in Tables 5.1 and 5.2.

REFERENCES

Achenbach, T.M., & Edelbrock, C.S. (1981). Behavioural problems and competencies reported by parents of normal and disrupted children aged four through sixteen. *Monographs of the Society for Research in Child Development*, **46**, 1–82.

Achenbach, T.M., & Edelbrock, C.S. (1983). *Manual for the Child Behaviour Checklist*. Burlington: University of Vermont, Department of Psychiatry.

Al-Issa, I., & Oudji, S. (1998). Culture and anxiety disorders. In S. Kazarian & D.R. Evans (Eds), *Cultural Clinical Psychology* (pp. 127–151). New York: Oxford University Press.

American Psychiatric Association (1968). *Diagnostic and statistical manual of mental disorders* (2nd edn). Washington, DC: Author.

American Psychiatric Association (1994). *Diagnostic and statistical manual of mental disorders* (4th edn). Washington, DC: Author.

Arcia, E., Skinner, M., Bailey, D., & Correa, V. (2001). Models of acculturation and health behaviours among Latino immigrants to the US. *Social Science and Medicine*, **53**, 41–53.

Barrett, P.M., Lowry-Webster, H., & Turner, C. (2000a). *FRIENDS program for children: Group leaders manual*. Brisbane: Australian Academic Press.

Barrett, P.M., Lowry-Webster, H., & Turner, C. (2000b). *FRIENDS program for children: Participants workbook*. Brisbane: Australian Academic Press.

Barrett, P.M., Lowry-Webster, H., & Turner, C. (2000c). *FRIENDS program for youth: Group leaders manual*. Brisbane: Australian Academic Press.

Barrett, P.M., Lowry-Webster, H., & Turner, C. (2000d). *FRIENDS program for youth: Participants workbook*. Brisbane: Australian Academic Press.

Barrett, P.M., Moore, A.F., & Sonderegger, R. (2000). The Friends program for young former-Yugoslavian refugees in Australia: A pilot study. *Behaviour Change*, **17**, 124–133.

Barrett, P.M., & Sonderegger, R. (2001a). *Multicultural life skills program for new young Australians: Group leaders manual*. Brisbane: Griffith University and the State of Queensland through the Queensland Transcultural Mental Health Centre (QTCMH), Division of Mental Health.

Barrett, P.M., & Sonderegger, R. (2001b). *Multicultural life skills program for new young Australians: Workbook for youth*. Brisbane: Griffith University and the State of Queensland through the Queensland Transcultural Mental Health Centre (QTCMH), Division of Mental Health.

Barrett, P.M., Sonderegger, R., & Sonderegger, N.L. (2001a). Evaluation of an anxiety prevention and positive-coping program (FRIENDS) for children and adolescents of non-English speaking background. *Behaviour Change*, **18**, 78–91.

Barrett, P.M., Sonderegger, R., & Sonderegger, N.L. (2001b). *Universal supplement to FRIENDS for children: Group leaders manual for participants from non-English speaking backgrounds*. Brisbane: Griffith University and the State of Queensland through the Queensland Transcultural Mental Health Centre (QTCMH), Division of Mental Health.

Barrett, P.M., Sonderegger, R., & Sonderegger, N.L. (2001c). *Universal supplement to FRIENDS for youth: Group leaders manual for participants from non-English speaking backgrounds*. Brisbane: Griffith University and the State of Queensland through the Queensland Transcultural Mental Health Centre (QTCMH), Division of Mental Health.

Barrett, P.M., Sonderegger, N.L., & Sonderegger, R. (2003). *The Bridge Program: For migrant and refugee families of Non-English Speaking Background*. Brisbane: Griffith University and the Commonwealth of Australia as represented by the Department of Families and Community Services.

Barrett, P.M., Sonderegger, R., & Sonderegger, N.L. (in press). Assessment of child and adolescent migrants to Australia: A cross-cultural comparison. *Behaviour Change*.

Barrett, P.M., Sonderegger, R., & Xenos, S. (2003). Using FRIENDS to combat anxiety and adjustment problems among young migrants to Australia: A national trial. *Clinical Child Psychology and Psychiatry*, **8**, 241–260.

Berry, J.W. (1998). Acculturation and health: Theory and research. In S. Kazarian & D.R. Evans (Eds), *Cultural Clinical Psychology* (pp. 39–57). New York: Oxford University Press.

Berry, J.W., & Kim, U. (1987). Acculturation and mental health. In P. Dasen, J.W. Berry, & N. Sartorius (Eds), *Cross-cultural psychology and health: Towards applications*. London: Sage.

Berry, J.W., Kim, U., Minde, T., & Mok, D. (1988). Comparative studies of acculturative stress. *International Migration Review*, **21**, 491–511.

Bird, H.R. (1996). Epidemiology of childhood disorders in a cross-cultural context. *Journal of Child Psychology and Psychiatry*, **37**, 35–49.

Butcher, J.N., Nezami, E., & Exner, J. (1998). Psychological assessment of people in diverse cultures. In S. Kazarian & D.R. Evans (Eds), *Cultural Clinical Psychology* (pp. 61–105). New York: Oxford University Press.

Chen, X., Rubin, K.H., & Sun, Y. (1992). Social reputation and peer relationships in Chinese and Canadian children: A cross-cultural study. *Child-Development*, **63**, 1336–1343.

Cheung, F.M. (1998). *Cross-cultural psychopathology*. Hong Kong: Elsevier Science.

Closser, M., & Blow, F. (1993). Special populations women, ethnic minorities, and the elderly. *Psychiatric Clinics of North America*, **16**, 199–208.

Evans, B., & Lee, B.K. (1998). Culture and child psychopathology. In S. Kazarian & D.R. Evans (Eds), *Cultural Clinical Psychology* (pp. 289–315). New York: Oxford University Press.

Farooq, S., Gahir, M.S., Okyere, E., Sheikh, A.J., & Oyebode, F. (1995). Somatization: A transcultural study. *Journal of Psychosomatic Research*, **39**, 883–888.

Friedman, S., Paradis, C.M., & Hatch, M.L. (1994). Issues of misdiagnosis in panic disorder with agoraphobia. In S. Freidman (Ed.), *Anxiety disorders in African-Americans* (pp. 128–146). New York: Springer.

Gutierrez, D.G. (1995). *Walls and mirrors: Mexican Americans, Mexican immigrants, and the politics of ethnicity*. Berkeley, CA: University of California Press.

Ho, D.Y.F. (1986). Chinese patterns of socialization: A critical review. In M.H. Bond (Ed.), *The psychology of the Chinese people* (pp. 1–37). Hong Kong: Oxford University Press.

Iwata, N., & Buka, S. (2002). Race/ethnicity and depressive symptoms: A cross-cultural/ethnic comparison among university students in East Asia, North and South America. *Social Science and Medicine*, **55**, 2243–2252.

Iwata, N., Saito, K., & Roberts, R.E. (1994). Responses to a self-administered depression scale among younger adolescents in Japan. *Psychiatry Research*, **53**, 275–287.

Jablensky, A., Sartorius, N., Ernberg, G., Ankar, M., Korten, A., Cooper, J.E., Day, R., & Bertelsen, A. (1992). Schizophrenia: manifestations, incidence and course in different cultures. *Psychology and Medicine*, **20**, 1–97.

Jablensky, A., Sartorius, N., Gulbinat, W., & Ernberg, G. (1981). Characteristics of depressive patients contacting psychiatric services in four countries. *Acta Psychiatrica Scandinaviea*, **68**, 367–383.

Jenkins, J.H., Kleinman, A., & Good, B.J. (1991). Cross-cultural studies in depression. In J. Becker & A. Kleinman (Eds), *Psychological aspects of depression* (pp. 67–99). Hillsdale, NJ: Erlbaum.

Jones, A.C., & Chao, C.M. (1997). Racial, ethnic and cultural issues in couples therapy. In W.K. Halford & H.J. Markman (Eds), *Clinical handbook of marriage and couples interventions*. New York: John Wiley & Sons.

Kaiser, A.S., Katz, R., & Shaw, B.F. (1998). Cultural issues in the management of depression. In S.S. Kazarian & D.R. Evans (Eds), *Cultural clinical psychology: Theory, research and practice* (pp. 177–214). New York: Oxford University Press.

Lopez, S.R. (2000). Cultural psychopathology: Uncovering the social world of mental illness. *Annual Reviews*: www.AnnualReviews.org

McGoldrick, J.G., Pearce, J.K. & Giordano, J (Eds) (1982) *Ethnicity and family therapy*. New York: Guilford Press.

Michaud, P.A., Blum, R.W., & Slap, G.B. (2001). Cross-cultural surveys of adolescent health and behaviour: Progress and problems. *Social Science and Medicine*, **53**, 1237–1246.

Ma, J.L. (2000). Treatment expectations and treatment experience of Chinese families towards family therapy: Appraisal of a common belief. *Journal of Family Therapy*, **22**, 296–307.

Markham, R., & Wang, L. (1996). Recognition of emotion by Chinese and Australian children. *Journal of Cross-Cultural Psychology*, **27**, 616–643.

Martinez, K. (1994). Cultural sensitivity in family therapy gone awry. *Hispanic Journal of Behavioural Sciences*, **16**, 75–89.

Matthews, A. (1997). A guide to case conceptualisation and treatment planning with minority group clients. *The Behaviour Therapist*, **20**, 35–39.

Munakata, T. (1989). The socio-cultural significance of the diagnostic label "neurasthenia" in Japan's mental health system. *Culture, Medicine and Psychiatry*, **13**, 203–213.

Nguyen, H.H., Messé, L.A., & Stollak, G.E. (1999). Toward a more complex understanding of acculturation and adjustment: Cultural involvement and psychological functioning in Vietnamese youth. *Journal of Cross-Cultural Psychology*, **30**, 5–31.

Parsons, C. (1990). Cross-cultural issues in health care. In J. Reid & P. Trompf (Eds), *The health of immigrant Australia: A social perspective* (pp. 108–153). Sydney: Harcourt Brace Javanovich.

Pfeiffer, W. (1982). Culture-bound syndromes. In I. Al-Issa (Ed.), *Culture and psychopathology* (pp. 201–218). Baltimore: University Park Press.

Ponterotto, J.G., Baluch, S., & Carielli, D. (1998). The Suinn-Lew Asian self-identity acculturation scale (SL-ASIA): Critique and research recommendations. *Measurement and Evaluation in Counselling and Development*, **31**, 109–124.

Prince, R., & Tcheng-Laroche, F. (1987). Culture-bound syndromes and international disease classification. *Culture, Medicine and Psychiatry*, **11**, 3–20.

Rice, N., & O'Donohue, W. (2002). Cultural sensitivity: A critical examination. *New Ideas in Psychology*, **20**, 35–48.

Roberts, C.M., & Schnieder, W. (1999). Self-concept and anxiety in immigrant children. *International Journal of Behavioural Development*, **23**, 125–147.

Rogler, L. (1994). International migration: A framework for directing research. *American Psychologist*, **49**, 701–708.

Sam, D.L. (2000). Psychological adaptation of adolescents with immigrant backgrounds. *Journal of Social Psychology*, **140**, 5–25.

Selvamanickam, S., Zgryza, M., & Gorman, D. (2001). *Coping in a new world: The social and emotional wellbeing of young people from culturally and linguistically diverse backgrounds.* Brisbane: Queensland Transcultural Mental Health Centre, Queensland Health, and Youth Affairs Network of Queensland, Inc.

Storer, D. (1985). *Ethnic family values in Australia.* Sydney: Prentice Hall.

Stuart, G.W., Minas, I.H., Klimidis, S., & O'Connell, S. (1996). English language ability and mental health service utilisation: A census. *Australian and New Zealand Journal of Psychiatry*, **30**, 270–277.

Takahashi, T. (1989). Social phobia syndrome in Japan. *Comprehensive Psychiatry*, **30**, 45–52.

Takeuchi, D.T., Sue, S., & Yeh, M. (1995). Return rates and outcomes from ethnicity-specific mental health programs in Los Angeles. *American Journal of Public Health*, **85**, 638–643.

Thakker, J., & Ward, T. (1998). Culture and classification: The cross-cultural application of the DSM-IV. *Clinical Psychology Review*, **18**, 501–529.

Thakker, J., Ward, T., & Strongman, K.T. (1999). Psychopathology and cross-cultural psychology: A constructivist perspective. *Clinical Psychology Review*, **19**, 843–874.

Ulusahin, A., Basoglu, M., & Paykel, E.S. (1994). A cross-cultural comparative study of depressive symptoms in British and Turkish clinical samples. *Social Psychiatry and Psychiatry Epidemiology*, **29**, 31–39.

Waxer, P. (1985). Nonverbal aspects of intercultural counseling: Interpersonal issues. In R.J. Samuda & A. Wolfgang (Eds), *Intercultural counseling and assessment: Global perspectives* (pp. 49–66). Toronto, Ontario, Canada: Hogrefe.

Weiss, M.G., Raguram, R., & Channabasavanna, S.M. (1995). Cultural dimensions of psychiatric illness: A comparison of the DSM-III-R and illness explanatory models in South India. *British Journal of Psychiatry*, **166**, 353–359.

Williams, K.E., & Chambless, D.L. (1990). The relationship between therapist characteristics and outcome *in vivo* exposure treatment of agoraphobia. *Behaviour Therapy*, **21**, 111–116.

Winter, K.A., & Young, M.Y. (1998). Biopsychosocial considerations in refugee mental health. In S. Kazarian & D.R. Evans (Eds), *Cultural clinical psychology* (pp. 348–376). New York: Oxford University Press.

World Health Organization (1973). *Report of the international pilot study of schizophrenia.* Geneva, Switzerland: Author.

World Health Organization (1979). *Schizophrenia: An international follow-up study.* Chichester, UK: John Wiley & Sons.

World Health Organization (1983). *Depressive disorders in different cultures: Report of the WHO collaborative study of standardized assessment of depressive disorders.* Geneva, Switzerland: Author.

Wyspianski, J.O., & Fournier-Ruggles, L.A. (1985). Counselling European immigrants: Issues and answers. In R.J. Samuda & A. Wolfgang (Eds), *Intercultural counseling and assessment* (pp. 225–234). Toronto: Hogrefe.

Xenos, S., & Hudson, A. (1999). *Cultural diversity in parenting: Parent training outcomes in Anglo-Australian, Vietnamese-Australian, Turkish-Australian, Spanish-Australian, and Greek-Australian families.* Auckland: Paper presented at Triple P "Changing Families" Conference.

Xenos, S., Hudson, A., & Gavidia-Payne, S. (1997). *Cross-cultural beliefs as predictors of parent-training outcomes in Vietnamese-Australian, Spanish-Australian, Turkish-Australian, and Greek-Australian families.* Melbourne: Paper presented at the 7th State Conference of the Australian Association for Cognitive and Behaviour Therapy (AACBT).

Xenos, S., Hudson, A., & Gavidia-Payne, S. (1998). *Parenting beliefs and parenting practices in Vietnamese-Australian, Spanish-Australian, Turkish-Australian, and Greek-Australian families.* Melbourne: Presented at the National Conference of the Australian Psychological Society.

Zvolensky, M.J., McNeil, D.W., Porter, C.A., & Stewart, S.H. (2001). Assessment of anxiety sensitivity in young American Indians and Alaska Natives. *Behaviour Research and Therapy,* **39**, 477–493.

PART II

Treatment Status for Specific Emotional and Behavioural Disorders

CHAPTER 6

Treatment of Generalized Anxiety Disorder in Children and Adolescents

Jennifer L. Hudson

Macquarie University, Australia

Alicia A. Hughes

Temple University, USA

and

Philip C. Kendall

Temple University, USA

INTRODUCTION

Phenomenology of GAD

The predominant feature of Generalized Anxiety Disorder (GAD) is excessive anxiety and uncontrollable worry about a variety of events or activities. Children with GAD commonly report worries about school, family, friends, performance, health, and world issues. For this worry to reach diagnostic levels, according to the DSM-IV (APA, 1994), excessive and uncontrollable worry in children must be accompanied by at least one physical symptom (e.g., muscle tension, sleep difficulties, restlessness, difficulty concentrating) and must occur on more days than not for a minimum of six months. Moreover, the worry or accompanying physical symptoms must cause significant distress or impairment in important areas of functioning (e.g., school, home, peer relationships) for the child to meet diagnostic criteria. Some of the more common physical symptoms reported by children with GAD,

Correspondence to Jennifer L. Hudson, Department of Psychology, Macquarie University, Sydney, NSW, 2109, Australia; email: jhudson@psy.mq.edu.au

Handbook of Interventions that Work with Children and Adolescents: Prevention and Treatment.
Edited by P.M. Barrett and T.H. Ollendick. © 2004 John Wiley & Sons, Ltd. ISBN 0-470-84453-1.

although not listed among the DSM-IV criteria, are stomach-ache or headache. Pimentel and Kendall (2003) found that parents reported significantly more somatic symptoms in their GAD children than the children themselves. Also, older children (11–13 year olds) with GAD endorsed significantly more somatic symptoms than younger children (9–11 year olds).

Parents of children with GAD have described their children as "worriers" who worry about "everything and anything." Children with GAD have reported worrying about novel situations and often require excessive or even constant reassurance to approach uncertain situations. School can provide a number of anxiety-provoking situations for the child with GAD—being on time, remembering to bring the correct books, not getting into trouble, correctly completing a homework or classroom task, performing on a test, having enough friends, and class trips. Perhaps in response to the worry, children with GAD avoid school-related situations such as excursions, camp, less-structured school days or days in which there may be a new or substitute teacher. Frequent visits to the school nurse or absentee days may be common for a child with GAD. Children with GAD may also worry excessively about their health or their family's health or become preoccupied with adult concerns such as family finances, family relationships, and even world or community events such as war or political issues. Not unlike adults, youth with GAD worry excessively (beyond normal for their age) and try to avoid provoking situations.

Our current understanding of GAD in children and adolescents is based largely on studies of youth with what was previously labelled Overanxious Disorder (OAD). OAD was included in previous editions of DSM but was subsumed under the modified GAD diagnostic criteria in DSM-IV (APA, 1994). The predominant feature of OAD, like GAD, was pervasive anxiety and excessive worry about future and past events as well as overconcern about performance or evaluation by others (Strauss et al., 1988). Research indicates that there is a high degree of consistency between DSM-III-R and DSM-IV diagnostic criteria for anxiety disorders in youth with very high agreement between DSM-III-R and DSM-IV criteria for parent report of OAD/GAD and child report (Kendall & Warman, 1996). These findings suggest that modifications made to the diagnostic categories do not interfere with our ability to generalize from past research.

Studies on children and adolescents with OAD suggest that it has a relatively early age of onset. The reported average age of onset ranges from 8.8 to 10 years with the average age at intake for treatment occurring between 10.8 and 13.9 years (Keller et al., 1992; Last et al., 1992).

The course of GAD in children and adolescents tends to be chronic. Cohen, Cohen, and Brook (1993) found that nearly half of the children and adolescents diagnosed with OAD continued to have this diagnosis 2.5 years later, suggesting a relatively stable and chronic course. Keller et al. (1992) reported a mean duration of 4.5 years in children and adolescents diagnosed with OAD. Conversely, Cantwell and Baker (1989) found that over 50% of youth with an OAD diagnosis received a diagnosis other than OAD at 4-year follow-up suggesting that OAD may be unstable over time. However, findings from this study are limited due to the fact the study only had eight children with a diagnosis with OAD. In a prospective study, Last et al. (1996) followed 84 youth with anxiety disorders over a three to four year period and reported that 35% received an alternative diagnosis most often another anxiety disorder or major depressive disorder. Findings from this study suggest children and adolescents with OAD/GAD may be at risk for developing other anxiety disorders or depression over time.

Age may influence the experience and presentation of GAD. Findings from Strauss and colleagues (1988) suggest that younger and older children with OAD differ in symptom expression, comorbid conditions, and severity of self-reported anxiety and depression. They found that older clinic-referred children (ages 12–19 years) reported a greater number of OAD symptoms and were more likely to express unrealistic concern about the appropriateness of past behaviour compared to younger children (ages 5–11 years). Younger children were more likely to receive a concurrent diagnosis of Separation Anxiety Disorder (SAD) or Attention Deficit Disorder (ADD) compared to older children. Older children were more likely than their younger cohorts to have coexisting depression or a specific phobia diagnosis. In addition, older children reported significantly more anxiety, worry, and depression compared to younger children with OAD. Inconsistent with findings from Strauss and colleagues (1988), recent research on children and adolescents with GAD did not find significant differences in the number of GAD symptoms between younger (ages 7–11 years) and older children (ages 12–18 years) diagnosed with GAD (Masi et al., 1999). However, Masi and colleagues found that brooding was reported significantly more often by adolescents than children, whereas the need for reassurance was more frequently expressed by children than by adolescents.

Comorbidity runs high with GAD. Studies indicate that the majority of youth with OAD are comorbid with at least one anxiety disorder (e.g., Last, Strauss, & Francis, 1987; Masi et al., 1999; Verduin & Kendall, 2003). Furthermore, Masi et al. reported that 62% of the children and adolescents with GAD were comorbid with a depressive disorder and 9% were comorbid with an externalizing disorder. Consistent with Masi et al. (1999), Last, Strauss, and Francis (1987) found that 9% of children diagnosed with OAD met DSM-III criteria for a concurrent behaviour disorder. In a clinic-referred sample of anxiety-disordered children, Verduin and Kendall (2003) reported that youth with GAD were very likely to be comorbid with another anxiety disorder and 18.3% were comorbid with ADHD, 10.1% with ODD and 6.4% with MDD.

One of the related features of anxiety disorders in children (and adults) is the presence of a cognitive processing bias towards personal, interpersonal and physical threat (see also Kendall et al., 1992). Barrett and colleagues (1996) conducted a study wherein children were given a number of hypothetical ambiguous situations. For example, children were asked about approaching a group of children playing a game. The children were told that as they approach the other children they notice that the other children are laughing. The results showed that anxious (as well as oppositional) children were more likely to interpret the situation in terms of perceived threat compared to non-clinical children (e.g., the children are laughing at me). Further studies have also indicated that anxiety-disordered children interpret situations as more threatening than normal control children (Bogels & Zigterman, 2000; Chansky & Kendall, 1997). Using a homograph task, Taghavi et al. (2000) found an interpretation bias in GAD children (ages 8 to 17 years) compared to children without a history of a psychiatric disorder. In this task, children were presented with homographs (i.e., words that are written the same but have different meanings) that had threatening and neutral meanings one by one on a card. The children were instructed to use each word in a sentence. Relative to children without a psychiatric diagnosis, children with GAD were more likely to generate a threatening versus a neutral meaning. In general, these findings support the presence of a cognitive processing bias for threat-related information in children with anxiety disorders.

Epidemiology

The reported prevalence rates for GAD in children and adolescents are based on the DSM-III and DSM-III-R diagnosis of OAD and, therefore, are an approximation of the prevalence of GAD in children and adolescents. A number of studies have explored the prevalence of OAD in children and adolescents and have produced variable estimates. In community studies, OAD has been found to be among the most prevalent anxiety disorders in children and adolescents (Werry, 1991). Epidemiological studies have reported fairly discrepant rates of OAD in youth ranging from 2.9% to 12.4% (e.g., Anderson et al., 1987; Kashani et al., 1990). The 12-month prevalence rates of OAD have been reported as 2.9% to 4.6% in children (Anderson et al., 1987; Benjamin, Costello, & Warren, 1990) and 4.2% in adolescents (Fergusson, Horwood, & Lynskey, 1993). In addition, the six-month prevalence rate for adolescents has been reported at 2.4% (Bowen, Offord, & Boyle, 1990). A recent community study of children and adolescents reported that the six-month prevalence of either OAD or GAD was 6.7% with 4.1% of the youth meeting criteria for both disorders (Muris et al., 1998). Varying prevalence rates of OAD/GAD in youth may be the result of methodological differences such as sample type, age of participants, informant, and assessment measures used across these studies.

The relationship between demographic factors and the prevalence of anxiety disorders in youth has been explored. With respect to age, epidemiological data suggest that the prevalence of OAD (as well as most other anxiety disorders) increases with age (e.g., Anderson et al., 1987; Cohen, Cohen, & Brook, 1993). Studies exploring the relation between gender and prevalence rates suggest that OAD appears to be as prevalent in males as in females until adolescence, after which it becomes more common in females than in males (Werry, 1991). In contrast, one study found that OAD was more prevalent in males (e.g., Anderson et al., 1987) while another found that OAD was more prevalent in females (Muris et al., 1998). This latter finding is consistent with studies on adults wherein GAD has been found to be more prevalent in women than in men (Kessler et al., 1994). Prevalence rates of anxiety disorders in African-American compared to Caucasian children are comparable (Last & Perrin, 1993) and similar results were found when comparing the prevalence rates of anxiety disorders in Hispanic-American compared to Caucasian youth (Ginsburg & Silverman, 1996).

AETIOLOGY

The aetiology of GAD can be understood in terms of equifinality and mutlifinality (Cicchetti & Rogosch, 1996). That is, there are many pathways that lead a child to develop GAD (equifinality). Similarly, the pathway that leads one child to develop

GAD may lead another child to alternative outcomes (multifinality). Indeed, the pathways toward GAD are complex and not defined by a single course.

Much of our understanding of these pathways comes from research examining anxiety disorders in general and research using adult populations with fewer studies examining the factors that may place a child at risk or protect a child against the development of GAD. Integrative models have begun to emerge that attempt to explain, given current knowledge, the interaction between key factors in the aetiology of GAD (e.g., Hudson & Rapee, in press). Research identifying these key factors will be reviewed.

Evidence suggests a heritable component to GAD. Twin studies indicate that 30–40% of anxiety symptoms are associated with genetic factors (Hettema, Neale, & Kendler, 2001) but the research suggests that what is inherited is not a specific heritability towards GAD but rather a general predisposition towards anxiety and perhaps other psychopathology such as depression. The existence of a genetic contribution to anxiety and depression in a sample of female twins has been reported (Andrews et al., 1990). Other studies suggest that perhaps there may be more to the heritability of anxiety disorders. For example, Kendler and colleagues (1992, 1995) found that GAD and depression were influenced by similar genetic factors in a sample of female twins, while other psychiatric disorders such as panic disorder were influenced by a different set of genetic factors. In contrast, Scherrer et al. (2000) showed that GAD was in fact influenced by the same genetic factors as panic disorder. Rapee (2001) suggests that the variable results may be accounted for by the different diagnostic criteria used to assess GAD across these studies (e.g., duration of one month versus six months).

Interestingly, Noyes and colleagues (1987) showed that in first-degree relatives of individuals with GAD there is an increased risk for GAD but not other anxiety disorders, indicating specific familial transmission. However, such family studies not only account for genetic heritability but also include influence from environmental factors (such as social environment shared by family members). Although twin studies indicate heritability towards anxiety in general, the findings from this family study indicate specific familial transmission of GAD.

Research examining the link between temperament and later anxiety disorders may help to understand the genetic contribution. One temperamental factor that has been showing promise with respect to its link with the anxiety disorders is "Behavioural Inhibition". Behavioural Inhibition (BI) is a categorical variable defined by the presence of inhibition to the unfamiliar, avoidance, or withdrawal of novel situations (Garcia Coll, Kagan, & Reznick, 1984). These children are shown in infancy to have higher levels of physiological arousal. Through a number of longitudinal studies conducted by Kagan and colleagues a clear link has been established between the presence of BI in children and the presence of later anxiety disorders. Infants identified as behaviourally inhibited at 21 months have been shown to have an increased risk for an anxiety disorder later in childhood (Biederman et al., 1993, 2001). In particular, those children whose behavioural inhibition remains stable are most likely to develop an anxiety disorder.

Consistent with this finding, parents of children with anxiety disorders (including GAD) have reported greater difficulties with their anxious children in the first year of life (crying, difficulties sleeping, pain and gas), more fears between the ages of 1 and 2 years, and more difficulties adjusting to transitions than children not seeking treatment for an anxiety disorder (Rapee & Szollos, 1997).

The accumulating evidence points to the role of the child's temperamental vulnerability, placing the child at greater risk for an anxiety disorder. However, not all children identified as temperamentally at risk will develop an anxiety disorder. Clearly, other environmental factors come into play that shape a child's trajectory toward an anxiety disorder.

One factor that has received increasing attention over the past five years is the role of the family in the aetiology and maintenance of anxiety disorders in children (Rapee, 1997). There may be a number of ways in which parents may be involved in the aetiologic or maintenance of the child's anxiety. Parental influence is likely to be exerted primarily through support of avoidance behaviour or modelling of anxious behaviours. In a study that clearly demonstrated the impact parents may have on the child's avoidance behaviour, Barrett and colleagues (1996) asked children with anxiety disorders (AD), oppositional defiant disorder (ODD) and non-clinical children (NC) to discuss hypothetical situations of ambiguous threat with their parents and decide what to do. Although ODD and NC children chose less avoidant solution following the discussion, AD children chose more avoidant solutions following the discussion with their parents. Closer evaluation of these discussions revealed that parents, in response to the child's avoidant suggestions, provided support and agreement of these choices, thereby reinforcing the avoidance (Dadds et al., 1996).

Other studies examining the role of parents in the development of anxiety have shown that mothers of anxious children may in fact be overinvolved during stressful situations and provide more help to the anxious child than necessary (see Hudson & Rapee, 2001; Siqueland, Kendall, & Steinberg, 1996). As to whether this parenting behaviour occurs in response to the child's more anxious style or whether this is a general parenting style remains under question. A more inhibited, sensitive child is likely to elicit certain parenting behaviours such as greater degrees of protection, overinvolvement and less autonomy granting (Hudson & Rapee, in press). This parenting trap is also likely to be further influenced by the parent's own anxiety level.

Alternately, it is possible that parenting which encourages approach behaviour rather than avoidance may alter an at-risk child's trajectory and protect the child from developing an anxiety disorder. A parent who encourages the approach of novel situations may teach the child that he or she is capable of coping with and conquering novel situations.

Parents may also be important in the modelling of anxious behaviour. Children learn through observation of others. Parents who worry may unknowingly pass this behaviour on to their child. There has been strong evidence in human infant research and animal research showing the impact of modelling on the fearful behaviour of offspring. For example, Gerull and Rapee (2002) showed that mothers of 15–20-month-old infants could influence their child's approach of novel threatening stimuli (e.g., rubber snake) depending on the facial expression shown to the child. If a mother provided a fearful rather than a happy face, 10 minutes later when the child was shown the object again, the child was less likely to approach the object in comparison to children whose mothers showed a happy face in response to the threatening object.

Another factor that may play a role in the development of GAD is the infant's attachment to his or her caregiver (Bowlby, 1973, 1974). There has been some preliminary evidence that children with an ambivalent attachment (i.e., children who have extreme difficulty separating from their caregiver and have difficulty being soothed on reunion) may be more likely to develop an anxiety disorder. One study examining later anxiety disorders and infant attachment (as measured by the Ainsworth Strange Situation; Ainsworth et al., 1978) showed that 28% of infants categorized as having ambivalent attachment were likely to have an anxiety disorder in adolescence compared to 12% of children with a secure attachment (Warren et al., 1997). Ambivalent attachment was a significant predictor of anxiety disorder in adolescence after accounting for the mother's anxiety and the child's temperament.

In addition to parents, other significant individuals in the child's life may play an important role in the development of GAD. Just as parents may provide support of the child's avoidance behaviour, so too may the child's peer group, siblings or teachers. Anxious children who affiliate with similarly anxious peers may be more likely to avoid taking certain risks or venturing into novel situations. This may further shape the child's anxious and avoidance behaviour and prevent the child from learning contrary information to his or her anxious beliefs. In comparison, anxious children who mix with confident non-anxious peers may, in fact, be pressured to take risks and try out situations that they otherwise would have avoided. The study of peer and sibling influences on anxiety is less developed and requires further investigation.

Another of the multiple pathways that may lead an individual to develop GAD is the experience of stressful events during childhood. There has been some evidence pointing to the specific role of stressful life events in the aetiology of GAD and not other anxiety disorders. In a study by Manassis and Hood (1998), psychosocial adversity predicted the degree of impairment in children with GAD but not in children with phobic disorders. Furthermore, studies with adult populations have found that individuals with GAD are more likely to report a traumatic event than individuals without GAD (Roemer et al., 1997; Torgersen, 1986).

Taking this further, Chorpita and Barlow (1998) have proposed that it is the experience of uncontrollability of one's environment, particularly in early childhood, that is central to the development of anxiety, and evidence from animal studies provides direct support of this thesis. Infant Rhesus monkeys reared in an environment in which they could control the delivery of food, water, and treats displayed significantly less fear and more exploratory behaviour in novel situations than monkeys reared in environments of reduced control (Mineka, Gunnar, & Champoux, 1986).

In addition to the beneficial effects of having control over one's environment, other factors have been investigated that may protect the child against the development of anxiety. For instance, social support appears to moderate the relationship between negative life events and the development of anxiety (e.g., Cowen, Pedro-Carroll, & Alpert-Gillis, 1990; Hill et al., 1996). The greater social support, the greater the buffer provided and the impact of the stressful event(s) is lowered.

Assessment

The importance of multimethod assessment—an assessment process that should include multiple methods and perspectives—is continually stressed in the child and adolescent literature (Kendall & Morris, 1991; Ollendick, 1986). This section will review some of the more widely used methods for the assessment of GAD in children and adolescents.

Structured Diagnostic Interviews

Structured diagnostic interviews are important with respect to treatment planning, research, and outcome evaluation. Research suggests that diagnostic reliability is improved with the use of these structured interviews (McClellan & Werry, 2000). Nevertheless, research indicates that the level of agreement between children and their parents is modest at best (e.g., Grills & Ollendick, 2003) and varies across structured diagnostic interviews (Schniering, Hudson, & Rapee, 2000). In general, children tend to report fewer symptoms and when disagreement exists between child and parent reports, the parent reports are often weighted more heavily when making a diagnosis (Rapee et al., 1994).

Widely used structured diagnostic interview for children and adolescent disorders include the Diagnostic Interview Schedule for Children (DISC; Schwab-Stone et al., 1993; Shaffer et al., 1993), the Diagnostic Interview for Children and Adolescents (DICA-IV; Shaffer et al., 2000), the Child and Adolescent Psychiatric Assessment (CAPA; Angold & Costello, 2000), and the Anxiety Disorders Interview Schedule for Children (ADIS-C/P; Silverman & Albano, 1996). Of these interview schedules, only the DICA-IV and ADIS-C/P are based on DSM-IV criteria.

The ADIS-C/P was designed specifically to diagnose anxiety disorders in children and adolescents and is the most widely used structured diagnostic interview to assess GAD and other anxiety disorders in youth. Recent research suggests that the ADIS-C/P has good reliability in symptom scale scores for GAD and good to excellent reliability for other anxiety disorders (Silverman, Saavedra, & Pina, 2001).

Self-Report Questionnaires

Self-report questionnaires are frequently used to assess anxiety in children and adolescents (see Table 6.1 for a summary of child report measures). Recent research suggests that measures such as the RCMAS and STAI-C cannot adequately discriminate children with anxiety disorders from children with other internalizing and externalizing disorders (e.g., Dierker et al., 2001; Lonigan, Carey, & Finch, 1994). The MASC, SCAS, and the SCARED were more recently developed to address criticisms in the literature that have questioned the diagnostic validity of the RCMAS, STAI-C, and other anxiety measures. In contrast to the above measures, the PSWQ-C is a method that is specifically designed to measure the tendency of children and adolescents to engage in excessive, generalized, and uncontrollable worry. Item examples include: "Once I start worrying, I can't stop"; "I am always worrying about

Table 6.1 Common self-report measures used to assess anxiety in children and adolescents

Measure	Comments
Revised Children's Manifest Anxiety Scale (RCMAS; Reynolds & Richmond, 1985)	Assesses chronic anxiety: physiological, social concern-concentration, worry/oversensitivity, and lie scales. Acceptable reliability and validity.
State-Trait Anxiety Inventory for Children (STAI-C; Spielberger, 1973)	Assesses state and trait anxiety. Has been shown to correlate with other self-report measures of anxiety in children and adolescents.
Multidimensional Anxiety Scale for Children (MASC; March et al., 1997)	Assesses physical symptoms, social anxiety, harm avoidance, separation anxiety. Excellent retest reliability and adequate convergent and divergent validity.
Spence Children's Anxiety Scale (SCAS; Spence, 1998)	Assesses generalized anxiety, separation anxiety, social phobia, obsessive compulsive, panic-agoraphobia, and physical injury symptoms. Acceptable six-month retest reliability, strong convergent reliability, and can discriminate between clinically anxious and non-anxious control children.
Screen for Child Anxiety Related Emotional Disorders (SCARED; Birmaher et al., 1997)	Child and parent report versions. Good retest reliability, internal consistency, and discriminant validity. Moderate child and parent agreement.
Penn State Worry Questionnaire for Children (PSWQ-C; Chorpita et al., 1997)	Assesses excessive, generalized and uncontrollable worry. Good convergent and discriminate validity and excellent test–retest reliability.

something". Chorpita and colleagues (1997) found that children with GAD reported significantly more worry on the PSWQ-C compared to children diagnosed with other anxiety disorders. In addition, Muris, Meesters, and Gobel (2001) reported that PSWQ-C scores were significantly associated with all types of anxiety disorders symptoms, but in particular with symptoms of GAD.

Behavioural Observations

Behavioural observations are generally used to assess anxiety symptoms in general rather than specific symptoms of GAD in children and adolescents. Examples of behavioural observations include: speech tasks, behavioural avoidance tasks (BATs), interactions in same sex or different sex dyads, and family interaction tasks. The anxiety symptoms typically include behaviours such as fingernail biting, leg shaking, absence of eye contact, trembling voice, fidgeting, crying, task avoidance, and inaudible voice.

There are several potential advantages to using behavioural observation as an assessment tool. First, behaviours observed in anxiety-inducing situations provide information on those situations that are most anxiety-inducing for the child and how the child reacts in these situations. Second, behavioural observations are an additional source of information typically obtained from a person who can provide information about how the child behaves in a different environment (e.g., a teacher). Third, some behavioural indices of anxiety (e.g., totals of several codes) have been shown to be sensitive to treatment effects and therefore can be used to evaluate treatment outcome for youth with anxiety disorders (e.g., Kendall, 1994; Kendall et al., 1997).

Two disadvantages temper the advantages. First, the coding systems used across studies vary and therefore limit our ability to generalize. Second, there is scant research on the reliability and validity of behavioural observation coding systems used with anxious youth. Lastly, behavioural observations are time-consuming and often difficult to implement in community settings.

Parent and Teacher Report Questionnaires

Like behavioural observations, parent and teacher report questionnaires are important because they provide information about how the child behaves in settings outside the clinic or research setting and how the child is observed by significant people in his or her life. Unfortunately, parent and teacher report questionnaires do not measure GAD symptoms specifically. The Trait portion of the State-Trait Anxiety Inventory for Children has been modified by Strauss for use by parents and the psychometric properties are acceptable (Southam-Gerow, Flannery-Schroeder, & Kendall, 2002).

Several questionnaires contain an anxiety-withdrawn dimension such as the Child Behavior Checklist (CBCL; Achenbach, 1991a) and the Teacher Report Form (TRF; Achenbach, 1991b). The CBCL has broadband internalizing and externalizing factors and eight specific scales (e.g., one is anxiety depression). The CBCL has been reported to have high retest reliability, interparent agreement, validity, high correlations with other similar parent measures, and the ability to discriminate between referred and non-referred children (Achenbach, 1991a). The TRF mirrors the CBCL but provides a picture of the child's behaviour and functioning within the classroom. The TRF has been shown to have high retest reliability over a two-week interval, moderate inter-teacher agreement, and the ability to discriminate between referred and non-referred children (Achenbach, 1991b). Using items from the CBCL and TRF, a parent and teacher report measure has been developed specifically for use with anxiety-disordered children. The CBCL-A consists of 16 items and has been found to have internal consistency, retest reliability, and to distinguish anxiety-disordered youth from non-disordered and normal control children (Kendall et al., 1998). Similarly, the TRF-A (Choudhury, 2001), an 18-item teacher report measure of anxiety, has shown very good internal consistency and retest reliability. Both measures show moderate to high correlations with other reliable anxiety measures.

There are several advantages to using parent and teacher rating scales such as the CBCL and the TRF. First, the reliability and validity of these measures has been supported by several research studies (e.g., Kendall et al., 1992; Southam-Gerow et al., 2002). Second, rating scales such as the CBCL and the TRF have normative data that are developmentally sensitive based on the gender and age of the child. Third, the rating scales are easy to administer and score wherein normalized T scores can be derived and compared to both clinical and non-clinical children and adolescents. One potential limitation inherent in parent and teacher report questionnaires is that the raters (i.e., the child's teacher and parents) are neither trained nor reliable with regard to the behaviour they are rating (Kendall et al., 1992).

TREATMENT

In the past decade, the treatment for GAD in children and adolescents has witnessed several significant advancements. Although the majority of treatment research has focused on anxiety disorders more generally, studies examining treatment of anxiety disorders have included children and adolescents with GAD. The approach that has received empirical support in the treatment of GAD is Cognitive Behaviour Therapy (CBT). According to several literature reviews, (Kazdin & Weisz, 1998; Ollendick & King, 1998, 2000) when judged against the criteria for determining whether or not a treatment has received empirical support (Chambless & Hollon, 1998) CBT for child and adolescent generalized anxiety disorder warrants designation as a "probably efficacious" treatment. The first randomized clinical trial evaluating child-focused CBT for children with anxiety disorders (including generalized anxiety disorder) was reported in Kendall (1994). Subsequently, there have been conceptual replications of child-focused CBT at multiple sites and the addition of a family component (e.g., Barrett et al., 1996) and the conduct of the therapy in group format (e.g., Flannery-Schroeder & Kendall, 2000).

Description of the "Coping Cat" Program

The following describes the individual cognitive behavioural treatment program designed specifically for anxiety-disordered children (i.e., the Coping Cat) and adolescents (i.e., the C.A.T. Project). The program consists of approximately 16 sessions wherein the first half of the program involves teaching the basic concepts and coping skills (education component) and the second half involves practicing the coping skills acquired in the first half of the treatment in both imaginal and *in vivo* exposures to anxiety-producing situations (practice component). In the education component, four concepts are taught to the child and summarized by the acronym FEAR. This mnemonic is a tool for children to use when they are tackling situations in which they feel anxious. FEAR stands for:

F   Feeling frightened? (awareness of physical symptoms of anxiety)
E   Expecting bad things to happen? (recognition of anxious self-talk)

A   Attitudes and Actions that will help (problem-solving)

R   Results and Rewards (self-evaluation and self-reward for effort).

During the first part of the program, skills such as cognitive restructuring, relaxation, problem-solving, self-evaluation, and self-reward are taught using a progressive approach. The children are first taught to recognize the physical symptoms related to anxiety (F-step) and to use the symptoms as cues to implement the remainder of the plan. However, before the skill building begins the therapist devotes the majority of the first session to building rapport with the child (e.g., playing a game the child enjoys, learning more about the child and his or her shared interests).

The therapist employs a number of strategies to ensure the greatest learning opportunity: coping modelling, tag-along procedures, and role-play. Throughout the treatment the therapist serves as a "coping model", that is, when a new skill is introduced the therapist first demonstrates the skill for the child. The term "coping" is used to reinforce that the aim is not perfection, rather, the therapist demonstrates how to overcome obstacles as they arise. Role-plays are frequently used in the treatment program as another method to demonstrate and practice newly acquired skills. Tag-along procedures are also useful to encourage the child's skill development without overwhelming the child. Once the therapist has modelled for the child, the child can then participate in the role-play by assisting the therapist. The role-play is repeated, this time with increased child involvement. Tag-along, coping modelling and role-play strategies are used to different degrees according to the child's skill level and understanding of concepts. For instance, the therapist may not need to use the "tag-along" strategy for an older child who quickly grasps the skill.

Homework assignments are an important component of the Coping Cat program (Hudson & Kendall, 2002). To reinforce learning and generalization of skills from the therapy room to the home and school environment, tasks that relate to the information covered are set at the end of each session. To avoid the negative connotations associated with homework, the tasks are referred to as "Show That I Can" or "STIC" tasks. The purpose of the task is for the child to practice—show off—the skills he or she has learned.

Awareness of Physical Symptoms

For the child with GAD, learning to identify physical symptoms accompanying their worry is an important step. In response to asking the question "Am I feeling frightened?" the child may identify a number of somatic symptoms (heart racing, nausea) associated with feeling worried. Awareness of physical symptoms related to anxiety alerts the child to address the arousal in some way. At this point in the program children are taught diaphragmatic breathing and progressive muscle relaxation. The body's major muscle groups are sequentially relaxed through a series of tension-releasing exercises designed to teach the child to identify states of tension and states of relaxation in their muscles. Relaxation scripts can be found in Ollendick and Cerny (1981) and Rapee et al. (2000). Children are given weekly homework assignments to practice the relaxations skills in anxiety-producing situations at school, home, or other relevant situations.

Recognition of Anxious Self-Talk

Children also learn to identify their anxious self-talk and understand that anxiety is associated with "Expecting bad things to happen". Cartoons and thought bubbles are used to help the child to identify their cognitions (see Figure 6.1). Having identified their anxious self-talk, together the therapist and the child test out and challenge the beliefs about the situation—and, over time, the child develops more

Figure 6.1   Identifying anxious cognitions (Illustrations by Peter J. Mikulka, PhD).

realistic, coping self-talk. The therapist can demonstrate by first providing non-stressful and low-stressful examples to which the child may relate (or use photos from a magazine). Often it is useful to begin with examples that do not involve the child (and hence are less threatening), perhaps a friend or a cartoon character. The child can help the therapist to generate possible anxious thoughts as well as more helpful, realistic thoughts. The aim is to generate, through practice, more realistic self-talk, not overly positive or negative self-talk. Questions like the following can help the child to gain a perspective on the situation: "How likely is it (i.e., the feared outcome) to happen?"; "What happened last time when you forgot your home-work?"; "What did you think of your friends when they answered the question incorrectly?".

Problem-Solving

Problem-solving is the key to the third step, "Actions and Attitudes that will help". The child and therapist brainstorm alternative adaptive behaviour and cognitions that will help the child to cope in the anxiety-provoking situation and also in every-day life. The child is encouraged to consider many possible solutions to the problem and select an optimal solution or two to implement. Rather than choosing the initial often maladaptive response (e.g., avoiding the situation), the child is encouraged to generate alternative more adaptive solutions. For example, the therapist and child might develop a plan of action about how to manage an upcoming school excursion to the museum. The child's initial response may be to avoid school on the day the trip is planned. Instead, the therapist and child generate a list of other things the child could do. Some of the child's responses may not be ideal but it is important, in order for the child to develop problem-solving abilities, to withhold judgment until the list of possible solutions has been exhausted. The therapist and child may suggest visiting the museum the weekend before to check it out, on the day, arrange to sit on the bus with a friend. At the end of the list, the child then evaluates each response, anticipating the advantages and disadvantages of each solution and chooses the most appropriate solution.

Self-Evaluation and Self-Reward

The final skill the child is taught is based on self-monitoring and contingent rein-forcement. Courageous behaviour is reinforced through appropriate reward. Chil-dren are taught to accurately reward ongoing effort and coping, not simply for successful outcomes. Anxious children tend to be highly critical of the performance, thus these skills teach the child to appropriately evaluate effort and not just outcome. Children are taught to use self-talk (e.g., "I am pleased with how I played"), as well as tangible rewards to reinforce effort. Throughout the program, the therapist models the use of appropriate rewards by rewarding the child's con-tribution in session and in STIC tasks with praise, sticker rewards or prizes (e.g., toys, books).

Practice

The second part of the therapy—the active engagement of the skills in the actual provocative situation—has been considered a potent ingredient in therapy. The child and therapist create a hierarchy starting with low anxiety-provoking situations moving to situations that produce high levels of anxiety. The gradual exposure to these situations allows the child to gain confidence in using the skills in easier situations first. The speed with which the child works through the hierarchy depends on the child's anxiety level. The next step in the hierarchy should be taken when the child has successfully tackled the previous step and experienced some reduction of anxiety. The next step should not produce too high an anxiety level but the aim is for the child to experience some distress and learn to manage it. To enable the child to tackle the *in vivo* exposures, practice can take the form of role-plays, tag-alongs and imaginal exposures. For all exposure tasks the child and the therapist collaborate to design the task and the FEAR plan.

Typical exposures for children with GAD may include the following: answering a question in class (correctly or incorrectly), not checking the book bag before going to school, not asking Mum for reassurance, starting a new after-school activity, asking a stranger for directions. In constructing exposures both in and out of the office, the therapist makes sure that the situation provides an opportunity for the child to face the feared situation. For example, if the child is worried about being late to school, then the exposure may involve having the child deliberately come late to school. By doing this the child can learn that even if late, the child is able to use problem-solving skills to handle this situation. The child practices the newly acquired skills repeatedly in situations until his or her anxiety has reduced and the child has learned that a negative expectation is an unlikely prediction.

Finally, the child creates a "commercial", usually completed in the form of a video, booklet, or cartoon, summarizing his or her experiences in the program. Importantly, this is in the child's own words—his or her own creation. For example, the child may write a song about the FEAR plan or direct a play in which the child's parents and the therapist act out a scenario depicting a character conquering his or her fears. The purpose of the commercial is to document the child's success and give him or her an opportunity to be the expert and "show off" what has been learned to help to tell other children about strategies for coping with anxiety.

Involving the Family

Throughout the program, the therapist works with the child's parents as collaborators (not as patients): the therapist meets with the child's parents on two specific occasions, usually after the third and eighth sessions. These sessions are relatively unstructured and allow concerns to be raised that the parents or the therapist may have about the child. The therapist can use these opportunities to provide the parents with alternative ways of understanding or managing their anxious child. The parents may have fallen into patterns of responding to the child's anxiety that may not be the most helpful. For example, the therapist may have noticed that in response to the child's barrage of "what if?" questions, the parents respond with reassuring phrases such as "It will be okay". By continually reassuring the child, the behaviour is reinforced and he or she is not given the opportunity to learn that the situation is "okay" without the parents' reassurance. The parents and the therapist would need to develop a plan to change the parents' response by gradually reducing the amount of reassurance they give to their child.

Table 6.2 provides a session-by-session guideline of the individual treatment program. For more details about the treatment, readers are referred to the second edition of the treatment manual (Kendall, 2000).

Table 6.2 Session by session outline of treatment content

Session	Content outline
1	To build rapport and provide an orientation to the treatment.
2	To help the child identify different types of feelings and to distinguish anxious, worried feelings from other types of feelings; to normalize feelings of fear and anxiety; to begin to develop a hierarchy of anxiety-provoking situations.
3	To review Session 2 content; to learn more about somatic responses to anxiety and to identify specific somatic responses to anxiety; the "F" Step.
4	Parent session: to provide additional information about the treatment; to give parents an opportunity to discuss their concerns about the child; to learn more about the situations in which the child becomes anxious; to give specific ways the parents can be involved in the program.
5	To introduce relaxation training and its use in controlling tension associated with anxiety; to review the somatic cues which show that the child is tense and anxious.
6	To introduce the function of personal thoughts and their impact on the child's response in anxiety-provoking situations; to help the child to begin to recognize self-talk (expectations, automatic questions, and attributions) in anxious situations; and to help the child to begin to develop and use less anxiety-provoking self-talk; the "E" step; to review relaxation training.
7	To review the concept of anxious self-talk and reinforce changing anxious self-talk into coping self-talk; to review relaxation training; to introduce the concept of developing and using strategies that will help the child better manage his anxieties; the "A" step.
8	To introduce the concept of evaluating or self-rating performance and rewarding based on performance; the "R" step; to review all previously introduced skills by formalizing the 4-step "FEAR plan" for the child to use when feeling anxious and practicing its use in non-stressful situations.
9	Parent session (see Session 4): to acknowledge that the next portion of the treatment may invoke greater anxiety in the child and normalize this reaction.
10–16	Practice FEAR steps in increasingly anxiety provoking situations; to practice the 4-step coping plan under low anxiety-provoking conditions, both *imaginal* and *in vivo*; commercial (Session 16 only).

Child-Focused CBT

The first randomized-controlled clinical trial designed to evaluate the efficacy of child-focused individual CBT (ICBT) was reported in 1994. Using child, parent, and teacher reports, structured diagnostic interviews, and behavioural observations, the "Coping Cat" program (Kendall, 2000; see "Description of the 'Coping Cat' Program" above) was compared to a wait-list control condition (WLC) for 47 youth (ages 9–13 years) diagnosed with DSM-III-R overanxious, separation anxiety, and avoidant disorders. Children were randomly assigned to ICBT or WLC. Sixty-three percent of the children in the study were diagnosed with OAD as their primary disorder. With regard to the demographic characteristics of the sample, 60% were male (40% female); 76% were Caucasian (24% minority); and 47% were 9–10 years old (53% 11–13 years old).

Findings revealed that treated children displayed greater improvements on child and parent reports as well as behavioural observations. Importantly, based on diagnostic interviews, 64% of the treated children at post-treatment no longer met diagnostic criteria for their primary diagnosis compared to 5% (or one child) in the wait-list control condition. Furthermore, the gains displayed at post-treatment were maintained at one-year follow-up.

Kendall and Southam-Gerow (1996) conducted a 2 to 5 year (average 3.35 years) follow-up study on 36 of the 47 children in the Kendall (1994) study. Ninety-one percent of the children with an initial OAD diagnosis no longer met criteria for this diagnosis. Treatment gains measured by self-report and parent report questionnaires of anxiety, self-reported anxious self-talk and depression were also maintained at the long-term follow-up.

A second randomized clinical trial (Kendall et al., 1997) compared ICBT to WLC for 94 youth (aged 9–13 years) diagnosed with DSM-III-R overanxious, separation anxiety, and avoidant disorders. The children were randomly assigned to treatment and to a therapist. Greater than 58% of the children in the study were diagnosed with OAD as their primary disorder. With regard to the demographic characteristics of the sample, 62% were male (38% female); 85% were Caucasian (15% minority); and 52% were 9–10 years old (48% 11–13 years old).

Based on diagnostic interviews with the parent(s) about the child, 50% of the children no longer met criteria for their primary disorder at post-treatment. Compared to the WLC children, children receiving ICBT displayed greater improvements on child and parent reports of anxiety symptoms, internalizing problems, coping behaviours, negative self-statements as well as behavioural observations (no significant differences emerged between the two groups on child self-report of depression and teacher report of internalizing problems). Also, a significantly greater number of children in ICBT displayed clinically meaningful change on both parent and teacher reports of internalizing problems compared to children in WLC. Clinically meaningful change is defined as changes that return deviant individuals to within non-deviant limits and can be examined using normative comparison such as those on the CBCL and TRF (Kendall et al., 1999). The supportive results displayed at post-treatment were maintained at one-year follow-up.

Child-Focused Group Treatment

Group treatment is often considered cost-effective, and may be a stage for multiple peer modelling and social exposure tasks. Recent research suggests that CBT for children and adolescents with anxiety disorders can be effective in a child-focused group format. A randomized-controlled clinical trial (Flannery-Schroeder & Kendall, 2000) evaluated the efficacy of a child-focused group CBT (GCBT) with that of individual CBT (ICBT) and a wait-list control condition (WLC) for 37 youths (ages 8–14 years) diagnosed with DSM-IV GAD, SAD, and social phobia (SP). Children were randomly assigned to GCBT, ICBT, or WLC. Fifty-six percent of the children in the study were diagnosed with GAD as their primary disorder. With regard to the demographic characteristics of the sample, 51% were male (49% female); 89% were Caucasian (11% minority); and 57% were 8–10 years old (43% 11–14 years old).

The GCBT condition (see Flannery-Schroeder & Kendall, 1996) was adapted from the Coping Cat manual and consisted of 18 weekly sessions of 90 minutes, whereas the ICBT had 18 weekly sessions of 50–60 minutes. The cognitive and behavioural treatment components (i.e., using coping self-talk, developing coping plans, role-playing, modelling, relaxation training, exposures, contingent reinforcements) and weekly homework assignments in GCBT were similar to those used in ICBT.

Treatment outcome was evaluated using structured diagnostic interviews as well as child, parent, and teacher reports. Analysis of diagnostic status revealed that 73% of the children in ICBT, and 50% of the GCBT children no longer met criteria for their primary disorder at post-treatment. This difference between the two conditions was not statistically significant. Sixty-four percent of the children in ICBT and 50% of the GCBT children no longer met criteria for GAD, SAD, or SP at post-treatment and the data revealed that children in both ICBT and GCBT displayed greater improvements on anxiety symptoms than the WLC children. Both child and parent reports revealed that both ICBT and GCBT displayed improvements of coping with anxiety-producing situations from pre- to post-treatment, whereas WLC children did not. The treatment gains displayed at post-treatment were maintained at three-month follow-up.

Family CBT

With accumulating evidence that parents play an important role in maintaining the child's anxiety (e.g., Barrett et al., 1996) the potential added benefits of increasing the level of parental involvement in the treatment of anxiety-disordered youth was considered. Several programs have adapted the child-focused program by including a family component (e.g., Barrett et al., 1996; Rapee et al., 2000). The extent to which the parents are involved, and the exact content of the family treatment, differs across these studies. For example, the content varies from providing the parent with skills to deal with their own anxiety to providing parents with skills to deal with their child's anxiety. The structure of the parental involvement differs also with additional parent-alone sessions accompanying the child sessions, family sessions or, in some cases, only parent sessions. Let us now examine the research on family-focused CBT.

In an Australian adaptation of the Coping Cat program, Barrett and colleagues (1996) compared the child-focused program alone to the child-focused program with an added family anxiety management (FAM) component. The CBT program used in this study was reduced to 12 weeks: basically the same CBT but within fewer sessions. Seventy-nine children (ages 7–14) with a primary diagnosis of overanxious disorder, separation anxiety disorder, or social phobia were randomly assigned to CBT, CBT+FAM, or wait-list control.

Although not family therapy in a traditional sense, the FAM did include (a) parental training in contingency management strategies, (b) communication and problem-solving skills, and (c) recognition/management of parents' own emotional and anxious responses to stimuli. In the contingency management component of the program parents are encouraged to reward courageous behaviour using descriptive praises while planned ignoring techniques and the use of privilege removal are used to extinguish inappropriate anxiety responses. Parents are taught to communicate and problem-solve more effectively as a couple and to be consistent in their approach to their child. Finally, parents are instructed on how to recognize and manage their own anxiety and stress. By learning how to manage their own anxiety more effectively, it can be argued, parents can then serve as more appropriate and effective models for their child.

At the completion of the program, both CBT conditions led to results better than wait-list and children receiving the CBT+FAM conditions were significantly more likely to no longer meet criteria for an anxiety diagnosis than children in the CBT alone or in the wait-list condition (84% vs 57% vs 26%). Differences between CBT alone and CBT+FAM were not present at the six-month follow-up, a meaningful difference was present at one-year follow-up with 95% of children in the CBT+FAM condition no longer meeting criteria compared to 70% in the CBT alone. These findings held true primarily for younger children (7–10 years) and female children. Within the younger age group (7–10 years), children were more likely to be diagnosis-free at post-treatment in the CBT+FAM condition (100%) than the CBT condition (56%). In contrast, for the older group (aged 11–14), there were non-significant post-treatment differences between the CBT (60%) and the CBT+FAM (60%) conditions. At one-year follow-up the same age effects were observed. Females, who participated in the CBT+FAM condition, were more likely to have no anxiety diagnosis at post-treatment (83%) compared to females who participated in the CBT alone condition (37%). Parent training may be more beneficial for younger female than for older male children. In any event, the percentages of cases not meeting diagnostic criteria after CBT or CBT+FAM are quite impressive and contribute to the efficacy associated with CBT.

Given our present focus on GAD, we can consider the outcomes specifically for the cases diagnosed as OAD. For children with OAD ($n = 30$; 38%) the findings were similar to the findings for the overall group: 68.2% were diagnosis free at post-treatment (SAD 77.8%; SP 61.5%) and at 12-month follow-up; 75% of children with OAD at pre-treatment were diagnosis free (SAD 94%; SP 77%). The results are impressive when one further notes that these children were assessed again on average six years following treatment (Barrett et al., 2001) and the findings continued to be supportive: CBT and CBT+FAM produced equivalent changes in the long term (86% CBT and 86% CBT+FAM not meeting diagnostic criteria). Again, given our focus on GAD, note that Barrett et al. (2001) compared the efficacy of the treatment for the children presenting with OAD and reported that 81% of OAD children were diagnosis free at the six-year follow-up. The comparable results from self-report and parent report questionnaires further buttressed the overall positive outcomes.

Using a group treatment, however, resulted in a different pattern of outcomes. Barrett (1998) compared CBT alone and CBT+FAM in a group format and reported that the differences between the two conditions were no longer present regardless of age or sex of the child. In this study 60 children with a primary anxiety disorder (50% with OAD) were randomized to group CBT alone, group CBT+FAM, or wait-list. At post-treatment, 60% of children in the CBT alone condition and 71% in the CBT+FAM condition compared to 25% in the wait-list condition no longer met criteria for an anxiety diagnosis, and at one-year follow-up the findings were maintained (65% in the CBT alone condition compared to 85% in the CBT+FAM condition no longer meeting criteria for an anxiety diagnosis). The favourable results add to the mounting body of support for CBT for childhood GAD.

A number of studies have also examined the efficacy of family CB treatments conducted in group format (Mendlowitz et al., 1999; Rapee, 2000; Shortt, Barrett, & Fox, 2001; Silverman et al., 1999; Toren et al., 2000). For example, Shortt, Barrett, and Fox (2001) compared a 10-session group family CBT with a wait-list control. The sample consisted primarily of children with overanxious disorder ($n = 42$), and children with separation anxiety ($n = 19$) and social phobia ($n = 10$). The treatment consisted of 10 sessions (40 minutes each) with the children and 4 sessions ($1^{1}/_{2}$ hours each) with the parents. The parent component included skills to help parents to recognize and manage their own anxiety, as well as contingency management training to help parents to manage their child's anxiety as communication and problem-solving skills. Children in the family group CBT showed significant improvements compared to the wait-list group at post-treatment (69% vs 6% not meeting diagnostic criteria) and at 12-month follow-up (68%). Other studies have also reported favourable results for children receiving group CBT plus additional parent sessions (Rapee, 2000; Silverman et al., 1999).

Mendlowitz et al. (1999) examined the efficacy of group family CBT in a sample of 68 children (aged 7–12 years) who met the criteria for one or more anxiety diagnosis.[1] In this study cases were randomly assigned to one of three 12-week treatment conditions: parent + child intervention, child-only intervention, and parent-only intervention. Change in the number of anxious and depressive symptoms and use of coping strategies occurred for all three groups, however, children in the combined parent + child intervention employed more active coping strategies and showed greater gains in parental reports of emotional well-being compared to either parent alone or child alone. This study suggests that the concurrent

---

[1] Number of GAD children not reported.

parental + child involvement provides additional benefit in improving the child's use of coping strategies.

Cobham, Dadds, and Spence (1998) investigated the effectiveness of a 10-session child-alone CBT and CBT + parent anxiety management (PAM) component. In the PAM condition parents were given skills to deal with their own anxiety and their child's anxiety during four additional sessions, including psychoeducation about the aetiology of childhood anxiety and the role of the family, cognitive restructuring, relaxation and contingency management. In this study, 67 anxiety-disordered children (ages 7–14) were separated into two groups based on their parents' anxiety level, measured via the State-Trait Anxiety Inventory (STAI; Spielberger, Gorsuch, & Lushene, 1970) either (i) a child-anxiety-only group if the parents were classified as non-anxious ($n = 32$) or (ii) the child + parental anxiety group ($n = 35$) if one or both parent(s) reported high levels of anxiety. Children from both of these groups were then randomly assigned either to child-focused CBT or to the child-focused CBT and parental-anxiety management (CBT+PAM). At post-treatment, results indicated that within the child-anxiety-only group, 82% of the children in the CBT-alone condition versus 80% of children in the CBT+PAM condition no longer met criteria for an anxiety disorder. Within the child + parental anxiety group, 39% in the CBT-alone condition versus 77% in CBT+PAM condition no longer met anxiety disorder criteria. The findings from this study indicate that children with anxious parents respond poorly at post-treatment when only the child receives treatment. The inclusion of the PAM increased the efficacy of child-focused CBT for children, but only for children who had at least one anxious parent. Interestingly, at 6- and 12-month follow-ups, the differential effects for children with anxious parents in the CBT-alone or CBT+PAM condition were no longer evident.

Comparing Treatment Components

Although the accumulating evidence points to the promising efficacy of CBT for children with GAD, the next important steps are to try to understand the treatment at a more conceptual level and to determine the effective elements of the complex/multifaceted treatment package. We encouraged future child anxiety treatment research to focus on understanding "which features of the treatment contribute most to the observed gains" (Kendall et al., in press). The data indicate that CB treatments work for approximately two-thirds of cases but we do not know which components or facets of the treatment bring about what types of change for GAD children.

A limited number of studies have attempted to determine the effective components of CBT and, unfortunately, those that have addressed the issue are preliminary. For instance, using a multiple baseline design, Eisen and Silverman (1993) compared the use of cognitive restructuring skills (plus exposure), relaxation skills (plus exposure) and a combination of cognitive restructuring and relaxation (plus exposure) with four children diagnosed with overanxious disorder. The three treatments produced equivalent changes; however, with only four subjects any conclusions must be considered preliminary. More recently, Eisen and Silverman (1998) examined the efficacy of CBT for children with GAD. Two children were assigned to prescriptive treatments (cognitive therapy plus exposure, or relaxation training plus exposure) based on problematic response classes (cognitive or somatic symptoms). The remaining two children first received non-prescriptive treatments followed by prescriptive treatments. Both treatments showed significant improvements, however the results suggested enhanced benefits of the prescriptive treatments over the non-prescriptive treatments with respect to the positive end-state functioning. But, again, the small number of cases requires caution.

Although a randomized clinical trial was used (Kendall et al., 1997), only a preliminary evaluation of the two components of the program was permitted because this was not the primary aim of the study. According to questionnaire measures, change did not occur until after the completion of the exposure part of the program. These data, albeit preliminary, suggest that exposure preceded by skills training brings about change. Theoretical and applied questions about the active ingredients within CBT persist and require research attention.

CONCLUSION

Only a few studies have examined the phenomenology and epidemiology of GAD in children and adolescents, with most of current understanding based on studies of youth with OAD. Nevertheless, the research suggests that the disorder is among the most prevalent disorders in children and adolescents is a relatively early onset, tends to be chronic in nature, is highly comorbid with other disorders, and may vary with developmental level. Reliable and valid self-, parent, and teacher report measures have been developed to assess anxiety in children as well as structured interviews to diagnose anxiety disorders.

A number of factors have been identified in the aetiology of anxiety disorders. Although the nature of the genetic transmission is not yet clear, it does not appear to be specific to GAD but may be shared with other anxiety disorders or depression. Manifestation of this heritability may occur in the form of an inhibited temperament. Interaction between an anxious, inhibited temperament and the presence or absence of certain environmental factors (environmental support of avoidance, modelling of anxious behaviour, parental anxiety, stressful life events, insecure attachment, or lack of social support) may shape the anxious temperament toward or away from disorder (see Hudson & Rapee, in press). Alternately, these environmental factors may be sufficient to result in disorder in the absence of an anxious temperament. Much of our understanding of aetiological processes in GAD comes from research across the anxiety disorders. Future research that helps to understand the specific GAD pathways and the interaction of the variables discussed is warranted.

CBT for anxiety disorders in youth has been found to show significant promise. Having been declared a "probably efficacious" treatment by multiple reviewers of the literature, CBT for children with anxiety disorders nevertheless still requires evaluation against an alternative treatment to elevate it to an "established efficacious" treatment. In a multitude of studies and across several sites, it is clear that compared to wait-list, anxiety-disordered children receiving CB treatment show significant improvements not only in diagnostic status but also on self- and parent report measures of symptomatology. Although there has been variability across the findings, there is some evidence to suggest the added benefits of including a family component to the treatment, particularly for younger, female children, or children with anxious parents. These results come from studies examining a heterogeneous group of anxiety-disordered children, with virtually no studies evaluating treatments for only children with GAD. The treatment studies that have compared outcome across diagnostic groups indicate that CB treatments are equally effective for children with a primary diagnosis of GAD and for children with other anxiety disorders such as Social Phobia and Separation Anxiety Disorder.

The majority (approximately two-thirds) of children and adolescents with GAD benefit from CBT. Yet, there are cases for whom the outcomes are not as favourable. Future research would be well spent developing and enhancing the current CB treatments to better service non-responders. The enhancement of treatments for children and adolescents with GAD relies on the advancement of our knowledge of the ingredients in therapy (both therapeutic content and process) that bring about the greatest change. Some studies have examined pre-treatment variables as potential moderators and other variables as potential mediators of treatment outcome (e.g., Treadwell & Kendall, 1996). However, relatively little research has been conducted on either client or therapist variables within the therapy process (Shirk & Russell, 1996). Analysis of the therapeutic process will likely contribute meaningfully to our conceptual understanding of treatment outcomes.

The consideration and investigation of developmental variables as they impact on treatment outcome may also help to increase the percentage of treatment responders. Some evidence indicates that older anxious children do not do as well in CBT as younger children (Southam-Gerow, Kendall, & Weersing, 2001). As a result, we have developed a treatment manual and workbook specifically designed for the anxious adolescent (see Kendall et al., 2002). The investigation of developmental variables other than age and gender effects (e.g., cognitive, social, emotional, or physical development) may also assist in maximizing treatment outcomes for children at variable developmental stages (Hudson et al., 2002).

Given that CBT for children with GAD has shown favourable results in clinics that have a research focus, one can then ask whether or not these results are transportable to community-based non-research-oriented settings (Kendall & Southam-Gerow, 1995). The availability of treatment manuals facilitates the transportability of CBT (see Kendall, 2000; Rapee et al., 2000). However, it may be the case that more than access to a therapy manual is needed for training of an effective therapist. Another concern regarding transportability is the potentially different comorbidity patterns encountered in research versus non-research settings. However, recent findings suggest that comorbidity did not affect treatment outcome in children with anxiety disorders (Kendall, Brady, & Verduin, 2001). Nonetheless, there is the continued need for future research examining the outcomes of children with GAD receiving CBT in community clinic settings.

REFERENCES

Achenbach, T.M. (1991a). *Manual for the Child Behavior Checklists/4–18 and 1991 Profile*. Burlington: University of Vermont.

Achenbach, T.M. (1991b). *Manual for the Teacher Report Form and 1991 Profile*. Burlington: University of Vermont, Department of Psychiatry.

Ainsworth, M.D.S., Blehar, M.C., Waters, E., & Wall, E. (1978). *Patterns of attachment: A psychological study of the strange situation*. Hillsdale, NJ: Lawrence Erlbaum Associates.

American Psychiatric Association (1994). *Diagnostic and statistical manual of mental disorders* (4th edn., rev.). Washington, DC: Author.

Anderson, D.J., Williams, S., McGee, R., & Silva, P.A. (1987). DSM-III disorders in preadolescent children: Prevalence in a large sample from the general population. *Archives of General Psychiatry*, **44**, 69–76.

Andrews, G., Stewart, G.W., Morris-Yates, A., Holt, P., & Henderson, A.S. (1990). Evidence for a general neurotic syndrome. *British Journal of Psychiatry*, **157**, 6–12.

Angold, A., & Costello, E. (2000). The Child and Adolescent Psychiatric Assessment (CAPA). *Journal of the American Academy of Child and Adolescent Psychiatry*, **39**, 39–48.

Barrett, P.M. (1998). Evaluation of cognitive-behavioural group treatments for childhood anxiety disorders. *Journal of Clinical Child Psychology*, **27**, 459–468.

Barrett, P.M., Duffy, A.L., Dadds, M.R., & Rapee, R.M. (2001). Cognitive-behavioural treatment of anxiety disorders in children: Long-term (6 year) follow-up. *Journal of Consulting and Clinical Psychology*, **69**, 1–7.

Barrett, P.M., Rapee, R.M., Dadds, M.M., & Ryan, S.M. (1996). Family enhancement of cognitive style in anxious and aggressive children. *Journal of Abnormal Child Psychology*, **24**, 187–203.

Benjamin, R.S., Costello, E.J., & Warren, M. (1990). Anxiety disorders in a pediatric sample. *Journal of Anxiety Disorders*, **4**, 293–316.

Biederman, J., Hirshfeld-Becker, D.R., Rosenbaum, J.F., Herot, C., Friedman, D., Snidman, N., Kagan, J., & Faraone, S.V. (2001). Further evidence of association between behavioral inhibition and social anxiety in children. *American Journal of Psychiatry*, **158**, 1673–1679.

Biederman, J., Rosenbaum, J.F., Bolduc-Murphy, E.A., Faraone, S.V., Chaloff, J., Hirshfeld, D.R., & Kagan, J. (1993). A 3-year follow-up of children with and without behavioral inhibition. *Journal of the American Academy of Child and Adolescent Psychiatry*, **32**, 814–821.

Birmaher, B., Brent, D.A, Chiappetta, L., Bridge, J., Monga, S., & Baugher, M. (1999). Psychometric properties of the Screen for Child Anxiety Related Emotional Disorders (SCARED): A replication study. *Journal of the American Academy of Child and Adolescent Psychiatry*, **38**, 1230–1236.

Birmaher, B., Khetarpal, S., Brent, D., Cully, M., Balach, L., Kaufman, J., & Neer, S.M. (1997). The Screen for Child Anxiety Related Emotional Disorders (SCARED): Scale construction and psychometric characteristic. *Journal of American Academy of Child and Adolescent Psychiatry*, **36**, 545–553.

Bogels, S.M., & Zigterman, D. (2000). Dysfunctional cognitions in children with social phobia, separation anxiety, and generalized anxiety disorder. *Journal of Abnormal Child Psychology*, **28**, 205–211.

Bowen, R.C., Offord, D.R., & Boyle, M.H (1990). The prevalence of overanxious disorder and separation disorder. *Journal of the American Academy of Child and Adolescent Psychiatry*, **29**, 753–758.

Bowlby, J. (1973). *Attachment and Loss: (Vol. 2): Separation*. London: The Hogarth Press and the Institute of Psycho-Analysis.

Bowlby, J. (1974). *Attachment and Loss (Vol. 1): Attachment*. London: The Hogarth Press and the Institute of Psycho-Analysis (originally published in 1969).

Cantwell, D.P., & Baker, L. (1989). Stability and natural history of DSM-III childhood diagnoses. *Journal of the American Academy of Child and Adolescent Psychiatry*, **29**, 691–700.

Chansky, T.E., & Kendall, P.C. (1997). Social expectancies and self-perceptions in anxiety-disordered children. *Journal of Anxiety Disorders*, **11**, 347–363.

Chambless, D., & Hollon, S. (1998). Defining empirically supported treatments. *Journal of Consulting and Clinical Psychology*, **66**, 5–17.

Chorpita, B.F., & Barlow, D.H. (1998). The development of anxiety: The role of control in the early environment. *Psychological Bulletin*, **124**, 3–21.

Chorpita, B.F., Tracey, S.A., Brown, T.A., Collica, T.J., & Barlow, D.H. (1997). Assessment of worry in children and adolescents: An adaptation of the Penn State Worry Questionnaire. *Behaviour Research and Therapy*, **35**, 569–581.

Choudhury, S.M. (2001). *Teacher ratings of anxiety in children: Development and validation of the teacher report form-anxiety scale.* Unpublished Masters Thesis. Philadelphia, Temple University.

Cicchetti, D., & Rogosch, F.A. (1996). Equifinality and multifinality in developmental psychopathology. *Development and Psychopathology*, **8**, 597–600.

Cobham, V.E., Dadds, M.R., & Spence, S.H. (1998). The role of parental anxiety in the treatment of childhood anxiety. *Journal of Consulting and Clinical Psychology*, **66**, 893–905.

Cohen, P., Cohen, J., & Brook, J.S. (1993). An epidemiological study of disorders in late childhood and adolescence: II Persistence of disorders. *Journal of Child Psychology and Psychiatry*, **34**, 867–875.

Cowen, E.L., Pedro-Carroll, J.L., & Alpert-Gillis, L.J. (1990). Relationships between support and adjustment among children of divorce. *Journal of Child Psychology and Psychiatry and Allied Disciplines*, **31**, 727–735.

Dadds, M.R., Barrett, P.M., Rapee, R.M., & Ryan, S. (1996). Family process and child anxiety and aggression: An observational analysis. *Journal of Abnormal Child Psychology*, **24**, 715–734.

Dierker, L.C., Albano, A.M., Clarke, G.N., Heimberg, R.G., Kendall, P.C., Merikangas, K.R., Lewinsohn, P.M., Offord, D.R., Kessler, R., & Kupfer, D.J. (2001). Screening for anxiety and depression in early adolescence. *Journal of the American Academy of Child and Adolescent Psychiatry*, **40**, 929–936.

Eisen, A.R., & Silverman, W.K. (1993). Should I relax or change my thoughts? A preliminary examination of cognitive therapy, relaxation training, and their combination with overanxious children. *Journal of Cognitive Psychotherapy: An International Quarterly*, **7**, 265–279.

Eisen, A.R., & Silverman, W.K. (1998). Prescriptive treatment for generalized anxiety disorder in children. *Behavior Therapy*, **29**, 105–121.

Fergusson, D.M., Horwood, L.J., & Lynskey, M.T. (1993). Prevalence and comorbidity of DSM-III-R diagnoses in a birth cohort of 15 year olds. *Journal of the American Academy of Child and Adolescent Psychiatry*, **32**, 1127–1134.

Flannery-Schroeder, E., & Kendall, P.C. (1996). *Cognitive-behavioural therapy for anxious children: Therapist manual for group treatment.* Ardmore, PA: Workbook Publishing.

Flannery-Schroeder, E., & Kendall, P.C. (2000). Group and individual cognitive-behavioral treatments for youth with anxiety disorders: A randomized clinical trial. *Cognitive Therapy and Research*, **24**, 251–278.

Garcia Coll, C., Kagan, J., & Reznick, J.S. (1984). Behavioral inhibition in young children. *Child Development*, **55**, 1005–1019.

Gerull, F.C., & Rapee, R.M. (2002). Mother knows best: Effects of maternal modelling on the acquisition of fear and avoidance behaviour in toddlers. *Behaviour Research and Therapy*, **40**, 279–287.

Ginsburg, G.S., & Silverman, W.K. (1996). Phobic and anxiety disorders in Hispanic and Caucasian youth. *Journal of Anxiety Disorders*, **10**, 517–528.

Glennon, B., & Weisz, J.R. (1978). An observational approach to the assessment of anxiety in young children. *Journal of Consulting and Clinical Psychology*, **46**, 1246–1257.

Grills, A.E., & Ollendick, T.H. (2003). Multiple informant agreement and the Anxiety Disorders Interview Schedule for Parents and Children. *Jorunal of the American Academy of Child and Adolescent Psychiatry*, **42**, 30–40.

Hettema, J.M., Neale, M.C., & Kendler, K.S. (2001). A review and meta-analysis of the genetic epidemiology of anxiety disorders. *American Journal of Psychiatry*, **158**, 1568–1578.

Hill, H.M., Levermore, H., Twaite, J., & Jones, L.P. (1996). Exposure to community violence and social support as predictors of anxiety and social and emotional behaviour among African American children. *Journal of Child and Family Studies*, **5**, 399–414.

Hudson, J.L., & Kendall, P.C. (2002). Showing you can do it: Homework in therapy for children and adolescents with anxiety disorders. *Journal of Clinical Psychology/In Session: Psychotherapy in Practice*, **58**, 525–534.

Hudson, J.L., & Rapee, R.M. (2001). Parent–child interactions and the anxiety disorders: An observational analysis. *Behaviour Research and Therapy*, **39**, 1411–1427.

Hudson, J.L., & Rapee, R.M. (in press). From temperament to disorder: An etiological model of Generalized Anxiety Disorder. In R.G. Heimberg, C.C. Turk, & D.S. Menin (Eds), *Generalized Anxiety Disorder: Advances in Research and Practice*. New York: Guilford Press.

Hudson, J.L., Kendall, P.C., Coles, M., Robin, J., & Webb, A. (2002). The other side of the coin: Using intervention research in child anxiety disorders to inform developmental psychopathology. *Development and Psychopathology*, **14**, 819–841.

Kagan, J. (1997). Temperament and the reactions to unfamiliarity. *Child Development*, **68**, 139–143.

Kashani, J.H., Vaidya, A.F., Soltys, S.M., Dandoy, A.C., Katz, L.M., & Reid, J.C. (1990). Correlates of anxiety in psychiatrically hospitalized children and their parents. *Journal of Psychiatry*, **143**, 319–323.

Kazdin, A.E. (1986). Research designs and methodology. In S. Garfield & A. Bergin (Eds), *Handbook of psychotherapy and behavior change* (3rd edn; pp. 85–99). New York: John Wiley & Sons.

Kazdin, A., & Weisz, J. (1998). Identifying and developing empirically supported child and adolescent treatments. *Journal of Consulting and Clinical Psychology*, **66**, 100–110.

Keller, M.B., Lavori, P., Wunder, J., Beardslee, W.R., Schwartz, C.E., & Roth, J. (1992). Chronic course of anxiety disorders in children and adolescents. *Journal of the American Academy of Child and Adolescent Psychiatry*, **31**, 595–599.

Kendall, P.C. (1994). Treating anxiety disorders in children: Results of a randomized clinical trial. *Journal of Consulting and Clinical Psychology*, **62**, 100–110.

Kendall, P.C. (2000). *Cognitive behavioral therapy for anxious children: Treatment manual. Second Edition*. Aramore, PA: Workbook Publishing. (Available from Philip C. Kendall, Department of Psychology, Temple University, Philadelphia, PA 19122.)

Kendall, P.C., & Morris, R. (1991). Child therapy: Issues and recommendations. *Journal of Consulting and Clinical Psychology*, **59**, 777–784.

Kendall, P.C., & Southam-Gerow, M.A. (1996). Long-term follow-up of a cognitive-behavioral therapy for anxiety disordered youths. *Journal of Consulting and Clinical Psychology*, **64**, 724–730.

Kendall, P.C., & Southam-Gerow, M. (1995). Issues in the transportability of treatment: The case of anxiety disorders in youths. *Journal of Consulting and Clinical Psychology*, **63**, 702–708.

Kendall, P.C., & Warman, M.J. (1996). Anxiety disorders in youth: Diagnostic consistency across DSM-III-R and DSM-IV. *Journal of Anxiety Disorders*, **10**, 452–463.

Kendall, P.C., Brady, E., & Verduin, T. (2001). Comorbidity in childhood anxiety disorders and treatment outcome. *Journal of the American Academy of Child and Adolescent Psychiatry*, **40**, 787–794.

Kendall, P.C., Chansky, T.E., Kane, M.T., Kim, R., Kortlander, E., Ronan, K., Sessa, F.M., & Siqueland, L. (1992). *Anxiety disorders in youth: Cognitive-behavioural interventions*. New York: Macmillan.

Kendall, P.C., Choudhury, M.S., Hudson, J.L., & Webb, A. (2002). *The C.A.T. Project*. Ardmore, PA: Workbook Publishing.

Kendall, P.C., Flannery-Schroeder, E., Panichelli-Mindel, S.M., Southam-Gerow, M., Henin, A., & Warman, M. (1997). Therapy for youths with anxiety disorders: A second randomized clinical trial. *Journal of Consulting and Clinical Psychology*, **65**, 366–380.

Kendall, P.C., Henin, A., MacDonald, J.P., & Treadwell, K.R.H. (1998). *Parent ratings of anxiety in children: Development and validation of the CBCL-A*. Unpublished manuscript. Philadelphia, Temple University.

Kendall, P.C., Hudson, J.L., Choudhury, M.S., Webb, A., & Pimentel, S. (in press). Cognitive behavioral treatment for childhood anxiety disorders. In E.D. Hibbs & P.S. Jensen (Eds), *Psychosocial treatments for child and adolescent disorders: Empirically based strategies for private practice*. American Psychological Association.

Kendall, P.C., Marrs-Garcia, A., Nath, S., & Sheldrick, R.C. (1999). Normative comparisons for the evaluation of clinical significance. *Journal of Consulting and Clinical Psychology*, **67**, 285–299.

Kendler, K.S., Neale, M.C., Kessler, R.C., Heath, A.C., & Eaves, L.J. (1992). Major depression and generalized anxiety disorder: Same genes, (partly) different environments? *Archives of General Psychiatry*, **49**, 716–722.

Kendler, K.S., Walters, E.E., Neale, M.C., Kessler, R.C., Heath, A.C., & Eaves, L.J. (1995). The structure of the genetic and environmental risk factors for six major psychiatric disorders in women: Phobia, generalized anxiety disorder, panic disorder, bulimia, major depression, and alcoholism. *Archives of General Psychiatry*, **52**, 374–383.

Kessler, R.C., McGonagle, K., Zhao, S., Nelson, C.B., Hughes, M., Eshleman, S.M., Wittchen, H.U., & Kendler, K.S. (1994). Lifetime and 12-month prevalence of DSM-III-R psychiatric disorders in the United States. *Archives of General Psychiatry*, **51**, 8–19.

Last, C.G., Hersen, M., Kazdin, A.E., Francis, G., & Grubb, H.J. (1987). Psychiatric illness in the mothers of anxious children. *American Journal of Psychiatry*, **144**, 1580–1583.

Last, C.G., & Perrin, S. (1993). Anxiety disorders in African-American and white children. *Journal of Abnormal Child Psychology*, **2**, 153–164.

Last, C.G., Strauss, C.C., & Francis, G. (1987). Comorbidity among childhood anxiety disorders. *Journal of Nervous and Mental Disease*, **175**, 726–730.

Last, C.G., Perrin, S., Hersen, M., & Kazdin, A.E. (1992). DSM-III-R anxiety disorders in children: Sociodemographic and clinical characteristics. *Journal of the American Academy of Child and Adolescent Psychiatry*, **31**, 1070–1076.

Last, C.G., Perrin, S., Hersen, M., & Kazdin, A.E. (1996). A prospective study of childhood anxiety disorders. *Journal of the American Academy of Child and Adolescent Psychiatry*, **35**, 1502–1510.

Lonigan, C.J., Carey, M.P., & Finch, A.J. (1994). Anxiety and depression in children and adolescents: Negative affectivity and the utility of self-reports. *Journal of Consulting and Clinical Psychology*, **62**, 1000–1008.

Manassis, K., & Hood, J. (1998). Individual and familial predictors of impairment in childhood anxiety disorders. *Journal of the American Academy of Child and Adolescent Psychiatry*, **37**, 428–434.

March, J.S., & Albano, A.M. (1998). Advances in the assessment of pediatric anxiety disorders. *Advances in Clinical Child Psychology*, **20**, 213–241.

March, J.S., Parker J.D.A., Sullivan, K., Stallings, P., & Conners, K. (1997). The Multidimensional Anxiety Scale for Children (MASC): Factor structure, reliability, and validity. *Journal of the American Academy of Child and Adolescent Psychiatry*, **36**, 554–565.

Masi, G., Mucci, M., Favilla, L., Romano, R., & Poli, P. (1999). Symptomatology and comorbidity of generalized anxiety disorder in children and adolescents. *Comprehensive Psychiatry*, **40**, 210–215.

McClellan, J.M., & Werry, J.S. (2000). Research on psychiatric interviews for children and adolescents: Introduction. *Journal of the American Academy of Child and Adolescent Psychiatry*, **39**, 19–27.

Mendlowitz, S.L., Manassis, K., Bradley, S., Scapillato, D., Miezitis, S., & Shaw, B.F. (1999). Cognitive-behavioral group treatments in childhood anxiety disorders: The role of parental involvement. *Journal of the American Academy of Child and Adolescent Psychiatry*, **38**, 1223–1229.

Mineka, S., Gunnar, M., & Champoux, M. (1986). Control and early socioemotional development: Infant rhesus monkeys reared in controllable versus uncontrollable environments. *Child Development*, **57**, 1241–1256.

Muris, P., Meesters, C., & Gobel, M. (2001). Reliability, validity, and normative data of the Penn State Worry Questionnaire in 8–12 year-old children. *Journal of Behavior Therapy and Experimental Psychiatry*, **32**, 63–72.

Muris, P., Meesters, C., Merkelbach, H., Sermon, A., & Zwakhalen, S. (1998). Worry in normal children. *Journal of the American Academy of Child and Adolescent Psychiatry*, **37**, 703–710.

Noyes, R., Jr., Clarkson, C., Crowe, R.R., Yates, W.R., & McChesney, C.M. (1987). A family study of generalized anxiety disorder. *American Journal of Psychiatry*, **144**, 1019–1024.

Ollendick, T. (1986). Behavior therapy with children. In S. Garfield & A. Bergin (Eds), *Handbook of psychotherapy and behavior change* (3rd edn; pp. 97–113). New York: John Wiley & Sons.

Ollendick, T.H., & Cerny, J.A. (1981). *Clinical behavior therapy with children*. New York: Plenum Press.

Ollendick, T.H., & King, N.J. (1998). Empirically supported treatments for children with phobic and anxiety disorders: Current status. *Journal of Clinical Child Psychology*, **27**, 156–167.

Ollendick, T.H., & King, N.J. (2000). Empirically support treatments for children and adolescents. In P.C. Kendall (Ed.), *Child and adolescent therapy: Cognitive-behavioural procedures* (2nd edn; pp. 386–425). New York: Guilford.

Pimentel, S.S., & Kendall, P.C. (2003). On the physiological symptom constellation in youth with Generalized Anxiety Disorder (GAD). *Journal of Anxiety Disorders*, **17**, 211–221.

Rapee, R.M. (1997). The potential role of childrearing practices in the development of anxiety and depression. *Clinical Psychology Review*, **17**, 47–67.

Rapee, R.M. (2000). Group treatment of children with anxiety disorders: Outcomes and predictors of treatment response. *Australian Journal of Psychology*, **52**, 125–130.

Rapee, R.M. (2001). The development of generalized anxiety. In M.W. Vasey & M.R. Dadds (Eds), *The developmental psychopathology of anxiety* (pp. 481–503). New York: Oxford University Press.

Rapee, R.M., & Szollos, A. (1997, November). *Early life events in anxious children*. Paper presented at the 31st annual meeting of the Association for Advancement of Behavior Therapy, Miami, FL.

Rapee R.M., Barrett, P.M., Dadds, M.R., & Evans, L. (1994). Reliability of the DSM-III-R childhood anxiety disorders using structured interview: Interrater and parent–child agreement. *Journal of the American Academy of Child and Adolescent Psychiatry*, **33**, 984–992.

Rapee, R.M., Wignall, A., Hudson, J.L., & Schniering, C.A. (2000). *Evidence-based treatment of child and adolescent anxiety disorders*. Oakland, CA: New Harbinger Publications.

Reynolds, C.R., & Richmond, B.O. (1978). A revised measure of children's manifest anxiety scale. *Journal of Abnormal Child Psychology*, **6**, 271–280.

Reynolds, C.R., & Richmond, B.O. (1985). *Revised Children's Manifest Anxiety Scale*. Los Angeles, CA: Western Psychological Services.

Roemer, L., Molina, S., Litz, B.T., & Borkovec, T.D. (1997). Preliminary investigation of the role of previous exposure to potentially traumatizing events in generalized anxiety disorder. *Depression and Anxiety*, **4**, 134–138.

Rynn, M.A., Siqueland, L., & Rickels, K. (2001). Placebo-controlled trial of Sertraline in the treatment of children with generalized anxiety disorder. *American Journal of Psychiatry*, **158**, 2008–2014.

Scherrer, J.F., True, W.R., Xian, H., Lyons, M.J., Eisen, S.A., Goldberg, J., Lin, N., & Tsuang, M.T. (2000). Evidence for genetic influences common and specific to symptoms of generalized anxiety and panic. *Journal of Affective Disorders*, **57**, 25–35.

Schniering, C.A., Hudson, J.L., & Rapee, R.M. (2000). Issues in the diagnosis and assessment of anxiety disorders in children and adolescents. *Clinical Psychology Review*, **20**, 453–478.

Schwab-Stone, M., Fisher, P., Piacentini, J., Shaffer, D., Davies, M., & Briggs, M. (1993). The Diagnostic Interview Schedule for Children-Revised Version (DISC-R), II: Test–retest reliability. *Journal of the American Academy of Child and Adolescent Psychiatry*, **32**, 651–657.

Shaffer, D., Fisher, P., Lucas, C.P., Dulcan, M.K., & Schwab-Stone, M.E. (2000). NIMH Diagnostic Interview Schedule for Children Version IV (NIMH DISC-IV): Description, differences from previous versions, and reliability of some common diagnoses. *Journal of the American Academy of Child and Adolescent Psychiatry*, **39**, 28–39.

Shaffer, D., Schwab-Stone, M., Fisher, P., Cohen, P., Piacentini, J., Davies, M., Conners, C., & Regier, D. (1993). The Diagnostic Interview Schedule for Children Revised Version

(DISC-R): I. Preparation, field testing, interrater reliability, and acceptability. *Journal of the American Academy of Child and Adolescent Psychiatry,* **32** (7), 643–650.

Shirk, S.R., & Russell, R.L. (1996). *Change processes in child psychotherapy: Revitalizing treatment and research.* New York: Guilford Press.

Shortt, A.L., Barrett, P.M., & Fox, T.L. (2001). Evaluating the FRIENDS Program: A cognitive-behavioral group treatment for anxious children and their parents. *Journal of Community Psychology,* **30**, 525–535.

Silverman, W.K., & Albano, A.M. (1996). *The Anxiety Disorders Interview Schedule for DSM-IV-Child and Parent Versions.* San Antonio, TX: Graywind Publications; a Division of the Psychological Corporation.

Silverman, W.K., Saavedra, L.M., & Pina, A.A. (2001). Test–retest reliability of anxiety symptoms and diagnoses with the Anxiety Disorders Schedule for DSM-IV: Child and parent versions. *Journal of the American Academy of Child and Adolescent Psychiatry,* **40**, 937-944.

Silverman, W.K., Kurtines, W.M., Ginsburg, G.S., Weems, C.F., Lumpkin, P.W., & Carmichael, D.H. (1999). Treating anxiety disorders in children with group cognitive-behavioural therapy: A randomized clinical trial. *Journal of Consulting and Clinical Psychology,* **67**, 995–1003.

Siqueland, L., Kendall, P.C., & Steinberg, L. (1996). Anxiety in children: Perceived family environments and observed family interactions. *Journal of Clinical Child Psychology,* **25**, 225–237.

Southam-Gerow, M., Flannery-Schroeder, E., & Kendall, P.C. (2002). A psychometric evaluation of the Parent Report Form of the State-Trait Anxiety Inventory for Children—Trait version. *Journal of Anxiety Disorders* (in press).

Southam-Gerow, M., Kendall, P.C., & Weersing, V.R. (2001). Examining outcome variability: Correlates of treatment response in a child and adolescent anxiety clinic. *Journal of Clinical Child Psychology,* **30**, 422–436.

Spence, S.H. (1998). A measure of anxiety symptoms among children. *Behaviour Research and Therapy,* **36**, 545–566.

Spielberger, C.D. (1973). *State-Trait Anxiety Inventory for Children: Preliminary manual.* Palo Alto, CA: Consulting Psychologists Press.

Spielberger C.D., Gorsuch, R.L., & Lushene, R.E. (1970). *Manual for the State-Trait Anxiety Inventory.* Palo Alto, CA: Consulting Psychologists Press.

Strauss, C.C., Lease, C.A., Last, C.G., & Francis, G. (1988). Overanxious disorder: An examination of developmental differences. *Journal of Abnormal Child Psychology,* **16**, 433–443.

Taghavi, M.R., Moradi, A.R., Neshat-Doost, H.T., Yule, W., & Dalgleish, T. (2000). Interpretation of ambiguous emotional information in clinically anxious children and adolescents. *Cognition and Emotion,* **14**, 809–822.

Toren, P., Wolmer, L., Rosental, B., Eldar, S., Koren, S., Lask,, M., Weizman, R., & Laor, N. (2000). Case series: Brief parent–child group therapy for childhood anxiety disorders using a manual-based cognitive-behavioural technique. *Journal of the American Academy of Child and Adolescent Psychiatry,* **39**, 1309–1312.

Torgersen, S. (1983). Genetic factors in anxiety disorders. *Archives of General Psychiatry,* **40**, 1085–1089.

Torgersen, S. (1986). Childhood and family characteristics in panic and generalized anxiety disorders. *American Journal of Psychiatry,* **143**, 630–632.

Treadwell, K.H., & Kendall, P.C. (1996). Self-talk in youth with anxiety disorders: States of mind, content specificity, and treatment outcome. *Journal of Consulting and Clinical Psychology,* **64**, 941–950.

Verduin, T.L., & Kendall, P.C. (2003). Differential patterns of comorbidity in childhood anxiety disorders. *Journal of Clinical Child and Adolescent Psychology,* **32**, 290–295.

Warren, S.L., Huston, L., Egeland, B., & Sroufe, L.A. (1997). Child and adolescent anxiety disorders and early attachment. *Journal of the American Academy of Child and Adolescent Psychiatry,* **36**, 637–644.

Werry, J.S. (1991). Overanxious disorder: A review of its taxonomic properties. *Journal of the American Academy of Child and Adolescent Psychiatry,* **30**, 533–543.

CHAPTER 7

Treatment of SAD and Panic Disorder in Children and Adolescents

Sara G. Mattis

and

Donna B. Pincus

Boston University, USA

INTRODUCTION

Phenomenology

Separation anxiety is well recognized as one of the normal, developmentally related fears that arise and dissipate at reasonably predictable times during childhood (Pianta, 1999). Separation fears are said to peak between the ages of 9 and 13 months, and occur among children all over the world (Barlow, 1988; Marks, 1987). For most children, separation anxiety begins to decrease after about 2 years of age. With the passage of time, most children become less fearful of separations from significant caregivers, and show increasing levels of autonomy beginning at about 3 years of age (Bernstein & Borchardt, 1991). Although separation anxiety has been recognized and studied as a characteristic of normal development for many years, it was not treated as a clinical diagnostic category until the publication of the third edition of the *Diagnostic and Statistical Manual of Mental Disorders* (DSM-III; APA, 1980), which described Separation Anxiety Disorder (SAD) as one of three distinct anxiety disorders of childhood. Given that separation anxiety is a normal developmental phenomenon in infancy and toddlerhood, the SAD diagnosis is only given if the child's level of anxiety during separation is inappropriate, given the child's age and developmental level.

Correspondence to Sara G. Mattis, Boston University, The Center for Anxiety and Related Disorders at Boston University, 648 Beacon St., 6th Floor, Boston, MA 02215-2015; e-mail: smattis@bu.edu

Handbook of Interventions that Work with Children and Adolescents: Prevention and Treatment.
Edited by P.M. Barrett and T.H. Ollendick. © 2004 John Wiley & Sons, Ltd. ISBN 0-470-84453-1.

The defining feature of SAD is an excessive and unrealistic fear of separation from an attachment figure, usually a parent. This fear is expressed through excessive and persistent worry about separation, behavioural and somatic distress when faced with separation situations, and persistent avoidance of, or attempts to escape from, such situations (Albano, Chorpita, & Barlow, 1996; Bell-Dolan, 1995). Common separation worries include worries about harm befalling either an attachment figure or themselves, worry that a parent will leave and never return, or worries that they themselves will be lost, kidnapped, or killed. Particularly for younger children, repeated nightmares with themes of separation are common (Francis, Last, & Strauss, 1987). Separation anxiety is often manifested by crying, wailing, and protesting upon the departure of the parent or other significant caregiver, and seeking/searching in the caregiver's absence (Thyer, Himle, & Fischer, 1993). Children often complain of physical symptoms, such as headaches or gastrointestinal upset. These symptoms may occur in the separation situations, as well as in anticipation of such situations.

Developmental differences in the expression of separation anxiety symptoms in children and adolescents have been demonstrated. Francis, Last, and Strauss (1987) evaluated 45 children and adolescents (aged 5–16) with SAD. There were no differences between boys and girls on each of the nine criteria for SAD. However, there were differences among age groups with regard to which criteria were most frequently endorsed. Young children (aged 5–8) were most likely to report fears of unrealistic harm, nightmares about separation, or school refusal; older children (aged 9–12) endorsed excessive distress at the time of separation; and adolescents (aged 13–16) most often endorsed somatic complaints and school refusal. Younger children (aged 5–8) endorsed the greatest number of symptoms relative to the older children and adolescents.

While SAD has long been viewed as an anxiety disorder with childhood onset, controversy has existed regarding the extent to which panic attacks and panic disorder occur in children and adolescents (see Nelles & Barlow, 1988). However, recent clinical research investigating the nature and prevalence of panic disorder prior to adulthood suggests that this disorder does occur in a young population, although far less frequently prior to the peripubertal period (Bernstein, Borchardt, & Perwien, 1996). Indeed, the fourth edition of the *Diagnostic and Statistical Manual of Mental Disorders* (DSM-IV; APA, 1994) suggests that late adolescence may be the initial peak period for onset of panic disorder.

A panic attack is defined in the DSM-IV as a sudden episode of intense fear, apprehension, or discomfort which is accompanied by at least four of 13 physical or cognitive symptoms (e.g., palpitations, sweating, shortness of breath, dizziness, fear of dying). Panic attacks may be present across a variety of anxiety disorders. For instance, a child with SAD may experience a situationally bound or cued panic attack each morning when he or she is faced with leaving his or her mother to go to school. However, to receive a diagnosis of panic disorder, a child or adolescent must evidence repeated unexpected or uncued panic attacks that are not associated with a situational trigger but occur spontaneously or "out of the blue". Furthermore, such panic attacks must be followed by at least one month of persistent concern about having additional attacks, worry about the implications or consequences of the attacks, or a significant change in behaviour related to the panic attacks (APA, 1994). Children and adolescents with panic disorder may also develop agoraphobia, defined as anxiety about being in situations from which escape might be difficult or embarrassing or help might not be readily available in the event of a panic attack.

Following the general consensus that panic disorder exists prior to adulthood, attention has increasingly shifted to questions regarding the phenomenology of this disorder in children and adolescents (Kearney et al., 1997). Kearney and colleagues conducted the first empirical study to examine the primary clinical features of panic in a sizable outpatient sample of youngsters with panic disorder compared to a group with non-panic anxiety disorders. Specifically, 20 youngsters aged 8–17 years ($M = 12.90$) were diagnosed with panic disorder with or without agoraphobia and compared to a group of 20 youngsters aged 8–16 years ($M = 10.85$) diagnosed with one or more anxiety disorders other than panic disorder. The most frequent and severe symptoms of youngsters with panic disorder included accelerated heart rate, nausea, hot/cold flashes, shaking, and shortness of breath. Settings most commonly avoided by this group included restaurants, crowds, small and large rooms, elevators, parks, and stores, although the level of avoidance was reported as generally moderate in most cases.

In comparison to the non-panic anxiety group, youngsters with panic disorder displayed significantly more diagnoses of depression as well as somewhat greater trait anxiety and significantly greater anxiety sensitivity. Specifically, the panic disorder group reported significantly more concern regarding changes in bodily function, especially breathing difficulties. Based on these findings, Kearney and colleagues (1997) recommended that depression and anxiety sensitivity should be assessed in youngsters with panic disorder, and suggested that future research should include physiological data, direct observation of escape and avoidance, and parent and teacher ratings. These researchers further recommended the use of cognitive therapy and techniques commonly used to treat panic disorder in adults (e.g., interoceptive exposure), although they noted that only one systematic, controlled treatment for panic disorder in adolescents had been evaluated empirically at the time of their own research (Ollendick, 1995).

Epidemiology

In the past 10 years, there have been a number of epidemiological studies reporting the prevalence rates of various anxiety disorders in the community. Overall, the results of these studies indicate that anxiety disorders are one of the most common, if not the most prevalent category of childhood disorders (Bernstein & Borchardt, 1991; Bernstein, Borchardt, & Perwien, 1996). SAD has been said to be the most common anxiety disorder seen in children and adolescents, with epidemiological studies reporting that as many as 41% of children experience separation concerns, while 5–10% show a clinical level of separation anxiety (Costello & Angold, 1995). Most clinical researchers agree that it is quite common for even very young children (aged 3 and older) to experience separation distress that causes significant interference in social, academic, and family functioning.

Prevalence estimates for early onset SAD are less well established, although the current consensus indicates a prevalence rate ranging from 3 to 5%. SAD appears to be slightly more common in females than in males, and has been shown to be frequently comorbid with overanxious disorder, depression, and somatic complaints

(Last, 1991; Last et al., 1987). Overall, although our knowledge of epidemiological aspects of SAD are still limited, it is clear that it is one of the most common mental health problems of childhood.

The prevalence of panic disorder in children and adolescents has attracted much recent interest and attention in the clinical child psychology literature (Kearney et al., 1997). Although controversy has existed regarding the extent to which panic attacks and panic disorder occur in children and adolescents (Kearney & Silverman, 1992; Nelles & Barlow, 1988), most clinical researchers now agree that panic disorder not only occurs prior to adulthood, but that its initial peak period of onset may occur in adolescence. In a recent review of anxiety disorders in children and adolescents, Bernstein, Borchardt, and Perwien (1996) reported that, while panic disorder is uncommon prior to the peripubertal period, retrospective reports of adults suggest that panic disorder typically begins by adolescence or young adulthood (Moreau & Follett, 1993; Von Korff, Eaton, & Keyl, 1985). Indeed, Bernstein, Borchardt, and Perwien (1996) concluded that adolescence is the peak period for the onset of panic disorder.

Similarly, in a comprehensive review of the literature on panic in children and adolescents, Ollendick, Mattis, and King (1994) concluded that panic attacks are common in adolescents and that panic disorder occurs not infrequently in this population. Among adolescent community samples, for example, 36% to 63% report panic attacks (King et al., 1993, 1996; Macaulay & Kleinknecht, 1989), and 1% to 5% report past or present symptoms sufficient to meet DSM criteria for panic disorder (Warren & Zgourides, 1988; Whitaker et al., 1990). Moreover, Last and Strauss (1989) reported that approximately 10% of adolescents referred to an outpatient anxiety disorders clinic met diagnostic criteria for panic disorder, whereas Alessi, Robbins, and Dilsaver (1987) reported that 15% of hospitalized adolescents received this diagnosis.

The occurrence of panic attacks and panic disorder prior to adolescence is less well established, although several clinical studies and case reports have identified panic in children (Alessi & Magen, 1988; Ballenger et al., 1989; Biederman, 1987; Garland & Smith, 1991; Herskowitz, 1986; Last & Strauss, 1989; Moreau, Weissman, & Warner, 1989; Van Winter & Stickler, 1984; Vitiello et al., 1990). Based on such research, the current consensus is that panic disorder does occur in adolescents, with an overall prevalence of about 1% (Lewinsohn et al., 1993), while the frequency of panic disorder in children remains controversial. It is also generally believed that panic disorder is relatively more common in females than in males, with a modal age of onset in mid-adolescence, particularly after 14 years of age (Kearney et al., 1997; Thyer et al., 1985; Von Korff, Eaton, & Keyl, 1985).

AETIOLOGY

Panic Disorder

There is no simple explanation for why some children and adolescents develop panic disorder, with existing evidence suggesting a "complex biopsychosocial process" (Barlow, 1988). Such a process requires consideration of the biological, psychological, and social systems of the child or adolescent, including how these systems interact and influence development. Hirshfeld and colleagues (1998) concluded that anxiety disorders often run in families, with family and twin studies suggesting a notable genetic influence (heritability estimates range from 32% to 46%). Based on the results of the Virginia Twin Registry Study, Kendler and colleagues (1993) reported that panic disorder appears to result from the additive effects of genetic and individual-specific environmental factors. Finally, research has suggested a link between behavioural inhibition, or the tendency to withdraw from novel stimuli (Kagan, Reznick, & Snidman, 1988), and the development of anxiety disorders, including panic.

Mattis and Ollendick (1997) proposed a pathway, rooted in Barlow's (1988) model of the aetiology of panic, through which a child's temperament, patterns of attachment to significant adults, and response to the stress of separation experiences might lead to the development of panic. This pathway is based in part on reports suggesting an association between stressful experiences of separation in childhood and the later development of panic (for review, see Mattis & Ollendick, 1997). For instance, Faravelli and colleagues (1985) found that 65% of adult patients with panic attacks and agoraphobia reported experiencing a traumatic separation experience (e.g., death of a parent, parental divorce) before the age of 15. Similarly, studies of high school students have found relatively high rates of early loss experiences, including parental divorce, among adolescents reporting panic attacks (Hayward, Killen, & Taylor, 1989; Warren & Zgourides, 1988). Finally, clinical studies of children and adolescents have reported high rates of comorbidity between separation anxiety and panic disorder (Alessi & Magen, 1988; Biederman, 1987; Moreau, Weissman, & Warner, 1989).

The developmental pathway proposed by Mattis and Ollendick (1997) suggests that a child's response to stressful separation experiences is related to temperament as well as the nature of attachment relationships with significant adults. For some children, temperament serves as an initial biological vulnerability within Barlow's (1988) model, setting the stage for the possible development of panic. For instance, a young child who is highly reactive to negative events (e.g., cries inconsolably and is not easily soothed) will be most at risk of experiencing intense, prolonged distress, combined with physiological arousal, when faced with the stress of separation. Such children may begin, over time, to associate distress with internal physical sensations (e.g., pounding heart, trembling), setting the stage for the development of panic. Furthermore, Mattis and Ollendick (1997) suggest that young children who show insecure attachment behaviours, such as intense distress when separated from the caregiver combined with difficulty being comforted after separation, may be most at risk for the development of panic. Such children are likely to feel a lack of safety and security, develop anxious apprehension over the possible recurrence of frightening experiences, and begin to avoid situations as a way of coping with stress.

SAD: Genetic and Family Factors

Although there is a relative dearth of research data in this area, there is evidence that separation anxiety selectively aggregates in families (Granell de Aldaz et al.,

1987). In a recent study, Silove and colleagues (1995) utilized the Separation Anxiety Symptom Inventory (SASI; Silove et al., 1993) to examine the familial aggregation of juvenile separation anxiety in 200 twin pairs drawn from the national twin register. Using structural equation modelling, the study demonstrated that 39% of variance in SASI scores were due to genetic effects, with even higher rates among women (41%). In addition, studies on infant temperament have indicated that the trait of "behavioural inhibition" (Kagan et al., 1984; Kagan, Reznick, & Snidman, 1987) may be a risk factor for the development of several anxiety disorders in children. Young children who are behaviourally inhibited tend to act shy, inhibited, and introverted and are reluctant to attend school—characteristics that may overlap with those of SAD. However, to date, little specific information is known about the degree to which behavioural inhibition relates specifically to the onset of SAD.

"Top-down" studies, which identify anxious adult probands and investigate psychopathology in their offspring, have provided tentative support for the familial aggregation of separation anxiety (Silove & Manicavasagar, 1993; Capps et al., 1996). In one example, in a study of 74 volunteers with histories of school fears, those who reported heightened levels of juvenile separation anxiety were more likely to have a sibling or child who suffered from similar symptoms. "Bottom-up" studies, or studies that examine psychiatric morbidity in parents and relatives of an identified proband with a specific disorder, generally have demonstrated increased rates of psychiatric disturbance in the parents of children with school phobia or heightened levels of separation anxiety, but parental diagnoses appeared to lack specificity (Last et al., 1991). Thus, there is strong evidence that anxiety aggregates in families, but few specific associations have been found linking specific anxiety disorders in parents and their children.

SAD: Parental Factors

Parental control and protectiveness have both been identified as core characteristics that may lead to psychopathology in offspring (Parker, Tupling, & Brown, 1979). Bowlby (1970, 1977), in his studies of attachment, asserted that early maternal overprotectiveness was a key influence in generating heightened separation anxiety in a child. Bowlby has described several variants of overprotective parent–child interactions; in some situations, the mother's own fears led to overprotective parenting, thereby provoking separation anxiety in the child, whereas in others, heightened separation anxiety in the child elicited overprotectiveness in the concerned parent. More recently, there have been numerous studies examining the role of family factors and their influence on the development of separation anxiety in childhood (e.g., Ginsburg, Silverman, & Kurtines, 1995). Research indicates that parenting styles characterized by high control and low warmth are more prevalent in families with anxious children than in families in which the child does not have a psychiatric diagnosis (Hudson & Rapee, 2000; Siqueland, Kendall, & Steinberg, 1996). Compared to the parents of children without psychiatric disorders, parents of anxious children tend to grant less psychological autonomy and evidence less warmth and acceptance. This parental control and lack of warmth may contribute to the child's experience of diminished control, leading to greater anxiety in the child. It has been suggested that child anxiety researchers begin to integrate parent–child interaction strategies and incorporate interventions that attempt to directly alter this parenting style and promote warmth, acceptance, and positive interactions between parents and children.

ASSESSMENT

A thorough assessment of child anxiety, including separation anxiety or panic disorder, should incorporate several elements, such as a diagnostic interview, behavioural observations, self-report measures, parent and teacher ratings, and physiological measures. By obtaining information from a variety of sources, the clinician is more likely to gain a multifaceted understanding of a child's anxiety disorder and to formulate an appropriate treatment plan.

Diagnostic Interview

Although there are numerous clinical interviews available, the Anxiety Disorders Interview Schedule for Children (ADIS-IV, Child Version; Silverman & Albano, 1997), the Schedule for Affective Disorders and Schizophrenia for School-Aged Children (K-SADS; Chambers, Puig-Antich, & Hirsch, 1985), the Diagnostic Interview Schedule for Children (DISC; Costello, Edelbrock, & Kalas, 1984), and the Child Assessment Schedule (CAS; Hodges, 1987) are among the most commonly utilized. Research has shown adequate reliability and validity for each of these interview schedules (e.g., Last et al., 1987).

Of the measures listed above, the Anxiety Disorders Interview Schedule for DSM-IV, Child Version (ADIS-IV, Child Version; Silverman & Albano, 1997) is the only diagnostic interview designed to exclusively assess anxiety and related disorders (e.g., depression) in children and adolescents. The interview consists of separate child and parent components. Typically, the child is interviewed first, followed by a separate interview with the parent(s). The interview is divided into several sections which correspond to the various anxiety and related disorders (e.g., Social Phobia, SAD, Panic Disorder, Dysthymia). Each section is introduced by a "screening question" which determines whether the interviewer should proceed with the entire section. For instance, when enquiring about panic disorder, the interview asks whether the child or adolescent has ever felt really scared "out of the blue". If the child has not had this experience, a diagnosis of panic disorder can be ruled out. However, if the child or parent answers affirmatively, the interviewer will go on to assess the nature of this anxiety, where and how often it has occurred, the presence of panic attack symptoms, feelings of apprehension following any unexpected panic attacks, and the degree to which panic has interfered in the child's life. The interviewer will then determine whether the child meets diagnostic criteria for panic disorder. A composite diagnosis which includes all information from both the child and parent is assigned, and each diagnosis is given a clinical severity rating (CSR) from 0 to 8, reflecting mild, moderate, severe, or very severe levels of distress and interference. Diagnoses receiving a CSR of 4 or above are considered clinically significant, and will typically be addressed during the course of treatment.

Behavioural Assessment

As a semistructured diagnostic interview, the ADIS-IV, Child Version (Silverman & Albano, 1997) not only yields information on the presence and severity of anxiety disorders, it also provides an important opportunity for behavioural observation. For instance, a child with SAD may experience difficulty separating from his or her parent(s) for the child portion of the interview. Behaviours such as tearfulness, clinginess, or pleading with the parent not to leave provide important information regarding the child's symptomatology and its impact on his or her life.

The direct observation of a child's behaviour within the setting where it occurs has been described as the "hallmark of behavioural assessment" (Ollendick & King, 1990). In order to gain a full understanding of a child's separation anxiety or panic, the therapist may need to observe the child in a natural environment, such as home, school, or an agoraphobic situation (e.g., crowds). For instance, the therapist may visit the child's home on a school morning in order to observe and record behaviours associated with separation anxiety (e.g., verbal protests about leaving home, whining or crying, physical complaints). Before beginning treatment with an adolescent who experiences panic disorder, the therapist might observe him or her in a crowded shopping centre, noting avoidance behaviours and physical symptoms reported by the adolescent.

The Behavioural Avoidance Task (BAT; Lang & Lazovik, 1963) provides a unique opportunity to gather behavioural data as well as self-ratings of anxiety within the clinic setting. During the BAT, the therapist constructs a situation in which the child is exposed in a controlled way to the focus of his or her fear. For example, a child with SAD might be observed initially while in the same room with the parent, then with the parent outside the room but within sight, and finally, with the parent out of sight (Wachtel & Strauss, 1995). Similarly, an adolescent with panic disorder may be asked to engage in exercises that elicit the feared physical sensations associated with panic (e.g., breathing through a straw, spinning in a chair). Throughout the BAT the child or adolescent is asked to rate his or her anxiety periodically on a Subjective Units of Distress Scale (SUDS) ranging from 0 to 100 (where 0 is completely relaxed and 100 is as anxious as the child can imagine being).

In conjunction with behavioural assessment, there is currently a burgeoning interest in the physiological assessment of anxious mood in children. Some recent work has supported the use of measuring heart rate and/or blood pressure when evaluating anxiety in children and adolescents (Beidel, 1988; Choate et al., 2000; Matthews, Manuck, & Saab, 1986; Pincus & Friedman, 1995). For instance, Choate and colleagues (2000) reported increased heart rate in adolescents with panic disorder during two tasks designed to simulate the physical sensations of a panic attack. Physiological assessment has not yet been studied empirically among children with SAD, but it may be useful to consider the role of physiological and somatic symptoms associated with this disorder.

Self-Report Measures

In addition to clinical interviews and behavioural assessment, self-report measures can also assist in the evaluation of separation anxiety and panic disorder in children and adolescents (see Table 7.1). For example, the Multidimensional Anxiety Scale for Children (MASC; March et al., 1997), the Childhood Anxiety Sensitivity Index (CASI; Silverman et al., 1991), the Revised Children's Manifest Anxiety Scale (RCMAS; Reynolds & Richmond, 1978), the State-Trait Anxiety Inventory for Children (STAIC; Spielberger, 1973), the Revised Fear Survey Schedule for Children (FSSC-R; Ollendick, 1983), and the School Refusal Assessment Scale (SRAS; Kearney & Silverman, 1993) are among the most commonly used measures for this population. The MASC may be particularly useful in the assessment of separation anxiety and panic symptomatology due to its inclusion of a Separation/Panic sub-scale which assesses the tendency to be scared when alone or in an unfamiliar place, and to want to stay close to family or home. However, it should be noted that several limitations with self-report measures have been reported, including their focus on general symptoms of anxiety rather than specific situations and their generally limited use with children under 7 years old due to reading requirements.

Parent and teacher rating forms and checklists are also quite valuable assessment instruments. Two questionnaires that assess symptomatology particularly related to separation anxiety include the Fear Scale of the Louisville Behavior Checklist (Miller et al., 1971) and the Parent Anxiety Rating Scale (Doris et al., 1971). Other questionnaires assess general anxiety symptomatology, such as the Child Behavior Checklist (CBCL; Achenbach & Edelbrock, 1983) and the Conners' Teacher Rating Scale (Conners, 1969).

TREATMENT

Separation Anxiety Disorder

Over the past decade, there has been burgeoning interest in the study of the treatment of Separation Anxiety Disorder (SAD). SAD is not only distressing to the child and family, but has also been associated with later risk of anxiety disorders such as panic disorder in adolescence and adulthood (Lease & Strauss, 1993). Despite the growing evidence that SAD is so prevalent in early childhood and may be linked to the presence of later psychopathology, there has been a paucity of empirical studies investigating the effectiveness of interventions for SAD in young children. The majority of treatment research of SAD has been limited to case reports with expected methodological limitations (Ollendick, Hagopian, & Huntzinger, 1991; Thyer & Sowers-Hoag, 1988). Currently, the majority of interventions utilized with older children are individual, child-focused treatments consisting of teaching children self-control skills (e.g., relaxation, cognitive-restructuring) to use during graded exposures to feared situations (Eisen & Kearney, 1995). The few treatment studies that have been conducted have included children in middle childhood (aged 7 and older) and adolescence (aged 13 and older), but have typically not included children in pre-school and early childhood

Table 7.1 Assessment instruments for SAD and panic disorder in children and adolescents

Instrument	Type	Description
Anxiety Disorders Interview Schedule for DSM-IV, Child Version (ADIS-IV, Child Version; Silverman & Albano, 1997)	Diagnostic interview	Assesses anxiety and related disorders in children and adolescents, aged 7–17. Consists of separate child and parent components.
Behavioral Avoidance Task (BAT; Lang & Lazovik, 1963)	Behavioural assessment	Child is exposed to anxiety-provoking stimuli in a controlled manner. Assesses behaviour (e.g., approach) and self-report of anxiety.
Multidimensional Anxiety Scale for Children (MASC; March et al., 1997)	Self-report measures	Assess anxiety and related constructs (e.g., anxiety sensitivity, fear, school refusal). The MASC may be particularly useful in the assessment of SAD and panic due to its inclusion of a Separation/Panic subscale.
Childhood Anxiety Sensitivity Index (CASI; Silverman et al., 1991)		
Revised Children's Manifest Anxiety Scale (RCMAS; Reynolds & Richmond, 1978)		
State-Trait Anxiety Inventory for Children (STAIC; Spielberger, 1973)		
Revised Fear Survey Schedule for Children (FSSC-R; Ollendick, 1983)		
School Refusal Assessment Scale (SRAS; Kearney & Silverman, 1993)		
Fear Scale of the Louisville Behavior Checklist (Miller et al., 1971)	Parent and teacher rating scales	Assess symptomatology related to separation anxiety as well as general anxiety symptoms as perceived by parents and teachers in different settings (e.g., school vs home).
Parent Anxiety Rating Scale (Doris et al., 1971)		
Child Behavior Checklist (CBCL; Achenbach & Edelbrock, 1983)		
Conners' Teacher Rating Scale (Conners, 1969)		

years (aged 4–8), despite the frequent early onset of SAD prior to age 6 (Eisen & Kearney, 1995; Eisen, Engler, & Geyer, 1998; Last, 1989; Ollendick & King, 1998). To date, there are currently no known interventions that have been designed or tested specifically to treat SAD in the pre-school and early childhood years.

Thus, although case reports of treatment of severe separation anxiety first appeared over 30 years ago, the literature in this area remains surprisingly sparse.

In a review of the literature on the behavioural treatment of SAD (Thyer & Sowers-Hoag, 1988), only 11 published studies were uncovered, some of which were among the earliest clinical reports of the application of behavioural methods to resolve psychosocial problems, conducted between 1957 and 1984. The majority of these case studies employed imaginal systematic desensitization (e.g., Bornstein & Knapp, 1981) or *in vivo* graduated exposure (Garvey & Hengrenes, 1966; Montenegro, 1968; Neisworth, Madle, & Goeke, 1975) or a combination of these two approaches (e.g., Butcher, 1983) to treat separation anxiety in children between the ages of 7 and 12 years. In addition, operant techniques have been employed successfully to shape independent behaviour in SAD children (e.g., Miller, 1972). Although case studies of successful cognitive or behavioural group treatment of children with SAD have continued to appear in the literature, very few controlled studies have been completed (Kendall et al., 1991). This is surprising, considering that SAD is considered to be the most frequently occurring anxiety disorder in childhood. To date, most empirical research that does exist has focused primarily on interventions for anxiety-based school refusal, which can be related to a range of anxiety disorders, including SAD, generalized worry, or a phobia of some aspect of the school environment (Last & Strauss, 1990). However, many researchers have cautioned that SAD should not be confused with school phobia, although many clinicians and researchers have tended to use the two terms synonymously. Research has demonstrated that a substantial proportion of school refusers do not show SAD and a sizable percentage of SAD children do not have difficulties attending school (Last et al., 1987; Last & Strauss, 1990).

The most recent review conducted of empirically supported treatments for children with phobic and anxiety disorders (Ollendick & King, 1998) indicates that only four between-group studies have been undertaken in recent years; all have evaluated the efficacy of cognitive behavioural therapy (CBT) for children aged 9 and above with anxiety disorders. Cognitive-behavioural treatment for anxiety disorders in children, as pioneered by Kendall and colleagues (e.g., Kendall et al., 1991) is focused on teaching children four major cognitive components: (a) recognizing anxious feelings and somatic reactions to anxiety, (b) clarifying cognitions in anxiety-provoking situations, (c) developing a plan to cope with the situation, and (d) evaluating the success of the coping strategies and utilizing self-reinforcement. In addition, behavioural strategies such as modelling, *in vivo* exposure, role-playing, relaxation training, and reinforced practice are used (Kane & Kendall, 1989; Kendall et al., 1997).

In one manualized between-group study, Kendall (1994) compared the outcome of a 16-session CBT program to a wait-list control condition. Forty-seven 9–13 year olds meeting diagnoses for overanxious disorder ($n = 30$), SAD ($n = 8$), and avoidant disorder ($n = 9$) were randomly assigned either to treatment or wait-list conditions. The allocation process resulted in 27 children receiving active treatment, and 20 children receiving a wait-list control condition. All control subjects were treated after the wait-list period. Approximately equal numbers of children with each diagnosis were represented in both the treatment and wait-list conditions. In addition, treatment and wait-list subjects did not differ across age, gender, or ethnicity at pre-treatment. For the assessment of sample representativeness, ANOVAs and chi squares were used to compare the treatment completers ($n = 47$) as well as the dropouts ($n = 13$) on demographic variables as well as frequency of diagnoses. For all variables, there were no significant differences between completers and dropouts.

By the end of treatment, 64% of treated cases did not meet diagnostic criteria for an anxiety disorder, versus 5% of the wait-list. Further, on the majority of measures administered, treated children fared better than the wait-list children. One- and three-year follow-ups revealed maintenance of treatment gains. Kendall and colleagues (1997) further confirmed the efficacy of this CBT program for use with anxious children. In this study, 94 anxious children, aged 9–13, were randomly assigned to CBT or a wait-list control condition. Seventy-one percent of children treated with CBT did not meet diagnostic criteria for an anxiety disorder at the end of treatment, compared to 5.8% of those in the wait-list condition. While these findings support the efficacy of cognitive-behavioural procedures with children aged 9 and above, the existing controlled treatment studies have typically not included younger children.

Thus, there is some evidence that various cognitive and behavioural techniques can be helpful when used, either individually or in combination, to treat SAD (Wachtel & Strauss, 1995). Systematic desensitization is one technique often employed, whereby a child creates a fear avoidance hierarchy focused on activities resulting in increasing levels of separation from the caregiver. Children are taught relaxation strategies, such as progressive muscle relaxation, to teach them to tense and release various muscle groups throughout the body to produce relaxation. Children are instructed in how to employ such techniques while entering feared situations ranging from those that elicit very mild levels of anxiety to those provoking extreme anxiety or panic. Children then are given homework assignments, negotiated with the therapist and parent, to conduct "exposure" exercises where the child enters the previously avoided situations. Children's successes are rewarded with praise or small treats.

There is also some evidence that modelling can be useful in the treatment of SAD. For example, a child might learn to overcome a fear of separation by watching other children separate from parents successfully. Children can be shown films of successful departures from parents, or they can observe a live model. Of all the modelling approaches with children, participant modelling (having the child attempt to confront the anxiety-provoking situation soon after watching a model) has been shown to be the most effective, followed by live modelling (Ollendick & Cerny, 1981). Taped modelling appears to be the least effective. However, while modelling has been utilized in investigations of various childhood fears, it has not yet been tested specifically on children with SAD.

Cognitive procedures have been found to be extremely helpful, especially to older children with SAD who have already developed the cognitive abilities to be able to learn to identify and change their maladaptive thoughts about separation. The assumption behind cognitive techniques is that the child's maladaptive thoughts, beliefs, attitudes, or self-statements lead to or maintain anxious behaviours. Children are taught to identify maladaptive thoughts, and to evaluate whether there is any "evidence" to support their fearful thoughts. Children are then taught how to generate more positive, competence-related coping statements, and "coping thoughts" to be used when anticipating or confronting anxiety-provoking situations.

These statements emphasize the child's competence (e.g., "I can do this by myself!"), and the fact that the child and parents are safe. Children are also taught to praise themselves for their bravery.

In addition to modelling procedures and cognitive procedures, contingency management procedures have been shown to be a highly effective component in treating SAD. Contingency management involves creating rewards and punishments to help children increase their ability to enter previously avoided situations and to behave independently. Typically, the child is reinforced with either verbal or tangible reinforcers, such as praise, stickers, or small treats, when he or she is able to separate from a caregiver or is able to perform activities independently. Rewards are also given as children accomplish each item on their fear and avoidance hierarchy of feared situations involving separation. Extinction procedures are also sometimes employed, such as removing consequences that reinforce avoidant behaviour (e.g., being allowed to stay home from school or receiving extra attention from parents by staying home).

The treatment studies/case reports that have been conducted on children with SAD have included children in middle childhood (aged 9 and older) and adolescence (aged 13 and older), but have typically not included children in pre-school and early childhood years (aged 4–7), despite the frequent early onset of SAD prior to age 6. To date, there are currently no known interventions that have been designed or tested specifically to treat SAD in the pre-school and early childhood years.

Many of the intervention strategies currently being evaluated for use with older children are likely to be developmentally inappropriate for the young pre-schooler with SAD. For example, young children aged 4–7 typically have not developed the meta-cognitive or representational abilities to allow them to engage in cognitive restructuring or imaginal exposure techniques. Further, the young pre-schooler may not yet have developed the cognitive and communicative abilities to verbalize their fears or to engage in self-control procedures that would often be taught to older children for use during graded exposures to feared situations (Eisen & Kearney, 1995). For this reason, the need for intensive parental involvement in young children's treatment is indicated.

Parent Training Approaches to the Treatment of SAD

Recent research has suggested that incorporating parents more centrally into the treatment of children with anxiety disorders can be extremely useful in reducing children's anxious behaviour (e.g., Knox, Albano, & Barlow, 1996) and may enhance treatment effectiveness and maintenance (Ginsburg, Silverman, & Kurtines, 1995). Ollendick and King (1998), in their review of treatments for children's fears, highlight the need for intensive parental involvement for treating children with fears and anxiety. They suggest that parents might be regarded as co-therapists, responsible for the implementation of procedures developed by the therapist, and responsible for giving children ample praise and positive reinforcement for brave behaviour. There have been several recent model programs currently being explored that involve parents more centrally in the treatment of children's fears.

The "transfer of control" model (Ginsburg, Silverman, & Kurtines, 1995) emphasizes the gradual fading of control from therapist to parent, and then to child. The Family Anxiety Management model (FAM; Dadds, Heard, & Rapee, 1992), like the transfer of control model, involves training parents in contingency management strategies to deal with their child's fears and anxieties and to facilitate the child's exposure to the phobic situation. These approaches explicitly recognize and target parental anxiety, problematic family relationships, and parent–child communication skills.

In one of the most recent controlled trials of child anxiety treatment, Barrett, Dadds, and Rapee (1996) compared CBT to a condition that included CBT plus a parent-training component. In the parent-training component, parents were taught how to reward courageous behaviour and extinguish excessive anxiety in their child. They were trained in reinforcement strategies including verbal praise, privileges, and tangible rewards to be made contingent on facing feared situations. Ignoring was taught as a method for dealing with excessive complaining and anxious behaviour. Parents were also taught to deal with their own emotional upsets and to model problem-solving responses to feared situations. In this study, 79 children (aged 7–14 years) were randomly assigned to CBT, CBT+FAM, and a wait-list control condition. Children had principal diagnoses of overanxious disorder ($n = 30$), social phobia ($n = 30$), and SAD ($n = 30$). At post-treatment, 74% of wait-list children and 43% of the CBT children still met criteria for an anxiety disorder, however, only 16% of the children in the CBT+FAM condition met diagnostic criteria for an anxiety disorder at post-treatment. Thus, CBT plus a parent-training component was better than CBT alone. CBT plus parent training was found to be superior even at one year post-treatment for reducing children's anxious behaviours.

It has been suggested that parent-training approaches can be useful for working with children with SAD in particular. Eisen, Engler, and Geyer (1998) indicated that parents of children with SAD can fall prey to three "traps" that can inadvertently facilitate childhood anxiety: (1) overprotection; (2) excessive reassurance; and (3) aversive parent–child interactions. Parental overprotection occurs when a parent limits a child's opportunities to be exposed to anxiety provoking stimuli. Parents may conceal sources of information (television shows) and restrict activities such as participation in clubs or sports. Further, a child's preoccupation with potential harm befalling a parent may fuel caregiver's protectiveness. Parents of children with SAD may also frequently resort to the use of excessive reassurance to reduce children's fears of tragic outcomes. In doing so, a parent may limit a child's opportunities to develop independent coping skills. Finally, parents may begin to view a child's anxious behaviour as manipulative, attention-seeking behaviour, which can result in aversive parent–child interactions, such as yelling or reprimands. Each of these "traps" could encourage child anxiety because the parent provides attention (positive or negative) during a child's fearful displays. It has been suggested that aversive parent–child interactions can be minimized, and maintenance and generalization of treatment effects can be enhanced, when parents serve as co-therapists (Eisen & Kearney, 1995; Foote, Eyberg, & Schumann, 1998; Kendall, 1991).

In developing effective parent-training programs for children with anxiety, researchers have begun to draw upon empirically validated parenting treatments that have been shown to be effective for childhood behaviour disorders (Eisen,

Engler, & Geyer, 1998). The following strategies have been viewed as important components to include in a parent-training program to reduce child anxiety: (1) enhancing parent attention (teaching parents to be more effective monitors of children's behaviours), (2) command training (teaching parents to deliver clear, direct commands), (3) differential reinforcement (teaching parents to ignore or minimize attention for fearful displays), and (4) shaping (positively rewarding children for brave behaviours) (Ginsburg, Silverman, & Kurtines, 1995; Lease & Strauss, 1993). There is growing evidence suggesting that parent-training approaches may be extremely useful for young children with SAD.

Panic Disorder

Although panic disorder has been extensively studied in adults, and effective cognitive-behavioural and pharmacological treatments have been developed and evaluated (cf. Barlow et al., 1989; Beck & Emery, 1985; Clark, Salkovskis, & Chalkley, 1985; Clum, 1989; Marks, 1987; Öst, Westling, & Hellström, 1993), relatively little research has focused on the treatment of panic disorder in children and adolescents. Indeed, only one controlled, multiple baseline study has evaluated its efficacy in the treatment of adolescents (Ollendick, 1995), while the first randomized-controlled treatment outcome study is currently underway (Mattis et al., 2001; Mattis & Kiel, 2002).

In a multiple-baseline design analysis of the cognitive-behavioural treatment of panic disorder in adolescents, Ollendick (1995) combined elements of the cognitive-behavioural treatments developed by Barlow and colleagues (e.g., Barlow et al., 1989) and Öst and colleagues (e.g., Öst, Westling, & Hellström, 1993). Participants were three females and one male, ranging in age from 13 to 17 years, and meeting DSM-III-R criteria for panic disorder with agoraphobia. Treatment duration ranged from 6 to 9 sessions, with termination contingent on panic-free status for two consecutive weeks. The initial treatment session focused on information regarding the nature of panic and the treatment strategy. The focus of the second session was progressive muscle relaxation and breathing retraining, while cue-controlled and applied relaxation was taught during the third session. The fourth treatment session focused on the development of positive self-statements, cognitive coping procedures, and self-instruction strategies. Exposure trials were then instituted, based on an individualized hierarchy of agoraphobic situations, and the remaining sessions were devoted to review of exposure trials, progress, and continued rehearsal of relaxation and self-instruction.

Cognitive-behavioural treatment resulted in a decrease in the frequency of panic attacks for all participants, with the average number of attacks per week during baseline ranging from 1.5 to 2, and all participants achieving two consecutive panic-free weeks before termination of treatment. Improvement was also evidenced in reduction of agoraphobic avoidance and self-efficacy ratings in agoraphobic situations. Specifically, at post-treatment participants rarely avoided agoraphobic situations, were able to remain in such situations alone for extended periods of time, and evidenced self-efficacy ratings which reflected feeling "very sure" to "absolutely sure" that they could cope with both agoraphobic situations and panic attacks.

Reductions in frequency of panic attacks and agoraphobic avoidance as well as increases in self-efficacy were maintained at six-month follow-up, with none of the participants meeting diagnostic criteria for panic disorder either at termination or follow-up. Furthermore, self-report measures of anxiety sensitivity, trait anxiety, fear, and depression reflected improvements at post-treatment which were, for the most part, maintained at follow-up. Based on these findings, Ollendick (1995) concluded that combined cognitive-behavioral treatment procedures found to be efficacious in the treatment of panic disorder in adults may be successfully applied to the treatment of adolescents.

At the Center for Anxiety and Related Disorders at Boston University, Mattis and colleagues (Mattis et al., 2001; Mattis & Kiel, 2002) are currently conducting a randomized-controlled trial evaluating the efficacy of cognitive-behavioural treatment of panic disorder in adolescents between the ages of 14 and 17. The treatment used in this study is a developmental adaptation of Panic Control Treatment (PCT; Barlow et al., 1989) which incorporates interoceptive exposure (exposure to feared bodily sensations associated with panic), situational exposure, breathing retraining, psychoeducation, and cognitive restructuring over the course of 11 treatment sessions. Barlow and colleagues (1989) have reported that PCT is highly efficacious in reducing the frequency and severity of panic attacks, panic disorder, and associated anxiety in an adult population.

Panic Control Treatment for Adolescents (PCT-A), similar to its adult counterpart, focuses on three aspects of panic attacks and related anxiety: the cognitive/misinterpretational aspect, the hyperventilatory response, and conditioned reactions to physical sensations (see Hoffman & Mattis, 2000, for a detailed description of the PCT-A protocol). Initial sessions target the cognitive/misinterpretational aspect through psychoeducation in which the adolescent is given accurate information about the physical sensations of anxiety and panic and their relationship to the fight/flight response. Through such information, the adolescent learns that such sensations are harmless, and that a panic attack represents a fearful reaction to normal physical sensations. Adolescents are also taught strategies for identifying and challenging anxiety-provoking thoughts (e.g., "I might faint") by evaluating the evidence (e.g., "How many times have I actually fainted as a result of panic") as well as their ability to cope (e.g., "Even if I did faint, would it be the end of the world or could I get through it?"). The role of hyperventilation in panic attacks is discussed, and adolescents are taught slow, diaphragmatic breathing in order to reduce the frequency and intensity of physical sensations that trigger and maintain panic. Conditioned reactions to physical sensations are addressed during the second half of treatment through interoceptive exposure which utilizes exercises and naturalistic activities to decondition fear reactions through gradual, repeated exposure to the physical sensations associated with panic. For instance, the adolescent is asked to breathe through a thin straw or to go running in order to elicit feelings of breathlessness. Through such exercises, the adolescent begins to separate physical sensations from an automatic reaction of fear, and to learn that such sensations are not truly dangerous. Finally, the adolescent develops a hierarchy of agoraphobic situations at the beginning of treatment, and situational exposure is incorporated as homework throughout treatment in order to encourage adolescents to approach situations associated with panic in their daily lives.

Currently, 20 adolescents, ages 14–17, with a principal diagnosis of panic disorder have participated in this randomized-controlled trial. Of these, 11 have been randomly assigned to receive immediate PCT-A, while nine have been assigned to a self-monitoring control group and asked to wait eight weeks before receiving PCT-A. Diagnostic interviews utilizing the Anxiety Disorders Interview Schedule, Child and Parent Versions (ADIS-IV-C/P; Silverman & Albano, 1997) are conducted with subjects prior to participation and following the treatment or control period. Subjects in the treatment group are also assessed three months following PCT-A. Interviewers assign clinical severity ratings (CSRs) for panic disorder on a 9-point scale reflecting level of distress and interference. A CSR of 4 or above is considered clinical, while a CSR less than 4 is subclinical. Subjects also complete the following self-report measures at each assessment point: the Multidimensional Anxiety Scale for Children (MASC; March et al., 1997), the Revised Children's Manifest Anxiety Scale (RCMAS; Reynolds & Richmond, 1978), the Childhood Anxiety Sensitivity Index (CASI; Silverman et al., 1991), and the Children's Depression Inventory (CDI; Kovacs & Beck, 1977).

Initial analyses have revealed significant improvement on CSR and all of the self-report measures for adolescents receiving PCT-A, with the control group showing improvement only on the CDI. These findings provide support for the efficacy of cognitive-behavioural treatment of panic disorder in adolescence. Specifically, they reveal significant reduction in severity of panic disorder, as well as associated anxiety and anxiety sensitivity, among adolescents receiving PCT-A relative to a control group. Notably, mean CSR remained in the clinical range for the control group, but fell to the subclinical range following PCT-A. Furthermore, analyses suggest that treatment gains are maintained at three-month follow-up. Enrolment continues and 3-, 6-, and 12-month follow-up assessments are in progress to further assess the efficacy of PCT-A. Hopefully, by continuing to study the efficacy of cognitive-behavioural treatment in a larger sample of adolescents, we will gain a better understanding of the treatment of panic disorder at its earliest stages, and will reduce the interference it causes in the lives of many adolescents and young adults.

Pharmacological Treatment

While the pharmacological treatment of panic disorder has been the focus of research with adults, no randomized-controlled trials have yet been conducted in a child or adolescent population (Ollendick, Birmaher, & Mattis, in press). In a review of the adult literature, Ollendick, Birmaher, and Mattis (in press) reported that the selective serotonin reuptake inhibitors (SSRIs), the tricyclic antidepressants (TCAs), and the high potency benzodiazepines have all been found to be relatively effective in the treatment of adults with panic disorder compared to a placebo control. Despite the absence of randomized-controlled trials with children or adolescents, case reports have suggested that benzodiazepines and the SSRIs may be efficacious treatments for panic disorder in a younger population. For instance, Renaud and colleagues (1999) conducted an open trial in which they used SSRIs to treat 12 children and adolescents with panic disorder over a 6–8 week period. The authors reported that nearly 75% of the youth showed "much to very much" improvement without significant side effects, and that 67% no longer met criteria for panic disorder by the end of the trial. Based on such research, Ollendick, Birmaher, and Mattis (in press) concluded that SSRIs are currently the most promising psychopharmacological treatment for panic disorder in children/adolescents, although randomized-controlled trials are clearly needed. A summary of treatment protocols for SAD and panic disorder in children and adolescents are presented in Table 7.2.

SUMMARY AND FUTURE DIRECTIONS

Anxiety disorders have been suggested as the most common category of childhood disorders (Bernstein & Borchardt, 1991). Of this category, SAD is the most common anxiety disorder in children and adolescents, with 5–10% of youngsters evidencing a clinical level of separation anxiety (Costello & Angold, 1995). While the prevalence of panic among prepubertal children is still a matter of dispute, recent research suggests that mid to late adolescence may be the peak period of onset for panic disorder with an overall prevalence of about 1% in this population (APA, 1994; Lewinsohn et al., 1993).

Both the prevalence and characteristics of SAD and panic disorder suggest that these disorders cause notable interference and distress in the lives of children and adolescents. The defining feature of SAD is excessive, unrealistic fear of separating from an attachment figure. Such fear often has the debilitating effect of limiting a child's exposure to experiences that may be critical to normal development (e.g., independently attending school or playdates). Similarly, adolescents who experience unexpected panic attacks may avoid situations that trigger physical sensations associated with anxiety (e.g., physical exercise), and often develop agoraphobia in which they avoid situations (e.g., movie theatres, crowds) for fear of having a panic attack. Again, such avoidance often interferes with the course of normal development.

Given the level of interference and distress associated with SAD and panic disorder, future research should be committed to advancing understanding of the aetiology, assessment, and treatment of these disorders in children and adolescents. While good aetiological models have been developed (see Mattis & Ollendick, 1997), longitudinal research which seeks to elucidate the complex interaction between genetic factors, temperament, attachment patterns, and environmental influences is sorely needed in understanding the development of both SAD and panic disorder. Similarly, future research should focus on the further development of robust assessment instruments that differentiate between the anxiety disorders, as well as the role of innovative assessment techniques (e.g., physiological measurements). Finally, treatment outcome research is critical in reducing the distress and interference caused by SAD and panic disorder. The research that has been conducted thus far suggests that treatment which incorporates cognitive and behavioural techniques (e.g., recognizing and changing anxious thoughts, facing feared situations and/or sensations, reinforcing coping behaviour) is quite promising in reducing the symptoms and distress associated with both SAD and panic disorder. However, many more controlled treatment studies are needed, particularly with younger children. Furthermore, the role of pharmacological treatment either alone

Table 7.2 Treatment protocols for SAD and panic disorder in children and adolescents

Study/protocol	Type of treatment	Description
Ollendick (1995)	Cognitive-behavioural treatment of panic disorder in adolescents aged 13–17.	Treatment combined information re panic, relaxation, cognitive strategies, and exposure over 6–9 sessions. Participants showed improvement on a number of variables, including number of panic attacks per week, agoraphobic avoidance, self-efficacy ratings, and self-report measures of anxiety sensitivity, trait anxiety, fear, and depression.
Mattis et al. (2001)	Panic Control Treatment for Adolescents (PCT-A) aged 14–17.	Treatment combines psychoeducation, cognitive-restructuring, diaphragmatic breathing, interoceptive exposure and situational exposure. Initial results show significant improvement on clinical severity of panic disorder as well as self-report measures of anxiety, anxiety sensitivity, and depression.
Renaud et al. (1999)	Pharmacological treatment of panic disorder in children and adolescents.	SSRIs were used to treat 12 children and adolescents with panic disorder over a 6–8 week period; 75% showed "much to very much" improvement without significant side effects; 67% no longer met criteria for panic disorder.
Kendall (1994) Kendall et al. (1997)	Cognitive-behavioural treatment of separation anxiety in children aged 9–13.	Treatment consisted of psychoeducation, cognitive restructuring, and situational exposure. Participants showed improvement on the majority of measures administered, and children in treatment fared better than those in the wait-list; the majority of treated children did not meet diagnostic criteria for an anxiety disorder at post-treatment. Gains maintained at post-treatment and one- and three-year follow-up.
Barrett et al. (1996)	Combined cognitive-behavioural treatment of anxiety with a parent training component in children aged 7–14 years.	Compared CBT to a condition including CBT + a parent-training component. Parents were taught how to reward courageous behaviour and extinguish excessive anxiety; parents also taught verbal praise, behavioural contingencies. Children who received CBT plus parent-training component fared significantly better than those receiving CBT alone.
Pincus et al. (2003) Pincus et al. (2001)	Parent–Child Interaction Therapy (PCIT, Eyberg & Matarazzo, 1980) applied to children with SAD aged 4–8 years and their parents.	Initial results show significant improvement on clinical severity of SAD as well as parent self-report measures of anxiety, child behaviour, and improved warmth in the parent–child interaction.

or in combination with cognitive-behavioural strategies must be the focus of further investigation.

While much has been learned in recent years regarding the nature, prevalence, and associated features of SAD and panic disorder, additional research is needed to further understanding of these disorders and their impact on children and adolescents. Through such study, we will be in a better position of truly understanding interventions that work in alleviating the distress associated with these disorders, thus attenuating their disruptive effects on the course of child and adolescent development.

REFERENCES

Achenbach, T.M., & Edelbrock, C.S. (1983). *Manual for the Child Behavior Checklist and Revised Child Behavior Profile.* Burlington, VT: University Associates in Psychiatry.

Albano, A.M., Chorpita, B.F., & Barlow, D.H. (1996). Childhood anxiety disorders. In E.J. Mash & R.A. Barkley (Eds), *Child psychopathology.* New York: Guilford Press.

Alessi, N.E., & Magen, J. (1988). Panic disorder in psychiatrically hospitalized children. *American Journal of Psychiatry,* **145**, 1450–1452.

Alessi, N.E., Robbins, D.R., & Dilsaver, S.C. (1987). Panic and depressive disorders among psychiatrically hospitalized adolescents. *Psychiatry Research,* **20**, 275–283.

American Psychiatric Association (1980). *Diagnostic and statistical manual of mental disorders* (3rd edn). Washington, DC: Author.

American Psychiatric Association (1994). *Diagnostic and statistical manual of mental disorders* (4th edn). Washington, DC: Author.

Ballenger, J.C., Carek, D.J., Steele, J.J., & Cornish-McTighe, D. (1989). Three cases of panic disorder with agoraphobia in children. *American Journal of Psychiatry,* **146**, 922–924.

Barlow, D.H. (1988). *Anxiety and its disorders.* New York: Guilford Press.

Barlow, D.H., Craske, M.G., Cerny, J.A., & Klosko, J.S. (1989). Behavioral treatment of panic disorder. *Behavior Therapy,* **20**, 261–282.

Barrett, P.M., Dadds, M.R., & Rapee, R.M. (1996). Family treatment of childhood anxiety: A controlled trial. *Journal of Consulting and Clinical Psychology,* **64** (2), 333–342.

Beck, A.T., & Emery, G. (1985). *Anxiety disorders and phobias: A cognitive perspective.* New York: Basic Books.

Beidel, D.C. (1988). Psychophysiological assessment of anxious emotional states in children. *Journal of Abnormal Psychology,* **97**, 80–82.

Bell-Dolan, D. (1995). Separation anxiety disorder. In R.T. Ammerman & M. Hersen (Eds), *Handbook of child behavior therapy in the psychiatric setting* (pp. 217–298). New York: John Wiley & Sons.

Bernstein, G.A., & Borchardt, C.M. (1991). Anxiety disorders of childhood and adolescence: A critical review. *Journal of the American Academy of Child and Adolescent Psychiatry,* **30** (4), 519–532.

Bernstein, G.A., Borchardt, C.M., & Perwien, A.R. (1996). Anxiety disorders in children and adolescents: A review of the past 10 years. *Journal of the American Academy of Child and Adolescent Psychiatry,* **35**, 1110–1119.

Biederman, J. (1987). Clonazepam in the treatment of prepubertal children with panic-like symptoms. *Journal of Clinical Psychiatry,* **48**, 38–41.

Bornstein, P.H., & Knapp, M. (1981). Self-control desensitization with a multi-phobic boy: A multiple baseline design. *Journal of Behavior Therapy and Experimental Psychiatry,* **12** (3), 281–285.

Bowlby, J. (1970). Disruption of affectional bonds and its effects on behavior. *Journal of Contemporary Psychotherapy,* **2** (2), 75–86.

Bowlby, J. (1977). The making and breaking of affectional bonds: II. Some principles of psychotherapy. *British Journal of Psychiatry*, **130**, 421–431.

Butcher, P. (1983). The treatment of childhood-rooted separation anxiety in an adult. *Journal of Behavior Therapy and Experimental Psychiatry*, **14** (1), 61–65.

Capps, L., Sigman, M., Sena, R., & Henker, B. (1996). Fear, anxiety and perceived control in children of agoraphobic parents. *Journal of Child Psychology and Psychiatry and Allied Disciplines*, **37** (4), 445–452.

Chambers, W.J., Puig-Antich, J., & Hirsch, M. (1985). The assessment of affective disorders in children and adolescents by semistructured interview: Test–retest reliability of the Schedule for Affective Disorders and Schizophrenia for School-Age Children, Present Episode Version. *Archives of General Psychiatry*, **42** (7), 696–702.

Choate, M.L., Mattis, S.G., Pincus, D.B., & Borrow, J.A. (November, 2000). *Physiological measures of treatment response in adolescents with panic disorder.* Poster presented at the Association for Advancement of Behavior Therapy Annual Convention in New Orleans, LA.

Clark, D.M., Salkovskis, P.M., & Chalkley, A.J. (1985). Respiratory control as a treatment for panic attacks. *Journal of Behavior Therapy and Experimental Psychiatry*, **16**, 23–30.

Clum, G.A. (1989). Psychological interventions vs. drugs in the treatment of panic. *Behavior Therapy*, **20**, 429–457.

Costello, E.J., & Angold, A. (1995). Epidemiology. In J. March (Ed.), *Anxiety disorders in children and adolescents* (pp. 109–124). New York: Guilford Press.

Costello, A.J., Edelbrock, C.S., & Kalas, R. (1984). *Development and Testing of the NIMH Diagnostic Interview Schedule for Children (DISC) in a Clinical Population: Final Report.* Rockville, MD: Center for Epidemiological Studies, NIMH.

Conners, C.K. (1969). A teacher rating scale for use in drug studies with children. *American Journal of Psychiatry*, **126**, 884–888.

Dadds, M.R., Heard, P.M., & Rapee, R.M. (1992). The role of family intervention in the treatment of child anxiety disorders: Some preliminary findings. *Behaviour Change*, **9** (3), 171–177.

Doris, J., McIntyre, A., Kelsey, C., & Lehman, E. (1971). Separation anxiety in nursery school children. *Proceedings of the Annual Convention of the American Psychological Association*, **6** (Pt 1), 145–146.

Eisen, A.R., & Kearney, C.A. (1995). *Practitioner's guide to treating fear and anxiety in children and adolescents: A cognitive-behavioral approach.* Northvale, NJ: Jason Aronson.

Eisen, A.R., Engler, L.B., & Geyer, B. (1998). Parent training for separation anxiety disorder. In J.M. Briesmeister & C.E. Schaefer (Eds), *Handbook of parent training: Parents as co-therapists for children's behavior problems* (2nd edn; pp. 205–224). New York: John Wiley & Sons.

Eyberg, S.M., & Matarazzo, R.G. (1980). Training parents as therapists: A comparison between individual parent–child interaction training and parent group didactic training. *Journal of Clinical Child Psychology,* **36** (2), 492–499.

Faravelli, C., Webb, T., Ambonetti, A., Fonnesu, F., & Sessarego, A. (1985). Prevalence of traumatic early life events in 31 agoraphobic patients with panic attacks. *American Journal of Psychiatry*, **142**, 1493–1494.

Foote, R., Eyberg, S.M., & Schumann, E. (1998). Parent–child interaction approaches to the treatment of child behavior disorders. In T.H. Ollendick & R.J. Prinz (Eds), *Advances in clinical child psychology* (vol. 20). New York: Plenum Press.

Francis, G., Last, C.G., & Strauss, C.C. (1987). Expression of separation anxiety disorder: The roles of age and gender. *Child Psychiatry and Human Development*, **18** (2), 82–89.

Garland, E.J., & Smith, D.H. (1991). Simultaneous prepubertal onset of panic disorder, night terrors, and somnambulism. *Journal of the American Academy of Child and Adolescent Psychiatry*, **30**, 553–555.

Garvey, W.P., & Hengrenes, J.R. (1966). Desensitization techniques in the treatment of school phobia. *American Journal of Orthopsychiatry*, **36** (1), 147–152.

Ginsburg, G.S., Silverman, W.K., & Kurtines, W.K. (1995). Family involvement in treating children with phobic and anxiety disorders: A look ahead. *Clinical Psychology Review*, **15** (5), 457–473.

Granell de Aldaz, E., Vivas, E., Gelfand, D.M., & Feldman, L. (1987). Estimating the prevalence of school refusal and school-related fears: A Venezuelan sample. *Journal of Nervous and Mental Disease*, **172** (12), 722–729.

Hayward, C., Killen, J.D., & Taylor, C.B. (1989). Panic attacks in young adolescents. *American Journal of Psychiatry*, **146**, 1061–1062.

Herskowitz, J. (1986). Neurologic presentations of panic disorder in childhood and adolescence. *Developmental Medicine and Child Neurology*, **28**, 617–623.

Hirshfeld, D.R., Rosenbaum, J.F., Smoller, J.W., Fredman, S.J., & Bulzacchelli, M.T. (1998). Early antecedents of panic disorder. In J.F. Rosenbaum & M.W. Pollack (Eds), *Panic disorder and its treatment* (pp. 93–151). New York: Marcel Dekker, Inc.

Hodges, K. (1987). Assessing children with a clinical research interview: The Child Assessment Schedule. In R.J. Prinz (Ed.), *Advances in behavioral assessment of children and families* (vol. 3). Greenwich, CT: JAI Press.

Hoffman, E.C., & Mattis, S.G. (2000). A developmental adaptation of panic control treatment for panic disorder in adolescence. *Cognitive and Behavioral Practice*, **7**, 253–261.

Hudson, J.L., & Rapee, R.M. (2000). The origins of social phobia. *Behaviour Modification*, **24** (1), 102–129.

Kagan, J., Reznick, J.S., & Snidman, N. (1987). The physiology and psychology of behavioral inhibition in children. *Child Development*, **58** (6), 1459–1473.

Kagan, J., Reznick, J.S., & Snidman, N. (1988). Biological bases of childhood shyness. *Science*, **240**, 167–171.

Kagan, J., Reznick, J.S., Clarke, C., Snidman, N., & Garcia-Coll, C. (1984). Behavioral inhibition to the unfamiliar. *Child Development*, **55** (6), 2212–2225.

Kane, M.T., & Kendall, P.C. (1989). Anxiety disorders in children: A multiple-baseline evaluation of a cognitive-behavioral treatment. *Behavior Therapy*, **20** (4), 499–508.

Kearney, C.S., & Silverman, W.K. (1992). Let's not push the "panic" button: A critical analysis of panic and panic disorder in adolescents. *Clinical Psychology Review*, **12**, 293–305.

Kearney, C.A., & Silverman, W.K. (1993). Measuring the function of school refusal behavior: The School Assessment Scale. *Journal of Clinical Child Psychology*, **22** (1), 85–96.

Kearney, C.A., Albano, A.M., Eisen, A.R., Allan, W.D., & Barlow, D.H. (1997). The phenomenology of panic disorder in youngsters: An empirical study of a clinical sample. *Journal of Anxiety Disorders*, **11**, 49–62.

Kendall, P.C. (Ed.) (1991). *Child and adolescent therapy: Cognitive-behavioral procedures*. New York: Guilford Press.

Kendall, P.C. (1994). Treating anxiety disorders in children: Results of a randomized clinical trial. *Journal of Consulting and Clinical Psychology*, **62** (1), 100–110.

Kendall, P.C., Chansky, T.E., Freidman, M., Kim, R., Kortlander, E., Sessa, F.M., & Siqueland, L. (1991). Treating anxiety disorders in children and adolescents. In P.C. Kendall (Ed.), *Child and adolescent therapy: Cognitive-behavioral procedures* (pp. 131–164). New York: Guilford Press.

Kendall, P.C., Flannery-Schroeder, E., Panichelli-Mindel, S.M., & Southam-Gerow, M. (1997). Therapy for youths with anxiety disorders: A second randomized clinical trial. *Journal of Consulting and Clinical Psychology*, **65** (3), 366–380.

Kendler, K.S., Neale, M.C., Kessler, R.C., Heath, A.C., & Eaves, L.J. (1993). Panic disorder in women: A population-based twin study. *Psychological Medicine*, **23**, 397–406.

King, N.J., Gullone, E., Tonge, B.J., & Ollendick, T.H. (1993). Self-reports of panic attacks and manifest anxiety in adolescents. *Behaviour Research and Therapy*, **31**, 111–116.

King, N.J., Ollendick, T.H., Mattis, S.G., Yang, B., & Tonge, B. (1996). Nonclinical panic attacks in adolescents: Prevalence, symptomatology, and associated features. *Behaviour Change*, **13**, 171–183.

Knox, L.S., Albano, A.M., & Barlow, D.H. (1996). Parental involvement in the treatment of childhood compulsive disorder: A multiple-baseline examination incorporating parents. *Behavior Therapy*, **27** (1), 93–114.

Kovacs, M., & Beck, A.T. (1977). An empirical-clinical approach toward a definition of childhood depression. In J.G. Schulterbrandt & A. Raskin (Eds), *Depression in childhood: Diagnosis, treatment, and conceptual models* (pp. 1–25). New York: Raven Press.

Lang, P.J., & Lazovik, A.D. (1963). Experimental desensitization of a phobia. *Journal of Abnormal and Social Psychology*, **66**, 519–525.

Last, C.G. (1989). Anxiety disorders of childhood or adolescence. In C.G. Last & M. Hersen (Eds), *Handbook of child psychiatric diagnosis* (pp. 156–169). New York: John Wiley & Sons, Inc.

Last, C.G. (1991). Somatic complaints in anxiety disordered children. *Journal of Anxiety Disorders*, **5** (2), 125–138.

Last, C.G., & Strauss, C.C. (1989). Panic disorder in children and adolescents. *Journal of Anxiety Disorders*, **3**, 87–95.

Last, C.G., & Strauss, C.C. (1990). School refusal in anxiety-disordered children and adolescents. *Journal of the American Academy of Child and Adolescent Psychiatry*, **29** (1), 31–35.

Last, C.G., Hersen, M., Kazdin, A.E., Finkelstein, R., & Strauss, C.C. (1987). Comparison of DSM-III separation anxiety and overanxious disorders: Demographic characteristics and patterns of comorbidity. *Journal of the American Academy of Child and Adolescent Psychiatry*, **26** (4), 527–531.

Last, C.G., Hersen, M., Kazdin, A.E., Orvaschel, H., & Perrin, S. (1991). Anxiety disorders in children and their families. *Archives of General Psychiatry*, **48** (10), 928–934.

Lease, C.A., & Strauss, C.C. (1993). Separation anxiety disorder. In R.T. Ammerman & M. Hersen (Eds), *Handbook of behavior therapy with children and adults*: *A developmental and longitudinal perspective* (vol. 171; pp. 93–107). Needham Heights, MA: Allyn & Bacon.

Lewinsohn, P.M., Hops, H., Roberts, R.E., Seeley, J.R., & Andrews, J.A. (1993). Adolescent psychopathology: I. Prevalence and incidence of depression and other DSM-III-R disorders in high school students. *Journal of Abnormal Psychology*, **102**, 133–144.

Macaulay, J.L., & Kleinknecht, R.A. (1989). Panic and panic attacks in adolescents. *Journal of Anxiety Disorders*, **3**, 221–241.

March, J.S., Parker, J.D.A., Sullivan, K., & Stallings, P. (1997). The Multidimensional Anxiety Scale for Children (MASC): Factor Structure, reliability, and validity. *Journal of American Academy of Child and Adolescent Psychiatry*, **36**, 554–565.

Marks, I.M. (1987). The development of normal fear: A review. *Journal of Child Psychiatry and Allied Disciplines*, **28** (5), 667–697.

Matthews, K.A., Manuck, S.B., & Saab, P.G. (1986). Cardiovascular responses of adolescents during a naturally occurring stressor and their behavioral and psychophysiological predictors. *Psychophysiology*, **23** (2), 198–209.

Mattis, S.G., & Kiel, E. (March, 2002). Cognitive-behavioral treatment of panic disorder in adolescence and the role of comorbid depression. In D.B. Pincus (Chair), *Recent advances in the cognitive behavioral assessment and treatment of anxiety disorders in children and adolescents*. Symposium presented at the meeting of the Eastern Psychological Association, Boston, MA.

Mattis, S.G., & Ollendick, T.H. (1997). Panic in children and adolescents: A developmental analysis. In T.H. Ollendick & R.J. Prinz (Eds), *Advances in clinical child psychology* (vol. 19; pp. 27–74). New York: Plenum Press.

Mattis, S.G., Hoffman, E.C., Cohen, E.M., Pincus, D.B., Choate, M.L., & Micco, J.A. (March, 2001). Cognitive-behavioral treatment of panic disorder in adolescence. In C.L. Masia & E.A. Storch (Chairs), *Treatment of childhood anxiety: Innovative interventions and future directions*. Symposium presented at the meeting of the Anxiety Disorders Association of America, Atlanta, GA.

Miller, P.M. (1972). The use of visual imagery and muscle relaxation in the countercondition of a phobic child: A case study. *Journal of Nervous and Mental Disease*, **154** (6), 457–460.

Miller, L.C., Barrett, C.L., Hampe, E., & Noble, H. (1971). Revised anxiety scales for the Louisville Behavior Check List. *Psychological Reports*, **29** (2), 503–511.

Montenegro, H. (1968). Severe separation anxiety in two preschool children: Successfully treated by reciprocal inhibition. *Journal of Child Psychology and Psychiatry and Allied Disciplines*, **9** (2), 93–103.

Moreau, D., & Follett, C. (1993). Panic disorder in children and adolescents. *Child and Adolescent Psychiatric Clinics of North America*, **2**, 581–602.

Moreau, D.L., Weissman, M., & Warner, V. (1989). Panic disorder in children at high risk for depression. *American Journal of Psychiatry*, **146**, 1059–1060.

Neisworth, J.T., Madle, R.A., & Goeke, K.E. (1975). "Errorless" elimination of separation anxiety: A case study. *Journal of Behavior Therapy and Experimental Psychiatry*, **6** (1), 79–82.

Nelles, W.B., & Barlow, D.H. (1988). Do children panic? *Clinical Psychology Review*, **8**, 359–372.

Ollendick, T.H. (1983). Reliability and validity of the Revised Fear Survey Schedule for Children (FSSC-R). *Behaviour Research and Therapy*, **21**, 685–692.

Ollendick, T.H. (1995). Cognitive-behavioral treatment of panic disorder with agoraphobia in adolescents: A multiple baseline design analysis. *Behavior Therapy*, **26**, 517–531.

Ollendick, T.H., & Cerny, J.A. (1981). Clinical behavior therapy with children. New York: Plenum.

Ollendick, T.H., & King, N.J. (1990). School phobia and separation anxiety. In H. Leitenberg (Ed.), *Handbook of social anxiety* (pp. 179–214). New York: Plenum Publishing Corp.

Ollendick, T.H., & King, N.J. (1998). Empirically supported treatments for children with phobic and anxiety disorders: Current status. *Journal of Clinical Child Psychology*, **27** (2), 156–167.

Ollendick, T.H., Birmaher, B., & Mattis, S.G. (in press). Panic disorder. In T.L. Morris & J.S. March (Eds), *Anxiety disorders in children and adolescents* (2nd edn). New York: Guilford.

Ollendick, T.H., Mattis, S.G., & King, N.J. (1994). Panic in children and adolescents: A review. *Journal of Child Psychology and Psychiatry*, **35**, 113–134.

Ollendick, T.H., Hagopian, L.P., & Huntzinger, R.M. (1991). Cognitive behavioral therapy with nighttime fearful children. *Journal of Behavior Therapy and Experimental Psychiatry*, **22** (2), 113–121.

Öst, L.G., Westling, B.E., & Hellström, K. (1993). Applied relaxation, exposure *in vivo* and cognitive methods in the treatment of panic disorder with agoraphobia. *Behaviour Research and Therapy*, **31**, 383–394.

Parker, G., Tupling, H., & Brown, L.B. (1979). A parental bonding instrument. *British Journal of Medical Psychology*, **52** (1), 1–10.

Pianta, R.C. (1999). Early childhood. In W.K. Silverman & T.H. Ollendick (Eds), *Developmental issues in the clinical treatment of children* (pp. 88–107). Needham Heights, MA: Allyn & Bacon.

Pincus, D.B., & Friedman (1995). *Differential effects of home monitoring and cognitive behavioral treatment for decreasing children's maladaptive nighttime fears.* Master's Thesis, Binghamton University Library.

Pincus, P., Eyberg, S.M., & Barlow, D.H. (2003). Childhood Separation Anxiety Disorder Treatment Program: Using Parent–Child Interaction Therapy for treatment of separation anxiety disorder in young children. Ongoing study, Center for Anxiety and Related Disorders at Boston University.

Pincus, P., Choate, M.L., Eyberg, S.M., & Barlow, D.H. (2001). Treatment of young children with separation anxiety disorder using Parent–Child Interaction Therapy. In J. Hudson and D. Pincus (co-chairs), Parents and their Role in the Etiology, Assessment, and Treatment of Anxiety Disorders in Children. Symposium conducted at the meeting of the 2001 World Congress of Behavioral and Cognitive Therapies, Vancouver, Canada.

Renaud, J., Birmaher, B., Wassick, S.C., & Bridge, J. (1999). Use of selective serotonin reuptake inhibitors for the treatment of childhood panic disorder: A pilot study. *Journal of Child and Adolescent Psychopharmacology*, **9**, 73–83.

Reynolds, C.R., & Richmond, B.O. (1978). What I think and feel: A revised measure of children's manifest anxiety. *Journal of Abnormal Child Psychology*, **6**, 271–280.

Silove, D., & Manicavasagar, V. (1993). Adults who feared school: Is early separation anxiety specific to the pathogenesis of panic disorder? *Acta Psychiatrica Scandinavica*, **88** (6), 385–390.

Silove, D., Manicavasagar, V., O'Connell, D., & Blaszczynski, A. (1993). Reported early separation anxiety symptoms in patients with panic and generalised anxiety disorder. *Australian and New Zealand Journal of Psychiatry*, **27** (3), 489–494.

Silove, D., Manicavasagar, V., O'Connell, D., & Morris-Yates, A. (1995). Genetic factors in early separation anxiety: Implications for the genesis of adult anxiety disorders. *Acta Psychiatrica Scandinavica*, **92** (1), 17–24.

Silverman, W.K., & Albano, A.M. (1997). *Anxiety Disorders Interview Schedule for DSM-IV, Child and Parent Versions*. San Antonio, TX: Psychological Corporation.

Silverman, W.K., Fleisig, W., Rabian, B., & Peterson, R.A. (1991). Childhood Anxiety Sensitivity Index. *Journal of Clinical Child Psychology*, **20**, 162–168.

Siqueland, L., Kendall, P.C., & Steinberg, L. (1996). Anxiety in children: Perceived family environments and observed family interaction. *Journal of Clinical Child Psychology*, **25** (2), 225–237.

Spielberger, C.D. (1973). *State-Trait Anxiety Inventory for Children*. Palo Alto, CA: Consulting Psychologists Press.

Thyer, B.A., & Sowers-Hoag, K.M. (1988). Behavior therapy for separation anxiety disorder. *Behavior Modification*, **12** (2), 205–233.

Thyer, B.A., Himle, J., & Fischer, D.J. (1993). Separation anxiety disorder. In R.T. Ammerman, M. Hersen, & C.G. Last (Eds), *Handbook of prescriptive treatments for children and adolescents*. (pp. 144–158). Needham Heights, MA: Allyn & Bacon.

Thyer, B.A., Parrish, R.T., Curtis, G.C., Nesse, R.M., & Cameron, O.G. (1985). Ages of onset of DSM-III anxiety disorders. *Comprehensive Psychiatry*, **26**, 113–122.

Van Winter, J.T., & Stickler, G.B. (1984). Panic attack syndrome. *The Journal of Pediatrics*, **105**, 661–665.

Vitiello, B., Behar, D., Wolfson, S., & McLeer, S.V. (1990). Diagnosis of panic disorder in prepubertal children. *Journal of the American Academy of Child and Adolescent Psychiatry*, **29**, 782–784.

Von Korff, M.R., Eaton, W.W., & Keyl, P.M. (1985). The epidemiology of panic attacks and panic disorder: Results of three community surveys. *American Journal of Epidemiology*, **122**, 970–981.

Wachtel, J.R., & Strauss, C.C. (1995). Separation anxiety disorder. In A.R. Eisen & C.A. Kearney (Eds), *Clinical handbook of anxiety disorders in children and adolescents*. (pp. 53–81). Northvale, NJ: Jason Aronson, Inc.

Warren, R., & Zgourides, G. (1988). Panic attacks in high school students: Implications for prevention and intervention. *Phobia Practice and Research Journal*, **1**, 97–113.

Whitaker, A., Johnson, J., Shaffer, D., Rapoport, J., Kalikow, K., Walsh, B.T., Davies, M., Braiman, S., & Dolinsky, A. (1990). Uncommon troubles in young people: Prevalence estimates of selected psychiatric disorders in a nonreferred adolescent population. *Archives of General Psychiatry*, **47**, 487–496.

CHAPTER 8

Treatment of Social Phobia in Children and Adolescents

Tracy L. Morris

West Virginia University, USA

INTRODUCTION

Social anxiety is a common, perhaps universal experience. For most children and adolescents, social anxiety is a mere transitory experience. For others it is a pervasive component of their social experience. When social anxiety causes extreme discomfort or results in impairment in interpersonal relations or academic performance, the diagnosis of social phobia should be considered. Social phobia is defined as a "marked and persistent fear of one or more social or performance situations in which the person is exposed to unfamiliar people or to possible scrutiny by others" (American Psyciatric Association, 1994, p. 416). In social phobia, the feared social stimuli (e.g., public performance situations; informal social interactions) elicit characteristic patterns of responding. The classic triple response mode of anxiety includes overt and covert (cognitive and physiological) behaviours. Overt behaviours include escape (e.g., leaving a party early) and avoidance (e.g., school refusal, reluctance to participate in classroom discussions). Characteristic cognitions include a negative evaluation component (e.g., "they are going to think I am stupid"). Typical physiological responses are increased heart rate, muscle tension, trembling, sweating, and blushing. Although all three response modes may be represented to a certain extent, individuals vary greatly as to the primary mode of response. For children and adolescents for whom cognitive or physiologic modes predominate, it may be difficult for others to note the extent of their social distress. Likewise, the overt behaviour of socially anxious children may be misinterpreted by others. Clinging, tantrums, and non-compliance with parental or teacher requests may be evident

Correspondence to Tracy L. Morris, West Virginia University, Department of Psychology, 1124 Life Sciences Building, Morgantown, WV 26506-6040; email: tracy.morris@mail.wvu.edu

Handbook of Interventions that Work with Children and Adolescents: Prevention and Treatment.
Edited by P.M. Barrett and T.H. Ollendick. © 2004 John Wiley & Sons, Ltd. ISBN 0-470-84453-1.

when children are unable to avoid feared social situations. Such responses may be mistaken as merely oppositional behaviour to the untrained observer.

In order to receive a diagnosis of social phobia, children must demonstrate capacity for age-appropriate social relationships (e.g., with family members). For children who appear to lack all capacity for social relatedness, the possibility of a pervasive developmental disorder should be explored. Further, the diagnosis of social phobia requires that the anxiety-related symptoms also occur in the presence of other children (not merely adult authority figures). Note that the term *social anxiety disorder* was introduced in the *Diagnostic and Statistical Manual of Mental Disorders*, 4th Edition (DSM-IV) as an alternative label for social phobia. The terms may be considered interchangeable.

Given the amount of time spent in school, it is not surprising that children and adolescents with social phobia report attending school to be a significant source of social distress (Beidel, 1991; Strauss & Last, 1993). In particular, informal peer interactions (e.g., having to talk to another child, joining peers at recess) have been cited as the most frequently occurring situations provoking anxiety in children and adolescents with social phobia (Beidel, 1991). Among adolescents with social phobia, 60% reported significant impairment at school (Essau, Conradt, & Petermann, 1999). Many children and adolescents with social phobia demonstrate concomitant social skills deficits. In an investigation by Beidel, Turner, and Morris (1999), children with social phobia were judged by independent observers to have significantly poorer social skills than age-matched controls in informal social interaction and public performance tasks. Similar findings were reported by Spence, Donovan, and Brechman-Toussaint (1999) for direct observation of children's performance in a role-play task, and for self- and parent reports of social skills. At this point, it is unclear whether impairments in social skills are a cause or consequence of social phobia. Reciprocal interactions are probably at play.

The DSM-IV provides for specification of a "generalized" subtype of social phobia if the child's fears include most social situations. Similarly, a "specific" subtype has been described in the literature (Heimberg et al., 1990b) referring to social fears and avoidance that occur only in limited contexts such as formal speaking or performing in public. The generalized subtype has been found to have an earlier onset, to be of greater severity, and to be associated with more pervasive affective symptoms (e.g., depression) than the specific subtype (Bruch & Heimberg, 1994; Turner, Beidel, & Townsley, 1992). Among clinic samples, the generalized form is the most prevalent type in children (89%; Beidel, Turner, & Morris, 1999).

Epidemiology

Lifetime prevalence estimates for social phobia vary widely depending on sampling procedures, method of assessment, and diagnostic criteria employed. A rate of 2.4% was found in the Epidemiological Catchment Area Survey (Schneier et al., 1992), versus 13.3% for the National Comorbidity Survey (NCS; Kessler et al., 1994). Comparison with international investigations (e.g., Lepine & Lellouch, 1995; Stein, Walker, & Ford, 1994) and evaluation of methodological procedures suggests that the NCS data may be most representative of lifetime prevalence for the full spectrum of social phobia.

The distribution of social phobia among clinic populations has been reported to be approximately equal for males and females (Last et al., 1992; Turner & Beidel, 1989). Among epidemiological samples, slightly more females than males meet criteria for the disorder, for example, NCS lifetime prevalence estimates were 11.1% for males versus 15.5% for females (Kessler et al., 1994; Mannuzza et al., 1992; Pollard & Henderson, 1988). This is in contrast to the underlying construct of social anxiety that has been found to be slightly higher among girls than boys in community samples (Epkins, 2002; Morris & Masia, 1998). No consistent racial or ethnic differences in the prevalence of social phobia have emerged in the literature (Beidel & Turner, 1998).

The mean age of onset for social phobia ranges from early- to mid-adolescence (Amies, Gelder, & Shaw, 1983; Last et al., 1992; Liebowitz et al., 1985; Öst, 1987; Turner et al., 1986). However, it is quite common for adults seeking treatment for social phobia to report that they have been shy and socially anxious nearly all their lives. Increased social demands (e.g., recitals, parties, dating) coupled with heightened self-awareness during adolescence may account for the peak progression of social anxiety to social phobia during this developmental stage. In the absence of direct intervention, social phobia is considered to be a chronic disorder. A longitudinal investigation of adults with social phobia indicated complete remission for only 38% of women and 32% of men over an eight-year period (Yonkers, Dyck, & Keller, 2001).

High comorbidity rates have been reported for social phobia. The most prevalent comorbid conditions are other anxiety disorders (particularly generalized anxiety disorder) and depression (Schneier et al., 1992; Turner et al., 1991). Although more research is needed on developmental progression, it does appear that severe social anxiety may increase risk for the development of other disorders. For instance, Stein and colleagues (1990) found that in the majority of comorbid cases, depression began *after* the onset of social phobia. Avoidance of social activities in an attempt to decrease social anxiety hinders the development of interpersonal. Children and adolescents who experience extreme levels of social anxiety have fewer close friendships and lower levels of acceptance within the peer group (Morris, 2001). Not surprisingly, social withdrawal sets up a vicious downward spiral leading to depression. Social phobia also has been associated with substance abuse (Essau, Conradt, & Petermann, 1999). As with depression, social phobia has been found to precede alcohol abuse in the majority of comorbid cases (Kushner, Sher, & Beitman, 1990). The "self-medication" hypothesis has been proposed to explain the association. That is, adolescents who experience high levels of social anxiety may find that alcohol and other substances lower their sense of inhibition and general physiological arousal in social situations. With disinhibiting substances as a social lubricant, these adolescents may find themselves much more outgoing when under the influence. Their more gregarious behaviour in that state is often reinforced by others, thus increasing the likelihood that they will use alcohol (or other substances) to confront social situations in the future. Unfortunately, this can often lead to a pattern of abuse and dependence.

AETIOLOGY

Unitary causal models have not been identified for social phobia, but numerous potential causative agents have been suggested. Morris (2001) provides a review of aetiological factors and presents an exploratory model for the development of social phobia. This proposed framework is consistent with a developmental psycho-pathology perspective in which the principles of multifinality (any single factor may lead to diverse outcomes) and equifinality (a diversity of paths may lead to the same outcome) are emphasized (see also Ollendick & Hirshfeld-Becker, 2002). The model suggests multiple entry points that may place a child on the path toward social phobia and, conversely, multiple points at which the course may be diverted. Associations among aetiological factors are not necessarily linear and great diversity may be found in individual aetiological pathways.

As with most disorders, the development of social phobia is probably influenced by a complex interplay of biological and environmental factors. Empirical information on the potential role of genetic transmission in the development of social anxiety is extremely limited. However, family studies indicate increased rates of social phobia among first-degree relatives (Fyer et al., 1993; Perugi et al., 1990; Reich & Yates, 1988). This is particularly the case for the generalized subtype (Mannuzza et al., 1995). Although the specific mechanisms of any biological components of social phobia remain to be determined, there is growing evidence to support an association with inhibited temperament. Behavioural inhibition refers to a generally shy demeanour and tendency to approach new situations with restraint, avoidance, and distress. Inhibition is thought to have a biological component. Increased rates of anxiety disorders in general, and social phobia in particular, have been found among behaviourally inhibited children (Biederman et al., 1990, 1993; Hirshfeld et al., 1992).

Inhibited temperament most likely is neither a sufficient nor a necessary factor in the development of social phobia. The interaction between the family environment and any underlying disposition of the child is paramount. Parents may promote the adaptive development of their inhibited infants, or interact in a manner that may increase the likelihood of future dysfunction in otherwise uninhibited offspring (see Masia & Morris, 1998 for review of parental factors associated with social anxiety). Parents play the central role in providing young children with opportunities for social contacts (Bhavnagri & Parke, 1991; Bryant & DeMorris, 1992; Putallaz & Hefflin, 1990), and parents who experience social anxiety may model social avoidance and be less likely to facilitate their children's social interaction (Daniels & Plomin, 1985). This hypothesis has received support in that adults with social phobia have described their parents as engaging in limited social interaction and fostering family isolation (Bruch et al., 1989; Bruch & Heimberg, 1994; Rapee & Melville, 1997). Of course, retrospective investigations lend themselves to criticisms of possible biased recall. To address this concern, Greco and Morris (2002) conducted a study with children and found similar associations between perceived parenting style and social anxiety. Although more extended observational research is needed, recent laboratory investigations have found parents of socially anxious children to demonstrate more controlling and rejecting behaviour toward their children during joint interaction tasks than parents of non-anxious children (Greco & Morris, in press; Morris 2002).

Dadds and his colleagues have conducted a series of studies demonstrating that parents of anxious children are more likely to model threat interpretations to ambiguous cues and to provide and reinforce avoidant solutions in response to hypothetical social scenarios than parents of aggressive or non-clinical control children (Barrett et al., 1996; Dadds, Barrett, & Rapee, 1996). Further, parents may foster social anxiety by communicating information that promotes hypervigilance and concerns about negative social evaluation. For example, the mother who says to her child "Don't spill that ice cream on your clothes or all the kids will think you are a slob" or the father who says "You don't really want to go out for basketball do you? You know you are not very good at it".

Factors related to the development of social anxiety are not limited to the home environment. Children's peer interactions provide unique opportunities for learning specific skills that are not realized through adult–child contact. The nature and quality of children's peer relationships may play a contributing role in social phobia. Reciprocal associations have been found for peer acceptance and social anxiety in children and adolescents (La Greca et al., 1988; La Greca & Lopez, 1998; La Greca & Stone, 1993; Morris, 2001).

Specific traumatic social conditioning experiences (e.g., vomiting in front of the class and seeing classmates laugh or scream out in revulsion) also have been cited as a possible cause or trigger for social phobia. However, most children who have had traumatic social experiences do not develop social phobia, and a sizable proportion of those diagnosed with social phobia do not recall any specific traumatic conditioning experiences. It is possible that reports of traumatic social conditioning triggering the onset of social phobia are an artefact of selective recall among those already sensitized by pre-existing social anxiety. Some research suggests that children and adolescents with social phobia demonstrate self-defeating cognitive biases, underestimate their own level of social skill, and focus excessively on perceived errors in social behaviour (Chansky & Kendall, 1997; Vasey et al., 1995; Zatz & Chassin, 1985). The role of social cognition in social anxiety merits further investigation. In sum, there appear to be multiple pathways to the development of social anxiety. Multiple biological and environmental factors have been implicated and each factor may interact with others to ameliorate or exacerbate its effect.

ASSESSMENT OF SOCIAL PHOBIA

Comprehensive assessment of social phobia requires a multimethod, multimodal approach. When working with children and adolescents, it is important to solicit information from multiple sources, such as parents, teachers, and peers. Parents cannot be considered the gold standard for all information about their children. Information should be obtained from the relevant individuals who have access to the situations in which the problem behaviours occur (e.g., teachers may provide a wealth of data on the child's performance in school and interactions with peers). It is not uncommon to find inconsistencies in information provided by parents, teachers, and children—and the bases for such discrepancies should be explored. Cognitive, behavioural, and somatic responses should be assessed in a variety of social contexts (e.g., home and school). Implementation of a multicontextual assessment strategy will help guide case conceptualization and treatment planning. The most commonly utilized assessment methods are noted below.

Structured Interviews

The Anxiety Disorders Interview Schedule for DSM-IV Child Version (ADIS-C/P; Silverman & Albano, 1996) is a semistructured interview developed to assist with the differential diagnoses of DSM-IV anxiety disorders. Even though the ADIS-C/P focuses primarily on childhood anxiety disorders, interview questions are also included to screen for affective and externalizing disorders. The child and parent(s) are interviewed separately and the resulting information is combined to determine diagnostic status. The ADIS-C/P includes items assessing children's cognitive, behavioural, and physiological responses across a range of potentially anxiety-provoking situations (e.g., interacting with peers, being separate from a parent). The social phobia section of the ADIS-C/P asks the child and parent(s) to provide fear, avoidance, and interference ratings across 13 social and performance situations.

To assess clinical significance, intensity ratings are obtained to indicate the extent to which particular fears interfere with daily functioning.

Self-Report Measures

Self-report questionnaires are routinely employed to obtain information on anxiety symptoms from children over 8 years of age. The most widely used (and psychometrically sound) measures of social anxiety are the Social Phobia and Anxiety Inventory for Children (SPAI-C), the Social Anxiety Scale for Children—Revised (SASC-R), and the Social Anxiety Scale for Adolescents (SAS-A).

The SPAI-C (Beidel, Turner, & Morris, 1995, 1998) is an empirically derived self-report measure developed to assess the frequency and range of social fears experienced by children and adolescents (8–14 years) in multiple social settings, such as home and school. The SPAI-C consists of 26 items evaluating cognitions (e.g., "what if I make a mistake and look stupid"), overt behaviour (e.g., avoiding social situations), and somatic responses (e.g., "feel sweaty", "heartbeat fast") across a range of potentially fear-inducing situations (e.g., school play, parties). The measure has demonstrated excellent internal consistency and high test–retest reliability across 2-week and 10-month intervals.

Beidel and coworkers (2000) provide data on the external and discriminative validity of the SPAI-C among 254 children aged 8–14 years. Behavioural validation was examined through read-aloud and role-play tasks. Independent observer's ratings of the children's anxiety and effectiveness in the behavioural tasks and the children's ratings of their own distress were significantly associated with SPAI-C scores. More importantly, the measure successfully discriminated not only between children with social phobia and normal controls, but also between children with social phobia and children with other anxiety disorders. This is quite notable given that other anxiety assessment instruments generally have failed to differentiate among children of varying diagnostic groups.

The SASC-R (La Greca & Stone, 1993) is a 22-item measure of social anxiety that focuses on both subjective experiences and behavioural consequences (e.g., avoidance, withdrawal) associated with social anxiety. The SASC-R comprises three factors: Fear of Negative Evaluation (FNE), and two subscales reflecting Social Avoidance and Distress (SAD) with new or unfamiliar peers (SAD-New) and more generalized social avoidance and distress (SAD-G). Scores on the SASC-R have been associated with peer relationship difficulties, such as peer rejection and neglect, and low self-esteem (e.g., La Greca & Stone, 1993). The measure has been shown to have good reliability and validity. An adolescent version (SAS-A; La Greca & Lopez, 1998) also has been developed.

Morris and Masia (1998) examined the association of the SPAI-C and the SASC-R among 277 grade school children. A moderate association was found indicating that the measures assess overlapping, but not identical constructs. One consideration is that the SPAI-C was developed specifically to assess the construct of social phobia as defined in the DSM-IV whereas the SASC-R was designed to assess the general construct of social anxiety. Epkins (2002) also examined the association between the SPAI-C and SASC-R for community ($n = 178$) and clinic ($n = 57$) samples. Results were consistent with those of Morris and Masia.

Behavioural Observation

Behavioural observation is an important component of the assessment of anxiety. Ideally, the child will be observed in the natural setting in which the anxiety manifests. For example, in the case of social phobia, it may be particularly useful to observe the child in the classroom and during school recess periods. However, with consideration and preparation, the clinician may set up situations in and around the office that will provide the proper setting events in which relevant behaviours may be displayed (e.g., reading aloud, delivering a speech).

Peer Report

A child's peer status typically is identified using sociometric nomination methods. The classic sociometric nomination procedure involves asking each child in a classroom to name three children with whom he or she most likes to play, and three with whom he or she least likes to play. Categorization of social status generally is based on two dimensions: how much a child is liked or disliked by his or her peers (social preference) and the child's visibility within the peer group (social impact; see Coie, Dodge, & Coppotelli, 1982). Other forms of peer report include sociometric rating procedures and the Revised Class Play (Matsen, Morrison, & Pelligrini, 1985). Sociometric rating procedures involve asking children to rate their classmates on various dimensions of liking and acceptance using a Likert-type scale. The Revised Class Play (RCP), asks children to assign their peers to various roles (usually positive and negative roles) in an imaginary play. Children might, for example, be asked to name which classmates are very shy. In addition to peer report, direct observation of children's interactions with classmates and friends can provide clinicians with valuable data regarding social interaction style and friendship quality.

TREATMENT OF SOCIAL PHOBIA

Behavioural Treatment

Behavioural approaches to the treatment of childhood anxiety have received strong empirical support. The most commonly employed strategies to decrease social anxiety and improve social functioning are presented below. Formulation of specific intervention goals and methods should follow from a functional analysis of each individual case. However, comprehensive treatment of social phobia in children and adolescents generally involves the integration of several techniques within an organized framework.

Relaxation Training

The most widely used procedures to promote relaxation are progressive muscle relaxation (systematic training involving tensing and relaxing of each major muscle group), positive visual imagery, or a combination of both. When working with very young children, presenting the relaxation skills in the form of a game—such as having the child pretend she is a turtle, stretching out her neck and limbs, and then pulling them back into the shell—may be most effective. Although relaxation training in itself is not considered sufficient for the treatment of social phobia, when practiced regularly relaxation techniques may be useful in lowering the child's overall level of arousal.

Exposure Therapy

The literature suggests that exposure is a necessary component to the successful treatment of all anxiety disorders including social phobia. Exposure-based approaches require that the child face the feared situation(s) and remain in the presence of feared stimuli for a sufficient period of time to allow for habituation and extinction of anxious responding. Such approaches include systematic desensitization and graduated exposure. Systematic desensitization involves relaxation training and the development of a fear hierarchy. Once the child is able to learn to put herself in a relaxed state, items from the fear hierarchy are presented (from least to most anxiety producing). These pairings may be presented through imagery or live in a clinic or natural setting. With repeated pairings, the child is able to remain in the presence of successively more salient fear stimuli for progressively longer periods of time. Graduated exposure is similar to systematic desensitization, but relaxation procedures are not implemented during the presentation of the feared objects or situations. Most clinicians prefer to use a graduated exposure approach when working with children (rather than sustained flooding), working slowly through a hierarchy, gradually exposing children to more challenging situations for increasingly longer periods of time. No evidence is available to suggest that the inclusion of relaxation training (as in systematic desensitization) is a necessary component or even adds incrementally to the success of exposure in the treatment of social phobia. However, when working with an extremely fearful child the clinician may find that the process of relaxation training helps to establish rapport and as such may foster more cooperation among children during subsequent exposure work.

Contingency Management

Contingency management involves arranging specific consequences for performance of target behaviours. The therapist works with the child (and parents) to develop a contract that explicitly states what the child is to do in order to receive reinforcement, as well as how and when the reinforcement will be delivered. Contracts often include a response cost for failure to meet a given goal. Parents and/or teachers generally are relied upon to administer consequences, although some adolescents may be able to self-contract. An example of a simple contract may be as follows: "If Jane initiates an interaction with a peer during recess on three of five days in a school week, the family will go to a movie of her choice on Friday evening. In addition, if Jane attempts to refuse to attend school on any day, she will forfeit her allotted video-game playing time for two days." Contingency management can be an important adjunct to exposure-based strategies in maintaining a system of reinforcement for completion of generalization or "homework" assignments detailed in the treatment plan.

Social Skills Training

Many anxious children exhibit social skills deficits, which is particularly the case with social phobia. These children often avoid social situations in which they may miss out on opportunities to learn age-appropriate skills. Most social skills training (SST) programs involve coaching, modelling, and social problem-solving components. Typical skills trained include joining in activities with peers, establishing and maintaining conversations, developing friendships, and communicating assertiveness. SST components are commonly included in systematic intervention programs for social phobia (see section on multicomponent treatment packages below).

Peer Involvement

Children's peer relationships provide important contexts for social, emotional, and interpersonal growth, and children who experience interpersonal difficulties with their peers are at substantial risk for further complications. It is important, therefore, to identify children's prominent socialization agents (e.g., parents, siblings, peers, teachers) and to solicit their active participation throughout the course of therapy. In peer-mediated or "peer-helper" interventions, children's peers serve as change-change agents and are trained to initiate, model, and reinforce desired change. In contrast, peer-pairing interventions involve strategically matching children with more socially skilled peers and providing opportunities for them to engage in activities together, but no formal training is provided to the peer. For example, a socially withdrawn child would be paired with a popular, socially adept "buddy". This peer pair could be asked to sit together, play with one another during recess, and be assigned to work together on an upcoming classroom project. In general, peer-pairing techniques are less time-consuming than peer-mediated interventions because the peers do not undergo specialized training prior to or during participation in the program. An advantage of peer-paring is the naturalistic nature of the activities, thus facilitating generalization. Outcome data suggest that peer-mediated and peer-pairing interventions lead to improved sociometric status, increased rates of positive interactions, and decreased rates of solitary behaviour (e.g., Morris, Messer, & Gross, 1995).

Multicomponent Treatment Packages

Cognitive-Behavioural Group Treatment for Adolescents

Albano and Barlow (1996) have developed a cognitive-behavioural group treatment for adolescents diagnosed with social phobia. Cognitive-Behavioural Group Treatment for Adolescents (CBGT-A) is a modified version of CBGT for adults (see Heimberg et al., 1990a). CBGT-A is a 16-week program consisting of psychoeducation, skill-building (e.g., social skills, problem-solving, and assertiveness training), cognitive restructuring, and behavioural exposure to socially distressing or fearful situations.

The short-term efficacy of CBGT-A has been evaluated in two studies. Albano and colleagues (1995) reported 3- and 12-month follow-up data for five adolescents; four were completely diagnosis free at both follow-up evaluations, and substantial improvements were noted for the fifth adolescent. In a subsequent investigation, Hayward et al. (2000) randomly assigned 35 adolescent girls ($M = 15.8$ years) with social phobia to treatment ($n = 12$) or control ($n = 23$) conditions. Significantly fewer of the adolescents who participated in CBGT-A met diagnostic criteria for social phobia following intervention. Notably, however, there were no diagnostic differences between the treated and untreated groups at one-year follow-up or in mean scores on a self-report measure of social phobia.

Social Effectiveness Therapy for Children

Beidel, Turner, and Morris (2000) have published the first controlled trial of behavioural treatment for social phobia in pre-adolescent children. Social Effectiveness Therapy for Children (SET-C) is a manualized behavioural intervention that incorporates both peer-generalization and friendship-making components. SET-C is a 12-week, multicomponent program developed specifically to treat children diagnosed with social phobia. Components of SET-C include parent education, social skills training (SST), peer generalization, and graduated *in vivo* exposure. One group social skills training (SST) session and one individual graduated *in vivo* exposure session are held each week. The individual *in vivo* exposure sessions last approximately 60 minutes each and involve exercises constructed to address each child's unique pattern of social fears. The SST sessions (conducted in small groups of 4–6 children and of 60 minutes' duration) focus on conversational and friendship-making skills. Instruction, modelling, behaviour rehearsal, feedback, and social reinforcement are used to teach and reinforce appropriate social behaviour. A unique and essential component of SET-C is the use of peer interaction experiences (developmentally appropriate group recreational activities, e.g., pizza parties, skating, bowling) to assist in the generalization of social skills to situations outside the clinic. Similar to peer-pairing approaches, non-anxious "peer facilitators" are recruited to participate in the treatment on a voluntary basis and asked to initiate and maintain interactions with the target children.

Fifty children (ages 8–12) were randomized to Social Effectiveness Therapy for Children (SET-C) or an active treatment for improving test taking and study skills. The SET-C and study skills programs each lasted 12 weeks and were equivalent in terms of therapist/participant contact. Following treatment, children receiving SET-C demonstrated statistically and clinically significant improvements across multiple domains (e.g., decreased levels of social and general anxiety, increased social skill and performance ratings, and more adaptive functioning in daily situations). These improvements were maintained six months post-treatment. Notably, 67% of children who participated in the SET-C program no longer met diagnostic criteria for social phobia post-treatment compared to only 5% of those receiving the active control treatment.

Cognitive-Behavioural Treatment plus Parental Involvement

Incorporation of parents in the treatment process is a valuable strategy, particularly given the accumulating evidence that many parents may (unwittingly) play a role in maintaining anxious behaviour. Spence, Donovan, and Brechman-Toussaint (2000) investigated the effectiveness of a cognitive-behavioural treatment (CBT) program with or without parental involvement for children and adolescents diagnosed with social phobia. Fifty children (aged 7–14 years) were randomly assigned to CBT, CBT plus parental involvement (CBT-PI), or a wait-list control condition. The CBT components included SST, relaxation training, positive self-instruction, cognitive challenge, and graded exposure. The purpose of the parent involvement component was to help parents to learn to model and reinforce the social skills taught in CBT; to ignore avoidance and socially anxious behaviour; to encourage child participation in social activities; and to reinforce homework completion. Parents observed the children's group sessions behind a one-way mirror and participated in a 30-minute weekly training session while their children were practicing skills in another room. Both interventions included 12 weekly group sessions and two booster sessions (occurring three and six months post-treatment). Although there was a trend for greater improvement in the CBT-PI group, differences were not statistically significant. Both treatment groups showed improvement in social skills from pre-treatment to 12-month follow-up based on parent report. However, neither treatment (in comparison to one another or to a control group) yielded significant differences for children's total number of peer interactions, parental report of competence with peers, or independent observer ratings of assertiveness during behavioural observation from pre- to post-treatment. The findings indicate that the CBT and CBT-PI approaches were effective in reducing social anxiety symptoms, but did not substantially affect social behaviour, thus providing further support for the inclusion of peers in the treatment process.

Pharmacological Treatment

A substantive review of pharmacological approaches to the treatment of social phobia is beyond the scope of this chapter. The reader is referred to Beidel et al. (2001) and Federoff and Taylor (2001) for more thorough discussion of the topic. Selective serotonin reuptake inhibitors (SSRIs) are the most frequently prescribed medications for the treatment of social phobia in children and adolescents. The most common SSRIs include paroxetine (Paxil), fluoxetine (Prozac), sertraline (Zoloft), and fluvoxamine (Luvox). These drugs generally are well tolerated, with only minimal side-effects (Velosa & Riddle, 2000). It has been a long-held contention by many clinicians that when anxiolytic medication is used, treatment success will be enhanced if the pharmacological approach is implemented in conjunction with cognitive-behavioural intervention. Chavira and Stein (2002) provide initial data in support of such a combined approach.

SUMMARY AND FUTURE DIRECTIONS

Social phobia is a prevalent, often chronic, disorder affecting large numbers of children and adolescents. Temperament, parent–child attachment, peer relations, and traumatic conditioning all have been implicated in the development of social phobia, and the condition is probably influenced by the interplay of multiple factors. Knowledge regarding the assessment, treatment, and correlates of social phobia in children and adolescents is expanding at an accelerated pace. In terms of assessment, the last decade has seen a shift from mere reliance on broad band measures of anxiety to the development of specific measures of social anxiety and phobia. The treatment literature has followed suit, with the advent of intervention programs designed specifically for the treatment of social phobia rather than anxiety in general. Great strides have been made in recent years, although the overall database remains relatively limited. Much work remains to be done with respect to controlled trials of behavioural, pharmacological, and combined interventions.

A commonly stated clinical position is that treatment tends to be more effective when implemented earlier, as opposed to later, in an individual's lifespan. Behaviour patterns generally are regarded as less well established in young children and thus more responsive to change. No doubt, certain approaches will be found to be more effective for specific age periods than will others. For too long, efforts toward intervention with children reflected mere downward extensions of work with adults. The trend toward inclusion of parents and peers in the treatment process suggests increasing developmental sensitivity to the needs of children and adolescents.

Early onset social phobia appears to be a chronic condition. However, one would be remiss without noting the vast opportunities for early intervention. At virtually any point in the lifespan a naturally occurring experience or targeted intervention may alter the individual's course. As the effect of risk factors tends to compound as time progresses, making it more difficult to return to a more adaptive path, intervention efforts may have a greater likelihood for success the earlier that they occur. Given this state of affairs, it is crucial that we expand our knowledge with respect to aetiological factors and developmental pathways. It is important that we determine which intervention strategies will be most successful, cost-effective, and practical for which behaviours, at which point in the child's development. The next decade promises much progress toward this goal.

REFERENCES

Albano, A.M., & Barlow, D.H. (1996). Breaking the vicious cycle: Cognitive behavioural group treatment for socially anxious youth. In E.D. Hibbs & P.S. Jensen (Eds), *Psychosocial treatments for child and adolescent disorders: Empirically based strategies for clinical practice* (pp. 43–62). Washington, DC: American Psychological Association.

Albano, A.M., Marten, P.A., Holt, C.S., Heimberg, R.G., & Barlow, D.H. (1995). Cognitive-behavioural group treatment for social phobia in adolescents: A preliminary study. *Journal of Nervous and Mental Disease,* **183**, 649–656.

American Psychiatric Association (1994). *Diagnostic and statistical manual of mental disorders* (4th edn). Washington, DC: Author.

Amies, P.L., Gelder, M.G., & Shaw, P.M. (1983). Social phobia: A comparative clinical study. *British Journal of Psychiatry,* **142**, 174–179.

Barrett, P.M., Rapee, R.M., Dadds, M.M., & Ryan, S.M. (1996). Family enhancement of cognitive style in anxious and aggressive children. *Journal of Abnormal Child Psychology,* **24**, 187–203.

Beidel, D.C. (1991). Social Phobia and overanxious disorder in school-age children. *Journal of the American Academy of Child and Adolescent Psychiatry,* **30**, 545–552.

Beidel, D.C., & Turner, S.M. (1998) *Shy children, phobic adults: The nature and treatment of social phobia.* Washington, DC: American Psychological Association.

Beidel, D.C., Turner, S.M., & Morris, T.L. (1995). A new inventory to assess child social phobia: The Social Phobia and Anxiety Inventory for Children. *Psychological Assessment,* **7**, 73–79.

Beidel, D.C., Turner, S.M., & Morris, T.L. (1998). *Social Phobia and Anxiety Inventory for Children.* North Tonawanda, NY: Multi-Health Systems, Inc.

Beidel, D.C., Turner, S.M., & Morris, T.L. (1999). Psychopathology of childhood social phobia. *Journal of the American Academy of Child and Adolescent Psychiatry,* **38**, 643–650.

Beidel, D.C., Turner, S.M., & Morris, T.L. (2000). Behavioral treatment of childhood social phobia. *Journal of Consulting and Clinical Psychology,* **68**, 1072–1080.

Beidel, D.C., Ferrell, C., Alfano, C.A., & Yeganeh, R. (2001). The treatment of childhood social anxiety disorder. *Psychiatric Clinics of North America,* **24**, 831–846.

Beidel, D.C., Turner, S.M., Hamlin, K., & Morris, T.L. (2000). The Social Phobia and Anxiety Inventory for Children (SPAI-C): External and discriminative validity. *Behavior Therapy,* **31**, 75–87.

Bhavnagri, N.P., & Parke, R.D. (1991). Parents as direct facilitators of children's peer relationships: Effects of age of child and sex of parent. *Journal of Social and Personal Relationships,* **8**, 423–440.

Biederman, J., Rosenbaum, J.F., Bolduc-Murphy, E.A., Faraone, S.V., Chaloff, J., Hirshfeld, D.R., & Kagan, J. (1993). A 3-year follow-up of children with and without behavioural inhibition. *Journal of the American Academy of Child and Adolescent Psychiatry*, **32**, 814–821.

Biederman, J., Rosenbaum, J.F., Hirshfeld, D.R., Faraone, S.V., Bolduc, E.A., Gersten, M., Meminger, S.R., Kagan, J., Snidman, N., & Reznick, J.S. (1990). Psychiatric correlates of behavioural inhibition in young children of parents with and without psychiatric disorders. *Archives of General Psychiatry*, **47**, 21–26.

Bruch, M.A., & Heimberg, R.G. (1994). Difference in perceptions of parental and personal characteristics between generalized and nongeneralized social phobics. *Journal of Anxiety Disorders*, **8**, 155–168.

Bruch, M.A., Heimberg, R.G., Berger, P., & Collins, T.M. (1989). Social phobia and perceptions of early parental and personal characteristics. *Anxiety Research*, **2**, 57–65.

Bryant, B.K., & DeMorris, K.A. (1992). Beyond parent–child relationships: Potential links between family environments and peer relations. In R.D. Parke & G.W. Ladd (Eds), *Family-Peer Relationships* (pp. 159–189). Hillsdale, NJ: Erlbaum.

Chansky, T.E., & Kendall, P.C. (1997). Social expectancies and self-perceptions in anxiety-disordered children. *Journal of Anxiety Disorders*, **11**, 347–363.

Chavira, D.A. & Stein, M.B. (2002). Combined psychoeducation and treatment with selective serotonin reuptake inhibitors for youth with generalized social anxiety disorder. *Journal of Child and Adolescent Psychopharmacology*, **12**, 47–54.

Coie, J.D., Dodge, K.A., & Coppotelli, H. (1982). Dimensions and types of social status: A cross-age perspective. *Developmental Psychology*, **18**, 557–570.

Dadds, M.M., Barrett, P.M., & Rapee, R.M. (1996). Family process and child anxiety and aggression: An observational analysis. *Journal of Abnormal Child Psychology*, **24**, 715–734.

Daniels, D., & Plomin, R. (1985). Origins of individual differences in infant shyness. *Developmental Psychology*, **21**, 118–121.

Epkins, C.C. (2002). A comparison of two self-report measures of children's social anxiety in clinic and community samples. *Journal of Clinical Child and Adolescent Psychology*, **31**, 69–79.

Essau, C.A., Conradt, J., & Petermann, F. (1999). Frequency and comorbidity of social phobia and social fears in adolescents. *Behaviour Research and Therapy*, **17**, 831–843.

Federoff, I.C., & Taylor, S. (2001). Psychological and pharmacological treatments of social phobia: A meta-analysis. *Journal of Clinical Psychopharmacology*, **21**, 311–324.

Fyer, A.J., Mannuzza, S., Chapman, T.F., Liebowitz, M.R., & Klein, D.F. (1993). A direct interview family study of social phobia. *Archives of General Psychiatry*, **50**, 286–293.

Greco, L.A., & Morris, T.L. (in press). Father–child interaction and child social anxiety: A preliminary observational investigation. *Journal of Psychopathology and Behavioral Assessment*.

Greco, L.A., & Morris, T.L. (2002). *Child report on the parental bonding instrument: Perceived parental style and internalizing problems in a community sample*. Manuscript under review.

Hayward, C., Varady, S., Albano, A.M., Thienemann, M., Henderson, L., Schatzberg, A.F. (2000). Cognitive-behavioral group therapy for social phobia in female adolescents. Results of a pilot study. *Journal of the American Academy of Child and Adolescent Psychiatry*, **39**, 721–726.

Heimberg, R.G., Dodge, C.S., Hope, D.A., Kennedy, C.R., & Zollo, L.J. (1990a). Cognitive behavioural group treatment for social phobia: Comparison with a credible placebo control. *Cognitive Therapy Resource*, **14**, 1–23.

Heimberg, R.G., Hope, D.A., Dodge, C.S., & Becker, R.E. (1990b). DSM-III-R subtypes of social phobia: Comparison of generalized social phobics and public speaking phobics. *Journal of Nervous and Mental Disease*, **178**, 172–179.

Hirshfeld, D.R., Rosenbaum, J.F., Biederman, J., Bolduc, E.A., Faraone, S.V., Snidman, N., Reznick, J.S., & Kagan, J. (1992). Stable inhibition and its association with anxiety disorder. *Journal of the American Academy of Child and Adolescent Psychiatry*, **31**, 103–111.

Kessler, R.C., McGonagle, K.A., Zhao, S., Nelson, C.B., Hughes, M., Eshelman, S., Wittchen, H., & Kendler, K.S. (1994). Lifetime and 12-month prevalence of DSM-III-R psychiatric disorders in the United States. *Archives of General Psychiatry*, **51**, 8–19.

Kushner, M.G., Sher, K.J., & Beitman, B.D. (1990). The relation between alcohol problems and the anxiety disorders. *American Journal of Psychiatry*, **147**, 685–695.

La Greca, A.M., & Lopez, N. (1998). Social anxiety among adolescents: Linkages with peer relations and friendships. *Journal of Abnormal Child Psychology*, **29**, 83–94.

La Greca, A.M., & Stone, W.L. (1993). Social anxiety scale for children—revised: Factor structure and concurrent validity. *Journal of Clinical Child Psychology*, **22**, 17–27.

La Greca, A.M., Dandes, S.K., Wick, P., Shaw, K., & Stone, W.L. (1988). Development of the social anxiety scale for children: Reliability and concurrent validity. *Journal of Clinical Child Psychology*, **17**, 84–91.

Last, C.G., Perrin, S., Hersen, M., & Kazdin, A.E. (1992). DSM-III-R anxiety disorders in children: Sociodemographic and clinical characteristics. *Journal of the American Academy of Child and Adolescent Psychiatry*, **31**, 928–934.

Lepine, J.P., & Lellouch, J. (1995). Classification and epidemiology of social phobia. *European Archives of Psychiatry and Clinical Neuroscience*, **244**, 290–296.

Liebowitz, M.R., Gorman, J., Fyer, A.J., & Klein, D.F. (1985). Social phobia: Review of a neglected anxiety disorder. *Archives of General Psychiatry*, **42**, 729–736.

Mannuzza, S., Fyer, A.J., Liebowitz, M.R., & Klein, D.F. (1992). Delineating the boundaries of social phobia: Its relationship to panic disorder and agoraphobia. *Journal of Anxiety Disorders*, **4**, 41–59.

Mannuzza, S., Schneier, F.R., Chapman, T.F., Liebowitz, M.R., Klein, D.F., & Fyer, A.J. (1995). Generalized social phobia: Reliability and validity. *Archives of General Psychiatry*, **52**, 230–237.

Masia, C.L., & Morris, T.L. (1998). Parental factors associated with social anxiety: Methodological limitations and suggestions for integrated behavioural research. *Clinical Psychology Science and Practice*, **5**, 211–228.

Matsen, A.S., Morrison, P., & Pelligrini, D.S. (1985). A revised class play method of peer assessment. *Developmental Psychology*, **21**, 523–533.

Morris, T.L. (2001). Social phobia. In M.W. Vasey & M.R. Dadds (Eds), *The developmental psychopathology of anxiety*, (pp. 435–458). Oxford: University Press.

Morris, T.L. (2002). Family interaction and social anxiety in children. Manuscript in progress.

Morris, T.L., & Masia, C.L. (1998). Psychometric evaluation of the social phobia and anxiety inventory for children: Concurrent validity and normative data. *Journal of Clinical Child Psychology*, **27** (4), 459–468.

Morris, T.L., Messer, S.C., & Gross, A.M. (1995). Enhancement of the social interaction and status of neglected children: A peer-pairing approach. *Journal of Clinical Child Psychology*, **24**, 11–20.

Ollendick, T.H., & Hirshfeld-Becker, D.R. (2002). The developmental psychopathology of social anxiety disorder. *Biological Psychiatry*, **51**, 4–58.

Öst, L.-G. (1987). Age of onset in different phobias. *Journal of Abnormal Psychology*, **96**, 223–229.

Perugi, G., Simonini, E., Savino, M., Mengali, F., Cassano, G.B., & Akiskal, H.S. (1990). Primary and secondary social phobia: Psychopathologic and familial differentiations. *Comprehensive Psychiatry*, **31**, 245–252.

Pollard, C.A., & Henderson, J.G. (1988). Four types of social phobia in a community sample. *Journal of Nervous and Mental Disease*, **176**, 440–445.

Putallaz, M., & Hefflin, A.H. (1990). Parent–child interaction. In S.R. Asher & J.D. Coie (Eds), *Peer Rejection in Childhood* (pp. 189–216). New York: Cambridge University Press.

Rapee, R.M., & Melville, L.F. (1997). Recall of family factors in social phobia and panic disorder: Comparison of mother and offspring reports. *Depression and Anxiety*, **5**, 7–11.

Reich, J., & Yates, W. (1988). Family history of psychiatric disorders in social phobia. *Comprehensive Psychiatry*, **29**, 72–75.

Schneier, F.R., Johnson, J., Hornig, C.D., Liebowitz, M.R., & Weissman, M.M. (1992). Social phobia: Comorbidity and morbidity in an epidemiologic sample. *Archives of General Psychiatry*, **49**, 282–288.

Silverman, W.K., & Albano, A.M. (1996). *Anxiety disorders interview schedule for DSM-IV child version*. San Antonio: Psychological Corporation.

Spence, S.H., Donovan, C., & Brechman-Toussaint, M. (1999). Social skills, social outcomes and cognitive features of childhood social phobia. *Journal of Abnormal Psychology*, **108**, 211–221.

Spence, S.H., Donovan, C., & Brechman-Toussaint, M. (2000). The treatment of childhood social phobia: The effectiveness of a social skills training-based, cognitive-behavioural intervention, with and without parental involvement. *Journal of Child Psychology and Psychiatry and Allied Disciplines*, **41**, 713–726.

Stein, M.B., Tancer, M.E., Gelernter, C.S., Vittone, B.J., & Uhde, T.W. (1990). Major depression in patients with social phobia. *American Journal of Psychiatry*, **147**, 637–639.

Stein, M.B., Walker, J.R., & Ford, D.R. (1994). Setting diagnostic thresholds for social phobia: Considerations from a community survey of social anxiety. *American Journal of Psychiatry*, **151**, 408–412.

Strauss, C.C., & Last, C.G. (1993). Social and simple phobias in children. *Journal of Anxiety Disorders*, **1**, 141–152.

Turner, S.M., & Beidel, D.C. (1989). Social phobia: Clinical syndrome, diagnosis, and comorbidity. *Clinical Psychology Review*, **9**, 3–18.

Turner, S.M., Beidel, D.C., & Townsley, R.M. (1992). Social phobia: A comparison of specific and generalized subtypes and avoidant personality disorder. *Journal of Abnormal Psychology*, **101**, 326–331.

Turner, S.M., Beidel, D.C., Borden, J.W., Stanley, M.R., & Jacob, R.G. (1991). Social phobia: Axis I and Axis II correlates. *Journal of Abnormal Psychology*, **100**, 102–106.

Turner, S.M., Beidel, D.C., Dancu, C.V., & Keys, D.J. (1986). Psychopathology of social phobia and comparison to avoidant personality disorder. *Journal of Abnormal Psychology*, **95**, 389–394.

Vasey, M.W., Daleiden, E.L., Williams, L.L., & Brown, L.M. (1995). Biased attention in childhood anxiety disorders: A preliminary study. *Journal of Abnormal Child Psychology*, **23**, 267–279.

Velosa, J.F., & Riddle, M.A. (2000). Pharmacologic treatment of anxiety disorders in children and adolescents. *Psychopharmacology*, **9**, 119–133.

Yonkers, K.A., Dyck, I.R., & Keller, M.B. (2001). An eight-year longitudinal comparison of clinical course and characteristics of social phobia among men and women. *Psychiatric Services*, **52**, 637–643.

Zatz, S., & Chassin, L. (1985). Cognitions of test-anxious children under naturalistic test-taking conditions. *Journal of Consulting and Clinical Psychology*, **53**, 393–401.

CHAPTER 9

Obsessive-Compulsive Disorder in Childhood and Adolescence: Description and Treatment

Paula M. Barrett *and* **Lara Healy-Farrell**

Griffith University, Australia

John Piacentini

University of California, USA

and

John March

Duke University, USA

INTRODUCTION

Childhood Obsessive-Compulsive Disorder (OCD), a sometimes perplexing anxiety condition, has received significant attention in the research literature in recent years. OCD, once considered as solely an adult disorder, is much more common in children than once thought, effecting as many as 2–3% of children (Rapoport et al., 2000; Zohar, 1999). Often described as *the secret problem* (e.g., Wever & Phillips, 1994), this childhood psychological disorder is becoming increasingly more recognized and accepted by professionals and the community alike as a genuine and severe childhood condition. The result of the recent surge in research attention, research funding and the subsequent development of empirically supported treatments that work, has led to this *secret problem* being identified earlier in children and treated more effectively. Given the chronic nature of childhood OCD and its

Correspondence to Paula Barrett, School of Applied Psychology, Griffith University, Mount Gravatt, Queensland, 4122, Australia; email: p.barrett@griffith.edu.au.

Handbook of Interventions that Work with Children and Adolescents: Prevention and Treatment.
Edited by P.M. Barrett and T.H. Ollendick. © 2004 John Wiley & Sons, Ltd. ISBN 0-470-84453-1.

associated negative impact on school performance (Toro et al., 1992), peer relationships (Allsopp & Verduyn, 1990), and on parents and siblings (Calvocoressi et al., 1995; Cooper, 1996; Barrett, Rasmussen, & Healy, 2001), the current challenge for researchers, clinicians, and the community is to disseminate expert knowledge and transfer efficacious treatment guidelines into clinical practice.

This chapter will present a description of this disorder as it presents in childhood, and review information on the phenomenology of childhood OCD, examining the clinical features, course of the disorder, comorbidity and the cognitive theory of its maintenance. A review of the most popular and psychometrically valid assessment strategies will be provided, together with information related to psychometric properties and clinical utility. Components of family-based cognitive-behavioural treatment will be presented, detailing specific strategies and guidelines for clinical implementation.

Description of OCD in Childhood

The diagnostic criteria for childhood OCD are nearly identical to those of the adult disorder (Swedo et al., 1989), which have changed very little during the last three revisions of the *Diagnostic and Statistical Manual of Mental Disorders* (DSM). According to the fourth edition of the DSM (DSM-IV; APA, 1994), OCD is characterized by the presence of recurrent obsessions and/or compulsions that are significantly time-consuming (i.e., occur for more than one hour per day) and cause significant distress. Obsessions are defined as intrusive and repetitive thoughts, images or impulses that may be perceived as senseless or inappropriate, and cause marked anxiety and distress. Compulsions are defined as repetitive behaviours or rituals performed to reduce or eliminate anxiety or distress (APA, 1994). The criteria for childhood OCD differs from that of the adult criteria in that children do not have to demonstrate insight into the excessive or senseless nature of their symptoms.

In terms of symptomatology, children and adolescents with OCD represent a heterogeneous group with a wide range of clinical presentations. The content of a given child's obsessive and compulsive symptoms often varies over time; however, the overall number of symptoms typically remains constant (Hanna, 1995; Rettew et al., 1992). For example, Rettew and colleagues (1992) followed the individual symptoms of 79 children and adolescents with OCD over an average of 7.9 years (range 2–16 years) and found that most patients' symptoms varied over time and most endorsed all of the common symptoms at some point.

Like the adult presentation of this disorder, the most common symptoms of OCD in childhood are obsessive contamination fears, often accompanied by ritualized and compulsive washing or avoidance of contaminated objects (Riddle et al., 1990; Swedo et al., 1989). Aggressive obsessions are also common in child and adolescent sufferers, with fear of harm to self or others, usually parents, being the predominant theme (Swedo et al., 1989). Geller and colleagues (2001a) examined developmental differences across age groups and found that aggressive obsessions were the most common obsessions in both their child and adolescent samples, and these occurred significantly more than in adults. Furthermore, in Geller et al.

(2001a), religious obsessions were over-represented in adolescents compared with children and adults, and sexual obsessions were under-represented in children, compared with adolescents and adults. Other common compulsions include checking, repetitive counting, arranging, touching in patterns, re-reading or re-writing, and mental rituals (including praying, counting or repetition; Swedo et al., 1989). One study found that hoarding occurs more frequently in children and adolescents compared with adults (Geller et al., 2001a). In Swedo and colleagues' study (1989), it was found that although some compulsions may be tied to a specific worry, many compulsions in childhood consist of actions being repeated until they feel "*just right*".

In the majority of cases (over 90% in one study), sufferers of OCD manifest both obsessions and compulsions (Foa et al., 1995); however, young children with comorbid tic disorder often report a number of compulsions with an absence of obsessions (Swedo et al., 1989). Only a small minority of children with OCD experience pure obsessions without accompanying compulsive behaviours or mental acts. Unlike many adults, children with OCD are often unable to specify the dreaded consequences that their compulsive rituals are intended to avert, beyond a vague premonition of something bad happening (Swedo et al., 1989). This might be a result of developmental limitations, such as language and cognitive development, or it may be that the nature of intrusive thoughts associated with this disorder varies across the developmental trajectory. Obsessional slowness is an even less common, but frequently disabling presentation in which a child or adolescent moves dramatically slowly. In these cases, careful assessment often reveals preoccupation with multiple mental rituals that interfere profoundly with normal activities (AACAP, 1998). In addition, clinical experience reveals that children often develop obsessional slowness in an attempt to prevent making mistakes when completing routine activities (i.e., tooth-brushing, bathing, showering) out of fear of having to engage in excessive rituals. Nonsensically, their slow and meticulously careful routines and rituals are engaged in to prevent *getting stuck* doing other rituals.

Onset and Course of the Disorder

Children and adolescents with OCD vary in the type of onset and the course of their illness. Onset may be abrupt or insidious and may or may not involve precipitating trigger events (Allsopp & Verduyn, 1990; Flament et al., 1988; Hanna, 1995). Triggering events tend to be traumatic in nature for the child and often involve common OCD-related threat themes including, serious illness, death of an extended family member or school-related stress, such as the transition from primary to high school. Studies have found that precipitating psychosocial events might be associated with the onset of the disorder in 38–54% of juvenile (i.e., child and adolescent) OCD cases (see Geller et al., 1998). Age of onset also varies, with reports of children as young as 2 or 3 years of age developing OCD, although the majority of cases appear to have their onset between 8 and 11 years of age (Allsopp & Verduyn, 1990; Hanna, 1995; Rapoport, Swedo, & Leonard, 1992; Riddle et al., 1990; Toro et al., 1992). Research suggests that boys may be more likely to have prepubertal onset, whereas girls may have a pubertal or adolescent onset. Most studies note a male predominance in children (3 : 2), with the gender distribution becoming more equal in adolescence (Swedo et al., 1989).

The course of the illness varies greatly from chronic with some fluctuations to severe exacerbations with periods of remission (AACAP, 1998). One longitudinal study demonstrated that 43–68% of children continue to meet diagnostic criteria for OCD 2 to 14 years after initial diagnosis (Leonard et al., 1993). The prognostic outlook may be a bit better with the advent of refined CBT and pharmacotherapy, however, exacerbations in OCD symptoms are often associated with stressors such as psychosocial change or illness (Swedo et al., 1989).

Comorbidity

Although OCD in children may occur without significant comorbidity, obsessions and compulsions are accompanied by other symptoms and syndromes in the majority of cases (AACAP, 1998). In a study by NIMH, only 26% of the cohort of childhood onset OCD had OCD as their sole diagnosis (Swedo et al., 1992). The most common comorbid diagnoses are other anxiety disorders, with one-third to one-half of children with OCD having a current or past history of another anxiety disorder (Geller et al., 1996; Swedo et al., 1989). A comorbid diagnosis of depression is also common with OCD, with prevalence rates of comorbid mood disorders ranging from 20% to 73% (Flament et al., 1990; Geller et al., 1996).

Tourettes disorder and tics also frequently co-occur with OCD, more so in children than in adolescents and adults. One study found that Tourettes disorder occurred in 25% of children with OCD in comparison to only 9% of adolescents and 6% of adults with OCD (Geller et al., 2001a). One study demonstrated that at least 50% of children with Tourettes disorder develop OC symptoms or disorder by adulthood (Leckman, 1993). Similarly, a second study showed that nearly 60% of children and adolescents seeking treatment for OCD had a lifetime history of tics, ranging from simple and transient through to Tourettes disorder (Leonard et al., 1992). Hanna et al. (2002) found that youngsters with OCD and tics have a different constellation of OC symptomatology than youngsters with OCD only. Although the two groups did not differ in the prevalence of obsessive symptoms, the OCD-only group evidenced a higher rate of ordering, washing, and hoarding symptoms compared to those with OCD plus tics.

There is inconsistency between studies reporting the rate of comorbid disruptive behaviour disorders in children with OCD. Some studies report relatively low rates of co-occurrence, for example 10% of children meeting criteria for a disruptive behaviour disorder, such as attention deficit hyperactivity disorder (ADHD) or oppositional defiant disorder (ODD) (Swedo et al., 1992; Thomsen, 1994). Other studies by Geller and colleagues (1996, 2001a, 2001b) report co-occurrence of OCD and disruptive behaviour disorders (including ADHD and ODD) as high as 57% for children and 47% for adolescents. Geller and colleagues (2001b) suggest that the much lower rates of comorbidity found in older studies might be a result of the exclusion criteria used in these previous studies. Geller et al. (2001b) argue that previous studies often use strict exclusion criteria, including comorbid Tourettes Syndrome, which is frequently associated with ADHD; therefore, the lower rates of

ADHD comorbidity in previous investigations might be the result of the under-representation of children and adolescents with comorbid Tourettes Syndrome and associated ADHD. Other common co-occurrences for childhood OCD include pervasive developmental disorders, body dysmorphic disorder, trichotillomania, anorexia nervosa, neurological disorders, and general pediatric conditions (AACAP, 1998).

OCD and the Family

While childhood OCD appears to profoundly affect the family, causing marked distress and frustration for concerned parents and confused siblings, childhood OCD also appears to be largely effected by specific family factors. However, to date very limited research has actually examined childhood OCD within the context of the family.

It is widely recognized that OCD has a strong genetic component, whereby OCD tends to run in families. A recent study by Nestadt et al. (2000) examined the familial nature of OCD by comparing the prevalence of OCD in the first-degree relatives of 80 OCD patients and 73 community controls. The relatives of the OCD patients were found to have higher rates of OCD compared to relatives of the controls (i.e., 11.7% in comparison to 2.7%). The demonstrated higher than average prevalence rates for OCD in immediate relatives raises the question of how parents might influence the development and/or maintenance of childhood OCD symptoms. Researchers have speculated that parents may model caution, avoidance or fearfulness, which may predispose a vulnerable child to develop OC symptoms (Henin & Kendall, 1997). Furthermore, parental personality characteristics such as perfectionism and cleanliness might also contribute to the development of OCD (Honjo et al., 1989; McKeon & Murray, 1987; Rachman, 1976; Rasmussen & Tsuang, 1986). Other authors have speculated that the parents of OC youngsters may be strict and over-involved (Merkel et al., 1993), lack warmth (Ehiobuche, 1988; Hoover & Insel, 1984), and have higher expectations for their children (Hollingsworth et al., 1980). To date few studies have systematically evaluated these behaviours within families who have a child with OCD.

In a study by Hibbs et al. (1991), investigating parental behaviours in a sample of 128 families who had a child with either disruptive behaviour problems, OCD, or no clinical disorder, results revealed that 82% of children with OCD came from families with high expressed emotion (EE; i.e., criticism and over-involvement). Parents of OCD children showed significantly higher levels of criticism and/or over-involvement than parents of non-clinic children. In a similar study, Valleni-Basile et al. (1995) examined adolescents' perceptions of their family environment using a self-report questionnaire. Adolescents with OCD reported significantly less emotional support, warmth and closeness in their family compared to non-clinic controls.

In a recent observational study examining parent and child behaviours during family interactions, Barrett, Shortt, and Healy (2001) compared observed parent and child behaviours across families whose child had OCD, another anxiety disorder, an externalizing disorder, or no clinical disorder. Results indicated that parents and children in the OCD group could be differentiated from families in the other groups based on parent and child behaviour. Specifically, mothers and fathers of OCD children were less confident in their child's ability, less rewarding of independence, and less likely to use positive problem solving. Children in the OCD group showed less positive problem-solving, less confidence in their ability to solve the problem, and displayed less warmth during their interactions with their parents.

Families also may serve to maintain the symptoms of childhood OCD through their involvement and accommodation to a child's rituals and OC demands. Parents and siblings often become involved in a child's OCD demands as an attempt to try to stop the child from performing rituals, or to decrease the child's distress, or in an effort to hurry the child along. Cooper (1996) investigated the effect of OCD on parents and siblings, and found that family members reported that OCD-related behaviours caused them personal distress, particularly depression, rumination, and being drawn unwittingly into the rituals. Results from this study also found evidence that family involvement in, and accommodation to, OCD was higher in the caregivers of children and adolescents than in family members of adults with OCD. The overall effect of the disorder on family members was profoundly negative with the large majority of respondents reporting at least some disturbance in their personal and social lives. Approximately two-thirds of families noted hardship to siblings and marital discord as a result of the child's OCD.

In a recent qualitative study investigating the effects of childhood OCD on sibling relationships and sibling distress, Barrett, Rasmussen, and Healy (2001) found that siblings of OCD children also accommodated to the OC symptoms and were distressed by the presence of OCD in their brother or sister. Furthermore, anxiety and depression were higher in siblings of an OCD child or adolescent, compared to siblings in a non-clinic comparison group. And finally, this study found that the quality of sibling relationships in OCD families improved with successful CBT treatment of OCD. Taken together, these studies offer preliminary evidence suggesting that OCD during childhood frequently occurs within families characterized by familial aggregation of anxiety and/or OCD, negative family interactions including involvement in OCD symptomatology, and is often associated with heightened negative emotion and distress in parents and siblings. The results of the above investigations examining the impact of OCD on families, and the comparable impact of the family on the maintenance of OCD, highlight the importance of involving families in the assessment and treatment of childhood OCD.

Cognitive Conceptualization of OCD

Cognitive theory offers one of the most widely accepted psychological accounts of the maintenance of OCD in adults. This theory postulates that distorted cognitive appraisals of risk (including perceived severity and probability of risk) and responsibility for harm are central to understanding the development of OC symptoms (Rachman, 1976, 1993; Salkovskis, 1985, 1989). Salkovskis (1985, 1989) contributed significantly to the advancement of the cognitive theory of OCD and proposed that the interpretation of intrusive thoughts as indicating personal *responsibility* for harm to self or others, leads to increased discomfort and anxiety, increased salience of the intrusive thoughts, and neutralizing behaviours. A number of studies using adult samples, including idiographic, psychometric, and experimental designs, have tested central components of the cognitive theory and have found moderate to strong support for cognitive biases of increased responsibility, probability, and severity of harm associated with OC characteristics (i.e., Carr, 1974; Clark & Purdon, 1993; Foa & Kozak, 1986; Freeston & Ladouceur, 1993; Freeston et al., 1993, Frost & Steketee, 1991; Lopatka & Rachman, 1995; Rheaume et al., 1994, 1995; Shafran, 1997; Steketee & Frost, 1994).

Other cognitive processes thought to be important in the maintenance of OCD are thought-action fusion (TAF; Rachman, 1993), self-doubt (i.e., O'Kearney, 1998), and cognitive control (i.e., Clark & Purdon, 1993). TAF, as described by Rachman (1993), is a cognitive process whereby obsessive-compulsive individuals experience thoughts and actions concerning harm as equivalent and see themselves as equally responsible for thinking as for acting. O'Kearney (1998) described self-doubt as a distinctive feature of the disorder in that it accounts for the indecisiveness that is often associated with OCD. He argued that OC individuals are motivated to repeat neutralizing behaviours as a result of the high levels of self-doubt that they experience related to their actions. The concept of cognitive control has been supported by researchers (i.e., Clark & Purdon, 1993) who argue beliefs relating to controlling one's thoughts in an attempt to avoid harm and reduce distress are characteristic features of individuals with OCD.

Only two studies to date have investigated the role of cognitive processes in the maintenance of childhood OCD. Barrett and Healy (in press-a) compared cognitive interpretations of threat in a sample of children with OCD (aged 7–13 years), with comparison samples of anxious children and non-clinic children. Using an idiographic approach, as proposed by the Obsessive-Compulsive Cognitions Working Group (1997), this study assessed cognitive appraisals of responsibility, probability, severity, thought-action fusion, self-doubt, and cognitive control. Results revealed that OCD children reported significantly higher ratings of responsibility, severity, TAF, and less cognitive control in comparison to non-clinic children. However, OCD children could only be clearly differentiated from anxious children on ratings of cognitive control. These findings provide only preliminary support for a cognitive conceptualization of OCD in childhood. Our results suggest that these cognitive processes might become more pronounced as children continue through the cognitive stages of development into adolescence.

In the second study examining cognitive processing of threat in childhood OCD, Barrett and Healy (in press-b) investigated the role of perceived responsibility in OC symptomatology. In a sample of children and adolescents with OCD, perceived responsibility of threat was experimentally manipulated during a behavioural avoidance task (BAT). The effects of high responsibility on levels of perceived probability of harm, severity of harm, distress, ritualizing and avoidance was examined. Based on studies by Lopatka and Rachman (1995) and Shafran (1997), this study manipulated levels of perceived responsibility by varying the presence of others during a BAT and assigning responsibility using signed contracts between the child and the experimenter. Results indicated that the experimental manipulation was successful in inflating perceived responsibility in children and adolescents with OCD, however an increase in perceived responsibility for harm did not lead to an increase in perceived probability for harm, severity for harm, or levels of distress, as hypothesized. The second part of this study involved examining whether cognitive-behavioural treatment (CBT) would decrease ratings across these cognitive processes, related distress, avoidance and ritualizing during a high responsibility BAT at post-treatment. In terms of treatment outcome, there were significant reductions on all the cognitive measures for children who completed a CBT family intervention. These studies suggest that children with OCD report inflated levels of these cognitive biases when compared with non-clinic children, and that CBT is effective in reducing these perceptions of threat. However, the first experimental study (Barrett & Healy, in press-b) investigating the cognitive processes in children and adolescents with OCD failed to find support for the critical role of responsibility, as proposed by Salkovskis (1985, 1989). These findings suggest that the current cognitive explanation of OCD in adulthood may not adequately explain and account for the disorder as it presents in children and adolescents. Continued research attempting to bridge the gap between the adult cognitive model of OCD and childhood OCD is warranted and will advance the current status of treatments available for children and adolescents.

ASSESSMENT OF CHILDHOOD OCD

Accurate assessment of diagnostic status and symptom severity is necessary to inform individualized and targeted treatment development, and for systematic and precise evaluation of treatment outcome. There are several methods of assessment for evaluating childhood OCD, including structured clinical interviews, rating scales and inventories, and behavioural observation systems; however, adequate analyses of the psychometric properties are still lacking for many of the assessment devices. At present, the most frequently used and validated measures in treatment outcome research for childhood OCD are the Anxiety Disorders Interview Schedule for Children/Parents (ADIS-C/P; Silverman & Albano, 1996); the National Institute of Mental Health Global Obsessive-Compulsive Scale (NIMH GOCS; Insel, Hoover, & Murphy, 1983); and the Child Yale–Brown Obsessive-Compulsive Scale (CY-BOCS; Goodman et al., 1989).

The ADIS-C/P, NIMH GOCS, and the CY-BOCS have been the assessments of choice in many childhood OCD treatment outcome studies. Table 9.1 provides a description of these assessment instruments and provides summary information on psychometric data. In addition to assessing diagnostic status and severity, previous research has suggested that it is important to assess and monitor specific symptoms, functional impairment (e.g., across home and school) and symptomatic distress (March, 1995). The devices that are currently relied on assess symptomatology and severity; however, functional impairment and symptomatic distress have typically not been assessed in treatment trials of childhood OCD. More recently, a number of alternative procedures have been utilized in treatment outcome studies of childhood OCD. These studies have introduced an innovative approach to assessing aspects of childhood OCD that have been neglected in previous treatment studies. These measures include the Multidimensional Anxiety Scale for Children (MASC; March et al., 1997b), the Child OCD Impact Scale (COIS; Piacentini et al., 2001),

Behavioural Avoidance Tasks (BAT; e.g., see Barrett, Healy, & March, in press), and an idiographic approach to the cognitive assessment of OCD in children and adolescents (e.g., see Barrett & Healy, in press-a). Given the significant role that the family plays in our understanding of childhood OCD, assessments of parental and sibling distress and involvement in OCD are also necessary, particularly when treatment involves parents and siblings. Table 9.1 presents further information on the above-mentioned assessment approaches, including psychometric data where available.

TREATMENT OF CHILDHOOD OCD

Evaluations of CBT for Childhood OCD

The OCD Expert Consensus Guidelines (March et al., 1997b) for treating childhood OCD, recommend exposure-based CBT as the first-line treatment of choice for all prepubertal children who present with primary OCD and for adolescents with mild or moderate OCD (i.e., CY-BOCS score <19). It is also generally agreed among experts in the field of childhood OCD that, depending on the extent to which OCD impairs family functioning or family dysfunction interferes with treatment for OCD, treatment should involve family members (i.e., March, 1995). A number of open trial evaluations of individual CBT for childhood OCD, involving parents, have been conducted over the past decade. These trials have consistently shown significant improvements in OC symptoms, with mean reductions in CY-BOCS ratings ranging from 50 to 60% (i.e., Franklin et al., 1998; March, Mulle, & Herbel, 1994; Piacentini et al., 1994; Scahill et al., 1996; Waters, Barrett, & March, 2001; Wever & Rey, 1997). Furthermore, these trials have indicated that treatment gains have been maintained at follow-up assessments, ranging in mean time of follow-up from three months (i.e., Scahill et al., 1996; Waters, Barrett, & March, 2001) to 24 months post-treatment (i.e., Wever & Rey, 1997). More recently, two studies (Fischer, Himle, & Hanna, 1998; Thienemann et al., 2001) have examined group CBT for adolescents with OCD in open trial designs. These studies found less dramatic improvements in OC symptomatology, with mean CY-BOCS reductions of 25% (Thienemann et al., 2001) and 32% (Fischer, Himle, & Hanna, 1998).

These open trials have improved remarkably on previous single-case treatment evaluations by utilizing standardized protocols for treatment, including reliable and valid measures of assessment, involving parents in treatment, and conducting follow-up assessments to evaluate treatment durability. Although these trials have provided preliminary evidence for the efficacy of CBT as the treatment of choice for childhood OCD, there are a number of limitations in the trials conducted to date. These limitations apply to methodological flaws within these investigations and include variability in treatment intensity (i.e., number of sessions per client), variability in timing of follow-up, absence of structured diagnostic interviews, absence of blind raters in conducting assessments, and relatively small sample sizes. Of particular note is the absence of randomized control groups in trials to date. Moreover, small sample sizes have limited the ability of researchers to identify potential

Table 9.1 Description and psychometric properties of assessment devices for child OCD

Instrument	Description	Subscales/procedural comments	Psychometric properties
Anxiety Disorders Interview Schedule—Child/Parent (Silverman & Albano, 1996)	Structured diagnostic clinical interview, child and parent versions	Screens for childhood internalizing and externalizing disorders of DSM-IV	• Inter-rater reliability 0.98 ADIS-C, 0.93 ADIS-P (Silverman & Nelles, 1988) • Retest reliability 0.76 ADIS-C, 0.67 ADIS-P (Silverman & Eisen, 1992). • Sensitivity to treatment effects for childhood anxiety (Barrett et al., 1996; Kendall, 1994) & OCD (Albano et al., 1995; Waters et al., 2001)
Child Yale–Brown Obsessive-Compulsive Scale (Goodman et al., 1989a, 1989b)	Semistructured clinician administered interview, assessing symptom severity of OCD	5 scales; time occupied, distress, interference, resistance, and control. Additional scales include; doubt, responsibility, slowness, indecisiveness, and avoidance	• High internal consistency for 10 items (0.87; Scahill et al., 1997) • Inter-rater reliability good to excellent; Total score 0.84, Obsess. score 0.91, Comp. Score 0.66 (Scahill et al., 1997) • Good construct validity (i.e., Leyton survey 0.62; Scahill et al., 1997)
NIMH Global Obsessive-Compulsive Scale (GOCS; Insel et al., 1983)	Single item, Likert scale, measuring overall severity of OCD symptoms, clinician rated	15 points of severity (1 = minimal symptoms to 15 = extreme) on Likert scale, clustered into 5 main groups with detailed descriptions (i.e., 1–3, 4–6, 7–9, 10–12, and 13–15)	• Retest reliability of 0.98 (Kim et al., 1992) and 0.87 (Kim et al., 1993) • Good convergent validity with Y-BOCS (range = 0.63–0.77; Black et al., 1990; Goodman et al., 1989; Kim et al., 1992, 1993)
Multidimensional Anxiety Scale for Children (MASC; March et al., 1997b)	Measures wide range of anxiety symptoms, Likert scale (4-point) self-report, 39-items, age range 8–18 years	Four factors with subfactors including—physical symptoms (tense/somatic), harm avoidance (anxious coping/perfectionism), social anxiety (humiliation/performance), and separation anxiety	• Internal reliability of total score is 0.9 (March et al., 1997b) • Satisfactory to excellent retest reliability (0.79 at 3 weeks, 0.93 at 3 months; March et al., 1997b) • Good convergent validity with RCMAS (0.63; March et al., 1997b) • Excellent discriminative validity between anxious and normal controls with 87% correct classification (March, 1998)

Measure	Description	Comments
Child OCD Impact Scale—Child/Adolescent Report; Parent Report (COIS-C/P; Piacentini et al., 2001)	Impact of OCD on psychosocial functioning, Likert scale (4-point) self-report, 20 items, child and parent parallel forms. Three domains of impairment; school, social, family/home. Four additional items of global impairment; school, home, socially and going out	COIS-P • Excellent internal consistencies for 3 subscales and total score (range 0.78–0.85; Piacentini et al., 2001) • Good convergent validity with CY-BOCS 0.46, and CBCL internalizing 0.40 (Piacentini et al., 2001) • COIS-C sensitive to psychopharmacological treatment (Geller et al., 2001c)
Idiographic Cognitive Assessment in children (see Barrett & Healy, in press-a)	Uses a standardized expectancy format to assess beliefs about harmful outcomes. For example, "If I think _____, and don't do _____, then _____" Uses Likert-scale fear thermometers to rate cognitive processes (0–10). Intrusive thoughts, rituals and expected outcomes are added into the sentence stem for each respondent. These are then rated on dimensions, including; perceived probability, severity, responsibility, SUDS, avoidance, etc.	• Sensitive to detecting differences across groups (i.e., anxious, OCD, and normal controls; Barrett & Healy, in press-a) • Used to assess how idiosyncratic beliefs change over time • Assessment strategy proposed by Obsessive Compulsive Cognitions Working Group (1997) • No studies examining psychometric properties
Behavioural Avoidance Task for children with OCD (see Barrett et al., in press)	Home-based observation task, individualized for child's most severe OCD symptom. Involves exposure to feared stimuli with response prevention. Child is exposed to feared stimuli for a period of 5 minutes without engaging in rituals, obtain ratings of distress, avoidance, and ritualizing using thermometer ratings in Likert-style format, clinician obtains child's ratings either during actual task or immediately following task	• Based on adult OCD studies; • moderate convergent validity of SUDs, fear and avoidance during BAT with YBOCS and MOCI (0.21–0.43; Steketee et al., 1996; Woody et al., 1995) • good discriminant validity with measures of depression and OCPD (Steketee et al., 1996) • sensitivity of detecting treatment effects, comparable to self-report measures and observer rating scales (Taylor, 1998)
Family/Sibling Accommodation Scale (Calvocoressi et al., 1995; Barrett, Rasmussen & Healy, 2001).	13-item self-report questionnaire to be completed by family members of OCD sufferer. Rates participation in symptoms and modification of personal or family routines on 5-point Likert scale from (0) never/none to (4) daily/extreme. Sum of items 1–9 provides a total accommodation score; item 10 rates level of distress experienced when accommodating to OCD; and items 11–13 measure consequences of not accommodating to OCD demands	• Data from preliminary questionnaire development study: • inter-rater reliability and intraclass correlations between 0.72 and 1.00 (Calvocoressi et al., 1995)

predictors of response to CBT for children with OCD. Nevertheless, two studies have shown that baseline medication status is not related to treatment outcome (Franklin et al., 1998; Piacentini et al., 2002) and that a poorer response to CBT is associated with a higher baseline CY-BOCS obsessions score and poorer pre-treatment social functioning (Piacentini et al., 2002).

To date, there has been only one controlled treatment outcome trial of family-based CBT for childhood OCD (Barrett, Healy, & March, 2002). This study, conducted at Griffith University, Australia, evaluated a family-based CBT protocol with random assignment of participants to individual treatment, group treatment, or a wait-list control condition. This treatment study is the first to include randomly assigned comparison groups, following a standardized cognitive-behavioural family-based treatment (CBFT) protocol for children and adolescents with OCD.

In Barrett, Healy, and March's (2002) study, 77 children and adolescents with OCD from throughout Brisbane and the Gold Coast, Australia, were randomized to individual CBFT, group CBFT, or a 4–6 week wait-list control condition. Children were assessed at pre- and post-treatment, and at three- and six-month follow-up by means of diagnostic interviews, symptom severity interviews, and self-report measures. Parental distress, family functioning, sibling distress and levels of accommodation to OCD demands were also assessed at pre- and post-treatment. Active treatment involved a manualized 14-week cognitive-behavioural protocol with parental and sibling components (i.e., FOCUS program). Results indicated statistically and clinically significant pre-treatment/post-treatment change on OCD diagnostic status and severity for both individual and group CBFT. There were no significant differences in improvement ratings between individual or group CBFT, and there were no significant changes across measures for the wait-list condition. Significant improvements occurred as early as Week 6 in the treatment, and continued across time to Week 11 and to post-treatment on ratings of OCD severity, depression and anxiety. Improvements in child diagnostic status and OC symptoms were maintained up to six months post-treatment. Further, there were significant reductions across time for both the active CBFT and the wait-list condition on sibling levels of depression and accommodation to OCD demands. Contrary to previous findings and expectations, group CBFT was found to be equally effective in reducing OCD symptoms for children and adolescents as individual treatment.

Similar to previous studies, these results demonstrate that individual and group cognitive-behaviour therapy, including an active family component, is effective in reducing OCD in children and adolescents. This study offers empirical support to previous investigations by applying a randomized-controlled design, including a wait-list control group; utilizing reliable and valid measures of treatment outcome to a large number of participants across pre-treatment, post-treatment and follow-up; and evaluating a standardized treatment protocol across individual and group psychotherapy conditions. Findings from this study support the short-term durability of CBFT in treating childhood OCD, however longer-term follow-up is necessary to adequately assess the durability of CBFT over the years to follow treatment.

Table 9.2 outlines 11 treatment trial evaluations of the CBT for childhood OCD involving parents, and describes each study sample, design, outcome measures,

Table 9.2 Child cognitive-behavioural treatment studies including parental involvement

Study	Sample	Design	Outcome measures	Results	Strengths (+) and limitations (−)
March et al., 1994	N = 15 8–18 yrs 10 female 5 male	Open trial CBT ± drug or other treatment M = 10 sessions	• Diagnostic • Y-BOCS • NIMH GOCS • CGI scale	• *50% mean reduction Y-BOCS* • *6 patients asymptomatic* • gains maintained 18-month f/u • medication discontinuation in 6 patients with booster sessions	+ protocol driven + reliable, valid assessments + parental involvement − varied treatment intensity (3–21 sessions) and content − f/u ranged from 3–21 months − no control condition − no structured diagnostic interviews
Piacentini et al., 1994	N = 3 9–13 yrs 3 female	Open trial CBT + family only 10 sessions	• Kiddie-SADS diagnostic • CY-BOCS • NIMH GOCS • CGI Scale	• 56% mean reduction CY-BOCS gains maintained at 12-month f/u • 51% mean reduction in NIMH	+ standardized 10 wk protocol + reliable, valid assessments + concurrent family sessions − f/u for only 2 patients − only CGI ratings at f/u − very small sample − no control group
Knox et al., 1996	N = 4 8–13 yrs 1 female 3 males	Open trial E/RP + parent involvement ± drugs Multiple baseline 24 sessions (3/wk)	• ADIS-C/P • Leyton Obsessional Inventory— Child • monitoring	• No clinical diagnosis of OCD at post or 3-month f/u • 1 diagnosis OCD at 12-month f/u • Leyton results varied/inconclusive • Improvements following parental involvement in E/RP	+ protocol driven + standardized parental involvement + structured clinical diagnostic interview − outcome assessment not sufficient − design does not allow for comparative effects of E/RP with/without parental involvement
Scahill et al., 1996	N = 7 10–15 yrs 5 males 2 females	Open trial BT ± drug M = 14 sessions	• Diagnostic • CY-BOCS • RCMAS • CDI	• 61% mean reduction CY-BOCS gains maintained 3-month f/u • 6 patients received 2–3 booster sessions before 6-month f/u • 3 patients w/out BT showed no change	+ family component + protocol driven − no structured diagnostic interviews − rater not blind to intervention − non-random assignment to control group

continues overleaf

Table 9.2 (continued)

Study	Sample	Design	Outcome measures	Results	Strengths (+) and limitations (−)
Wever & Rey, 1997	N = 57	Open trial CBT alone, Drug alone, CBT ± drug 2 wkly sessions 12 daily sessions	• CY-BOCS • CBCL • Global Family Environ. Scale (GFES)	• CBT + Drug • 60% mean reduction in CY-BOCS • gains maintained at f/u (M = 24 months) • 68% remission at post • 39% weaned off drug • comorbid ODD (21% of sample) demonstrated poorer outcome	+ large sample size + family involvement + protocol driven − no control group/random assign − no structured diagnostic interviews − f/u varied (8–60 months) − results for CBT + medication group only (other groups too small)
Franklin et al., 1998	N = 14 10–17 yrs 10 males 4 females	Open trial CBT ± drug or other treatment M = 16–18 sessions	• Diagnostic • Y-BOCS • O-C symptom ratings • Hamilton Depression Scale	• 67% mean reduction Y-BOCS • gains maintained at f/u (M = 9 months) • CBT alone as effective as CBT + drug • No difference between intensive vs weekly sessions • No difference in depression	+ reliable, valid assessments + intensive vs weekly delivery + parental involvement − small sample for comparisons − no control condition − no structured diagnostic interviews − non-random assign. to conditions (CBT/CBT + Med)
Fischer et al., 1998	N = 15 12–17 yrs 9 males 6 females	Open trial group CBT ± drug 7 wkly sessions	• CY-BOCS: obsessions, compulsions, total score	• 32% mean reduction in CY-BOCS • 50% mean reduction in CY-BOCS at 6-month f/u • significant reductions maintained at 6-month f/u for obsessions and total score	+ examined efficacy of group CBT + protocol driven − insufficient assessment − only 1 family session − no control group − assessment raters not blind
Thienemann et al., 2001	N = 18 13–17 yrs 12 males 6 females	Open trial Group CBT ± drug or other treatment 14 wkly sessions	• Diagnostic • CY-BOCS • CGI Scale • CDI • MASC • CBCL • Parenting Stress Index	• 25% mean reduction in CY-BOCS reductions in MASC, CDI, CBCL • no change on PSI pre- to post-treatment • 1 patient did not complete treatment	+ thorough assessment + family involvement + examined efficacy of group CBT + protocol driven − no control group − concurrent other treatments − no f/u − assessment raters not blind

Study	Sample	Design	Measures	Outcomes	Strengths/Limitations
Waters et al., 2001	N = 7 10–14 yrs 4 females 3 males	Open trial CBT 14 wkly sessions	• ADIS-C/P • CY-BOCS • NIMH GOCS • CGAS • MASC OC • CDI • FAD • Family accommodation scale	• 86% success rate (diagnosis free) • 60% mean reduction in NIMH GOCS • 60% mean reduction in CY-BOCS improvements maintained at 3-month f/u • reductions in family accommodation • no change in family functioning as measured by FAD	+ Protocol driven family based CBT + Standardized treatment delivery + inclusion and exclusion criteria + reliable and valid assessments of child and family functioning + structured diagnostic interviews + no concurrent treatment − no control group − small sample
Piacentini et al., 2002	N = 42 5–17 yrs 25 female 17 male	Open trial CBT ± drug M = 12.5 sessions	• ADIS-C/P • CY-BOCS • NIMH GOCS • CGI Scale • COIS • CDI • MASC • CBCL	• 45% mean reduction in NMH GOCS • no difference between CBT alone or CBT + drug • 79% significantly improved (i.e. CGI < 2) • severity of obsessions and OCD related academic impairment associated with poorer outcome	+ protocol driven + family involvement + large sample size + reliable and valid assessments − post raters not blind − no control group − assessments at post did not include all measures − no f/u assessments
Barrett et al., in preparation	N = 77 6–17 yrs 39 female 38 male	Controlled outcome trial individual CBT, Group CBT, wait-list ± drug	• ADIS-C • CY-BOCS • NIMH GOCS • CDI • MASC • FAD • DASS • Sibling CDI, MASC, sibling accommodation	• 88% diagnosis free in individual • 76% diagnosis free in group • 65% mean reduction in CY-BOCS for individual • 61% mean reduction in CY-BOCS for group • no differences between individual and group • no change in severity for wait-list gains maintained 3- and 6-month f/u • no difference between CBT alone or CBT + drug	+ randomized control groups + protocol driven & standardized + inclusion and exclusion criteria + family involvement including siblings + large sample sizes + reliable and valid assessment + assessors blind + f/u across variety of measures − structured diagnostic interviews with parents only − no follow-up of wait-list group − f/u to only 6 months post

results and methodological strengths and limitations. In general, these treatments have been found to be highly effective.

Psychopharmacological Treatment of Childhood OCD

A number of controlled multisite trials have demonstrated the efficacy of antiserotonergic agents for OCD in children and adolescents. Large multicentre trials of the tricyclic antidepressant clomipramine (DeVeaugh-Geiss et al., 1992), and the selective serotonin reuptake inhibitors (SSRIs), sertraline (March et al., 1998), fluvoxamine (Riddle et al., 2001), and fluoxetine (Geller et al., 2001c) have established the efficacy of these medications for childhood OCD with the first three compounds currently approved by the FDA for use in the United States in children and adolescents with the disorder. Paroxetine and Citalopram have demonstrated similar benefit in recent open trials (Rosenberg et al., 1999; Thomsen, 1997). The controlled studies have yielded response rates ranging from 40% to 55% and reductions in symptom severity ranging from 20% to 50%; thus, a significant proportion of medication responders remain mild to moderately ill after the completion of treatment (Grados, Scahill, & Riddle, 1999). The most common adverse effects for the SSRIs include nausea, insomnia, hyperstimulation, agitation, headache, and sexual side-effects; however, these side-effects are typically transient in nature, and the medications are generally well tolerated (Albano, March, & Piacentini, 1999). Unfortunately, an evidence base for guiding medication combination and augmentation strategies in children with OCD does not yet exist. However, given the observed efficacy of CBT in medication non-responsive youngsters (March, Mulle, & Herbel, 1994; Franklin et al., 1998; Piacentini et al., 2002), combined medication plus high quality CBT should be offered to patients prior to attempting complex medication strategies (Albano, March, & Piacentini, 1999).

Only one direct, controlled comparison of medication and CBT for childhood OCD has been published to date (de Haan et al., 1998). In this study, 22 children were assigned to either 12 weeks of the SRI medication clomipramine (mean dose = 2.5 mg/kg) or E/RP. Although both treatments were successful, E/RP was significantly more effective than medication in terms of both response rate (66.7% vs 50%) and reduction in symptom severity (59.9% vs 33.4%). The results of the de Haan et al. study, along with findings from medication discontinuation trials (e.g., Leonard et al., 1991) suggesting that relapse is likely upon medication withdrawal, have led to the consensus treatment recommendation that CBT should be the first-line treatment of choice for children and most adolescents with OCD (March et al., 1997a).

March, Foa, Franklin, and Leonard have just completed the final year of subject recruitment for a five-year NIMH-funded randomized-controlled trial of initial treatments for children and adolescents with a DSM-IV diagnosis of OCD. The Pediatric OCD Treatment Study (POTS), which was the first *investigator-initiated* comparative treatment trial in pediatric psychiatry, is likely to be the definitive study of initial treatment for childhood OCD. POTS Stage I is a balanced 1 × 4 comparison of CBT, sertraline (SER), their combination (COMB), and a control condition (pill PBO). Stage II is a discontinuation trial in Stage I responders to assess treatment durability. Beyond assessing comparative efficacy and durability of treatment approaches, this study will also examine time-action affects; differential effects of treatment on specific aspects of OCD, including functional impairment; and predictors of treatment response.

Family-Based CBT Treatment Protocol

Treatment protocols are universal components of well-designed clinical trials evaluating treatment efficacy. Although treatment protocols have a clear and undisputedly important role in research, the role of treatment protocols in clinical practice is also undeniably important. Once a particular treatment has shown relative efficacy as the treatment of choice for a particular disorder in a particular population, treatment protocols need to be exportable to clinical practice if clinicians are to offer appropriate and efficacious interventions.

One treatment protocol for childhood OCD is the FOCUS program (i.e., Freedom from Obsessions and Compulsions Using Special tools; Barrett, Healy, & March, in preparation). This protocol is a manualized CBT program for children, adolescents, and parents fighting OCD, based on March's pioneering treatment program "How I ran OCD off My Land" (March & Mulle, 1996). The FOCUS program has been adapted from March's original work and includes a structured parent and sibling protocol, and allows for both individual and group treatment delivery.

The FOCUS protocol involves 14 weekly sessions, plus booster sessions as required over the 12 months following treatment. Each session typically runs for approximately 1.5 hours. Sessions include individual or group CBT with the child/group (50 minutes), parent/sibling skills training (30 minutes), and a family review of progress (10 minutes). There are broadly three different treatment components of the FOCUS program, including (1) psychoeducation, anxiety management, and cognitive therapy, (2) intensive exposure/response prevention, and (3) maintenance of gains, including resiliency building and relapse prevention. Component 1 is delivered across weeks 1–5, component 2 is delivered intensely across weeks 6–10 and then is monitored and reviewed throughout treatment, and component 3 is delivered in weeks 11–14. The child CBT sessions focus on psychoeducation, cognitive training, anxiety management training, developing stimulus hierarchies, graded exposure and response prevention, building buffer zones with support networks, and relapse prevention. Parent and sibling sessions focus on psychoeducation, problem-solving skills, strategies to reduce parental and sibling involvement in the child's symptoms, and encouraging family support of home-based exposure and response prevention. Booster sessions provide additional opportunities for children to gain assistance in generalizing the skills learnt in previous sessions. The FOCUS protocol includes manualized therapist guidelines, child and youth workbooks, and parent supplements to treatment (Barrett, Healy, & March, in preparation). Table 9.3 presents a session-by-session outline of the FOCUS program, which was used in Barrett, Healy, and March's (2002) controlled treatment outcome trial of childhood OCD.

Table 9.3   The FOCUS program: Session outline of a CBT family treatment protocol

Session number	Child session	Parent/sibling session	
1	Psychoeducation Developing a neurobehavioural framework Forming an expert team Externalizing OCD		
2	Introducing tool kit Mapping OCD Introduce step plans and E/RP	Psychoeducation continued Physiology of anxiety E/RP	
3	More mapping and step plans Understanding anxiety and body clues Relaxation games	Psychoeducation of OCD How OCD impacts on siblings	
4	Practice E/RP Thoughts and feelings Self talk and bossing back	Parental anxiety management Thoughts and feelings Parents as co-therapists for E/RP	
5	Thought traps of OCD Probability and responsibility Responses to OCD thoughts Review E/RP	Cognitive biases of OCD Rational responses to OCD	
6	More thought traps Ignoring/suppressing thoughts Thoughts = Actions Review E/RP	Sibling anxiety management Mapping parental and sibling involvement and accommodation	
7	Mapping OCD OCD disguises —doubt, slowness, avoidance	Identifying disguises of OCD and ways of managing them	
8	Family problem-solving Negotiating disengagement of parental and sibling accommodation and involvement		
9	Develop step plans for new activities to replace OCD	Rewards for sibling support Review problem-solving	
10	Mapping Support Networks Reviewing E/RP	Overcoming obstacles in withdrawal of accommodation	
11	Mapping what OCD might look like in the future	Planning futures without OCD	
12	Reviewing tool kit Reward ceremonies	Reviewing tool kit Reward ceremonies	
13	Booster 1 (1 month) Review tool kit and prepare step plans	Parental support	Sibling support
14	Booster 2 (3 month) Review tool kit and prepare step plans	Parental support	Sibling support
15	Booster 3 (6 month) Review tool kit and prepare step plans	Parental support	Sibling support
16–18	Booster 4 (12 months) Review tool kit and prepare step plans	Parental support	Sibling support

Note: Shaded sessions denote sibling sessions. Typically, sibling session 1 is sibling alone, session 2 is sibling with parent and session 3 is sibling with OCD child. This can be varied to suit the individual family.

The following section of this chapter presents a description of the key treatment components involved in a family-based CBT protocol for children and adolescents with OCD.

Psychoeducation and Mapping OCD

The primary goal of *psychoeducation* is to normalize OCD as a condition similar to any other medical condition, and develop a neurobehavioural understanding of how OCD works. Stories and metaphors are the most effective way of describing OCD to children, using examples such as a "wiring problem, like in a computer", or "brain hiccups". Stories should attempt to describe what OCD is (i.e., a neurobehavioural condition, involving special brain chemicals), why it happened to the child (i.e., familial aggregation, stressful triggers), how many children it affects (i.e., how many other kids at a child's school/in their soccer club who might have OCD), how it interferes with a child's life (i.e., at school, with school work, with friends, at home), how it is maintained and worsened by avoidance and ritualizing (through negative reinforcement), and what can be done about it (i.e., CBT and/or psychopharmacology). Comparisons of OCD to other chronic illnesses of childhood such as asthma, high blood pressure, and diabetes can be useful in helping families to understand the fluctuating, yet typically chronic, nature of the illness, and the role of environmental stress in exacerbating symptoms. These comparisons are especially helpful for shifting common familial perceptions of the child's OCD behaviour from wilful opposition to a problem that is, at least prior to treatment, beyond the child's ability to control.

Psychoeducation should involve an extensive discussion with the child and the parents of what the treatment will involve. It is important for the family to clearly understand the goals of treatment, and for all family members to agree on being active participants in the treatment. The treatment components are briefly described to the family, using the metaphor of developing a *"tool box"* of strategies for the child to use in fighting the OCD. Exposure and response prevention (E/RP) should be described to the child and parents, so that the family has an accurate expectation of what treatment will involve. An accurate understanding of E/RP and the habituation process by the child and other family members is essential for addressing anticipatory fears and resistance to the initial exposure sessions. As an example, swimming in an unheated pool or lake can be used to describe the habituation of anxiety during E/RP. Initially the water will feel very cold and uncomfortable. However, after swimming for a few minutes, the discomfort will disappear and the water will feel fine. The clinician discusses the role of the family in therapy, formulating an expert team approach with the family. Parents and siblings are described as co-therapists at home, and the child is set up as the captain of the treatment team, setting the pace of the therapy.

In addition to psychoeducation, sessions 1–2 also involve introducing the first tool in treatment, namely, *externalizing* the OCD (i.e., March & Mulle, 1996), which is based on the principles of narrative therapy. Externalizing OCD requires the child and parents to begin to see OCD as a separate entity to the child, an entity that the child and family are fighting against. To help the child and family achieve this, the child is encouraged to give OCD a nickname (i.e., March & Mulle, 1996) and draw a picture of what it might look like. Externalizing OCD is effective as it takes responsibility for OCD behaviour away from the child, reducing blaming behaviour by parents and siblings. In addition, describing OCD as a separate entity to the child, allows for the child, family and therapist to be allies working together against the OCD. Referring to OCD by its nickname allows the child and family to describe detailed information about OCD with the child feeling less embarrassed and defensive about his or her behaviour.

In these initial treatment sessions, the clinician introduces another tool, which is referred to as *mapping* OCD. Mapping OCD refers to self-monitoring, as well as parental monitoring, of OCD symptomatology. Using a fear thermometer, a Likert-type scale, ranging in intensity of anxiety/distress from 0 (no distress) to 10 (extreme distress) and illustrated as a thermometer, the child and family practices within the sessions and between sessions, identifying different habits/rituals and thoughts associated with OCD, and rates these symptoms in severity using the fear thermometer. Mapping OCD allows for the development of a stimulus hierarchy that is used when developing E/RP tasks. Through mapping OCD symptoms at home, school and with friends, the child becomes an expert detective at identifying what is and is not OCD-related behaviour and thinking.

Anxiety Management Strategies

Anxiety management strategies, such as relaxation and breathing, are introduced to the child, usually prior to E/RP, as tools to help the child to reduce his anxiety during E/RP tasks. The child first learns to identify his *body clues*, which are the physiological reactions that occur as a result of heightened anxiety. For example, butterflies in the tummy, red faces, sweaty palms, shaky knees, and feelings of needing to go to the toilet are common body clues associated with feelings of anxiety. Once the child can identify his own body clues, he has a strategy of detecting when OCD might be sneaking up on him, and has an understanding of how anxiety manifests in his body. Following this, the child is taught diaphragmatic breathing, progressive-muscle relaxation and a number of fun relaxation games that can be used when he is feeling anxious, as well as during actual E/RP tasks.

Cognitive Therapy

Drawing on the cognitive theory of OCD in adults (Rachman, 1976, 1993; Salkovskis, 1985, 1989), cognitive therapy for OCD typically involves cognitive restructuring of faulty threat appraisals. For children, however, who are limited by their level of cognitive development, cognitive therapy aims to teach them how to identify their thoughts and "boss back" OCD using more appropriate and positive self-talk. Cognitive therapy begins with teaching the child the connection between thoughts, feelings and behaviours, and illustrating the cycle of obsessions, anxiety or discomfort and compulsions. Children learn to identify thoughts and feelings, and change the way they think using *"self-talk"*. Using their self-talk, children are able to "boss back" OCD (i.e., March & Mulle, 1996) and change the way they respond to threat, replacing the false messages that OCD tells them with real and rationale responses.

Other cognitive strategies involve teaching children to identify the thought traps of OCD, including threat biases of increased perceived probability of harm. Exercises in teaching children to "check the chances" of threat occurring are incorporated into cognitive treatment. These exercises give children a strategy for testing the accuracy of what OCD is telling them. For example, OCD often tells children that if they don't do their rituals, then something terrible will *definitely* happen. Children with OCD tend to believe these false messages, unless they are taught an effective way to actually calculate the real likelihood of threat occurring. Children are taught to break down all the possible steps that would have to happen leading up to the dreaded consequence. For example, a child who fears becoming very sick from touching water taps would break down the steps actually leading to the child getting very sick, as follows; (1) the taps must have germs on them, (2) the germs must get on my hands, (3) washing my hands under water doesn't get the germs off, (4) the germs jump from my hands into my mouth, (5) my body/immune system is not able to fight the germs, (6) I get really sick. This exercise demonstrates that you don't get sick immediately after touching taps, but rather a number of other events have to happen. Once the child can see that a number of events have to take place before the dreaded consequence will occur, the clinician then goes through the likelihood of each step actually occurring. The child then rates the chances of each step occurring as a percentage or a fraction (i.e., 80% or 8/10). Once all likelihoods are estimated for each step, the actual probability of the dreaded consequence is discussed, highlighting the degree of exaggeration in OCD messages. For the OCD child to *definitely* get sick from touching the taps, all of the above steps have to *definitely* happen (i.e., 100% chance) or else the child couldn't possibly get sick.

Other traps of OCD include thought suppression, or ignoring obsessive thoughts, obsessive slowness, doubt and avoidance. Thought suppression (Salkovskis, 1996) is a cognitive process often occurring in OCD sufferers, and refers to the sufferers attempt to suppress or ignore OCD thoughts, which in turn leads to the "paradoxical effect" of increased frequency of the OCD thoughts and consequently, heightened anxiety and increased ritualizing (i.e., Salkovskis & Campbell, 1994; Trinder & Salkovskis, 1994). Cognitive therapy addressing thought suppression, obsessional slowness, doubt and avoidance, involves engaging children in discussions about how OCD traps them into using these cognitive and behavioural strategies. Therapy further requires the child to engage in activities and exercises aimed at disconfirming these OCD traps in thinking and behaving.

Exposure plus Response Prevention

Development of the Fear Hierarchy

In order to facilitate the delivery of E/RP in graded fashion, the next step in treatment is the development of a detailed inventory of the patient's obsessions and compulsions, rank ordered by the degree of distress associated with each symptom.

Distress is assessed using a "fear thermometer" in which patients rate each symptom from 0 (no distress) to 10 (highest distress). The scaling of the fear thermometer can be adjusted according to the developmental needs of the child (e.g., 0–3 scale for a younger child). Symptoms are then arranged according to distress levels with the resulting hierarchy serving as the template for designing specific exposures and determining the order in which they are to be addressed. The stimulus hierarchy is called a "step plan", where children are encouraged to take small, achievable steps with each exposure task to ultimately overcome OCD. Table 9.4 presents two examples of step plans for OCD.

Exposure and Response Prevention

In E/RP, youngsters are systematically exposed to a series of fear-eliciting situations or stimuli and instructed to not engage in any ritualistic or avoidant behaviour to reduce the resulting increases in anxiety. As noted above, E/RP progresses in graded fashion with less distressing symptoms addressed first, followed by more difficult exposures as treatment progresses. Exposures are typically developed and initially practiced in the therapy session; however, most treatment gains accrue from ongoing practice in the natural environment. The most commonly proposed mechanism for the effectiveness of E/RP is that with repeated exposures, associated anxiety dissipates through the process of autonomic habituation. In addition, as youngsters realize that the feared consequence of not ritualizing are not going to occur, their expectations of harm disappear, which reduces anxiety even further (Foa & Kozak, 1986).

Youngsters are asked to graph their distress ratings both in session and during assigned exposures outside of the clinic. Graphing provides an excellent means for children to visualize their habituation to anxiety and allows for immediate and easily understood feedback regarding treatment successes or potentially difficult areas. Following each session, youngsters are given homework assignments to facilitate continued habituation of anxiety and foster generalization of in-session gains to the natural environment. Homework usually consists of practicing the exposure and anxiety management techniques learned in session that week. The child should practice the homework assignments as consistently as possible (typically at least 4–5 times per week) and ensure that assigned exposures endure long enough for habituation to occur (typically 15–45 minutes).

Imaginal Exposure

Imaginal exposures are typically used when the feared situation is internal or not reproducible in the treatment setting. For example, a child obsessed with the fear of failing in school because he didn't check his classwork enough times would be asked to imagine this actually happening. Subsequent exposures can take many forms and might include writing the fears on paper, describing the fears out loud, drawing a picture of the feared situation or outcome, or any other method that serves to habituate the distress associated with the symptom. As treatment

Table 9.4 Example stimulus hierarchies for various faces of OCD

Step	Face of OCD: Contamination obsessions and washing rituals — Exposure and response prevention task	SUDS[a]
6	Take foreign or new objects straight into bedroom and place on bed or drawers. Only wash hands after going to the toilet.	6
5	Only leave foreign or new objects in de-contamination boxes for 1 day instead of 3–4 days. Wash hands only after going to toilet and before eating.	6
4	Don't wash mouth out after eating and don't wash hands after eating. Instead, wipe hands on napkin only.	5
3	Walk around the house without shoes on and don't wash feet other than in shower before going to bed.	4
2	Open fridge door with hand, using the door handle and don't wash hands afterwards.	3
1	Don't wash mouth out after having a drink. Make sure I drink juice, cordial and soft drink in addition to water.	2

Step	Face of OCD: Feeling "just right" compulsions — Exposure and response prevention task	SUDS[a]
6	Do not lick my fingers after I have dried off from a shower or after I have dried off from the pool.	6
5	Dry my toes with my bath towel after I have had my shower and after I have had a swim in the pool, and do not lick my fingers.	6
4	Do not answer questions for other people. Do not answer for my brother when mum asks him something and do not say answers out loud in the classroom unless the teacher asks me the question.	5
3	Wear my school shirt tucked in and do not adjust it until after I go to the toilet and I have to tuck it in again. Do not kick my feet into my school shoes when my feet feel funny.	4
2	Screw up paper and do not lick my fingers. Wear under pants instead of satin boxer shorts and do not lick my fingers after putting them on.	3
1	Do not adjust any doors or windows at home. Leave doors as they are, and at night leave my bedroom door open, with the latch on it, and have my bedroom window either fully open or closed.	3

[a] SUDS: subjective units of distress, 0 = none at all; 6 = worst imaginable.

progresses, imaginal exposures are often recorded on endless loop audiotapes for youngsters to listen to in between therapy sessions. It is important to note that the stated goal of treating obsessions is typically not to eliminate the obsession entirely, but rather to reduce the emotional intensity and negative valence of the thought to the point that it is no longer bothersome or anxiety provoking to the youngster.

Behavioural Reward Program

A behavioural reward program in which children are systematically rewarded for completing in-session tasks and homework assignments is often useful for maximizing treatment compliance. However, given the variable nature of response to treatment for some cases, youngsters should be rewarded for attempting or completing therapy assignments rather than for actual levels of symptom reduction.

SUMMARY AND FUTURE DIRECTIONS

Childhood OCD is characterized by recurrent, chronic and often disabling symptoms. This disorder in childhood is often complicated by high comorbidity with other emotional disorders, typically anxiety and depressive disorders; elevated family distress and in some cases dysfunction; and is often associated with significant disruption in a child's academic and social life. Research into this childhood disorder has advanced considerably over the past decade, with particular progress being made in treatment efficacy research. Over the past decade a number of open trial evaluations of exposure-based CBT have been published, supporting the effectiveness of this treatment approach. More recently Barrett, Healy, and March's (2002) controlled evaluation of CBT for childhood OCD has been completed, demonstrating strong support for a developmentally sensitive, family-based individual and group CBT protocol.

Although we have made considerable advances in knowledge and the development of treatment guidelines that work, research into childhood OCD remains conspicuously limited in comparison to research into adult OCD. The exportability of treatment protocols to other clinical settings, and with more complex clients (i.e., with comorbid Tourettes syndrome, tic disorder, obsessional slowness) requires further research, including studies conducted across multiple sites. Further research is also necessary to evaluate the relative efficacy of CBT with and without medication in a controlled trial. Given the potentially significant role that families play in the maintenance of childhood OCD, treatments need to address family interactions and involvement in OCD symptoms, to improve the quality of family relationships and to improve treatment response and durability of treatment outcomes. Although results of treatment trials to date appear encouraging, it remains to be shown whether treatment gains are maintained at longer follow-up assessments. Factors that predict treatment responsiveness and treatment resistance are also yet to be systematically evaluated. As research continues to address these areas of uncertainty, the exportability of research-based treatment protocols into community clinical settings will surely pursue and be of great benefit to youngsters with OCD and their families.

REFERENCES

AACAP (1998). Practice parameters for the assessment and treatment of children and adolescents with obsessive-compulsive disorder. *Journal American Academy of Child and Adolescent Psychiatry*, **37** (suppl. 10), 27s–45s.

Albano, A., Knox, L.S., & Barlow, D.H. (1995). Obsessive-compulsive disorder. In A.E. Eisen, C.A. Kearney, & C.H. Schaefer (Eds), *Clinical handbook of anxiety disorders in children and adolescents* (pp. 282–316). New Jersey: Jason Aronson.

Albano, A., March, J., & Piacentini, J. (1999). Cognitive-behavioural treatment of obsessive-compulsive disorder. In R. Ammerman, M. Hersen, & C. Last (Eds), *Handbook of prescriptive treatments for children and adolescents* (pp. 193–215). Boston: Allyn & Bacon.

Allsopp, M., & Verduyn, C. (1990). Adolescents with obsessive-compulsive disorder: A case note review of consecutive patients referred to a provincial regional adolescent psychiatry unit. *Journal of Adolescence*, **13**, 157–169.

American Psychiatric Association. (1994). *Diagnostic and statistical manual of mental disorders* (4th edn). Washington, DC: Author.

Barrett, P.M., & Healy, L.J. (in press-a). An examination of the cognitive processes involved in childhood obsessive-compulsive disorder. *Behaviour, Research and Therapy.*

Barrett, P.M., & Healy, L.J. (in press-b). An examination of the cognitive processes involved in childhood obsessive-compulsive disorder. *Journal of Child and Adolescent Psychology.*

Barrett, P.M., Dadds, M.R., & Rapee, R.M. (1996). Family treatment of childhood anxiety: A controlled trial. *Journal of Consulting and Clinical Psychology*, **64**, 333–342.

Barrett, P.M., Healy, L.J., & March, J.S. (in press). Behavioural avoidance task for childhood obsessive-compulsive disorder: A home based observation. *American Journal of Psychotherapy.*

Barrett, P.M., Healy, L.J., & March, J.S. (2002). *Cognitive-behavioural family treatment of childhood obsessive-compulsive disorder: A controlled trial.* Manuscript Submitted.

Barrett, P.M. Healy, L.J., & March, J.S. (in preparation). *FOCUS: Freedom from obsessions and compulsions using skills. Therapist Manual and Workbooks*. Mount Gravatt, Brisbane: Griffith University.

Barrett, P.M., Rasmussen, P.J., & Healy, L. (2001). The effect of obsessive-compulsive disorder on sibling relationships in late childhood and early adolescence: Preliminary findings. *The Australian Educational and Developmental Psychologist*, **17** (2), 82–102.

Barrett, P.M., Shortt, A.L., & Healy, L.J. (2001). Does parent and child behaviours differentiate families whose children have obsessive-compulsive disorder from other clinic and non-clinic families? *Journal of Child Psychology and Psychiatry and Allied Disciplines*, **43** (5), 597–607.

Black, D.W., Kelly, M., Myers, C., & Noyes, R. (1990). Tritiated imipramine binding in obsessive-compulsive volunteers and psychiatrically normal controls. *Biological Psychiatry*, **27** (3), 319–327.

Calvocoressi, L., Lewis, B., Harris, M., Trufan, S.J., Goodman, W.K., McDougle, C.J., & Price, L.H. (1995). Family accommodation of obsessive-compulsive disorder. *American Journal of Psychiatry*, **152**, 441–443.

Carr, A.T. (1974). Compulsive neurosis: A review of the literature. *Psychological Bulletin*, **81**, 311–318.

Clark, A.C., & Purdon, C. (1993). New perspective's for a cognitive theory of obsessions. *Australian Psychologist*, **28** (3), 161–167.

Cooper, M. (1996). Obsessive compulsive disorder: Effects on family members. *American Journal of Orthopsychiatry*, **66**, 296–304.

de Haan, E., Hoogduin, K.A., Buitelaar, J., & Keijser, S. (1998). Behavior therapy versus clomipramine for the treatment of obsessive-compulsive disorder. *Journal of the American Academy of Child & Adolescent Psychiatry*, **37**, 1022–1029.

DeVeaugh-Geiss, J., Moroz, G., Biederman, J., Cantwell, D., Fontaine, R., Greist, J.H., Reichler, R., Katz, R., & Landau, P. (1992). Clomipramine hydrochloride in childhood and adolescent obsessive-compulsive disorder—a multicenter trial. *Journal of American Academy of Child and Adolescent Psychiatry*, **31**, 45.

Ehiobuche, I. (1988). Obsessive-compulsive neurosis in relation to parental child-rearing patterns amongst Greek, Italian, and Anglo-Australian subjects. *Acta Psychiatrica Scandinavica*, **78**, 115–120.

Fischer, D.J., Himle, J.A., & Hanna, G.L. (1998). Group behavioural therapy for adolescents with obsessive-compulsive disorder: Preliminary outcomes. *Research on Social Work*, **8** (6), 629–636.

Flament, M.F., Koby, E., Rapoport, J.L., Berg, J., Zahn, T., Cox, C., Denckla, M., & Lenane, M. (1990). Obsessive-compulsive disorder: A prospective follow-up study. *Journal of Child Psychology and Psychiatry*, **31**, 363–380.

Flament, M.F., Rapoport, J.L., Berg, C.Z., Screery, W., Whitaker, A., Davies, M., Kalikow, K., & Shaffer, D. (1988). Obsessive-compulsive disorder in adolescence: An epidemiological study. *Journal of the American Academy of Child and Adolescent Psychiatry*, **27**, 764–771.

Foa, E.B., & Kozak, M.J. (1986). Emotional processing of fear: Exposure to corrective information. *Psychological Bulletin*, **99**, 20–35.

Foa, E.B., Kozak, M.J., Goodman, W.K., Hollander, E., Jenike, M.A., & Rasmussen, S.A. (1995). DSM-IV field trial: Obsessive-compulsive disorder. *American Journal of Psychiatry*, **152** (4), 654.

Franklin, M.E., Kozak, M.J., Cashman, L.A., Coles, M.E., Rheingold, A.A., & Foa, E.B. (1998). Cognitive-behavioural treatment of pediatric obsessive-compulsive disorder: An open clinical trial. *Journal of American Academy of Child and Adolescent Psychiatry*, **37** (4), 412–419.

Freeston, M.H., & Ladouceur, R. (1993). Appraisals of cognitive intrusions and response style: replication and extension. *Behaviour Research and Therapy*, **31** (2), 185–191.

Freeston, M., Ladouceur, R., Gagnon, F., & Thibodeau, N. (1993). Beliefs about obsessional thoughts. *Journal of Psychopathology and Behavioural Assessment*, **15**, 1–21.

Frost, R.O., & Steketee, G. (1991, November). *Familial and background characteristics of nonclinical compulsives.* Paper presented at the annual meeting of the Association for Advancement of Behaviour Therapy, New York.

Geller, D., Beiderman, J., Griffin, S., Jones, J., & Lefkowitz, T.R. (1996). Comorbidity of juvenile obsessive-compulsive disorder with disruptive behaviour disorders: A review and a report. *Journal American Academy of Child and Adolescent Psychiatry*, **35**, 1637–1646.

Geller, D., Biederman, J., Jones, J., Park, K., Schwartz, S., Shapiro, S., & Coffey, B. (1998). Is juvenile obsessive-compulsive disorder a developmental subtype of the disorder? A review of the pediatric literature. *Journal of the American Academy of Child and Adolescent Psychiatry*, **37** (4), 420–427.

Geller, D., Biederman, J., Faraone, S., Agranat, A., Cradlock, K., Hagermoser, L., Kim, G., Frazier, J., & Coffey, B. (2001a). Developmental aspects of obsessive-compulsive disorder: Findings in children, adolescents and adults. *The Journal of Nervous and Mental Disease*, **189** (7), 471–477.

Geller, D., Biederman, J., Faraone, S., Bellordre, C.A., Kim, G.S., Hagermoser, L., Cradlock, K., Frazier, J., & Coffey, B.J. (2001b). Disentangling chronological age from age of onset I children and adolescents with obsessive-compulsive disorder. *International Journal of Neuropsychopharmacology*, **4**, 169–178.

Geller, D.A., Hoog, S.L., Heiligenstein, J.H., Ricardi, R.K., Tamura, R., Kluszynski, S., & Jacobson, J.G. (2001c). The fluoxetine pediatric OCD study team, US fluoxetine treatment for obsessive-compulsive disorder in children and adolescents: A placebo-controlled clinical trial. *Journal of the American Academy of Child and Adolescent Psychiatry*, **40** (7), 773–779.

Goodman, W.K., Price, L.H., Rasmussen, S.A., Mazure, C., Fleischmann, R.L., Hill, C.L., Heninger, G.R., & Charney, D.S. (1989a). The Yale–Brown Obsessive-Compulsive Scale (Y-BOCS): Development, use and reliability. *Archives of General Psychiatry*, **46**, 1006–1011.

Grados, M., Scahill, L., & Riddle, M. (1999). Pharmacotherapy in children and adolescents with obsessive-compulsive disorder. *Child and Adolescent Psychiatric Clinics of North America*, **8**, 617.

Hanna, G.L. (1995). Demographic and clinical features of obsessive-compulsive disorder in children and adolescents. *Journal of the American Academy of Child and Adolescent Psychiatry*, **34**, 19–27.

Hanna, G., Piacentini, J., Cantwell, D., Fischer, D., Himle, J., & Van Etten, M. (2002). Obsessive-compulsive disorder with and without tics in a clinical sample of children and adolescents, *Depression and Anxiety*, **16**, 59–63.

Henin, A., & Kendall, P.C. (1997). Obsessive-compulsive disorder in childhood and adolescence. *Advances in Clinical Child Psychology*, **19**, 75–131.

Hibbs, E.D., Hamburger, S.D., Lenane, M., Rapoport, J.L., Kruesi, M.J.P., Keysor, C.S., & Goldstein, M.J. (1991). Determinants of expressed emotion in families of disturbed and normal children. *Journal of Child Psychology and Psychiatry*, **32**, 757–770.

Hollingsworth, C.E., Tanguay, P.E., Grossman, L., & Pabst, P. (1980). Long-term outcome of obsessive compulsive disorder in childhood. *Journal of the American Academy of Child and Adolescent Psychiatry*, **19**, 134–144.

Honjo, S., Hirano, C., Musase, S., Kaneko, T., Sugiyama, T., Ohtaka, K., Aoyama, T., Takei, Y., Inoko, K., & Wakabayashi, S. (1989). Obsessive-compulsive disorder symptoms in childhood and adolescence. *Acta Psychiatrica Scandinavica*, **80**, 83–91.

Hoover, C.F., & Insel, T.R. (1984). Families of origin in obsessive-compulsive disorder. *Journal of Nervous and Mental Disease*, **172**, 207–215.

Insel, T.R., Hoover, C., & Murphy, D.L. (1983). Parents of patients with obsessive-compulsive disorder. *Psychological Medicine*, **13** (4), 807–811.

Kendall, P.C. (1994). Treating anxiety disorders in children: Results of a randomised clinical trial. *Journal of Consulting and Clinical Psychology*, **62**, 100–110.

Kim, S.W., Dysken, M.W., & Kuskowski, M. (1992). The Symptom Checklist-90: Obsessive-Compulsive Subscale: A reliability and validity study. *Psychiatry Research*, **41** (1), 37–44.

Kim, S.W., Dysken, M.W., Kuskowski, M., & Hoover, K.M. (1993). The Yale-Brown Obsessive Compulsive Scale and the NIMH Global Obsessive Compulsive Scale (NIMH-GOCS): A reliability and validity study. *International Journal of Methods in Psychiatric Research*, **3** (1), 37–44.

Knox, L., Albano, A., & Barlow, D. (1996). Parental involvement in the treatment of childhood obsessive-compulsive disorder: A multiple baseline examination involving parents. *Behaviour Therapy*, **27**, 93–114.

Leckman, J.F. (1993). Tourette's Syndrome. In E. Hollander (Ed.), *Obsessive-compulsive related disorders* (pp. 113–138). Washington, DC: American Psychiatric Press.

Leonard, H.L., Lenane, M.C., Swedo, S.E., Rettew, D.C., Hamburger, S.D., Bartko, J.J., & Rapoport, J.L. (1992). Tics and Tourette's disorder: A 2- to 7-year follow-up of 54 obsessive-compulsive children. *American Journal of Psychiatry*, **149**, 1244–1251.

Leonard, H.L., Swedo, S.E., Lenane, M.C., Rettew, D.C., Cheslow, D.L, Hamburger, S.D., & Rapoport, J.L. (1991). A double-blind desipramine substitution during long-term clomipramine treatment in children and adolescents with obsessive-compulsive disorder. *Archives of General Psychiatry*, **48** (10), 922–927.

Leonard, H., Swedo, S., Lenane, M., Rettew, D.C., Hamburger, S.D., Bartko, J.J., & Rapoport, J.L. (1993). A two to seven year follow-up study of 54 obsessive compulsive children and adolescents. *Archives of General Psychiatry*, **50**, 429.

Lopatka, C., & Rachman, S. (1995). Perceived responsibility and compulsive checking: An experimental analysis. *Behaviour Research and Therapy*, **33** (6), 673–684.

March, J.S. (1995). Cognitive behavioural psychotherapy for children and adolescents with OCD: A review and recommendations for treatment. *Journal of the American Academy of Child and Adolescent Psychiatry*, **34**, 7–18.

March, J. (1998). Manual for the Multidimensional Anxiety Scale for Children (MASC). Toronto: MultiHealth Systems.

March, J.S., & Mulle, K. (1996). Banishing OCD: Cognitive-behavioural psychotherapy for obsessive-compulsive disorders. In E.D. Hibbs & P.S. Jensen (Eds), *Psychosocial treatments for child and adolescent disorders: Empirically based strategies for clinical practice* (pp. 83–102). Washington, DC: American Psychological Association.

March, J.S., Mulle, K., & Herbel, B. (1994). Behavioural psychotherapy for children and adolescents with obsessive-compulsive disorder: An open clinical trial of a new protocol driven treatment package. *Journal of American Academy of Child and Adolescent Psychiatry*, **33** (3), 333–341.

March, J., Biederman, J., Wolkow, R., Safferman, A., Mardekian, J., Cook, E.H., Cutler, N., Dominguez, R., Ferguson, J., Muller, B., Riesenberg, R., Rosenthal, M., Sallee, F.R., & Wagner, K. (1998). Sertraline in children and adolescents with obsessive-compulsive disorder: A multicenter randomized controlled trial. *Journal of the American Medical Association*, **280**, 1752.

March, J., Frances, A., Carpenter, D., & Kahn, D. (1997a). Expert consensus guidelines: treatment of obsessive-compulsive disorder. *Journal of Clinical Psychology*, **58**, 1.

March, J.S., Parker, J.D.A., Sullivan, K., Stallings, P., & Conners, C.K. (1997b). The Multidimensional Anxiety Scale for Children (MASC): Factor structure, reliability, and validity. *Journal of the American Academy of Child and Adolescent Psychiatry*, **36**, 554–565.

McKeon, P., & Murray, R. (1987). Familial aspects of obsessive-compulsive neurosis. *British Journal of Psychiatry*, **151**, 528–534.

Merkel, W.T., Pollard, C.A., Wiener, R.L., & Staebler, C.R. (1993). Perceived parental characteristics of patients with obsessive-compulsive disorder, depression, and panic disorder. *Child Psychiatry and Human Development*, **24**, 49–57.

Nesdadt, G., Samuels, J., Riddle, M., Beinvenu, J.O., Llang, K.Y., LaBuda, M., Walkup, J., Grados, M., & Hoehn-Saric, R. (2000). A family study of obsessive compulsive disorder. *Archives of General Psychiatry*, **57**, 358–363.

Obsessive-Compulsive Cognitions Working Group (1997). Cognitive assessment of obsessive-compulsive disorder. *Behaviour Research and Therapy*, **35** (7), 667–681.

O'Kearney, R. (1998). Responsibility Appraisals and Obsessive-Compulsive Disorder: A critique of Salkovskis's cognitive theory. *Australian Journal of Psychology*, **50**, 43–47.

Piacentini, J., Bergman, R.L., Jacobs, C., McCracken, J., & Kretchman, J. (2002). Cognitive-behaviour therapy for childhood obsessive-compulsive disorder: Efficacy and predictors of treatment response. *Journal of Anxiety Disorders*, **16**, 207–219.

Piacentini, J., Gitow, A., Jaffer, M., Graae, F., & Whitaker, A. (1994). Outpatient behavioural treatment of child and adolescent obsessive-compulsive disorder. *Journal of Anxiety Disorders*, **8**, 277–289.

Piacentini, J., Jaffer, M., Bergman, R.L., McCracken, J., & Keller, M. (2001). Measuring impairment in childhood OCD: Psychometric properties of the COIS. *Proceedings of the American Academy of Child and Adolescent Psychiatry Meeting*, **48**, 146.

Rachman, S. (1976). Obsessive-compulsive checking. *Behaviour Research and Therapy*, **14**, 169–277.

Rachman, S. (1993). Obsessions, responsibility, and guilt. *Behaviour Research and Therapy*, **31** (2), 149–154.

Rapoport, J.L., Swedo, S.E., & Leonard, H.L. (1992). Childhood obsessive-compulsive disorder. *Journal of Clinical Psychiatry*, **53**, 11–16.

Rapoport, J.L., Inoff-Germain, G., Weissman, M.M., Greenwald, S., Narrow, W.E., Jensen, P.S., Lahey, B.B., & Canino, G. (2000). Childhood obsessive-compulsive disorder in the NIMH MECA Study: Parent versus child identification of cases. *Journal of Anxiety Disorders*, **14**, 535–548.

Rasmussen, S.A., & Tsuang, M.T. (1986). Clinical characteristics and family history in DSM-IV obsessive-compulsive disorder. *American Journal of Psychiatry*, **143**, 317–322.

Rettew, D.C., Swedo, S.E., Leonard, H.L., Lenane, M.C., & Rapoport, J.L. (1992). Obsessions and compulsions across time in 79 children and adolescents with obsessive-compulsive disorder. *Journal American Academy of Child and Adolescent Psychiatry*, **31**, 1050–1056.

Rheaume, J., Ladouceur, R., Freeston, M., & Letarte, H. (1994). Inflated responsibility in obsessive-compulsive disorder: Psychometric studies of a semi-idiographic measure. *Journal of Psychopathology and Behavioural Assessment*, **16**, 265–276.

Rheaume, J., Ladouceur, R., Freeston, M., & Letarte, H. (1995). Inflated responsibility in obsessive-compulsive disorder: Validation of an operational definition. *Behavioural Research and Therapy*, **88**, 159–169.

Riddle, M.A., Reeve, E.A., Yaryura-Tobias, J.A., Yang, H.M., Claghorn, J.L., Gaffney, G., Greist, J.H., Holland, D., McConville, B.J., Pigott, T., & Walkup, J.T. (2001). Fluvoxamine for children and adolescents with obsessive-compulsive disorder: A randomized, controlled, multicenter trial. *Journal of the American Academy of Child and Adolescent Psychiatry*, **40**, 222–229.

Riddle, M.A., Scahill, L., King, R., Hardin, M.T., Toublin, K.E., Ort, S.I., Leckman, J.F., & Cohen, D.J. (1990). Obsessive-compulsive disorder in children and adolescents. Phenomenology and family history. *Journal American Academy of Child and Adolescent Psychiatry*, **29**, 766–772.

Rosenberg, D., Steward, C., Fitzgerald, K., Tawile, V., & Carroll, E. (1999). Paroxetine open-label treatment of pediatric outpatients with obsessive-compulsive disorder. *Journal of the American Academy of Child and Adolescent Psychiatry*, **38**, 1180.

Salkovskis, P.M. (1985). Obsessional compulsive problems: A cognitive-behavioural analysis. *Behaviour Research and Therapy*, **23** (5), 571–583.

Salkovskis, P.M. (1989). Cognitive behavioural factors and the persistence of intrusive thoughts in obsessional problems. *Behaviour Research and Therapy*, **27** (6), 677–682.

Salkovskis, P.M. (1996). Cognitive-behavioural approaches to the understanding of obsessional problems. In R.M. Rapee (Ed.), *Current controversies in the anxiety disorders*. New York: Guilford Press.

Salkovskis, P.M., & Campbell, P. (1994). Thought suppression in naturally occurring negative intrusive thoughts. *Behaviour, Research and Therapy*, **32**, 1–8.

Scahill, L., Riddle, M.A., McSwiggan-Hardin, M.T., Ort, S.I., King, R.A., Goodman, W.K., Cicchetti, D., & Leckman, J.F. (1997). The Children's Yale–Brown Obsessive-Compulsive Scale: Preliminary report of reliability and validity. *Journal American Academy of Child and Adolescent Psychiatry*, **36**, 844–853.

Scahill, L., Vitulano, L.A., Brenner, E.M., Lynch, K.A., & King, R.A. (1996). Behavioural therapy in children and adolescents with obsessive-compulsive disorder: A pilot study. *Journal of Child and Adolescent Psychopharmacology*, **6** (3), 191–202.

Shafran, R. (1997). The manipulation of responsibility in obsessive-compulsive disorder. *British Journal of Clinical Psychology*, **36**, 397–407.

Silverman, W.K., & Albano, A.M. (1996). *Anxiety Disorders Interview Schedule for DSM-IV: Parent Version*. San Antonio, USA: Graywing.

Silverman, W.K., & Eisen, A. (1992). Age differences in the reliability of parent and child reports of child anxious symptomatology using a structured interview. *Journal of Child and Adolescent Psychiatry*, **31**, 117–124.

Silverman, W.K., & Nelles, W.B. (1988). The Anxiety Disorders Interview Schedule for Children. *Journal of the American Academy of Child and Adolescent Psychiatry*, **27** (6), 772–778.

Steketee, G., & Frost, R.O. (1994). Measurement of risk-taking in obsessive-compulsive disorder. *Behavioural and Cognitive Psychotherapy*, **22**, 287–298.

Steketee, G., Chambless, D.L., Tran, G.Q., Worden, H., & Gillis, M.M. (1996). Behavioural Avoidance Test for obsessive compulsive disorder. *Behaviour Research and Therapy*, **34** (1), 73–83.

Swedo, S.E., Leonard, H.L., Kruesi, M.J., Rettew, D.C., Listwak, S.J., Berrettini, W., Stipetic, M., Hamburger, S., Gold, P.W., Potter, W.Z., & Rapoport, J.L. (1992). Cerebrospinal fluid neurochemistry in children and adolescents with obsessive-compulsive disorder. *Archives of General Psychiatry*, **49**, 29–36.

Swedo, S.E., Rapoport, J.L., Leonard, H., Lenane, M., & Cheslow, D. (1989). Obsessive-compulsive disorder in children and adolescents: Clinical phenomenology of 70 consecutive cases. *Archives of General Psychiatry*, **46**, 335–341.

Taylor, S. (1998). Assessment of obsessive-compulsive disorder. In R.P. Swinson & M.M. Antony (Eds), *Obsessive-compulsive disorder: Theory, research, and treatment* (pp. 229–257). New York: Guilford Press.

Thienemann, M., Martin, J., Cregger, B., Thompson, H.B., & Dyer-Freidman, J. (2001). Manual driven group cognitive-behavioural therapy for adolescents with obsessive-compulsive disorder: A pilot study. *Journal of American Academy of Child and Adolescent Psychiatry*, **40** (11), 1254–1260.

Thomsen, P.H. (1994). Obsessive-compulsive disorder in children and adolescents. A 6–22 year follow-up study. Clinical descriptions of obsessive-compulsive phenomenology and continuity. *European Journal of Child and Adolescent Psychiatry*, **3**, 82–96.

Thomsen, P. (1997). Child and adolescent obsessive-compulsive disorder treated with citalo-pram: Findings from an open trial of 23 cases. *Journal of Child and Adolescent Psycho-pharmacology*, **7**, 157.

Toro, J., Cervera, M., Osejo, E., & Salamero, M. (1992). Obsessive compulsive disorder in childhood and adolescence: A clinical study. *Journal of Child Psychology and Psychiatry and Allied Disciplines*, **33**, 1025–1037.

Trinder, H., & Salkovskis, P.M. (1994). Personally relevant intrusions outside the laboratory: Long term suppression increases intrusion. *Behaviour Research and Therapy*, **32**, 833–842.

Valleni-Basile, L.A., Garrison, C.Z., Jackson, K.L., Waller, J.L., McKeown, R.E., Addy, C.L., & Cuffe, S.P. (1995). Family and psychosocial predictors of obsessive compulsive disorder in a community sample of young adolescents. *Journal of Child and Family Studies*, **4**, 193–206.

Waters, T., Barrett, P., & March, J. (2001). Cognitive-behavioural family treatment of childhood obsessive-compulsive disorder: An open clinical trial. *American Journal of Psychotherapy*, **55**, 372–387.

Wever, C., & Phillips, N. (1994). *The secret problem*. Sydney: Shrink-Rap Press.

Wever, C., & Rey, J.M. (1997). Juvenile obsessive-compulsive disorder. *Australian and New Zealand Journal of Psychiatry*, **31**, 105–113.

Woody, S.R., Steketee, G., & Chambless, D.L. (1995). Reliability and validity of the Yale–Brown Obsessive-Compulsive Scale. *Behaviour Research and Therapy*, **33** (5), 597–605.

Zohar, A.H. (1999). The epidemiology of obsessive-compulsive disorder in children and ado-lescents. *Child and Adolescent Psychiatric Clinics of North America*, **8** (3), 445–460.

CHAPTER 10

Treatment of PTSD in Children and Adolescents

Sean Perrin

Patrick Smith

and

William Yule

Institute of Psychiatry, London, England

INTRODUCTION

The purpose of the present chapter is to provide an overview of the PTSD litera-ture on children. Of course, PTSD *is not* the only outcome of interest following a traumatic event but is arguably the most frequent and well understood. PTSD as a diagnostic entity, even with its flaws, has proven to be a valid and useful framework for understanding the effects of traumatic events. It also serves as a useful entry point and limiting factor for approaching the trauma literature, which has grown so rapidly in the past 20 years that it is beyond the scope of one chapter to give it a full and comprehensive review. A heavy emphasis is also placed here on cognitive-behavioural models of aetiology and treatment. Other models and treatments do exist, but few have been more fruitful in terms of both our scientific understanding and treatment of PTSD. With this in mind, we hope the reader will appreciate that any chapter on PTSD in children can only speak to a small part of the complex effects of trauma in this age group.

Phenomenology

Table 10.1 lists the diagnostic criteria for PTSD as set forth in DSM-IV (APA, 1994). The criteria have been the subject of much criticism, particularly as they apply to

Correspondence to Sean Perrin, Institute of Psychiatry, De Crespigny Park, Denmark Hill, London SE5 8AF UK; email: s.perrin@iop.kcl.ac.uk

Handbook of Interventions that Work with Children and Adolescents: Prevention and Treatment.
Edited by P.M. Barrett and T.H. Ollendick. © 2004 John Wiley & Sons, Ltd. ISBN 0-470-84453-1.

Table 10.1   DSM-IV Criteria for Post-traumatic Stress Disorder

A. The person has been exposed to a traumatic event in which both of the following have been present:
   1. The person has experienced, witnessed, or been confronted with an event or events, that involve actual or threatened death or serious injury, or a threat to the physical integrity of oneself or others.
   2. The person's response involved intense fear, helplessness, or horror. Note: In children, it may be expressed by disorganized or agitated behaviour.

B. The traumatic event is persistently re-experienced in at least one of the following ways:
   1. Recurrent and intrusive distressing recollections of the event, including images, thoughts, or perceptions. Note: In young children, repetitive play may occur in which themes or aspects of the trauma are expressed.
   2. Recurrent distressing dreams of the event. Note: In children, there may be frightening dreams without recognizable content.
   3. Acting or feeling as if the traumatic event were recurring (includes a sense of reliving the experience, illusions, hallucinations, and dissociative flashback episodes, including those that occur upon awakening or when intoxicated). Note: In young children, trauma specific re-enactment may occur.
   4. Intense psychological distress at exposure to internal or external cues that symbolize or resemble an aspect of the traumatic event.
   5. Physiological reactivity upon exposure to internal or external cues that symbolize or resemble an aspect of the traumatic event.

C. Persistent avoidance of stimuli associated with the trauma and numbing of general responsiveness (not present before the trauma), as indicated by at least three of the following:
   1. Efforts to avoid thoughts, feelings, or conversations associated with the trauma.
   2. Efforts to avoid activities, places, or people that arouse recollections of the trauma.
   3. Inability to recall an important aspect of the trauma.
   4. Markedly diminished interest or participation in significant activities.
   5. Feelings of detachment or estrangement from others.
   6. Restricted range of affect (e.g., unable to have loving feelings).
   7. Sense of a foreshortened future (e.g., does not expect to have a career, marriage, children, or a normal life span).

D. Persistent symptoms of increased arousal (not present before the trauma), as indicated by at least two of the following:
   1. Difficulty falling or staying asleep.
   2. Irritability or outbursts of anger.
   3. Difficulty concentrating.
   4. Hypervigilance.
   5. Exaggerated startle response.

E. Duration of the disturbance (symptoms in B, C, and D) is more than 1 month.

F. The disturbance causes clinically significant distress or impairment in social, occupational, or other important areas of functioning.

Specify if:
Acute: If duration of symptoms is less than 3 months.
Chronic: If duration of symptoms is 3 months or more.
With delayed onset: Onset of symptoms at least 6 months after the stressor.

children. However, the core PTSD symptom clusters (intrusion, avoidance, and hyperarousal) as defined in DSM have been found repeatedly in school-age children and adolescents, across cultures, and following a variety of traumatic events (see Fletcher, 1996, and McNally, 1993, for reviews of the relevant literature). What follows is a brief description of how the DSM-IV symptom criteria manifest in children, and how the DSM compares with other diagnostic approaches to the disorder.

Criterion A

The Traumatic Event. There is no distinction between what constitutes a traumatic event for an adult as opposed to a child. What defines the event as traumatic is its potential life-threatening nature and the immediate reaction of the individual exposed to it (i.e., distress). However, DSM does take into account that children may express distress quite differently from adults with the child's initial reaction including the possibility of *disorganized or agitated behaviour* (e.g., crying, clinging, or hyperkinesis).

Criterion B

Re-experiencing. Intrusive and distressing thoughts of the trauma are frequent in traumatized children of all ages. However, very young children may not have the ability to verbally describe such recollections (if present). Re-experiencing in the young child may also be expressed as *repetitive and trauma-thematic play*. Such play (including drawing) may reflect an attempt by the child to better understand the event or to gain mastery over the recollections. Likewise vivid nightmares involving the theme of the trauma are common in children of all ages but younger children may also experience frightening dreams without any recognizable content, or dreams involving monsters, rescuing others, and threats to the self or loved ones. Upon awakening from nightmares, children often become panicky and run to their parent's bedroom, and find it difficult to describe or recall what has been dreamt. Parents often find that they are unable to get the child back to bed, and it is not unusual to learn from the parents that their traumatized child has not slept alone in months or even years.

In contrast to other forms of intrusions, flashbacks appear to be less common in very young children, but this matter has been the subject of some debate (see Spiegel, 1984; Perry et al., 1995; Scheeringa & Zeanah, 1995; Putnam, 1997). By contrast, young children often display signs of re-experiencing through vivid re-enactment of the trauma in the form of drawings, stories, and play (Scheeringa & Zeanah, 1995; Scheeringa et al., 1995). While not specifically stated in DSM-IV, it is reasonable to assume that *traumatic re-enactment* differs in quality from *repetitive traumatic play*, with the former taking on a more distressing and/or dissociative aspect (like a flashback). Of course, not all children have explicit memories of the traumatic event but the appearance of upset in the presence of traumatic reminders is sufficient for the child to meet the re-experiencing criterion.

Criterion C

Persistent Avoidance and Numbing of General Responsiveness. Avoidance of trauma-related thoughts, feelings, conversations, and external traumatic reminders is common in traumatized children of all ages. Nevertheless, it is important to recognize how parental attitudes and reactions to the trauma may influence the topography of avoidance in the child. For example, overprotective parents often prohibit their traumatized child from engaging in any discussion of the trauma or from having contact with physical reminders. By contrast, some parents may not permit the child *to avoid* (e.g., making them sleep in their own bed, go to school, visit friends, ride in cars after a road traffic accident, etc.). We have found it useful to ask the child what they *would avoid* if given the opportunity. A related issue is the fact that the child may want to talk about the trauma but refrain from doing so because they do not want to upset their parents.

The cognitive and verbal capacity of the child is another important factor to consider when assessing avoidance. For example, *the inability to recall important aspects of the trauma* counts as a symptom under the avoidance criterion in PTSD, but this needs to be weighed against the ability of the child to process and verbally recall the trauma. Also, when assessing for the presence of *diminished interest or participation in significant activities* one needs to be aware that changes in preferred playmates and activities is part of normal childhood development. In the case of adolescents, this presents as "feeling misunderstood" and a degree of detachment or estrangement from adults. When assessing for this symptom, it is important to listen for statements indicating that they feel different from others as a result of their traumatic experiences. Such beliefs are common in traumatized children of all ages, particularly those left with visible scars or who have lost a parent.

A *restricted range of affect* is thought to reflect a general state of emotional numbing, but the symptom description in DSM is rather vague and has proven a difficult phenomenon to assess (Litz, 1992). Children may report that they are beset with feelings of guilt, anger, or fear that seem to crowd out all other emotional experiences. In our experience, a more generalized state of emotional numbing (e.g., no or little feelings at all) is rare, particularly in young children.

Finally, older children and adolescents may develop a view of life as quite fragile after a traumatic event, particularly if they sustained a permanent injury or witnessed the death of another. This can lead to a *sense of a foreshortened future*, often expressed as a loss of any thoughts about the future. Very young children report the loss of future-related thoughts less often, and instead may develop the belief that they can foresee untoward events in the future (omen formation).

Criterion D

Persistent Symptoms of Increased Arousal (not present before the trauma). Arousal-related symptoms are common in traumatized children of all ages. Very young children often report an increase in somatic complaints like headaches and stomach pains. Not surprisingly, difficulties around bedtime are common. Intense fears of the dark often appear (or return) in the aftermath of a trauma, with some children becoming quite panicky at bedtime. They may have fears of having nightmares, finding it difficult to fall or stay asleep, leaving them tired during the day. It is not unusual for parents to report that their child sleeps during the day, or in the case of the very young, takes prolonged daytime naps. Irritability and outbursts of anger are common in some children, and is often manifested as hypersensitivity in response to the slightest mishap or perceived criticism. Older children will often directly acknowledge that they are getting into more arguments with others since the trauma.

Concentration difficulties often arise as a result of frequent traumatic intrusion and efforts to avoid thoughts and feelings with decreases in school performance and more frequent accidents resulting. Hypervigilance in children is often evidenced by compulsive checking of locks and doors, overprotectiveness of others, and frequent requests for reassurance that everything is okay. Prolonged and excessive upset in response to loud noises and arguing (which then prompt clingy, worrisome, or irritable reactions) is common in traumatized children.

DSM-IV states that individuals who meet the symptom criteria for PTSD must have marked impairment in at least one area of functioning for a period of at least one month. In certain cases, objective evidence of impairment in school and social functioning may be difficult to obtain. Some children may be reluctant to admit that they are not performing to their usual standard or may feel obliged to work harder at school so as not to disturb their parents. In other cases, adults may simply not recognize or accept that the child has been affected and downplay the degree of impairment. As stated above, some parents do not allow the child to engage in behaviours that might give evidence of impairment (e.g., avoiding or doing poorly at school, staying indoors most of the time, or sleeping with parents/siblings). In such cases, it is not unusual for the traumatized child to suffer in silence while giving an outward appearance of normal functioning.

The Scheeringa Criteria for Very Young Children. In light of the many limitations of the DSM criteria as they apply to those under 4 years of age, Scheeringa et al. (1995) have developed an alternate set of PTSD criteria based on DSM-IV for infants and young children. While currently under investigation, they may prove useful in guiding the reader toward some of the developmental issues of importance to traumatized children (see also Vernberg & Varela, 2001, for a discussion of this topic). Scheeringa et al. suggest that the child need only have experienced a traumatic event and not the intense fear at the time of the event that DSM-IV requires under Criterion A. As to re-experiencing, they suggest that only one of the following is needed: (1) post-traumatic play that is compulsively repetitive, represents part of the trauma, fails to relieve anxiety, and is less elaborate and imaginative than usual play; (2) play re-enactment that represents part of the trauma but lacks the monotonous repetition and other characteristics of post-traumatic play; (3) recurrent recollections of the traumatic event other than what is revealed in play and is not necessarily distressing; (4) nightmares that may have obvious links to the trauma or be of increased frequency with unknown content; (5) episodes with objective features of a flashback or dissociation; (6) distress at exposure to traumatic reminders.

Under Criterion C, Scheeringa et al. (1995) suggest that only one of the following symptoms is needed (DSM-IV requires three): (1) constriction of play, even in the presence of post-traumatic play or play re-enactment; (2) socially more withdrawn; (3) restricted range of affect; (4) loss of acquired developmental skills, especially language regression and toilet training. They suggest a change in the criteria for arousal (Criterion D) to accept any one of the following [DSM-IV requires at least two]: (1) night terrors; (2) difficulty going to sleep which is not related to being afraid of having nightmares or a fear of the dark; (3) night-waking not related to nightmares or night terrors; (4) decreased concentration: marked decrease in concentration or attention span compared to before the trauma; (5) hypervigilance; (6) exaggerated startle response. A new cluster of symptoms is introduced by Scheeringa et al. titled "New Fear and Aggression" of which only one is needed: (1) new aggression; (2) new separation anxiety; (3) fear of toilet training alone; (4) fear of the dark; (5) any new fears of things or situations not obviously related to the trauma. Scheeringa et al. (1995) suggest that the requirement of impairment in social, occupational, or other important areas of functioning be omitted.

Scheeringa et al.'s alternative set of PTSD criteria requires only four symptoms in addition to the experience of a traumatic event, whereas DSM-IV requires at least six, distress at the time of the trauma, and evidence of impairment. While the risk of false positives is certainly higher, this needs to be weighted against the likely risk of a "false negative" diagnosis of PTSD in this age group. While some of the Scheeringa criteria are equally vague as those set out in DSM-IV, they underline the need for more developmentally sensitive criteria in children and the need for further research on this topic. In the interim, it is useful to consider PTSD as described in the widely used *International Classification of Diseases* (ICD-10; WHO, 1992). ICD-10 lists symptoms similar to those in DSM-III-R (APA, 1987), however it emphasizes the presence of repetitive and intrusive memories as characteristic of the disorder. Specifically, ICD-10 states:

> ... conspicuous emotional detachment, numbing of feeling, and avoidance of stimuli that might arouse recollections of the trauma are often present but are not essential for the diagnosis. The autonomic disturbances, mood disorder, and behavioural abnormalities are all contributory to the diagnosis but not of prime importance. (WHO, 1992, p. 148)

Epidemiology

Most community-based epidemiological studies conducted to date have been carried out with older adolescents or adults (see Fairbanks et al., 1995, for a review). Nevertheless, the available evidence suggests that PTSD is not a rare condition during childhood. Giaconia and coworkers (1994) found a lifetime-prevalence of 6% in a community sample of older adolescents, while Kessler et al. (1995) found a lifetime-prevalence rate of 10% using data collected from older adolescents and adults in the National Comorbidity Survey.

Studies of children and adolescents selected because they were exposed to a traumatic event report higher rates of PTSD than that found in community studies. Pynoos and colleagues (1987) examined the occurrence of PTSD in 159 children one month after an attack by a sniper on a school playground. Seventy-seven percent of the children on the playground and 67% at school on the same day had moderate or severe PTSD, as measured by the PTSD Reaction Index (PTSD-RI). Similarly, Schwarz and Kowalski (1991) administered the PTSD-RI to 64 pre-adolescent children, nearly six months after a shooting spree in their school. Using "conservative" symptom thresholds (i.e., symptoms occurring "much" or "most of the time"), the prevalence of PTSD under DSM-III was 16%, but only 8% under DSM-III-R, and 9% under DSM-IV. Using "liberal" symptom threshold levels (i.e., symptoms occurring at least "a little of the time"), prevalence rates were 91% under DSM-III, 50% under DSM-III-R, and 26% under DSM-IV. These data point out the risk for under-identification of PTSD in very young children when using the DSM-III-R and DSM-IV criteria as compared to DSM-III.

Kinzie and colleagues (1986) conducted one of the first investigations using diagnostic criteria to assess the effects of war on children. Of 40 Cambodian refugees living in Oregon, 50% met criteria for DSM-III PTSD nearly four years after leaving their country. Sack and colleagues (1994) reported much lower rates (lifetime = 21.5%, current = 18%) in 200 Cambodian refugees living in the United States. Similarly, in a study of 840 Lebanese children, Saigh (1989a) observed a much lower rate of current PTSD (32.5%). Interestingly, Saigh (1991) found that the rates of PTSD were consistent across various categories of war-exposure (i.e., direct, observation, and indirect).

Several studies have reported on the prevalence of PTSD following natural, accidental, or inflicted disasters. Milgram and coworkers (1988) observed a 40% prevalence rate for PTSD in children one month after a bus accident. Bradburn (1991) reported prevalence rates of 27% for moderate PTSD and 36% for mild PTSD in 22 children aged 10–12 years, some six to eight months after the San Francisco earthquake. Of 179 children aged 2–15 years who were examined two years after the Buffalo Creek disaster, 37% received probable PTSD diagnoses based on a retrospective examination of relevant records (Green et al., 1991).

Several large-scale investigations of PTSD were conducted following Hurricane Hugo that struck the South Carolina coast in 1989. Based on self-report data obtained from over 5000 hurricane survivors, Lonigan et al. (1991) reported PTSD prevalence rates of 5.1% in a no-exposure group, 10.4% in those with mild-exposure, 15.5% for those with moderate-exposure, and 28.9% in the high-exposure group. The overall prevalence rate for PTSD for the same sample was 5% nearly three months after the hurricane (Shannon et al., 1994). Similarly, Garrison and colleagues (1993) reported current prevalence rates ranging from 1.5% to 6.2% one year after Hurricane Hugo in a sample of 11 to 17 year olds.

AETIOLOGY

As is clear from the preceding review, not everyone exposed to a traumatic event develops PTSD. Thus PTSD must result from some combination of personal vulnerability factors, characteristics of the traumatic event itself, the individual's appraisal of that event, and post-trauma factors.

Personal Vulnerability

PTSD shares many of the same personal risk factors as other disorders. Specifically, being female, from a lower socioeconomic background, and having a previous history of trauma or psychiatric illness are all associated with an increased risk of PTSD following a traumatic event (Breslau & Davis, 1987; Brewin, Andrews, & Valentine, 2000; Earls et al., 1988; Helzer, Robins, & McEnvoy, 1987). However, Udwin et al. (2000) found that these same person-centred variables (as well as pre-trauma educational attainment) were more strongly related to PTSD duration and severity than onset of the disorder in a large prospective study of traumatized adolescents. At present, there is no clear evidence that age is a specific risk factor for PTSD, although some have suggested that pre-schoolers may be protected from the effects of trauma by their inability to fully appreciate the dangers associated with the event (Keppel-Benson & Ollendick, 1993).

Objective Characteristics of the Trauma

Trauma proximity, severity, and duration have all been found to be related to PTSD development in adults and children (Bradburn, 1991; Breslau & Davis, 1987; Brewin, Andrews, & Valentine, 2000; Foy et al., 1987; Lonigan et al., 1991; Pynoos et al., 1987, 1993; Schwarz & Kowalski, 1991; Udwin et al., 2000). Another important aspect of the trauma appears to be its degree of *predictability* and *controllability*. A large animal literature suggests that unpredictable and uncontrollable events (usually electric shocks) are more likely to produce stable PTSD-like symptoms (Foa, Zinbarg, & Olasov-Rothbaum, 1992). How these two factors relate to PTSD in humans is as yet unclear. For example, Resnick and colleagues (1993) found that traumatic events inflicted by others (e.g., physical assaults) were more likely to produce PTSD than were natural disasters (e.g., hurricanes and earthquakes) in a nationally representative sample of American women. Natural disasters are clearly uncontrollable but not necessarily unpredictable, whereas assaults may vary considerably in terms of both their predictability and controllability.

Subjective Experience During the Trauma

The degree of perceived life-threat experienced during the trauma has been found to be related to the development of PTSD in adults (Clohessy & Ehlers, 1999; Dunmore, Clark, & Ehlers, 2001; Ehlers, Maercker, & Boos, 2000; Ehlers, Mayou, & Bryant, 1998; Kilpatrick et al., 1989; Steil & Ehlers, 2000) and in children (Ehlers, Mayou, & Bryant, 2001; Foy et al., 1996; Stallard, Velleman, & Baldwin, 1998; Udwin et al., 2000). The experience of having "given up control" during the traumatic event (also referred to as mental defeat) has been shown to be associated with PTSD onset, duration, and severity in adults (Brewin, Andrews, & Valentine, 2000; Ehlers, Maercker, & Boos, 2000; Koopman, Classen, & Speigel, 1994; Murray, Ehlers, & Mayou, 2000; Shalev et al., 1996) but its impact on children is as yet unknown.

Post-Trauma Factors

Avoidance and emotional numbing symptoms in the immediate aftermath of the trauma predict the later development of PTSD in adults (Brewin et al., 1999; North et al., 1999). Studies with children have found that a high degree of distress in the immediate aftermath of the trauma is associated with later PTSD severity (DiGallo, Barton, & Parry-Jones, 1997; Nader et al., 1990; Yule & Udwin, 1991). In a follow-up study of traumatized children, Ehlers et al. (2001) found that mental confusion during the trauma, and in its immediate aftermath, along with negative appraisals of one's symptoms, avoidance, and dissociation all predicted later PTSD severity. Interestingly, having a parent with an avoidant style was associated with more severe PTSD reactions in children after a road traffic accident (Ehlers, Mayou, & Bryant, 2001). Parental adjustment post-trauma has elsewhere been shown to be associated with the child's PTSD symptomatology (McFarlane, 1987).

Cognitive-Behavioural Approaches to PTSD

Central to a cognitive-behavioural understanding of PTSD is the notion that emotional and behavioural responses, which are normal in the context of a life-threatening event, become maladaptive when they generalize and occur in non-threatening contexts. Many attempts have been made to explain how this process of generalization occurs invoking conditioning theories, information-processing models, and cognitive neuroscience (e.g., Brewin, 2001; Ehlers & Clark, 2000; Foa & Kozak, 1986; Foa, Zinbarg, & Olasov-Rothbaum, 1992; Keane, Zim-mering, & Caddell, 1985; Foa, Steketee, & Olasov-Rothbaum, 1989).

From a learning theory perspective, a traumatic event involves the presentation of any number of unconditioned stimuli (USs) (e.g., damage to bodily tissues, loud noises, seeing others being hurt). These USs elicit any number of unconditioned responses (URs) during the traumatic event (e.g., startle response, autonomic arousal, fear, freezing, tonic immobility, analgesia to pain) (Foa, Zinbarg, & Olasov-Rothbaum, 1992; Southwick et al., 1994). The traumatic event occurs in a context and against the background of a variety of other neutral stimuli. These neutral stimuli become conditioned such that they elicit the same URs as the trauma itself. These *conditioned stimuli* (CSs) (along with contexts similar to the traumatic event) elicit avoidance or escape responses which are then maintained by their effect on distress (Keane, Zimmering, & Caddell, 1985). In support of this basic learning-theory view of PTSD is a large experimental literature demonstrating PTSD-like symptoms in animals following conditioning trials with neutral and aversive stimuli (see Foa, Zinbarg, & Olasov-Rothbaum, 1992, and Mineka, 1985, for a review).

The re-experiencing phenomena, which are so central to our understanding of PTSD, may simply be analogous to a conditioned fear response and share similar underlying mechanisms of acquisition (Foa, Zinbarg, & Olasov-Rothbaum, 1992). Such a view is consistent with modern conditioning theories which hold that the CS–US/UR representation in memory is triggered by subsequent presentations of the CS alone (Bouton & Nelson, 1998; Falls, 1998; Wagner, 1979, 1981). Thus, in the aftermath of a traumatic event, recollections occur because they are activated by encounters with trauma-related CSs. The recollections are experienced as *unintentional* because the individual is not consciously aware of the stimuli that elicit them. Indeed, studies have repeatedly shown that people do quite poorly when asked to identify the CSs to which they have been exposed in conditioning trials (Bouton,

Mineka, & Barlow, 2001; Morgan & Riccio, 1998). The recollections are experienced as *intrusive* because they include the trauma-related stimuli that elicit unpleasant emotional and physiological reactions (Keane, Zimmering, & Caddell, 1985).

Conditioning theory asserts that repeated exposure to a CS in the absence of a US should produce a gradual decrease in the conditioned responses (i.e., the responses are extinguished) (Pavlov, 1927). In this way, extinction can be seen as the way in which an organism's learned behaviours are corrected to fit with current circumstances (Falls, 1998). Arguably, extinction of traumatic responses occurs naturally in the majority of trauma-exposed individuals. However, in those individuals who do go onto develop PTSD, conditioning theory holds that avoidance of the trauma-related CSs blocks the extinction process (Keane, Zimmering, & Caddell, 1985).

However, extinction is not the simple procedure it appears to be, and avoidance may not be the only explanation for why extinction of the traumatic responses fails to occur. For example, a very powerful CS (like those associated with traumatic events) can act like a US—constantly conditioning new stimuli with which it is paired—and prevent extinction from occurring (Falls, 1998). Also, extinction appears to be largely *context-dependent*. In other words, extinction is much more likely to occur if the CS is encountered in a context that closely resembles the original conditioning experience (Bouton & Nelson, 1998). Thus, repeated encounters with trauma-related CSs in contexts different from the traumatic event prevents extinction of the PTSD symptoms.

A final consideration in the persistence of PTSD is the robustness of memory. There is a growing body of evidence that the CS–US/UR associations laid down in memory during conditioning trials are not actually erased with extinction (Falls, 1998). A modern view of extinction holds that it actually results from a discrimination being made between situations in which the CS is followed by the US and situation in which it is not—and that discrimination appears to be dependent upon context (Falls, 1998). In simple terms, individual's with PTSD need to learn that the presence of a CS (e.g., a traumatic reminder) in a non-threatening context does not mean that the traumatic event will necessarily follow.

Conditioning models of PTSD have traditionally had little to say about the role of appraisal and meaning in people's reaction to events. Today most cognitive-behavioural accounts of PTSD incorporate principles about the role of appraisals from information-processing theory (e.g., Lang, 1977, 1985). One such account is the emotional processing model put forward by Foa and colleagues (Foa & Kozak, 1986; Foa, Steketee, & Olasov-Rothbaum, 1989) wherein traumatic events are seen to lead to the development of fear networks in memory that act to prevent further traumatization. These fear networks contain information about the objective characteristics of the trauma, the individual's responses to the trauma, and his or her subjective appraisal of the dangerousness and meaningfulness of the event (Foa & Kozak, 1986). This network is activated in memory by encounters with trauma-related stimuli, bringing about increases in arousal, re-experiencing, and avoidant behaviours.

The emotional processing model also argues that traumatic events produce changes in one's fundamental assumptions about safety and self-efficacy. These changes lead, in turn, to the development of new assumptions that, in turn, cause an increase in the threat-value attached to a variety of previously neutral or even safety-signalling stimuli (Foa & Kozak, 1986). Consequently, many stimuli in the current environment of the traumatized individual can activate the fear network, making it more readily accessible in memory than other potentially adaptive emotion networks, and diverting attention resources from other non-trauma related cues. In support of this view is a growing body of literature indicating that individuals with PTSD show an attentional bias for threat-cues (McNally, 1998). The fear network can only be consolidated in long-term memory when corrective information (both cognitive and affective) is incorporated and a new information structure develops (Foa & Kozak, 1986). Foa, Steketee, & Olasov-Rothbaum (1989) suggest that *in-vivo* and imaginal exposure sessions provide the type of corrective feedback necessary for consolidation of the fear network. Specifically, increased contact with feared stimuli leads to habituation or extinction of the anxiety response, which they argue is a form of corrective feedback. Such corrective exposure also leads to changes in the individual's beliefs about the likelihood of being re-traumatized in the presence of neutral cues and safety signals (Foa, Steketee, & Olasov-Rothbaum, 1989).

Salmon and Bryant (2002) have taken the information-processing account described above and added several developmental considerations. They note that very young children tend to encode less information and to do it more slowly—and thus may be more susceptible to forgetting. They suggest that such early memories may require trauma-specific cues to facilitate retrieval. Salmon and Bryant (2002) also point out that as children have less prior knowledge about how the world works, their appraisals are influenced by parental appraisals of the same event.

The emotional-processing model posited by Foa and Kozak (1986) has generated many testable hypotheses regarding the development of PTSD. However, some have argued that it does not fully account for dissociative or flashback phenomena, nor the apparent discontinuity in emotional responding during intrusive traumatic recollections and voluntary recall of the event (Power & Dalgleish, 1999). Brewin and colleagues (Brewin, 2001; Brewin, Dalgleish, & Joseph, 1996) take a cognitive neuroscience approach to the development of PTSD. They argue that "traumatic" memories are encoded with little or no input from the hippocampus (the neural structure believed to be responsible for encoding memories within a spatial and temporal context) (Brewin, Dalgleish, & Joseph, 1996). In bypassing the hippocampus, the sensory, physiological and motor aspects of the traumatic experience become represented in "situationally accessible memories" (SAMs) (Brewin, 2001). SAMs contain little verbal information and are not readily accessible through conscious means. They are triggered off by cues that have become associated with the trauma via classical conditioning. Once the SAMs are triggered, intense and distressing physical sensations and emotions present during the trauma return, and to such a degree that the person may become dissociative or report a flashback. In Brewin's model (2001), therapy works by accessing these SAMs and elaborating upon them verbally so that they may be represented (stored) as Verbally Accessible Memories (VAMs). VAMs can be deliberately retrieved from autobiographical memory, and subject to deliberate editing such that the threatening aspects of the event are placed into a temporal and spatial context, and the entire event more fully assimilated (Brewin, 2001).

Ehlers and Clark (2000) take a similar approach as Brewin and colleagues, but in addition they stress the role of certain maladaptive cognitive strategies, appraisals, and meta-cognitions in the maintenance of PTSD. Specifically, they propose that the PTSD sufferers attach dysfunctional meaning to the PTSD symptoms (e.g., intrusive recollections mean I am going crazy). The PTSD sufferer may also have developed beliefs consistent with a sense of mental defeat (helplessness), permanent and global change (e.g., my life is ruined and the world is a horrible place), and alienation from others (e.g., people will think I am weak because I cannot cope on my own) (Ehlers & Clark, 2000). Such dysfunctional beliefs motivate maladaptive coping strategies like avoidance, thought suppression, rumination and distraction that block full emotional processing of the traumatic event. They also contribute to the individual's sense that the trauma continues to have damaging implications in the present and generate a sense of "current threat" (Ehlers & Clark, 2000). As cited above, there is a growing body of evidence that such beliefs do predict PTSD duration and severity, intrusion frequency, and general anxiety, independently of the objective characteristics of the traumatic event.

The above review, albeit brief, has attempted to outline how cognitive-behaviourists have attempted to model the complex phenomenon that is PTSD. There are clear points of overlap between the models, but there are also important differences. Perhaps what is most important to remember is that across the various models, they all suggest the use of some form of exposure to trauma-related stimuli or memories to bring about more effective emotional processing of the event (Foa & Meadows, 1997).

ASSESSMENT

The assessment of PTSD is a potentially threatening experience and must be conducted with sensitivity and respect for the child's developmental abilities. A good example of a sensitive and developmentally appropriate interview for children has been described by Pynoos and Eth (1986). In addition, direct interviews of the child need to be supplemented with information gathered from parents, teachers, witnesses, news reports, medical and school records. It is important for the interviewer to gather as much information regarding the traumatic event as possible in order to facilitate more accurate recall of the event, and symptoms not readily admitted or remembered (Nader, 1995).

Overview of the Assessment

We have found it useful to see the entire family together first to give an overview of the interview process. This is followed by an interview with the parents and then the child (separately). During the parental interview, the child completes self-report questionnaires. It is important to remember that whereas children often minimize the extent and severity of their own disruptive behaviours, parents often over-emphasize these symptoms, while remaining unaware of particular fears or negative emotions (Nader, 1995). Finally, the interviewer should also be alert to the possibility that some parents may be inclined to minimize the effect of a trauma on their child and thus under-report symptoms (Sternberg et al., 1993). Therefore, it is useful to find out what, if any, reaction the parents may have had to the trauma and their views about discussion of the trauma and contact with traumatic reminders.

Interviewing the Child

While potentially time-consuming, a semistructured diagnostic interview based on DSM-IV criteria is helpful to the accurate diagnosing of PTSD. There are numerous semistructured interviews available (see Nader, 1995, and March, 1998, for a review), although many do not have any published data supporting their validity or reliability with respect to DSM-IV PTSD. Those that do include: the Diagnostic Interview for Children and Adolescents Revised (DICA; Reich, Shakya, & Taibelson, 1991), the Schedule for Affective Disorders and Schizophrenia for School-Age Children—Present and Lifetime Version, PTSD Scale (K-SADS-PL: Kaufman et al., 1997), the Childhood PTSD Interview—Child Form (Fletcher, 1997), the Children's PTSD Inventory (Saigh et al., unpublished manuscript), the PTSD Reaction Index (PTSD-RI; Pynoos et al., 1993), and the Clinician Administered PTSD Scale—Child and Adolescent Version (CAPS-C; Nader et al., 1994). Most semistructured PTSD interviews can be administered in approximately 90 minutes, but usually require some training in administration.

Self-Report Measures of PTSD

Many of the self-report measures for childhood PTSD were adapted from semistructured interviews or measures originally designed for adults, and have limited usefulness with young children (see Nader, 1995, and McNally, 1991, for a review). Nevertheless, the Children's Post Traumatic Stress Reaction Index (CPTS-RI; Frederick, 1985) has been used in a number of major studies (Pynoos et al., 1987, 1993; Pynoos & Nader, 1988) and has been shown to have good internal consistency and to relate well to clinical judgment of PTSD severity (Yule & Udwin, 1991). The Children's Impact of Traumatic Events Scale—Revised (CITES-R; Wolfe et al., 1991) was developed to assess the impact of sexual abuse on children and also has good psychometric properties. March and coworkers (1998) developed the Kiddie Posttraumatic Symptomatology Scale (K-PTS) for use in epidemiological studies and the measure has been shown to have good internal consistency and to correlate well with a diagnostic measure of PTSD (March, 1998).

One of the most widely used measures of PTSD is the Impact of Events Scale (IES; Horowitz, Wilner, & Alvarez, 1979). The IES is a 15-item scale that assesses intrusion and avoidance and can be used with older children and adolescents (Yule & Udwin, 1991; Yule & Williams, 1990). Yule, Udwin, and Murdoch (1990) have reduced the number of intrusion and avoidance items to 8, added 5 relating to arousal, and reworded all of the items for use with children aged 8 and above. This 13-item version of the IES has been used in a number of different countries and has proven to be a valid and reliable measure of PTSD (Smith et al., 2001, 2002).

Self-report measures of PTSD are best used in conjunction with measures of anxiety, fear, and depression (Stallard & Law, 1993; Yule & Udwin, 1991). Such measures might include the Birleson Depression Inventory (Birleson, 1981), the Children's Manifest Anxiety Scale (Reynolds & Richmond, 1978), and the Fear Survey Schedule for Children (Ollendick, 1983). An additional supplemental measure for use with children is the Post traumatic Cognitions Inventory (PTCI) (Foa et al., 1999). The PTCI is an empirically derived measure of cognitions about PTSD symptoms, and generalized beliefs about safety that have been shown to predict PTSD development and severity. The 47-item measure has been adapted for use with school-age children and adolescents and is likely to prove useful in treatment planning and evaluation.

TREATMENT

Cognitive-Behaviour Therapy (CBT) is the most frequently studied psychosocial treatment and has been subjected to the greatest number of rigorously controlled investigations of PTSD in adults (see Foa & Meadows, 1997; Olasov-Rothbaum et al., 2000, for reviews). In their review of the literature, Foa and Meadows (1997) found that therapies involving prolonged exposure to traumatic cues and treatments aimed at anxiety management were reported to be effective in reducing PTSD symptoms. While few randomized-controlled trials of CBT with children have been published, there is evidence supporting the use of this treatment in traumatized children (see Cohen, Berliner, & March, 2000, for a review of this literature).

Some of the most rigorously controlled investigations of CBT published to date have been carried out with sexually abused children. In the first study (Berliner & Saunders, 1996), 80 sexually abused children were randomized to either a traditional treatment group that addressed abuse issues through discussion, activities, games, and role-play, or to a treatment group using the same techniques plus relaxation, cognitive restructuring, and graduated exposure. Marked improvements were found in both groups across parent and child measures, however the addition of CBT interventions did not improve the effectiveness of the more traditional group therapy. By way of contrast, Deblinger, Lippman, and Steer (1996) found group-administered CBT to be superior to traditional group therapy. In their study, 100 sexually abused children were randomly assigned to either a community treatment control group or one of three trauma-focused CBT conditions: individual treatment with the child, treatment with the parent, and treatment through the parent only. The two CBT treatments that included the child were found to be superior to all other treatment conditions. Interestingly, the CBT condition involving both the parent and child produced significantly more improvement in externalizing and depressive symptoms (Deblinger, Lippman, & Steer, 1996).

Cohen and Mannarino (1996, 1998) have conducted two randomized-controlled trials of CBT in sexually abused children. In the first study (Cohen & Mannarino, 1996), they randomly assigned 68 sexually abused pre-schoolers to either a trauma-focused CBT intervention for the child and parent together or to a non-directive supportive therapy condition involving the pre-schooler only. The CBT condition was markedly superior to the non-directive therapy in this sample of pre-schoolers, and the gains in the CBT group were maintained at 6- and 12-month follow-ups (Cohen & Mannarino, 1997). The authors partially replicated their findings in a subsequent randomized trial with 49 children aged 7 to 14 years in that CBT was superior to non-directive supportive therapy in reducing depression and improving social competence. However, they found no group differences on their measure of PTSD (Cohen & Mannarino, 1998). Similarly, Celano et al. (1996) randomly assigned 32 sexually abused, school-age children to an 8-session CBT group or treatment as usual, and found no group differences in PTSD symptoms.

Goenjian et al. (1997) compared CBT to no treatment for traumatized children following an earthquake in Armenia. Children in two of four schools near the earthquake epicentre received a school-based intervention involving group discussion about the trauma, relaxation and desensitization, grief work, and normalization of responses. Children in the remaining two schools were not treated (no randomization to treatment conditions was performed). The school-based treatment was found to be superior to no-treatment on self-report measures of PTSD and distress. Indeed, children in the no-treatment, comparison schools became more depressed over the period of study.

Several uncontrolled studies have been conducted which also provide support for the use of CBT for childhood PTSD. March et al. (1998) tested the efficacy of an 18-week, group-administered CBT package for PTSD in 17 older children and adolescents who had suffered a single incident trauma. Eight of the 14 subjects who completed the treatment (57%) were free of PTSD at the end of treatment and another four were free of PTSD at six-month follow-up (an overall recovery rate of 86%). In an uncontrolled trial of a 12-session CBT program (comprising coping skills training, gradual exposure, and educative/preventative work) for 19 sexually abused children, Deblinger, McLeer, and Henry (1990) found that every major category of PTSD symptoms improved, with no child still meeting diagnostic criteria post-treatment. Saigh has produced a series (1987, 1987a, 1989a) of single-case, multiple-baseline studies demonstrating the effectiveness of prolonged imaginal exposure for children with PTSD arising from interpersonal violence and war.

Finally, the most recent addition to the armamentarium of individual treatment techniques for PTSD is Eye Movement Desensitisation and Reprocessing (EMDR; Shapiro, 1989). While some would not include EMDR under the broad rubric of CBT, its reliance on prolonged imaginal exposure suggests greater overlap than differences between the two approaches. In addition to imaginal exposure, EMDR employs dual attention tasks, most notably saccadic eye movements, to facilitate accelerated processing of traumatic memories (see Shapiro, 1995, for a description). Considerable controversy surrounds EMDR and the research purported to show its efficacy with adults. As yet, only one controlled trial with children has been published. Chemtob et al. (in press, cited in Cohen, Berliner, & March, 2000) randomly assigned 32 children exposed to a hurricane to either three sessions of EMDR or a wait-list control condition. The authors found this very brief intervention to be more

effective in reducing PTSD symptoms (56% free of a PTSD diagnosis) than no treatment. Interestingly, the children in this study were non-responders to a previous
trial of CBT. Further research is clearly needed.

In the remainder of the chapter, we devote our attention to a brief description of
the main components of a 10-session, CBT treatment manual for children and adolescents with PTSD (Smith, Perrin, Yule, & Clark, unpublished manuscript). This
manual is currently undergoing evaluation as part of a randomized-controlled trial
by the authors and is broadly based on the cognitive-behavioural model of PTSD
set forth by Ehlers and Clark (2000). The treatment has five main goals. First, traumatic memories need to be elaborated and integrated into autobiographical
memory so that re-experiencing symptoms are reduced. Second, misappraisals of
the trauma and/or any PTSD symptoms need to be modified so that the sense of
current threat is reduced. Third, dysfunctional coping strategies that prevent
memory elaboration, exacerbate symptoms, or hinder a reassessment of problematic appraisals need to be eliminated. Fourth, maladaptive beliefs of the parents with
respect to the traumatic event and its sequelae need to be identified and modified.
Finally, parents need to be recruited as co-therapists in their child's treatment. These
goals are achieved through a combination of interventions, which are briefly
described below.

Engaging the Child and Parents in Treatment

Initial sessions are focused on engaging the child and parents in therapy and normalizing the traumatic responses. Attempts are made to reduce any apparent separation anxiety by encouraging a good working relationship between the therapist,
child, and parents. During this part of treatment, the therapist encourages the child
to *reclaim their life* that has been disturbed by the presence of PTSD symptoms.
This is done by helping the child to reappraise any trauma-related belief (e.g., life
will never be the same again, the world is a dangerous place), so that any current
sense of threat and avoidance is reduced. It is important to counter any reduced
levels of activity early in therapy to help to lift the child's low mood, reduce overprotectiveness on the part of parents, and to give the whole family a sense that
normal life is progressing and moving forward. Pleasant activities are scheduled,
taking care that they are enjoyable and not concerned with confronting traumatic
reminders. Overprotective parents may require assistance to reduce any fears about
allowing the child more independence.

Relaxation and Sleep Hygiene

The child is instructed in the use of relaxation and sleep hygiene techniques. A
relaxation audiotape is also prepared for use at home. The child is instructed in
the use of a SUDS scale (e.g., 0 = *very calm* to 100 = *really, really scared*) for self-
monitoring of distress. For younger children, a visual feelings-thermometer can be
used. SUDS ratings should be used often to encourage children to monitor and
report anxiety feelings.

Imaginal Exposure

Central to the treatment will be the use of imaginal exposure, termed *reliving*. Reliving is preceded by a careful age-appropriate rationale, linked to a discussion of the role of cognitive and behavioural avoidance in maintaining PTSD, and is always taken at the child's own pace. The child is asked to sit comfortably, relax, and if comfortable, close their eyes. They are then asked to talk about the trauma from its beginning until the point when they felt safe again. The therapist prompts for SUDS' ratings throughout, and asks the child to describe any sights, sounds, smells, thoughts and feelings in a first-person present tense. Prompting for sensory memories is useful at "hotspots" or points where the child seems to rush through or have difficulty in recall. At hotspots, the therapist may ask the child to "rewind and hold" or "stop the tape" to enable them to give a more detailed description. In order to bring new information into the trauma memory, the child can be asked to relive the event from another perspective. For example, they may relive a car accident from a bird's eye view, or their parents point of view. Reliving can also be combined with new information after cognitive restructuring (see below).

After reliving, the therapist prompts for SUDS rating and continues to do so periodically. In this way the decline in SUDS is used to demonstrate that the child can learn to tolerate the memories and that the associated anxiety declines very quickly. Thus, it is important to allow plenty of time for anxiety levels to return to normal. Once the reliving is completed, the child should be praised for their efforts and asked to share their experience of the exercise, and what they though were the worst parts of the trauma. The therapist will then help the child to reappraise any trauma-based distortions or beliefs. Finally, all reliving exercises should be audiotaped and given to the child to listen to as homework.

In-Vivo Exposure

Direct or *in-vivo* exposure to the site of the trauma or other external reminders can help the child to elaborate and integrate their traumatic memories and thus reduce re-experiencing and behavioural avoidance. *In-vivo* exposure also allows the child to distinguish between "then" and "now" (i.e., to discriminate between their memory of the scene or reminders and how the scene is now in reality) and should be long enough to allow habituation of the anxiety response to occur.

In-vivo exposure sessions are typically set up as behavioural experiments. The child is asked why they are avoiding reminders and what would happen if they confronted them. It is important to obtain testable, concrete predictions that the therapist can help the child to re-evaluate feared consequences. If spontaneous intrusive memories occur when they are exposed to reminders, the child is asked to discriminate between "then" and "now" in detail. Where there are differences between the memory and reality, these are highlighted and the therapist emphasizes that the traumatic event is in the past and that things have moved on. The therapist will also emphasize that the child is making great efforts to win back lost activities and is succeeding in that attempt. Finally, it is important that the child is not dependent on the therapist to confront avoided reminders. *In-vivo* exposures can be set up for homework, in conjunction with parents (see below).

Undermining Avoidance

Several techniques are used to undermine avoidance. First, the child is asked to allow any intrusions to come and go naturally, without trying to push them away. Alternatively, the child may be asked to deliberately hold on to traumatic images but then move the image in and out of focus, close and far away. A third technique is to ask the child to find the triggers for their intrusions and when their intrusions occur, to evaluate how the trigger differs from the trauma. For example, following a noise that triggers a traumatic memory, the child should look around and see how their current environment differs from the traumatic one. Finally, they may use positive self-talk in conjunction with the above techniques (e.g., It's just a memory, even though it feels real, and things are different now).

Cognitive Restructuring

Children may show maladaptive cognitions about the trauma itself and/or about symptoms of PTSD. The former may be to do with responsibility (I caused the accident), or guilt (I should have been able to save my mother), or shame (I wet myself). Some children may show magical thinking or omen formation (I just knew something bad would happen that day). Misappraisals of symptoms are commonly to do with "going crazy". Also, many children have an unrealistically heightened sense of danger (I will have another crash if I go in a car). When asked, children often say that they thought they were going to die at the time of the trauma. Many cognitions can be altered through sharing of factual information about the traumatic event that was learned from parents or witnesses. Normalizing also helps to change maladaptive symptom appraisals (e.g., all these memories mean I am going crazy).

As well as self-blame, children may mistakenly perceive blame from parents, and this can impede recovery. Such beliefs may be changed through giving information in joint sessions with parents. A heightened sense of danger may also be tackled by giving information about the relative risk of calamitous events (e.g., earthquakes are very rare). With older teenagers, traditional cognitive therapy techniques may be used. In relation to guilt, for example, children can be asked to look at the evidence for their belief through questioning (e.g., What else could you have done at the time?).

Finally, maladaptive cognitions may also be changed through behavioural experiments. For example, reliving may be set up as a test of the prediction that the child will lose control or go mad if they allow themselves to think about the trauma in all its detail. *In-vivo* exposure might be set up as a test of the prediction that another trauma will happen if the child engages physical reminders (e.g., travelling in a car again after an accident). After cognitive restructuring, new information or adaptive cognitions may be combined with reliving. Here, the child is asked to say out loud the new information or realistic cognition, along with evidence, *during reliving*. The latter assists the child in integrating more adaptive cognitions into the memory that facilitate its long-term storage.

Involving Parents in Treatment

The extent to which parents are involved in treatment will depend on whether they have been affected by the trauma themselves, and how they have reacted to their child's PTSD. Minimal involvement might consist of participating in assessment and receiving education about the effects of trauma on children. Most parents should be encouraged to help children with homework, and helped to change the way they cope with their child's distress. Some parents may be more closely involved in therapy, with joint parent–child sessions used to help to challenge the child's misappraisals of symptoms or to model talking and expressing feelings in a safe environment. With younger children, parents will always be asked to join the end of the session so that the therapist and child can explain what has been done in therapy and plan homework assignments. For some children, it will be useful to see parents alone briefly to reassess difficulties that the child may be under-reporting (e.g., bedwetting and aggression).

Wherever possible, the therapist should draw out any similarities between the child and parent reactions. This will help parents to better understand their child's reaction and the rationale for treatment. When the parents are seen alone, it is helpful to ask about their attitudes to treatment and to "talking/processing" compared with avoiding. If necessary, the therapist may start to change maladaptive beliefs through education and behavioural experiments. If parents minimize their child's difficulties, the parent may be asked to join the end of a session where a child speaks directly about his or her difficulties. Some parents become overprotective following a trauma and, at times, it can amount to parental separation anxiety. This will usually require individual sessions with the parent.

Finally, given the cascade of events that may follow a traumatic incident, treatment formulation will also address secondary adversities, with the aim of preventing further complications. Often, these may be traumatic reminders, ongoing legal processes, and anniversaries. It is common, for example, that academic attainment drops following exposure and this in turn may potentially impact on the child's functioning in other areas and later into adulthood. Therefore, a comprehensive treatment plan may include "pulsed intervention" at times of expected stress such as changing schools and anniversaries (e.g., James, 1989).

SUMMARY AND FUTURE DIRECTIONS

In this chapter we have tried to highlight the current literature on the nature and treatment of PTSD in children and adolescents. This literature is growing but clearly lags behind its adult counterpart. However, the current research supports the conclusion that children and adolescents exposed to severe and life-threatening traumas can and do develop PTSD. While PTSD as a diagnostic category has significant limitations for capturing all the effects of trauma in both children and adults, it is a useful guide for both clinical and research purposes.

The study of post-traumatic stress reactions in children remains wide open with regard to areas in need of additional research. However, five main areas appear particularly important: (1) descriptive studies of young people's reactions across trauma types and age/developmental stages; (2) neurobiological correlates of PTSD in children; (3) psychophysiological assessment of PTSD; (4) follow-up studies of treated and untreated children with PTSD; and (5) randomized-controlled trials of CBT versus other active treatments (including EMDR). In addition, effective treatments need to be adapted for use in countries where large number of children have been exposed to wars and natural disasters, and where mental health services are either poorly resourced or non-existent. As such, treatment packages need to be modular and flexible enough for use with groups or in school settings by teachers and other paraprofessionals. They must be simple and contain translatable outcome measures.

REFERENCES

American Psychiatric Association (1987). *Diagnostic and statistical manual of mental disorders* (3rd edn—revised). Washington, DC: Author.

American Psychiatric Association (1994). *Diagnostic and statistical manual of mental disorders* (4th edn). Washington, DC: Author.

Berliner, L., & Saunders, B.E. (1996). Treating fear and anxiety in sexually abused children: Results of controlled 2-year follow-up study. *Child Maltreatment*, **1**, 294–309.

Birleson, P. (1981). The validity of depressive disorder in childhood and the development of a self-rating scale: A research report. *Journal of Child Psychology and Psychiatry*, **22**, 73–88.

Bouton, M.E., & Nelson, J.B. (1998). The role of context in classical conditioning: some implications for cognitive behavior therapy. In W. O'Donohue (Ed.), *Learning and Behavior Therapy* (pp. 59–84). Massachusetts: Allyn & Bacon.

Bouton, M.E., Mineka, S., & Barlow, D.H. (2001). A modern learning theory perspective on the etiology of panic disorder. *Psychological Review*, **1**, 4–32.

Bradburn, L.S. (1991). After the earth shook: Childrens stress symptoms 6–8 months after a disaster. *Advances in Behavioural Research and Therapy*, **13**, 173–179.

Breslau, N., & Davis, G.C. (1987). Posttraumatic stress disorder: The stressor criterion. *Journal of Nervous and Mental Diseases*, **175** (5), 255–264.

Brewin, C.R. (2001). A cognitive neuroscience account of posttraumatic stress disorder and its treatment. *Behaviour Research and Therapy*, **39**, 373–393.

Brewin, C.R., Andrews, B., & Valentine, J.D. (2000). Meta-analysis of risk factors for post-traumatic stress disorder in trauma-exposed adults. *Journal of Consulting and Clinical Psychology*, **68**, 747–766.

Brewin, C.R., Dalgleish, T., & Joseph, S. (1996). A dual representation theory of posttraumatic stress disorder. *Psychological Review*, **103**, 670–686.

Brewin, C.R., Andrews, B., Rose, S., & Kirk, M. (1999). Acute stress disorder and posttraumatic stress disorder in victims of violent crime. *American Journal of Psychiatry*, **156**, 360–366.

Celano, M., Hazzard, A., Webb, C., & McCall, C. (1996). Treatment of traumagenic beliefs among sexually abused girls and their mothers: an evaluation study. *Journal of Abnormal Child Psychology*, **24**, 1–16.

Chemtob, C.M., Nakashima, J., Hamada, R., & Carlon, J. (in press). Brief treatment for elementary school children with disaster-related posttraumatic stress disorder: A field study. *Journal of Clinical Psychology*.

Clohessy, S., & Ehlers, A. (1999). Ptsd symptoms, response to intrusive memories, and coping in ambulance services workers. *British Journal of Clinical Psychology*, **38**, 251–265.

Cohen, J.A., & Mannarino, A.P. (1996). A treatment outcome study for sexually abused preschool children: Initial findings. *Journal of the American Academy of Child and Adolescent Psychiatry*, **35**, 42–50.

Cohen, J.A., & Mannarino, A.P. (1997). A treatment study for sexually abused children: Outcome during a one-year follow-up. *Journal of the American Academy of Child and Adolescent Psychiatry*, **36**, 1228–1235.

Cohen, J.A., & Mannarino, A.P. (1998). Interventions for sexually abused children: Initial treatment outcome findings. *Child Maltreatment*, **3**, 17–26.

Cohen, J.A., Berliner, L., & March, J.S. (2000). Treatment of children and adolescents. In E. Foa, T. Keane, & M. Freidman (Eds), *Effective Treatments for PTSD: Practice Guidelines from the International Society for Traumatic Stress Studies* (pp. 106–138). New York: Guilford.

Deblinger, E., McLeer, S.V., & Henry, D. (1990). Cognitive behavioural treatment for sexually abused children suffering posttraumatic stress: Preliminary findings. *Journal of the American Academy of Child and Adolescent Psychiatry*, **19**, 747–752.

Deblinger, E., Lippman, J., & Steer, R. (1996). Sexually abused children suffering posttraumatic stress symptoms: Initial treatment findings. *Child Maltreatment*, **1**, 310–321.

DiGallo, A., Barton, J., & Parry-Jones, G. (1997). Road traffic accidents: Early psychological consequences in children and adolescents. *British Journal of Psychiatry*, **170**, 358–362.

Dunmore, E., Clark, D.M., & Ehlers, A. (2001). Cognitive factors involved in the onset and maintenance of PTSD. *Behaviour Research and Therapy*, **37**, 809–829.

Earls, F., Smith, E., Reich, W., & Jung, K.G. (1988). Investigating psychopathological consequences of disaster in children: A pilot study incorporating a structured diagnostic approach. *Journal of the American Academy of Child and Adolescent Psychiatry*, **27**, 90–95.

Ehlers, A., & Clark, D.M. (2000). A cognitive model of posttraumatic stress disorder. *Behaviour Research and Therapy*, **38**, 319–345.

Ehlers, A., Maercker, A., & Boos, A. (2000). PTSD following political imprisonment: the role of mental defeat, alienation, and permanent change. *Journal of Abnormal Psychology*, **109**, 45–55.

Ehlers, A., Mayou, R.A., & Bryant, B. (1998). Psychological predictors of chronic PTSD after motor vehicle accidents. *Journal of Abnormal Psychology*, **107**, 508–519.

Ehlers, A., Mayou, R.A., & Bryant, B. (2001). Cognitive predictors of posttraumatic stress disorder in children: results of a prospective longitudinal study. *Behaviour Research and Therapy*.

Ehlers, A., Clark, D.M., Dunmore, E., Jaycox, L., Meadows, E., & Foa, E.B. (1998). Predicting response to exposure treatment in PTSD. The role of mental defeat and alienation. *Journal of Traumatic Stress*, **11**, 457–471.

Fairbanks, J.A., Schlenger, W.E., Saigh, P.A., & Davidson, J.R.T. (1995). An epidemiologic profile of post-traumatic stress disorder: Prevalence, comorbidity, and risk factors. In M.J. Friedman, D.S. Charney, & A.Y. Deutch (Eds), *Neurobiological and clinical consequences of stress: From normal adaptation to PTSD* (pp. 415–427). Philadelphia: Lippincott-Raven Publishers.

Falls, W.A. (1998). Extinction: A review of theory and evidence suggesting that memories are not erased with nonreinforcement. In W. O'Donohue (Ed.), *Learning and behavior therapy* (pp. 205–229). Massachusetts: Allyn & Bacon.

Fletcher, K.E. (1996). Child Posttraumatic Stress Disorder. In E.J. Mash & R. Barkley (Eds), *Child psychopathology* (pp. 242–276). New York: Guilford Press.

Fletcher, K. (1997). Childhood PTSD Interview-Child Form. In E. Carlson (Ed.), *Trauma assessments: A clinician's guide* (pp. 248–250). New York: Guilford Press.

Foa, E.B., & Kozak, M.J. (1986). Emotional processing of fear: Exposure to corrective information. *Psychological Bulletin*, **99**, 220–235.

Foa, E.B., & Meadows, E.A. (1997). Psychosocial treatments for posttraumatic stress disorder: a critical review. *Annual Review of Psychology*, **48**, 449–480.

Foa, E.B., Steketee, G., & Olasov-Rothbaum, B. (1989). Behavioural/cognitive conceptualisations of post-traumatic stress disorder. *Behavior Therapy*, **20**, 155–176.

Foa, E.B., Zinbarg, R., & Olasov-Rothbaum, B. (1992). Uncontrollability and unpredictability in post-traumatic stress disorder: An animal model. *Psychological Bulletin*, **112**, 218–232.

Foa, E.B., Ehlers, A., Clark, D.M., Tolin, D., & Orsillo, S.M. (1999). The posttraumatic cognitions inventory (PCTI): Development and validation. *Psychological Assessment*, **11**, 303–314.

Foy, D.W., Madvig, B.T., Pynoos, R.S., & Camilleri, A.J. (1996). Etiologic factors in the development of posttraumatic stress disorder in children and adolescents. *Journal of School Psychology*, **34**, 133–145.

Foy, D.W., Resnick, H.S., Sipprelle, R.C., & Carroll, E.M. (1987). Etiology of posttraumatic stress disorder in Vietnam Veterans: Analysis of premilitary, military, and combat exposure influences. *Journal of Consulting and Clinical Psychology*, **52**, 79–87.

Frederick, C. (1985). Selected foci in the spectrum of post traumatic stress disorders. In L.J. Murphy (Ed.), *Perspectives on disaster recovery* (pp. 110–130). East Norwalk, CT: Appleton-Century-Crofts.

Garrison, C.Z., Weinrich, M.W., Hardin, S.B., Weinrich, S., & Wang, L. (1993). Post-traumatic stress disorder in adolescents after a hurricane. *American Journal of Epidemiology*, **138**, 522–530.

Giaconia, R., Reinherz, H.Z., Silverman, A.B., Pakiz, B., Frost, A.K., & Cohen, E. (1994). Ages of onset of psychiatric disorders in a community population of older adolescents. *Journal of the American Academy of Child and Adolescent Psychiatry*, **33**, 706–717.

Goenjian, A. (1993). A mental health relief programme in Armenia after the 1988 earthquake. *British Journal of Psychiatry*, **163**, 230–239.

Goenjian, A.K., Karayan, I., Pynoos, R., Steinberg, A., Najarian, L., Asarnow, J., Ghurabi, M., & Fairbanks, L. (1997). Outcome of psychotherapy among early adolescents after trauma. *American Journal of Psychiatry*, **154**, 536–542.

Green, B.L., Korol, M., Grace, M.C., Vary, M.G., Leonard, A.C., Glesser, G.C., & Smithson-Cohen, S. (1991). Children and disaster: Age, gender, and parental effects on PTSD symptoms. *Journal of the American Academy of Child and Adolescent Psychiatry*, **30**, 945–951.

Handford, H.A., Mayes, S.O., Mattison, R.E., Humphrey, F.J., Bagnato, S., Bixler, E.O., & Kales, J.D. (1986). Child and parent reaction to the TMI nuclear accident. *Journal of the American Academy of Child Psychiatry*, **25**, 346–355.

Helzer, J.E., Robins, L.N., & McEnvoy, M.A. (1987). Posttraumatic stress disorder in the general population: Findings of the epidemiological catchment area survey. *The New England Journal of Medicine*, **317**, 1630–1634.

Horowitz, M.J., Wilner, N., & Alvarez, W. (1979). Impact of event scale: A measure of subjective stress. *Psychosomatic Medicine*, **41**, 209–218.

James, B. (1989). *Treating traumatized children: New insights and creative interventions*. Massachusetts: Lexington Books.

Kaufman, J., Birmaher, B., Brent, D., Rao, U., Flynn, C., Moreci, P., Williamson, D., & Ryan, N. (1997). Schedule for Affective Disorders and Schizophrenia for School-Age Children-Present and Lifetime version (K-SADS-PL): Initial reliability and validity data. *Journal of the American Academy of Child and Adolescent Psychiatry*, **36**, 980–988.

Keane, T.M., Fairbank, J.A., & Caddell, J.M. (1989). Implosive (flooding) therapy reduces symptoms of PTSD in Vietnam combat veterans. *Behavior Therapy*, **20**, 245–260.

Keane, T.M., Zimmering, R.T., & Caddell, J.M. (1985). A behavioural formulation of PTSD in Vietnam veterans. *The Behavior Therapist*, **8**, 9–12.

Keppel-Benson, J.M., & Ollendick, T.H. (1993). Posttraumatic stress disorders in children and adolescents. In C.F. Saylor (Ed.), *Children and disasters* (pp. 29–43). New York: Plenum.

Kessler, R.C., Sonnega, A., Bromet, E., Hughes, M., & Nelson, C.B. (1995). Posttraumatic stress disorder in the National Comorbidity Survey. *Archives of General Psychiatry*, **52**, 1048–1060.

Kilpatrick, D., Saunders, B., Amick-McMullan A., Best, C., Veronen, L., & Resnick, H. (1989). Victim and crime factors associated with the development of crime-related posttraumatic stress disorder. *Behavior Therapy*, **20**, 177–198.

Kinzie, J.D., Sack, W.H., Angell, R.H., Manson, S., & Rath, B. (1986). The psychiatric effects of massive trauma on Cambodian children: I. The children. *Journal of the American Academy of Child and Adolescent Psychiatry*, **25**, 370–376.

Koopman, C., Classen, C., & Spiegel, D. (1994). Predictors of posttraumatic stress symptoms among survivors of the Oakland/Berkely California firestorm. *American Journal of Psychiatry*, **151**, 888–894.

Lang, P.J. (1977). Imagery in therapy: An information processing analysis of fear. *Behavior Therapy*, **8**, 862–886.

Lang, P.J. (1985). The cognitive psychophysiology of emotion: Fear and anxiety. In A.H. Turner & J. Maser (Eds), *Anxiety and the anxiety disorders* (pp. 131–170). Hillsdale, NJ: Lawrence Erlbaum Associates.

Litz, B.J. (1992). Emotional numbing in combat-related post-traumatic stress disorder: A critical review and reformulation. *Clinical Psychology Review*, **12**, 417–432.

Lonigan, C.J., Shannon, M.P., Finch, A.J., Daugherty, T.K., & Saylor, C.M. (1991). Children's reactions to a natural disaster: Symptom severity and degree of exposure. *Advances in Behaviour Research and Therapy*, **13**, 135–154.

March, J.S. (1998). Assessment of pediatric posttraumatic stress disorder. In P. Saigh & J. Bremner (Eds), *Posttraumatic stress disorder: A comprehensive approach to assessment and treatment* (pp. 199–218). Needham Heights, MA: Allen & Bacon.

March, J., Amaya-Jackson, L., Terry, R., & Constanzo, P. (1998). Posttraumatic symptomatology in children and adolescents after an industrial fire. *Journal of the American Academy of Child and Adolescent Psychiatry*, **36**, 1080–1088.

March, J.S., Amaya-Jackson, L., Murray, M.C., & Schulte, A. (1998). Cognitive-behavioural psychotherapy for children and adolescents with posttraumatic stress disorder after a single-incident stressor. *Journal of the American Academy of Child and Adolescent Psychiatry*, **37**, 585–593.

McAllister, W. R., & McAllister, D. E. (1998). Two-factor theory: Implications for understanding anxiety based clinical phenomena. In W. O'Donohue & L. Krasner (Eds), *Theories of Behaviour change: Exploring Behaviour change* (pp. 145–171). Washington, DC: American Psychological Association.

McFarlane, A.C. (1987). Family functioning and overprotection following a natural disaster: The longitudinal effects of post-traumatic morbidity. *Australia and New Zealand Journal of Psychiatry*, **21**, 210–218.

McLeer, S.V., Deblinger, E., Henry, D., & Orvaschel, H. (1992). Sexually abused children at high risk for post-traumatic stress disorder. *Journal of the American Academy of Child and Adolescent Psychiatry*, **31**, 875–879.

McNally, R.J. (1991). Assessment of posttraumatic stress disorder in children. *Psychological Assessment*, **3**, 531–537.

McNally, R.J. (1993). Stressors that produce posttraumatic stress disorder in children. In J.R.T. Davidson & E.B. Foa (Eds), *Posttraumatic stress disorder: DSM-IV and beyond* (pp. 55–74). Washington: American Psychiatric Press.

McNally, R.J. (1998). Experimental approaches to cognitive abnormality in posttraumatic stress disorder. *Clinical Psychology Review*, **18**, 971–982.

Milgram, N.A., Toubiana, Y., Klingman, A., Raviv, A., & Goldstein, I. (1988). Situational exposure and personal loss in children's acute and chronic reactions to a school bus disaster. *Journal of Traumatic Stress*, **1**, 339–532.

Mineka, S. (1985). Animal models of anxiety based disorders. In R. Tuma & J. Maser (Eds), *Anxiety and anxiety disorders* (pp. 199–244). Hillsdale, NJ: Erlbaum.

Morgan, R.E., & Riccio, D.C. (1998). Memory retrieval processes. In W. O'Donohue & L. Krasner (Eds), *Theories of behaviour change: Exploring behaviour change* (pp. 464–482). Washington, DC: American Psychological Association.

Murray, J., Ehlers, A., & Mayou, R.A. (2000). *Dissociation and posttraumatic stress disorder:*

Two prospective studies of motor vehicle accident survivors. Manuscript submitted for publication.

Nader, K.O. (1995). Assessing traumatic experiences in children. In J.P. Wilson & T.M. Keane (Eds), *Assessing psychological trauma and PTSD: A handbook for practitioners* (pp. 217–244). New York: Guilford Press.

Nader, K.O., & Fairbanks, L. (1994). The suppression of reexperiencing: Impulse control and somatic symptoms in children following traumatic exposure. *Anxiety, Stress, and Coping: An International Journal*, **7**, 229–239.

Nader, K.O., & Pynoos, R.S. (1989). *Child posttraumatic stress disorder inventory: Parent Interview*. An unpublished manuscript. University of California, Los Angeles.

Nader, K., Blake, D., Kriegler, J., & Pynoos, R. (1994). *Clinician Administered PTSD Scale: Child and Adolescent Version (CAPS-C), Current and Lifetime Version, and Instruction Manual*. UCLA Neuropsychiatric Institute and National Center for PTSD.

Nader, K., Pynoos, R.S., Fairbanks, L., & Frederick, C. (1990). Childhood PTSD reactions one year after a sniper attack. *American Journal of Psychiatry*, **147**, 1526–1530.

North, C.S., Nixon, S.J., Shariat, S., Mallonee, S., McMillen, J.C., Spitznagel, E.L., & Smith, E.M. (1999). Psychiatric disorders among survivors of the Oklahoma City Bombing. *Journal of the American Medical Association*, **282**, 755–762.

Olasov-Rothbaum, B., Meadows, E.A., Resick, P., & Foy, D.W. (2000). Cognitive-behavioural therapy. In E. Foa, T. Keane, & M: Freidman (Eds), *Effective Treatments for PTSD: Practice Guidelines from the International Society for Traumatic Stress Studies* (pp. 60–83). New York: Guilford.

Ollendick, T.H. (1983). Reliability and validity of the Revised Fear Survey Schedule for Children (FSSC-R). *Behaviour Research and Therapy*, **21**, 685–692.

Pavlov, I.P. (1927). *Conditioned reflexes*. London: Oxford University Press.

Perry, B.D., Pollard, R.A., Blakley, T.L., Baker, W.L., & Vigilante, D. (1995). Childhood trauma, the neurobiology of adaptation, and "use-dependent" development of the brain: How "states" become "traits". *Infant Mental Health Journal*, **16**, 271–291.

Power, M.J., & Dalgleish, T. (1999). Two routes to emotion: Some implications of mulit-level theories of emotion for therapeutic practice. *Behavioural and Cognitive Psychotherapy*, **27** (2), 129–141.

Putnam, F.W. (1997). *Dissociation in children and adolescents: A developmental perspective*. New York: Guilford Press.

Pynoos, R.S., & Eth, S. (1986). Witness to violence: The child interview. *Journal of the American Academy of Child and Adolescent Psychiatry*, **25**, 306–319.

Pynoos, R.S., & Nader, K. (1988). Psychological first aid and treatment approaches for children exposed to community violence: Research implications. *Journal of Traumatic Stress*, **1**, 243–267.

Pynoos, R.S., & Nader, K. (1993). Issues in the treatment of posttraumatic stress in children and adolescents. In J. Wilson & B. Raphael (Eds), *International handbook of traumatic stress syndromes* (pp. 535–549). New York: Plenum Press.

Pynoos, R.S., Frederick, C., Nader, K., Arroyo, W., Steinberg, A., Eth, S., Nunez, F., & Fairbanks, L. (1987). Life threat and posttraumatic stress in school-age children. *Archives of General Psychiatry*, **44**, 1057–1063.

Pynoos, R.S., Goenjian, A., Karakashian, M., Tashjian, M., Manjikian, R., Manoukian, G., Steinberg, A.M., & Fairbanks, L.A. (1993). Posttraumatic stress reactions in children after the 1988 Armenian earthquake. *British Journal of Psychiatry*, **163**, 239–247.

Rachman, S. (1980). Emotional processing. *Behaviour Research and Therapy*, **18**, 51–60.

Reich, W., Shakya, J.J., & Taibelson, C. (1991). *Diagnostic Interview for Children and Adolescents (DICA)*. St Louis, MO: Washington University.

Resnick, H., Kilpatrick, D., Dansky, B., Saunders, B., & Best, C. (1993). Prevalence of civilian trauma and posttraumatic stress disorder in a representative national sample of women. *Journal of Consulting and Clinical Psychology*, **61**, 984–991.

Reynolds, C.R., & Richmond, B.O. (1978). What I think and feel: A revised measure of children's manifest anxiety. *Journal of Abnormal Child Psychology*, **6**, 271–280.

Sack, W.H., McSharry, S., Clarke, G.N., Kinney, R., Seeley, M.S., & Lewinsohn, P. (1994). The Khmer Adolescent Project: I. Epidemiologic findings in two generations of Cambodian refugees. *Journal of Nervous and Mental Diseases*, **182**, 387–395.

Saigh, P.A. (1987). In-vitro flooding of an adolescent's posttraumatic stress disorder. *Journal of Clinical Child Psychology*, **16**, 147–150.

Saigh, P.A. (1987a). In-vitro flooding of a childhood posttraumatic stress disorder. *School Psychology Review*, **16**, 203–211.

Saigh, P.A. (1989). The validity of DSM-III posttraumatic stress disorder classification as applied to children. *Journal of Abnormal Psychology*, **198**, 189–192.

Saigh, P.A. (1989a). The use of in-vitro flooding in the treatment of a traumatized adolescent. *Journal of Behavioural and Developmental Paediatrics*, **10**, 17–21.

Saigh, P.A. (1991). The development of posttraumatic stress disorder following four different types of traumatization. *Behaviour Research and Therapy*, **29**, 213–216.

Saigh, P.A. (1992) The behavioural treatment of child and adolescent posttraumatic stress disorder. *Advances in Behaviour Research and Therapy*, **14**, 247–275.

Saigh. P.A., Yasik, A.E., Oberfield, R., Indamar, S., Rubenstien, H., & Nester, J. (unpublished manuscript). *The development and validation of the DSM-IV version of the Children's Posttraumatic Stress Disorder Inventory*.

Salmon K., & Bryant, R.A. (2002). Posttraumatic stress disorder in children: The influence of developmental factors. *Clinical Psychology Review*, **22**, 163–188.

Scheeringa, M.S., & Zeanah, C.H. (1995). Symptom expression and trauma variables in children under 48 months of age. *Infant Mental Health Journal*, **16** (4), 259–270.

Scheeringa, M.S., Zeanah, C.H., Drell, M.J., & Larrieu, J.A. (1995). Two approaches to diagnosing posttraumatic stress disorder in infancy and early childhood. *Journal of the American Academy of Child and Adolescent Psychiatry*, **34**, 191–200.

Schwarz, E.D., & Kowalski, J.M. (1991). Posttraumatic stress disorder after a school shooting: Effects of symptom threshold selection and diagnosis by DSM-III, DSM-III-R, or proposed DSM-IV. *American Journal of Psychiatry*, **148**, 592–597.

Schwarz, E.D., & Perry, B.D. (1994). The post-traumatic response in children and adolescents. *Psychiatric Clinics of North America*, **17**, 311–326.

Shalev, A., Peri, T., Cannetti, L., & Schrieber, S. (1996). Predictors of PTSD and injured trauma survivors: A prospective study. *American Journal of Psychiatry*, **153**, 219–225.

Shannon, M.P., Lonigan, C.J., Finch, A.J., & Taylor, C.M. (1994). Children exposed to disaster. I: Epidemiology of posttraumatic symptoms and symptom profiles. *Journal of the American Academy of Child and Adolescent Psychiatry*, **33**, 80–93.

Shapiro, F. (1989). Eye movement desensitization: A new treatment for post traumatic stress disorder. *Journal of Behaviour Therapy and Experimental Psychiatry*, **20**, 211–217.

Shapiro, F. (1995). *Eye movement desensitization and reprocessing: Basic principles, protocols and procedures*. New York: Guilford Press.

Smith, P., Perrin, S., Dyregov, A., & Yule W. (2002). Principal components analysis of the Impact of Event Scale with children in war. *Personality and Individual Differences*.

Smith, P., Perrin, S., Yule, W., & Rabe-Hesketh, S. (2001). War-exposure and maternal reactions in the psychological adjustment of children from Bosnia-Hercegovina. *Journal of Child Psychology and Psychiatry*, **42** (3), 395–404.

Southwick, S.M., Bremner, D., Krystal, J.H., & Charney, D.S. (1994). Psychobiologic research in post-traumatic stress disorder. *Psychiatric Clinics of North America*, **17**, 251–264.

Spiegel, D. (1984). Multiple personality as posttraumatic stress disorder. *Psychiatric Clinics of North America*, **7**, 101–110.

Stallard, P., & Law, F. (1993). Screening and psychological debriefing of adolescent survivors of life threatening events. *British Journal of Psychiatry*, **163**, 660–665.

Stallard, P., Velleman, R., & Baldwin, S. (1998). Prospective study of posttraumatic stress disorder in children involved in road traffic accidents. *British Medical Journal*, **317**, 1619–1623.

Steil, R., & Ehlers, A. (2000). Dysfunctional meaning of posttraumatic intrusions in chronic PTSD. *Behaviour Research and Therapy*, **38**, 537–558.

Sternberg, K.J., Lamb, M.E., Greenbaum, C., Cichetti, D., Dawud, S., Cortes, R.M., Krispin, O., & Lorey, F. (1993). Effects of domestic violence on children's behavior problems and depression. *Developmental Psychology*, **29**, 44–52.

Udwin, O., Boyle, S., Yule, W., Bolton, D., & O'Ryan, D. (2000). Risk factors for long-term psychological effects of a disaster experienced in adolescence: Predictors of posttraumatic stress disorder. *Journal of Child Psychology and Psychiatry*, **41**, 969–979.

Vernberg, E.M., & Varela, R.E. (2001). PTSD: A developmental perspective. In M. Vasey & M.R. Dadds (Eds), *The developmental psychopathology of anxiety* (pp. 386–406). New York: Oxford University Press.

Wagner, A.R. (1979). Habituation and memory. In A. Dickinson & R.A. Boakes (Eds), *Mechanisms of learning and motivation* (pp. 5–47). Hillsdale, NJ: Erlbaum.

Wagner, A.R. (1981). SOP: A model of automatic memory processing in animal behaviour. In N. Spear & R. Miller (Eds), *Information processing in animals: Memory mechanisms* (pp. 301–336). California: Academic Press.

WHO (1992). *International classification of diseases* (10th revised edn). Geneva: World Health Organization.

Wolfe, V.V., Gentile, C., Sas, L., & Wolfe, D.A. (1991). Children's Impact of Traumatic Events Scale: A measure of post-sexual abuse PTSD symptoms. *Behavioural Assessment*, **13**, 359–338.

Wolfe, V.V., Gentile, C., & Wolfe, D.A. (1989). The impact of sexual abuse on children: A PTSD formulation. *Behavior Therapy*, **20**, 215–228.

Yule, W. (1992). Post traumatic stress disorder in child survivors of shipping disasters: The sinking of the "Jupiter". *Psychotherapy and Psychosomatics*, **57**, 200–205.

Yule, W. (1994). Post traumatic stress disorders. In M. Rutter, E. Taylor, & L. Hersov (Eds), *Child and adolescent psychiatry: Modern approaches* (3rd edn; pp. 392–406). Oxford: Blackwells.

Yule, W., & Udwin, O. (1991). Screening child survivors for post-traumatic stress disorders: Experiences from the "Jupiter" sinking. *British Journal of Clinical Psychology*, **30**, 131–138.

Yule, W., & Williams, R. (1990). Post traumatic stress reactions in children. *Journal of Traumatic Stress*, **3**, 279–295.

Yule, W., Udwin, O., & Murdoch, K. (1990). The "Jupiter" sinking: Effects on children's fears, depression and anxiety. *Journal of Child Psychology and Psychiatry*, **31**, 1051–1061.

CHAPTER 11

Treatment of School Refusal

David Heyne

Leiden University, The Netherlands

and

Neville J. King

Monash University, Australia

INTRODUCTION

School refusal can be a severely disruptive and disabling condition which jeopardizes a young person's social, emotional, academic, and vocational development. As well as causing difficulties for the young person, school refusal contributes to distress for concerned parents and school staff, and it may provoke family disruption and conflict. Moreover, successful management of the problem often presents a real challenge to education and mental health professionals (Kahn, Nursten, & Carroll, 1996).

An initial challenge surrounds correct classification of non-attendance problems. There are different terms such as separation anxiety and school phobia that have been used interchangeably to refer to similar constructs (Phelps, Cox, & Bajorek, 1992). Conversely, similar terms such as school refusal and school refusal behaviour have been defined differently by some authors. Kearney and Silverman (1996) use the term *school refusal behaviour* to describe cases of "child-motivated refusal to attend school or difficulties remaining in classes for an entire day" (p. 345), including problems of truancy. Others draw a distinction between truancy and school refusal, preferring to use the more focused term *school refusal* for cases where difficulty attending school is associated with emotional distress (cf. King & Bernstein, 2001; Martin et al., 1999; Okuyama et al., 1999), is not associated with serious antisocial behaviour (cf. Heyne et al., 2002; Honjo et al., 2001; McShane, Walter, & Rey, 2001), and involves the child usually staying at home versus being absent from home (cf. Hansen et al., 1998; Kameguchi & Murphy-Shigematsu, 2001).

Correspondence to David Heyne, Faculty of Social and Behavioural Sciences, Depertment of Developmental and Educational Psychology, P.O. Box 9555, 2300 RB Leiden, The Netherlands; email: heyne@fsw.LeidenUniv.nl

Handbook of Interventions that Work with Children and Adolescents: Prevention and Treatment.
Edited by P.M. Barrett and T.H. Ollendick. © 2004 John Wiley & Sons, Ltd. ISBN 0-470-84453-1.

In this chapter we prefer the term *school refusal* rather than *school phobia* or *separation anxiety*. School refusal implies a difficulty with school attendance, without identifying the problem as exclusively related to a phobia of something in the school environment or to separation anxiety. Furthermore, we use it to distinguish between school refusal and truancy—two reasonably distinct types of attendance problems often requiring different approaches to intervention (Berg, 2002). Berg and colleagues' initial criteria (Berg, Nichols, & Pritchard, 1969) and revised criteria (Berg, 1997, 2002; Bools et al., 1990) help to identify school refusal and distinguish it from truancy. The criteria include: (1) reluctance or refusal to attend school, often (but not necessarily) leading to prolonged absence; (2) the child usually remaining at home during school hours, rather than concealing the problem from parents; (3) displays of emotional upset at the prospect of attending school, which may be reflected in excessive fearfulness, temper tantrums, misery, or possibly in the form of unexplained physical symptoms; (4) an absence of severe antisocial tendencies, beyond the child's resistance to parental attempts to get the child to school; and (5) reasonable parental efforts to secure the child's attendance at school, at some stage in the history of the problem. These criteria also help to distinguish between school refusal and another type of attendance problem, that of school withdrawal, which is associated with parental ambivalence or opposition toward the child attending school regularly (Kahn & Nursten, 1962). Blagg (1987) similarly identified cases of non-attendance that were associated more with the family's covert support for non-attendance than with school refusal or truancy.

Phenomenology

The onset of school refusal may be sudden (e.g., occurring immediately after school holidays) or gradual (e.g., progressing over weeks or months from vague complaints of dislike of school, through slowness in getting ready for school, to outright refusal to attend). For some school refusers, absenteeism may be sporadic or non-existent. Others display pervasive absenteeism, consistently absent from school for weeks, months, or even years at a time.

The emotional distress associated with school refusal may be manifest in a wide variety of ways, with varying degrees of severity, at varying times, and in various settings. Behaviourally, when pressured to attend school, there may be complaints about school, whining, and temper tantrums, and some young people threaten to run away or to harm themselves (Berg, 2002; Blagg, 1987). The young person may seek to avoid the distress associated with school attendance by refusing to get out of bed or to get ready for school, or refusing to get into the car to travel to school. Some set out for school but instead return home in a state of anxiety, and others appear to behave normally after arriving at school, their fear seeming to have rapidly dissipated, only to recur the next day when it is time for school again (Berg, 2002).

Somatic symptoms are commonly associated with school refusal. In an investigation of outpatient adolescent school refusers with comorbid anxiety and depressive disorders (Bernstein et al., 1997), the most common self-reported symptoms were feeling faint or dizzy, feeling sick in the stomach, backpain, stomach pains, and frequent vomiting.[1] Among Japanese school refusers, common symptoms have been categorized as gastrointestinal symptoms (e.g., diarrhoea, nausea, vomiting), pain symptoms (e.g., headaches, back pain), cardiopulmonary symptoms (e.g., palpitation, shortness of breath), and other autonomic symptoms (e.g., fever, vertigo) (Honjo et al., 2001).

The cognitive component of school refusal involves irrational or dysfunctional thoughts associated with school attendance. Hersov (1985) observed that "many children insist that they want to go to school and prepare to do so but cannot manage it when the time comes" (p. 384). In these situations young people may, for example, overestimate the likelihood of anxiety-provoking situations occurring at school or harm befalling their parents, underestimate their own ability to cope with anxiety-provoking situations, magnify the unpleasant aspects of school attendance, or misinterpret the thoughts and actions of others at school (e.g., Kearney, 2001; King et al., 1998a).

While diagnoses are not applicable in all cases of school refusal (e.g., Berg et al., 1993; Bernstein & Borchardt, 1996), many school refusers meet criteria for anxiety disorders and to a lesser extent depressive disorders, the latter often overlapping with anxiety disorders (e.g., Bernstein, 1991; Last & Strauss, 1990; Martin et al., 1999; McShane, Walter, & Rey, 2001). A broad range of anxiety disorders have been reported in studies of clinically-referred school refusers. In Bernstein et al.'s (1999) sample of 46 anxious-depressed school refusers, DSM-III-R (APA, 1987) anxiety disorders included overanxious disorder (91%), simple phobia (89%), social phobia (71%), avoidant disorder (52%), agoraphobia (39%), separation anxiety disorder (30%), obsessions (20%), compulsions (13%), panic disorder (7%), and post-traumatic stress disorder (7%). In our own study of 61 anxiety-disordered school refusers (Heyne et al., 2002), primary DSM-IV (APA, 1994) diagnoses included adjustment disorder with anxiety (39%), anxiety disorder not otherwise specified (15%), separation anxiety disorder (10%), social phobia (10%), generalized anxiety disorder (3%), specific phobia (3%), obsessive-compulsive disorder (2%), agoraphobia without history of panic disorder (2%), and panic disorder with agoraphobia (2%).

Increasing attention is being paid to the relationship between school refusal and depression. Questions include: the extent to which depression is a specific feature of school refusal, separate from it, or part of the anxiety associated with school refusal (Elliott, 1999; Honjo et al., 2001); the causal relationship between school refusal and depression (Bernstein & Garfinkel, 1986; Kearney, 1993); and the impact of depression on the outcome of treatments for school refusal (Bernstein et al., 2000; Okuyama et al., 1999). Notwithstanding this uncertainty, it is likely that many young people with school refusal will meet criteria for a depressive disorder or will experience problematic depressive symptoms (cf. Kearney, 1993), especially adolescent school refusers (Baker & Wills, 1978; McShane, Walter, & Rey, 2001).

School refusal is also associated with externalizing behaviour. School refusers may become stubborn, argumentative, and display aggressive behaviours when their parents attempt to get them to go to school (Berg, 2002; Hersov, 1985; Hoshino et

---

[1] The self-report instrument (Diagnostic Interview for Children and Adolescents—Revised—Adolescent Version) did not assess for headaches.

al., 1987; King & Ollendick, 1989b), although more severe antisocial behaviours such as stealing and destructiveness are not characteristically shown (Berg, 2002). As well as being an expression of a young person's anxiety, externalizing behaviour has been hypothesized to represent an exaggeration of distress to induce parental guilt or to intimidate parents, with the aim of avoiding anxiety-provoking situations (Kearney, 2001). School refusers who consistently display multiple externalizing behaviours over time may be diagnosed with oppositional defiant disorder.

Epidemiology

In a review of prevalence rates reported in the literature, Granell de Aldaz et al. (1984) found rates as disparate as 0.01% and 25%, varying according to the population studied, the methodology employed, and the criteria for defining school refusal. In their own study of Venezuelan pre-school and school-age children aged between 3 and 14 years, Granell de Aldaz and colleagues used a range of criteria to estimate the prevalence of school refusal. When using the criteria of children's reports of fear together with frequent non-attendance, the prevalence rate was 1.2%. In the USA, Ollendick and Mayer (1984) used the Berg, Nichols, and Pritchard (1969) criteria to investigate the occurrence of school refusal among school-age children, yielding an incidence rate of 0.4%. In a 1973 survey of children in England and Wales, 1.3% were reportedly absent during the week of the survey due to school refusal (Kahn, Nursten, & Carroll, 1996). Overall, it appears that somewhere between 1 and 2% of all school-age children will exhibit school refusal at some point.

Among clinic-referred young people, early estimates of the incidence of school refusal were around 5% (Burke & Silverman, 1987; Hersov, 1985), and probably higher among secondary school students (Hersov, 1985). In a recent Australian study McShane, Walter, and Rey (2001) reported that adolescent school refusal cases constituted 7% of the clinic population. According to a Japanese study, approximately 16% of young people aged under 18 and attending an outpatient clinic were unable to "make himself/herself go to school because of some psychological factor" (Honjo, Kasahara, & Ohtaka, 1992, p. 29). Some reports suggest that the rate of school refusal cases is increasing (e.g., Honjo, Kasahara, & Ohtaka, 1992; Kameguchi & Murphy-Shigematsu, 2001; Ollendick & Mayer, 1984), although Gordon and Young (1976) pointed out early on that the notion of an increase may be reflective of a greater awareness of the problem and propensity to refer for treatment. A recent study of non-referred young people indicated an increase in attendance problems (Iwamoto & Yoshida, 1997), although there was no report of time-related changes in incidence according to the different types of non-attendance problems (i.e., distinguishing between school refusal and truancy).

Reviews generally indicate that school refusal is equally common in both sexes (Kearney, 2001; King & Ollendick, 1989b; Ollendick & Mayer, 1984; Timberlake, 1984). School refusal can occur throughout the entire range of school years, and there are reports of referral-related peaks at certain ages and transition points. Hersov (1985) suggested that it is more prevalent between 5 and 7 years of age, at 11 years of age, and at 14 years of age and older, roughly corresponding to early schooling, change of school, and nearing the end of compulsory education. In a study of 63 school refusers with diagnosed anxiety disorders, Last and Strauss (1990) observed that the peak age range for referral was from 13 to 15 years, with some elevation also noted at 10 years of age. Others have similarly suggested that school refusal has a higher prevalence in pre-adolescence and adolescence relative to early or middle childhood (Kearney, Eisen, & Silverman, 1995; Last, 1992).

An important consideration with respect to age-related trends is the distinction between the young person's age when he or she is ultimately referred for help, and the age at onset of the first episode of school refusal. In a review of 63 school refusers' case files, Smith (1970) observed two peaks for age at onset: 5 to 6 years and 11 to 12 years. In a large sample of clinic-referred school refusers aged 10 to 17 years ($N = 192$), the majority (78%) first exhibited school refusal in the first or second year of secondary school, with a mean age of onset of 12.3 years (s.d. = 2.6) (McShane, Walter, & Rey, 2001).

Some early reports suggested that school refusers frequently are of above-average intelligence (e.g., Davidson, 1960; Nursten, 1958; Rodriguez, Rodriguez, & Eisenberg, 1959), while other studies suggested that school refusers show a fairly normal distribution of intelligence (e.g., Baker & Wills, 1978; Chazan, 1962; Hampe et al., 1973). Naylor et al. (1994) found that hospitalized adolescent school refusers had a significantly higher incidence of language impairments and learning difficulties relative to diagnosis-, age-, and sex-matched psychiatric controls, but in another sample of inpatient school refusers there was no evidence of "educational backwardness" (Berg, 1980, p. 242). In their study of a more representative sample of school refusers, Hampe et al. (1973) suggested that academic achievement is distributed much as it is in the general population.

Overall, the available literature provides no clear evidence that socioeconomic status is directly associated with the incidence of school refusal, and the relationship between race and school refusal is also unclear (Kearney, 2001). Reports on the occurrence of single-parent families in school refusal cases vary. For example, fathers were absent or deceased in none of Talbot's (1957) sample of 24 clinic-referred school refusers and in 16% of Hersov's (1960) clinic-referred sample, whereas 38% and 51% of children came from single-parent households in the studies by Bernstein, Svingen, and Garfinkel (1990) and Last and Strauss (1990), respectively. Data from controlled studies (e.g., Bernstein & Borchardt, 1996; Lang, 1982) suggest that single-parent families are in fact over-represented among cases of school refusal. Regarding family position, Kearney's (2001) review suggested that school refusers tend to be the only, or the eldest, or the youngest child in the family.

AETIOLOGY

The range of clinical presentations and diagnoses that may be associated with school refusal points to its aetiological complexity. A helpful way to organize the range of potentially relevant aetiological factors is to consider the domains of predisposing, precipitating, and perpetuating factors.

Much of the discussion and research to date highlights the potential role of parent and family factors in predisposing young people to the development of school refusal. Early reports suggested that the child's dependency is fostered or condoned by the mother (e.g., Berg & McGuire, 1974; Eisenberg, 1958). Recent reports similarly emphasize the overprotection and over-involvement of mothers in the families of some school refusers (e.g., Kameguchi & Murphy-Shigematsu, 2001; Kearney & Silverman, 1995), and suggest that parents may give mixed messages to their children about school attendance and independence (Bernstein, Svingen, & Garfinkel, 1990). Detached family relationships have also been associated with school refusal (Bernstein et al., 1999; Kearney & Silverman, 1995). For example, Bernstein et al. (1999) proposed that adolescent school refusers may seek to rebel following a childhood in which enmeshment was prominent. Regarding family constellation, Bernstein and Borchardt (1996) speculated that the characteristics of single parent family situations may predispose the young person to school refusal. Conversely, in dual parent families characterized by marital conflict, the child may learn that, in his or her absence, the family structure will disintegrate (Valles & Oddy, 1984). Parental psychopathology may also be linked to the development of school refusal (cf. Kameguchi & Murphy-Shigematsu, 2001; Martin et al., 1999).

At the individual level, young people prone to anxiety, depression, and associated social difficulties may be particularly susceptible to school refusal (Elliott, 1999). However, questions about whether school refusal precedes other problems such as anxiety or depression or is an outcome of those other problems are often unanswered (Kearney, 2001). The frustration and impairment in academic performance as a result of language disorders and learning difficulties may also contribute to the development of school refusal (cf. Naylor et al., 1994). At a community level, increasing social pressure for students to achieve academically and the associated competitiveness of school environments is held to contribute to non-attendance problems in Japan (Iwamoto & Yoshida, 1997; Kameguchi & Murphy-Shigematsu, 2001). More research is required to identify those school-based factors that are associated with school refusal (Okuyama et al., 1999).

Many precipitating factors have been associated with the onset of school refusal. In Smith's (1970) review of the files of 63 inpatient and outpatient school refusers, common precipitants included: a change of school, especially from primary school to secondary school; an absence due to illness; an upsetting family event; and a frightening event at school. Among a sample of 17 non-referred school refusers, Place et al. (2000) noted that all but one completely attributed their non-attendance to bullying. Place and colleagues suggested that this may have been "an explanation of convenience" for some young people but that, clearly, "events were traumatic" for others (p. 350). Among a referred sample of 192 adolescent school refusers, McShane, Walter, and Rey (2001) identified conflict with family or peers, academic difficulties, family separation, change of home or school, and physical illness as key stressors associated with the onset of school refusal.

Specific school-based situations that might be avoided by some young people include tests, oral presentations, athletic performance, undressing for showers, having to complete homework, and the reactions of teachers (Kearney & Beasley, 1994; Leung, 1989; Ollendick & Mayer, 1984). Other high-risk times for the onset of school refusal might include the times following major holidays (King et al., 2001b), mother's commencing work (Ollendick & Mayer, 1984), and the death of someone in the close or extended social network of the young person (Davidson, 1960). More unique precipitants have included the development of a fear at a movie (Smith, 1970) and neurological aetiology such as a brain tumour (Stein et al., 1996). For some school refusers, precipitating events are not identifiable (e.g., Baker & Wills, 1978; Smith, 1970); identification of precipitating events is more likely in those cases where the onset of school refusal is more recent (cf. Baker & Wills, 1978). In many cases, a combination of precipitating events is reported (e.g., Silove & Manicavasagar, 1993).

A vicious cycle may set in once young people stay away from school, and for this reason Okuyama et al. (1999) described school refusal as "a serious psychiatric emergency" (p. 462). A range of factors may be involved in the perpetuation of the problem, and much discussion relates to parent and family functioning. For example, in reporting on parent–child relationships in the families of school refusers relative to a normative sample, Bernstein, Svingen, and Garfinkel (1990) suggested that the parents of school refusers may be ineffective in their role to facilitate a return to school, and that the child may assume a hostile, defiant and controlling role within the family. Likewise, King, Ollendick, and Tonge (1995) suggested that overly dependent mothers and uninvolved fathers may lack effective parenting strategies important to the management of school refusal. The psychopathology that is frequently evidenced in parents of school refusers (e.g., Bernstein & Garfinkel, 1988; Bools et al., 1990; Last et al., 1987; Martin et al., 1999) may perpetuate the problem, inasmuch as the parents' own anxiety or depression may make it difficult for them to appropriately support their child.

The secondary gain associated with not being at school is a common factor in school refusers' ongoing avoidance of school (Burke & Silverman, 1987; Kearney, 2001). This might be in the form of parental attention and tangible reinforcement such as access to the television, the computer, pets, toys, food, etc. Negative reinforcement of school refusal may be another significant factor in its continuation, in that the young person's non-attendance is reinforced by the avoidance of negative affect associated with being at school (Kearney, 2001). The cognitions of the young person are also linked to the perpetuation of school refusal; the more time that is spent away from school, the more likely it is that some young people will think that they cannot cope with the social and academic aspects of school (Okuyama et al., 1999). In particular, they may expect difficulty in answering peers' or teacher's questions about their absence (Heyne et al., 1998). Once school refusers have cut themselves off from regular attendance, they may become increasingly anxious and depressed (Berg, 2002).

ASSESSMENT

Having determined that the problem is principally one of school refusal, and not truancy or school withdrawal, a multi-source and multi-method assessment is conducted. The diversity of aetiological factors and clinical presentations associated with school refusal invalidates the use of a single informant or assessment method. Data are used to form and test hypotheses about the development and maintenance of school refusal and thus to plan appropriate treatment. During (or even prior to)

assessment, a medical examination should be conducted to rule out physical aeti-
ologies, given that school refusal is often associated with somatic complaints and
sometimes follows a genuine physical illness. Throughout assessment, much support
needs to be provided to families and to school staff, because of the distress associated with the crisis-like presentation of school refusal (Heyne & Rollings, 2002;
Kearney, 2001).

Clinical-Behavioural Interviews

Clinical-behavioural interviews are conducted to obtain detailed information about
target behaviours and the variables that occasion and maintain the behaviours. They
also inform the selection of additional assessment methods as required (e.g., psychoeducational testing). Given that the young people and their parent(s) will often
have different perspectives on the school refusal problem, we spend considerable
time conducting separate interviews, allowing each the opportunity to freely discuss
their views (cf. Blagg, 1987).

Blagg's (1987) guidelines for conducting interviews with school-refusing children
and parents provide an efficient way to obtain pertinent information. Another set
of interview schedules for use with school refusers and their parents is presented in
Heyne and Rollings (2002). In addition to questioning around central areas (e.g.,
history of school refusal; stressors inside and outside of school; prior efforts to
address the school refusal), the interviews encourage close inquiry regarding the
household routine on school mornings, the child's activities when not at school, attitudes toward school and school attendance, and attributions regarding the maintenance of school refusal. When interviewing the young person, we refrain from asking
about non-attendance too early in the process to avoid jeopardizing the establishment of a working relationship. Often, school refusers have already been asked
"why can't you go to school?" by a host of well-meaning people, leading to the young
people's increased frustration or resistance if they are unable or unwilling to identify contributing factors.

Stemming from the work of Mansdorf and Lukens (1987), we supplement the
clinical-behavioural interviews with self-statement assessments. Separate self-
statement assessments are conducted with the school refuser and his or her parents,
using a series of standardized questions (see Heyne & Rollings, 2002). This form of
assessment helps to systematically identify child and parent cognitions that may be
associated with the development and maintenance of school refusal and may
warrant attention during treatment.

We also visit the school to interview relevant staff about the young person's social,
emotional, behavioural, and academic functioning, with a particular focus on the
manifestation of anxious and depressive symptomatology. When feasible, direct
observations of the young person and parents are conducted in the home and school
settings, providing a source of detailed information about the antecedents and consequences of the young person's reluctance and resistance. When this is not feasible, parents and school staff are supported in the process of making and recording
behavioural observations, using tailored monitoring diaries. (See Kearney, 2001, for
a discussion of direct behavioural observations.)

Diagnostic Interviews

Diagnostic interviews assist in the development of a comprehensive profile of the range and severity of difficulties for the young person. Notwithstanding problems in differentiating among diagnostic categories, efforts to develop a diagnostic profile allow for use of the knowledge base for treating specific disorders (cf. Evans, 2000). Silverman and Albano's (1996) Anxiety Disorders Interview Schedule for Children facilitates differential diagnosis among major DSM-IV disorders. It was designed around anxiety-related disorders in children and adolescents, but includes sections on mood disorders and behaviour disorders. Separate interview schedules are available for use with the child (ADIS-C) and with the parents (ADIS-P), and composite diagnoses are developed based on the reports of both parties. The ADIS-C/P have demonstrated adequate inter-rater reliability (Rapee et al., 1994) and satisfactory test–retest reliability at the symptom level (Silverman & Rabian, 1995) and disorder level (Silverman & Eisen, 1992). The benefits of employing this reliable method for diagnostic assessment need to be weighed up against the time required for use of a diagnostic interview schedule and the clinician's competence in diagnosis.

Self-Report Measures

There is a wide range of psychometrically sound self-report measures that may be used to efficiently assess levels of fear, anxiety, and depression in the school-refusing child or adolescent. Measures of fear and anxiety include: the Fear Survey Schedule for Children—Revised (FSSC-R; Ollendick, 1983) and its later version, the Fear Survey Schedule for Children—II (FSSC-II; Gullone & King, 1992); the Revised Children's Manifest Anxiety Scale (RCMAS; Reynolds & Richmond, 1978) and a newer measure of anxiety, the Spence Children's Anxiety Scale (SCAS; Spence, 1998); and more focused measures such as the Social Anxiety Scale for Children—Revised (SASC-R; La Greca & Stone, 1993). While depression should not be assumed, it should be assessed (Kearney, 2001), and the Children's Depression Inventory (CDI; Kovacs, 1992) is commonly employed.

A self-report measure which focuses upon the cognitions of school refusers was developed by Heyne et al. (1998). The Self-Efficacy Questionnaire for School Situations (SEQ-SS) assesses young people's efficacy expectations regarding their ability to cope with potential anxiety-provoking situations such as doing school work, handling peers' questions about absence from school, and being separated from parents during school-time. Recent reviews provide detailed discussion of these and other self-report measures for use in the assessment of school refusal (see Kearney, 2001; Ollendick & King, 1998).

Self-Monitoring

In self-monitoring, the young person is asked to report on clinically relevant target behaviours at the time of their occurrence, facilitating a more focused assessment.

We frequently ask the young person to monitor their emotional distress on successive school mornings using an index card for recording feelings and symptoms. Depending on the young person's age and compliance, self-monitoring procedures can be used to help to identify antecedents and consequences that maintain school refusal (Ollendick & King, 1998). For example, diaries might be tailored to experiences such as attending certain subjects or being in the school-yard during lunchtimes. Beidel, Neal, and Lederer (1991) developed a daily diary for the assessment of anxiety in school children, and this may also be usefully employed with school refusers.

Parent- and Teacher-Completed Measures

Parents are often asked to monitor the young person's daily attendance, emotional distress, and levels of cooperation and resistance. Information on levels of partner support, parental responses to the young person's emotional distress and noncompliance, and levels of stress experienced by the family may also be included in monitoring diaries completed by parents (cf. Kearney & Albano, 2000a, 2000b). At a more general level, a variety of parent- and teacher-completed measures have been used in the assessment of school-refusing children and adolescents. For example, the Child Behavior Checklist (CBCL; Achenbach, 1991a) assesses the competencies and behaviour problems of children aged 4 to 18 years from the perspective of the parent. The Teacher's Report Form (TRF; Achenbach, 1991b) is a corresponding measure for gaining the perspective of school staff. The CBCL and TRF yield scores for two broad-band behavioural dimensions (internalizing and externalizing) together with scores for subscales including withdrawal, social problems, anxiety/depression, somatic complaints, attention problems, aggressive behaviours, and delinquent behaviours. There is much research support for the psychometric properties of these measures (Daugherty & Shapiro, 1994), and their clinical utility is enhanced by the extensive normative data for boys and girls of varying ages (King & Ollendick, 1989a).

Assessment of parent and family functioning is also important in understanding the situation surrounding the young person's school refusal (cf. Kearney, 2001). We ask parents to complete the Beck Depression Inventory (Beck, Steer, & Brown, 1996), the Brief Symptom Inventory (Derogatis, 1993), and the Abbreviated Dyadic Adjustment Scale (Sharpley & Rogers, 1984). Parents and adolescent school refusers are also asked to complete the general functioning subscale of the McMaster Family Assessment Device (Epstein, Baldwin, & Bishop, 1983), incorporating items which address areas such as problem-solving, roles, and affective involvement. (See Kearney, 2001, for a review of parent and family measures that might be employed in the assessment of school refusal.)

Review of Attendance Record

A review of the school's attendance record can provide useful information about the extent and pattern of non-attendance. Regular absences associated with certain activities (e.g., school excursions), classes (e.g., physical education classes or language classes), or days of the week (e.g., following paternal access visits) may help to shed light on factors maintaining the school refusal. In some chronic cases, parents are only fully cognizant of the overall extent of their child's non-attendance when presented with the attendance record for the past months or years.

Systematic Functional Analysis

The School Refusal Assessment Scale (SRAS; Kearney & Silverman, 1993) warrants specific attention. It is a child self-report measure (SRAS-C) with a corresponding parent-completed measure (SRAS-P), both of which facilitate a rapid, systematic functional analysis for school refusal behaviour (i.e., including school refusal and truancy). The SRAS-C and SRAS-P contain 16 items assessing four functions hypothesized to maintain school refusal behaviour: (1) avoidance of stimuli that provoke a sense of general negative affectivity; (2) escape from aversive social or evaluative situations; (3) attention-seeking behaviour; and (4) pursuit of tangible reinforcement outside of school. Scores for the four functional conditions are computed on the basis of the combined child and parent reports, and the functional condition with the highest score is deemed to be the primary factor maintaining the school refusal behaviour.

Prescribed treatments are indicated for each of the functional conditions identified by the SRAS (see Kearney & Albano, 2000a, 2000b). For example, systematic desensitization is recommended for young people motivated by a desire to avoid anxiety and other negative affectivity, as in the first functional condition. However, to determine the most appropriate form of treatment, initial hypotheses arising from the SRAS functional analysis system ought to be further developed in the light of other information gathered during the assessment (cf. Kearney, 2001; Meyer, Hagopian, & Paclawskyj, 1999). According to Daleiden and colleagues (1999), there is preliminary support for the utility of the SRAS, and it is most likely beneficial as a decision aid in the broader process of developing a treatment plan.

Integration of Assessment Information

Table 11.1 summarizes the process issues and the resources relevant to the assessment of school refusal. Information gathered from the aforementioned components of assessment is used by the clinician(s) to develop a diagnostic profile of the young person and a case formulation. Discrepant information (e.g., disparate child and parent reports on the SRAS regarding the function of the school refusal) is evaluated in reference to other sources of information and according to clinician judgment about the reliability of informant reports (cf. Kearney, 2001). The case formulation identifies individual, family, and school factors associated with the development and maintenance of the young person's refusal to attend school, together with the strengths of the individual, the family, and the school setting. This information informs the targets and process for intervention. Of course, a myriad of other complexities must be considered during assessment and treatment such as

Table 11.1   Key process issues and resources in the assessment of school refusal

Identification
- Consider school-based systems for monitoring attendance and early detection of young people with problematic attendance levels.
- Distinguish between school refusal and different forms of non-attendance such as truancy or school withdrawal (cf. Berg, 2002).
- Bear in mind the distinction sometimes made between "self-corrective" school refusal (often remitting within two weeks of onset) and "substantial" school refusal (Kearney & Silverman, 1996).

Assessment
Issues
- Provide close support to family members who are often highly distressed by the problem of school non-attendance.
- Make arrangements for an investigation of the young person's physical health.
- Employ a multi-source, multi-method approach to assessment, making use of the range of measures and procedures presented here, in view of the complex nature of school refusal. When a more efficient assessment is necessary, the clinician may select the measures and procedures most likely to yield essential information about the development and maintenance of the problem, based upon an initial clinical-behavioural interview.
- Weigh up the benefits of employing a reliable method for diagnostic assessment (e.g., ADIS-C/P) against the time required for use of a diagnostic interview schedule and the clinician's competence in diagnosis.
- Employ sensitive timing and approach in asking young people about reasons for non-attendance.
- Explore the young person's school functioning and examine the school attendance record during a visit with school staff.
- Consult with all professionals who are currently involved; this is important in understanding the problem and in arranging a cohesive management plan (cf. Coulter, 1995).
- Prepare a case formulation incorporating predisposing, precipitating, perpetuating, and protective factors. Conduct a family feedback session, which helps to provide clarification and aims to promote collaboration between the clinician and family members.
- Provide assessment feedback to school staff and other professionals involved, facilitating understanding and collaboration at the school level.

Resources
- *Interviews*
  Clinical-behavioural interviews (e.g., Blagg, 1987; Heyne & Rollings, 2002)
  Self-Statement Assessments (Heyne & Rollings, 2002)
  Anxiety Disorders Interview Schedule for Children (Silverman & Albano, 1996)
- *Child Self-Report Measures*
  Fear Survey Schedules (e.g., Gullone & King, 1992; Ollendick, 1983)
  Fear Thermometers (e.g., Heyne & Rollings, 2002)
  Anxiety Scales (e.g., Reynolds & Richmond, 1978; Spence, 1998)
  Depression Inventories (e.g., Kovacs, 1992)
  Self-Efficacy Questionnaire for School Situations (Heyne et al., 1998)
  School Refusal Assessment Scale—Child (Kearney & Albano, 2000a, 2000b)
- *Self-Monitoring Diaries* (e.g., Beidel et al., 1991; Ollendick & King, 1998)

Table 11.1   *(continued)*

- *Parent-Completed Measures*
  Monitoring diaries/Behavioural observations (e.g., Kearney & Albano, 2000a, 2000b)
  Child Behavior Checklist (Achenbach, 1991a)
  School Refusal Assessment Scale—Parent (Kearney & Albano, 2000a, 2000b)
  Measures of parental distress (e.g., Beck et al., 1996; Derogatis, 1993)
  Measures of family functioning and dyadic adjustment (e.g., Epstein et al., 1983; Sharpley & Rogers, 1984)
- *Teacher-Completed Measures*
  Teacher's Report Form (Achenbach, 1991b)

the impact of socioeconomic disadvantage, single parent households, and ethnocultural diversity.

TREATMENT

Some cases of school refusal are self-corrective, spontaneously remitting within a few weeks of onset (Kearney & Silverman, 1996). In many instances, school refusal is more intractable. The prompt implementation of an intervention program is prudent, as clinical experience and research suggest that young people who do not receive help early are much more difficult to treat (e.g., Okuyama et al., 1999). During intervention, the aim of early return to school is often emphasized (Blagg, 1987), even in approaches with more of a family focus (Place et al., 2000). For this reason, temporary home tuition is usually contraindicated (Howlin, 1994; King & Bernstein, 2001). Of the range of psychosocial treatment approaches used with school refusers (e.g., play therapy, psychodynamic psychotherapy, family therapy, cognitive-behaviour therapy), nearly all are of unknown efficacy and acceptability (Blagg, 1987; Gullone & King, 1991). Only cognitive-behaviour therapy (CBT) has been subjected to rigorous evaluation in randomized-controlled clinical trials, and it is regarded as having sparse but encouraging empirical support (King & Bernstein, 2001).

In a study by Last, Hansen, and Franco (1998), school refusers aged 6 to 17 years were randomly assigned to 12 weekly sessions of CBT or to educational support therapy (EST). The two major components of CBT with the child consisted of graduated *in-vivo* exposure and coping self-statement training. The EST condition controlled for the non-specific effects of treatment, incorporating educational presentations, encouragement for children to talk about their fears, and a daily diary for recording feared situations and associated thoughts and feelings. All of the children met the criteria for an anxiety disorder diagnosis.

There were 20 completers in the CBT group and 21 in the EST group. Both the CBT and EST groups displayed improvements in attendance and self-reports of fear (FSSC-R), anxiety (Modified State-Trait Anxiety Inventory for Children; Fox & Houston, 1983), and depression (CDI). At post-treatment, 65% of the CBT group and 50% of the EST group no longer met criteria for their primary anxiety disorder, but the difference was not significant. Last, Mansen, and Franco (1998) concluded that the structured CBT approach might not be superior to the less structured treatment encompassed in EST. At the same time, the details of the study suggest disparate non-response rates at four-week follow-up: the attendance of 40% of the EST group had not improved, compared with 14% of the CBT group. Moreover, the CBT group experienced a significantly greater reduction in depression relative to the EST group. On the basis of the study by Last et al., it may be premature to argue that a less-structured approach is equally effective as CBT for school refusal, particularly in view of possible overlap between the two approaches used in this study. That is, the EST condition included self-monitoring of thoughts and feelings, and a focus upon maladaptive thinking.

King et al. (1998b) randomly allocated the families of 34 school refusers aged 5 to 15 years to a four-week CBT program or to a wait-list control. The manual-based CBT program comprised, on average, six child sessions, five parent sessions, and one school consultation. Most of the school refusers in the study (79%) experienced a principal diagnosis associated with anxiety or phobia. Relative to wait-list controls, more of the children who received therapy exhibited a clinically significant improvement in school attendance—nearly all (15/17) were attending school at least 90% of the time. Treated children also underwent significant improvements on self-reports of fear (FSSC-II), anxiety (RCMAS), depression (CDI), and self-efficacy (SEQ-SS). A parent-completed measure (CBCL) provided further confirmation of the beneficial effects of treatment. For 13 out of the 16 treated young people who were able to be located at three- to five-year follow-up, improvements in school attendance were maintained and no new psychological problems were evidenced (King et al., 2001c).

Heyne and colleagues (2002) dismantled the aforementioned CBT program, evaluating the relative efficacy of child therapy and parent/teacher training. The families of 61 school refusers aged between 7 and 14 years were randomly allocated to: (i) eight sessions of child therapy, or (ii) eight sessions of parent therapy and teacher training, or (iii) a combination of child therapy and parent/teacher training. All of the young people had an anxiety disorder diagnosis, and 15% had a comorbid mood disorder. By 4.5-month follow-up, all three CBT approaches were found to be effective in increasing school attendance and self-efficacy (SEQ-SS), and in reducing the school refusers' fear (FSSC-II), anxiety (RCMAS), and depression (CDI); no between-group differences were observed. Although the design of this component analysis study did not include a control group, the results are supportive of the use of CBT in the treatment of school refusal.

Following, we outline our CBT program for school refusal, comprising child therapy and caregiver training (Heyne et al., 2002; King et al., 1998b). Child therapy involves the use of behavioural and cognitive procedures directly with the young person, helping them to acquire and employ skills and strategies for coping with school return and regular attendance. Caregiver training focuses on the role that parents and teachers can play in managing environmental contingencies at home and school—contingencies that are maintaining the school refusal problem and those that facilitate the young person's regular and voluntary school attendance. The child-, parent-, and school-based interventions involve the judicious selection of and emphasis upon intervention components. This individualized approach rests upon the complex array of possible factors involved in the development and maintenance of school refusal, together with the need to be sensitive to the individuality of each child, family, and school situation (cf. Barrett, Dadds, & Rapee, 1996; Kendall, 1994).

The primary treatment goals are the resumption of regular and voluntary attendance and the reduction of emotional distress. The diagnostic profile and case formulation guide the clinician towards individual factors (e.g., somatic symptoms; particular type of anxiety disorder; comorbid mood disorders; learning difficulties), family factors (e.g., secondary gain associated with being at home during the schoolday; parental depression), and school factors (e.g., bullying in the school-yard; conflict with teachers) requiring attention in order to achieve the treatment goals. Between assessment and treatment, a feedback session is conducted with the young person and their parents, often separately. We explain the findings of the assessment, relate these to the plans for treatment, and invite comment, clarification, and questions. By consulting with the young person and parents regarding the findings, we aim to develop a shared understanding of the problem and to foster a collaborative approach to treatment. Relevant school staff are also contacted and briefed on the assessment findings.

Treatment is often conducted across four weeks, including between six and eight sessions with the young person, five and eight sessions with the parents, and one consultation and regular telephone contact with school staff. The young person and his or her parents are encouraged to engage in specially tailored between-session practice tasks to reinforce and generalize skills beyond the clinical setting and to effect change in the young person's behaviour in the home and school environments. Table 11.2 summarizes central issues and resources to be considered in the cognitive-behavioural treatment of school refusal.

Child Therapy

CBT with school-refusing children and adolescents draws upon four major components: relaxation training, enhancement of social competence, cognitive therapy, and exposure. Indications for the use of each component are addressed in turn.

Relaxation Training

Training in relaxation provides the young person with a means of countering feelings of physiological arousal associated with school attendance (e.g., approaching the school grounds on the day of school return; giving class talks). In learning to manage discomforting feelings, young people are better placed to confront challenging situations and to employ other skills and strategies in the process of coping with school attendance. Indications for relaxation training include elevated scores on the subscales of selected measures (e.g., the physiological subscale of the RCMAS and the somatic complaints subscales of the CBCL and TRF), together with reports of somatic complaints during clinical-behavioural and diagnostic interviews. Relaxation training may also occur as a stress management procedure for a young person with generalized anxiety disorder, or in preparation for desensitization procedures to be employed with the young person (see below).

Table 11.2 Key process issues and resources in a cognitive-behavioural intervention for school refusal

---

Intervention with the young person

Issues
- Indicated use of relaxation training, social skills training, and cognitive therapy with the young person, in preparation for exposure to challenging situations (e.g., separation from parents; answering peers' questions about absences; staying at school for a full day).
- Flexible, developmentally sensitive engagement of young people in learning the skills for coping with regular school attendance.
- Use of educational materials, clinician modelling, behaviour rehearsal, and between-session practice tasks.
- Foster the young person's development and use of problem-solving skills (e.g., brainstorming ways of handling challenging social situations; reviewing the advantages and disadvantages of full-time versus graded return to school).
- Include a rich schedule of reinforcement for the young person's successive efforts and achievements in acquiring skills and increasing attendance.

Resources
- *Relaxation training*
  Educational materials (e.g., Barrett et al., 2000; Kendall, 1992b)
  Progressive Muscle Relaxation Training for Older Children (e.g., Ollendick & Cerny, 1981)
  Progressive Muscle Relaxation Training for Younger Children (e.g., Koeppen, 1974)
  Robot-Ragdoll Technique for Younger Children (Kendall et al., 1992)
  Autogenic Relaxation Training (e.g., Davis et al., 1995)
  Guided Imagery (e.g., Rapee et al., 2000)
  Breathing Retraining (e.g., Andrews et al., 1994)

- *Enhancing social competence*
  Educational materials (e.g., Kelly, 1996; Matthews, 2001; McGrath & Francey, 1991; Spence, 1995)
  Further reading (Bloomquist, 1996; Chazan et al., 1998)

- *Cognitive therapy*
  'Seven Ds' aid in conducting cognitive therapy (Heyne & Rollings, 2002)
  Educational materials (e.g., Clarke et al., 1990; Kearney & Albano, 2000a, 2000b; Kendall, 1992a, 1992b)
  Examples of cognitive therapy for school refusal (King et al., 1995; Mansdorf & Lukens, 1987)
  Further reading (Beck, 1995; Bernard & Joyce, 1984; Wilkes et al., 1994; Zarb, 1992)

- *Exposure*
  Examples of hierarchies for exposure (imaginal and *in vivo*) (e.g., Heyne & Rollings, 2002; Kearney & Albano, 2000a, 2000b; King et al., 1995)
  Examples of emotive imagery for school refusal (e.g., Heyne & Rollings, 2002; King et al., 1995)
  Further reading (Kendall et al., 2000; King et al., 2001b; Silverman & Kurtines, 1996)

- 'Secrets to Success' activity aimed at reducing the likelihood of relapse (e.g., Heyne & Rollings, 2002; Kendall et al., 1992)

Intervention with the parents

Issues
- In dual parent families, emphasize the involvement of both parents and the development of a united approach. In single-parent families, identify people who can support the process of school return.
- Initial attention to issues of school/classroom placement and the timing and approach to school return (e.g., graduated versus full-time return).

Table 11.2   *(continued)*

- Systematic introduction to, and training in, parent behaviour management strategies aimed at facilitating school attendance. The time taken to adequately address each strategy will vary from one family to the next.
- The training process draws on educational materials, clinician modelling, behaviour rehearsal, and between-session practice tasks. Cognitive therapy is used to facilitate parental engagement in the training process.
- Provide information on the research support for the efficacy of the proposed treatment and its components, to help build a realistically positive expectation of treatment success (cf. Ronan & Deane, 1998).
- Foster and prompt close communication between parents and school staff about each step in the plan for school return.
- Attend to the parents' own emotional distress.
- Acknowledge and respond to the impact of the school non-attendance upon siblings.

Resources
- Exploring factors contributing to behaviour problems (e.g., Sanders, 1992)
- Behaviour management strategies for school refusal (e.g., Heyne & Rollings, 2002; Kearney & Albano, 2000a, 2000b; Kearney & Roblek, 1998)
- Effective use of instructions (e.g., Forehand & McMahon, 1981; Sanders, 1992)
- Effective use of planned ignoring (e.g., Forehand & McMahon, 1981; Sanders, 1992)
- Using positive reinforcement and contingency contracts (e.g., Forehand & McMahon, 1981; Kearney & Albano, 2000a, 2000b; Sanders, 1992)
- Addressing parent cognitions (e.g., Heyne & Rollings, 2002; McMullin, 2000)
- Strategies for managing parental distress (e.g., Davis et al., 1995)

Intervention at the school
Issues
- Identification of supportive school staff who can attend to school-based issues that will facilitate the young person's return to regular attendance.
- Staff preparations in the lead-up to the young person's return to school (e.g., briefing peers; selecting suitable "buddies"; arranging a time and place for the young person to be met by welcoming staff).
- Consideration of short- or long-term modifications to the young person's academic program.
- Special school arrangements for accommodating young people with somatic complaints, and for assessing missed or incomplete work.
- Close monitoring by staff of the young person's attendance and adjustment upon return to school.
- Ensure the young person's access to supportive staff or a special mentor figure.
- Encourage a rich schedule of school-based reinforcement for the young person's efforts and achievements, however small these may be initially.
- Staff adopting an attitude of being "kind but firm, and more kind than firm," avoiding the use of ultimatums.
- Close communication between staff and parents regarding progress and successive steps in the plan for increasing attendance.

Resources
- Strategies at the school level (e.g., Blagg, 1987; Heyne & Rollings, 2002; Want, 1983)
- Further reading (Kearney & Hugelshofer, 2000; Reynolds, 1996; Rutter & Maughan, 2002)

Several scripts have been developed for conducting progressive muscle relaxation training with children of different ages (e.g., Koeppen, 1974; Ollendick & Cerny, 1981). The clinician must be creative in teaching relaxation to young people, aiming to engage them sufficiently to ensure that some form of cue-controlled relaxation is ultimately acquired. Alternative forms of relaxation training that may be used include guided imagery (e.g., Rapee et al., 2000), autogenic relaxation training (e.g., Davis, Eshelman, & McKay, 1995), and breathing retraining (e.g., Andrews et al., 1994).

Enhancement of Social Competence

Social skills training aimed at enhancing the young person's social competence is employed in two predominant situations. First, many school refusers report anxiety about handling questions from peers or teachers regarding their absence from school. Such reports are elicited via the SEQ-SS or arise through the clinical-behavioural interview. Second, some children's skills in making and maintaining friendships or handling teasing and bullying may be underdeveloped, leaving them vulnerable to isolation and seeking to avoid the school situation. Social competencies, social withdrawal, and social problems are assessed via subscales on the CBCL, TRF, SRAS, and RCMAS; through interviews with parents, children, and school staff; and through observation in the clinical setting. More specific measures such as the SASC-R may also be used to assess aspects of social functioning.

Enhancement of the young person's social competence involves the use of educational handouts (e.g., McGrath & Francey, 1991; Spence, 1995), clinician modelling of desired social behaviours, and having the young person rehearse the behaviours through role-plays. The young person receives reinforcing and corrective feedback from the clinician. We aim to have the young person gradually experience increasingly challenging social situations during the training sessions, so that the range of social reactions that may occur outside of the clinic can be experienced. The young person's success in responding to more challenging role-play situations can build his or her sense of self-efficacy in readiness for facing real-life social situations.

Cognitive Therapy

A vital aspect of school refusal intervention is a focus on the young person's cognitions. Emotionally distressed school refusers may, for example, process events in a distorted manner (e.g., "I know the teacher doesn't like me because she raises her voice"), overestimate the probability of negative events occurring (e.g., "Mum will fall ill while I'm at school"), underestimate coping resources (e.g., "I won't know what to do if the teacher asks me a question"), and engage in negative self-evaluations (e.g., "I'm hopeless at sport"). During assessment, indicators of the importance of cognitive therapy may come from the clinical-behavioural interview with the child (including the adjunctive self-statement assessment), the diagnostic interview, self-efficacy expectations assessed via the SEQ-SS, the worry/oversensitivity subscale of the RCMAS, and items in the CDI. Of course, many more indications will arise through the course of intervention with the young person, especially during the process of detecting and evaluating the young person's cognitions.

Cognitive therapy with school refusers is aimed at modifying maladaptive cognitions in order to effect a change in the young person's emotions and behaviour, mobilizing them toward school attendance. The "Seven Ds" is an aid in the process of conducting cognitive therapy, emphasizing key components involved in Describing the cognitive therapy model, Detecting cognitions, Determining maladaptive cognitions, Disputing maladaptive cognitions, Discovering adaptive cognitions or coping statements, Doing a between-session practice task, and Discussing the outcome of the task (Heyne & Rollings, 2002). Cartoon materials are often useful in helping younger children to understand the connection between thoughts, feelings, and actions, and in engaging them in the process of detecting their maladaptive cognitions and discovering more adaptive cognitions (e.g., Kendall, 1992a; Kendall et al., 1992). Disputational procedures more suited to adolescent school refusers with a greater capacity for examining their thoughts are presented elsewhere (e.g., Beck, 1995; Wilkes et al., 1994; Zarb, 1992).

Exposure

Naturally, exposure to school attendance constitutes a key component of CBT for school refusal. In conjunction with the above preparatory strategies, school-return arrangements must be negotiated with the young person, parents, and school staff. When young people have been fully absent from school (as opposed to attending sporadically), we aim for school return to occur mid-way through the intervention. This allows sufficient time for the young person to develop the above-mentioned skills during the lead up to the exposure associated with school return (cf. Kendall et al., 1997), and allows opportunities for collaboratively trouble-shooting difficulties that arise during and after the return to school.

For many school refusers exhibiting high levels of anxiety, a graduated return to school is usually negotiated, constituting *in-vivo* desensitization. This involves a step-by-step approach to conquering the anxiety elicited by school return (e.g., attending for one class on the first day, two classes the next day, etc.). The young person draws on his or her relaxation skills and cognitive coping statements to manage the anxiety associated with the successive steps. The young person's input into the development of the graded attendance plan is ultimately important (see Heyne & Rollings, 2002). When the child's anxiety is very high, imaginal desensitization may need to occur prior to the planned school return, perhaps incorporating emotive imagery with younger children (cf. King, Ollendick, & Tonge, 1995; King et al., 2001a).

Some young people and their families prefer that the process of school return be rapid, involving full-time attendance as soon as the young person returns to school. This is usually more stressful than a graduated return to school, but it is intended to prevent or minimize the embarrassment for young people of having to explain why they are leaving school part way through the day. We believe that rapid school return is probably more appropriate for young children with mild or recent onset school refusal.

Concluding Sessions with the Child

In an effort to prevent relapse, the young person may participate in a "Secrets to Success" activity toward the end of treatment (cf. "My Commercial"; Kendall et al., 1992). In such an activity, the young person is given an opportunity to share his or her ideas about how to respond effectively to school refusal. This may be in the form of a poster, playing the "expert in the field" during an audiotaped or videotaped mock interview or commercial, or conducting a "motivational talk" for another clinician or family members. This activity helps to reinforce what the child had learned, celebrates the achievements, and builds up a coping template (Kendall et al., 1992) and self-esteem (Kearney & Hugelshofer, 2000). In the future, the poster or tape may serve as a prompt for the young person's successful management of setbacks.

Parent/Teacher Training

Key aspects of work with the parents include: initial attention to issues of school placement and the date and process for school return; the development of behaviour management strategies; and implementing the plan for school return. Work with school staff focuses upon preparation for the young person's school return and the use of behaviour management strategies to support the young person at school.

Initial Phase with Parents

Parents are encouraged to discuss any doubts about their child's current school or classroom placement, so that the plans for facilitating school return do not come unstuck because of the parents' ambivalence about such matters. When doubts about school or classroom placement do emerge, a problem-solving discussion takes place to consider all of the advantages and disadvantages of making changes. Also in the initial phase, anxious and sceptical parents may benefit from educational handouts addressing the development and nature of school refusal, emotional problems, and behaviour problems, together with information about the effectiveness of current approaches to treatment.

As mentioned, school return is generally scheduled for mid-way through treatment, and parents are helped to make a decision about the best day for the child's school return. Important factors include the availability of two adults to facilitate the young person's attendance, and a knowledge of the young person's timetable. In an effort to create a positive experience for the child on the first day of school return, it is helpful to plan for return on a day with, for example, the least number of disliked subjects or teachers.

Parent-Based Strategies for Facilitating Attendance

In the lead up to school return, the clinician helps parents to plan and institute smooth morning routines for the young person (e.g., waking up; getting showered and dressed), and to manage the young person's access to reinforcing events and experiences when at home during school hours. This serves to reduce the secondary gain that may otherwise strengthen the child's resolve not to attend school. Assessment of secondary gain occurs through clinical-behavioural interviews and via subscale 4 on the SRAS.

Parents might receive training in command giving, where emphasis is upon gaining the young person's attention and using clear and specific instructions (cf. Forehand & McMahon, 1981). This is particularly important for those parents who give vague and imprecise instructions about school-related issues. Consistent with operant principles, parents are instructed in the recognition and reinforcement of the young person's appropriate coping behaviours and school attendance, and in the planned ignoring of inappropriate behaviours such as tantrums, arguments, and somatic complaints without known organic cause (Blagg, 1987; Kearney & Roblek, 1998). The challenge that comorbid disruptive behaviour disorders can present to treatment (cf. McShane, Walter, & Rey, 2001) highlights the importance of training in behaviour management strategies. Performance-based methods of modelling, rehearsal, and feedback are employed during the training. This provides parents with opportunities to gain confidence and increase their competence in the use of the strategies, especially the calm and consistent use of planned ignoring.

Parents may also utilize exposure-based principles and behaviour management strategies to help address specific problems in the lead up to school return. For example, the young person with separation anxiety may be exposed to progressively longer periods of separation from parents before a school return is attempted. The parents of a socially anxious child may facilitate an increase in their child's social involvement during the first half of treatment, prior to instituting a return to school.

Implementation Phase with Parents

During treatment, if the child does not come to the point of attending school voluntarily, parents are encouraged to consider being firmer with the child. Having issued clear expectations and instructions regarding attendance, parents may be required to escort their child to school physically, a role that necessitates good planning and support (Kearney & Roblek, 1998; Kennedy, 1965). This process of "professionally informed parental pressure" (cf. Gittelman-Klein & Klein, 1971) is an important aspect of treatment, allowing parents to deal with a young person's entrenched avoidance of school. Considerable time is spent devising a plan for handling each potentially problematic situation (i.e., helping the child to get out of bed and ready for school; escorting the child to school; leaving the child at school; dealing with running away). Parents will often benefit from cognitive and behavioural strategies aimed at helping themselves to remain calm and committed during management of their child's non-attendance (cf. Kearney & Roblek, 1998), also allowing them to model confidence in the child's ability to cope with school return. Through blocking the child's avoidance, exposure to school attendance can ultimately lead to a reduction in emotional distress and to the experience of naturally occurring positive events at school. Attention to school-based strategies will increase the likelihood that voluntary school attendance will ultimately be achieved.

School-Based Strategies for Facilitating Attendance

Working with school staff (e.g., classroom teachers, home room teachers, and counsellors) can ensure the integration of the young person into the classroom, as well as the school wide system. A supportive staff member is identified, who might help the young person to settle in on arrival at school and familiarize him or her with the routine for the day, and closely monitor the young person's attendance and emotional well-being while settling back into school. It may also be helpful to have the young person or school staff select one or two students to act as "buddies" who will provide peer support during the early stages of school re-entry, and who could make contact with the young person during subsequent absences.

Depending on the young person's preference, classmates may be advised of the school return and encouraged to be supportive and to refrain from probing about non-attendance. The clinician and school staff can also explore arrangements to temporarily or permanently accommodate the young person's special needs (e.g., reduced homework requirements; academic remediation; change of classroom; modified curriculum). We have found it critical, on many occasions, to ensure that school staff are fully informed about the special needs of the young person and the arrangements that have been made to accommodate them. A memo to relevant staff reduces the possibility that an uninformed staff member inadvertently singles out the distressed young person for attention or questions about prior absences.

Engineering positive experiences for the young person can help to make the school environment a more reinforcing place to be. Specific reinforcement of the young person's attendance and efforts at coping is desirable, and staff have often been creative in developing a menu of possible reinforcers (e.g., special classroom responsibilities; choosing an activity for the class; extra recess time or video-watching privileges with friends; canteen vouchers; mentoring time with a favoured teacher). Staff are also encouraged to use planned ignoring of inappropriate behaviours such as pleading to go home or tantrums, employing the same supportive yet consistent approach as outlined for parents.

Further Treatment Considerations

School staff and parents are encouraged to develop close communication during the treatment process. This ensures a clear understanding and consistency during the implementation of plans such as a graded return to school or graded reintroduction to the completion of homework, it serves to reduce parent anxiety about how the young person is coping through the day, and it allows for prompt and appropriate responses to events such as the young person running away from school or signs of a setback. Parents and school staff are encouraged to contact the clinician when setbacks become more frequent or enduring. To prevent relapse, the clinician may conduct booster sessions or telephone follow-ups at times known to be difficult, such as the return to school after a holiday period, a change of school, and examinations (cf. Kearney & Hugelshofer, 2000).

While CBT is often instrumental in reducing young people's emotional distress and helping them to attend school regularly and voluntarily, alternative or adjunctive treatments are sometimes required. In line with a stages of treatment model (cf. Heyne, King, & Tonge, in press), we propose that treatment might begin with CBT, and that if there is only a partial response, CBT may be continued in modified form or medication may be added. For example, greater clinical attention may need to be given to parental psychopathology and broader family problems, or CBT might be further adapted to the specific needs of the depressed young person (cf. Kearney, 1993). If medication is used, the current state of knowledge suggests that it should be in conjunction with CBT, and not in place of it (American Academy of Child and Adolescent Psychiatry, 1997; Tonge, 1998). Extrapolating from the work of Bernstein and colleagues (Bernstein et al., 2000, 2001), it may be helpful to consider the combined use of CBT and medication as a first stage of treatment for school refusers with comorbid severe depressive and anxiety disorders.

If, following reasonable trials (in delivery, duration, and dose) of CBT or CBT plus routinely employed pharmacological treatments, there is still no response to treatment, alternative psychosocial or pharmacological treatments need to be considered. For example, family therapy might be necessary to improve motivation for participation in behaviourally oriented programs (Kearney & Albano, 2000b) and to reduce the severity and course of school refusal (Bernstein et al., 1999). Off-site educational units may also be considered for young people who have great difficulty attending mainstream school (Place et al., 2000). (For a review of pharmacological treatments for school refusal, see Heyne, King, & Tonge, in press, and Tonge, 1998.)

SUMMARY AND FUTURE DIRECTIONS

Although the central feature of school refusal is always the same—difficulty in attending school regularly and voluntarily—it can be associated with a broad range of symptoms or disorders of varying severity, and can be determined by as broad a range of contributing and maintaining factors. Appropriately, school refusers have been described as "one of the most amorphous populations in clinical child psychology" (Kearney, 2001). Using a robust but flexible multi-source and multi-method approach to assessment, the clinician derives a diagnostic profile and case formulation that describes the likely predisposing, precipitating, and perpetuating factors.

Of the treatments commonly employed for school refusal, CBT has the most research support. Moreover, the clinical utility of CBT is enhanced by its brevity, and it is regarded as an acceptable approach by families and school staff (Gullone & King, 1991; Heyne, 1999; Kearney & Beasley, 1994; King et al., 1998b). Based on the assessment information, the clinician selects from and differentially emphasizes the various components of CBT in working with the young person, the parents, and school staff. A recent study by Heyne et al. (2002) suggested that it may not always be necessary to work with both the young person and their caregivers in order to effectively treat school refusal. The more economical approach of working solely with parents and school staff may be sufficient when the child is younger and displays minimal emotional distress. School refusers with more disturbed behavioural and emotional functioning may more likely benefit from direct clinical work.

Future research needs to explore which individual, family, and school factors differentially mediate outcomes in child therapy programs, parent/teacher training programs, and combined programs. Special attention should be paid to the causal relationship between school refusal and depression, and the impact of depression on treatment outcome (Honjo et al., 2001; Kearney, 1993; King et al., 2000). Parental and family functioning have received considerable research attention, but the cause-and-effect relationship between parental psychopathology, family functioning, and school refusal requires further investigation. Just as parental difficulties may contribute to a young person's school refusal, the stress for parents in having to manage school refusal may sometimes contribute to parental anxiety, depression, and marital distress. Future research also needs to explore which factors help to mitigate against the development of school refusal. Beyond a knowledge of predisposing, precipitating, and perpetuating factors, what can be learned about protective factors?

Finally, there is a need to compare the efficacy of CBT, pharmacological treatment, and their combination (cf. Bernstein et al., 2000). Pharmacological treatments are regularly employed in the treatment of school refusal, but there has been no evaluation of their role relative to psychosocial treatments. Treatment effectiveness studies conducted in clinical settings as opposed to research settings will help to inform the fine-tuning of subsequent assessment and treatment recommendations (cf. Weisz, 2000).

REFERENCES

Achenbach, T.M. (1991a). *Manual for the Child Behavior Checklist/4–18 and 1991 Profile*. Burlington, VT: University of Vermont Department of Psychiatry.

Achenbach, T.M. (1991b). *Manual for the Teacher's Report Form and 1991 Profile*. Burlington, VT: University of Vermont Department of Psychiatry.

American Academy of Child and Adolescent Psychiatry (1997). Practice parameters for the assessment and treatment of children and adolescents with anxiety disorders. *Journal of the American Academy of Child and Adolescent Psychiatry*, **36** (suppl.), 69S–84S.

American Psychiatric Association (1987). *Diagnostic and statistical manual of mental disorders* (3rd edn—revised). Washington, DC: Author.

American Psychiatric Association (1994). *Diagnostic and statistical manual of mental disorders* (4th ed.). Washington, DC: Author.

Andrews, G., Crino, R., Hunt, C., Lampe, L., & Page, A. (1994). *The treatment of anxiety disorders: Clinician's guide and patient manuals*. Melbourne: Cambridge University Press.

Baker, H., & Wills, U. (1978). School phobia: Classification and treatment. *British Journal of Psychiatry*, **132**, 492–499.

Barrett, P.M., Dadds, M.R., & Rapee, R.M. (1996). Family treatment of childhood anxiety disorders: A controlled trial. *Journal of Consulting and Clinical Psychology*, **64**, 333–342.

Barrett, P.M., Lowry, H., & Turner, C. (2000). *FRIENDS Program: Participant workbook for youth*. Brisbane, QLD: Australian Academic Press.

Beck, A.T., Steer, R.A., & Brown, G.K. (1996). Beck Depression Inventory (2nd edn). New York: Psychological Corporation.

Beck, J. (1995). *Cognitive therapy: Basics and beyond*. New York: Guilford Press.

Beidel, D.C., Neal, A.M., & Lederer, A.S. (1991). The feasibility and validity of a daily diary for the assessment of anxiety in children. *Behavior Therapy*, **22**, 505–517.

Berg, I. (1980). School refusal in early adolescence. In L. Hersov & I. Berg (Eds), *Out of School—Modern Perspectives* (pp. 231–249). Chichester: John Wiley & Sons.

Berg, I. (1997). School refusal and truancy. *Archives of Disease in Childhood*, **76**, 90–91.

Berg, I. (2002). School avoidance, school phobia, and truancy. In M. Lewis (Ed.), *Child and adolescent psychiatry: A comprehensive textbook* (3rd edn; pp. 1260–1266). Sydney: Lippincott Williams & Wilkins.

Berg, I., & McGuire, R. (1974). Are mothers of school-phobic adolescents overprotective? *British Journal of Psychiatry*, **124**, 10–13.

Berg, I., Nichols, K., & Pritchard, C. (1969). School phobia: Its classification and relationship to dependency. *Journal of Child Psychology and Psychiatry*, **10**, 123–141.

Berg, I., Butler, A., Franklin, J., Hayes, H., Lucas, C., & Sims, R. (1993). DSM-III-R disorders, social factors and management of school attendance problems in the normal population. *Journal of Child Psychology and Psychiatry*, **34**, 1187–1203.

Bernard, M., & Joyce, M. (1984). *Rational-emotive therapy with children and adolescents: Theory, treatment strategies, preventative methods*. New York: Wiley Interscience.

Bernstein, G.A. (1991). Comorbidity and severity of anxiety and depressive disorders in a clinic sample. *Journal of the American Academy of Child and Adolescent Psychiatry*, **30**, 43–50.

Bernstein, G.A., & Borchardt, C.M. (1996). School refusal: Family constellation and family functioning. *Journal of Anxiety Disorders*, **10**, 1–19.

Bernstein, G., & Garfinkel, B.D. (1986). School phobia: The overlap of affective and anxiety disorders. *Journal of the American Academy of Child Psychiatry*, **25**, 235–241.

Bernstein, G.A., & Garfinkel, B.D. (1988). Pedigrees, functioning, and psychopathology in families of school phobic children. *American Journal of Psychiatry*, **145**, 70–74.

Bernstein, G.A., Svingen, P.H., & Garfinkel, B.D. (1990). School phobia: Patterns of family functioning. *Journal of the American Academy of Child and Adolescent Psychiatry*, **29**, 24–30.

Bernstein, G.A., Borchardt, C.M., Perwien, A.R., Crosby, R.D., Kushner, M.G., Thuras, P.D., & Last, C.G. (2000). Imipramine plus cognitive-behavioural therapy in the treatment of school refusal. *Journal of the American Academy of Child and Adolescent Psychiatry*, **39**, 276–283.

Bernstein, G.A., Hektner, J.M., Borchardt, C.M., & McMillan M.H. (2001). Treatment of school refusal: One-year follow-up. *Journal of the American Academy Child and Adolescent Psychiatry*, **40**, 206–213.

Bernstein, G.A., Massie, E.D., Thuras, P.D., Perwien, A.R., Borchardt, C.M., & Crosby, R.D. (1997). Somatic symptoms in anxious-depressed school refusers. *Journal of the American Academy of Child and Adolescent Psychiatry*, **36**, 661–668.

Bernstein, G.A., Warren, S.L., Massie, E.D., & Thuras, P.D. (1999). Family dimensions in anxious-depressed school refusers. *Journal of Anxiety Disorders*, **13**, 513–528.

Blagg, N. (1987). *School phobia and its treatment*. New York: Croom Helm.

Bloomquist, M. (1996). *Skills training for children with behaviour disorders*. New York: Guilford Press.

Bools, C., Foster, J., Brown, I., & Berg, I. (1990). The identification of psychiatric disorders in children who fail to attend school: A cluster analysis of a non-clinical population. *Psychological Medicine*, **20**, 171–181.

Burke, A.E., & Silverman, W.K. (1987). The prescriptive treatment of school refusal. *Clinical Psychology Review*, **7**, 353–362.

Chazan, M. (1962). School phobia. *British Journal of Educational Psychology*, **32**, 209–217.

Chazan, M., Laing, A., Davies, D., & Phillips, R. (1998). *Helping socially withdrawn and isolated children and adolescents*. London: Cassell.

Clarke, G., Lewinsohn, P., & Hops, H. (1990). *Student workbook: Adolescent coping with depression course*. Eugene, OR: Castalia Publishing Company.

Coulter, S. (1995). School refusal, parental control and wider systems: Lessons from the management of two cases. *Irish Journal of Psychological Medicine*, **12**, 146–149.

Daleiden, E.L., Chorpita, B.F., Kollins, S.H., & Drabman, R.S. (1999). Factors affecting the reliability of clinical judgements about the function of children's school-refusal behaviour. *Journal of Clinical Child Psychology*, **28**, 396–406.

Daugherty, T.K., & Shapiro, S.K. (1994). Behavior checklists and rating forms. In T.H. Ollendick, N.J. King, & W.R. Yule (Eds), *International handbook of phobic and anxiety disorders in children and adolescents* (pp. 331–346). New York: Plenum Press.

Davidson, S. (1960). School phobia as a manifestation of family disturbance: Its structure and treatment. *Journal of Child Psychology and Psychiatry*, **1**, 270–287.

Davis, M., Eshelman, E., & McKay. M. (1995). *The relaxation and stress reduction workbook*. Oakland, CA: New Harbinger Publications.

Derogatis, L.R. (1993). *The Brief Symptom Inventory* (2nd edn). Riderwood, MD: Clinical Psychometric Research.

Eisenberg, L. (1958). School phobia: Diagnosis, genesis and clinical management. *Pediatric Clinics of North America*, **5**, 645–666.

Elliott, J.G. (1999). Practitioner review: School refusal: Issues of conceptualisation, assessment, and treatment. *Journal of Child Psychology and Psychiatry*, **40**, 1001–1012.

Epstein, N.B., Baldwin, L.M., & Bishop, D.S. (1983). The McMaster Family Assessment Device. *Journal of Marital and Family Therapy*, **9**, 171–180.

Evans, L.D. (2000). Functional school refusal subtypes: Anxiety, avoidance, and malingering. *Psychology in the Schools*, **37**, 183–191.

Forehand, R.L., & McMahon, R.J. (1981). *Helping the noncompliant child: A clinician's guide to parent training*. New York: Guilford Press.

Fox, J.E., & Houston, B.K. (1983). Distinguishing between cognitive and somatic trait and state anxiety in children. *Journal of Personality and Social Psychology*, **45**, 862–870.

Gittelman-Klein, R., & Klein, D.F. (1971). Controlled imipramine treatment of school phobia. *Archives of General Psychiatry*, **25**, 204–207.

Gordon, D.A., & Young, R.D. (1976). School phobia: A discussion of aetiology, treatment and evaluation. *Psychological Reports*, **39**, 783–804.

Granell de Aldaz, E., Vivas, E., Gelfand, D.M., & Feldman, L. (1984). Estimating the prevalence of school refusal and school-related fears. A Venezuelan sample. *Journal of Nervous and Mental Disease*, **172**, 722–729.

Gullone, E., & King, N.J. (1991). Acceptability of alternative treatments for school refusal: Evaluations by students, caregivers and professionals. *British Journal of Educational Psychology*, **61**, 346–354.

Gullone, E., & King, N.J. (1992). Psychometric evaluation of a revised fear survey schedule for children and adolescents. *Journal of Child Psychology and Psychiatry*, **33**, 987–998.

Hampe, E., Miller, L., Barrett, C., & Noble, H. (1973). Intelligence and school phobia. *Journal of School Psychology*, **11**, 66–70.

Hansen, C., Sanders, S.L., Massaro, S., & Last, C.G. (1998). Predictors of severity of absenteeism in children with anxiety-based school refusal. *Journal of Clinical Child Psychology*, **27**, 246–254.

Hersov, L. (1960). Refusal to go to school. *Journal of Child Psychology and Psychiatry*, **1**, 137–145.

Hersov, L. (1985), School refusal. In M. Rutter & L. Hersov (Eds.), *Child and adolescent psychiatry: Modern approaches* (2nd edn; pp. 382–399). Oxford: Blackwell Scientific Publications.

Heyne, D. (1999). *Evaluation of child therapy and caregiver training in the treatment of school refusal* [dissertation]. Melbourne: Monash University.

Heyne, D., & Rollings, S. (2002). *School refusal*. Oxford: Blackwell Scientific Publications.

Heyne, D., King, N.J., & Tonge, B. (in press). School refusal. In T.H., Ollendick & J. March (Eds), *Phobic and anxiety disorders in children and adolescents: A clinicians guide to effective psychosocial and pharmacological interventions*. Oxford University Press.

Heyne, D., King, N.J., Tonge, B., Rollings, S., Pritchard, M., Young, D., & Myerson, N. (1998). The Self-Efficacy Questionnaire for School Situations: Development and psychometric evaluation. *Behaviour Change*, **15**, 31–40.

Heyne, D., King, N.J., Tonge, B.J., Rollings, S., Young, D., Pritchard, M., & Ollendick, T.H. (2002). Evaluation of child therapy and caregiver training in the treatment of school refusal. *Journal of the American Academy of Child and Adolescent Psychiatry*, **41**, 687–695.

Honjo, S., Kasahara, Y., & Ohtaka, K. (1992). School refusal in Japan. *Acta Paedopsychiatrica*, **55**, 29–32.

Honjo, S., Nishide, T., Niwa, S., Sasaki, Y., Kaneko, H., Inoko, K., & Nishide, Y. (2001). School refusal and depression with school inattendance in children and adolescents: Comparative assessment between the Children's Depression Inventory and somatic complaints. *Psychiatry and Clinical Neurosciences*, **55**, 629–634.

Hoshino, Y., Nikkuni, S., Kaneko, M., Endo, M., Yashima, Y., & Kumashiro, H. (1987). The application of DSM-III diagnostic criteria to school refusal. *The Japanese Journal of Psychiatry and Neurology*, **41**, 1–7.

Howlin, P. (1994). Special educational treatment. In M. Rutter, E. Taylor, & L. Hersov (Eds), *Child and adolescent psychiatry: Modern approaches* (3rd edn; pp. 1071–1088). Oxford: Blackwell Scientific Publications.

Iwamoto, S., & Yoshida, K. (1997). School refusal in Japan: The recent dramatic increase in incidence is a cause for concern. *Social Behavior and Personality*, **25**, 315–320.

Kahn, J., & Nursten, J. (1962). School refusal: A comprehensive view of school phobia and other failures of school attendance. *American Journal of Orthopsychiatry*, **32**, 707–718.

Kahn, J., Nursten, J., & Carroll, H.C.M. (1996). An overview. In I. Berg & J. Nursten (Eds), *Unwillingly to school* (pp. 159–173). London: Gaskell.

Kameguchi, K., & Murphy-Shigematsu, S. (2001). Family psychology and family therapy in Japan. *American Psychologist*, **56**, 65–70.

Kearney, C.A. (1993). Depression and school refusal behaviour: A review with comments on classification and treatment. *Journal of School Psychology*, **31**, 267–279.

Kearney, C.A. (2001). *School refusal behaviour in youth: A functional approach to assessment and treatment*. Washington, DC: American Psychological Association.

Kearney, C.A., & Albano, A.M. (2000a). *When children refuse school: A cognitive-behavioural therapy approach—Parent Workbook*. The Psychological Corporation, United States of America: Graywind Publications Incorporated.

Kearney, C.A., & Albano, A.M. (2000b). *When children refuse school: A cognitive-behavioural therapy approach—Therapist Guide*. The Psychological Corporation, United States of America: Graywind Publications Incorporated.

Kearney, C.A., & Beasley, J.F. (1994). The clinical treatment of school refusal behaviour: A survey of referral and practice characteristics. *Psychology in the Schools*, **31**, 128–132.

Kearney, C.A., & Hugelshofer, D.S. (2000). Systemic and clinical strategies for preventing school refusal behaviour in youth. *Journal of Cognitive Psychotherapy: An International Quarterly*, **14**, 51–65.

Kearney, C.A., & Roblek, T.L. (1998). Parent training in the treatment of school refusal behaviour. In J.M. Briesmeister & C.E. Schaefer (Eds), *Handbook of parent training: Parents as co-therapists for children's behaviour problems* (pp. 225–256). New York: John Wiley & Sons, Inc.

Kearney, C.A., & Silverman, W.K. (1993). Measuring the function of school refusal behaviour: The School Refusal Assessment Scale. *Journal of Clinical Child Psychology*, **22**, 85–96.

Kearney, C.A., & Silverman, W.K. (1995). Family environment of youngsters with school refusal behaviour: A synopsis with implications for assessment and treatment. *The American Journal of Family Therapy*, **23**, 59–72.

Kearney, C.A., & Silverman, W.K. (1996). The evolution and reconciliation of taxonomic strategies for school refusal behaviour. *Clinical Psychology: Science and Practice*, **3**, 339–354.

Kearney, C.A., Eisen, A.R., & Silverman, W.K. (1995). The legend and myth of school phobia. *School Psychology Quarterly*, **10**, 65–85.

Kelly, A. (1996). *Talkabout: A social communication skills package*. Oxon: Winslow Press.

Kendall, P.C. (1992a). Childhood coping: Avoiding a lifetime of anxiety. *Behaviour Change*, **9**, 229–237.

Kendall, P.C. (1992b). *Coping cat workbook*. Ardmore, PA: Workbook Publishing.

Kendall, P.C. (1994). Treating anxiety disorders in children: Results of a randomized clinical trial. *Journal of Consulting and Clinical Psychology*, **62**, 100–110.

Kendall, P.C., Chansky, T.E., Kane, M.T., Kim, R.S., Kortlander, E., Ronan, K.R., Sessa, F.M., & Siqueland, L. (1992). *Anxiety disorders in youth: Cognitive-behavioural interventions.* Boston: Allyn & Bacon.

Kendall, P.C., Chu, B.C., Primentel, S.S., & Choudbury, M. (2000). Treating anxiety disorders in youth. In P.C. Kendall (Ed.), *Child and adolescent therapy: Cognitive-behavioural procedures* (2nd edn; pp. 235–287). New York: Guilford Press.

Kendall, P.C., Flannery-Schroeder, E., Panichelli-Mindel, S.M., Southam-Gerow, M., Henin, A., & Warman, M. (1997). Therapy for youths with anxiety disorders: A second randomized clinical trial. *Journal of Consulting and Clinical Psychology,* **65**, 366–380.

Kennedy, W.A. (1965). School phobia: Rapid treatment of fifty cases. *Journal of Abnormal Psychology,* **70**, 285–289.

King, N.J., & Bernstein, G.A. (2001). School refusal in children and adolescents: A review of the past ten years. *Journal of the American Academy of Child and Adolescent Psychiatry,* **40**, 197–205.

King, N.J., & Ollendick, T.H. (1989a). Children's anxiety and phobic disorders in school settings: Classification, assessment, and intervention issues. *Review of Educational Research,* **59**, 431–470.

King, N.J., & Ollendick, T.H. (1989b). School refusal: Graduated and rapid behavioural treatment strategies. *Australian and New Zealand Journal of Psychiatry,* **23**, 213–223.

King, N.J., Ollendick, T.H., & Tonge, B.J. (1995). *School refusal: Assessment and treatment.* Boston: Allyn & Bacon.

King, N.J., Heyne, D., Gullone, E., & Molloy, G.N. (2001a). Usefulness of emotive imagery in the treatment of childhood phobias: Clinical guidelines, case examples and issues. *Counselling Psychology Quarterly,* **14**, 95–101.

King, N.J., Heyne, D., Tonge, B., Gullone, E., & Ollendick, T.H. (2001b). School refusal: Categorical diagnoses, functional analysis and treatment planning. *Clinical Psychology and Psychotherapy,* **8**, 352–360.

King, N.J., Ollendick, T.H., Tonge, B.J., Heyne, D., Pritchard, M., Rollings, S., Young, D., & Myerson, N. (1998a). School refusal: An overview. *Behaviour Change,* **15**, 5–15.

King, N.J., Tonge, B.J., Heyne, D., & Ollendick, T.H. (2000). Research on the cognitive-behavioural treatment of school refusal: A review and recommendations. *Clinical Psychology Review,* **20**, 495–507.

King, N.J., Tonge, B.J., Heyne, D., Pritchard, M., Rollings, S., Young, D., Myerson, N., & Ollendick, T.H. (1998b). Cognitive-behavioural treatment of school-refusing children: A controlled evaluation. *Journal of the American Academy of Child and Adolescent Psychiatry,* **37**, 375–403.

King, N.J., Tonge, B.J., Heyne, D., Turner, S., Pritchard, M., Young, D., Rollings, S., Myerson, N., & Ollendick, T.H. (2001c). Cognitive-behavioural treatment of school-refusing children: Maintenance of improvements at 3- to 5-year follow-up. *Scandinavian Journal of Behaviour Therapy,* **30**, 85–89.

Koeppen, A.S. (1974). Relaxation training for children. *Elementary School Guidance and Counseling,* 14–21.

Kovacs, M. (1992). *Children's Depression Inventory.* New York: Multi-Health Systems, Inc.

La Greca, A.M., & Stone, W.L. (1993). Social Anxiety Scale for Children—Revised: Factor structure and concurrent validity. *Journal of Clinical Child Psychology,* **22**, 17–27.

Lang, M. (1982). School refusal: An empirical study and system analysis. *Australian Journal of Family Therapy,* **3**, 93–107.

Last, C.G. (1992). Anxiety disorders in childhood and adolescence. In W.M. Reynolds (Ed.), *Internalizing disorders in children and adolescents* (pp. 61–106). New York: John Wiley & Sons.

Last, C.G., & Strauss, C.C. (1990). School refusal in anxiety-disordered children and adolescents. *Journal of the American Academy of Child and Adolescent Psychiatry,* **29**, 31–35.

Last, C.G., Hansen, C., & Franco, N. (1998). Cognitive-behavioural treatment of school phobia. *Journal of the American Academy of Child and Adolescent Psychiatry,* **37**, 404–411.

Last, C.G., Francis, G., Hersen, M., Kazdin, A.E., & Strauss, C.C. (1987). Separation anxiety and school phobia: A comparison using DSM-III criteria. *American Journal of Psychiatry*, **144**, 653–657.

Leung, A.K.C. (1989). School phobia: Sometimes a child or teenager has a good reason. *Postgraduate Medicine*, **85**, 281–282, 287–289.

Mansdorf, I.J., & Lukens, E. (1987). Cognitive-behavioural psychotherapy for separation anxious children exhibiting school phobia. *Journal of the American Academy of Child and Adolescent Psychiatry*, **26**, 222–225.

Martin, C., Cabrol, S., Bouvard, M.P., Lepine, J.P., & Mouren-Simeoni, M.C. (1999). Anxiety and depressive disorders in fathers and mothers of anxious school-refusing children. *Journal of the American Academy of Child and Adolescent Psychiatry*, **38**, 916–922.

Matthews, J. (2001). *Digging Deep—Activities Book/Teacher's Manual: A practical program to encourage young people to name, own, and deal with their emotions*. Melbourne: Australian Council for Educational Research.

McGrath, H., & Francey, S. (1991). *Friendly kids, friendly classrooms: Teaching social skills and confidence in the classroom*. Melbourne: Longman Cheshire.

McMullin, R. (2000). *The new handbook of cognitive therapy techniques*. New York: W.W. Norton & Company.

McShane, G., Walter, G., & Rey, J.M. (2001). Characteristics of adolescents with school refusal. *Australian and New Zealand Journal of Psychiatry*, **35**, 822–826.

Meyer, E.A., Hagopian, L.P., & Paclawskyj, T.R. (1999). A function-based treatment for school refusal behaviour using shaping and fading. *Research in Developmental Disabilities*, **20**, 401–410.

Naylor, M.W., Staskowski, M., Kenney, M.C., & King, C.A. (1994). Language disorders and learning disabilities in school-refusing adolescents. *Journal of the American Academy of Child and Adolescent Psychiatry*, **33**, 1331–1337.

Nursten, J.P. (1958). The background of children with school phobia: A study of twenty-five cases. *The Medical Officer*, **100**, 340–342.

Okuyama, M., Okada, M., Kuribayashi, M., & Kaneko, S. (1999). Factors responsible for the prolongation of school refusal. *Psychiatry and Clinical Neurosciences*, **53**, 461–469.

Ollendick, T.H. (1983). Reliability and validity of the Revised Fear Survey Schedule for Children (FSSC-R). *Behaviour Research and Therapy*, **21**, 685–692.

Ollendick, T.H., & Cerny, J.A. (1981). *Clinical behaviour therapy with children*. New York: Plenum Press.

Ollendick, T.H., & King, N.J. (1998). Assessment practices and issues with school-refusing children. *Behaviour Change*, **15**, 16–30.

Ollendick, T.H., & Mayer, J.A. (1984). School phobia. In S.M. Turner (Ed.), *Behavioral treatment of anxiety disorders* (pp. 367–411). New York: Plenum Press.

Phelps, L., Cox, D., & Bajorek, E. (1992). School phobia and separation anxiety: Diagnostic and treatment comparisons. *Psychology in the Schools*, **29**, 384–394.

Place, M., Hulsmeier, J., Davis, S., & Taylor, E. (2000). School refusal: A changing problem which requires a change of approach? *Clinical Child Psychology and Psychiatry*, **5**, 345–355.

Rapee, R., Barrett, P.M., Dadds, M.R., & Evans, L. (1994). Reliability of the DSM-III-R childhood anxiety disorders using structured interview: Interrater and parent–child agreement. *Journal of the American Academy of Child and Adolescent Psychiatry*, **33**, 984–992.

Rapee, R., Spence, S., Cobham, V., & Wignall, A. (2000). *Helping your anxious child: A step-by-step guide for parents*. Oakland, CA: New Harbinger Publications.

Reynolds, C.R., & Richmond, B.O. (1978). What I think and feel: A revised measure of children's manifest anxiety. *Journal of Abnormal Child Psychology*, **6**, 271–280.

Reynolds, D. (1996). School factors. In I. Berg & J. Nursten (Eds), *Unwillingly to school* (pp. 38–56). London: Gaskell.

Rodriguez, A., Rodriguez, M., & Eisenberg, L. (1959). The outcome of school phobia: A follow-up study based on 41 cases. *American Journal of Psychiatry*, **116**, 540–544.

Ronan, K.R., & Deane, F.P. (1998). Anxiety disorders. In P. Graham (Ed.), *Cognitive-behaviour therapy for children and families* (pp. 74–94). Melbourne: Cambridge University Press.

Rutter, M., & Maughan, B. (2002). School effectiveness findings. *Journal of School Psychology*, **40**, 451–475.

Sanders, M.R. (1992). *Every parent: A positive approach to children's behaviour*. Sydney: Addison-Wesley.

Sharpley, C.F., & Rogers, H.J. (1984). Preliminary validation of the abbreviated Spanier Dyadic Adjustment Scale: Some psychometric data regarding a screening test of marital adjustment. *Educational and Psychological Measurement*, **44**, 1045–1050.

Silove, D., & Manicavasagar, V. (1993). Adults who feared school: Is early separation anxiety specific to the pathogenesis of panic disorder? *Acta Psychiatrica Scandinavica*, **88**, 385–390.

Silverman, W.K., & Albano, A.M. (1996). *Anxiety Disorders Interview Schedule for DSM-IV, Child and Parent Versions*. San Antonio, TX: Psychological Corporation.

Silverman, W.K., & Eisen, A.R. (1992). Age differences in the reliability of parent and child reports of child anxious symptomatology using a structured interview. *Journal of the American Academy of Child and Adolescent Psychiatry*, **31**, 117–124.

Silverman, W.K., & Kurtines, W.M. (1996). *Anxiety and phobic disorders: A pragmatic approach*. New York: Plenum Press.

Silverman, W.K., & Rabian, B. (1995). Test–retest reliability of the DSM-III-R childhood anxiety disorder symptoms using the Anxiety Disorders Interview Schedule for Children. *Journal of Anxiety Disorders*, **9**, 139–150.

Smith, S.L. (1970). School refusal with anxiety: A review of sixty-three cases. *Canadian Psychiatric Association Journal*, **15**, 257–264.

Spence, S. (1995). *Social skills training: User's guide*. Windsor: NFER-Nelson.

Spence, S. (1998). A measure of anxiety symptoms among children. *Behaviour Research and Therapy*, **36**, 545–566.

Stein, M., Duffner, P.K., Werry, J.S., & Trauner, D.A. (1996). School refusal and emotional lability in a 6-year-old boy. *Developmental and Behavioral Pediatrics*, **17**, S29–S32.

Talbot, M. (1957). Panic in school phobia. *American Journal of Orthopsychiatry*, **27**, 286–295.

Timberlake, E.M. (1984). Psychosocial functioning of school phobics at follow-up. *Social Work Research and Abstracts*, **20**, 13–18.

Tonge, B. (1998). Pharmacotherapy of school refusal. *Behaviour Change*, **15**, 98–106.

Valles, E., & Oddy, M. (1984). The influence of a return to school on the long-term adjustment of school refusers. *Journal of Adolescence*, **7**, 35–44.

Want, J.H. (1983). School-based intervention strategies for school phobia: A ten-step "common sense" approach. *The Pointer*, **27**, 27–32.

Weisz, J.R. (2000). Agenda for child and adolescent psychotherapy research: On the need to put science into practice. *Archives of General Psychiatry*, **57**, 837–838.

Wilkes, T.C.R., Belsher, G., Rush, A.J., & Frank, E. (1994). *Cognitive therapy for depressed adolescents*. New York: Guilford Press.

Zarb, J. (1992). *Cognitive-behavioural assessment and therapy with adolescents*. New York: Bruner/Mazel.

CHAPTER 12

Treatment of Specific Phobia in Children and Adolescents

Thomas H. Ollendick

Virginia Polytechnic Institute and State University, USA

Thompson E. Davis III

Virginia Polytechnic Institute and State University, USA

and

Peter Muris

Maastricht University, The Netherlands

INTRODUCTION

Fear is a normal part of life. Whether one believes we learn to fear or come "prepared" to develop certain fears, the result is the same. It is common for children sitting around a camp fire to become entranced by ghost stories, for teenagers at the movies to recoil in their seats from slasher horror films, and for adults to enthusiastically read mystery books. As may be evident in these everyday examples, at times we do not avoid becoming scared or frightened. Moreover, or at least so it seems, we actually invite it. In fact, most times, fears can be shaken off by pulling the covers tight, checking under the bed or around the corner, and making sure to turn the locks on our doors. We tell ourselves the feared event is unlikely to happen and muster enough reserve to go on with the business of life. Not so with a phobia.

Specific phobia is a particularly crippling disorder, at least in part because it is frequently misunderstood. A specific phobia, like so many psychological disorders, is characterized by cognitive, behavioural, and physiological responses whose intensity is sufficient to cause significant distress. As suggested some years ago by Marks

Correspondence to Thomas H. Ollendick, Virginia Polytechnic Institute and State University, Blacksburg, Virginia 24061-0436; email: tho@vt.edu

Handbook of Interventions that Work with Children and Adolescents: Prevention and Treatment.
Edited by P.M. Barrett and T.H. Ollendick. © 2004 John Wiley & Sons, Ltd. ISBN 0-470-84453-1.

(1969), a phobia is out of proportion to the demands of the situation and cannot be dismissed easily or reasoned away. Intense fear can paralyze those with a phobia to the point that their quality of life is affected markedly. Adults, at least, have some measure of insight into their phobia and recognize it as excessive or unreasonable, even though the fear may become so intense that it leads to avoidance behaviours or extreme anxiety if it cannot be avoided. Children, by contrast, may not have this awareness. All a child may know is that he or she is scared of a dog, getting a shot at the doctor's office, or thunderstorms and wants to get away and to avoid the event or situation as much as possible, and as soon as possible (Ollendick, Hagopian, & King, 1997; Ollendick, King, & Muris, 2002).

Phenomenology

A child's successful development is characterized by meeting and completing diverse developmental milestones, and subsequently integrating each successive achievement into increasingly adaptive outcomes. Unfortunately, the converse is also true; maladaptations in the form of incomplete milestones, trauma, or insult can impede development and the successful integration of key cognitive abilities and competencies (Toth & Cicchetti, 1999). In the instance of a specific phobia, developmental circumstances have coalesced into an intense fear. This fear presentation is described and diagnosed based upon clinical judgment of how closely a child's clinical presentation matches select diagnostic criteria such as those embodied in the *Diagnostic and statistical manual of mental disorders*—4th edition (DSM-IV; APA, 1994). More precisely, the DSM-IV (pp. 410–411) specifies that a specific phobia is characterized by:

A. Marked and persistent fear that is excessive or unreasonable, and that is cued by the presence or anticipation of a specific object or situation (e.g., flying, heights, animals, receiving an injection, seeing blood).
B. Exposure to the phobic stimulus almost invariably provokes an immediate anxiety response, which may take the form of a situationally bound or situationally predisposed Panic Attack. (In children, anxiety might be expressed by crying, tantrums, freezing, or clinging behaviours.)
C. The person recognizes that the fear is excessive or unreasonable. (However, in children, this feature may be absent.)
D. The phobic situation(s) is avoided or else is endured with intense anxiety or distress.
E. The avoidance, anxious anticipation, or distress in the feared situation(s) interferes significantly with the person's functioning and their relationships, or there is marked distress about having the phobia.
F. In individuals under age 18 years, the duration is at least six months.
G. The anxiety, Panic Attacks, or phobic avoidance associated with the specific object or situation are not better accounted for by another mental disorder, such as Obsessive-Compulsive Disorder, Post-Traumatic Stress Disorder, Separation Anxiety Disorder, Social Phobia, Panic Disorder with Agoraphobia, or Agoraphobia without History of Panic Disorder.

In addition, five subtypes of specific phobia are defined: Animal Type, Natural Environment Type, Blood-Injection-Injury Type, Situational Type, and Other Type (e.g., phobic avoidance of situations that may lead to choking, vomiting, or contracting an illness; in children, avoidance of loud sounds or costumed characters).

Moreover, from a developmental perspective, a specific phobia is not simply a constellation of categorical criteria surrounding an intense fear; rather, it also consists of several developmental impediments. A child suffering from a specific phobia not only suffers from the disorder, but also from the limitations that the disorder imposes on the developmental process. For example, a child who cannot go to a friend's house for fear of the friend's dog or an adolescent who cannot leave the house after dusk for fear of the dark are both impacted by the direct effects of the phobia and also by the resulting lack of experiences which would afford them important developmental experiences (e.g., being able to socialize with friends). In this way, there is a reciprocal interaction that takes place in which avoidance of the fear is negatively reinforced and the resulting interference on the child's quality of life is made more severe. Taken from this perspective, avoidance of a phobic stimulus reinforces future avoidance behaviour and also impedes the course of normal development.

According to the DSM-IV, as noted above, a specific phobia is characterized by the "marked and persistent fear of circumscribed objects or situations (criterion A)" (p. 405). However, the DSM-IV also acknowledges the possibility of developmental differences in presentation. Specifically, it has been suggested that whereas adults are aware of the excessive nature of their fears and subsequent responses, children may not have this degree of cognitive insight into their phobias—essentially, children may just know they are afraid and not know or appreciate that their fear is an over-reaction or that their fear is unreasonable and out of proportion to the danger involved. In addition, the DSM-IV specifies specific anxiety behaviours in children of which the clinician should be aware in making a determination—particularly relevant are "crying, tantrums, freezing, or clinging" (p. 410). Implicit within these considerations is the importance of development in the understanding of a phobic reaction and also in the child's ability to understand what has transpired. In adults, a marked distinction associated with a specific phobia is the knowledge that the fear is irrational and out of proportion to the risk—a presentation to the contrary would be better encapsulated as a delusional disorder. However, in children there is a realization that these fears may transcend a child's cognitive ability to conceptualize or even determine what is happening to him or her—there may simply just be an intense physiological response to an object or situation that defies the child's understanding (Forsyth & Chorpita, 1997; Ollendick, Grills, & King, 2001).

Adding to this level of complexity are findings which suggest that underlying a specific phobia are usually a number of other fears and, very likely, a comorbid anxiety disorder and possibly a major depressive disorder. Although fear is the defining characteristic of phobia, Curtis et al. (1998) found that multiple fears are typically involved in and part and parcel of most phobic presentations. Interestingly, their findings also suggest that an increased number of specific fears, regardless of the content of those fears (i.e., if they were similar or not), increased the likelihood of a diagnosis of specific phobia and predicted a more severe presentation with greater impairment and subsequent disability.

In addition, physiological arousal is also discernibly different among the different phobia subtypes. Based on the type of phobia—animal, blood-injection-injury (BII), natural environment, or situational—the physiological response of the child may differ. Most dramatically are comparisons between BII phobias and the three other subtypes. Physiological responses in children with animal, situational, and natural environment phobias are typically elevated upon presentation of the phobic stimuli, as evidenced by increases in heart rate, blood pressure, norepinephrine, and epinephrine (Fyer, 1998; Öst, 1987). However, physiological responses in children with BII phobia have been observed to be markedly different. Typically, children with blood phobia experience a slight arousal after encountering the phobic stimulus that is then followed by a dramatic drop in blood pressure and heart rate leading to fainting spells (Fyer, 1998). Of additional importance, these findings impact treatment options and therapeutic concerns, which will be taken into account later.

Epidemiology

The DSM-IV reports a lifetime prevalence rate of 10 to 11.3%, and a 9% one-year incidence rate, for specific phobia in community samples (p. 408). Specific phobias, then, affect approximately 10% of the total community population. But, what about children? How many of them develop phobias? The extant literature distils down to prevalence rates of approximately 5% of children in community samples and approximately 15% of children in outpatient or other mental health settings (Ollendick, Hagopian, & King, 1997; Ollendick & Hirshfeld-Becker, 2002).

Even so, a more subtle distinction needs to be made to determine the true epidemiological patterns involved. To this end, Ollendick, Hagopian, and King (1997) suggested a relatively "pure" presentation for specific phobia in community samples of children, citing low levels of comorbidity when compared to other anxiety disorders in community samples, and citing data that suggested that "30% of children with a phobic disorder at a later point in time also had one at an earlier point in time" (p. 204). In short, specific phobias in children from community samples tend to be long-lasting at least for a significant minority of these youth. Moreover, they tend to be comorbid with other phobias, but not necessarily with other anxiety or affective disorders. However, clinical samples suggest a high degree of comorbidity among all the anxiety disorders. Here, Ollendick, Hagopian, and King (1997) point to findings that suggest that comorbidity is as high as 61.9% for anxiety disorders and other internalizing and externalizing disorders. Similarly, Silverman et al. (1999) reported that 72% of their 104 clinic-referred, phobic children (ages 6–16 years) had at least one additional comorbid diagnosis. The most prevalent comorbid diagnoses included an additional specific phobia (19%), separation anxiety disorder (16%), overanxious disorder (14%), and attention deficit hyperactivity disorder (6%). In sum, these findings indicate that phobic children presenting to clinics are more likely to present with comorbid disorders than children in community samples.

These rates take on added importance when considered in the appropriate context—the reported age of onset of adult phobias. Öst (1987) studied a sample of 370 adult phobic patients to determine the mean age of onset for particular phobic types and for additional prevalence information. He found that for specific phobias, animal phobia had the earliest age of onset (7 years) followed by blood phobia (9 years) and dental phobia (12 years), with claustrophobia having the latest age of onset (20 years). Of note, most specific phobias had their age of onset in childhood or adolescent years.

Finally, prevalence rates differ for the two sexes and for different specific phobias. Again, according to the DSM-IV, 75 to 90% of individuals presenting with an animal phobia, a natural environment phobia, or a situational phobia are female. In contrast, persons with BII phobia are approximately 55 to 70% female. These rates are consistent with those shown in the child literature suggesting that girls and younger boys report a higher number of specific fear symptoms (Ollendick, King, & Frary, 1989; Muris, Schmidt, & Merckelbach, 1999) and in the adult literature suggesting that females are more likely to suffer from phobias (Curtis et al., 1998). Additionally, fears of animals have been found to be the most common specific phobia in women, while fear of heights has been found to be the most common specific phobia in men (second most common in women) (Muris et al., 1999).

AETIOLOGY

The underlying causes of specific phobia are poorly understood and currently the source of considerable debate—probably due in no small way to the developmental principle of equifinality, the notion that many different pathways may lead to the same endpoint, and due to the general heterogeneity of the diagnosis (Muris & Merckelbach, 2001; Ollendick & Hirshfeld-Becker, 2002; Toth & Cicchetti, 1999). An in-depth discussion of the aetiological pathways to fear is beyond the scope of this chapter (interested parties are directed to a series of recent articles in *Behaviour Research and Therapy,* **40**, 2002). Even so, four distinct pathways for the acquisition of specific phobia have been suggested: phobic acquisition by way of conditioning, acquisition by way of vicarious learning, acquisition by way of information about the feared stimulus, and acquisition by non-associative means (Rachman, 2002).

Associative models have traditionally been based on conditioning theory. In other words, a phobic child has been conditioned to respond with fear to certain stimuli. This conditioning is suggested to take place by one of three avenues: direct classical conditioning, vicarious conditioning, and information/instruction (Ollendick & King, 1991; Rachman, 1977). In its simplest form, a phobia can be learned through actual classical conditioning experience: the development of an association between a conditioned stimulus and a conditioned response. For example, a child becomes afraid of dogs after having been chased, knocked down, and perhaps bitten by a dog. A phobia can also be learned, however, through seeing someone else display fear to a particular stimulus in a vicarious conditioning paradigm. To wit, a child can become afraid of dogs after seeing another child chased and bitten by a dog. Finally, a phobia can be learned by simply having someone instruct another person to be afraid—in other words, specific instructions (perhaps inadvertently in most cases, but not all) are given by influential adults to be afraid of dogs, snakes, water, etc. For example, a child might become afraid of dogs after being told by a parent to be very careful around dogs and to be wary of them because they might knock them down and bite them.

In contrast to associative models of phobia acquisition, non-associative models have relied on a combination of temperament, biology, and failure to habituate to explain the development of a phobia. Essentially, these models are built upon the idea that different species have predisposed inborn fears that presently serve or, at least at one point in evolutionary time, served an adaptive purpose. In the instance of a phobia, the reaction that is seen has become out of place with the adaptation observed over time. For example, Fyer (1998) points to stranger anxiety, fear of the visual cliff, and separation anxiety as adaptive forms of temperamental fear. In each of these instances, and others, a phobia may result from a failure to successfully habituate to these inborn fears. As discussed by Menzies and Clarke (1995), such a failure to habituate likely results from a lack of opportunity for safe exposure, dishabituation in response to increased demands and stress, or a deficiency in the individual precluding the ability to habituate. Even so, the precise mechanisms accounting for this failure to habituate have not been explicated. Interestingly, Forsyth and Chorpita (1997) emphasize that even if a non-associative account were viable, there is no treatment that follows logically from this paradigm. Whether therapists embrace this model or not, the treatment of choice has been that prescribed by a notably associative model.

Aetiological evidence has been summarized recently by Ollendick, Hagopian, and King (1997) and Ollendick, King, and Muris (2002) who report that not only does conditioning play a role, but that multiple modes of conditioning may be necessary and may be specific to the type of phobic outcome. For instance, in a study comparing high- and low-fearful children, they point out that the primary difference between high- and low-fearful snake-phobic children was that the high-fearful children were more likely to endorse a combination of influences including modelling, information/instruction, and direct conditioning. Essentially, they suggest, a single conditioning event may not be sufficient to trigger a phobia; rather, and more consistent with the developmental principle of equifinality, many events and modes of conditioning seem to occasion the development of any one phobia.

ASSESSMENT

According to Forsyth and Chorpita (1997), most individuals presenting with specific phobia simply want to change the way they feel toward the phobic stimulus. In children, as noted earlier, there may not be the recognition that the fear is unreasonable or out of proportion to the demands of the situation and, as a result, the child may not believe it is necessary to change his or her "phobia." This lack of understanding by a phobic child requires the clinician to be doggedly thorough and exacting while completing the assessment process. Reasons for this level of care on the part of the clinician are implicit, and simply a part of being a conscientious practitioner, but such a degree of evaluation should also indicate a desire on the part of the clinician to be informed by developmental theory. In this way, the clinician remains aware that responses that are adaptive at one stage may become pathological when evidenced at other stages. Therefore, in children especially, clinicians need to remain current on the child's developmental sequelae. For instance, all children exhibit periods of fear during their early development; however, persistence of excessive fear into middle childhood and adolescence is unusual.

Elaborating more fully, Ollendick, Grills, and King (2001) have suggested four dictums to guide a developmentally informed evaluation. First, the developmentally aware clinician refers to cognitive theory and guidelines created from socio-emotional development to select appropriate assessment measures. Second, the adaptive nature of a behaviour or cognition, or lack thereof, should be considered within the larger context of comparable normative data. Third, a clinician should be aware of psychopathological phenotypes; essentially, a clinician must be aware of the different ways a disorder presents at different ages (i.e., what a disorder "looks like" at different ages). And, fourth, a clinician must be conscious of the plasticity of behaviour and its potential to change over time. Overall, it is assumed that most clinicians implicitly strive for such a comprehensive and developmentally informed assessment. Ollendick, Grills, and King (2001), however, assert that these previously implicit assessment guidelines need to become explicit and that they need to be moved to the forefront of clinical practice.

As a result, the assessment of a phobic child or adolescent should be detailed and developmentally informed. We suggest the use of three primary arenas of assessment to provide insight into a child's behaviour, affect, and cognition. Specifically, phobias are typically assessed by behavioural avoidance tasks, clinical interviews, and self- and other-report measures (see Table 12.1).

Behavioural Tasks

There are two primary types of behavioural tasks: Behavioural Avoidance Tasks (BATs) and Direct Observation of Anxiety (DOA) tasks. BATs have been a commonly used means of phobia assessment. Early use of BATs included Lang and Lazovik's (1963) method in which fearful adults were asked to approach caged snakes and to indicate their degree of avoidance on a 3-point scale (i.e., looking, touching, or holding). Basically, in its simplest form, a BAT is a clinician engineered and controlled situation in which a person is exposed to the potentially phobic stimulus so that a behavioural assessment of the degree of avoidance can be observed objectively. For instance, a BAT for a potential spider phobia might involve having a spider enclosed in a clear jar at the end of the room. A child is then instructed to walk to the jar, open the lid, and pick up the spider and hold it for 5 seconds. The degree to which the child complies or avoids the therapist's instructions can provide an elegant measure of phobic avoidance. In addition, information about the degree of experienced fear can be obtained by asking the child to report subjective units of distress (SUDs) ratings periodically throughout the BAT. Such ratings can vary from 0 to 100 but we have frequently found ratings of 0 to 8 to be quite sufficient. Typically, the measure of BAT performance is the percentage of steps completed and the SUDs experienced in that process. When used properly, the BAT is a mainstay of phobic assessment as it can be conveniently arranged and allows for direct observation of the child's difficulty and phobic response.

In addition to BATs, there exist several protocols for the Direct Observation of Anxiety (DOA). This process involves the systematic coding of a child's anxious

Table 12.1 Summary of specific phobia assessment options: description and psychometric properties

Instrument	Description	Subscales/Procedural comments	Psychometric properties
Anxiety Disorders Interview Schedule-Child/Parent (ADIS-C/P; Silverman & Albano, 1996)	Structured diagnostic clinical interview, child and parent versions	Screens for childhood internalizing and externalizing disorders of DSM-IV	• Interrater reliability 0.98 ADIS-C, 0.93 ADIS-P (Silverman & Nelles, 1988). • Retest reliability 0.76 ADIS-C, 0.67 ADIS-P (Silverman & Eisen, 1992). • Sensitivity to treatment effects for childhood anxiety (Barrett et al., 1996; Kendall, 1994)
Behavioural Avoidance Tasks (BAT; *in-vivo*, exposure-based assessment of approach/avoidance of a phobic stimulus)	Although heterogeneity for BAT procedures exists in the literature, typically a child is asked to enter a room containing the relevant phobic stimulus at the opposite end. The child's approach toward the stimulus is documented and a percentage of steps or stages completed out of the total possible is calculated	Differing opinions regarding the number of steps, as well as differing steps for different stimuli. For example, our Phobia Project currently uses 10 steps for dog phobia and 13 steps for snake phobia	• For a more detailed discussion of the pros/cons the reader should see Dadds et al., 1994. • Briefly, BAT performance seems to be reliable for any one type of BAT for any one child; however, the heterogeneity of procedures makes large comparisons difficult. • Issues of test–retest reliability and standardization of procedures are currently being addressed by our Phobia Project.
Child Behaviour Checklist (CBCL; Achenbach, 1991b)	Measure typically filled out by a child's parent/guardian. Inquires generically into a child's skills, behaviours, interactions, and hobbies. Age range 4 to 18 years	Separates internalizing and externalizing difficulties into various Problem Scales which can be useful: Withdrawn, Somatic Complaints, Anxious/Depressed, Social Problems, Thought Problems, Attention Problems, Delinquent Behaviour, and Aggressive Behaviour	• Satisfactory to excellent retest reliability (approx. 0.89 at 1 week, 0.75 at 1 year, 0.71 at 2 years; Achenbach, 1991b). • Inter-rater agreement approx. 0.65 to 0.75 for parents (Achenbach, 1991b). • Scaled scores can be interpreted such that there is an 89.1% correct classification rate (Achenbach, 1991b)

Direct Observation of Anxiety (DOA)	A child's anxious behaviours (e.g., shaking, sweating, clinging, trembling, crying) are typically coded by an observer based upon a predetermined scale	Various protocols exist for the observation of many different types of anxiety. These differing methodologies also incorporate differing numbers of behaviours to be recorded (e.g., Glennon & Weisz, 1978, 30 behaviours selected and designed to reflect levels of fear and anxiety). Perhaps most famous, Ainsworth et al.'s, 1978 Strange Situation	• Diverse methodologies and coding systems exist. For a brief review, we recommend Dadds et al. (1994); and particularly for anxiety, Barrett et al. (1996). • Reliabilities are reported to range from low to very high depending on the coding protocol
Fear Survey Schedule for Children-Revised (FSSC-R; Ollendick, 1983)	Self-report measure consisting of 80 specific phobia items, Likert scale (3-point)	Consists of a Total Score and five subscales: Fear of Failure, Fear of the Unknown, Fear of Injury and Small Animals, Fear of Danger and Death, and Medical Fears	• Excellent to satisfactory retest reliability (approx. 0.82 at 1 week, 0.55 at 3 months; Ollendick, 1983) • Has been demonstrated that school phobic children have significantly higher Total Scores than school phobic matched controls (Ollendick, 1983) • Has been shown to discriminate, significantly, between different types of specific phobia when completed by parent or child (Weems et al., 1999)
Multidimensional Anxiety Scale for Children (MASC; March et al., 1997)	Measures wide range of anxiety symptoms, Likert scale (4-point) self-report, 39-items, age range 8 to 18 years	Four factors with subfactors including: physical symptoms (tense/somatic), harm avoidance (anxious coping/perfectionism), social anxiety (humiliation/ performance), and separation anxiety	• Internal reliability of total score is 0.90 (March et al., 1997) • Satisfactory to excellent retest reliability (0.79 at 3 weeks, 0.93 at 3 months; March et al., 1997) • Good convergent validity with RCMAS (0.63; March et al., 1997)

continues overleaf

Table 12.1 *(continued)*

Instrument	Description	Subscales/Procedural comments	Psychometric properties
Revised Children's Manifest Anxiety Scale (RCMAS; Reynolds & Richmond, 1978)	Self-report measure consisting of 37 items related to anxiety, age range 6 to 19 years, response is "yes" or "no"; 9 of 37 items measure social desirability	Consists of a Total Anxiety score and four subscale scores: Physiological Anxiety, Worry/Oversensitivity, Social Concerns/Concentration, and Lie/Social Desirability	• Excellent discriminative validity between anxious and normal controls with 87% correct classification (March et al., 1997) • Satisfactory retest reliability (approx. 0.68 at 9 months; Reynolds & Richmond, 1985) • Has been suggested to discriminate significantly between state and trait anxiety when compared to the STAIC (RCMAS scores associated with "chronic manifest anxiety"; Reynolds & Richmond, 1985)
Screen for Child Anxiety Related Emotional Disorders-Revised (SCARED-R; Muris et al., 1999)	Self-report measure consisting of 66 items related to DSM-IV anxiety disorders, age range 8 to 18 years, response is on a 3-point Likert scale	Consists of a Total Scale score and seven subscales: Separation Anxiety Disorder, Generalized Anxiety Disorder, Panic Disorder, Social Phobia, Obsessive-Compulsive Disorder, Traumatic Stress Disorder, and Specific Phobias	• Internal reliability of total score is 0.94 (Muris & Steerneman, 2001) • Internal reliability of Specific Phobia scale is 0.58–0.71 (Muris & Steerneman, 2001) • Good convergent validity with FSSC-R (Total Scale correlates 0.64; Muris & Steerneman, 2001). Has been suggested to discriminate significantly between anxious and disruptive disorders (Muris & Steerneman, 2001)

Specific Phobia Questionnaires (Instruments designed to inquire about certain specific phobias). For example, the Spider Phobia Questionnaire for Children (SPQ-C; Kindt et al., 1996)	Self-report measure consisting of 29 spider phobia related items, response is "true" or "not true"	Scores on all items are summed to create a Total Score that suggests the degree of spider fear	• Satisfactory retest reliability (approx. 0.61 at 6–7 weeks; Kindt et al., 1996) • Has been suggested to discriminate significantly between spider phobic and non-phobic girls (Kindt et al., 1996)
Teacher Report Form (TRF; Achenbach, 1991c)	Measure typically filled out by a child's teacher. Inquires generically into a child's skills, interactions, and hobbies, as well as maladaptive behaviours	Separates internalizing and externalizing difficulties into various Problem Scales which can be useful: Withdrawn, Somatic Complaints, Anxious/ Depressed, Social Problems, Thought Problems, Attention Problems, Delinquent Behaviour, and Aggressive Behaviour	• Satisfactory to excellent retest reliability (approx. 0.9 at 2 weeks, 0.75 at 2 months, 0.66 at 4 months; Achenbach, 1991c) • Inter-rater agreement approx. 0.54 for teachers seeing students in different conditions (Achenbach, 1991c) • Scaled scores can be interpreted such that there is a 79.3% correct classification rate (Achenbach, 1991c)
Youth Self-Report (YSR; Achenbach, 1991d)	Measure typically filled out by the child. Inquires generically into a child's skills, interactions, and hobbies, as well as problematic behaviours	Separates internalizing and externalizing difficulties into various Problem Scales which can be useful: Withdrawn, Somatic Complaints, Anxious/ Depressed, Social Problems, Thought Problems, Attention Problems, Delinquent Behaviour, and Aggressive Behaviour	• Satisfactory retest reliability (approx. 0.72 at 1 week, 0.49 at 7 months; Achenbach, 1991d) • Scaled scores can be interpreted such that there is a 71.9% correct classification rate (Achenbach, 1991d)

behaviours and outward physiological signs of anxiety as they actually occur in the clinical setting. For instance, a coding system designed by Glennon and Weisz (1978) examined 30 different fear-related behaviours in young children (e.g., crying, nail-biting, trembling, rigid body posture) as they approached the school setting and upon separation from their parents. Perhaps the best-known example of DOA is the Strange Situation detailed early on by Ainsworth et al. (1978). This observational system has spawned many studies on parent–child interactions.

The Clinical Interview

Clinical interviews are also a crucial component of the assessment of any disorder, including phobias. During the initial clinical interview, assessment should involve detailing the precise nature of the specific phobia. Specific phobias represent a heterogeneous disorder and the treatment for a blood phobia, applied muscle tension, would be inappropriate for an animal phobia, applied relaxation. Additionally, the severity of the phobia and any comorbid disorders or additional underlying fears can be ascertained with the clinical interview.

In addition, a detailed functional analysis of the phobia should be obtained. A functional analysis involves the clinician detailing the origins of the phobia, cognitions about the phobia, and the behaviours that come about in response to the phobic stimulus (see Table 12.2). In essence, this interview should be an expedition or foray into a child's cognitions during which the clinician makes use of a hypothesis-testing process to determine the circumstances in which phobic behaviour occurs (Ollendick & Ollendick, 1997). This information should then be examined by the clinician in an attempt to determine the cognitions and behaviours that maintain and exacerbate the child's phobic symptoms. An excerpt from a functional analysis prompt is presented in Table 12.2. Each of the child's cognitions should

Table 12.2   Excerpt from a functional analysis prompt

"We are going to try to work together to figure out exactly what is scary for you so that we can find the most accurate and helpful way to help you with it. We will be detectives together on the trail of the phobia trying to find the exact thoughts you have that make you so scared. I will be asking you lots of questions, and you will need to help me understand all about this fear so that we can tackle it together."

"What is it about (phobic stimulus) that leads you to be afraid?"

Is it the size?	It might bite or sting?
The way it moves?	The colour?
The noise it makes?	Its body parts (e.g., teeth, claws, etc.)?

"What do you think will happen when you are exposed to the phobic stimulus?"

At home? Both inside and outside the house.	With family?
With friends?	At school?

be evaluated. We have found it helpful to ask three follow-up questions in particular for each phobic belief. How likely is it that (what the child believes) will happen? How bad would it be for the child if it actually happened? How sure are you (the child) that you could handle it or deal with it (i.e., cope) if it did happen? These key cognitions and behaviours then become targets for therapeutic intervention.

In addition to the clinical analytical interview, we have found the Anxiety Disorders Interview Schedule for DSM-IV (Silverman & Albano, 1996) to be a useful tool at this stage in the assessment process. This semistructured interview allows for a detailed and comprehensive assessment of phobias and other major diagnosable DSM-IV Axis I disorders. In addition, this measure has two versions, one for children and one for parents about their child. In this way, clinicians may conduct careful assessments of phobias and comorbid anxiety disorders and then compare parent and child reports (Grills & Ollendick, 2002). From a developmental perspective, this comparison can be crucial as children frequently have a skewed perception of the normalcy of their fear and degree of avoidance. Taken together, however, the parents' interview can supplement and further evaluate the degree of normalcy and circumstances surrounding the phobia by allowing the clinician to make use of the parents' greater cognitive facilities and experience with both their phobic and non-phobic children.

Self-Report Measures

Standardized self-report measures also aid in the determination of the scope and type of phobia. Specifically, the Fear Survey Schedule for Children—Revised (FSSC-R; Ollendick, 1983) provides a window into a variety of phobias including social phobia, specific phobias, and specific phobia of shots and doctors. Recently, Weems et al. (1999) have shown that the FSSC-R discriminated well among specific phobias and also allowed for parent-report assessments to be differentiated. Additionally, the reliability and validity of the FSSC-R have been found to be acceptable, making this measure an excellent assessment tool for practicing the continued vigilance required of keeping up with a developing child. It also provides normative information for boys and girls of varying ages and nationalities, and it has been translated into several languages.

Additional self-report measures have also been found to be helpful. Particular questionnaires devoted to the assessment of individual phobias also exist. For example, the Spider Phobia Questionnaire for Children is a 29-item instrument that provides the clinician with an overall spider fear score (SPQ-C; Kindt, Brosschot, & Muris, 1996). Additionally, more general measures of anxiety and functioning may prove useful. For instance, Muris et al. (1999) revised the Screen for Child Anxiety Related Emotional Disorders. This 66-item self-report measure focuses on measuring anxiety disorders as defined by the DSM-IV. March et al.'s (1997) Multidimensional Anxiety Scale for Children (MASC) and Reynolds and Richmond's (1978) Revised Children's Manifest Anxiety Scale (RCMAS) have also been found to be suitable measures of general anxiety and fear. Additionally, the Youth Self-Report

(YSR; Achenbach, 1991a) is an excellent measure of an older child's general internalizing and externalizing behaviours (appropriate for children 11 years of age and older). While these diverse measures contain some individual items addressing phobia specifically, they are also invaluable in that they provide information on general functioning and a variety of other types of anxiety disorders. This added information is crucial in informing assessment due, in part, to the comorbidity issues discussed above.

In a similar fashion, other-report measures of functioning can be critical to the developmentally aware therapist. In order to form a complete assessment picture of a child's phobia, it is important to determine how the child is perceived to function outside of the therapy room in other areas and in other situations. To this end, we have found the checklists developed by Achenbach (1991b) to be the most helpful. These checklists require parents, teachers, and other relevant adults to indicate the degree to which a child has certain thoughts, feelings, or behaviours. When properly scored, the Child Behaviour Checklist (CBCL) and Teacher Report Form (TRF) allow a clinician to evaluate a child's functioning across eight different behavioural dimensions: withdrawn, somatic complaints, anxious/depressed, social problems, thought problems, attention problems, delinquent behaviour, and aggressive behaviour. This information can then be incorporated into a more comprehensive assessment picture, allowing for standardized measurement of parents' and teachers' input.

As a whole, a developmental perspective on assessment should take a dynamic approach. By this, we mean that assessment should be an ongoing interactive process both prior to and throughout therapy. A child can change in myriad ways during treatment through the experiences obtained in and out of therapy. Assessment, then, should be used to inform and then monitor efficacious treatment (Ollendick & Hersen, 1984; Ollendick & Ollendick, 1997).

TREATMENT

Given the four distinct pathways to phobia acquisition described above and their general dependence upon variants of learning theory (except non-associative for which no treatment paradigm exists at this time), several treatments building upon and expanding basic concepts in learning theory and social cognitive theory have been developed. Historically, methodologies developed for the treatment of specific phobia have been systematic desensitization, emotive imagery, flooding, contingency management, modelling, behavioural family intervention, and cognitive-behavioural treatment (Ollendick, Hagopian, & King, 1997; Ollendick & King, 1998, 2000). Additionally, a cognitive-based intensive exposure treatment developed by Öst (1989) called one-session treatment is recently being applied to children and appears promising (Muris et al., 1998; Öst et al., 2001). Given, however, the complexity of factors affecting and maintaining a phobic presentation, these treatments have evolved beyond simple learning principles in their sophistication to incorporate other useful paradigms and techniques as well (e.g., the incorporation of cognitive theory and information processing theory). Even so, the cornerstone to these techniques is found in Marks' observation that "an important mechanism shared by all of these methods is exposure of the frightened subject to a frightening situation until he acclimatizes" (1975, p. 67).

Systematic Desensitization

Developed from classical conditioning theory, systematic desensitization is based on the idea that two hedonically opposed states cannot occur simultaneously. Wolpe (1958) elaborated upon the work of early theorists (e.g., Pavlov, Watson, Jones, & Masserman) and developed the procedure that is generally understood as systematic desensitization. According to his theory, counterconditioning of the classically conditioned phobia is achieved through a process of reciprocal inhibition. Systematic desensitization, then, is a process by which anxiety created by the phobic stimulus is suppressed and subverted by a simultaneous and incompatible learned response (e.g., relaxation). As such, systematic desensitization is generally composed of three steps: (1) progressive muscle relaxation training, (2) the creation and elaboration of a fear-producing stimulus hierarchy by the therapist and child, and (3) the systematic pairing of relaxation with increasingly intense items in the hierarchy.

To this end, treatment begins by teaching the child some form of progressive muscle relaxation. This procedure involves instructing the child to tense and then relax various muscle groups sequentially up and down the body until a state of relative quiescence or relaxation is obtained. Presently, a variety of relaxation scripts exist, generally developed for use with adults. Developmental concerns should be the deciding factor among them. Specifically, younger children may have more difficulty attending to and learning relaxation than adults and adolescents. As a result, simplified relaxation protocols of a briefer duration may be necessitated (see Ollendick & Cerny, 1981, for such a script). Also, the use of imagery and fantasy may help to spark a younger child's continued interest (Koeppen, 1974). For example, providing additional imagery by instructing the child to pretend that he is squeezing a whole lemon in his hand and trying to get out the last drop of juice may capture a younger child's attention more than the simple instruction to squeeze the hand firmly into a fist.

After the child is sufficiently skilled in relaxation, a hierarchy of the child's phobic stimuli is created. Essentially, a continuum of increasingly more stressful and anxiety-provoking fears is created and rank-ordered from least to greatest. In this portion of treatment, parental input is advised with the child contributing as much as he or she is able. Parental input is crucial, especially for younger children, as children may not always be aware of the various gradations of stimuli that trigger their phobic responses.

Finally, systematic desensitization begins by moving up the hierarchy, either *in vivo* or by way of imagery, until a point of anxiety is reached. At this point, the child is relaxed and the process begins over again until he or she can reach the highest level of the continuum with only minimal to no fear. Ollendick, Hagopian, and King (1997) point out that while systematic desensitization has, at least historically, been the treatment of choice, its use with children is difficult and highly dependent on the child's cognitive abilities. As a result, a therapist should determine if a child has the capability to allow systematic desensitization to be the best treatment option (e.g., is able to become skilled at relaxation, is cognitively able to imagine stimuli or tolerate *in-vivo* presentations).

Emotive Imagery

Emotive imagery follows from systematic desensitization theory utilizing the same concept of reciprocal inhibition—just not by way of relaxation. This technique was developed by Lazarus and Abramowitz (1962) for use with younger children who, presumably, had difficulties with the demands of systematic desensitization proper. Emotive imagery, however, while similar to systematic desensitization in principle, does not make use of relaxation techniques and instead seeks to elicit "positive affect". The treatment still necessitates the development of a hierarchy of items. However, treatment progresses in a storytelling fashion such that the child and a favourite hero are linked, supportive, and interacting to overcome the fear. In this way, the child and imaginary hero overcome fear-evoking obstacles systematically along the hierarchy under the direction of the therapist. Together, the two are imagined to battle or in some way become exposed to or overcome the fears. For example, Batman may accompany a phobic child, deemed Batman's special agent, through a graduated storyline that exposes the child to his fears (Jackson & King, 1981).

As with systematic desensitization, caution is recommended because this technique must be tailored to the imaginative capabilities of the child. The delicate goal should be to take development into consideration so as to be neither over- nor under-stimulating. Additionally, use of the child's own favourite heroes or heroines and fantasies should be encouraged and anxiety levels should be carefully monitored (e.g., by using SUDs ratings) and attended to (King, Hamilton, & Ollendick, 1988; Rosenstiel & Scott, 1977).

Flooding

Flooding is yet another technique involving imagined or, preferably, *in-vivo* exposure. Central to the concept of flooding is the behavioural phenomenon of extinction—prolonged exposure to a conditioned stimulus in the absence of the aversive outcome leads to an extinction of the response. Flooding differs significantly from systematic desensitisation or emotive imagery because prolonged exposure is "forced" upon the child until the extinction of the response is complete. In this way, reinforcement for the avoidance of the phobic stimulus does not occur (i.e., the child is not allowed to escape his or her anxiety by avoiding the stimulus). For example, a child evidencing a fear of heights may be subtly "forced" to go up on top of a building with the therapist and stay until the fear subsides. By its very nature, flooding is initially aversive and unpleasant, which may reflect its being used infrequently in children. It is not recommended at this time.

Contingency Management

Contingency management procedures are based upon a different area of learning theory than the previous treatments. The goal of treatment using contingency management strategies is to reinforce a child for approaching the phobic stimulus. This operant-based treatment forgoes classical conditioning paradigms, and instead focuses on the principles of shaping, reinforcement, and extinction. Generally, this process requires three steps: (1) initial assessment and functional analysis, (2) shaping and reinforcement, and (3) extinction.

As introduced above, a detailed assessment of the phobic response is required in order to identify effective reinforcers and to determine exactly what happens when the child is exposed to the fearful object. To this end, a functional analysis should be conducted to determine how the child acts when confronted by the phobic stimulus in different situations with different individuals present or not present. The goal of such an analysis should be to determine the factors that are maintaining the avoidance behaviour.

Following the functional analysis, the therapist should determine the reinforcers necessary to change a phobic child's behaviour, keeping in mind that particularly powerful reinforcers will be needed to overcome the avoidance response. After determining the appropriate reinforcers, a plan designed to shape approach behaviour through positive reinforcement should be enacted. As with most forms of learning, reinforcement will be most effective when the goal of the exercise is clear and specific (i.e., specific progress in approaching the phobic stimulus), the reinforcer is something that the child finds sufficiently desirable, the child is aware of the reinforcer and the necessary steps required to obtain reinforcement, and the reinforcer is presented as quickly after successful completion of the steps as is possible (King, Hamilton, & Ollendick, 1988). Additionally, an initial continuous reinforcement schedule should be modified into a partial reinforcement schedule after mastery is evidenced. Simultaneously with shaping and reinforcement, extinction protocols should be put in place with the goal being to no longer reward avoidance behaviours. This step requires the therapist to identify the reinforcing elements of the avoidance behaviour in the functional analysis and remove or alter them. In some instances, this may translate into the therapist altering parents' behaviours in order to be supportive of their child when he or she becomes afraid, but not allow gross avoidance or manipulation.

A recent study conducted by Silverman et al. (1999) examined the benefits of contingency management treatment and self-control treatment against an education support control group. In this study, 81 phobic children and their parents were evaluated using child, parent, and clinician measures. The children were assigned to one of the three 10-week manualized conditions (i.e., self-control, contingency management, or education support). Interestingly, all three conditions were found to impart substantial improvement in the child's functioning as measured by child, parent, and clinician measures; however, slightly more gains were evident in the two active treatment conditions. Additionally, treatment gains were maintained in subsequent follow-ups at 3, 6, and 12 months.

Modelling

Although it has been shown that observing a model interact with an object can create a phobia in an observer, modelling successful interactions with phobic stimuli has also been found to be a successful method of treating a phobia. The process of modelling, as described by Bandura (1969), involves vicarious conditioning. Modelling in this way involves a child's observation of a model's non-phobic approach toward a stimulus and subsequent ability to cope successfully without fear. In this way, fear is reduced and the skills needed for navigating the anxiety-provoking situation are observed and acquired.

Three different types of modelling have been found to be effective: filmed modelling, live modelling, and participant or guided modelling. As suggested by its name, filmed modelling involves having a phobic child watch a similar model (i.e., a model with physical characteristics approximately similar to child viewing the film) gradually cope with a phobic encounter and interact with the phobic stimulus. Live modelling entails having the phobic child observe a real model interact and cope with the phobic stimulus (again, having the model be as similar to the phobic child as is possible). Participant modelling, or guided modelling, imparts learning by having the child interact with the model one-on-one while the model demonstrates ways of successfully dealing with the phobic stimulus. In this particular case, the model and observer (i.e., the phobic child) are in close physical contact as the model intimately demonstrates how to approach the phobic stimulus and then physically and verbally instructs the observer. This method of modelling allows the child to experience more support while encountering the anxiety-provoking stimulus.

In an effort to determine the relative merits of the three different types of modelling, Ollendick (1979) examined the effectiveness of treatments with filmed, live, and participant modelling on the subsequent reduction of fearfulness in children and adolescents. He suggested a clear progression in treatment effectiveness from filmed modelling (effective in about 25–50% of cases) to live modelling (effective in about 50–67% of cases) to participant modelling (effective in about 80–92% of cases). While important to note that these were largely subclinical cases, Ollendick (1979) suggested a compelling argument for the use of live, participant modelling and instruction to overcome fear.

Behavioural Family Interventions

The impact and influence of parents and families on children cannot be over-emphasized. As implicitly and explicitly suggested above, parents take an active role in their phobic child's treatment with their involvement depending on the type of treatment decided upon. Parents provide crucial information during assessment, can help to form hierarchies for systematic desensitization or emotive imagery, can be supportive and caring during exposure, eventually take over contingency management practices at home and abroad, and act as potential models for coping behaviour and skills development. Even so, behavioural family interventions would suggest even more parental involvement to the extent of making the parents equal partners in the treatment of their child's phobia. Unfortunately, there are no good controlled outcome studies looking at treatment of specific phobias from this perspective.

That being the case, promising results have emerged from the "transfer of control" model (Ginsburg, Silverman, & Kurtines, 1995) and from the Family Anxiety Management model (FAM; Dadds, Heard, & Rapee, 1992). The transfer of control model emphasizes a systematic transfer of control from the therapist to the parent and, eventually, to the child. This approach and FAM engage parents actively in treatment by training them in contingency management strategies and then relinquishing the responsibility for anxiety management and phobic exposure to the parents themselves. Additionally, self-control strategies (e.g., relaxation, self-instruction) are frequently taught to the child so that he or she acquires the skills to eventually control and cope with any anxiety. In this way, treatment is seen as a strong and equal partnership between therapist, family, and child allowing the open targeting of dysfunctional dynamics related to parental anxiety, difficult family relationships, deficits in parenting skills, and parent–child relational and communicative problems. Encouragingly, a controlled group study of 79 anxiety-disordered children using FAM was found to be superior to a wait-list control condition and to an individually oriented cognitive-behaviour therapy condition, both after treatment and at one-year follow-up (Barrett, Dadds, & Rapee, 1996). Such positive effects, however, were limited to young children; for the older children, both treatments were found to be equally effective.

Cognitive-Behaviour Therapy

Affect, behaviour, and cognition are inextricably and reciprocally intertwined. As such, previous treatments have investigated the use of learning theory to change behaviour and alleviate subsequent fearful affect and terrifying cognitions (e.g., contingency management, modelling). Cognitive-behaviour therapy for specific phobia offers a slightly different perspective. Treatment following this model is based upon the assumption that inaccurate and maladaptive cognitions drive psychopathological affect and behaviour. As a result, interventions are specifically targeted at changing and adapting faulty cognitions that should, in turn, lead to a change in affect and behaviour.

To accomplish this change, a therapist can make use of a variety of techniques. Verbal self-instructional training has been the most commonly used cognitive-behavioural approach for reducing fears in young children. As developed by Meichenbaum and Goodman (1971), verbal self-instruction training essentially involves an elaborate participant modelling protocol. To begin the process, the therapist models appropriate interactions with a phobic stimulus while, at the same time, verbally self-instructing to facilitate coping. Next, the phobic child, who has been observing the stimulus encounter and coping self-talk, completes the same modelled behaviours while receiving verbal instruction from the therapist. Then, the child is instructed to perform the modelled behaviour just as the therapist did: without the therapist's external direction, but with the child verbally directing his or her own behaviour toward the goal. After these skills have been mastered, the child is then directed to gradually fade his or her self-instruction to a whisper and eventually to internalize the self-talk dialogue so as to be covertly directing his or her own actions.

While self-instructional training is an important part of cognitive-behaviour treatment, findings suggest that it alone may not be sufficient to create change (Hagopian, Weist, & Ollendick, 1990; Ollendick, 1995; Ollendick, Hagopian, & Huntzinger, 1991). As a result, cognitive-behaviour therapy for specific phobia typically, and rather elegantly, integrates components of relaxation training and reinforcement in concert with self-instructional training. For example, Graziano and Mooney (1980) conducted a between-group study of 6- to 13-year-old, severely night-time phobic children. These children were assigned to either a wait-list control condition or a cognitive-behavioural condition composed of relaxation training and verbal coping. Additionally, parents played a crucial role by operantly reinforcing the children's progress. Results suggested that the combined cognitive-behavioural treatment was effective. Also, maintenance of improvement was found to continue at a two- to three-year follow-up (Graziano & Mooney, 1982).

More recently, Kendall and his colleagues have pioneered an integrated cognitive and behavioural treatment program for phobic and anxious youth. Cognitive strategies are used to assist the child to recognize anxious cognitions, to use awareness of such cognitions as a cue for managing anxiety, and to help the child to cope more effectively in anxiety-producing situations. In addition, behavioural strategies such as modelling, *in-vivo* exposure, role-play, exercises, muscle relaxation, and reinforced practice are used. Thus, these cognitive-behavioural procedures are broad in scope and incorporate many of the elements of effective treatments used with such children. In the first randomized-controlled trial of this integrated treatment (using a treatment manual), Kendall (1994) compared the outcome of this intervention to a wait-list control condition with 47 children between 9 and 13 years of age. All the children met the diagnostic criteria for anxiety disorders and over half of them were comorbid with at least one other psychiatric disorder. Treated children improved on a number of relevant dimensions; perhaps the most dramatic difference was the percentage of children not meeting full criteria for an anxiety disorder at the end of treatment—64% versus 5% of the wait-list children. At follow-up one and three years later, improvements were maintained (Kendall & Southam-Gerow, 1996). Kendall et al. (1997) reaffirmed the efficacy of this integrated procedure with 94 children (ages 9–13) randomly assigned to cognitive-behavioural and wait-list conditions: 71% of the treated children no longer met full diagnostic criteria for an anxiety disorder compared to 5% of those in the wait-list condition. Furthermore, Barrett et al. (1996) also demonstrated that this combined cognitive and behavioural intervention was more effective than wait-list conditions (albeit less effective than FAM-based treatment—see above). Thus, considerable support exists for cognitive-behaviour therapy, at least in comparison to wait-list conditions.

One-Session Treatment

Finally, Öst and colleagues (Öst, 1989; Öst, Brandberg, & Alm, 1997; Öst, Ferebee, & Furmark, 1997) have developed a one-session treatment for specific phobias in adults that has recently been extended to the treatment of children (Öst et al., 2001). Their model involves a single session involving a combination of cognitive-behaviour techniques, exposure, modelling, and social reinforcement. The result is a treatment that appears very similar to participant modelling and the combined model of cognitive-behaviour therapy described above. In session, the therapist actively challenges maladaptive cognitions underlying the phobic avoidance by the child. This is accomplished by having the child openly discuss his or her beliefs about the phobic stimulus with the therapist while in the presence of the phobic stimulus. Treatment begins with an initial functional analysis and the development of a fear hierarchy. Once actual treatment begins, the therapist and child are distanced from the stimulus; however, as the child's beliefs are confronted and disproved, the therapist and child move closer to the stimulus. The hallmark, then, of one-session treatment is a graduated, systematic, prolonged exposure to the phobic stimulus combined with the active dissuading and repair of faulty cognitions. Importantly, this treatment is all done in a highly supportive and conscientious manner: the child must give assent before going on to the next step in the hierarchy and SUDs ratings are continuously monitored and considered before moving up to the next level. Notably, this treatment has been designed to be maximally effective in one session, approximately three hours in length.

Results from pilot studies with children show that the treatment produces significant gains immediately after treatment (Muris et al., 1998) and continue at one-year follow-up (Öst et al., 2001). Even more impressively, the treatment has been found to be comparable to other treatments, and perhaps superior to them. Currently, Ollendick and Öst have developed a manual and treatment program to systematically examine the effects of one-session treatment on children in a controlled trial. In this ongoing randomized trial, 120 children in Sweden and 120 in the United States are being randomly assigned to one-session treatment, an education support condition, and a wait-list control condition. Initial findings suggest that the one-session treatment is superior to the other conditions and the children "tolerate" the intense treatment well. That is, the interactive nature of the intervention appears to hold their attention and motivate them to succeed in treatment. Moreover, ample use of participant modelling and reinforcement for graduated steps in approaching and engaging the feared object appear instrumental in its efficacy. Moreover, the children seem to enjoy the sessions and to take pride and ownership in their new-found interactive skills and reduced levels of anxiety.

Empirical Status of Present Treatments and Predictors of Change

When considering the various treatments for specific phobia, two crucial questions need to be addressed: how efficacious is any one treatment, and what predicts successful treatment outcome? For some time, the Task Force on the Promotion and Dissemination of Psychological Procedures, commissioned by the Society of Clinical Psychology (a division of the American Psychological Association) has suggested the creation and use of three categories of treatment efficacy (see Chambless, 1996; Chambless & Hollon, 1998; Chambless & Ollendick, 2001). This categorization system is discussed in more detail in previous chapters (see Chapter 1 for a detailed discussion of the criteria for well-established treatments, probably efficacious treatments, and experimental treatments). Researchers have begun to meaningfully categorize the treatments for specific phobia according to the Task Force's guidelines for efficacy. Ollendick and King (1998, 2000), for example, completed reviews of the empirically supported treatments for specific phobias in children. Specifically, they suggested that imaginal and *in-vivo* systematic desensitization, live modelling and filmed modelling, and cognitive-behaviour therapy possessed probably efficacious status (i.e., they are more effective than wait-list conditions but not necessarily more effective than other treatments or credible placebo treatment). Of note, however, participant modelling and reinforced practice (e.g., contingency management) were suggested to be well-established treatments. Emotive imagery, however, was determined to be still in the experimental stage of evidence. One-session treatment for children, although highly effective with adults, must also be viewed as an experimental treatment at this time. The necessary research on its efficacy, as well as that of emotive imagery, has just not yet been conducted (but is underway). When these findings about the efficacy of existing interventions are compared to the previous descriptions and preferences for treatment interventions, it becomes evident that further research is necessary to establish the efficacy of several of these methods of treatment. Moreover, important effectiveness trials of these interventions in applied settings are largely unexplored at this time.

The second treatment-relevant issue concerns the prediction of treatment outcome. The few studies that have addressed this issue with phobic and anxious youth have not found many variables or sets of variables that are associated with treatment outcome. For example, child characteristics such as gender, age, and ethnicity were not related to treatment outcome in Kendall's randomized control trials of cognitive-behaviour therapy (Treadwell, Flannery-Schroeder, & Kendall, 1995). Nor were levels of comorbidity (Kendall et al., 1997). Moreover, Kendall (1994) reported that neither children's perceptions of the therapeutic relationship nor therapists' perceptions of parental involvement in treatment were related to outcome. Recently, however, Berman et al. (2000) suggest some additional important factors to consider when examining treatment outcome in the treatment of phobic and anxiety disorders in children and adolescents. Their study examined predictors of treatment outcome for 106 phobic and anxious youth (aged 6 to 17 years) and their parents. As with the findings reported by Kendall (1994), initial analyses examining treatment success and failure revealed no significant predictors of treatment outcome related to sociodemographic variables (e.g., gender, ethnicity, family income). Further analyses, however, revealed that children with comorbid diagnoses of depression were more likely to experience treatment failure. Additionally, higher levels of child self-reported depression and trait anxiety predicted treatment failure. Furthermore, parental indices of psychopathology also differentiated treatment success or failure: with higher global severity ratings on the Symptom Checklist (SCL-90) and elevated levels of depression (Beck Depression Inventory) and fear (Fear Questionnaire) all being predictive of treatment failure. Thus, in this more recent analysis, both diagnostic comorbidity and parental psychopathology were associated with adverse outcomes. Such findings suggest the need to address diagnostic comorbidity (especially that of co-occurring depression) and parental psychopathology both in the assessment process and the design of treatment interventions. Movements to include the parents in treatment (cf. Barrett et al., 1996; Cobham, Dadds, & Spence, 1998; Ginsburg, Silverman, & Kurtines, 1995) may shed some light on the important issue of parental psychopathology whereas recent efforts to examine the comorbidty of depression and anxiety may help sort out some of the issues associated with co-occurring disorders that impede treatment progress (cf. Berman et al., 2000; Brent et al., 1998; Seligman & Ollendick, 1998).

SUMMARY AND FUTURE DIRECTIONS

Specific phobias are complex, intense, irrational fears that are extensively intertwined in any one child with issues related to his or her own unique development, the presence of comorbid diagnoses, and his or her parents' psychological functioning and parenting practices. Specific phobias are present in approximately 5% of children from community settings and 15% of children referred to clinics or outpatient settings. Assessment of specific phobias is necessarily multi-modal and multi-informant. Assessment procedures that are empirically validated and developmentally sensitive are required. Although the models of phobia acquisition have been diverse, treatments based on exposure principles have remained the treatments of choice and, for the most part, enjoy "well established" status as effective interventions. Other interventions including systematic desensitization, self-instruction training, and various forms of modelling are less well established although evidence suggests that they are probably efficacious interventions as well. Still other treatments such as emotive imagery and one-session treatment appear promising but can only be viewed as experimental procedures at this point in time. Thus, a number of potential interventions are available for the treatment of specific phobias in children and adolescents.

Although much is known about the nature of specific phobias in children and adolescents, much remains to be learned. For example, although psychometrically sound assessment instruments have been developed, we really do not know the extent to which these assessment strategies are applicable to clinical practice settings or the frequency of their use in such settings. Similarly, although various treatment strategies have been developed and shown to be largely effective, we do not know how appropriate these interventions are for clinical practice or even if they are being used routinely in clinical practice settings. Issues such as these have been referred to as the "transportability" of effective assessment and treatment practices (Chambless & Ollendick, 2001). Moreover, we really know very little about the predictors of effective treatment. We need to know more about what treatments are effective for which children and "why" these treatments work or do not work for certain children. In pursuit of these questions, we will need to identify both the mediators and moderators of effective interventions. Although specific phobias were once identified as "simple" phobias, our review suggests that these disorders are hardly simple ones, nor is their assessment and treatment "simple", let alone easy or straightforward. Specific phobias are complex disorders that require complex solutions. Much work remains to be done in our pursuit of helping children and adolescents who present with these disorders in our clinical practice and research settings.

REFERENCES

Achenbach, T.M. (1991a). *Integrative guide for the 1991 CBCL/4-18, YSR, and TRF profiles.* Burlington: University of Vermont.

Achenbach, T.M. (1991b). *Manual for the Child Behavior Checklist/4–18 and 1991 profile.* Burlington: University of Vermont.

Achenbach, T.M. (1991c). *Manual for the Teacher's Report Form and 1991 profile.* Burlington: University of Vermont.

Achenbach, T.M. (1991d). *Manual for the Youth Self-Report Form and 1991 profile.* Burlington: University of Vermont.

Ainsworth, M.D., Blehar, M.C., Waters, E., & Wall, S. (1978). *Patterns of attachment: A psychological study of the strange situation.* Hillsdale, NJ: Erlbaum.

American Psychiatric Association. (1994). *Diagnostic and statistical manual of mental disorders* (4th edn). Washington, DC: Author.

Bandura, A. (1969). *Principles of behavior modification.* New York: Holt, Rinehart, & Winston.

Barrett, P.M., Dadds, M.R., & Rapee, R.M. (1996). Family treatment of childhood anxiety: A controlled trial. *Journal of Consulting and Clinical Psychology,* **64**, 333–342.

Barrett, P.M., Rapee, R.M., Dadds, M.R., & Ryan, S. (1996). Family enhancement of cognitive styles in anxious and aggressive children: The FEAR effect. *Journal of Abnormal Child Psychology,* **24**, 187–203.

Berman, S.L., Weems, C.F., Silverman, W.K., & Kurtines, W.M. (2000). Predictors of outcome in exposure-based cognitive and behavioral treatments for phobic and anxiety disorders in children. *Behavior Therapy,* **31**, 713–731.

Brent, D.A., Kolko, D.J., Birmaher, B., Baugher, M., Bridge, J., Roth, C., & Holder, D. (1998). Predictors of treatment efficacy in a clinical trial of three psychosocial treatments adolescent depression. *Journal of the American Academy of Child and Adolescent Psychiatry,* **37**, 906–914.

Chambless, D.L. (1996). In defense of dissemination of empirically supported psychological interventions. *Clinical Psychology: Science and Practice,* **3**, 230–235.

Chambless, D.L., & Hollon, S.D. (1998). Defining empirically supported theories. *Journal of Consulting and Clinical Psychology,* **66**, 7–18.

Chambless, D.L., & Ollendick, T.H. (2001). Empirically supported psychological interventions: Controversies and evidence. *Annual Review of Psychology,* **52**, 685–716.

Cobham, V.E., Dadds, M.R., & Spence, S.H. (1998). The role of parental anxiety in the treatment of childhood anxiety. *Journal of Consulting and Clinical Psychology,* **66**, 893–900.

Curtis, G.C., Magee, W.J., Eaton, W.W., Wittchen, H.U., & Kessler, R.C. (1998). Specific fears and phobias: Epidemiology and classification. *British Journal of Psychiatry,* **173**, 212–217.

Dadds, M.R., Heard, P.M., & Rapee, R.M. (1992). The role of family intervention in the treatment of child anxiety disorders: Some preliminary findings. *Behavior Change,* **9**, 171–177.

Dadds, M.R., Rapee, R.M., & Barrett, P.M. (1994). Behavioral observation. In T.H. Ollendick, N.J. King, & W. Yule (Eds), *International handbook of phobic and anxiety disorders in children and adolescents* (pp. 349–364). New York: Plenum Press.

Forsyth, J.P., & Chorpita, B.F. (1997). Unearthing the nonassociative origins of fears and phobias: A rejoinder. *Journal of Behavior Therapy and Experimental Psychiatry,* **28**, 297–305.

Fyer, A.J. (1998). Current approaches to etiology and pathophysiology of specific phobia. *Biological Psychiatry,* **44**, 1295–1304.

Ginsburg, G.S., Silverman, W.K., & Kurtines, W.K. (1995). Family involvement in treating children with phobic and anxiety disorders: A look ahead. *Clinical Psychology Review,* **15**, 457–473.

Glennon, B., & Weisz, J.R. (1978). An observational approach to the assessment of anxiety in young children. *Journal of Consulting and Clinical Psychology,* **46**, 1246–1257.

Graziano, A.M., & Mooney, K.C. (1980). Family self-control instruction for children's nighttime fear reduction. *Journal of Consulting and Clinical Psychology,* **48**, 206–213.

Graziano, A.M., & Mooney, K.C. (1982). Behavioral treatment of "nightfears" in children: Maintenance of improvement at $2^1/_2$- to 3-year follow-up. *Journal of Consulting and Clinical Psychology*, **50**, 598–599.

Grills, A.E., & Ollendick, T.H. (2002). Issues in parent–child agreement: The case of structured diagnostic interviews. *Clinical Child and Family Psychology Review*, **5**, 57–83.

Hagopian, L.P., Weist, M.D., & Ollendick, T.H. (1990). Cognitive-behavior therapy with an 11-year-old girl fearful of AIDS infection, other diseases, and poisoning: A case study. *Journal of Anxiety Disorders*, **4**, 257–265.

Jackson, H.J., & King, N.J. (1981). The emotive imagery treatment of a child's trauma-induced phobia. *Journal of Behavior Therapy and Experimental Psychiatry*, **12**, 325–328.

Kendall, P.C. (1994). Treating anxiety disorders in children: Results of a randomized clinical trial. *Journal of Consulting and Clinical Psychology*, **62**, 100–110.

Kendall, P.C., & Southam-Gerow, M.A. (1996). Long-term follow-up of a cognitive-behavioral therapy for anxiety-disordered youth. *Journal of Consulting and Clinical Psychology*, **64** (4), 724–730.

Kendall, P.C., Flannery-Schroeder, E., Panichelli-Mindel, S., Southam-Gerow, M., Henis, A., & Warman, M. (1997). Therapy for youths with anxiety disorders: A second randomized clinical trial. *Journal of Consulting and Clinical Psychology*, **65**, 366–380.

Kindt, M., Brosschot, J.F., & Muris, P. (1996). Spider phobia questionnaire for children (SPQ-C): A psychometric study and normative data. *Behavioral Research and Therapy*, **34**, 277–282.

King, N.J., Hamilton, D.I., & Ollendick, T.H. (1988). *Children's phobias: A Behavioral perspective*. London: John Wiley & Sons.

Koeppen, A.S. (1974). Relaxation training for children. *Elementary School Guidance and Counseling*, **9**, 14–21.

Lang, P.J., & Lazovik, A.D. (1963). Experimental desensitization of phobia. *Journal of Abnormal and Social Psychology*, **66**, 519–525.

Lazarus, A.A., & Abramowitz, A. (1962). The use of "emotive imagery" in the treatment of children's phobias. *Journal of Mental Science*, **108**, 191–195.

March, J., Parker, J., Sullivan, K., Stallings, P., & Conners, C.K. (1997). The Multidimensional Anxiety Scale for Children (MASC): Factor structure, reliability, and validity. *Journal of the American Academy of Child and Adolescent Psychiatry*, **36**, 554–565.

Marks, I.M. (1969). *Fears and phobias*. San Diego, CA: Academic Press.

Marks, I.M. (1975). Behavioral treatments of phobic and obsessive-compulsive disorders: A critical appraisal. In M. Hersen, R.M. Eisler, & P.M. Miller (Eds), *Progress in behavior modification* (vol. 1; pp. 65–158). New York: Academic Press.

Meichenbaum, D., & Goodman, J. (1971). Training impulsive children to talk to themselves: A means of developing self-control. *Journal of Abnormal Psychology*, **77**, 115–126.

Menzies, R.G., & Clarke, J.C. (1995). The etiology of phobias: A non-associative account. *Clinical Psychology Review*, **15**, 23–48.

Muris, P., & Merckelbach, H. (2001). The etiology of childhood specific phobias: A multifactorial model. In M.W. Vasey & M. Dadds (Eds), *The developmental psychopathology of anxiety* (pp. 355–385). New York: Oxford University Press.

Muris, P., & Steerneman, P. (2001). The revised version of the Screen for Child Anxiety Related Emotional Disorders (SCARED-R): First evidence for its reliability and validity in a clinical sample. *British Journal of Clinical Psychology*, **40**, 35–44.

Muris, P., Schmidt, H., & Merckelbach, H. (1999). The structure of specific phobia symptoms among children and adolescents. *Behaviour Research and Therapy*, **37**, 863–868.

Muris, P., Merckelbach, H., Holdrinet, I., & Sijsenaar, M. (1998). Treating phobic children: Effects of EMDR versus exposure. *Journal of Consulting and Clinical Psychology*, **66**, 193–198.

Muris, P., Merckelbach, H., Schmidt, H., & Mayer, B. (1999). The revised version of the Screen for Child Anxiety Related Emotional Disorders (SCARED-R): Factor structure in normal children. *Personality and Individual Differences*, **26**, 99–112.

Ollendick, T.H. (1979). Fear reduction techniques with children. In M. Hersen, R.M. Eisler, & P.M. Miller (Eds), *Progress in behavior modification* (vol. 8; pp. 127–168). New York: Academic.

Ollendick, T.H. (1983). Reliability and validity of the Revised Fear Survey Schedule for Children (FSSC-R). *Behaviour Research and Therapy*, **21**, 685–692.

Ollendick, T.H. (1995). Cognitive-Behavioral treatment of panic disorder with agoraphobia in adolescents: A multiple baseline design analysis. *Behavior Therapy*, **26**, 517–531.

Ollendick, T.H., & Cerny, J.A. (1981). *Clinical behavior therapy with children*. New York: Plenum.

Ollendick, T.H., & Hersen, M. (1984). *Child behavior assessment: Principles and procedures*. New York: Pergamon Press.

Ollendick, T.H., & Hirshfeld-Becker, D.R. (2002). The developmental psychopathology of social anxiety disorder. *Biological Psychiatry*, **51**, 44–58.

Ollendick, T.H., & King, N.J. (1991). Origins of childhood fears: An evaluation of Rachman's theory of fear acquisition. *Behaviour Research and Therapy*, **29**, 117–123.

Ollendick, T.H., & King, N.J. (1998). Empirically supported treatments for children with phobic and anxiety disorders: Current status. *Journal of Clinical Child Psychology*, **27**, 156–167.

Ollendick, T.H., & King, N.J. (2000). Empirically supported treatments for children and adolescents. In P.C. Kendall (Ed.), *Child and adolescent therapy* (2nd edn). New York: Guilford Press.

Ollendick, T.H., & Ollendick, D.G. (1997). Helping children handle stress and anxiety. *In Session: Psychotherapy in Practice*, **3**, 89–102.

Ollendick, T.H., Grills, A.E., & King, N.J. (2001). Applying developmental theory to the assessment and treatment of childhood disorders: Does it make a difference? *Clinical Psychology and Psychotherapy*, **8**, 304–314.

Ollendick, T.H., Hagopian, L.P., & Huntzinger, R.M. (1991). Cognitive-Behavioral therapy with nighttime fearful children. *Journal of Behavior Therapy and Experimental Psychiatry*, **22**, 113–121.

Ollendick, T.H., Hagopian, L.P., & King, N.J. (1997). Specific phobias in children. In G.C.L. Davey (Ed.), *Phobias: A handbook of theory, research and treatment* (pp. 201–223). London: John Wiley & Sons.

Ollendick, T.H., King, N.J., & Frary, R.B. (1989). Fears in children and adolescents: Reliability and generalizability across gender, age, and nationality. *Behaviour Research and Therapy*, **27**, 19–26.

Ollendick, T.H., King, N.J., & Muris, P. (2002). Fears and phobias in children: Phenomenology, epidemiology, and aetiology. *Child and Adolescent Mental Health*, **7**, 98–106.

Öst, L.G. (1987). Age onset in different phobias. *Journal of Abnormal Psychology*, **96**, 223–229.

Öst, L.G. (1989). One-session treatment for specific phobias. *Behaviour Research and Therapy*, **27**, 1–7.

Öst, L.G., Brandberg, M., & Alm, T. (1997). One versus five sessions of exposure in the treatment of flying phobia. *Behaviour Research and Therapy*, **35**, 987–996.

Öst, L.G., Ferebee, I., & Furmark, T. (1997). One-session group therapy of spider phobia: direct versus indirect treatments. *Behaviour Research and Therapy*, **35**, 721–732.

Öst, L.G., Svensson, L., Hellstrom, K., & Lindwall, R. (2001). One-session treatment of specific phobias in youths: A randomized clinical trial. *Journal of Consulting and Clinical Psychology*, **69**, 814–824.

Rachman, S. (1977). The conditioning theory of fear acquisition: A critical examination. *Behavior Research and Therapy*, **15**, 375–387.

Rachman, S. (2002). Fears born and bred: Non-associative fear acquisition? *Behaviour Research and Therapy*, **40**, 121–126.

Reynolds, C.R., & Richmond, B.O. (1978). What I think and feel: A revised measure of children's manifest anxiety. *Journal of Abnormal Child Psychology*, **6**, 271–280.

Reynolds, C.R., & Richmond, B.O. (1985). *Revised Children's Manifest Anxiety Scale manual*. Los Angeles: Western Psychological Services.

Rosenstiel, S.K., & Scott, D.S. (1977). Four considerations in using imagery techniques with children. *Journal of Behavior Therapy and Experimental Psychiatry*, **8**, 287–290.

Seligman, L.D., & Ollendick, T.H. (1998). Comorbidity of anxiety and depression in children: An integrative review. *Clinical Child and Family Psychology Review*, **1**, 125–144.

Silverman, W.K., & Albano, A.M. (1996). *Anxiety Disorders Interview Schedule for DSM-IV, Child and Parent Versions*. San Antonio, TX: Psychological Corporation.

Silverman, W.K., & Eisen, A. (1992). Age differences in the reliability of parent and child reports of child anxious symptomatology using a structured interview. *Journal of Child and Adolescent Psychiatry*, **31**, 117–124.

Silverman, W.K., & Nelles, W.B. (1988). The Anxiety Disorders Interview Schedule for Children. *Journal of the American Academy of Child and Adolescent Psychiatry*, **27**, 772–778.

Silverman, W.K., Kurtines, W.M., Ginsburg, G.S., Weems, C.F., Rabian, B., & Serafini, L.T. (1999). Contingency management, self-control, and education support in the treatment of childhood phobic disorders: A randomized clinical trial. *Journal of Consulting and Clinical Psychology*, **67**, 675–687.

Toth, S.L., & Cicchetti, D. (1999). Developmental psychopathology and child psychotherapy. In S.W. Russ & T.H. Ollendick (Eds), *Handbook of psychotherapies with children and families* (pp. 15–44). New York: Kluwer Academic/Plenum Publishers.

Treadwell, K.R., Flannery-Schroeder, E.C., & Kendall, P.C. (1995). Ethnicity and gender relation to adaptive functioning, diagnostic status, and treatment outcome in children from an anxiety clinic. *Journal of Anxiety Disorders*, **9**, 373–384.

Weems, C.F., Silverman, W.K., Saavedra, L.M., Pina, A.A., & Lumpkin, P.W. (1999). The discrimination of children's phobias using the Revised Fear Survey Schedule for Children. *Journal of Child Psychology and Psychiatry*, **40**, 941–952.

Wolpe, J. (1958). *Psychotherapy by reciprocal inhibition*. Stanford, CA: Stanford University Press.

CHAPTER 13

Treatment of Depression in Children and Adolescents

Laura D. Seligman

University of Toledo, USA

Amanda B. Goza

Northern Virginia Mental Health Institute, USA

and

Thomas H. Ollendick

Virginia Polytechnic Institute and State University, USA

INTRODUCTION

Depression in youth may be characterized by the intense dsyphoria or irritability of major depression or the long-term melancholy of dysthymia. Additionally, it is increasingly accepted that children and adolescents can be diagnosed with bipolar disorder, with some reports suggesting that rapid cycling between depressed and manic states is often characteristic in youth (see, for review, NIMH Developmental Psychopathology and Prevention Research Branch, 2001). Our focus, however, will be limited to unipolar depression including major depression and dysthymia.

Early onset depression has been linked to a number of negative life outcomes both during childhood and adolescence and also later in adulthood. Depressed youth have been found to be at risk for suicide attempts (Lewinsohn, Rohde, & Seeley, 1998), more likely not to complete high school (Kessler et al., 1995), and to bear children in the teenage years (Kessler et al., 1997). In addition, formerly depressed adolescents typically retain some depressive symptomatology and are at increased risk for future episodes of mood disturbance (Lewinsohn, Rohde, & Seeley, 1998). Increased understanding of how to treat mood disorders in youth is therefore imperative not only because of the frequency with which these disorders

Correspondence to Laura D. Seligman, Department of Psychology, University of Toledo, Toledo, OH 43606; email: LSeligm@UTNet.UToledo.edu

Handbook of Interventions that Work with Children and Adolescents: Prevention and Treatment.
Edited by P.M. Barrett and T.H. Ollendick. © 2004 John Wiley & Sons, Ltd. ISBN 0-470-84453-1.

are encountered, but because, when present, they engender significant immediate distress and impairment and can lead to lifelong difficulties in functioning.

Despite the obvious significance of these disorders for the current functioning and future adjustment of children, our existing knowledge base is primarily the result of systematic study conducted over the past two decades. Although it is now generally accepted that children and adolescents can and do experience mood disorders, which is explicitly acknowledged in the current version of the *Diagnostic and Statistical Manual of Mental Disorders*, 4th edition (DSM-IV; American Psychiatric Association, 1994), historically this has not been the case. Developmental questions have caused theorists from a variety of perspectives to doubt the possibility of affective disturbances in youth or, alternatively, to conceptualize its occurrence as representing a normal developmental phase (e.g., attributed to the "moodiness" of adolescence). However, given the current evidence, a developmental psychopathology perspective is now focusing attention on more complex questions regarding the phenomenology of mood disturbances in youth and its implications for treatment.

Depression in adults is characterized by sad affect, lack of interest or pleasure in activities, feelings of worthlessness, and changes in appetite, weight, activity level, and sleep patterns. However, it has been widely assumed that depressed youth exhibit symptoms of depression that differ markedly from those observed in depressed adults. Consistent with this point of view, depressed adolescents have been found to be more likely to report worthlessness and guilt and less likely to evidence weight or appetite changes and thoughts of death or suicide than depressed adults (Lewinsohn, Rohde, & Seeley, 1998). In addition, depression in youth has been characterized by depressive symptomatology falling outside the accepted diagnostic criteria for the disorder, such as somatic complaints, social withdrawal, and hopelessness (Ryan et al., 1987). Further, in DSM-IV, irritability in children has become a diagnostic equivalent to sad or depressed mood, an explicit acknowledgment of this difference in presentation across age. These differences notwithstanding, several researchers have concluded, based on the body of research generated over the past 20 years, that depressive disorders are quite similar across the lifespan (Lewinsohn, Rohde, & Seeley, 1998; see however Luby et al., 2002; Ryan et al., 1987). Interestingly, in contrast, it has been demonstrated that, with regard to neurobiological correlates of depression, the differences between depressed children, adolescents and adults far outweigh the similarities (Kaufman et al., 2001), suggesting there is still much we do not understand in the developmental nature of mood disorders. However, as our understanding of depressive phenomena in childhood and adolescence and the impact of early depressive experiences on later functioning have increased, the need for effective treatments has become increasingly evident. This becomes especially clear when we examine the number of children and adolescents who suffer from these debilitating disorders.

Epidemiology

Estimates of the number of youth in need of effective treatment for depression and dysthymia vary widely. As can be seen in Table 13.1, prevalence rates for mood

Table 13.1 Epidemiological studies of depression in children and adolescents

Reference	Age	Source of information	Diagnostic system	Disorder	Prevalence		
					Boys	Girls	Total
Anderson et al., 1987	11	Parent, child, teacher	DSM-III	Depression/Dysthymia			1.8%
Bird et al., 1988	4–16	Parent, child	DSM-III	Depression/Dysthymia			5.9%
Cohen et al., 1993	10–20	Parent, child	DSM-III	Major Depression			
				10–13	1.8%	2.3%	2.0%
				14–16	1.6%	7.6%	4.7%
				17–20	2.7%	2.7%	2.7%
Costello et al., 1996	9, 11, 13	Parent, child	DSM-III-R	Major Depression	0%	0.1%	0%
				Dysthymia	0.2%	0.1%	0.1%
				Depression NOS	1.7%	1.2%	1.5%
Fergusson et al., 1993	15	Parent, child	DSM-III-R	*Child Report*			
				Major Depression			
				Current			0.7%
				Last Year			4.2%
				Dysthymia			0.4%
				Any mood disorder			4.9%
				Parent Report			
				Major Depression			
				Current			0.5%
				Last Year			2.2%
				Dysthymia			0.1%
				Any Mood Disorder			2.4%
Haarasilta et al., 2001	15–19	Adolescent	DSM-III-R	Major Depressive Episode	4.4%	6.0%	5.3%
Kashani et al., 1987	14–16	Child report to establish diagnosis, parent report to confirm presence of psychiatric disorder (caseness)	DSM-III	Depression/Dysthymia	2.7%	13.3%	8.0%

continues overleaf

Table 13.1 (continued)

Reference	Age	Source of information	Diagnostic system	Disorder	Prevalence		
					Boys	Girls	Total
Kashani et al., 1989	8, 12, 17	Parent, child	DSM-III	Depressive Disorder			
				Child Report			
				8			1.5%
				12			1.5%
				17			5.7%
				Parent Report			
				8			0%
				12			1.4%
				17			2.9%
Lewinsohn et al., 1993	Time 1: $M = 16.6$	Adolescent	DSM-III-R	*Time 1*			
				Unipolar Depression	2.0%	3.8%	2.9%
				Major Depression	1.7%	3.4%	2.6%
				Dysthymia	0.5%	0.6%	0.5%
				Time 2			
				Unipolar Depression	2.6%	3.7%	3.2%
				Major Depression	2.6%	3.6%	3.1%
				Dysthymia	0%	0.3%	0.1%
McGee et al., 1990	15	Adolescent, parent	DSM-III	Major Depressive Episode			
				Current	0.4%	0.7%	1.2%
				Past	0.4%	1.5%	1.9%
				Dysthymia	0.4%	1.1%	1.1%
Sawyer et al., 2001	6–17	Parent	DSM-IV	Depressive Disorder	3.2%	2.8%	3.0%
Steinhausen & Metzke, 1999	12–17	Adolescent	Score on Depression Scale	"Moderately or severely depressed" (at least 1 SD above mean)			23.6%

disorders range from a high of 8.0% (Kashani et al., 1987) to a low of 1.6% (Costello et al., 1996). Differences among studies in terms of case definitions, time intervals assessed, assessment techniques, and sample composition and size make comparison of prevalence rates across studies difficult. The range of ages of children included both within and across studies makes comparison of data particularly problematic, as prevalence rates tend to be lower in younger children than adolescents and increase across childhood and into adolescence (Lewinsohn, Rohde, & Seeley, 1998). In the studies reviewed here, prevalence rates for depression based on DSM criteria and including both depression and dysthymia were estimated as high as 5.9% in a sample of children 4–16 years old (Bird et al., 1988) and as high as 8% in a sample including only adolescents (Kashani et al., 1987). In contrast, studies including only younger children yield prevalence estimates as low as 1.5% (based on children's report). Prevalence rates for these children were even lower when only the parent's report was considered.

The rate of depression appears to peak in the mid-teen years, between the ages of 14 and 17 (Cohen et al., 1993; Kashani et al., 1989; Lewinsohn et al., 1993), although some studies suggest that this pattern is only evidenced in girls (Cohen et al., 1993). It is widely believed that the sex difference in prevalence rates for depression emerges during adolescence; that is, although boys and girls evidence similar rates of depression in early years, girls evidence a rise in depression during adolescence that overtakes prevalence rates in boys. There is some evidence to support this effect (e.g., Cohen et al., 1993; McGee et al., 1990; Steinhausen & Metzke, 1999), although not all studies are consistent with this conclusion (Lewinsohn et al., 1993).

Moreover, it appears that the number of youth evidencing significant depressive symptomatology may be considerably higher than that suggested by the typical epidemiological study employing DSM or International Classification of Diseases (ICD; World Health Organization, 1992) criteria. For example, Steinhausen and Metzke (1999) estimated the prevalence of clinically significant levels of depressive symptomatology at 23.6%, considerably higher than that obtained in the remaining studies listed in Table 13.1. These findings suggest that examining the rate of disorder alone may be misleading when anticipating the need for services.

AETIOLOGY

Aetiological theories of depression in children have been primarily derived from theories originally advanced to explain the development and maintenance of depression in adults, an extension that is reasonable given the similarities of many features of depression across age (Kaslow, Rehm, & Siegel, 1984; Kazdin, 1993; Ryan et al., 1987). Theoretical perspectives on childhood depression emerging from interpersonal and cognitive-behavioural conceptualizations of the disorder have been most clearly defined and have been the conceptual basis for the majority of treatment studies for depression in youth and are therefore our focus here. The interested reader can find explanations of psychodynamic and biological perspectives on depression in Ollendick (1998).

Interpersonal theory conceptualizes depression and depressive phenomena as arising from problems in interpersonal conflicts (Weissman, Markowitz, & Klerman,

2000). Within this framework, depression is seen as a reaction to grief, loss, or separation; stemming from recurrent or ongoing interpersonal disputes; difficulties in navigating role transitions such as divorce of parents, birth of siblings, change in school, or physical changes; or as a result of interpersonal deficits, which have resulted in the absence of lasting, close, and satisfying relationships (Mufson, Moreau, & Weissman, 1996). Treatments based on interpersonal theory are focused on current problems, important interpersonal relationships, and evaluating and solving the problematic situation (Weissman, Markowitz, & Klerman, 2000).

Cognitive-behavioural conceptualizations of childhood depression have been explicitly defined and have led to the development of a number of comprehensive treatment protocols. These also implicate relationship difficulties as contributing factors (primarily in the context of social, interpersonal, and intrapersonal coping skills deficits), but emphasize the importance of cognitive distortions and errors and environmental deficits in the development and maintenance of depression in youth.

The skills deficit hypothesis asserts that at the root of depressive phenomena are basic deficits in one or more critical areas of functioning. These deficits lead to negative interactions or events that serve to facilitate the development of depressive behaviours and maladaptive thinking. Critical skill deficits may occur in the areas of self-reinforcement, social interactions, interpersonal behaviours, coping, ability to engage in pleasant activities, or other specific domains of functioning (e.g., academics, sports), and lead to failure within these contexts. As a child experiences failure in a particular area of functioning, he or she begins to experience heightened aversive physiological arousal in those situations and begins to engage in negative thoughts about his or her performance. This, in turn, further heightens the child's arousal and discourages him or her from participating (Seligman, 1975), resulting in a lack of potential reinforcement opportunities which, in turn, contributes to the development of depressive symptoms.

The cognitive distortion hypothesis holds that distorted thinking processes are the foundation for depressive phenomena. Cognitive distortions that lead to the emergence of depression include negative distortions of information about oneself, others, and the future (Beck, 1967) and the tendency to make internal, stable, and global attributions for negative events (Abramson, Seligman, & Teasdale, 1978; Seligman, 1975). While an environmental or skills deficit may have initially contributed to the emergence of negative cognitions, it is the pervasive negative, distorted thinking processes that give rise to depressive symptomatology and help to maintain it.

The environmental deficit hypothesis holds that deficits in the child's environment are the basis for the emergence of depressive symptomatology. Environmental deficits include frequently occurring aversive events that are beyond the child's control and a lack of reinforcing contingencies for behaviour, either because contingencies are no longer reinforcing or because they are unavailable (Lewinsohn & Shaw, 1969). Examples of environmental deficits include insufficient parental praise and reinforcement, excess punishment, harsh or unpleasant environmental conditions, and under-involvement in enjoyable activities. Chronic exposure to punitive, harsh, unrewarding, unpleasant, or socially impoverished conditions contributes to the development of depression by fostering feelings of helplessness and hopelessness, negative thoughts, and low self-esteem.

Prominent treatment protocols based on cognitive-behavioural theory emphasize interactions among ineffective coping strategies, poor self-control and interpersonal skills, a dysfunctional style of thinking, and disturbances in family functioning in the development and maintenance of depression (Stark, Rouse, & Livingston, 1991).

Family dynamics and functioning are implicated in all major theories of childhood depression. It is primarily within the family context that children receive reinforcement, engage in pleasurable activities, learn to interpret situations, learn critical social, interpersonal and coping skills, and experience relationship difficulties, loss, and grief. Family therapies, therefore, are hypothesized to play an important role in the treatment of childhood depression; however, as will be seen shortly, little empirical evidence to date supports their utility.

ASSESSMENT

Beginning in the 1980s, as interest in depressive phenomena in youth flourished, a plethora of instruments to assess depression in children and adolescents began to emerge, including self-reports, clinician rating scales, diagnostic interviews, and parent and teacher reports (Myers & Winters, 2002).

Self-Reports/Questionnaires

Many instruments with sound psychometric properties and normative data exist for the clinician or researcher wishing to obtain a child's self-report of depression. Further, there are numerous advantages to using self-reports. For example, several of these questionnaires have been validated in diverse samples and translated into several languages (Myers & Winters, 2002). In addition, some instruments have equivalent forms for use with children and adolescents that can be useful when following a child over time. The Children's Depression Inventory (CDI; Kovacs, 1985), meant for use with children and early adolescents between the ages of 7 and 16, is similar to the Beck Depression Inventory (BDI-II; Beck, Steer, & Brown, 1996), appropriate for use with adolescents (Strober, Green, & Carlson, 1981) and adults. A child version of the BDI, the Beck Depression Inventory for Youth (BDI-Y; Beck, Beck, & Jolly, 2001), is now also available, making comparison across ages even easier. Similarly, Reynolds has two scales for measuring depression in youth, the Reynolds Children's Depression Scale (RCDS; Reynolds, 1989), for use with children between the ages of 8 and 12, and the Reynolds Adolescent Depression Scale (RADS; Reynolds, 1987a), for use with youth between the ages of 13 and 18. Moreover, the RCDS and RADS do not have a question that directly assesses suicidal ideation or intent, which may be preferable when screening non-clinical youth in school settings, where such an item may be perceived as possibly iatrogenic. Of course, the absence of data on suicidality may be an important disadvantage to consider when choosing an instrument intended for use with a patient sample; however, Reynolds provides a separate but related self-report to assess suicidal ideation (SIQ; Reynolds, 1987b).

Self-reports are easy to use and score, and many are short or have abbreviated forms, allowing clinicians to track and monitor response to treatment with little investment of the child's time. For example, some evidence suggests that the CDI may be sensitive to treatment change (Myers & Winters, 2002; see also below). Additionally, given that most self-reports provide information about a variety of affective symptoms (e.g., anhedonia, interpersonal problems/social isolation, somatic complaints) and associated problems (e.g., anxiety, aggression, oppositional behaviour), attention to patterns of responding can provide useful information for case conceptualization and treatment planning. For example, as will be seen shortly, both relaxation and social skills training have been found to be useful strategies for treating depression, but while relaxation training may prove useful for a depressed child reporting high levels of anxiety and somatic complaints, social skills training and activity scheduling may be more effective for youth reporting interpersonal problems and aggressive behaviours.

On the other hand, there are several disadvantages to using self-reports, especially when they are used in isolation. Discriminative validity is often problematic when using self-reports of depression, especially when attempting to differentiate depression from anxiety (Seligman & Ollendick, 1998). Instruments such as the CDI include items that are conceptually unclear, and items that may be more reflective of anxiety or externalizing problems. Additionally, as noted by Hodges (1990) and Myers and Winters (2002), self-reported depressive symptomatology is often equated with diagnosis, despite considerable evidence suggesting that self-reports do not perform well in identifying youth with an affective disorder. In fact, while Hodges found that the CDI correctly identified 84% of non-depressed youth, it only identified 54% of depressed youth correctly; this suggests that using the CDI in place of diagnosis would result in many missed cases. On the other hand, inspection of Table 13.1 clearly shows that use of a cutoff score on a self-report rating scale results in a much-inflated estimation (compared to diagnosis) of affective disorders in Steinhausen and Metzke's (1999) sample of adolescents.

The mismatch between self-report data and diagnosis is not surprising given that most of these instruments do not directly enquire about DSM criteria. Newer instruments, however, have attempted to resolve this problem by developing items that map directly onto the symptoms indicated for diagnosis by the DSM. For example, the Beck Youth Inventory for Depression was designed to assess the DSM-IV criteria for major depression (Beck, Beck, & Jolly, 2001; Steer et al., 2001). Similarly, Chorpita and colleagues recently revised the Spence Children's Anxiety Scale (Spence, 1998) to include items that correspond with DSM-IV's definition of major depression (Chorpita et al., 2000). Although innovations such as these may prove useful in providing efficient methods of diagnosis, data on these instruments' sensitivity and specificity in identifying clinically depressed youth are currently lacking.

Depression questionnaires designed to be completed by parents are not as common as self-reports, and the lack of convergent validity between parent and child reported depression is notorious. While clinical judgment has often led to the conclusion that, given the subjective nature of depression, children are the best reporters of their own affective state, little data exist to test this hypothesis. In fact, some data suggest that parents and children may attend to different information (Cole et al., 2000), indicating that the complete picture may be most aptly captured by using a combination of child and parent reports. Again, however, it is problematic that few instruments exist to specifically obtain information about parents' perceptions of their children's depression.

Achenbach's Child Behavior Checklist (CBCL; Achenbach, 1991) includes a subscale that contains items assessing both anxiety and depression; however, Rey and Morris-Yates (1991) created a depression factor derived from the CBCL and found it to differentiate youth with a DSM-III major depression diagnosis from those with other psychiatric diagnoses, separation anxiety disorder, and dysthymia at better than chance levels. Use of the depression factor resulted in moderate sensitivity (83%) but low specificity (55%). The fact that these results are almost the opposite of those obtained by Hodges (1990) when she compared the CDI to diagnosis (i.e., sensitivity = 54%; specificity = 84%) again suggests that a combination of parent and self-reports may be the method of choice when using rating scales to approximate diagnosis, with each report providing distinctly different information.

One of the clear limitations of the CBCL and similar measures, such as the Behavior Assessment System for Children (BASC; Reynolds & Kamphaus, 1992), which does provide a separate depression scale, is their length. Although these instruments provide a comprehensive evaluation, their parent versions contain over 100 items. Recently, Goodman (1997) developed the Strengths and Difficulties Questionnaire (SDQ) to address this concern. The SDQ contains only 25 items, 5 of which assess emotional problems. Goodman and Scott (1999) found that SDQ scores were highly correlated with those from the CBCL, and that the SDQ and CBCL were equally able to differentiate between a psychiatric and non-patient sample. Moreover, with the addition of the supplemental impact scale, the SDQ may be useful in identifying caseness (Goodman, 1999).

Clinician Rating Scales and Diagnostic Interviews

Several diagnostic interviews exist to assess the presence or absence of DSM diagnostic criteria, including mood disorders. Interviews range from highly structured to semistructured. The Diagnostic Interview Schedule for Children (DISC; Shaffer et al., 2000) and the Diagnostic Interview for Children and Adolescents (DICA; Welner et al., 1987) are highly structured interviews that may be reliably administered by laypeople or even via a computer. The Anxiety Disorders Interview Schedule for DSM-IV, Child Version (ADIS-IV/C; Silverman & Albano, 1996) and the Schedule for Affective Disorders and Schizophrenia for School-Age Children (K-SADS; Orvaschel & Puig-Antich, 1986) are semistructured interviews, intended to be administered by trained interviewers familiar with the DSM criteria. Structured and semistructured diagnostic interviews are generally considered the gold standard for determining diagnosis; however, they may be time-consuming. On the one hand, the costs may be worth while in research settings where demonstrably reliable diagnosis and complete assessment are required. On the other, in clinical settings it may be a better use of time to adapt these instruments for a more flexible clinical interview (Grills & Ollendick, 2002).

Clinician rating scales, such as the Hamilton Rating Scale for Depression (HRSD; Hamilton, 1960) and the Children's Rating Scale—Revised (CDRS-R; Poznanski et al., 1984) may be used in conjunction with a diagnostic interview. These instruments offer a dimensional rating of severity similar to those obtained by parent and child reports. Shain, Naylor and Alessi (1990) have demonstrated that both the HRSD and the CDRS-R are highly correlated with youths' self-reports of depression, although the correlations for girls were higher than those for boys.

Although a comprehensive evaluation would benefit from a combination of all of these methods (Ollendick & Hersen, 1984), practical limitations necessitate that most often we need to choose from among them, based on the specific purposes of the assessment. Moreover, in most cases, an assessment for depression must also include instruments designed to assess for associated symptomatology (e.g., anxiety, hopelessness, family dysfunction, cognitive distortions and deficits) to be useful in treatment conceptualization and planning, as well as assist in monitoring the efficacy of specific interventions.

TREATMENT

What Works?

Until recently, the one unequivocal statement that could be made about psychosocial treatments for childhood depression—what works, for whom, and why—was that we really did not know. Fortunately, in the late 1980s, we began to see advances that began to address some of these questions. Using the criteria for empirically supported treatments established by the Task Force on Promotion and Dissemination of Psychological Procedures (Chambless et al., 1996), Kaslow and Thompson (1998) found two treatment programs, Stark's Cognitive Behavioural Therapy (CBT) program for depressed children (Stark, Reynolds, & Kaslow, 1987; Stark, Rouse, & Livingston, 1991) and Lewinsohn's CBT treatment for depressed adolescents (Lewinsohn et al., 1990; Lewinsohn et al., 1996) to meet or approximate the requirements for a probably efficacious treatment. More recently, in a multidisciplinary review, Chorpita and colleagues (2002) found CBT to be a well-established treatment for depression in youth, and Interpersonal Therapy (IPT) and CBT with parental involvement to be probably efficacious treatments. (See Table 13.2 for the Task Force's definition of well-established and probably efficacious treatments.)

The discrepancies between the two groups' findings appear to be related to a number of factors. First, the groups varied in their definition for a given treatment; that is, while Kaslow and Thompson chose to define treatments at the level of the treatment manual, Chorpita's group chose to define treatment manuals that shared "a majority of components with similar clinical strategies and theoretical underpinnings" (p. 170) as the same treatment. Additionally, discrepancies may have arisen because Kaslow and Thompson considered treatments for children separately from treatments for adolescents, whereas Chorpita et al. considered the overall evidence for effectiveness in youth. Most importantly, advances in the field resulted in additional evidence for CBT and IPT not available at the time of Kaslow and Thompson's (1998) review.

One difficulty in using many of the extant treatment studies to answer the question of what works for depressed children is that, historically, few studies have tested

Table 13.2 Criteria for Well-Established and Probably-Efficacious Psychosocial Interventions for Childhood Disorders

Well-established

1. At least two well-conducted group-design studies, conducted by different investigatory teams, showing the treatment to be either
   (a) superior to pill placebo or alternative treatment
   OR
   (b) equivalent to an already established treatment in studies with adequate statistical power
   OR
2. A large series of single-case design studies (i.e., n > 9) that both:
   (a) use good experimental design
   AND
   (b) compare the intervention to another treatment.
   AND
3. Treatment manuals used for the intervention preferred.
   AND
4. Sample characteristics must be clearly specified.

Probably-efficacious

1. Two studies showing the intervention more effective than a no-treatment control group (e.g., a wait-list comparison group).
   OR
2. Two group-design studies meeting criteria for well-established treatment but conducted by the same investigator.
   OR
3. A small series of single-case design experiments (i.e., *n* > 3) that otherwise meet Criterion 2 for well-established treatments.
   AND
4. Treatment manuals used for the intervention preferred.
   AND
5. Sample characteristics must be clearly specified.

treatments with clinically depressed youth. Many have recruited samples of children with elevated levels of depressive symptomatology as obtained from self-reports of depression, such as those discussed previously, who may or may not have had an affective disorder as defined by DSM or ICD. Some evidence, however, suggests that there may be important differences between these children and those seen in clinical settings (Brent et al., 1998). Studies conducted with non-diagnosed samples leave questions about whether the treatments used would be as effective if conducted with a more severe sample. Notable exceptions to these problems are found in the research programs of Lewinsohn and Mufson.

While much of Lewinsohn's work has been with adults, his Coping with Depression Course for Adolescents (CWD-A), a developmentally scaled down version of his CBT treatment for adults, has been shown to be effective in treating adolescents with an affective disorder. CWD-A is a 16-session treatment delivered over 8 weeks in a group format. The program consists of both cognitive and behavioural components including social skills training, self-monitoring of mood states, planning of pleasant activities, anxiety reduction, and training in communication and conflict resolution (for a complete description see Lewinsohn et al., 1996).

In a randomized-controlled trial, Lewinsohn et al. (1990) investigated the effectiveness of a modified version of the CWD-A course with a group of 59 adolescents diagnosed with an affective disorder. CWD-A was compared to both a wait-list control and a version of the CWD-A course to which a parental component was added. In both active treatment groups, the adolescents met in groups for 14 two-hour sessions over a period of seven weeks. In the CWD-A + parent component condition, parents met in a separate group for seven sessions to learn skills, including coping skills and reinforcing positive changes in their children's behaviour, which were meant to complement the skills that youth were learning in their groups. At post-treatment, both active treatment groups showed significantly greater improvement as compared to the wait-list control. However, follow-up revealed that approximately 30% of youth who had recovered with treatment experienced a relapse within two years (Clarke et al., 1999).

In a more recent investigation, Clarke and colleagues (1999) attempted to address the issue of relapse prevention in a replication and extension of Lewinsohn et al.'s (1990) earlier work. One hundred and twenty-three adolescents diagnosed with an affective disorder were again randomly assigned to either the 16-session CWD-A group, the CWD-A group + 9 sessions for parents, or a wait-list control condition. A total of 96 adolescents completed this acute phase of treatment. At post-treatment, the youth in the two active treatment conditions were then randomly assigned to a booster session condition, a frequent assessment condition, or an annual assessment condition. Every four months for two years, the youth in the booster condition completed an assessment and participated in a booster session designed to reinforce the skills acquired during the acute phase of treatment. Likewise, youth in the frequent assessment condition completed an assessment every four months during the two-year follow-up period. Youth in the annual assessment completed just the assessment each year for the two-year follow-up period. Similar to earlier findings, results revealed that both active treatments were significantly better than the wait-list control but not significantly different from one another. This study resulted in an effect size ("Cohen's h") of 0.34 for the CBT treatment and 0.38 for the CBT + parent treatment, whereas the original trial resulted in an effect size of 0.98 for the CBT condition and 1.06 for the CBT + parent condition. Despite the smaller magnitude of the effect, which the authors attributed to a higher rate of recovery in the wait-list condition in this second study, youth in the active treatment conditions were over two times more likely to recover from their affective disorder when compared to youth in the wait-list condition.

Analyses at follow-up revealed that, at one year, recovery rates for those youth who were still depressed at the end of the acute treatment phase were significantly higher for those in the booster condition than for those in the assessment only conditions. At the end of the follow-up period, however, those youth in the assessment only conditions had "caught up" so that no significant differences in rates of recovery were evident at two years.

No significant differences between groups were found in terms of maintenance of treatment gains (i.e., relapse or recurrence rates) for those youth whose depression had remitted during the acute phase of treatment. That is, while youth who were still depressed at the end of treatment appeared to benefit from the booster sessions in that they recovered faster than those youth who only received the assessments, the booster sessions did not have the intended effect of decreasing the rate of recurrence of disorder. In fact while the rate of recurrence in the booster condition approached that of the original study (27%), no youth in the frequent assessment condition, and only 14% of youth in the annual assessment condition, experienced a recurrence of a major depressive episode. These results must be considered with caution, however, given that approximately 27% of participants assigned to one of the three follow-up conditions did not complete the assessments, and many of those in the booster treatment condition who did complete the follow-up assessments did not actually attend the booster sessions. In fact, the authors note that attendance at booster sessions was estimated to be approximately 50%; thus, in some ways, the booster condition may have been very similar to the frequent assessment condition, with the exception that participants may have perceived themselves as being non-compliant with treatment. Further, completion of follow-up assessment was related to BDI scores at post-treatment; those who dropped out at follow-up had higher BDI scores at post-treatment, suggesting that follow-up data may not be representative of the sample as a whole.

In another promising line of research, Mufson and colleagues have examined the effectiveness of Interpersonal Therapy for Adolescents (IPT-A) for diagnosed youth, first in an open trial and then in a randomized controlled trial (Mufson et al., 1994, 1999). Treatment was modelled on Klerman's IPT for adults but was modified to address developmental issues of importance to adolescents. Although the open clinical trial provided tentative support for the use of IPT with adolescents, the randomized clinical trial was able to make more definitive comparisons between IPT-A and a clinical monitoring condition. Youth in the clinical monitoring condition met with a therapist for 1–2 brief sessions a month. Adolescents in the IPT-A group were seen weekly for 12 weeks, with additional weekly telephone contacts during the first four weeks of the treatment program. Analysis of data for those who completed the treatment program showed generally positive but somewhat mixed results. Self-reported depressive symptoms were not significantly different for the two groups; however, clinician ratings on the HRSD were significantly lower for those in the IPT-A groups (ratings were made by an evaluator blind to treatment status). Further, the superiority of IPT-A extended to self-reported social adjustment and some aspects of problem-solving skills.

Aside from these two research programs, four additional studies have looked at the effectiveness of CBT and IPT in diagnosed youth. In general, these studies have supported the use of both CBT (Brent et al., 1997; Rosselló & Bernal, 1999) and IPT (Rosselló & Bernal, 1999) with depressed youth. However, Fine et al. (1990) found one component of CBT, social skills training, to be less effective than therapeutic support in the short term. However, at nine-month follow-up this was no longer true, as youth receiving social skills training continued to make progress, while no additional treatment benefit was noted for those in the therapeutic support group. Additionally, Kolko, Brent and colleagues investigated the use of Systemic Behaviour Family Therapy (SBFT) for adolescents with a mood disorder diagnosis, but found little support for its use (Brent et al., 1997; Kolko et al., 2000).

Studies including youth with depressive symptoms, mostly with schools samples, have primarily examined the use of various cognitive-behavioural treatments. For example, Weisz et al. (1997) found a brief (i.e., 8 session) group CBT treatment to be effective relative to a wait-list control condition. On the other hand, however, Liddle and Spence (1990) used an 8-session CBT group treatment for Australian youth with depressive symptoms and found that the treated group fared no better than either an attention placebo control group or the wait-list control group. Although both studies used the CDI and CDRS-R to determine eligibility, Weisz et al. employed more liberal criteria, suggesting perhaps that these brief treatments may work only with a less severe sample. Additionally, while both treatments included aspects of cognitive restructuring, Liddle and Spence's treatment also focused primarily on problem-solving and social skills training while Weisz et al.'s treatment focused more on behavioural techniques such as activity scheduling and developing skills that had the potential to increase the likelihood of positive reinforcement and decrease the likelihood of punishment. Although it is unclear what particular skills were the focus of treatment here, and it is likely that there was a good deal of overlap with the social skills training provided in the Liddle and Spence treatment package, it may have been that the skills training provided by Weisz and colleagues was more comprehensive and, thus, more effective. However, evidence from other non-clinical samples suggests that a variety of cognitive, behavioural, or cognitive-behavioural treatments can be effective in treating depressed youth. Relaxation training and various combinations of cognitive-behavioural interventions, sometimes labelled "self-control skills," that include interventions such as self-monitoring, modelling, role-plays, activity scheduling, problem-solving, self-evaluation, self-reinforcement, and cognitive restructuring have all been found to be effective (Butler et al., 1980; Kahn et al., 1990; Reynolds & Coats, 1986; Stark, Reynolds, & Kaslow, 1987; Stark, Rouse, & Livingston, 1991; Stark, 1990).

In fact, Stark and colleagues have developed a comprehensive treatment program for depressed youth and their parents (Stark et al., 1996) based on their treatment outcome research (Stark, Reynolds, & Kaslow, 1987; Stark, Rouse, & Livingston, 1991) and basic research in childhood mood disorders. Although Stark's original school-based treatment program was effective with youth in groups, his more recent adaptation employs a variety of CBT procedures in both a group and individual format. Interventions are delivered in such a way as to promote positive mood first and then to focus on altering the depressogenic self-focused cognitions that may be too difficult for the child to tackle without prior symptom relief. Individual sessions are used to engage the child and allow for discussion of material that may be too embarrassing for the child to bring up in the group format. Group sessions allow the therapist to assess the child's social skills and perceptions and also provide a safe social context in which the child can receive feedback inconsistent with his or her negative beliefs. The program is developmentally sensitive in that it includes concrete steps to teach skills before children try to apply the skills to their symptoms. Additionally, a transactional approach (Sameroff, 1995) appears to drive a social skills training component, which recognizes that depressed children's behavioural difficulties may create a social context that subsequently leads to depressed mood. The parent component, similar to that in Lewinsohn's program, appears to be largely psychoeducational in nature, although parents are taught CBT techniques to deal with the anger that characterizes families of depressed children.

This program, however, does not seem to address the fact that depressed children are more likely to have depressed parents and that parental psychopathology may more generally need to be addressed. In fact, Stark et al. note that their clinical experience suggests that this treatment program does not seem to work well when significant parental psychopathology is present (Stark et al., 1996), which is supported by other investigators (Brent et al., 1998).

What Works Best?

It should be noted that although Chorpita et al.'s (2002) review placed treatments in a multi-tiered classification, this cannot be interpreted as evidence of the superiority of one treatment over another. Rather, the difference between well-established and probably efficacious treatments is in the level of evidence supporting a treatment, not in the degree of efficacy that has been found for the treatment.

In order to compare the effects found for various treatments across studies, we calculated effect sizes for each study that focused on the treatment of diagnosed youth. Using only studies that included diagnosed children and adolescents represented an attempt on our part to ensure that samples were comparable across studies. These data can be seen in Table 13.3. We examined both the clinical effect found for a given treatment, the number of children and adolescents who were diagnosis free at post-treatment, and the statistical effect for each treatment, using dimensional measures of depression (i.e., self-reported depressive symptomatology on the BDI or CDI). It should be noted that in some cases the treated group could be compared to an attention control group and in other cases the only possible comparison was between the treated group and a wait-list control.

For studies in which CBT was compared to a wait-list control, effect sizes, both clinical and statistical, ranged from small to large. The one study that compared CBT to an attention control treatment, found medium effects. As previously noted, in an unusual finding, Fine et al. (1990) discovered that one component of CBT treatments, social skills training, when used alone, was inferior to a non-directive support treatment, resulting in an effect size favouring the therapeutic support group in the medium range. The two studies in which a parent treatment component was added to CBT found effect sizes in the small and large range.

Although the clinical effect size could not be computed for any study that compared IPT to a simple wait-list control, Mufson et al.'s clinical monitoring condition approximated a wait-list control and resulted in both a clinical and statistical effect size in the medium range; this finding is similar to the statistical effect found by Roselló and Bernal when they compared IPT to a wait-list. Brent et al. found small effects for Systematic Behaviour Family Therapy.

Table 13.3   Clinical and statistical effect, comparing treated groups with wait-list or attention control group, for treatments conducted with a diagnosed sample

Reference	Treatment	Control	Clinical effect[a]	Statistical effect[b]
Brent et al. (1997)	CBT	NST	0.56	0.40
	SBFT	NST	0.21	0.07
Clarke et al. (1999)	CBT	WL	0.34	0.58
	CBT + Parent	WL	0.38	0.24
Fine et al. (1990)[c]	Social skills	Support	—	−0.52
Lewinsohn et al. (1990)	CBT	WL	0.98	0.92
	CBT + Parent	WL	1.06	1.45
Mufson et al. (1999)	IPT	Clinical monitoring	0.70	0.57
Rosselló & Bernal (1999)[c]	CBT	WL	—	0.34
	IPT	WL	—	0.74

[a] Cohen's h, based on number of youth no longer having an affective disorder diagnosis at follow-up.
[b] Hedges d, based on post-treatment self-reported symptoms on either BDI or CDI.
[c] These studies did not report post-treatment diagnoses.

Although CBT + parent treatment resulted in the largest effect size in one study, it also resulted in one of the smallest effect sizes in another, highlighting the amount of variability for treatments across studies.[1] This, combined with the small number of studies examining each type of treatment, makes it difficult to calculate a reliable mean effect size that could be used to compare treatments across studies. On the other hand, in studies that directly compare one treatment to another (see Table 13.4) IPT appears to be superior to CBT treatments and CBT treatments appear to be superior to Systematic Behaviour Family Therapy. These results must be interpreted with caution, however, given the small number of studies and the particulars of the samples involved. For example, Roselló and Bernal tested CBT and IPT treatments in a sample of Puerto Rican youth and suggested that IPT might be more appropriate for these adolescents given the cultural emphasis on interpersonal relationships.

Why Do Treatments Work?

To our knowledge, only one study directly examined mediators of treatment changes in childhood depression (Kolko et al., 2000). Specifically, as discussed previously, Brent, Kolko and colleagues examined treatment effects of CBT, SBFT, and non-directive supportive therapy (NST) (Brent et al., 1997). In addition to treatment

---

[1] It should be noted, however, that the proportion of youth in the CBT + parent treatment condition that were diagnosis free at post-treatment in the Clarke et al. study was actually higher than that found by Lewinsohn and colleagues (1990), but the effect size is lower because almost half the youth in the wait-list condition studied by Clarke et al. were diagnosis free at post-treatment.

Table 13.4 Clinical and statistical effect, comparing treated groups for treatments conducted with a diagnosed sample

Reference	Treatment 1	Treatment 2	Clinical effect[a]	Statistical effect[b,d]
Brent et al. (1997)	CBT	SBFT	0.35	0.38
Clarke et al. (1999)	CBT	CBT + Parent	−0.09	0.32
Lewinsohn et al. (1990)	CBT	CBT + Parent	−0.08	−0.33
Rosselló & Bernal (1999)[c]	CBT	IPT	—	−0.34

[a] Cohen's h, based on number of youth no longer having an affective disorder diagnosis at follow-up.
[b] Hedges d, based on post-treatment self-reported symptoms on either BDI or CDI.
[c] Study did not report post-treatment diagnoses.
[d] Positive effect sizes indicate a better outcome for Treatment 1; negative effect sizes indicate a better outcome for Treatment 2.

outcome, they examined family and cognitive functioning to test the hypothesis that CBT and SBFT are effective because of the mechanisms of change theoretically proposed to account for their effects (Kolko et al., 2000). As predicted, they found that CBT had a greater acute effect on cognitive distortions than either SBFT or NST. Contrary to what might be expected, CBT also had a greater impact on marital satisfaction and behavioural control than NST, while the difference between SBFT and NST was not significant. Unfortunately, there were no significant differences between treatment groups on the specific outcome variables used in this study;[2] therefore, mediational analyses, examining changes in cognitive distortions, marital satisfaction, and behavioural control could not be conducted. Obviously, further research is required to identify the changes that are responsible for therapeutic gains when they do occur.

What Works in the Real World? Efficacy versus Effectiveness

Although the support for the treatments we have discussed come from efficacy as opposed to effectiveness trials, the distinctions between these types of studies are often not as clear cut as we may believe (Ollendick & King, 2000). Table 13.5 outlines some of the characteristics of the studies we have reviewed as they relate to the distinctions between clinic or real world treatment and research or laboratory treatments as outlined by Weisz, Huey, and Weersing (1998). In addition, we include sample and study characteristics, such as age and ethnicity, as well as attrition rates, to address related issues of generalizability.

As can be seen in Table 13.5, approximately 40% of the studies identified included help-seeking youth treated in outpatient clinics; however, these clinics were associated with academic centres. Although differences may exist between families that

---

[2] Note, however, that Brent et al. (1997) found significant differences for this same sample in terms of diagnosis and self-reported depression when making pairwise comparisons, supporting the superiority of CBT treatments.

Table 13.5 Indicators of generalizability from laboratory to clinic

Reference	Type of Sample	Setting	Format	Age	Ethnicity	Exclusionary Criteria	Dropout Rate
Brent et al., 1997	Clinic sample and recruited	Outpatient medical centre clinic	Individual	13–18	85% Caucasian 15% Other	Psychosis, Bipolar I or II disorder, OCD, eating disorders, substance abuse within past 6 months, ongoing physical or sexual abuse, pregnancy, or chronic medical illness	CBT: 11.8% SBFT: 17.2% NST: 20%
Butler et al., 1980	Recruited and teacher nominated	School	Group	5th–6th Graders	Not reported	Not reported	None
Clarke et al., 1999	Recruited	Not reported	Group	14–18	Not reported	Current mania/hypomania, PD, GAD, CD, substance abuse, organic brain syndrome, mental retardation, schizophrenia, currently receiving other treatment for depression (unwilling to discontinue), in need of immediate acute treatment	22%
Fine et al., 1990	Clinic sample	Outpatient hospital based clinic	Group	13–17	Primarily Caucasian, also North American Indian, Asian, mixed descent	Not aged 13–17, neurological damage, borderline intelligence or below	33%
Kahn et al., 1990	Recruited	School	Group	10–14	Not reported	Receiving antidepressant medication or any other treatment for depression	None

Lewinsohn et al., 1990	Recruited	Not reported	Group	14–18	Not reported	Current bipolar disorder with mania, bipolar disorder with hypomania, PD, GAD, CD, substance abuse, MDD/psychotic subtype, organic brain syndrome, mental retardation, history of schizophrenia, need for immediate treatment and/or actively suicidal and/or need for hospitalization	15%
Liddle & Spence, 1990	Recruited	School	Group	7–11	Not reported	Intellectually handicapped	Not reported
Mufson et al., 1999	Clinic sample	Outpatient medical centre clinic	Individual	12–18	71% Hispanic 29% Other	Actively suicidal, in another treatment for same condition, chronic medical illness, psychotic, bipolar, CD, substance abuse, eating disorders, OCD	12%
Mufson et al., 1994	Clinic sample	Outpatient medical centre clinic	Individual	12–18	Sample 1: Not reported Sample 2: 79% Hispanic; 21% African American	Actively suicidal, IQ less than 70, psychotic substance abuse, CD, bipolar disorder, concurrent treatment for same disorder	21%
Reynolds & Coats (1986)	Recruited	School	Group	High school students	100% Caucasian	Learning disability, mental retardation, emotional disturbance other than depression, current use of medication	CBT: 33% Relaxation: 27%

continues overleaf

Table 13.5 (continued)

Reference	Type of Sample	Setting	Format	Age	Ethnicity	Exclusionary Criteria	Dropout Rate
Rosselló & Bernal, 1999	Clinic sample referred from public schools	University outpatient clinic	Individual	13–17	Puerto Rican	Serious imminent suicidal, psychotic, bipolar, CD, substance abuse, organic brain syndrome, hyperaggression, need for immediate hospitalization, currently receiving psychotropic medication or psychotherapy legal issues	17% IPT 16% CBT
Stark et al., 1987	Recruited	School	Group	9–12	Not reported	1 child excluded because of "serious nondepressive pathology"	3% (condition not reported)
Stark et al., 1991	Recruited	School and home	Group	Grades 4–6	Not reported	None reported	Not reported
Weisz et al., 1997	Recruited and teacher/counsellor nominated	School	Group	Grades 3–6	63% Caucasian 37% Other, primarily African American	None reported	None

Note: CBT = Cognitive Behavioural Therapy; SBFT = Systemic Behaviour Family Therapy; IPT = Interpersonal Therapy; NST = Nondirective Supportive Treatment; MDD = Major Depressive Disorder; PD = Panic Disorder; GAD = Generalized Anxiety Disorder; CD = Conduct Disorder; OCD = Obsessive-Compulsive Disorder; BID = Bellevue Index of Depression; RADS = Reynolds Adolescent Depression Scale; CDI = Children's Depression Inventory; CDRS-R = Children's Depression Rating Scale—Revised.

seek treatment in university or medical centre-based clinics, as opposed to mental health clinics and private practices, we know of no data that explore whether or not these are meaningful differences in terms of treatment outcome (i.e., moderators of treatment outcome). Brent and colleagues (1998) highlight the role of moderating variables in providing evidence of the effectiveness of laboratory-based treatments, suggesting that robust treatments—i.e., those treatments that work despite the presence of potentially adverse predictors—have the greatest potential for application in real-life settings. Taking such an approach, they found support for the transportability of CBT. Further research is needed to address such questions and guide decisions regarding which variables we should focus on in studies testing possible moderators of treatment outcome.

As 60% of studies primarily treated youth who had been recruited for participation, we may be limited in our ability to generalize the results of these studies to clinic settings. Brent et al. (1998) found that treatment outcome was moderated by referral status (i.e., clinical referral versus advertisement), with poorer treatment outcome associated with clinical referral. Importantly, however, they found that the difference in outcome could be explained by the greater sense of hopelessness in clinic-referred youth, suggesting that hopelessness, as opposed to referral status, is a key variable to attend to in identifying how well recruited samples match those seen in clinical settings. Therefore, in order to increase the external validity of efficacy trials for childhood depression, it will be important when using recruited samples to select participants based not only on depressive symptomatology but also on the presence of an associated loss of hope.

Although the majority of participants have been drawn from Caucasian samples, some notable exceptions exist (e.g., Mufson et al., 1994, 1999; Rosselló & Bernal, 1999; Weisz et al., 1997), which suggest that both CBT and IPT treatments may be applicable for youth coming from a variety of cultural backgrounds. However, given that there may be ethnic differences in parents' views of treatment strategies (Tarnowski et al., 1992), it will be important to examine whether cultural or ethnic factors play a role in treatment dropout. Additionally, as indicated by the data in Table 13.5, it will be important to identify other possible factors related to dropout and develop methods to reduce attrition rates.

Some studies employed extensive exclusionary criteria, reducing the heterogeneity and comorbidity seen in clinic samples; however, others have used minimal exclusionary criteria and included youth with most comorbid conditions. Moreover, it appears that participants across studies probably represent a heterogeneous sample. Again, however, it will be important to identify participant characteristics that may affect outcome, rather than focus on heterogeneity itself, when designing studies to address questions of effectiveness.

Although it is true, as Weisz and colleagues suggest, that the focus of the treatments in these studies has been narrow in that they attempted to treat only symptoms of depression, several studies also examined the effect of treatment on associated symptoms and problems such as anxiety, interpersonal relationships, family dysfunction, social skills deficits, and self-esteem. In fact, some targeted depressive symptoms by addressing these other problems and, in that respect, could be considered broadly focused. In addition, although Weisz et al. correctly note that most research therapies are behavioural or cognitive-behavioural in nature and treatments delivered in a clinic setting are not (and many of the ones reviewed here are no exception[3]), it appears that this discrepancy may be due more to clinicians' orientations (Weersing, Weisz, & Donenberg, 2002) and beliefs about the superiority of psychodynamic-humanistic treatment rather than a lack of acceptability of cognitive or behavioural strategies on the part of families (Brent et al., 1997; Tarnowski et al., 1992) or the actual benefits of "treatment as usual" (Ollendick & King, 2000; Weersing & Weisz, 2002). Therefore, although it will be important to further investigate the treatments commonly used in clinical practice, it is imperative that we also focus on why efficacious treatments are not commonly used and on how we can transport treatments that work to clinical practice. One possible obstacle that can be seen from examination of Table 13.5 is that many of the treatments that have gained empirical support are delivered in a group format, which may not be feasible for the clinician in private practice or the typical outpatient mental health clinic. Therefore, it will be important to examine whether these treatments can be effectively delivered in an individual format.

In sum, while the efficacy trials for childhood depression do differ from everyday clinical practice in some of the ways outlined by Weisz and colleagues, there are more similarities than one might at first suspect. Moreover, the differences that do exist may or may not be meaningful ones, and meaningful differences (i.e., discrepancies between the treatments found to be efficacious and those actually used) highlight the need to modify not only clinical research but also clinical practice.

CONCLUSIONS

Comparing "the state of the art" for treating childhood depression today to only 20 years ago gives us much cause for hope. Not only are we beginning to get an idea of what works for treating depressed youth, we also have evidence of what does not work (i.e., treatment as usual) (Ollendick & King, 2000; Weersing & Weisz, 2002). We are now faced with the challenge of transporting efficacious treatments into clinical practice so that our best treatments are the ones being used.

The picture of treatment for depressed children today is not without complications, however, both in terms of identifying effective treatments and also in terms of improving treatment. Identifying efficacious treatments according to the APA's Task Force criteria is difficult in that, while the criteria require support from multiple studies across investigators, different investigatory teams make slight modifications to treatment protocols or use different names for very similar treatments, making it impossible to meet the most stringent criteria needed for a well-established treatment. Hopefully, identification of the essential and non-essential components of treatment packages, as well as the principles that underlie these treatments, will result in increasingly similar treatments being tested by different investigators. Alternatively, the value of replication may simply need to be resurrected so that we can easily come to agreement on what constitutes an efficacious treatment. Additionally, in identifying treatments that will generalize to multiple

---

[3] The studies of IPT treatment in this area are, however, exceptions.

cultural groups, we need to use theory to identify potentially important moderators and mediators of treatment outcome. While it could be suggested, and perhaps it would be ideal (although not feasible), that treatments need to be tested on each specific population to be deemed efficacious for that group, most evidence supports the contention that treatments are inherently flexible. This is not surprising given that treatments have to be able to work with multiple individuals and that a good deal of variability exists within a cultural group as well as across groups.

In terms of improving treatments, identifying moderators and mediators of treatment outcome would provide information on when treatments work, and why. Coupled with theory, this would not only help us develop the most efficient treatment programs but could also guide efforts in effectiveness trials. Moreover, despite the efficacy of current treatments in laboratory studies, and, we believe, potential effectiveness in the clinic, close inspection of response rates quickly reveals that a great many children and adolescents do not benefit from even our best treatments. One avenue that has been explored to improve treatment is to include parents and family members. This makes sense in light of evidence that the families of depressed children often exhibit family dysfunction (Dadds & Barrett, 1996) and are headed by parents who evidence their own psychopathology (Weissman et al., 1984, 1992), and findings that indicate that parental psychopathology is a significant moderator of treatment efficacy (Brent et al., 1998). To date, however, parent and family therapies have not been shown to be effective (Brent et al., 1997; Clarke et al., 1999; Kolko et al., 2000; Lewinsohn et al., 1990). Most attempts to include parents and families in treatment have taken a largely psychoeducational approach in dealing with family dysfunction and parental psychopathology. This, in effect, is saying that, while children and adolescents with emotional disturbances need CBT or IPT treatments, we can expect their parents and families to change by simply educating them. This seems to fly in the face of the evidence on empirically supported treatments for adults. A more consistent approach might include a truly comprehensive treatment for parents and families that uses similar treatment strategies for addressing the problems encountered by children and their family members and takes into account the reciprocal nature of the interactions (i.e., the transactions) within the family.

Additionally, rather than provide treatment to every family of a depressed child or adolescent, it may be more efficient and effective to use a prescriptive or case-conceptualization approach in which family dynamics, parental psychopathology, and developmental issues are assessed and considered in treatment planning (see, Goza & Ollendick, 2002; Persons, 1992). For example, the data on treatment outcome for anxious children supports adjunctive parent treatment for children but not for adolescents (Barrett, Dadds, & Rapee, 1996). Furthermore, it obviously makes sense to address the depressogenic cognitive style that depressed parents may model for their child when it is present, but it may damage treatment credibility and the therapeutic relationship to spend session time on such issues when it is not indicated.

Lastly, given the sometimes serious effects of childhood depression on both children and families, we applaud the efforts of those who are currently investigating preventive treatments (e.g., Clarke et al., 1995) and suggest that this is an important avenue for future research. In short, we have learned much about juvenile depression, its treatment, and its prevention in recent years; still, however, much remains to be accomplished for the many youth in our society who present with these disorders.

REFERENCES

Abramson, L.Y., Seligman, M.E.P., & Teasdale, J. (1978). Learned helplessness in humans: Critique and reformulation. *Journal of Abnormal Psychology*, **87**, 59–74.

Achenbach, T.M. (1991). *Manual for the Child Behavior Checklist/4–18 and 1991 Profile*. Burlington, VT: University of Vermont, Department of Psychiatry.

American Psychiatric Association. (1994). *Diagnostic and statistical manual of mental disorders* (4th edn.). Washington, DC: Author.

Anderson, J.C., Williams, S., McGee, R., & Silva, P.A. (1987). DSM-III disorders in preadolescent children: Prevalence in a large sample from the general population. *Archives of General Psychiatry*, **44**, 69–76.

Barrett, P.M., Dadds, M.R., & Rapee, R.M. (1996). Family treatment of childhood anxiety: A controlled trial. *Journal of Consulting and Clinical Psychology*, **64**, 333–342.

Beck, A.T. (1967). *Depression: Clinical, experimental, and theoretical aspects*. New York: Hoeber.

Beck, J.S., Beck, A.T., & Jolly, J.B. (2001). *Manual for the Beck Youth Inventories of Emotional and Social Impairment*. San Antonio, TX: Psychological Corporation.

Beck, A.T., Steer, R.A., & Brown, G.K. (1996). *Manual for the Beck Depression Inventory II*. San Antonio, TX: The Psychological Corporation.

Bird, H.R., Canino, G., Rubio-Stipec, M., Gould, M.S., Ribera, J., Sesman, M., Woodbury, M., Huertas-Gouldman, S., Pagan, A., Sanchez-Lacay, A., & Moscoso, M. (1988). Estimates of the prevalence of childhood maladjustment in a community survey in Puerto Rico: The use of combined measures. *Archives of General Psychiatry*, **45**, 1120–1126.

Brent, D.A., Holder, D., Kolko, D., Birmaher, B., Baugher, M., Roth, C., Iyengar, S., & Johnson, B.A. (1997). A clinical psychotherapy trial for adolescent depression comparing cognitive, family, and supportive therapy. *Archives of General Psychiatry*, **54**, 877–885.

Brent, D.A., Kolko, D.J., Birmaher, B., Baugher, M., Bridge, J., Roth, C., & Holder, D. (1998). Predictors of treatment efficacy in a clinical trial of three psychosocial treatments for adolescent depression. *Journal of the American Academy of Child and Adolescent Psychiatry*, **37**, 906–914.

Butler, L., Mietzitis, S., Friedman, R., & Cole, E. (1980). The effect of two school-based intervention programs on depressive symptoms in preadolescents. *American Educational Research Journal*, **17**, 111–119.

Chambless, D.L., Sanderson, W.C., Shoham, V., Bennett Johnson, S., Pope, K.S., Crits-Christoph, P., Baker, M., Johnson, B., Woody, S.R., Sue, S., Beutler, L., Williams, D.A., & McCurry, S. (1996). An update on empirically validated therapies. *The Clinical Psychologist*, **49**, 5–18.

Chorpita, B.F., Yim, L., Moffitt, C., Umemoto, L.A., & Francis, S.E. (2000). Assessment of symptoms of DSM-IV anxiety and depression in children: A revised child anxiety and depression scale. *Behaviour Research and Therapy*, **38**, 835–855.

Chorpita, B.F., Yim, L.M., Donkervoet, J.C., Arensdorf, A., Amundsen, M.J., McGee, C., Serrano, A., Yates, A., Burns, J.A., & Morelli, P. (2002). Toward large-scale implementation of empirically supported treatments for children: A review and observations by the Hawaii empirical basis to services task force. *Clinical Psychology: Science and Practice*, **9**, 165–190.

Clarke, G.N., Hawkins, W., Murphy, M., Sheeber, L.B., Lewinsohn, P.M., & Seeley, J.R. (1995). Targeted prevention of unipolar depressive disorder in an at-risk sample of high school adolescents: A randomized trial of group cognitive intervention. *Journal of the American Academy of Child and Adolescent Psychiatry*, **34**, 312–321.

Clarke, G.N., Rohde, P., Lewinsohn, P.M., Hops, H., & Seeley, J.R. (1999). Cognitive-Behavioural treatment of adolescent depression: Efficacy of acute group treatment and booster sessions. *Journal of the American Academy of Child and Adolescent Psychiatry*, **38** (1), 329–342.

Cohen, P., Cohen, J., Kasen, S., Velez, C.N., Hartmark, C., Johnson, J., Rojas, M., Brook, J., & Streuning, E.L. (1993). An epidemiological study of disorders in late childhood and adolescence—I. Age- and gender-specific prevalence. *Journal of Child Psychology and Psychiatry*, **34**, 851–867.

Cole, D.A., Hoffman, K., Tram, J.M., & Maxwell, S.E. (2000). Structural differences in parent and child reports of children's symptoms of depression and anxiety. *Psychological Assessment*, **12**, 174–185.

Costello, E.J., Angold, A., Burns, B.J., Erkanli, A., Stangl, D.K., & Tweed, D.L. (1996). The Great Smoky Mountains Study of Youth: Functional impairment and serious emotional disturbance. *Archives of General Psychiatry*, **53**, 1137–1143.

Dadds, M.R., & Barrett, P.M. (1996). Family processes in child and adolescent anxiety and depression. *Behaviour Change*, **13**, 231–239.

Fergusson, D.M., Horwood, J., & Lynskey, M.T. (1993). Prevalence and comorbidity of DSM-III-R diagnoses in a birth cohort of 15 years olds. *Journal of the American Academy of Child and Adolescent Psychiatry*, **32** (6), 1127–1134.

Fine, S., Forth, A., Gilbert, M., & Haley, G. (1990). Group therapy for adolescent depressive disorder: A comparison of social skills and therapeutic support. *Journal of the American Academy of Child and Adolescent Psychiatry*, **30**, 79–85.

Goodman, R. (1997). The Strengths and Difficulties Questionnaire: A research note. *Journal of Child Psychology and Psychiatry*, **38**, 581–586.

Goodman, R. (1999). The extended version of the Strengths and Difficulties Questionnaire as a guide to child psychiatric caseness and consequent burden. *Journal of Child Psychology and Psychiatry*, **40**, 791–801.

Goodman, R., & Scott, S. (1999). Comparing the Strengths and Difficulties Questionnaire and the Child Behavior Checklist: Is small beautiful? *Journal of Abnormal Child Psychology*, **27**, 17–24.

Goza, A.B., & Ollendick, T.H. (2002). *Cognitive-behavioural treatment for depression in children: The impact of case formulation on treatment selection*. Manuscript in preparation.

Grills, A.E., & Ollendick, T.H. (2002). Issues in parent–child agreement: The case of structured diagnostic interviews. *Clinical Child and Family Psychology Review*, **5**, 57–83.

Haarasilta, L., Marttunen, M., Kaprio, J., & Aro, H. (2001). The 12-month prevalence and characteristics of major depressive episode in a representative sample of adolescents and young adults. *Psychological Medicine*, **31** (7), 1169–1179.

Hamilton, M. (1960). A rating scale for depression. *Journal of Neurology, Neurosurgery, Psychiatry*, **12**, 56–62.

Hodges, K. (1990). Depression and anxiety in children: A comparison of self-report questionnaires to clinical interview. *Psychological Assessment*, **2**, 376–381.

Kahn, J.S., Kehle, T.J., Jenson, W.R., & Clark, E. (1990). Comparison of cognitive-behavioural, relaxation, and self-modeling interventions for depression among middle-school students. *School Psychology Review*, **19**, 196–211.

Kashani, J.H., Beck, N.C., Hoeper, E.W., Fallahi, C., Corcoran, C.M., McAllister, J.A., Rosenberg, T.K., & Reid, J.C. (1987). Psychiatric disorders in a community sample of adolescents. *American Journal of Psychiatry*, **144**, 584–589.

Kashani, J.H., Orvaschel, H., Rosenberg, T.K., & Reid, J.C. (1989). Psychopathology in a community sample of children and adolescents: A developmental perspective. *Journal of the American Academy of Child and Adolescent Psychiatry*, **28**, 701–706.

Kaslow, N.J., & Thompson, M.P. (1998). Applying the criteria for empirically supported treatments to studies of psychosocial interventions for child and adolescent depression. *Journal of Clinical Child Psychology*, **27**, 146–155.

Kaslow, N.J., Rehm, L.P., & Siegel, A.W. (1984). Social-cognitive and cognitive correlates of depression in children. *Journal of Abnormal Child Psychology*, **12**, 605–620.

Kaufman, J., Martin, A., King, R., & Charney, D. (2001). Are child-, adolescent-, and adult-onset depression one and the same disorder? *Society of Biological Psychiatry*, **49**, 980–1001.

Kazdin, A.E. (1993). Psychotherapy for children and adolescents: Current progress and future directions. *American Psychologist*, **48**, 644–657.

Kessler, R.C., Berglund, P.A., Foster, C.L., Saunders, W.B., Stang, P.E., & Walters, E.E. (1997). Social consequences of psychiatric disorders, II: Teenage parenthood. *American Journal of Psychiatry*, **154**, 1405–1411.

Kessler, R.C., Foster, C.L., Saunders, W.B., & Stang, P.E. (1995). Social consequences of psychiatric disorders I: Educational attainment. *American Journal of Psychiatry*, **152**, 1026–1032.

Kolko, D.J., Brent, D.A., Baugher, M., Bridge, J., & Birmaher, B. (2000). Cognitive and family therapies for adolescent depression: Treatment specificity, mediation, and moderation. *Journal of Consulting and Clinical Psychology*, **68**, 603–614.

Kovacs, M. (1985). Children's Depression Inventory. *Psychopharmacology Bulletin*, **21**, 995–998.

Lewinsohn, P., & Shaw, D. (1969). Feedback about interpersonal behavior as an agent of behavior change: A case study in the treatment of depression. *Psychotherapy and Psychosomatics*, **17**, 82–88.

Lewinsohn, P., Rohde, P., & Seeley, J. (1998). Major depressive disorder in older adolescents: Prevalence, risk factors, and clinical implications. *Clinical Psychology Review*, **18**, 765–794.

Lewinsohn, P.M., Clarke, G.N., Hops, H., & Andrews, J.A. (1990). Cognitive-behavioral treatment for depressed adolescents. *Behavior Therapy*, **21**, 385–401.

Lewinsohn, P.M., Clarke, G.N., Rohde, P., Hops, H., & Seeley, J. (1996). A course in coping: A cognitive-behavioural approach to the treatment of adolescent depression. In E.D. Hibbs & P.S. Jensen (Eds), *Psychosocial treatments for child and adolescent disorders: Empirically based strategies for clinical practice* (pp. 109–135). Washington, DC: American Psychological Association.

Lewinsohn, P.M., Hops, H., Roberts, R.E., Seeley, J.R., & Andrews, J.A. (1993). Adolescent psychopathology: I. Prevalence and incidence of depression and other DSM-III-R disorders in high school students. *Journal of Abnormal Psychology*, **102**, 133–144.

Liddle, B., & Spence, S.H. (1990). Cognitive-behaviour therapy with depressed primary school children: A cautionary note. *Behavioural Psychotherapy*, **18**, 85–102.

Luby, J.L., Heffelfinger, A.K., Mrakotsky, C., Hessler, M.J., Brown, K.M., & Hildebrand, T. (2002). Preschool Major Depressive Disorder: Preliminary validation for developmentally modified DSM-IV criteria. *Journal of the American Academy of Child and Adolescent Psychiatry*, **41**, 928–937.

McGee, R., Feehan, M., Williams, S., Partridge, F., Silva, P.A., & Kelly, J. (1990). DSM-III disorders in a large sample of adolescents. *Journal of the American Academy of Child and Adolescent Psychiatry*, **29**, 611–619.

Mufson, L., Moreau, D., & Weissman, M.M. (1996). Focus on relationships: Interpersonal psychotherapy for adolescent depression. In E.D. Hibbs & P.S. Jensen (Eds), *Psychosocial treatments for child and adolescent disorders: Empirically based strategies for clinical practice*. Washington, DC: American Psychological Association.

Mufson, L., Moreau, D., Weissman, M.M., Wickermaratne, P., Martin, J., & Somoilov, A. (1994). Modification of interpersonal psychotherapy with depressed adolescents (IPT-A): Phase I and II studies. *Journal of the American Academy of Child and Adolescent Psychiatry*, **33**, 695–705.

Mufson, L., Weissman, M.M., Moreau, D., & Garfinkel, R. (1999). Efficacy of interpersonal psychotherapy for depressed adolescents. *Archives of General Psychiatry*, **56**, 573–579.

Myers, K., & Winters, N.C. (2002). Ten-year review of rating scales. II: Scales for internalizing disorders. *Journal of the American Academy Child and Adolescent Psychiatry*, **41**, 634–659.

NIMH Developmental Psychopathology and Prevention Research Branch (2001). National Institute of Mental Health research roundtable on prepubertal bipolar disorder. *Journal of the American Academy of Child and Adolescent Psychiatry*, **40**, 871–878.

Ollendick, T.H. (Ed.) (1998). *Comprehensive clinical psychology: Vol. 5: Children and adolescents: Clinical formulation and treatment*. Oxford, England: Pergamon/Elsevier Science Ltd.

Ollendick, T.H., & Hersen, M. (1984). *Child behavioural assessment: Principles and procedures*. New York: Pergamon Press.

Ollendick, T.H., & King, N.J. (2000). Empirically supported treatments for children and adolescents. In P.C. Kendall (Ed.), *Child and adolescent therapy* (pp. 386–425). New York: Guilford Press.

Orvaschel, H., & Puig-Antich, J. (1986). *Schedule for Affective Disorders and Schizophrenia for School-Age Children, Epidemiologic Version: Kiddie-SADS-E (K-SADS-E) (4th version)* (Technical Report). Pittsburgh: Western Psychiatric Institute and Clinic.

Persons, J.B. (1992). A case formulation approach to cognitive-behavior therapy: Application to panic disorder. *Psychiatric Annals*, **22**, 470–473.

Poznanski, E.O., Grossman, J.A., Buchsbaum, Y., Banegas, M., Freeman, L., & Gibbons, R. (1984). Preliminary studies of the reliability and validity of the Children's Depression Rating Scale. *Journal of the American Academy of Child Psychiatry*, **23**, 191–197.

Rey, J.M., & Morris-Yates, A. (1991). Adolescent depression and the Child Behavior Checklist. *Journal of the American Academy of Child and Adolescent Psychiatry*, **30** (3), 423–427.

Reynolds, C.R., & Kamphaus, R.W. (1992). *Manual for the Behavior Assessment System for Children*. Circle Pines, MN: American Guidance Service.

Reynolds, W.M. (1987a). *Professional manual for The Reynolds Adolescent Depression Scale*. Odessa, FL: Psychological Assessment Resources.

Reynolds, W.M. (1987b). *Professional manual for The Suicidal Ideation Questionnaire*. Odessa, FL: Psychological Assessment Resources.

Reynolds, W.M. (1989). *Professional manual for the Reynolds Child Depression Scale*. Odessa, FL: Psychological Assessment Resources.

Reynolds, W.M., & Coats, K.I. (1986). A comparison of cognitive-behavioral therapy and relaxation training for the treatment of depression in adolescents. *Journal of Consulting and Clinical Psychology*, **54**, 653–660.

Rosselló, J., & Bernal, G. (1999). The efficacy of cognitive-behavioural and interpersonal treatments for depression in Puerto Rican adolescents. *Journal of Consulting and Clinical Psychology*, **67**, 734–745.

Ryan, N., Puig-Antich, J., Amborsini, P., Rabinovich, H., Robinson, D., Nelson, B., Iyengar, S., & Twomey, J. (1987). The clinical picture of major depression in children and adolescents. *Archives of General Psychiatry*, **44**, 854–861.

Sameroff, A.J. (1995). General systems theories and developmental psychopathology. *Developmental Psychology*, **1**, 659–695.

Sawyer, M.G., Arney, F.M., Baghurst, P.A., Clark, J.J., Graetz, B.W., Kosky, R.J., Nurcombe, B., Patton, G.C., Prior, M.R., Raphael, B., Rey, J.M., Whaites, L.C., & Zubrick, S.R. (2001). The mental health of young people in Australia: Key findings from the Child and Adolescent Component of the National Survey of Mental Health and Well-Being. *Australian and New Zealand Journal of Psychiatry*, **35** (6), 806–814.

Seligman, L.D., & Ollendick, T.H. (1998). Comorbidity of anxiety and depression in children and adolescents: An integrative review. *Clinical Child and Family Psychology Review*, **1**, 125–144.

Seligman, M.E. (1975). *Helplessness*. San Francisco: Freeman.

Shaffer, D., Fisher, P., Lucas, C.P., Dulcan, M.K., & Schwab-Stone, M.E. (2000). NIMH Diagnostic Interview Schedule for Children Version IV (NIMH DISC-IV): Description, differences from previous versions, and reliability of some common diagnoses. *Journal of the American Academy of Child and Adolescent Psychiatry*, **39**, 28–38.

Shain, B.N., Naylor, M., & Alessi, N. (1990). Comparison of self-rated and clinician-rated measures of depression in adolescents. *American Journal of Psychiatry*, **147**, 793–795.

Silverman, W.K., & Albano, A.M. (1996). *Anxiety Disorders Interview Schedule for DSM-IV, Child Version*. San Antonio: The Psychological Corporation.

Spence, S.H. (1998). A measure of anxiety symptoms among children. *Behaviour Research and Therapy*, **36**, 545–566.

Stark, K.D. (1990). *Childhood depression: School-based intervention.* New York: Guilford Press.

Stark, K., Reynolds, W.M., & Kaslow, N.J. (1987). A comparison of the relative efficacy of self-control therapy and a behavioural problem-solving therapy for depression in children. *Journal of Abnormal Child Psychology*, **15**, 91–113.

Stark, K., Rouse, L., & Livingston, R. (1991). Treatment of depression during childhood and adolescence: Cognitive-behavioural procedures for the individual and family. In P.C. Kendall (Ed.), *Child and adolescent therapy* (pp. 165–206). New York: Guilford.

Stark, K.D., Swearer, S., Kurkowski, C., Sommer, D., & Bowen, B. (1996). Targeting the child and the family: A holistic approach to treating child and adolescent depressive disorders. In E.D. Hibbs & P.S. Jensen (Eds), *Psychosocial treatments for child and adolescent disorders: Empirically based strategies for clinical practice* (pp. 207–238). Washington, DC: American Psychological Association.

Steer, R.A., Kumar, G., Beck, J.S., & Beck, A.T. (2001). Evidence for the construct validities of the Beck Youth Inventories with child psychiatric outpatients. *Psychological Reports*, **89**, 559–565.

Steinhausen, H., & Metzke, C. (1999). Adolescent self-rated depressive symptoms in a Swiss epidemiological study. *Journal of Youth and Adolescence*, **29**, 427–440.

Strober, M., Green, J., & Carlson, G. (1981). Utility of the Beck Depression Inventory with psychiatrically hospitalized adolescents. *Journal of Consulting and Clinical Psychology*, **49**, 482–483.

Tarnowski, K.J., Simonian, S.J., Bekeny, P., & Park, A. (1992). Acceptability of interventions for childhood depression. *Behavior Modification*, **16**, 103–117.

Weersing, V.R., & Weisz, J.R. (2002). Community clinic treatment of depressed youth: Benchmarking usual care against CBT clinical trials. *Journal of Consulting and Clinical Psychology*, **70**, 299–310.

Weersing, V.R., Weisz, J.R., & Donenberg, G.R. (2002). Development of the Therapy Procedures Checklist: A therapist-report measure of technique use in child and adolescent treatment. *Journal of Clinical Child Psychology*, **31**, 168–180.

Weissman, M., Markowitz, J., & Klerman, J. (2000). *Comprehensive guide to interpersonal psychotherapy.* New York: Basic Books, Inc.

Weissman, M.M., Fendrich, M., Warner, V., & Wickramaratne, P. (1992). Incidence of psychiatric disorder in offspring at high and low risk for depression. *Journal of the American Academy of Child and Adolescent Psychiatry*, **31**, 640–648.

Weissman, M.M., Prusoff, B.A., Gammon, D., Merikangas, K.R., Leckman, J.F., & Kidd, K.K. (1984). Psychopathology in the children (Ages 6–18) of depressed and normal parents. *Journal of the American Academy of Child Psychiatry*, **23**, 78–84.

Weisz, J.R., Huey, S.J., & Weersing, V.R. (1998). Psychotherapy outcome research with children and adolescents: The state of the art. In T.H. Ollendick & R.J. Prinz (Eds), *Advances in clinical child psychology* (vol. 20; pp. 49–91). New York: Plenum Press.

Weisz, J.R., Thurber, C.A., Sweeney, L., Proffitt, V.D., & LeGagnoux, G.L. (1997). Brief treatment of mild-to-moderate child depression using primary and secondary control enhancement training. *Journal of Consulting and Clinical Psychology*, **65**, 703–707.

Welner, Z., Reich, W., Herjanic, B., Jung, K.G., & Amando, H. (1987). Reliability, validity, and parent–child agreement studies of the Diagnostic Interview for Children and Adolescents (DICA). *Journal of the American Academy of Child and Adolescent Psychiatry*, **26**, 649–653.

World Health Organization (1992). *International classification of diseases* (10th revision edn). Geneva: Author.

CHAPTER 14

Treatment of Substance Abuse Disorders in Children and Adolescents

Holly Barrett Waldron

and

Sheryl Kern-Jones

Oregon Research Institute, USA

INTRODUCTION

Illicit substance use among adolescents has been persistently high over the past decade and remains one of the most pressing public health concerns in the United States (Johnston et al., 2001; Dennis et al., in press). Encouragingly, clinical research has yielded a number of empirically supported, efficacious treatments for adolescent drug abuse (Dennis et al., 2003; Henggeler et al., 2002; Liddle et al., 2001; Ozechowski & Liddle, 2000; Schoenwald & Henggeler, 2002; Szapocznik & Williams, 2000; Wagner & Waldron, 2001; Waldron & Kaminer, in press; Waldron et al., 2001). This increased research, examining substance abuse treatment effectiveness with adolescents, represents a much expanded focus on adolescent treatment outcome and a greater recognition of the important differences between adolescent and adult substance use patterns and the benefits they receive from different types of treatment (Deas et al., 2000). This recognition has fostered the development of treatments tailored to the unique developmental needs and use patterns of adolescents. Recent reviews of clinical trials evaluating adolescent interventions have noted consistencies in research findings and signalled initial steps toward consensus, albeit preliminary, regarding promising treatment models with demonstrated efficacy

Correspondence to Holly B. Waldron, Oregon Research Institute, 1715 Franklin Blvd. Eugene, Oregon 97403; email: hwaldron@ori.org

Handbook of Interventions that Work with Children and Adolescents: Prevention and Treatment.
Edited by P.M. Barrett and T.H. Ollendick. © 2004 John Wiley & Sons, Ltd. ISBN 0-470-84453-1.

across several studies (Deas & Thomas, 2001; Muck et al., 2001; Waldron, 1997; Williams, Chang, & colleagues, 2000; Winters, 1999).

This chapter will focus on interventions for adolescents who engage in problematic alcohol or drug use and meet diagnostic criteria for substance abuse or dependence. Major treatment approaches will be presented including traditional, cognitive-behavioural, family, pharmacotherapy, and other models along with a review of efficacy trials. Because the majority of youth receive outpatient treatment, which has been the focus of most controlled studies (Williams, Chang, & colleagues, 2000), outpatient interventions will be emphasized. Emerging findings and directions for future research will also be discussed.

Conceptualizing Adolescent Substance Abuse

No clear consensus exists regarding the definition of problematic alcohol and drug use and the diagnostic characteristics of substance abuse and dependence for adolescents (Bailey, 1989; Waldron, 1997; Winters, Latimer, & Stinchfield, 2001). Substance use can interfere with crucial developmental tasks and the development of coping skills for responding to stress (Baumrind, 1985; Bentler, 1992). Despite this, the majority of older adolescents who experiment with alcohol or hard drugs do not become addicted and appear to "mature out" of problem use as they transition into adulthood (Kouzis & Labouvie, 1992; Shedler & Block, 1990). However, habitual or heavy use among youth remains an urgent problem that has been conceptualized as part of a broad cluster of problem behaviour including school failure, juvenile delinquency, and high-risk sexual activity (Donovan & Jessor, 1985; Newcomb & Felix-Ortiz, 1992). Developmental factors are important and experimentation with drugs and alcohol by children and younger adolescents is a less frequent phenomenon associated with a much higher risk of developing long-term problems (Winters, Latimer, & Stinchfield, 2001).

National survey data show that experimentation with drugs and alcohol is normative for older adolescents, and regular use has increased in the past decade. Current US estimates indicate that about 25% of high school 12th graders, 20% of 10th graders, and 10% of 8th graders use illicit drugs each month, with nearly 6% of 12th graders and 4.5% of 10th graders using marijuana daily. In addition, about a third of high school seniors and one-fourth of sophomores use alcohol in binges at least once every two weeks (Johnston, O'Malley, & Bachman, 2000). Similarities and differences exist in patterns of use between adolescents and adults. Youth use a broader range of substances and drink less often, but they consume the same quantities of alcohol and develop dependence much more rapidly than adults (Deas et al., 2000). Adolescent substance abuse appears to result from multiple, interacting influences (Wagner et al., 1999; Waldron, 1998) from the society and local community, interpersonal influences (e.g., peer and parent use), and intrapersonal factors (e.g., physiological responsivity to drugs; cf. Hawkins, Catalano, & Miller, 1992). Each of the treatment models focuses on a different combination of risk and protective factors theorized to influence adolescent substance abuse.

TRADITIONAL THERAPY MODELS

Conceptualization of Traditional Models

Traditional interventions include supportive and psychodynamic models; however, the majority are based upon the 12-Step orientation of Alcoholics Anonymous/ Narcotics Anonymous (AA/NA; Kassel & Jackson, 2001). The AA/NA philosophy views alcohol and drug use as a disease with a progressive course and holds that successful treatment requires abstinence (cf. Kassel & Jackson, 2001). This perspective supports the belief that individuals must recognize a higher spiritual power to support change following a 12-Step recovery process. Youth appear to find 12-Step interventions less appealing, and some theorists have suggested that the tenets of 12-Step models may be inappropriate for adolescents without modification (Deas & Thomas, 2001; Wagner et al., 1999). The Minnesota Model, based upon AA/NA philosophy, conceptualizes substance abuse as a disease that is treated through group process and self-help strategies designed to promote behaviour change (Winters, Latimer, & Stinchfield, 1999).

Traditional Interventions

Twelve-Step interventions involve group meetings in community settings. Led by recovering members, most groups are open to anyone and often serve as an adjunct to other treatment. Treatment includes confession, restitution, sharing stories and recovery efforts with the group, self-help literature, and mentorship with a recovering sponsor. The Minnesota Model typically includes a 4–6 week inpatient therapeutic milieu, professional staff, 12-Step meetings, recreational activities, and aftercare (Kassel & Jackson, 2001; Williams, Chang, & colleagues, 2000).

Treatment Outcome

The nature of 12-Step interventions makes them difficult to study in well-controlled trials due to group anonymity, self-selection biases, and variability in content and process across groups (Montgomery, Tonigan, & Miller, 1993). Most studies have been conducted with inpatient populations and the majority of these studies have serious methodological weaknesses (Kassel & Jackson, 2001; Kownacki & Shadish, 1999). A number of studies have found poorer outcomes for individuals mandated or randomized to AA/NA (Kownacki & Shadish, 1999). However, Kennedy and Minami (1993) found lower relapse rates for youth attending AA/NA following residential treatment (cf. Godley, Godley, & Dennis, 2001). The few outcome studies with youth indicate that many benefit from Minnesota Model and 12-Step interventions when compared to untreated youth; however, the few comparisons with alternative interventions have yielded mixed results. Therefore, no conclusions can be drawn regarding the relative effectiveness of the 12-Step model at this time.

COGNITIVE-BEHAVIOURAL THERAPY MODELS

Conceptualization of the Model

Cognitive-behavioural therapy (CBT) models are based on learning theories that conceptualize substance use as a learned behaviour that is acquired and maintained by the principles of classical and operant conditioning and social learning theory (Waldron & Kaminer, in press). Classical conditioning principles posit that substance abuse is a result of conditioned responses to environmental triggers or cues. An operant conditioning perspective proposes that substance use behaviours are maintained by antecedents and consequences (i.e., social reinforcers, physiological effects). The social learning model incorporates cognitive processes into classical and operant perspectives, such as the perception and appraisal of environmental cues, in determining behaviour (Bandura, 1977). This perspective views substance use as a result of multiple factors, including learning about use through observation and imitation of social models (i.e., parents and peers), social reinforcement, self-efficacy beliefs, expectancies, and physiological influences (Abrams et al., 1986).

Cognitive-Behavioural Interventions

The focus of CBT is teaching skills for avoiding substance use and engaging in prosocial behaviours. Common components include self-monitoring, avoidance of triggers (i.e., stimulus cues which predict use), altering reinforcement contingencies, coping-skills training to manage and resist urges to use, drug refusal skills, problem-solving, mood regulation, and relapse prevention (Marlatt & Gordon, 1985; Monti et al., 1989). The behavioural targets of change (e.g., identification of contingencies) vary widely depending on the cognitive skills, emotional maturity, social functioning, and age of the adolescent. The CBT model is implemented within individual and group treatment modalities and CBT strategies are applied in behaviourally based family therapy.

Treatment Outcome for Cognitive-Behavioural Interventions

Over the past decade, numerous studies have provided strong support for the effectiveness of CBT in treating adult substance abuse and dependence (cf. Miller & Heather, 1998) and adolescents with disorders known to co-occur with substance abuse, such as conduct problems, depression, and anxiety (cf. Waldron & Kaminer, in press). Early research on CBT was plagued by methodological problems, however several recent well-designed efficacy trials have boosted efforts to provide empirical support for CBT in treating youth substance abuse.

The majority of research on CBT with adolescents has focused on individual or group modalities in outpatient settings. Kaminer and his colleagues conducted three clinical trials in which youth were randomly assigned to group CBT or an interactional group intervention. In one study, both interventions produced similar reductions in substance use problems and, in two studies, CBT led to post-treatment differential gains over the interactional group intervention (Kaminer & Burleson, 1999; Kaminer, Burleson, & Goldberger, 2002).

Liddle and his colleagues (2001) compared family therapy, a multifamily psycho-educational group, and an adolescent skills-based CBT group that included two motivational family sessions. All three conditions were associated with clinically significant reductions in substance use and acting out behaviours. Family therapy retained more youth and led to the greatest substance use reductions. The CBT group showed gradual decline in drug use from pre-treatment to follow-up, not apparent at post-treatment, and the authors suggested that the effect may have resulted from a delay between adolescents putting newly acquired skills into use and deriving benefit from their implementation. Liddle and his colleagues also compared individual CBT to family therapy (Liddle et al., 2003) and found significant reductions in drug use, internalizing and externalizing problems for both interventions.

Waldron and her colleagues have conducted a systematic program of research evaluating outpatient family therapy and CBT interventions designed to address specific risk and protective factors for substance-abusing youth. In one study, adolescents were randomly assigned to individual CBT, group CBT, or family therapy (Waldron et al., 2001). Youth in group CBT showed delayed positive outcomes, with no significant change at post-treatment followed by significant reductions in percent days of marijuana use at 7-month and 19-month follow-ups. For youth in family therapy, significant reductions in percent days of marijuana use were found at post-treatment, 7-month, and 19-month follow-ups. However, the percent days of marijuana use showed no significant change for youth in individual CBT.

A somewhat different pattern of findings emerged for individual CBT when clinically meaningful change was examined by the proportion of youth achieving abstinence or minimal levels of marijuana use (i.e., reported use on fewer than 10% of the days) as the outcome measure (Waldron & Kaminer, in press; Kern-Jones et al., 2001). A significant percentage of youth achieved minimal levels of use following the individual CBT intervention (30%) and, while the percentage dipped at 7-month follow-up (17%), a sizeable percentage of youth maintained abstinence or minimal use levels at 19-month follow-up (27%). An examination of clinically meaningful change for the family therapy and group CBT interventions produced the same results as in the previous analyses.

The Cannabis Youth Treatment study, funded by the Center for Substance Abuse Treatment, included a four-site clinical trial to evaluate CBT and family-based interventions for adolescent marijuana abuse and dependence (Dennis et al., in press). A total of 600 adolescents were randomly assigned to one of five interventions that included combinations of individual motivational enhancement, group CBT, family psychoeducation, individual Adolescent Community Reinforcement Approach (ACRA; Godley, Godley, & Dennis, 2001), and multidimensional family therapy (Liddle et al., 2001). All five interventions produced significant reductions in cannabis use and negative consequences of use from pre-treatment to the 3-month follow-up that were maintained at the 12-month follow-up (Dennis et al., in press). In addition, changes in marijuana use were accompanied by reductions in behavioural, family, and school problems, violence, and illegal activity. The findings provided support for CBT and family-based interventions and did not support a simple dose–response relationship.

Taken together, the findings from several studies provide initial support for the effectiveness of CBT in the treatment of adolescent substance abuse. Findings reported by Dennis, Kaminer, Liddle, and their colleagues indicate that both group and individual CBT interventions can be as effective as alternative treatments. The findings by Waldron and her colleagues suggest that about one-third of youth participating in individual CBT achieve substantial benefit. Further studies are needed to determine which youth are most likely to benefit from different types of treatment.

The consistent empirical support of group CBT for substance-abusing adolescents stands in contrast to the iatrogenic effects reported for other group interventions (Azrin et al., 1994; Dishion, McCord, & Poulin, 1999; Dishion, Poulin, & Barraston, 2001). Most studies with iatrogenic effects were of preventive interventions with high-risk youth. Dishion, McCord, and Poulin (1999) have suggested that peer deviancy training may have been the cause. Sufficient information is not yet available to determine if the structure or type of group treatment, adolescent population, therapist training, or other factors may be related to positive or negative outcome. A number of features associated with group approaches may facilitate cognitive, affective, and behavioural changes. These include the realization that others share similar problems, modelling, rehearsal, peer/therapist feedback, learning and practice of new social behaviours, and the development of trust. The evidence supporting group CBT suggests that the group treatment modality holds promise. Research is needed to determine the conditions under which group interventions are beneficial or detrimental for substance-abusing youth.

FAMILY THERAPY MODELS

Family Therapy Models: Conceptualizations and Interventions

Family therapy has been one of the most widely implemented and evaluated intervention approaches for adolescent substance abuse (Craig, 1993; Selekman & Todd, 1991). The majority of family-based interventions have been derived from General Systems Theory (Bertalanffy, 1968). Family approaches view the family as a basic social system consisting of individuals and the processes that characterize family relationships (e.g., roles, rules for behaviour) that are reciprocally interdependent. Family systems develop communication patterns and repeat behavioural sequences to regulate members and maintain equilibrium (i.e., homoeostasis). Substance abuse is conceptualized as a maladaptive behaviour that serves an important function in the family system, allowing the family to cope with stressors or maintain the system organization (Stanton, Todd, & Associates, 1982). For example, the attention required to cope with adolescent drug abuse may allow the family to avoid marital conflict or could reflect an inability to cope with the drug user's transition from childhood into adolescence.

Several distinct theoretical models have developed within the field of family therapy. Family systems theory provides an important conceptual basis for each of these models. Behavioural family therapy relies on operant and social learning theories to understand individual behaviour in the context of the family. Substance use is viewed as a pattern of responses learned in the context of social interactions (e.g., observing parents and peers) and established as a result of environmental contingencies, such as family-related consequences (Bry, 1988). The Functional Family Therapy model (FFT; Barton & Alexander, 1981) integrates family systems and cognitive-behavioural theories with the assumption that family members and their behaviours are mutually interdependent and that the meaning of behaviour resides in the context of relationships. FFT includes a motivational component and a systematic analysis of relational intimacy-distancing functions that guides the application of behavioural treatment techniques. Ecological models, such as multisystemic (MST; Henggeler et al., 1998) and multidimensional (MDFT; Liddle & Hogue, 2001) family therapies, emphasize intervening with extrafamilial social systems, such as the school and juvenile justice system. These approaches conceptualize substance use as deriving from sources of influence within the context of multiple systems inside and outside the family.

Family therapy is aimed at restructuring the interactional patterns associated with substance abuse, theoretically making the abuse unnecessary for the maintenance of system functioning. Treatment techniques include: (1) forming a therapeutic relationship (i.e., joining) which elicits recurring behavioural sequences (i.e., enactment) while destabilizing the dysfunctional behavioural exchanges, (2) helping family members to view their behaviour as interrelated and gain a perspective consistent with change (e.g., reframing), (3) restructuring interaction patterns and establishing new behaviours, and (4) intervening with multiple systems (cf. Stanton, Todd, & Associates, 1982; Szapocznik et al., 1983).

Treatment Outcome for Family Therapy Interventions

In the last decade, considerable advances have been made in family therapy research and evidence is mounting in support of the efficacy of family therapy for adolescent alcohol and drug abuse (Liddle & Dakof, 1995; Ozechowski & Liddle, 2000). Much of the impetus for family therapy research can be attributed to the pivotal work of Stanton, Todd, and Associates (1982) and to Szapocznik and his colleagues (Scopetta et al., 1979; Szapocznik et al., 1983, 1986), who conducted the first systematic studies of family therapy. Since these early investigations, nearly a dozen randomized trials of family therapy outcome have been completed or are underway. Recent reviews of the empirical support for family treatments (Liddle & Dakof, 1995; Ozechowski & Liddle, 2000; Waldron, 1997) have reported remarkable consistency with regard to findings in support of family-based interventions for substance-abusing youth.

Research has supported integrative models such as functional (Barton & Alexander, 1981), multisystemic (Henggeler et al., 1998), and multidimensional (Liddle et al., 2001) family therapies that combine elements of both systems and behavioural approaches. Family therapy has been found to be particularly successful with treatment engagement (Friedman, 1989). An early study by Scopetta et al. (1979) investigated whether family interventions are more beneficial if they are ecologically focused or whether intervention with the family is sufficient. A multisystems intervention was compared to family therapy alone. No differences between approaches were found, with both producing marked substance use reductions.

Research supports the efficacy of family therapy over process-oriented, supportive group therapy for substance-abusing youth. Joanning et al. (1992) found that family therapy was more effective than a process-oriented group therapy or family drug education in decreasing youth drug use and problem behaviours. Azrin et al. (1994) found that behavioural family therapy produced greater than 50% reductions in drug and alcohol use, whereas increases in use were found for a process-oriented group. Donohue and Azrin (2001) found a similar outcome when comparing behavioural family therapy to a problem-solving intervention.

Comparisons of ecologically based family therapy to alternative interventions have provided evidence supporting family therapy. As discussed above, Liddle and his colleagues (2001) compared the ecologically based multidimensional family therapy (MDFT), an intervention developed specifically for adolescent substance abusers, to a multifamily psychoeducational group and an adolescent CBT group intervention. Substance use reductions were found for all three treatments. Youth in family therapy had the highest levels of improvement and higher levels of retention in treatment. In another study, adolescents participating in MDFT and CBT evidenced significant decreases in substance use through a 12-month follow-up, although improvement appeared to continue after family therapy compared to some levelling off in substance-use reductions for the CBT intervention after the 6-month follow-up (Liddle et al., 2003).

In a study with substance-abusing juvenile delinquents, Henggeler et al. (1998) found that youth in multisystemic family therapy significantly reduced their substance use and had better overall outcomes than those in treatment-as-usual community services. The four-site Cannabis Youth Treatment trial (Dennis et al., 2003), presented above, provided evidence supporting the efficacy of multidimensional family therapy and several other interventions. All five treatments led to significant reductions in cannabis use and maintenance of change over 12 months. A clinical trial by Waldron and her colleagues (2001), discussed above, comparing functional family therapy (FFT; Barton & Alexander, 1981) to individual and group CBT therapy provided support for FFT and group CBT interventions. Significant reductions in substance use were found at the four-month follow-up, and maintained at 19 months, for youth who participated in family therapy.

Ozechowski and Liddle (2000) reviewed 12 clinical trials and all reported significant pre- to post-treatment improvement. In seven of the studies reviewed, family therapy was found to be more effective in reducing substance use than an individual CBT, group, and family psychoeducational interventions. Benefits of treatment were retained 6 to 12 months following treatment in 6 of the 7 studies. Additionally, in five of six studies reviewed by Williams, Chang, and colleagues (2000), family therapy was superior to other outpatient treatments. The trials support integrative, behavioural, and ecologically based family therapy models.

PHARMACOTHERAPY FOR SUBSTANCE ABUSE AND DEPENDENCE

While pharmacotherapy has become increasingly common in the treatment of adult substance abuse and dependence, the use of medications to treat children and adolescents remains controversial. Mechanisms for pharmacological treatments of substance abuse include treatments that make drug use aversive, provide an alternative substitute, block the reinforcing effects, relieve craving or withdrawal, and address comorbid disorders (Kaminer, 1994, 2001). The addictive properties and cardiotoxicity of medications must be evaluated and an assessment for depression, suicidality, and the likelihood for compliance is highly recommended. Additionally, the potential abusability of medications is an important consideration for substance-abusing youth.

Adolescents commonly use a variety of substances, and pharmacotherapy research is lacking on the treatment of youth polysubstance abuse (cf. Kaminer, 2001). Nevertheless, no evidence suggests that adolescents should be treated differently from adults. Kaminer (2001) has suggested that adult practice guidelines be followed for detoxification. No specific contraindications exist for nicotine gum or patches, heroin substitutes, methylphenidate or other stimulants for cocaine abuse (Kaminer, 1994) or substitution of methadone for heroin when detoxification is contraindicated. Disulfiram (Antabuse) is inappropriate because youth alcohol use is characterized by episodic binges and non-compliance can be medically dangerous.

The most common pharmacotherapy for adolescent substance abusers is the use of psychoactive medications to treat symptoms or disorders coexisting with the abuse. Deas and Thomas (2001) cite two controlled clinical trials: A double blind study by Geller and colleagues of lithium versus placebo in youth with bipolar disorder found fewer positive urine drug screens in the lithium group. Ten depressed adolescents participating in a CBT group were randomly assigned to Sertraline or a placebo. Both groups significantly decreased their drinking. While substance-abusing adolescents may benefit from pharmacotherapy, the main concern has been the lack of any empirical attention and future research is clearly needed on the safety and efficacy of medications for treating adolescent substance abuse (cf. Kaminer, 2001).

OTHER TREATMENTS

Drug court has become increasingly popular in the juvenile justice system. Youth are monitored through probation, drug urinalysis, and are required to participate in 12-Step or other interventions. To date, there is no research to support the effectiveness of such interventions beyond drug court completion with youth, and evaluations of effectiveness with adults have indicated mixed findings (Vito & Tewksbury, 1998).

School-based programs are common for both the prevention and treatment of adolescent substance use. Studies have provided preliminary support for Student Assistance Programs in the schools (Wagner, Kortlander, & Morris, 2001), and there is increasing diversity in school-based treatments including several of the models discussed above.

Residential treatment, based upon the therapeutic community model, typically involves six months to two years in a structured living environment. Treatment, commonly provided by paraprofessionals, promotes the acquisition of adaptive personal and social behaviours. One review found a median 75% dropout rate

(Williams, Chang, & colleagues, 2000). Jainchill, Bhattacharya, and Yagelka (1995) and Jainchill (1997) reviewed six programs in nine locations and found 44% of treatment completers had significant use reductions at six-month follow-up (as cited in Muck et al., 2001). While some youth appear to benefit, few appear to complete residential treatment.

Summary

Strong empirical support exists in the literature for the efficacy of family therapy for adolescent substance abuse (Liddle & Dakof, 1995; Ozechowski & Liddle, 2000; Waldron, 1998; Stanton & Shadish, 1997). Findings regarding group interventions have been mixed, and most studies have supported the efficacy of cognitive-behavioural group interventions. However, studies on process-oriented groups have shown a range of findings, from iatrogenic effects to benefits similar to other interventions. Research has provided modest support for the efficacy of individual CBT. Further research is needed on traditional, pharmacological, and other interventions before conclusions can be drawn regarding their effectiveness.

Consistent with literature reviews (Catalano et al., 1990–91; Deas & Thomas, 2001; Waldron & Kaminer, in press; Muck et al., 2001; Williams, Chang, & colleagues, 2000; Winters, 1999), the results show that outpatient family and CBT treatments can be effective in reducing adolescent substance use. In many trials, youth in family therapy reported more rapid substance use reductions than those in CBT, suggesting that family therapy may be particularly helpful in producing rapid change. However, despite advances in model development and clinical trials, none of the interventions sufficiently addressed the adolescents' problems. Relapse was a consistent problem across studies, and a significant percentage of youth needed intervention in the year following treatment. The single best predictor of 12-month outcomes was not baseline client characteristics or treatment components, but whether the adolescent initially responded to treatment at three months.

EMERGING EVIDENCE AND FUTURE DIRECTIONS

Further research is needed to examine the mechanisms of change associated with outcomes for family therapy and CBT models. In addition, the identification of intervention components that are most important for changing different targeted behaviours could be helpful in matching treatments to individual needs. Additional research is also needed on group-based treatment modalities to identify the conditions under which these treatments are most likely to be beneficial or detrimental. As noted by Williams, Chang, and colleagues (2000), trials are needed to compare the efficacy of the major treatment modalities (i.e., inpatient versus outpatient treatment, short-term inpatient versus long-term residential).

Most efficacy research focuses on substance use reductions despite the common coexistence of multiple problem behaviours in adolescents, such as polysubstance abuse, high-risk sexual behaviours, school failure, and illegal activity. There is an important need for the development of interventions that target multiple-risk behaviours and studies that assess multiple outcomes. Due to adolescents' rapid development of dependence (Deas et al., 2000), additional research is also needed on assessment and early intervention to recognize the early symptoms of substance abuse.

Relapse remains a common problem following treatment, even with those interventions identified as the most effective, and studies are beginning to identify youth who are at greatest risk for relapse (Latimer et al., 2000). Emerging findings are pointing to the role of tobacco and alcohol in relapse following drug treatment. Investigations are needed to improve treatment strategies that target the risk and protective factors associated with relapse. Aftercare programs show promise and studies are needed to evaluate their ability to increase the durability of behaviour change following treatment. In summary, researchers have made great strides in the identification and development of promising interventions for adolescent substance abuse and dependence, yet much work remains to be done to improve outcomes and their durability over time.

REFERENCES

Abrams, D.B., Carey, K.B., Monti, P.M., & Niaura, R.S. (1986). Understanding relapse and recovery in alcohol abuse. *Annals of Behavioral Medicine*, **8**, 27–32.

Azrin, N.H., Donohue, B., Besalel, V.A., Kogan, E.S., & Acierno, R. (1994). Youth drug abuse treatment: A controlled outcome study. *Journal of Child and Adolescent Substance Abuse*, **3**, 1–16.

Bailey, G.W. (1989). Current perspectives on substance use in youth. *Journal of the American Academy of Child and Adolescent Psychiatry*, **28**, 151–162.

Barton, C., & Alexander, J.F. (1981). Functional family therapy. In A.S. Gurman & D.P. Kniskern (Eds), *Handbook of family therapy* (pp. 403–443). New York: Brunner/Mazel.

Bandura, A. (1977). *Social learning theory*. Englewood Cliffs, NJ: Prentice Hall.

Baumrind, D. (1985). Familial antecedents of adolescent drug use: A developmental perspective. In C.L. Jones & R.J. Battjes (Eds), *Etiology of drug abuse: Implications for prevention* (pp. 13–44). National Institute on Drug Abuse Research Monograph 56. Rockville, MD: DHHS.

Bentler, P.M. (1992). Etiologies and consequences of adolescent drug use: Implications for prevention. *Journal of Addictive Diseases*, **11**, 47–61.

Bertalanffy, L. von (1968). *General systems theory: Foundation, development, applications*. New York: Braziller.

Bry, B.H. (1988). Family-based approaches to reducing adolescent substance use: Theories, techniques and findings. In E.R. Rahdert & J. Grabowski (Eds), *Adolescent drug abuse: Analyses of treatment research* (pp. 39–68). National Institute on Drug Abuse Research Monograph 77. Rockville, MD: DHHS.

Catalano, R.F., Hawkins, J.D., Wells, E.A., Miller, J., & Brewer, D. (1990–91). Evaluation of the effectiveness of adolescent drug abuse treatment, assessment of risks for relapse, and promising approaches for relapse prevention. *The International Journal of the Addictions*, **25**, 1085–1140.

Craig, R.J. (1993). Contemporary trends in substance abuse. *Professional Psychology: Research and Practice*, **24**, 182–189.

Deas, D., & Thomas, S.E. (2001). An overview of controlled studies of adolescent substance abuse treatment. *The American Journal on Addictions*, **10**, 178–189.

Deas, D., Riggs, P., Langenbucher, J., Goldman, M., & Brown, S. (2000). Adolescents are not adults: Developmental considerations in alcohol users. *Alcoholism: Clinical and Experimental Research*, **24**, 232–237.

Dennis, M.L., Funk, R., Godley, M.D., Godley, S.H., & Waldron, H.B. (in press). Measuring peak alcohol use among adolescents entering residential treatment: A comparison of estimates from the Form-90 and GAIN-1. *Addiction*.

Dennis, M.L. et al. (2003). Main findings of the Cannabis Youth Treatment (CYT) randomized field experiment. Manuscript submitted.

Dishion, T.J., McCord, J., & Poulin, F. (1999). When interventions harm: Peer groups and problem behaviour. *American Psychologist*, **54**, 755–764.

Dishion, T.J., Poulin, F., & Barraston, B. (2001). Peer group dynamics associated with iatrogenic effects in group interventions with high-risk young adolescents. *New Directions for Child and Adolescent Development*, **91**, 79–92.

Donohue, B., & Azrin, N. (2001). Family behaviour therapy. In E.F. Wagner & H.B. Waldron (Eds), *Innovations in adolescent substance abuse interventions* (pp. 205–227). Oxford: Elsevier Science.

Donovan, J.E., & Jessor, R. (1985). Structure of problem behaviour in adolescence and young adulthood. *Journal of Consulting and Clinical Psychology*, **56**, 890–904.

Friedman, A.S. (1989). Family therapy vs. Parent groups: Effects on adolescent drug abusers. *The American Journal of Family Therapy*, **17**, 335–347.

Godley, S.H., Godley, M.D., & Dennis, M.L. (2001). The assertive aftercare protocol for adolescent substance abusers. In E.F. Wagner & H.B. Waldron (Eds), *Innovations in adolescent substance abuse interventions* (pp. 313–331). Oxford: Elsevier Science.

Hawkins, J.D., Catalano, R.F., & Miller, J.Y. (1992). Risk and protective factors for alcohol and other drug problems in adolescence and early adulthood: Implications for substance abuse prevention. *Psychological Bulletin*, **112**, 64–105.

Henggeler, S.W., Schoenwald, S.K., Borduin, C.M., Rowland, M.D., & Cunningham, P.B. (1998). *Multisystemic treatment of antisocial behaviour in children and adolescents*. New York: Guilford Press.

Henggeler, S.W., Schoenwald, S.K., Liao, J.G., Letourneau, E.J., & Edwards, D.L. (2002). Transporting efficacious treatments to field settings: The link between supervisory practices and therapists fidelity in MST programs. *Journal of Clinical Child Psychology*, **31** (2), 155–167.

Jainchill, N. (1997). Therapeutic communities for adolescents: The same and not the same. In G. DeLeon (Ed.), *Community as method: Therapeutic communities for special populations and special settings* (pp. 161–177). New York: Praeger.

Jainchill, N., Bhattacharya, G., & Yagelka, J. (1995). Therapeutic communities for adolescents. In E. Rahdert & D. Czechowicz (Eds), *NIDA research monograph 156, Adolescent drug abuse: Clinical assessment and therapeutic interventions* (NIH Publication No. 95-3908, pp. 190–217). Rockville, MD: National Institute on Drug Abuse.

Joanning, H., Thomas, F., Quinn, W., & Mullen, R. (1992). Treating adolescent drug abuse: A comparison of family systems therapy, group therapy, and family drug education. *Journal of Marital and Family Therapy*, **18**, 345–356.

Johnston, L.D., O'Malley, P.M., & Bachman, J.G. (2000). *Monitoring the Future: National survey results on drug use, 1975–2000. Volume I: Secondary school students*. NIH Publication No. 01-4924. Bethesda, MD: National Institute on Drug Abuse.

Johnston, L.D., O'Malley, P.M., & Bachman, J.G. (2001). *Monitoring the Future: National survey results on drug use, 1975–2000. Volume I: Secondary school students*. NIH Publication No. 01-4924. Bethesda, MD: National Institute on Drug Abuse.

Kadden, R.M., Cooney, N.L., Getter, H., & Litt, M.B. (1989). Matching alcoholics to coping skills or interactional therapies: Posttreatment results. *Journal of Consulting and Clinical Psychology*, **57**, 698–704.

Kaminer, Y. (1994). *Adolescent substance abuse: A comprehensive guide to theory and practice*. New York: Plenum.

Kaminer, Y. (2001). Psychopharmacological therapy. In E.F. Wagner & H.B. Waldron (Eds), *Innovations in adolescent substance abuse interventions* (pp. 285–311). Oxford: Elsevier Science.

Kaminer, Y., & Burleson, J. (1999). Psychotherapies for adolescent substance abusers: 15-month follow-up. *American Journal of Addictions*, **8**, 114–119.

Kaminer, Y., Burleson, J., & Goldberger, R. (2002). Psychotherapies for adolescent substance abusers: Short- and long-term outcomes. *Journal of Nervous and Mental Disease*, **190**, 737–745.

Kassel, J.D., & Jackson, S.I. (2001). Twelve-step-based interventions for adolescents. In E.F. Wagner & H.B. Waldron (Eds), *Innovations in adolescent substance abuse interventions* (pp. 333–351). Oxford: Elsevier Science.

Kennedy, B.P., & Minami, M. (1993). The Beech Hill Hospital/Outward Bound adolescent chemical dependency treatment program. *Journal of Substance Abuse Treatment*, **10**, 395–406.

Kern-Jones, S., Waldron, H.B., Brody, J.L., Turner, C.W., & Peterson, T.R. (August, 2001). *Treatment efficacy and clinical significance of substance use reductions*. Paper presented at the 2001 American Psychological Association Annual Convention, San Francisco.

Kouzis, A.C., & Labouvie, E.W. (1992). Use intensity, functional elaboration, and contextual constraint as facets of adolescent alcohol and marijuana use. *Psychology of Addictive Behaviours*, **6**, 188–195.

Kownacki, R.J., & Shadish, W.R. (1999). Does Alcoholics Anonymous work? The results from a meta-analysis of controlled experiments. *Substance Use and Misuse*, **34**, 1897–1916.

Latimer, W.W., Winters, K.C., Stinchfield, R., & Traver, R.E. (2000). Demographic, individual, and interpersonal predictors of adolescent alcohol and marijuana use following treatment. *Psychology of Addictive Behaviours*, **14**, 162–173.

Liddle, H.A., & Dakof, G.A. (1995). Efficacy of family therapy for drug abuse: Promising but not definitive. *Journal of Marital and Family Therapy*, **21**, 511–543.

Liddle, H.A., & Hogue, A. (2001). Multidimensional family therapy for adolescent substance abuse. In E.F. Wagner & H.B. Waldron (Eds), *Innovations in adolescent substance abuse interventions* (pp. 229–261). Oxford: Elsevier Science.

Liddle, H.A., Dakof, G.A., Parker, G.S., Diamond, G.S., Barrett, K., & Tejeda, M. (2001). Multidimensional family therapy for adolescent substance abuse: Results of a randomized clinical trial. *American Journal of Drug and Alcohol Abuse*, **27**, 651–688.

Liddle, H.A., Dakof, G.A., Turner, R.M., & Tejeda, M. (2003). Treating adolescent substance abuse: A comparison of individual and family therapy interventions. Manuscript submitted for publication.

Marlatt, G.A., & Gordon, J.R. (Eds) (1985). *Relapse prevention: Maintenance strategies in the treatment of addictive behaviors*. New York: Guilford.

McGee, L., & Newcomb, M.D. (1992). General deviance syndrome: Expanded hierarchical evaluations at four ages from early adolescence to adulthood. *Journal of Consulting and Clinical Psychology*, **60**, 766–776.

Miller, W.R., & Heather, N. (1998). *Treating Addictive Behaviors*. New York: Plenum.

Montgomery, H.A., Tonigan, S., & Miller, W.R. (1993). Differences among AA groups: Implications for research. *Journal of Studies on Alcohol*, **54**, 502–504.

Monti, P.M., Abrams, D.B., Kadden, R.M., & Cooney, N.L. (1989). *Treating Alcohol Dependence: A coping skills guide*. New York: Guilford.

Muck, R., Zempolich, K.A., Titus, J.C., Fishman, M., Godley, M.D., & Schwebel, R. (2001). An overview of the effectiveness of adolescent substance abuse treatment models. *Youth and Society*, **33**, 143–168.

Newcomb, M.D., & Felix-Ortiz, M. (1992). Multiple protective and risk factors for drug use and abuse: Cross-sectional and prospective findings. *Journal of Personality and Social Psychology*, **63**, 280–296.

Ozechowski, T.J., & Liddle, H.A. (2000). Family-based therapy for adolescent drug abuse: Knowns and unknowns. *Clinical Child and Family Psychology Review*, **3**, 269–298.

Raveis, V.H., & Kandel, D.B. (1987). Changes in drug behaviour from middle to late twenties: Initiation, persistence, and cessation of use. *American Journal of Public Health*, **77**, 607–611.

Schoenwald, S.K., & Henggeler, S.W. (2002). Mental health services research and family-based treatment: Bridging the gap. In H.A. Liddle & D.A. Santisteban (Eds), *Family psychology: Science-based interventions* (pp. 259–282). Washington, DC: American Psychological Association.

Scopetta, M.A., King, O.E., Szapocznik, J., & Tillman, W. (1979). *Ecological structural family therapy with Cuban immigrant families*. Report to the National Institute on Drug Abuse: Grant #H81DA 01696.

Selekman, M.D., & Todd, T.C. (1991). *Family therapy approaches with adolescent substance abusers*. Needham Heights, MA: Allyn & Bacon.

Shedler, J., & Block, J. (1990). Adolescent drug use and psychological health: A longitudinal inquiry. *American Psychologist*, **45**, 612–630.

Stanton, M.D., & Shadish, W.R. (1997). Outcome, attrition, and family/couples treatment for drug abuse: A review of the controlled, comparative studies. *Psychological Bulletin*, **122**, 170–191.

Stanton, M.D., Todd, T.C., & Associates (1982). *The family therapy of drug abuse and addiction*. New York: Guilford Press.

Szapocznik, J., & Williams, R.A. (2000). Brief Strategic Family Therapy: Twenty-five years of interplay among theory, research and practice in adolescent behaviour problems and drug abuse. *Clinical Child and Family Psychology Review*, **3** (2), 117–134.

Szapocznik, J., Kurtines, W.M., Foote, F.H., Perez-Vidal, A., & Hervis, O. (1983). Conjoint versus one-person family therapy: Some evidence for the effectiveness of conducting family therapy through one person. *Journal of Consulting and Clinical Psychology*, **51**, 889–899.

Szapocznik, J., Kurtines, W.M., Foote, F.H., Perez-Vidal, A., & Hervis, O. (1986). Conjoint versus one-person family therapy: Further evidence for the effectiveness of conducting family therapy through one person with drug-abusing adolescents. *Journal of Consulting and Clinical Psychology*, **54**, 395–397.

Vito, G.F., & Tewksbury, R.A. (1998). The impact of treatment: the Jefferson County (Kentucky) drug court program. *Federal Probation*, **62**, 46–51.

Wagner, E.F., & Waldron, H. (Eds) (2001). *Innovations in adolescent substance abuse interventions*. New York: Pergamon.

Wagner, E.F., Brown, S.A., Monti, P.M., Myers, M.B., & Waldron, H.B. (1999). Innovations in adolescent substance abuse intervention. *Alcoholism: Clinical and Experimental Research*, **23**, 236–249.

Wagner, E.F., Kortlander, E., & Morris, S.L. (2001). The Teen Intervention Project: A school-based intervention for adolescents with substance use problems. In E.F. Wagner & H.B. Waldron (Eds), *Innovations in adolescent substance abuse interventions* (pp. 189–203). Oxford: Elsevier Science.

Waldron, H.B. (1997). Adolescent substance abuse and family therapy outcome: A review of randomized trials. In T.H. Ollendick & R.J. Prinz (Eds), *Advances in clinical child psychology* (vol. 19; pp. 199–234). New York: Plenum.

Waldron, H.B. (1998). Adolescent substance abuse disorders. In A. Bellack & M. Hersen (Eds), *Comprehensive clinical psychology. Vol. 5: Children and adolescents: Clinical formulation and treatment* (pp. 539–563). Elsevier Science.

Waldron, H.B., & Kaminer, Y. (in press). On the learning curve: The emerging evidence supporting cognitive-behavioural therapies for adolescent substance abuse. *Addiction*.

Waldron, H.R., Slesnick, N., Brody, J.L., Turner, C.W., & Peterson, T.R. (2001). Treatment outcomes for adolescent substance abuse at 4- and 7-month assessments. *Journal of Consulting and Clinical Psychology*, **69**, 802–813.

Williams, R.J., Chang, S.Y., & Addiction Centre Adolescent Research Group (2000). A comprehensive and comparative review of adolescent substance abuse treatment outcome. *Clinical Psychology: Science and Practice*, **7**, 138–166.

Winters, K.C. (1999). Treating adolescents with substance use disorders: An overview of practice issues and treatment outcome. *Substance Abuse*, **20**, 203–225.

Winters, K.C., Latimer, W.W., & Stinchfield, R. (1999). Adolescent treatment. In P.J. Ott, R.E. Tarter, & R.T. Ammerman (Eds), *Sourcebook on substance abuse: Etiology, epidemiology, assessment, and treatment*. Boston: Allyn & Bacon.

Winters, K.C., Latimer, W.W., & Stinchfield, R. (2001). Assessing adolescent substance use. In E.F. Wagner & H.B. Waldron (Eds), *Innovations in adolescent substance abuse interventions* (pp. 1–29). Oxford: Elsevier Science.

CHAPTER 15

Treatment of ADHD in Children and Adolescents

Karen C. Wells

Duke University Medical Center, USA

INTRODUCTION

Attention Deficit Hyperactivity Disorder (ADHD) is one of the most common and impairing of the childhood psychological disorders. Two recent epidemiological studies, conducted in the Great Smoky Mountains, as well as in four US communities (Atlanta, Georgia; New Haven, Connecticut; West Chester, New York; and San Juan, Puerto Rico) using independently administered, structured diagnostic interviews indicate that between 3% and 5% of youth meet the criteria for ADHD (Angold et al., 2000; Jensen et al., 1999). This means that at least one child in virtually every classroom in America is affected by this disorder. Data from the National Ambulatory Medical Care Survey indicated a 2.3% increase in the rate of office-based visits documenting a diagnosis of ADHD from 1990 to 1995 and a 2.9% increase in the rate of ADHD patients prescribed stimulant medication (2 million visits in 1995) (Hoagwood et al., 2000; Robison et al., 1999). Other recent studies indicate that ADHD is both under-diagnosed (i.e., some children who meet independently assessed diagnostic criteria do not receive the diagnosis in practice) and over-diagnosed (i.e., some children who do not meet independently assessed diagnostic criteria nevertheless are given the diagnosis in practice). In two of these, only 12–25% of independently assessed children who met criteria for diagnosis of ADHD received treatment (Jensen et al., 1999; Wolraich et al., 1998), whereas, in another recent study, the rate of stimulant treatment was almost twice the rate of parent-reported ADHD and the majority of stimulant-treated children did not meet diagnostic criteria for ADHD (Angold et al., 2000). The prevalence of ADHD tends to peak in middle childhood and to occur more frequently in lower SES groups.

Correspondence to Karen C. Wells, PO Box 3320, Duke University Medical Centre, Durham NC 27710; email: wells020@mc.duke.edu

Handbook of Interventions that Work with Children and Adolescents: Prevention and Treatment.
Edited by P.M. Barrett and T.H. Ollendick. © 2004 John Wiley & Sons, Ltd. ISBN 0-470-84453-1.

Cardinal Features

ADHD has a long and controversial history with many iterations in the psychiatric nosology with regard to labels used to describe the disorder as well as theories regarding its aetiology and primary deficits (Conners & Erhardt, 1998). However, clinical descriptions of the disorder have remained remarkably stable with regard to what are now considered its cardinal features (Inattention, Hyperactivity, Impulsivity) (APA, 1994). In the current version of the *Diagnostic and Statistical Manual of Psychiatric Disorders* (DSM-IV), there are three subtypes of the disorder: ADHD, Predominantly Inattentive Type; ADHD, Predominantly Hyperactive-Impulsive Type and ADHD-Combined Type (a combination of inattentive and hyperactive-impulsive symptoms). Validity of the distinction between the inattentive subtype and combined subtype can be found in studies of family history, gender distribution, neuropsychology and response to treatment (Hinshaw, 1994).

COMORBIDITY

In addition to its central features, ADHD is usually associated with one or more comorbid conditions, associated features or functional deficits, or combination of these, which add to the impairment picture and complicate the assessment and treatment strategy. Impairment from the central symptoms must be present in two or more settings, and clinically significant impairment in social, academic or occupational functioning is necessary to make the diagnosis (APA, 1994). Furthermore, despite the early prevailing view that ADHD was a time-limited disorder of pre-puberty, prospective studies on psychiatric clinic samples have revealed ADHD to be a chronic disorder in a substantial majority of children who receive the diagnosis, with antisocial outcomes, substance abuse, and continued attentional, family, interpersonal, and occupational difficulties persisting into adolescence and adulthood (Klein & Manuzza, 1991; Weiss & Hechtman, 1993).

The central symptoms of ADHD carry implications for treatment as there are now hundreds of treatment studies demonstrating the efficacy of stimulant medications on core symptoms (Greenhill & Ford, 2002; Spencer et al., 1996). In addition, the comorbid and associated conditions that add to the clinical complexity of ADHD have significant implications for both medication and psychosocial treatments. Chief among the complicating comorbid conditions are Oppositional Defiant Disorder (35–60% of ADHD cases in clinical and epidemiological samples); Conduct Disorder (30–50% of ADHD cases); Specific Learning Disabilities (10–26% of ADHD cases when conservative estimates of LD are employed); and Anxiety (25–40% of ADHD cases) (Barkley, 1996; Biederman, Faraone, & Lapey, 1992; Hinshaw, 1992; Conners & Erhardt, 1998). Demographic findings across several studies indicate that the disorder is predominantly a male disorder with male to female ratios in the 3:1 to 10:1 range.

Associated Features: School

Within the school domain, the vast majority of ADHD children have significant problems with school behaviour and performance, as noted by low rates of on-task behaviour in the classroom (Abikoff, Gittelman-Klein, & Klein, 1977), academic task completion (Pfiffner & Barkley, 1990) and low rates of positive exchanges with teachers and higher rates of negativity (Whalen, Henker, & Dotemoto, 1980). These patterns of behaviour contribute to high rates of academic underachievement, placement in special education services, grade retention and school dropout (Barkley, DuPaul, & McMurray, 1990; Barkley et al., 1990; Hinshaw, 1992). More than half of ADHD children may require tutoring, nearly one-third are retained at least one grade in school, and nearly one-third are placed in some form of special education setting. Negative school outcomes can occur even in the absence of a learning disability.

Associated Features: Family

Within the family domain, the parent–child interactions of ADHD children and adolescents with their mothers and fathers are frequently disturbed and conflictual, and family life is often characterized by discord and disharmony. Children with ADHD are less compliant to their parents' instructions, sustain their compliance for shorter time periods, are less likely to remain on task and display more "negative'" behaviour than their normal, same age counterparts. In what Johnston (1996) labelled a "negative-reactive" response pattern, mothers and fathers of ADHD children display more directive, commanding behaviour, more disapproval, less rewards that are contingent on the child's prosocial and compliant behaviours, and more overall negative behaviour than the parents of normal children (Anderson, Hinshaw, & Simmel, 1994; Barkley, Karlsson, & Pollard, 1985; Befera & Barkley, 1984; Cunningham & Barkley, 1979; Mash & Johnston, 1982; Tallmadge & Barkley, 1983).

Studies with ADHD adolescents and their parents show continuation of elevated levels of negative interactions, angry conflicts, and less positive and facilitative behaviour toward each other, relative to normal adolescents and their families (Barkley et al., 1991, 1992; Edwards et al., 2001). Elevated rates of reciprocal, negative behaviours characterize these teen–parent interactions.

Family life is characterized by more parenting stress and a decreased sense of parenting self-competence (Fischer, 1990; Mash & Johnston, 1990; Podolski & Nigg, 2001; Whalen & Henker, 1999), more parent alcohol consumption (Pelham & Lang, 1993, 1999), increased rates of maternal depression and marital conflict, separation, and divorce (Befera & Barkley, 1984; Barkley et al., 1990, 1991). Although the presence of comorbid ODD is associated with much of the parent–child interactional conflicts and stress in ADHD families (Barkley et al., 1992; Podolski & Nigg, 2001), parents and youth with ADHD alone still display interactions that are deviant from normal (Fletcher et al., 1996; Johnston, 1996; Johnston & Mash, 2001).

Recent evidence from longitudinal studies suggests that for some ADHD youth, dysfunctions in parenting may play a role in the origins of ADHD (Campbell, 1994;

Carlson, Jacobvitz, & Sroufe, 1995; Pierce, Ewing, & Campbell, 1999). In addition, the careful, systematic work of Patterson and his colleagues has clearly documented the aetiologic significance of disrupted parenting in childhood aggression and oppositional behaviour that have high comorbidity rates with ADHD (Dishion & Patterson, 1999; Patterson, Reid, & Dishion, 1992). There is evidence that aggression and other signs of conduct disorder mediate the increased risk for later substance abuse, criminality, and antisocial spectrum disorders in adulthood (Lynskey & Fergusson, 1995; Hinshaw, 1994; Klein & Manuzza, 1991). In addition, high rates of negativity in parent–child interactions are related to dysfunction across domains of function and settings (e.g., Anderson, Hinshaw, & Simmel, 1994).

Associated Features: Peer Relationships

In addition to disrupted school and family functioning, ADHD youth also display impairment in peer relationships. ADHD children are overwhelmingly rejected by their peers (Asarnow, 1988; Bagwell et al., 2001; Erhardt & Hinshaw, 1994). The disturbed peer relations do not appear to be related to non-behavioural variables such as physical attractiveness (Erhardt & Hinshaw, 1994), nor to social skills deficits *per se* (Whalen & Henker, 1992). While behavioural characteristics consistent with ADHD contribute uniquely to poor social functioning (Pope & Bierman, 1999), it is the socially noxious, aggressive, and uncooperative behaviours of ADHD youth that seem most responsible for provoking peer rejection, explaining up to 46% of the variance in negative peer nominations (Erhardt & Hinshaw, 1994). Furthermore, peer rejection of ADHD youth occurs very rapidly (i.e., within minutes or hours of introduction to a peer group) and remains stable across time, even after behavioural improvement (Granger, Whalen, & Henker, 1993), probably due to negative attributions by peers and reputational bias. Some of the peer rejection experienced by ADHD youth may be attributable to comorbid aggression, but even non-aggressive ADHD boys are significantly more rejected than non-aggressive, comparison youth (Hinshaw & Melnick, 1995). Given the strong predictive power of negative peer status for a variety of maladaptive outcomes in adolescence and adulthood (Ollendick et al., 1992; Parker & Asher, 1987) the importance of successful treatment in this domain has been strongly emphasized (Bagwell et al., 2001; Conners & Erhardt, 1998; Hinshaw, 1994).

AETIOLOGY AND TARGETS OF TREATMENT

While theories of aetiology of ADHD abound—including genetic, neurological, environmental, dietary, home environment consistency, and psychosocial factors (Arnold, 2002; Barkley, 1998; Conners & Erhardt, 1998)—there is little agreement in the field on causal mechanisms. Therefore, rather than basing treatments on underlying mechanisms, clinical researchers have tended to develop and evaluate treatments targeted at the clinical and prognostic characteristics of the syndrome, its symptoms, comorbidities, functional impairments and long-term risk factors, identified in the empirical literature and reviewed above. Thus, the evidence-based literature on treatment has focused primarily on psychopharmacology (usually the stimulant medications), on parenting and family interventions, on school-based intervention, and, to a lesser extent thus far, on peer interventions. The assumption has been that treatments that target the core symptoms of ADHD, as well as aggression, coercive family interactions, poor peer relations, and academic deficits and failure, will have the greatest chance of reducing the present clinical impairment(s), as well as the long-term outcome for youth who suffer from this disorder (Wells et al., 2000b).

ASSESSMENT AND TREATMENT PLANNING

Before discussing evidence-based treatment of ADHD, it is important briefly to consider assessment. While a comprehensive review of ADHD assessment is well beyond the scope of this chapter, treatment cannot proceed until an adequate and thorough assessment has taken place. The goal of assessment should be a careful diagnosis of ADHD as well as possible comorbid diagnoses, and other impairments in the family, school, and social domains since all of these have implications for treatment and prognosis. Multiple methods of assessment exist involving multiple informants (youth, parent, and teacher) across multiple settings (school, home). These include interviews, rating scales, psychological and performance tests, direct observational procedures, and medical evaluations, and the reader is referred to recent reviews of this literature and clinical recommendations (Anastopoulos & Shelton, 2001; Conners & Jett, 2001). Once assessment has occurred, and in the absence of empirical literature on matching patient characteristics to treatments in ADHD (Wells, 2001), clinicians may proceed on a rational basis by assigning evidence-based treatments that logically address symptom and impairment domains (e.g., Parent Management Training for parent–child interaction conflicts).

Issues of treatment palatability and acceptability by patients, parents, and schools, as well as side-effects monitoring, must be taken into account in designing and implementing treatment plans. These vary for medication and psychosocial treatments and may dictate which treatment(s) are implemented or in what order. While large group studies show that stimulant medication is more effective for core symptoms than behaviour therapy (MTA Cooperative Group, 1999a), some patients and parents may have negative feelings about medication. For example, in two large-scale clinical trials, 21% and 15% of potential participants either declined entry into the study because they did not want medication, or once in the study refused medication (Hechtman & Abikoff, 1995; MTA Cooperative Group, 1999b). Such families may wish to try behaviour therapy before considering drug treatment.

Other results of recent large-scale trials may also guide more refined treatment recommendations. For example, because a lower dose is needed to achieve a positive outcome when medication is combined with behaviour therapy than when medication is used alone (MTA Cooperative Group, 1999a), some patients and parents (especially those with negative medication side-effects) may wish to start with behaviour therapy and add low-dose medication later. Likewise, this important study (to be discussed in detail later) indicated that youth with ADHD and comorbid anxiety who receive behaviour therapy have equivalent positive effects on ADHD symptoms to ADHD/anxious children who receive medication alone. In addition, in this study, the combination of medication and behaviour therapy was superior to community-based treatment on anxiety/depressive symptoms for this subgroup, whereas medication treatment alone was not (MTA Cooperative Group, 1999a, 1999b). Thus, clinicians treating ADHD/anxious children may wish to recommend behaviour therapy alone, since it will be equally effective as medication on core symptoms. Alternatively, combination (medication plus behaviour therapy) treatment might be recommended, if maximum reduction in the comorbid anxious symptoms is also desirable. Studies such as this illustrate why documenting the comorbidity picture for ADHD children referred for evaluation is important and carries possible treatment implications.

In the final analysis, it is the response of individual ADHD children that is important in clinical practice, and responses of individuals can vary from those predicted by average group effects reported in clinical trials. Therefore, treatments ideally should be implemented sequentially and the effects of each treatment evaluated before adding additional treatments.

EVIDENCE-BASED TREATMENT

Psychopharmacology

The psychostimulant medications for treatment of ADHD are among the most well-researched treatment modalities in all of child psychiatry. Literally hundreds of studies have been conducted, at least 180 of which are placebo-controlled trials. It is clearly beyond the scope of this chapter to review all of these studies in detail and the reader is referred to several comprehensive reviews (Greenhill & Ford, 2002; Spencer et al., 1996) that present tables of the characteristics of individual, randomized, placebo-controlled studies. What follows is a summary of the major findings of the effects of controlled studies of stimulants with ADHD youth. By far, the majority of this research has been conducted with school age pre-pubertal children, usually Caucasian boys. Stimulant treatment studies with girls and with ethnic minority groups are sparse. A handful of studies now exist with adolescents and they will be summarized in a subsequent section.

There are three FDA-approved classes of stimulants in use with ADHD children: the amphetamines (Dexedrine, Adderall, and Dextrostat); the methylphenidates (Ritalin, Ritalin-SR, Ritalin-LA, Focalin, Concerta, Metadate-ER, Metadate-CD, and Methylin); and magnesium pemoline (Cylert). Most research has occurred using the short-acting forms of Dexedrine and Ritalin usually involving twice a day or, more rarely, three times a day dosing. Their onset of action is usually within 30 to 60 minutes of administration, peak clinical effect usually within 1 to 2 hours, and total duration of effects usually 2–5 hours (Spencer, Biederman, & Wilens, 2000). Currently, Ritalin is prescribed for about 88% of cases recognized by physicians whereas Dexedrine is prescribed for about 12% of cases, even though controlled comparisons have not indicated a difference in efficacy (Richters et al., 1995). The newer agents represent slow release, or long-acting preparations or delivery systems and have the advantage of allowing for once a day dosing. A renewal of interest in

ADHD has resulted in very recent evaluations of these newer preparations which appear to be showing positive and similar effects to the older forms (e.g., Wolraich et al., 2001), although individual responsiveness to long-acting forms of Dexedrine and methylphenidate is highly variable (Pelham et al., 1987).

These compounds tend to increase excitatory central nervous system activity in many brain regions (March, Wells, & Conners, 1996), hence the term, psychostimulants (but, it should be noted, the excitation can produce inhibitory effects). Dextroamphetamine and methylphenidate are structurally related to the catecholamines, dopamine and norepinephrine, whereas pemoline acts primarily through dopaminergic mechanisms. Concerns about liver toxicity and fulminant liver failure have resulted in a revision of indications for pemoline such that pemoline, though effective, should not be considered a first-line treatment (Pizzuti, 1996).

Effects of Stimulant Medication

Stimulant medications have large, immediate, salutary effects on a range of primary and comorbid symptoms and some functional domains in ADHD youth. Improvements in core features of motor overactivity, impulsivity, and inattentiveness have been demonstrated in a large number of studies (Spencer et al., 1996). With regard to specific core symptoms, studies have shown beneficial effects on sustained attention and persistence of effort, restlessness, motor activity, attention to assigned classroom tasks, attention during sports play, off-task behaviour, impulsive behaviour, academic productivity, classroom behaviour disturbances, disruptive verbal behaviour and teacher-rated and curriculum-based measures of academic performance (Abikoff & Gittelman, 1984; Barkley, 1977; Carlson et al., 1992; Elia et al., 1991; Milich et al., 1991; Pelham et al., 1991). Effects on laboratory measures of cognitive functions such as vigilance, cognitive impulsivity, reaction time, short-term memory, and learning of verbal and non-verbal material have also been demonstrated (Rapport & Kelly, 1991; Swanson, 1988). However, in spite of demonstrated acute, short-term effects on such classroom relevant symptoms and characteristics of ADHD, studies on enhancement on children's overall academic achievement have so far proved disappointing with little evidence of longer term achievement gains (Klein & Abikoff, 1997; Schachar & Tannock, 1993; Swanson et al., 1995).

Stimulants have also demonstrated positive impact on the social behaviours and interactions of youth with ADHD. Despite early assumptions that stimulant medications would not affect aggressive behaviour, studies conducted over the past decade have indicated positive effects on symptoms associated with ODD and CD (for review see McMahon & Wells, 1998). Reductions in both overt (aggressiveness, non-compliance) and covert (e.g., stealing) antisocial behaviours have been reported (Hinshaw, Heller, & McHale, 1992). In the most recent direct test of stimulant effects on Conduct Disorder and Oppositional Defiant Disorder, Klein et al. (1997) showed that specific symptoms of Conduct Disorder (measured by structured interviews, direct observations and teacher ratings) were reduced by methylphenidate in youth diagnosed with ODD/CD (two-thirds of whom also had ADHD).

In addition to salutary effects on child aggressive behaviours, studies have also shown that the parent–child interactions known to be associated with oppositional behaviour in children are also reduced when the children are treated with stimulant medication (Barkley & Cunningham, 1979; Wells et al., 2000a). Likewise, social interactions with peers show improvements. Stimulant treatment reduces negative verbalizations such as teasing and swearing. Treated youth are less dominating and annoying and initiate fewer negative social interactions with parents and peers. Nevertheless, the reduction in these negative social behaviours seems to be a function of the reductions in the core symptoms of ADHD (impulsivity and aggression) rather than an increase in prosocial skills *per se*. In fact, there may be an increase in social unresponsiveness and social withdrawal with stimulant treatment that may decrease the extent to which youth are liked by their peers (Buhrmester et al., 1992).

Evidence for the effects of stimulant medications on ADHD youth who have comorbid anxiety or depression is less clear cut than the picture for aggression. Spencer et al. (1996) reviewed all existing pediatric studies of ADHD with comorbid anxiety or depression and reported a lesser response to stimulants on ADHD symptoms in this comorbid subgroup compared to ADHD without anxiety in six out of nine studies. However, the effect of stimulants on the comorbid anxiety and depression symptoms was not assessed in any of these studies. In the MTA study (MTA Cooperative Group, 1999a), which did assess anxiety and depressive symptoms in addition to primary ADHD symptoms, the combination treatment group (medication management plus behaviour therapy) produced significantly greater decreases in anxiety and depressive symptoms than a community comparison group whereas medication management alone did not. Based on Spencer et al.'s (1996) review and the results of the MTA study, clinicians may be advised to recommend combination treatment (medication plus behaviour therapy) for ADHD youth who also have comorbid anxiety disorders, if beneficial effects on internalizing symptoms as well as ADHD symptoms are desirable. In addition, March et al. (2000) suggest that because anxiety is successfully treated with cognitive-behaviour therapy (CBT) (in contrast to pure ADHD in which no effects of CBT have been demonstrated), this may be a comorbid subgroup (ADHD plus anxiety) in which CBT should be considered as part of the behavioural treatment package.

Most studies of stimulants in youth are short duration studies (less than three months) and symptoms re-emerge as soon as the medication is withdrawn. Effect sizes for methylphenidate across studies range from 0.7 to 1.3 (Swanson et al., 1993) depending on the dose and outcome parameters. Generally there is a linear dose response effect but some youth display an inverted U response and some will have a threshold response (Rapport & Kelly, 1991).

A few longer duration studies now exist, showing positive effects of stimulants at 12 months (Gillberg et al., 1997), 14 months (MTA Cooperative Group, 1999a), and 24 months (Abikoff & Hechtman, 1998) of continuous treatment. Long-term follow-up studies of ADHD youth into adulthood do not show evidence of long-term benefit from medication treatment (Weiss & Hechtman, 1993). However, long-term compliance rates to stimulant medication appear to be low. In one survey of prescription practices, the majority of ADHD children for whom physicians prescribed stimulant medications, received only one or two prescriptions (Sherman & Hertzig, 1991). In a Canadian study, only 52% of children continued to take their medication at 3 years (Thiruchelvam, Charach, & Schachar, 2001). Thus, long-term outcome may be seriously confounded by medication non-compliance in longitudinal studies. Nevertheless, Biederman et al., (1996) documented that children with ADHD continued to have significant academic, social, and psychiatric impairment in adolescence despite substantial use of medications.

Effects in Adolescents

At least half of pre-pubertal children diagnosed with ADHD continue to meet criteria for the disorder in adolescence (Weiss & Hechtman, 1993) and many teens diagnosed in childhood continue to suffer from functional life impairments even if their primary symptoms drop to subclinical levels in adolescence (Barkley, 1998). Recognition that ADHD continues to be a significant problem in adolescence has resulted in a dramatic increase in the prevalence of stimulant treatment of adolescence in recent years (Safer & Krager, 1994). Despite this, there is a dearth of controlled studies on stimulant treatment of adolescents. Eight of nine published controlled trials were recently reviewed by Smith et al. (2000) who reported that while all studies showed statistically significant improvement, about half of the adolescents exhibited clinically significant improvement when treated with methylphenidate. This figure is less than the 70–90% range generally reported for pre-pubertal children treated with stimulants. However, the average effect size for adolescents was at the top of the range reported in studies with children. Beneficial effects have been found on primary symptoms as well as social, academic and classroom behaviours (Evans et al., 2001; Smith et al., 2000). A small number of dosage studies suggest essentially equivalent effects of methylphenidate at low and high doses in adolescence with an increased risk of negative side-effects at increasingly higher doses (Smith et al., 1998). Anecdotal reports suggest that some adolescents have a negative subjective experience while taking stimulants prompting medication non-compliance. The dosage question as well as the putative phenomenon of unpleasant subjective effects in adolescence need further study.

Non-Stimulant Medication

Although stimulant medication is considered the first-line drug treatment of ADHD, a number of other classes of medications have been used as possible treatment alternatives for ADHD children who do not respond to stimulants or have significant undesirable side-effects. These include tricyclic antidepressants, SSRI antidepressants, Bupropion, Clonidine, and carbamazepine. Because stimulants are so effective with the vast majority of cases, a review of these secondary drug classes will not be undertaken here but the interested reader is referred to excellent recent reviews (Schachar & Ickowicz, 1999; Spencer, Biederman, & Wilens, 1998).

Behaviour Therapy

The short-term efficacy of stimulant medication for ADHD is well established (Swanson et al., 1993), and some authors consider stimulant drug treatment to be the first-line treatment of choice for this disorder (Klein & Abikoff, 1997)—although others do not (Pelham & Waschbusch, 1999). Nevertheless, there are limitations to the exclusive use of pharmacological treatment alone for ADHD (Pelham & Hinshaw, 1992; Wells, 1987). First, not all ADHD children show a positive response to stimulant medication. In group studies, 10–30% show an adverse response or no response to a single stimulant (Swanson et al., 1995), although the response rate tends to be higher if two or more are tried (Spencer, Biederman, & Wilens, 1998). Of those who do respond, many do not show enough improvement for their behaviour to fall within the normal range on either rating scales or behavioural observations. Second, stimulant medication does not maximally affect the full range of symptomatology. Whereas positive effects are usually found on measures of attention, activity, and impulsivity (Conners & Erhardt, 1998) and to a lesser extent on conduct problems (McMahon & Wells, 1998; Hinshaw, 1994), salutary effects are more inconsistent for such crucial dimensions as academic achievement or poor peer relationships (Pelham & Hinshaw, 1992; Swanson et al., 1995; Whalen et al., 1989). Moreover, as noted previously, there is little evidence that treatment with stimulant medication alters the poor long-term course of ADHD (Weiss & Hechtman, 1993). Finally, one prominent leader in the field of ADHD has argued strongly that stimulant medications should be an adjunct to behavioural interventions, which should be implemented as the first-line treatment (Pelham & Waschbusch, 1999). In addition to the above limitations of stimulant medications, Pelham argues that higher doses of stimulants (and the risk of greater adverse side-effects) can be avoided, and the same positive effects on behaviour achieved, when behaviour therapy is implemented first and low-dose medication is added. Also, Pelham argues that when a child's core symptoms respond positively to stimulant medication as the first-line treatment, parents and teachers are less motivated to implement behavioural and psychoeducational treatments. The latter treatments are more likely to address the comorbid and functional impairments that are the most important risk factors for poor long-term outcome (e.g., aggression; academic failure; poor peer relationships). Failure to employ these treatments may contribute to the evidence suggesting poor long-term outcome for this disorder with medication treatment alone.

For all of these reasons, a number of psychosocial treatments have been investigated for ADHD. Of these, only behaviour therapy procedures, implemented in the home, classroom, and in specialized environments such as a summer camp, have an evidence base (Hinshaw, Klein, & Abikoff, 2002). Therefore, these procedures will be reviewed here. Cognitive-behaviour therapy has been demonstrated to be ineffective in the treatment of ADHD (Abikoff et al., 1988) and so it will not be reviewed (although see the earlier caveat regarding the possible use of CBT with ADHD/anxious youth).

As noted earlier, because there is little agreement in the field on underlying causal mechanisms in ADHD, treatment development has been guided by an empirical rather than a theoretical rationale. Because empirical research has identified core and comorbid symptoms as well as functional impairments (e.g., oppositional and aggressive behaviour; parent–child interaction problems; classroom and academic problems; poor peer relations), behaviour therapy procedures designed to address these problem areas have been evaluated with ADHD children. Thus, behavioural parent training, behavioural classroom management and other intensive child interventions utilizing skills practice and contingency management have been employed both alone and in combination. These treatments will be reviewed within three categories: (1) direct contingency management; (2) behavioural parent training, and (3) behavioural school interventions.

Direct Contingency Management

Direct contingency management studies typically employ single subject experimental designs implemented in special schools (e.g., Pfiffner, Rosen, & O'Leary, 1985), psychiatric inpatient settings (e.g., Wells et al., 1981), or intensive summer treatment programs (Hoza et al., 1992; Pelham & Hoza, 1996). In these studies, the contingency management strategies are generally more intensive than in clinical behaviour therapy (parent training and school intervention) and are implemented directly in the specialized setting by a paraprofessional, a consulting professional, or expert teacher rather than by a parent or teacher (Pelham et al., 1998). An example of this type of study was reported by Wells et al., (1981). In this single-subject experimental design conducted on a psychiatry inpatient unit, two children with ADHD were treated by a behaviour therapist who sat next to their desks in the unit classroom. The therapist placed a poker chip in bowls on the children's desks every time an audio-recorded tone sounded and the child was on-task. Over time, control of the program was faded from the therapist to the children who rewarded themselves with poker chips every time the tone sounded and they were on task. Poker chips were exchangeable for back-up rewards from the unit store. This direct contingency management strategy resulted in large improvements in on-task behaviour and reductions in other disruptive classroom behaviour in two children whose ADHD symptoms were so severe as to require psychiatric hospitalization.

There is a large number of highly controlled, experimental studies examining various types of contingencies in behavioural programs directed at youth with ADHD. Illustrative of these are studies examining response cost (Rapport, Murphy, & Bailey, 1980), verbal reprimands, time-out and loss of privileges (e.g., Abramowitz, O'Leary & Rosen, 1987; Pfiffner, Rosen & O'Leary, 1985; Pfiffner & O'Leary, 1987). The experimental control available in such studies often produces short-term behavioural gains larger than those obtained with clinical behaviour therapy. Nevertheless, treatment gains disappear when contingencies are removed in these short-term programs (just as effects of medication disappear after medication is withdrawn). Direct contingency management generally produces large improvements over baseline, with effects roughly equivalent to low-dose medication alone (Carlson et al., 1992). In addition, the combination of low-dose medication and direct contingency management can produce effects nearly identical to those produced with high-dose medication alone (Carlson et al., 1992).

Behavioural Parent Training

As reviewed in an earlier section, the parent–child interactions in families of ADHD youth are characterized by excessive levels of negative and controlling behaviours with their attendant effects on aetiology, escalation, and maintenance of symptoms as well as on family stress and disharmony. Although stimulant medication delivered to children has been demonstrated to reduce coercive behaviour in children *and in their parents* (Barkley & Cunningham, 1979; Barkley et al., 1985; Wells et al., 2000b), parent training approaches, directly target not just negative, coercive behaviours but a wide range of parenting skills and family variables relevant to management of ADHD youth in a wide variety of situations. Thus Parent Training (PT) has been considered a key clinical activity in behaviour therapy for these families (Hinshaw, Klein, & Abikoff, 2002; Pelham & Waschbusch, 1999).

Since 1980, there have been 15 experimental trials in the published literature that have examined PT as a single treatment or as a component of a clinical behaviour therapy package for youth with ADHD. In most of these studies a variation of the PT programs of Barkley (1997) and Forehand and McMahon (1981) have been utilized. Both of these programs are anchored in the original PT program developed by Connie Hanf (who trained both Barkley and Forehand). In these fundamental programs, PT usually runs from 8 to 12 sessions. However, in the most recent and largest evaluation of behaviour therapy with ADHD youth (MTA Cooperative Group, 1999a), PT was expanded to address many additional family and school issues and ran for 27 group sessions and 8 individual sessions over 14 months (Wells et al., 1996, 2000b).

The first 12 sessions from the PT program in the MTA study are presented in Table 15.1. These sessions reflect fundamental PT and were adapted from programs of Barkley (1997) and Forehand and McMahon (1981). As can be seen, parents are taught skills of positive reinforcement, giving effective commands and establishing home rules, use of effective punishment procedures (time-out and response cost),

Table 15.1 MTA Study Parent Training Sessions

Session 1	Structured Clinical Interview, Review of ADHD and Introduction to Treatment
Session 2	Setting up "School/Home Daily Report Card"
Session 3	Overview of Social Learning and Behaviour Management Principles and Review of DRC
Session 4	Attending and "Special Playtime"
Session 5	Rewarding and Ignoring Skills in "Special Playtime" and "Catch Your Child Being Good"
Session 6	Using Positive Skills and Premack Principle to Increase Targets: Catch Child Being Good and Independent Play
Session 7	Giving Effective Commands to Children, Establishing Behaviour Rules and Attending and Rewarding Compliance to Instructions
Session 8	Time-Out Procedure
Session 9	Home Token Economy 1
Session 10	Home Token Economy 2
Session 11	Response Cost
Session 12	Planned Activities Training and Setting Generalization

as well as using skills outside of home. In this version of PT, parents were also taught early in the program how to set up a cooperative, home-school Daily Report Card (DRC) with the child's teacher in the school. This is often done early in behavioural treatment of ADHD youth, especially for those who will not be treated with stimulant medication, due to the serious difficulties that these children have in school and the need to offer some help with these problems early in treatment.

While most clinical PT programs end with these fundamental interventions, expanded PT incorporates other interventions to address the multilevel problems often present in families with ADHD youth. Expanded sessions from the MTA study PT program are presented in Table 15.2. These sessions address stress, anger, and mood management in parents, and direct a great deal of attention to teaching, modelling, and role-playing with parents the skills necessary for becoming advocates for their child in the schools. Parents are taught how to contact relevant school personnel, how to ask for and conduct a meeting in school, how to work with the teacher to set up a home-school DRC, and how to set up homework structures and procedures for the child in the home. This work with parents complements and coordinates with school interventions (see next section). (For details and session by session outlines of PT see Barkley, 1997; Forehand & McMahon, 1981; and Wells et al., 1996.)

The experimental studies of parent training with ADHD youth have shown that parent training produces reductions in inattention and overactivity (Anastopoulos et al., 1993; Dubey, O'Leary, & Kaufman, 1983; Sonuga-Barke et al., 2001), in child non-compliance and conduct problems (Pisterman et al., 1989; Pollard, Ward, & Barkley, 1983; Sonuga-Barke et al., 2001), and in child aggression (Anastopoulos et al., 1993). As would be expected, improvements in parenting skills (Pisterman et al., 1989, 1992) have also been found. Notably, some studies have also reported reductions in parent stress, and improvements in parent self-esteem with parent training (Anastopoulos et al., 1993; Pisterman et al., 1992; Sonuga-Barke et al., 2001). Effect sizes for parent training of 1.2 have been reported on ADHD symptoms (assessed by rating scale) (Anastopoulos et al., 1993; Horn et al., 1991). Anastopoulos et al.

Table 15.2 MTA Parent Training Sessions (*continued*)

Session 13	Stress, Anger, and Mood Management 1
Session 14	Stress, Anger, and Mood Management 2
Session 15	Peer Programming in Home and School
Session 16	Preparing for the New School Year
Session 17	Parent Skills for Academic/School Support at Home
Session 18	Review of Attending, Rewarding, Ignoring Skills; review of "Special Time"
Session 19	Review of Commands, House Rules, and Time-Out
Session 20	Review of Home Token Economy and Response Cost
Session 21	Review of Academic Support/Homework Programs at Home
Session 22	Planning for the Second Summer
Session 23	Parent Skills for School Advocacy
Session 24	Parent Skills for School Advocacy
Session 25	Parent Skills for School Advocacy
Session 26	Parent Skills for School Advocacy
Session 27	Problem-Solving School Issues

(1993) stated that 64% of their sample reported clinically significant changes with PT compared with 27% for a wait-list control group.

Other studies have examined multicomponent behaviour therapy programs of which PT is one component. The most typical combination involves PT plus teacher consultation (TC). This is done because the effects of PT are centred on home behaviour and generalization of PT effects to the school would not be expected. The combination of these two interventions has been referred to as clinical behaviour therapy, as it fits best in a traditional outpatient, clinical model (Hinshaw et al., 2000; Pelham & Waschbusch, 1999). In TC, the therapist works with the teacher to set up a DRC focusing on classroom behaviour and academic performance, and may also consult with the teacher on classroom-wide behaviour management strategies (see section on Behavioral School Intervention below) if indicated and acceptable to the teacher. Several studies have combined PT and TC (Horn et al., 1990, 1991; Pelham et al., 1988) and compared them to medication with results generally showing that the combination of PT plus TC results in significant improvement in children's home and school behaviour. Even greater improvements are noted when PT and TC also are combined with stimulant medication (Pelham et al., 1988).

Effects in Adolescents

Only two studies have examined PT or other family-based interventions with adolescents. In the first, three family-based treatments were compared: PT, Family Problem-Solving and Communication Training, and Structural Family Therapy. All three treatments produced statistically significant improvements and none was superior to the others. However, only a few subjects showed clinically significant improvements and effect sizes, while moderate to large for ADHD symptoms, were relatively small for social and academic behaviour (Barkley et al., 1992). In the most recent study with adolescents, Family Problem-Solving and Communication Training alone was compared to PT followed by Family Problem-Solving Training. Both treatments produced significant improvements but did not differ. However, dropout rates were lower with the combination treatment.

In summary, PT has received empirical support as a treatment for youth with ADHD. Statistically and, to a lesser extent, clinically significant effects of PT alone are found primarily in the home setting on ratings by parents, which nevertheless have the potential for bias, even though the measures may be valid and treatment sensitive. Studies with objective assessments are needed in this field.

Behavioural School Interventions

Because of the dual problems of academic underachievement and disruptive classroom behaviour associated with ADHD, studies have addressed the effects of behavioural procedures in the classroom environment. Direct school-based treatment for youth with ADHD may consist of both academic interventions (e.g., peer tutoring and computer-assisted instruction) and behavioural interventions involving antecedent strategies such as the posting of classroom rules as well as consequence strategies such as teacher positive attention, classroom token programs such as point systems, as well as the use of negative consequences such as verbal reprimands, response cost, and time-out. These interventions require the behavioural consultant to work directly with the teacher in establishing a behavioural system in the classroom.

Many of the strategies used in school interventions were evaluated in the direct contingency management studies reviewed earlier and, subsequently, have been applied in the regular school environment by regular schoolteachers working with behavioural consultants. Research has shown that consequence-oriented strategies consisting only of positive reinforcement approaches are insufficient by themselves in reducing the disruptive behaviours and increasing the appropriate classroom behaviours with ADHD youth (Hoffman & DuPaul, 2000). As has also been shown in the PT literature, some form of mild punishment is necessary to achieve the greatest effects. Response cost strategies, in which children lose a privilege or point(s) on a token system, have been employed successfully in this regard and result in greater effects on behaviour than when response cost is not used (Pfiffner & O'Leary, 1993; Pfiffner, Rosen, & O' Leary, 1985).

Another form of school intervention used frequently in more traditional office-based behaviour therapy is the Daily Report Card (DRC). In the DRC approach, teachers report on specified academic and behavioural targets at predetermined intervals (e.g., at the end of every class period) on a daily note or index card. Children bring the card home every day and parents deliver predetermined rewards at home based on the teacher's report of the child's performance. At first, reports are done daily. Over time the course of the school year they may be faded to weekly, bi-weekly, or monthly, DRC approaches are often combined with and incorporated into Parent Training strategies in outpatient clinical behaviour therapy.

The literature on academic and behavioural classroom interventions with ADHD youth recently has been reviewed by DuPaul and Eckert (1998) and by Hoffman and DuPaul (2000). While much less voluminous than the literature on stimulant medication and relying largely on single-subject experimental design and small group experimental methods, these studies suggest that behavioural classroom interventions reduce many of the disruptive classroom behaviours of ADHD youth. In addition, peer tutoring and computer-assisted instruction can both produce decreases in inattentive, off-task behaviour and peer tutoring may produce significant gains in vocabulary performance and decreases in disruptive classroom behaviour, even though this is not a direct target of intervention. While promising, these latter conclusions are based primarily on a small number of studies. A meta-analysis of studies employing antecedent and consequence based behavioural interventions indicated that these interventions are effective in improving both behavioural and academic problems associated with ADHD, although effects are greater for reduction of disruptive behaviour than for improvement in academic performance (Hoffman & DuPaul, 2000). Effect sizes for these interventions are generally similar to those obtained in meta-analyses of stimulant intervention. However, as with stimulant medication, there is not yet evidence of long-term gains in academic achievement with these interventions.

Effects with Adolescents

Few studies have reported effects of behavioural interventions in the classroom with adolescent samples. One line of research has investigated structured note-taking, in which adolescents were taught to use a format for note-taking while listening to class lectures (Evans, Pelham, & Grudburg, 1994). Following this training, adolescents with ADHD showed improvements in comprehension, on-task behaviour, small reductions in disruptive behaviour, and improved quiz performance. This is a promising study and the method bears more investigation. While there is no reason to believe that the behaviour classroom interventions reported earlier would not also produce salutary effects with adolescents, implementation issues are more difficult in middle and high school when adolescents begin to change classes and have multiple teachers. Perhaps this is one reason that so little research has occurred specifically with the adolescent population.

Combination Treatment

Both stimulant medication and behavioural interventions produce statistically and clinically significant improvements in the primary symptoms, and many of the comorbidities and functional impairments for youth with ADHD as reviewed above. In head to head comparisons, medications alone have been shown to produce greater average effects than behaviour therapy alone (Carlson et al., 1992; Klein & Abikoff, 1997; Pelham et al., 1993; MTA Cooperative Group, 1999a). Even though significant improvements are obtained, neither stimulant medication alone nor behaviour therapy alone produces full normalization of symptoms or functional impairments. In addition, neither treatment alone has improved long-term outcome, and effects for both treatments typically diminish or disappear once the treatment is withdrawn. Therefore, investigators have been interested in the question of whether the combination of medication and behaviour therapy will produce better effects on multiple symptom domains, on normalization, and on long-term outcome than either treatment alone.

Two published between-subjects experiments have directly addressed the question of combined treatment relative to unimodal treatments. Because the results of these studies have important implications for treatment of youth with ADHD, they will be presented in some detail. In the first of these, Klein and Abikoff (1997) randomly assigned 89, 6–12-year-old children diagnosed with ADHD—none of whom had clinically significant anxiety or conduct disorders—to three experimental groups: Pill placebo plus clinical behaviour therapy (BT), that included parent training and teacher consultation on behavioural classroom interventions; methylphenidate (MTP) titrated gradually to a maximum of 60 mg/day for optimal efficacy; and methylphenidate plus clinical behaviour therapy. Children in the combination group received the same regimen of each treatment. Treatment was implemented for eight weeks in each condition. One criticism of this study has been that there was no attention placebo plus pill placebo or wait-list control group against which to evaluate the effects of active treatment. However, for the critical question regarding the effects of combined vs unimodal treatment, such a control is not needed. In addition to parent, teacher, psychiatrist, and psychologist ratings, the study also employed objective classroom assessment using blind observers who used an objective coding system.

Results of this study showed significantly greater improvement for MTP alone compared to BT alone on teacher rating scales and on psychiatrist ratings but not on parent rating scales. Teachers' and mothers' ratings of global overall improvement were not different between the unimodal groups but psychiatrists considered significantly more children to be improved globally on MTP compared to BT. On objective classroom observations, children receiving MTP showed significantly greater positive effects on 5 out of 14 coded behaviours.

With regard to combination treatment, parents', psychiatrists' and psychologists' ratings revealed no differences between MTP and MTP plus BT. Thus on these ratings, there was no benefit of adding behaviour therapy to MTP alone. However, some teacher ratings as well as the objective codes of minor and vigorous motor behaviour showed superior effects of combination treatment over MTP alone. In addition, significantly more children receiving combined treatment were considered globally improved by teachers (93%) and psychiatrists (97%) compared to MTP alone (69% and 79% for teachers and psychiatrists respectively). After eight weeks of treatment, the children who received combination treatment achieved full normalization on all objective classroom measures; that is, they did not differ from normal comparison children on any objective measures.

This study provided evidence that behaviour therapy alone is a viable alternative to medication treatment alone in the views of parents and global aspects of teachers' perceptions. In addition, some evidence for the superiority of combination treatment was found and full normalization was achieved only with combination treatment. There was no long-term follow-up in this study, so effects of combined vs unimodal treatment on longer-term prognosis are unknown.

A subsequent much more extensive and intensive study has also examined the effects of unimodal treatments vs their combination. At the time of its inception, the MTA study was the largest clinical trial ever launched by the NIMH. In this study, 579 youth, 7 to 9 years old, with DSM-IV diagnoses of combined type ADHD at six sites in the USA and Canada, were randomly assigned to four experimental groups: Medication Management (MedMgt) (see Greenhill et al., 1996 for full description of the MTA MedMgt strategy); Intensive Behaviour Therapy (Beh); their combination (Comb); or to a community comparison (CC) group which allowed a comparison of the first three conditions with treatment typically offered in the community. Treatment extended for 14 months in all conditions. Beh was intensive and consisted of 27 group and eight sessions of individual PT as described earlier (Wells et al., 1996, 2000b); an intensive eight-week summer day camp treatment program modelled on the Summer Treatment Program (STP) of Pelham and Hoza (1996); and an intensive school intervention, including regular teacher consultation throughout the school year and a paraprofessional aide program for 12 weeks (see Wells et al., 2000b, for a full description of MTA Beh). The participant sample contained multiple comorbidities, including comorbid anxiety and conduct disorders, and outcome was assessed across multiple symptom and impairment domains (see Hinshaw et al., 1997, for a description of assessment strategy). Results of this important study showed that all four groups had sizeable reductions in symptoms over the 14-month treatment period. MedMgt performed significantly better than Beh on parent- and teacher-rated core ADHD symptoms but not for any of the other measures of comorbid and functional impairment. For core ADHD symptoms, children in the Comb and MedMgt groups showed significantly greater improvement than those in the Beh and community care group (two-thirds of whom received medication in the community) which did not tend to differ from each other.

However, for oppositional-aggressive symptoms, for anxiety symptoms, for teacher-rated social skills, for one aspect of parent–child relations, and for reading achievement, combination treatment was more effective than community care, whereas medication management was not more effective than community care. In terms of overall satisfaction with treatment quality and their child's progress, parents preferred the combination treatment and the psychosocial treatment to MedMgt alone. Furthermore, secondary analyses (Conners et al., 2001; Swanson et al., 2001) showed that if composite outcome measures are used, combination treatment significantly outperformed MedMgt alone.

Combined treatment subjects were maintained on significantly lower daily doses of methylphenidate than MedMgt subjects. In addition, moderator analyses showed that for children with comorbid anxiety, behavioural treatment alone yielded significantly better outcomes than did routine community care on ADHD-related and internalizing symptoms (MTA Cooperative Group, 1999b) and did not differ from MedMgt and combined treatment in this regard. Likewise, in families receiving public assistance, medication alone produced a negative effect, decreased closeness in parent–child relationships (whereas the two groups that included behavioural treatment did not), and combined treatment yielded greater benefit for social skills (MTA Cooperative Group, 1999b).

The results of these two important studies, show that both behaviour therapy and medication are effective treatments for youth who have ADHD and that, especially for some secondary domains of function and for some comorbid subgroups, behaviour therapy or combination treatment may be equally or more effective than medication alone, certainly as it is prescribed in the community (Klein & Abikoff, 1997; MTA Cooperative Group, 1999a, 1999b). In addition, the results of the MTA are consistent with previous within-subjects and small group research, showing that lower doses of medication are required to achieve similar results when medication is combined with behaviour therapy compared to medication alone (e.g., Carlson et al., 1992). While these are important advances, much work remains to be done elucidating the mechanisms through which behavioural, medication, and combined treatment exert their effects, the long-term effects of these treatments and the extent to which the treatments evaluated in these studies can be transported to community settings and with what effect on immediate and long-term outcomes.

CONCLUSIONS

In this chapter, the major evidence-based approaches to treatment of Attention Deficit Hyperactivity Disorder—one of the most prevalent psychiatric disorders of childhood and adolescence—have been reviewed. Survey of this literature reveals hundreds of studies evaluating psychopharmacologic (mainly stimulant medication) approaches to treatment of this disorder, and considerably fewer, but many notably strong experimental studies of various approaches to behaviour therapy. Many leaders in the field (but not all) consider stimulant medication to be the front-line treatment for this disorder and the literature indicates that the strongest clinical effects for unimodality treatment are obtained with stimulant medication. Clinical behaviour therapy also produces important benefits but the clinical benefits of behaviour therapy alone are less than those achieved with medication alone. There is important evidence from two major published studies that the combination of behaviour therapy and stimulant medication is more effective than either alone on certain symptom domains and is the only treatment that produces normalization in youth diagnosed with ADHD. In addition, subgroups of ADHD children obtain benefits from behaviour therapy alone that are just as great as those obtained with medication alone. It is still unknown if any of these treatments improve long-term outcome of this disorder. At present it appears that ADHD should be thought of and treated as a chronic disorder that requires ongoing treatment over the course of development, as the evidence indicates that the effects of both behaviour therapy and stimulant medication reverse when the treatments are withdrawn.

REFERENCES

Abikoff, H., & Gittelman, R. (1984). Does behaviour therapy normalize the classroom behaviour of hyperactive children? *Archives of General Psychiatry*, **41**, 449–454.

Abikoff, H., & Hechtman, L., (1998). *Multimodal treatment for children with ADHD: Effects on ADHD and social behaviour and diagnostic status* (unpublished).

Abikoff, H., Gittelman-Klein, R., & Klein, D. (1977). Validation of a classroom observation code for hyperactive children. *Journal of Consulting and Clinical Psychology*, **45**, 772–783.

Abikoff, H., Ganeles, D., Reiter, G., Blum, C., Foley, C., & Klein, R.G. (1988). Cognitive training in academically deficient ADDH boys receiving stimulant medication. *Journal of Abnormal Child Psychology*, **16**, 411–432.

Abramowitz, A.J., O'Leary, S.G., & Rosen, L.A. (1987). Reducing off-task behaviour in the classroom: A comparison of encouragement and reprimands. *Journal of Abnormal Child Psychology*, **15**, 153–163.

American Psychiatric Association. (1994). *Diagnostic and statistical manual of mental disorders* (4th edn). Washington, DC: Author.

Anastopoulos, A.D., & Shelton, T.L. (2001). *Assessing attention-deficit/hyperactivity disorder*. New York: Kluwer Academic.

Anastopoulos, A.D., Shelton, T.L., DuPaul, G.J., & Guevremont, D.C. (1993). Parent training for attention-deficit hyperactivity disorder: Its impact on parent functioning. *Journal of Abnormal Child Psychology*, **21**, 581–595.

Anderson, C.A., Hinshaw, S.P., & Simmel, C. (1994). Mother–child interactions in ADHD and comparison boys: Relationships with overt and covert externalizing behaviour. *Journal of Abnormal Child Psychology*, **22**, 247–265.

Angold, A., Erkanli, A., Egger, H.L., & Costello, E.J. (2000). Stimulant treatment for children: A community perspective. *Journal of the American Academy of Child and Adolescent Psychiatry*, **39**, 975–994.

Arnold, L.E. (2002). Treatment alternatives for Attention-Deficit/Hyperactivity Disorder (ADHD). In P.J. Jensen & J. Cooper (Eds), *Attention Deficit/Hyperactivity Disorder: State of the Science: Best Practices*. Kingston, NJ: Civic Research Institute.

Asarnow, J.R. (1988). Peer status and social competence in child psychiatric inpatients: A comparison of children with depressive, externalizing, and concurrent depressive and externalizing disorders. *Journal of Abnormal Child Psychology*, **16**, 151–162.

Bagwell, C.L., Molina, B.S.G., Pelham, W.E., Jr, & Hoza, B. (2001). Attention-deficit hyperactivity disorder and problems in peer relations: Predictions from childhood to adolescence. *Journal of the American Academy of Child and Adolescent Psychiatry*, **40**, 1285–1292.

Barkley, R.A. (1977). A review of stimulant drug research with hyperactive children. *Journal of Child Psychology and Psychiatry*, **18**, 137–165.

Barkley, R.A. (1996). Attention-deficit/hyperactivity disorder. In E.J. Mash & R.A. Barkley (Eds), *Child psychopathology* (pp. 63–112). New York: Guilford Press.

Barkley, R.A. (1997). *ADHD and the nature of self-control*. New York: Guilford Press.

Barkley, R.A. (1998). *Attention-deficit hyperactivity disorder: A handbook for diagnosis and treatment* (2nd edn). New York: Guilford Press.

Barkley, R.A., & Cunningham, C.E. (1979). The effects of methylphenidate on the mother–child interactions of hyperactive children. *Archives of General Psychiatry*, **36**, 201–208.

Barkley, R.A., Karlsson, J., & Pollard, S. (1985). Effects of age on the mother–child interactions of hyperactive children. *Journal of Abnormal Child Psychology*, **13**, 631–638.

Barkley, R.A., Anastopoulos, A.D., Guevremont, D.G., & Fletcher, K.F. (1992). Adolescents with attention-deficit hyperactivity disorder: Mother–adolescent interactions, family beliefs and conflicts, and maternal psychopathology. *Journal of Abnormal Child Psychology*, **20**, 263–288.

Barkley, R.A., DuPaul, G.J., & McMurray, M.B. (1990). Attention deficit disorder with and without hyperactivity: Clinical response to three dose levels of methylphenidate. *Pediatrics*, **87**, 519–531.

Barkley, R.A., Fischer, M., Edelbrock, C.S., & Smallish, L. (1990). The adolescent outcome of hyperactive children diagnoses by research criteria: I. An 8-year prospective follow-up study. *Journal of the American Academy of Child and Adolescent Psychiatry*, **29**, 546–557.

Barkley, R.A., Fischer, M., Edelbrock, C.S., & Smallish, L. (1991). The adolescent outcome of hyperactive children diagnoses by research criteria: III. Mother–child interactions, family conflicts, and maternal psychopathology. *Journal of Child Psychology and Psychiatry*, **32**, 233–256.

Barkley, R.A., Guevremont, D.C., Anastopoulos, A.D., & Fletcher, K.E. (1992). A comparison of three family therapy programs for treating family conflicts in adolescents with attention-deficit hyperactivity disorder. *Journal of Consulting and Clinical Psychology*, **60** (3), 450–462.

Barkley, R.A., Karlsson, J., Pollard, S., & Murphy, J. (1985). Developmental changes in the mother–child interactions of hyperactive boys: Effects of two doses of Ritalin. *Journal of Child Psychology and Psychiatry*, **26**, 705–715.

Befera, M., & Barkley, R.A. (1984). Hyperactive and normal girls and boys: Mother–child interactions, parent psychiatric status, and child psychopathology. *Journal of Child Psychology and Psychiatry*, **26**, 439–452.

Biederman, J., Faraone, S.V., & Lapey, K. (1992). Comorbidity of diagnosis in attention-deficit hyperactivity disorder. In G. Weiss (Ed.), *Child and adolescent psychiatric clinics of North America: Attention-deficit hyperactivity disorder* (pp. 335–360). Philadelphia: Saunders.

Biederman, J., Faraone, S., Milberger, S., Guite, J., Mick, E., Chen, L., Mennin, D., Marrs, A., Ouellette, C., Moore, P., Spencer, T., Norman, D., Wilens, T., Kraus, I., & Perrin, J. (1996). A prospective 4-year follow up study of attention-deficit hyperactivity and related disorders. *Archives of General Psychiatry*, **53** (5), 437–446.

Buhrmester, D., Whalen, C.K., Henker, B., MacDonald, V., & Hinshaw, S.P. (1992). Prosocial behaviour in hyperactive boys: Effects of stimulant medication and comparison with normal boys. *Journal of Abnormal Child Psychology*, **20**, 103–121.

Campbell, S.B. (1994). Hard-to-manage preschool boys: Externalizing behaviour, social competence, and family context at two-year follow-up. *Journal of Abnormal Child Psychology*, **22**, 147–166.

Carlson, E.A., Jacobvitz, D., & Sroufe, L.A. (1995). A developmental investigation of inattentiveness and hyperactivity. *Child Development*, **66**, 37–54.

Carlson, C.L., Pelham, W.E., Milich, R., & Dixon, J. (1992). Single and combined effects of methylphenidate and behaviour therapy on the classroom performance of children with attention-deficit hyperactivity disorder. *Journal of Abnormal Child Psychology*, **20**, 213–232.

Conners, C.K., & Erhardt, D. (1998). Attention-deficit hyperactivity disorder in children and adolescents. In A.S. Bellack & M. Herse (Eds), *Comprehensive clinical psychology* (pp. 487–525). New York: Pergamon.

Conners, C.K., & Jett, J.L. (2001). *Attention deficit hyperactivity disorder (in adults and children): The latest assessment and treatment strategies*. Kansas City, MO: Compact Clinicals.

Conners, C.K., Epstein, J.N., March, J.S., Angold, A., Wells, K.C., Klaric, J., Swanson, J.M., Abikoff, H.B., Arnold, L.E., Elliott, G.R., Greenhill, L.L., Hechtman, L., Hinshaw, S.P., Hoza, B., Jensen, P.S., Kraemer, H.C., Newcorn, J., Pelham, W.E., Severe, J.B., Vitiello, B., & Wigal, T. (2001). Multimodal treatment of ADHD in the MTA: An alternative outcome analysis. *Journal of the American Academy of Child and Adolescent Psychiatry*, **40**, 159–167.

Cunningham, C.E., & Barkley, R.A. (1979). The interactions of hyperactive and normal children with their mothers during free play and structured tasks. *Child Development*, **50**, 217–224.

Dishion, T.J., & Patterson, G.R. (1999). Model building in developmental psychopathology: A pragmatic approach to understanding and intervention. *Journal of Clinical Child Psychology*, **28** (4), 502–512.

Dubey, D.R., O'Leary, S.G., & Kaufman, K.F. (1983). Training parents of hyperactive children in child management: A comparative outcome study. *Journal of Abnormal Child Psychology*, **11** (2), 229–246.

DuPaul, G.J., & Eckert, T.L. (1998). Academic interventions for students with attention-deficit/hyperactivity disorder: A review of the literature. *Reading and Writing Quarterly*, **14** (1), 59–83.

Edwards, G., Barkley, R.A., Laneri, M., Fletcher, K., & Metevia L. (2001). Parent–adolescent conflict in teenagers with ADHD and ODD. *Journal of Abnormal Child Psychology*, **29** (6), 557–572.

Elia, J., Borcherding, B.G., Rapoport, J.L., & Keysor, C.S. (1991). Methylphenidate and dextroamphetamine treatments of hyperactivity: Are there true nonresponders? *Psychiatry Research*, **36**, 141–155.

Erhardt, D., & Hinshaw, S.P. (1994). Initial sociometric impressions of attention-deficit hyperactivity disorder and comparison boys: Predictions from social behaviours and from nonbehavioural variables. *Journal of Consulting and Clinical Psychology*, **62**, 833–842.

Evans, S.E., Pelham, W.E., Jr., & Grudburg, M.V. (1994). The efficacy of notetaking to improve behaviour and comprehension of adolescents with attention-deficit hyperactivity disorder. *Exceptionality*, **5** (1), 1–17.

Evans, S.W., Pelham, W.E., Smith, B.H., Bukstein, O., Gnagy, E.M., Greiner, A.R., Altenderfer, L., & Baron-Myak, C. (2001). Dose–response effects of methylphenidate on ecologically valid measures of academic performance and classroom behaviour in adolescents with ADHD. *Experimental and Clinical Psychopharmacology*, **9** (2), 163–175.

Fischer, M. (1990). Parenting stress and the child with attention deficit hyperactivity disorder. *Journal of Clinical Child Psychology*, **19**, 337–346.

Fletcher, K.E., Fisher, M., Barkley, R.A., & Smallish, L. (1996). A sequential analysis of the mother–adolescent interactions of ADHD, ADHD/ODD, and normal teenagers during neutral and conflict discussions. *Journal of Abnormal Child Psychology*, **24**, 271–297.

Forehand, R., & McMahon, R. (1981). *Helping the non-compliant child: A clinician's guide to parent training*. New York: Guilford Press.

Gillberg, C., Melander, H., von Knorring, A.L., Janols, L.O., Thernlund, G., Hagglof, B., Eidevall-Wallin, L., Gustafsson, P., & Kopp, S. (1997). Long-term stimulant treatment of children with attention-deficit hyperactivity disorder symptoms. *Archives of General Psychiatry*, **54**, 857–864.

Granger, D.A., Whalen, C.K., & Henker, B. (1993). Perceptions of methylphenidate effects on hyperactive children's peer interactions. *Journal of Abnormal Child Psychology*, **21**, 535–549.

Greenhill, L.L., & Ford, R.E. (2002). Child attention-deficit hyperactivity disorder: Pharmacological treatments. In P.E. Nathan & J.M. Gorman (Eds), *A guide to treatments that work* (2nd edn; pp. 25–55). New York: Oxford University Press.

Greenhill, L.L., Abikoff, H.B., Arnold, L.E., Cantwell, D.P., Conners, C.K., Elliott, G., Hechtman, L., Hinshaw, S.P., Hoza, B., Jensen, P.S., March, J.S., Newcorn, J., Pelham, W.E., Severe, J.B., Swanson, J.M., Vitello, B., & Wells, K. (1996). Medication treatment strategies in the MTA study: Relevance to clinicians and researchers. *Journal of the American Academy of Child and Adolescent Psychiatry*, **34**, 1304–1313.

Hechtman, L., & Abikoff, H. (1995). Multi-modal treatment plus stimulants vs stimulant treatment in ADHD children: Results from a two-year comparative treatment study. *Proceedings of the Annual Meeting of the American Academy of Child and Adolescent Psychiatry*, p. 63, October, New Orleans, LA.

Hinshaw, S.P. (1992). Academic underachievement, attention deficits, and aggression: Comorbidity and implications for intervention. *Journal of Consulting and Clinical Psychology*, **60**, 893–903.

Hinshaw, S.P. (1994). *Attention deficits and hyperactivity in children*. Thousand Oaks, CA: Sage.

Hinshaw, S.P., & Melnick, S.M. (1995). Peer relationships in children with attention-deficit hyperactivity disorder with and without comorbid aggression. *Development and Psychopathology*, **7**, 627–647.

Hinshaw, S.P., Heller, T., & McHale, J.P. (1992). Covert antisocial behavior in boys with attention-deficit hyperactivity disorder: External validation and effects of methylphenidate. *Journal of Consulting and Clinical Psychology*, **60** (2), 274–281.

Hinshaw, S.P., Klein, R.G., & Abikoff, H.B. (2002). Childhood attention-deficit hyperactivity disorder: Nonpharmacological treatments and their combination with medication. In P.E. Nathan & J.M. Gorman (Eds), *A guide to treatments that work* (2nd edn; pp. 3–23). New York: Oxford University Press.

Hinshaw, S.P., March, J.S., Abikoff, H., Arnold, L.E., Cantwell, D.P., Conners, C.K., Elliott, G.R., Halperin, J., Greenhill, L.L., Hechtman, L.T., Hoza, B., Jensen, P.S., Newcorn, J.H., McBurnett, K., Pelham, W.E., Richters, J.E., Severe, J.B., Schiller, E., Swanson, J., Vereen, D., Wells, K.C., & Wigal, T. (1997). Comprehensive assessment of childhood attention-deficit hyperactivity disorder in the context of a multisite, multimodal clinical trial. *Journal of Attention Disorders*, **1**, 217–234.

Hinshaw, S.P., Owens, E.B., Wells, K.C., Kraemer, H.C., Abikoff, H.B., Arnold, L.E., Conners, C.K., Elliott, G., Greenhill, L.L., Hechtman, L., Hoza, B., Jensen, P.S., March, J.S., Newcorn, J., Pelham, W.E., Swanson, J.M., Vitiello, B., & Wigal, T. (2000). Family processes and treatment outcome in the MTA: Negative/ineffective parenting practices in relation to multimodal treatment. *Journal of Abnormal Child Psychology*, **28**, 555–568.

Hoagwood, K., Jensen, P.S., Feil, M., Vitiello, B., & Bhatara, V.S. (2000). Medication management of stimulants in pediatric practice settings: A national perspective. *Developmental and Behavioural Pediatrics*, **21** (5), 322–331.

Hoffman, J.B., & DuPaul, G.J. (2000). Psychoeducational interventions for children and adolescents with attention-deficit/hyperactivity disorder. *Child and Adolescent Psychiatric Clinics of North America*, **9** (3), 647–661.

Horn, W.F., Ialongo, N., Greenberg, G., Packard, T., & Smith-Winberry, C. (1990). Additive effects of behavioural parent training and self-control therapy with attention deficit hyperactivity disordered children. *Journal of Clinical Child Psychology*, **19**, 98–110.

Horn, W.F., Ialongo, N.S., Pascoe, J.M., Greenberg, G.A., Packard, T., Lopez, M., Wagner, A., & Puttler, L. (1991). Additive effects of psychostimulants, parent training, and self-control therapy with ADHD children. *Journal of the American Academy of Child and Adolescent Psychiatry*, **30**, 233–240.

Hoza, B., Pelham, W.E., Sams, S.E., & Carlson, C. (1992). An examination of the "dosage" effects of both behaviour therapy and methylphenidate on the classroom performance of two ADHD children. *Behavior Modification*, **16**, 164–192.

Jensen, P.S., Kettle, L., Roper, M.T., Sloan, M.T., Dulcan, M.K., Hoven, C., Bird, H.R., Bauermeister, J.J., & Payne, J.D. (1999). Are stimulants overprescribed? Treatment of

ADHD in four U.S. communities. *Journal of the American Academy of Child and Adolescent Psychiatry*, **38** (7), 797–804.

Johnston, C. (1996). Parent characteristics and parent–child interactions in families of nonproblem children and ADHD children with higher and lower levels of oppositional-defiant behavior. *Journal of Abnormal Child Psychology*, **24**, 85–104.

Johnston, C., & Mash, E.J. (2001). Families of children with attention-deficit/hyperactivity disorder: Review and recommendations for future research. *Clinical Child and Family Psychology Review*, **4** (3), 183–207.

Klein, R.G., & Abikoff, H. (1997). Behavior therapy and methylphenidate in the treatment of children with ADHD. *Journal of Attention Disorders*, **2**, 89–114.

Klein, R.G., & Manuzza, S. (1991). Long-term outcome of hyperactive children: A review. *Journal of the American Academy of Child and Adolescent Psychiatry*, **30**, 383–387.

Klein, R.G., Abikoff, H., Klass, E., Ganeles, D., Seese, L.M., & Pollack, S. (1997). Clinical efficacy of methylphenidate in conduct disorder with and without attention deficit hyperactivity disorder. *Archives of General Psychiatry*, **54** (12), 1073–1080.

Lynskey, M.T., & Fergusson, D.M. (1995). Childhood conduct problems, attention deficit behaviours, and adolescent alcohol, tobacco, and illicit drug use. *Journal of Abnormal Child Psychology*, **23**, 281–302.

March, J.S., Wells, K., & Conners, C.K. (1996). Attention-deficit/hyperactivity disorder: Part II. Treatment strategies. *Journal of Practical Psychiatry and Behavioral Health*, **2** (1), 23–32.

March, J.S., Swanson, J.M., Arnold, L.E., Hoza, B., Conners, C.K., Hinshaw, S.P., Hechtman, L., Kraemer, H.C., Greenhill, L.L., Abikoff, H.B., Elliott, L.G., Jensen, P.S., Newcorn, J.H., Vitiello, B., Severe, J., Wells, K.C., & Pelham, W.E. (2000). Anxiety as a predictor and outcome variable in the multimodal treatment study of children with ADHD (MTA). *Journal of Abnormal Child Psychology*, **28** (6), 527–541.

Mash, E.J., & Johnston, C. (1982). A comparison of the mother–child interactions of younger and older hyperactive and normal children. *Child Development*, **53**, 1371–1381.

Mash, E.J., & Johnston, C. (1990). Determinants of parenting stress: Illustrations from families of hyperactive children and families of physically abused children. *Journal of Clinical Child Psychology*, **19**, 313–328.

McMahon, R.J., & Wells, K.C. (1998). Conduct problems. In E.J. Mash & R.A. Barkley (Eds), *Treatment of childhood disorders* (2nd edn). New York: Guilford Press.

Milich, R., Carlson, C.L., Pelham, W.E., & Licht, B.G. (1991). Effects of methylphenidate on the persistence of ADHD boys following failure experiences. *Journal of Abnormal Child Psychology*, **19**, 519–536.

MTA Cooperative Group (1999a). A 14-month randomized clinical trial of treatment strategies for attention-deficit hyperactivity disorder (ADHD). *Archives of General Psychiatry*, **56**, 1073–1086.

MTA Cooperative Group (1999b). Effects of co-morbid anxiety disorder, family poverty, session attendance, and community medication on treatment outcome for attention-deficit hyperactivity disorder. *Archives of General Psychiatry*, **56**, 1088–1096.

Ollendick, T.H., Weist, M.D., Borden, M.C., & Green, R.W. (1992). Sociometric status and academic, behavioral, and psychological adjustment: A five year longitudinal study. *Journal of Consulting and Clinical Psychology*, **60**, 80–87.

Parker, J.G., & Asher, S.R. (1987). Peer relations and later personal adjustment: Are low-accepted children at risk? *Psychological Bulletin*, **102**, 357–389.

Patterson, G.R., Reid, J.B., & Dishion, T.J. (1992). *Antisocial boys.* Eugene, OR: Castalia.

Pelham, W.E., & Hinshaw, S.P. (1992). Behavioral intervention for ADHD. In S.M. Turner, K.S. Calhoun, & H.E. Adams (Eds), *Handbook of clinical behavior therapy* (2nd edn; pp. 259–283). New York: John Wiley & Sons.

Pelham, W.E., & Hoza, B. (1996). Intensive treatment: A summer treatment program for children with ADHD. In E.D. Hibbs & P.S. Jensen (Eds), *Psychosocial treatments for child and adolescent disorders: Empirically-based strategies for clinical practice* (pp. 311–340). Washington, DC: American Psychological Association.

Pelham, W.E., & Lang, A.R. (1993). Parental alcohol consumption and deviant child behaviour: Laboratory studies of reciprocal effects. *Clinical Psychology Review*, **13**, 763–784.

Pelham, W.E., & Lang, A.R. (1999). Can your children drive you to drink? Stress and parenting in adults interacting with children with ADHD. *Alcohol Research and Health*, **23** (4), 292–298.

Pelham, W.E., & Waschbusch, D.A. (1999). Behavioural intervention in attention-deficit/ hyperactivity disorder. In H.C. Quay & A.E. Hogan (Eds), *Handbook of disruptive behavior disorders* (pp. 255–278). New York: Kluwer Academic.

Pelham, W.E., Wheeler, T., & Chronis, A. (1998). Empirically supported psychosocial treatments for attention-deficit hyperactivity disorder. *Journal of Clinical Child Psychology*, **27** (2), 190–205.

Pelham, W.E., Carlson, C., Sams, S.E., Dixon, M.J., & Hoza, B. (1993). Separate and combined effects of methylphenidate and behavior modification on boys with attention-deficit hyperactivity disorder in the classroom. *Journal of Consulting and Clinical Psychology*, **61**, 506–515.

Pelham, W.E., Greenslade, K.E., Vodde-Hamilton, M., Murphy, D.A., Greenstein, J.J., Gnagy, E.M., Guthrie, K.J., Hoover, M.D., & Dahl, R.E. (1990). Relative efficacy of long-acting stimulants on children with attention-deficit hyperactivity disorder: A comparison of standard methylphenidate, sustained-release methylphenidate, sustained-release dextroamphetamine, and pemoline. *Pediatrics*, **86**, 226–237.

Pelham, W.E., Schnedler, R.W., Bender, M., Nilsson, D., Miller, J., Budrown, M., Ronnei, M., Paluchowski, C., & Marks, D. (1988). The combination of behavior therapy and methylphenidate in the treatment of attention deficit disorder: A therapy outcome study. In L.M. Bloomingdale (Ed.), *Attention deficit disorder* (vol. 3; pp. 29–48). Oxford, United Kingdom: Pergamon.

Pelham, W.E., Sturges, J., Hoza, J., Schmidt, C., Bijlsma, J.J., Milich, R., & Moorer, S. (1987). Sustained release and standard methylphenidate effects on cognitive and social behavior in children with attention deficit disorder. *Pediatrics*, **80**, 491–501.

Pelham, W.E., Vodde-Hamilton, M. Murphy, D.A., Greenstein, J., & Vallano, G. (1991). The effects of methylphenidate on ADHD adolescents in recreational, peer group and classroom settings. *Journal of Clinical Child Psychologist*, **20**, 293–300.

Pfiffner, L.J., & Barkley, R.A. (1990). Educational placement and classroom management. In R.A. Barkley (Ed.), *Attention-deficit hyperactivity disorder: A handbook for diagnosis and treatment* (pp. 498–539). New York: Guilford Press.

Pfiffner, L.J., & O'Leary, S.G. (1987). The efficacy of all-positive management as a function of the prior use of negative consequences. *Journal of Applied Behavior Analysis*, **20**, 265–271.

Pfiffner, L.J., & O'Leary, S.G. (1993). School-based psychological treatments. In J.L. Matson (Ed.), *Handbook of hyperactivity in children*. Boston, MA: Allyn & Bacon.

Pfiffner, L.J., Rosen, L.A., & O'Leary, S.G. (1985). The efficacy of an all-positive approach to classroom management. *Journal of Applied Behavior Analysis*, **18**, 257–261.

Pierce, E.W., Ewing, L.J., & Campbell, S.B. (1999). Diagnostic status and symptomatic behavior of hard-to-manage preschool children in middle childhood and early adolescence. *Journal of Clinical Child Psychology*, **28**, 44–57.

Pisterman, S., Firestone, P., McGrath, P., Goodman, J.T., Webster, I., Mallory, R., & Goffin, B. (1992). The role of parent training in treatment of preschoolers with ADDH. *American Journal of Orthopsychiatry*, **62**, 397–408.

Pisterman, S., McGrath, P., Firestone, P., Goodman, J.T., Webster, I., & Mallory, R. (1989). Outcome of parent-mediated treatment of preschoolers with attention deficit disorder with hyperactivity. *Journal of Consulting and Clinical Psychology*, **57**, 628–635.

Pizzuti, D. (1996). Letter to physicians. Abbott Laboratories Pharmaceutical Products Division, Medical Services Dept., Abbott Park, Chicago, IL, USA.

Podolski, C.L., & Nigg, J.T. (2001). Parent stress and coping in relation to child ADHD severity and associated child disruptive behavior problems. *Journal of Clinical Child Psychology*, **30**, 503–513.

Pollard, S., Ward, E., & Barkley, R.A. (1983). The effects of parent training and Ritalin on the parent–child interactions of hyperactive boys. *Child and Family Therapy*, **5**, 51–69.

Pope, A.W., & Bierman, K.L. (1999). Predicting adolescent peer problems and antisocial activities: The relative roles of aggression and dysregulation. *Developmental Psychology*, **35** (2), 335–346.

Rapport, M.D., & Kelly, K.L. (1991). Psychostimulant effects on learning and cognitive function: Findings and implications for children with attention-deficit hyperactivity disorder. *Clinical Psychology Review*, **11**, 61–92.

Rapport, M.D., Murphy, A., & Bailey, J.S. (1980). The effects of a response cost treatment tactic on hyperactive children. *Journal of School Psychology*, **18**, 98–111.

Richters, J.E., Arnold, L.E., Jensen, P.S., Abikoff, H., Conners, C.K., Greenhill, L.L., Hechtman, L., Hinshaw, S.P., Pelham, W.E., & Swanson, J.M. (1995). The NIMH collaborative multimodal treatment study of children with attention-deficit/hyperactivity disorder (MTA): Background and rationale. *Journal of the American Academy of Child and Adolescent Psychiatry*, **34** (8), 987–1000.

Robison, L.M., Sclar, D.A., Skaer, T.L., & Galin, R.S. (1999). National trends in the prevalence of attention-deficit/hyperactivity disorder and the prescribing of methylphenidate among school-age children: 1990–1995. *Clinical Pediatrics*, **38**, 209–217.

Safer, D.J., & Krager, J.M. (1994). The increased rate of stimulant treatment for hyperactive/inattentive students in secondary schools. *Pediatrics*, **94**, 462–464.

Schachar, R., & Ickowicz, A. (1999). Pharmacological treatment of attention-deficit/hyperactivity disorder. In H.C. Quay & A.E. Hogan (Eds), *Handbook of disruptive behavior disorders* (pp. 221–254). New York: Kluwer Academic.

Schachar, R., & Tannock, R. (1993). Childhood hyperactivity and psychostimulants: A review of extended treatment studies. *Journal of Child and Adolescent Psychopharmacology*, **3**, 81–97.

Sherman, M., & Hertzig, M.E. (1991). Prescribing practices of Ritalin: The Sulfolk County, New York study. In L.L. Greenhill & B.B. Osman (Eds), *Ritalin: Theory and patient management* (pp. 187–193). New York: Mary Ann Liebert, Inc.

Smith, B.H., Pelham, W.E., Gnagy, E., & Yudell, R.S. (1998). Equivalent effects of stimulant treatment for attention-deficit hyperactivity disorder during childhood and adolescence. *Journal of the American Academy of Child and Adolescent Psychiatry*, **37**, 314–321.

Smith, B.H., Waschbusch, D.A., Willoughby, M.T., & Evans, S. (2000). The efficacy, safety, and practicality of treatments for adolescents with attention-deficit/hyperactivity disorder (ADHD). *Clinical Child and Family Psychology Review*, **3** (4), 243–267.

Sonuga-Barke, E.J.S., Daley, D., Thompson, M., Laver-Bradbury, C., & Weeks, A. (2001). Parent-based therapies for preschool attention-deficit/hyperactivity disorder: A randomized, controlled trial with a community sample. *Journal of the American Academy of Child and Adolescent Psychiatry*, **40** (4), 402–408.

Spencer, T., Biederman, J., & Wilens, T (1998). Pharmacotherapy of ADHD with antidepressants. In Russell A. Barkley (Ed.), *Attention deficit hyperactivity disorder: A handbook for diagnosis and treatment* (2nd edn; pp. 552–563). New York: Guilford Press.

Spencer, T., Biederman, J., & Wilens, T. (2000). Pharmacotherapy of attention deficit hyperactivity disorder. *Child and Adolescent Psychiatric Clinics of North America*, **9** (1), 77–97.

Spencer, T., Biederman, J., Wilens, T., Harding, M., O'Donnell, D., & Griffin, S. (1996). Pharmacotherapy of attention-deficit/hyperactivity disorder across the life cycle. *Journal of the Academy of Child and Adolescent Psychiatry*, **35** (4), 409–432.

Swanson, J.M. (1988). What do psychopharmacological studies tell us about information processing deficits in ADDH? In L.M. Bloomingdale & J. Sergeant (Eds), *Attention deficit disorder: Criteria, cognition, intervention* (pp. 97–116). New York: Pergamon Press.

Swanson, J.M., McBurnett, K., Wigal, T. et al. (1993). Effect of stimulant medication on children with attention-deficit disorder: A review of reviews. *Exceptional Child*, **60** (2), 154–162.

Swanson, J.M., Kraemer, H.C., Hinshaw, S.P., Arnold, L.E., Conners, C.K., Abikoff, H.B., Clevenger, W., Davies, M., Elliott, G., Greenhill, L.L., Hechtman, L., Hoza, B., Jensen, P.S., March, J.S., Newcorn, J.H., Owens, E.B., Pelham, W.E., Schiller, E., Severe, J., Simpson, S., Vitiello, B., Wells, K.C., Wigal, T., & Wu, M. (2001). Clinical relevance of the primary findings of the MTA: Success rates based on severity of symptoms at the end of treatment. *Journal of the American Academy of Child and Adolescent Psychiatry*, **40**, 168–179.

Swanson, J.M., McBurnett, K., Christian, D.L., & Wigal, T. (1995). Stimulant medication and treatment of children with ADHD. In T.H. Ollendick & R. Prinz (Eds), *Advances in clinical child psychology* (vol. 17; pp. 265–322). New York: Plenum.

Tallmadge, J., & Barkley, R.A. (1983). The interactions of hyperactive and normal boys with their fathers and mothers. *Journal of Abnormal Child Psychology*, **11**, 565–580.

Thiruchelvam, D., Charach, A., & Schachar, R.J. (2001). Moderators and mediators of long-term adherence to stimulant treatment in children with ADHD. *Journal of the American Academy of Child and Adolescent Psychiatry*, **40** (8), 922–928.

Weiss, G., & Hechtman, L.T. (1993*). Hyperactive children grown up: ADHD in children, adolescents, and adults.* New York: Guilford Press.

Wells, K.C. (1987). What do we know about the use and effects of behaviour therapies in the treatment of ADD? In J. Loney (Ed.), *The young hyperactive child: Answers to questions about diagnosis, prognosis, and treatment* (pp. 111–122). New York: Haworth.

Wells, K.C. (2001). Comprehensive versus matched psychosocial treatment in the MTA study: Conceptual and empirical issues. *Journal of Clinical Child Psychology*, **30** (1), 131–135.

Wells, K.C., Abikoff, H., Abramowitz, A., Courtney, M., Cousins, L., Del Carmen, R., Eddy, M., Eggers, S., Fleiss, K., Heller, T., Hibbs, T., Hinshaw, S., Hoza, B., Pelham, W., & Pfiffner, L. (1996). *Parent training for attention deficit hyperactivity disorder: MTA study* (unpublished).

Wells, K.C., Conners, C.K., Imber, L., & Delameter, A. (1981). Use of a single-subject methodology in clinical decision-making with a hyperactive child on the psychiatric inpatient unit. *Behavioral Assessment*, **3**, 359–369.

Wells, K.C., Epstein, J.N., Hinshaw, S.P., Conners, C.K., Klaric, J., Abikoff, H.B., Abramowitz, A., Arnold, L.E., Elliott, G., Greenhill, L.L., Hechtman, L., Hoza, B., Jensen, P.S., March, J.S., Pelham, W., Jr, Pfiffner, L., Severe, J., Swanson, J.M., Vitiello, B., & Wigal, T. (2000a). Parenting and family stress treatment outcomes in attention deficit hyperactivity disorder (ADHD): An empirical analysis in the MTA study. *Journal of Abnormal Child Psychology*, **28** (6), 543–553.

Wells, K.C., Pelham, W.E., Jr, Kotkin, R.A., Hoza, B., Abikoff, H.B., Abramowitz, A., Arnold, L.E., Cantwell, D.P., Conners, C.K., Del Carmen, R., Elliott, G., Greenhill, L.L., Hechtman, L., Hibbs, E., Hinshaw, S.P., Jensen, P.S., March, J.S., Swanson, J.M., & Schiller E. (2000b). Psychosocial treatment strategies in the MTA study: Rationale, methods, and critical issues in design and implementation. *Journal of Abnormal Child Psychology*, **28** (6), 483–505.

Whalen, C.K., & Henker, B. (1992). The social profile of attention-deficit hyperactivity disorder: Five fundamental facets. *Child and Adolescent Psychiatric Clinics of North America*, **1**, 395–410.

Whalen, C.K., & Henker, B. (1999). The child with attention-deficit/hyperactivity disorder in family context. In H.C. Quay & A.E. Hogan (Eds), *Handbook of disruptive behavior disorders* (pp. 139–156). New York: Kluwer Academic.

Whalen, C.K., Henker, B., & Dotemoto, S. (1980). Methylphenidate and hyperactivity: Effects on teacher behaviors. *Science*, **208**, 1280–1282.

Whalen, C.K., Henker, B., Buhrmeister, D., Hinshaw, S.P., Huber, A., & Laski, K. (1989). Does stimulant medication improve the peer status of hyperactive children? *Journal of Consulting and Clinical Psychology*, **57**, 545–549.

Wolraich, M., Greenhill, L., Pelham, W., Swanson, J., Wilens, T., Palumbo, D., Atkins, M., McBurnett, K., Bukstein, O., & August, G. (2001). Randomized, controlled trial of OROS methylphenidate once a day in children with attention-deficit/hyperactivity disorder. *Pediatrics*, **108**, 833–892.

Wolraich, M.L., Hannah, J.N., Baumgaertel, A., & Feurer, I.D. (1998). Examination of DSM-IV criteria for ADHD in a county-wide sample. *Journal of Developmental and Behavioral Pediatrics*, **19**, 162–168.

CHAPTER 16

Treatment of Oppositional Defiant Disorder in Children and Adolescents

Ross W. Greene

Harvard Medical School, USA

J. Stuart Ablon

Harvard Medical School, USA

Jennifer C. Goring

Virginia Tech, USA

Vanessa Fazio

Suffolk University, USA

and

Lauren R. Morse

Massachusetts General Hospital, USA

INTRODUCTION

In this chapter we describe and evaluate interventions currently used to treat children and adolescents diagnosed with oppositional defiant disorder (ODD). We first present an overview of the behaviours comprising ODD, followed by a description of methods of assessment and treatment. We also discuss various child and family characteristics associated with the development of these behaviours and the importance of these characteristics in matching treatment to the needs of individual children and their adult caretakers.

Correspondence to Ross Greene, Collaborative Problem Solving Institute, Department of Psychiatry, Massachusetts General Hospital, 313 Washington Street, Suite 402, Newton, MA 02458, USA; email: greene@helix.mgh.harvard.edu

Handbook of Interventions that Work with Children and Adolescents: Prevention and Treatment.
Edited by P.M. Barrett and T.H. Ollendick. © 2004 John Wiley & Sons, Ltd. ISBN 0-470-84453-1.

Phenomenology of ODD

Oppositional defiant disorder (ODD) refers to a recurrent childhood pattern of developmentally inappropriate levels of negativistic, defiant, disobedient, and hostile behaviour toward authority figures (APA, 1994). Specific behaviours associated with ODD include temper outbursts; persistent stubbornness; resistance to directions; unwillingness to compromise, give in, or negotiate with adults or peers; deliberate or persistent testing of limits; and verbal (and minor physical) aggression. These behaviours are almost always present in the home and with individuals the child knows well, and often occur simultaneously with low self-esteem, mood lability, low frustration tolerance, and swearing (APA, 1994). Prevalence rates range from 2 to 16% (APA, 1994).

Until recently, ODD has received limited research attention, perhaps due to its relatively recent introduction into the diagnostic nomenclature. ODD has seldom been considered separately from conduct disorder (CD) (e.g., Hinshaw, 1994; Kuhne, Schachar, & Tannock, 1997; Lahey & Loeber, 1994), probably because ODD has heretofore been viewed merely as an early variant of CD (as noted by Schachar & Wachsmuth, 1990). Data have, in fact, shown that a majority of children diagnosed with CD exhibit the behaviours associated with ODD concurrently or at an earlier age (e.g., Frick et al., 1991; Hinshaw, Lahey, & Hart, 1993; Lahey et al., 1992; Loeber et al., 1992). Thus, to the degree that the behaviours associated with ODD often precede more serious forms of psychopathology—including not only CD but also adult antisocial behaviour (see Langbehn et al., 1998)—the manifestation of these behaviours represents an important window of opportunity for prevention efforts (Loeber, 1990; Lynam, 1996). However, the continuity between ODD and CD is by no means perfect: approximately two-thirds of children diagnosed with ODD do *not* subsequently develop CD (e.g., Biederman et al., 1996a; Hinshaw, Lahey, & Hart, 1993; Hinshaw, 1994; Lahey & Loeber, 1994), leading some researchers to question the practice of combining ODD and CD into a single generic category often called "conduct problems" (Kuhne, Schachar, & Tannock, 1997).

Although the association between ODD and the more serious behaviours comprising CD is indeed imperfect, the behaviours associated with ODD have nonetheless been shown to have potent and adverse effects on adult–child and child–peer interactions (Anastopoulos et al., 1992; Arnold & O'Leary, 1995; Barkley et al., 1992; Greene et al., 2002b; Stormschak et al., 1997), and recent findings demonstrate that this is true irrespective of whether ODD occurs in the presence of CD (Greene et al., 2002d). As described more fully below, ODD youths with and without CD have been found to have significantly elevated rates of comorbid disorders, significant social impairment, and family dysfunction (Greene et al., 2002d).

AETIOLOGY

There is some evidence to suggest that genetic factors may contribute to the development of ODD. Recent data provide evidence that both ODD and CD are familial, albeit with stronger association in CD than in ODD (Greene et al., 2002c). However, theorists have increasingly come to recognize the limitations of the "nature versus nurture" debate, and models of development have increasingly taken on a transactional emphasis that is not well captured by a mere diagnosis. This evolution presumably has been prompted by compelling data underscoring the reciprocal nature of interactions between parents and their difficult offspring (e.g., Anderson, Lytton, & Romney, 1986; Dumas & LaFreniere, 1993; Dumas, LaFreniere, & Serketich, 1995).

The transactional or reciprocal model (Bell, 1968; Belsky, 1984; Chess & Thomas, 1984; Cicchetti & Lynch, 1993, 1995; Gottlieb, 1992; see Sameroff, 1975, 1995) posits that a child's outcome is a function of the degree of "fit" or "compatibility" between child and adult characteristics. A higher degree of adult–child compatibility is thought to contribute to optimal outcomes (in both child and adult), whereas a lesser degree of compatibility is thought to contribute to less advantageous outcomes (in child and adult). Moreover, from a transactional perspective, oppositional behaviour would be viewed as only *one of many possible manifestations of adult–child incompatibility*, in which the characteristics of one interaction partner (e.g., the child) are poorly matched to the characteristics of the second interaction partner (e.g., the parent or teacher), thereby contributing to disadvantageous behaviour in both partners which, over time, contributes to more durable patterns of incompatibility (Greene, Ablon, & Goring, 2003). Such a conceptualization has important implications for the process and goals of treatment, because interventions aimed at reducing children's oppositional behaviour must take into account the transactional processes (incompatibilities between child and adult characteristics) giving rise to such behaviour. Therefore, effective treatment typically requires the active involvement of child *and* adult. Further, the primary goal of treatment is to understand, address, and resolve factors contributing to adult–child incompatibility (Greene, Ablon, & Goring, 2003).

It has been argued that, in its focus on inept parenting practices, research on non-compliance in children has historically overemphasized *adult* characteristics. In order to achieve a truly transactional perspective on ODD—in other words, to understand the myriad patterns of adult–child incompatibility that could contribute to a child's oppositional behaviour—significantly greater attention must be paid to *child* characteristics, with a specific emphasis on emotion regulation, frustration tolerance, adaptation, and problem-solving skills (Greene, Ablon, & Goring, 2003; Greene & Doyle, 1999). Developmental psychologists have long underscored these domains as related to a child's capacity to adapt to environmental changes or demands and internalize standards of conduct (e.g., Crockenberg & Litman, 1990; Harter, 1983; Kochanska, 1993, 1995; Kopp, 1982, 1989; Rothbart & Derryberry, 1981). The skill of compliance—defined as the capacity to defer or delay one's own goals in response to the imposed goals or standards of an authority figure—can be considered one of many developmental expressions of a young child's evolving capacities in these domains (e.g., Maccoby, 1980; Perry & Perry, 1983; Stifter, Spinrad, & Braungart-Rieker, 1999). The capacity for compliance is thought to develop in a sequence that includes, in infancy, managing the discomfort that can accompany hunger, cold, fatigue, and pain; modulating arousal while remaining engaged with the environment; and communicating with caregivers to signal that assistance is needed (e.g., Gottman, 1986; Kopp, 1989). With the development of language, more sophisticated mechanisms for self-regulation and affective modulation develop, as children learn to use language to label and communicate their thoughts and feelings, develop cognitive schemas related to cause-and-effect, and generate and internalize strategies aimed at facilitating advantageous interactions with the environment (e.g., Kopp, 1989; Mischel, 1983).

Researchers have underscored the frustration and emotional arousal that often accompany externally imposed demands for compliance (e.g., Amsel, 1990; Hoffman, 1975; Kochanska, 1993; Kopp, 1989; Stifter, Spinrad, & Braungart-Rieker, 1999). When compliance is viewed both as a complex skill and as a critical milestone on the trajectory of emerging self-regulation and affective modulation, then *non*-compliance (i.e., oppositional behaviour) can be conceptualized as one of many potential byproducts of what might best be described as a "compromised trajectory" in these domains. The finding that infants with poor emotional regulation later have higher rates of non-compliance during the toddler years (Stifter, Spinrad, & Braungart-Rieker, 1999) is not surprising within such a conceptual framework, and is consistent with evidence suggesting that psychopathology tends to occur within a developmental sequence in which less serious manifestations of deviance precede more serious ones (Cicchetti, 1990; Huizinga, 1995; Loeber, 1990).

Many of the psychiatric disorders that are commonly comorbid with ODD may set the stage for compromised skills in the domains of emotion regulation, problem-solving, frustration tolerance, and adaptation. Given that the child characteristics contributing to the development of ODD have been neglected in the literature, we believe it is useful to briefly examine these disorders. Of course, in reviewing these characteristics/disorders, it is not our intention to establish the primacy of child characteristics in the development of ODD. Thus, we discuss each characteristic/disorder in the context of a transactional conceptualization.

Child Characteristics Associated with ODD

Attention deficit/hyperactivity disorder (ADHD) is a diagnosis often applied to children compromised in the skills of self-regulation, deficiencies in higher-order problem-solving, and adjusting behaviour to fit shifting environmental demands (e.g., Hinshaw & Erhardt, 1991; Whalen, 1989), and the overlap and developmental continuity between ADHD and ODD is well established (e.g., Abikoff & Klein, 1992; Biederman et al., 1996b; Danforth, Barkley, & Stokes, 1991; Hinshaw, Lahey, & Hart, 1993; Lahey & Loeber, 1994; Loeber, 1990; Loeber & Keenan, 1994; Speltz et al., 1999; see Newcorn & Halperin, 1994). Current data show that approximately 65% of children diagnosed with ADHD have comorbid ODD, and that over 80% of children diagnosed with ODD have comorbid ADHD (Greene et al., 2002d).

Of late, researchers have focused on the specific cognitive skills deficits underlying ADHD, with particular emphasis on executive skills (e.g., Barkley, 1997a; Denckla, 1996; Fuster, 1995; Milner, 1995; Pennington & Ozonoff, 1996). While there is disagreement over the precise cognitive skills comprising the executive functions (see Lyon, 1996), there is little disagreement over the detrimental effects of executive skill deficits on adaptive human functioning (see Douglas, 1980; Eslinger, 1996). A variety of cognitive skills have been characterized as "executive", including *working memory*, defined as an individual's capacity to hold events in his or her mind while bringing to bear hindsight and forethought for the purpose of acting on the events (see Fuster, 1989, 1995; Pennington, 1994); *self-regulation*, defined as an individual's capacity to regulate arousal in the service of goal-directed action (see Barkley, 1997a); *shifting cognitive set*, which refers to the efficiency and flexibility by which an individual shifts from the rules and expectations of one situation to the rules and expectations of another (see Hayes, Gifford, & Ruckstuhl, 1996); and *problem-solving*, which refers to an individual's capacity to organize a coherent plan of action in response to a problem or frustration (see Borkowski & Burke, 1996).

It has been argued that deficits in executive skills have the potential to compromise a child's capacity to respond to adult directives in an adaptive (compliant) manner (Greene & Ablon, 2004; Greene & Doyle, 1999). For example, a child compromised in the domain of working memory might experience significant difficulty efficiently reflecting upon both the previous consequences of non-compliance (hindsight) and the anticipated consequences of potential actions (forethought). A child compromised in the capacity to regulate arousal might respond to the frustration that occurs in the context of imposed demands for compliance with a high level of emotional reactivity (e.g., screaming, crying, swearing) rather than an appropriate level of reflection (hindsight) and reason. In a child compromised in the skill of shifting cognitive set, one might reasonably expect that the capacity to comply rapidly with adult directives might also be compromised (directives typically require the recipient to shift from the mindset that immediately preceded the directive to the mindset being imposed by the environment).

How might a child's executive deficits be incorporated into a transactional conceptualization of ODD? It seems clear that executive deficits do not *guarantee* that a child will develop ODD (recall that 35% of children diagnosed with ADHD are *not* diagnosed with ODD). From a transactional perspective, it is the degree of compatibility between a child with ADHD and his or her adult caretakers that determines whether oppositional (or other maladaptive) behaviours are ultimately expressed. If, for example, a child with executive deficits were "paired" with an adult who, due to depression or irritability, frequently imposed demands for rapid shifting of cognitive set and exhibited little tolerance for or understanding of the child's poor impulse control, we would predict a low level of compatibility, at least in those interactions tapping into this aspect of their interactions. By contrast, if the child were "paired" with an adult who was aware of this area of incompatibility, cognizant of the situations in which this domain of interactions was likely to be most problematic, and interacted with the child in a way that minimized the adverse effects of such interactions, we would predict a higher level of compatibility and more optimal functioning in child and adult.

The overlap between ODD and mood and anxiety disorders is also increasingly documented. Researchers have shown extremely high rates of ODD in children diagnosed with depression and bipolar disorder (Angold & Costello, 1993; Biederman et al., 1996a; Geller & Luby, 1997; Wozniak & Biederman, 1996; Wozniak et al., 1995). In one study, nearly 70% of children diagnosed with severe major depression and 85% of children diagnosed with bipolar disorder were also diagnosed with ODD (Greene et al., 2002d). Indeed, it is youths with ODD with comorbid mood disorders who may be at particular risk for the development of conduct disorder (Greene et al., 2002d). Meaningful rates of anxiety disorders have also been found in youth with ODD: in one study, over 60% of youth diagnosed with ODD had a comorbid anxiety disorder and 45% of youth diagnosed with an anxiety disorder had comorbid ODD (Greene et al., 2002d). The overlap between ODD and obsessiveness may be particularly compelling (e.g., Garland & Weiss, 1996).

Emotion regulation skills develop in early infancy and increase in complexity and sophistication as a child matures. Children who fail to develop such skills at an expected or advantageous pace may be over- or under-reactive to a wide range of affectively charged situations (e.g., Stifter, Spinrad, & Braungart-Rieker, 1999). Children whose tendency is to over-react to affectively charged situations may find the physiological and emotional arousal associated with such situations difficult to regulate, and may become cognitively debilitated in the midst of such arousal (a phenomenon referred to as "cognitive incapacitation" by Zillman [1988]). Consequently, these children may respond to such situations with more affect (e.g., screaming, swearing) than reason (rational problem-solving) and a reduced capacity to inhibit aggression (Greene & Doyle, 1999). The "affective storms" (prolonged and aggressive temper outbursts) seen in children with bipolar disorder (described by Wozniak & Biederman, 1996) may be considered an example of such over-reactivity. Such outbursts—which may include threatening or attacking others—seem to be associated with a pervasive irritable mood (Wozniak & Biederman, 1996). The rage attacks seen in children with Tourette's disorder—explosive anger, irritability, temper outbursts, and aggression—appear to resemble this pattern as well (e.g., Budman et al., 1998). Children who tend to under-react to affectively charged situations may have difficulty mustering the requisite emotional and cognitive resources to respond to such situations adaptively and may respond to these situations in ways that reflect a similar level of debilitation (e.g., crying, withdrawing). Taken together, there would appear to be strong suggestion that compromised emotion regulation skills—in the form of depressed mood, irritability, mood instability, anxiety, or obsessiveness—has the potential to compromise a child's capacity to respond to adult requests in an adaptive (compliant) fashion.

How might a child's difficulties with emotion regulation inform a transactional conceptualization of ODD? As with executive deficits, it is clear that mood and anxiety disorders do not guarantee that a child will develop ODD. Once again, it is the degree of compatibility between an irritable or anxious child and characteristics of his or her adult caretakers that determines whether oppositional (or other maladaptive) behaviours are ultimately expressed. If an irritable or anxious child were "paired" with an adult who had a poor tolerance to irritability or anxiety and therefore responded to the child in an impatient, inflexible, perhaps hostile manner, we might predict a low level of compatibility, at least in regard to those interactions and situations tapping into this area of incompatibility. By contrast, if the child were "paired" with an adult who was knowledgable about the child (and adult) characteristics contributing to such incompatibility, was aware of the situations in which this incompatibility was likely to be most problematic, and was able to set the stage for interacting with the child in a way that minimized the adverse effects of this incompatibility, we would predict a higher level of compatibility and more optimal outcomes in both child and adult.

Language development is also crucial to the evolution of problem-solving, emotion regulation, frustration tolerance, and adaptability. Not surprisingly, there is a demonstrated association between oppositional defiant disorder and language impairment. Recent data indicate that over 20% of youth diagnosed with ODD have a comorbid language-processing disorder, and that 55% of youth with language-processing disorders are also diagnosed with ODD (Greene et al., 2002d). Cognitive skills such as labelling, categorizing, and communicating feelings and needs, and identifying and selecting corresponding behavioural strategies, are strongly mediated by language (e.g., Bretherton et al., 1986). Language permits children to obtain verbal feedback about the appropriateness of the behavioural strategies they select, thereby facilitating thinking about and reflecting on previous and future actions (e.g., Kopp, 1989). Those children compromised in the capacity to label emotions (such as frustration or anger) may have difficulty identifying and internalizing an adaptive repertoire of behavioural strategies for responding to such emotions. Children limited in the capacity to communicate their emotions and needs may have difficulty participating in give-and-take interactions in a flexible, facile, adaptive manner. Those who have difficulty reflecting on previous and future actions may fail to expand response repertoires, may exhibit delays in problem-solving skills, and may consequently respond to various situations in a manner reflective of a very narrow range of response options (Greene & Doyle, 1999).

As with executive deficits and mood and anxiety disorders, it is clear that while language impairment heightens a child's risk for oppositional behaviour, such an outcome is by no means guaranteed. At the risk of redundancy, it is the degree of compatibility between a child with linguistic delays and his or her adult caretakers that determines whether oppositional (or other maladaptive) behaviours are ultimately expressed. If a linguistically impaired child were, for example, to be paired with an adult who, perhaps because of executive deficits or anxiety, carried expectations for immediate responding to adult queries, we would predict a low level of compatibility, at least in those interactions tapping into this domain of incompatibility. By contrast, if the child were "paired" with an adult who was aware of this area of incompatibility, cognizant of the situations in which this domain of interactions was likely to be most problematic, and interacted with the child in a way that minimized the adverse effects of such interactions, we would predict a higher level of compatibility and more optimal outcomes in both child and adult.

Social cognition represents a very broad domain of skills overlapping significantly with ADHD, mood and anxiety disorders, and language impairment (Greene et al., 1997). Researchers have found a clear association between social information processing deficits and disruptive behaviour and mood disorders (e.g., Bloomquist et al., 1997; Dodge, 1993; Milich & Dodge, 1984; Moore, Hughes, & Robinson, 1992; Quiggle et al., 1992), and a well-established link exists between impaired social cognitive processes and aggressive behaviour (e.g., Vitiello & Stoff, 1997). Kendall (1993) has distinguished between cognitive *distortions* and cognitive *deficiencies*, with the former referring to dysfunctional thinking processes and the latter to an insufficient amount of cognitive activity in situations in which greater forethought prior to action is needed. Both factors are worthy of consideration as it relates to child characteristics which may contribute to the development of oppositional behaviour.

The notion that cognitive distortions may be implicated in aggression is supported by the work of Dodge and colleagues (e.g., Dodge, 1980; Dodge & Coie, 1987; Dodge et al., 1990) who have shown that children whose aggression is classified as "reactive" tend to misinterpret peers' behaviour as being hostile and tend to react to ambiguous provocation with aggression, whereas children whose aggression is classified as "proactive" show fewer signs of distorted social information processing. By what mechanism might the development of the cognitive distortions that typify reactive aggression occur? As noted above, the cognitive skills mediating affective modulation and self-regulation evolve in a developmental sequence beginning at birth and, in optimal circumstances, become increasingly broad and more sophisticated over time. Patterns of social responding are said to become increasingly automatic and rigid over time, whether adaptive or maladaptive, and early experience is thought to exert significant influence on the development of these automatic social responses. Indeed, mental representations of past social interactions and their outcomes are thought to govern the manner by which a child will respond to social stimuli in the immediate, ongoing stream of a social interaction. Emotional arousal may also play a significant role in the development and process of social cognition, as it influences a child's interpretation of a social interaction and the accessibility and selection of response options. The importance of self-regulation and affective modulation skills to this process is clear. Compromised skills in these domains are thought to impose limitations that contribute to incomplete, inaccurate, biased encoding and interpretations of social information; to confine the breadth, accessibility, and enactment of a child's response repertoire; and to set the stage for maladaptive automatic patterns of responding to specific social stimuli (e.g., Akhtar & Bradley, 1991; Dodge, 1993).

Cognitive deficiencies have also been implicated in ODD and aggression, particularly in the domain of problem-solving skills. Researchers have shown that aggressive children tend to have difficulties generating alternative solutions, making decisions about which solutions are most appropriate, and enacting solutions (e.g., Dodge et al., 1986; Kendall, 1993; Kendall, Ronan, & Epps, 1991; Lochman, White, & Wayland, 1991; Richard & Dodge, 1982). Indeed, recent research has shown boys with ADHD with comorbid ODD/CD to evidence greater impairment in problem-solving skills as compared to boys with ADHD alone (Matthys, Cuperus, & Van Egeland, 1999). Other conditions which co-occur with ODD may also set the stage for impaired problem-solving. For example, children with non-verbal learning disability often exhibit deficits in problem-solving skills (see Little, 1993; Rourke, 1989; Rourke & Fuerst, 1995; Semrud-Clikeman & Hynd, 1990), presumably due to rigid, literal, concrete processing.

If it is incompatibility that determines whether ODD-related behaviours are ultimately expressed, then it is once again necessary to consider the transactional processes by which a child's cognitive deficiencies and/or distortions might contribute to variable degrees of compatibility between the child and his or her adult caretakers. If a child who, for example, had difficulty rapidly evaluating response options were paired with an adult who, perhaps because of certain notions about discipline, insisted upon rapid compliance with adult commands, we might predict a lower level of compatibility, at least in those situations tapping into this domain of their interactions. By contrast, if the child were "paired" with an adult who was aware of the child's difficulties, was helped to have more flexible notions of adult discipline, cognizant of the situations in which incompatibility was most likely to present, and interacted with the child in a way that minimized the adverse effects of such incompatibility, we would predict a higher level of compatibility and more optimal outcomes in both child and adult.

Adult Characteristics Associated with ODD

As noted above, a transactional approach to ODD—truly understanding the areas of incompatibility that give rise to oppositional behaviour—requires an understanding of the characteristics of both child *and* adult. Let us turn our attention now to the adult contribution to child–adult compatibility. Alas, this is accomplished with some difficulty, for the majority of research examining adult characteristics flows from *unidirectional* theories emphasizing inept parenting practices as the primary factor influencing the development of oppositional or aggressive behaviour in children. In other words, such research has stemmed from a clear assumption about causality (i.e., parents are the primary agents influencing parent–child interactions) that is incongruent with a transactional perspective.

For example, the social interactional model (e.g., Patterson & Gullion, 1968; Patterson, Reid, & Dishion, 1992; see Taylor & Biglan, 1998) has focused on patterns of parental discipline that contribute to the development of "coercive" parent–child exchanges. As described by Chamberlain and Patterson (1995), four subtypes of "parent inadequate discipline" have been identified as contributing to the development of coercive parent–child interchanges. These subtypes include *inconsistent discipline* (parents who respond indiscriminately to a child's positive and negative behaviours, evidence poor or inconsistent follow-through with commands, give in when a child argues, and unpredictably change expectations and consequences for rule violations); *irritable explosive discipline* (parents who issue high rates of direct commands; frequently use high-intensity, high-amplitude strategies such as hitting, yelling, and threatening; frequently make humiliating or negative statements about the child; and in which there is an increased likelihood that the child will respond with aggressive or defiant behaviour); *low supervision and involvement* (parents who are unaware of their child's activities outside of their direct supervision, do not know with whom the child is associating, are unaware of their child's adjustment at school, rarely engage in joint activities with their child, and are unwilling or unable to provide supervision even when aware of the child's association with antisocial peers); and *inflexible rigid discipline* (parents who rely on a single or limited range of discipline strategies for all types of transgressions, fail to take contextual or extenuating factors into account, consistently fail to provide rationales or to use other induction techniques in the context of discipline confrontations, and fail to adjust the intensity of the discipline reaction to the severity of the child's infraction).

Interestingly, if one were truly determined to invoke unidirectional explanations for children's oppositional behaviour, an alternative unidirectional interpretation of the above adult characteristics is possible: children who evidence oppositional/aggressive behaviour cause any of a variety of maladaptive responses from their adult caretakers. Fortunately, in emphasizing compatibility, such "chicken versus egg" debates lose their appeal. The social interactional model has, in fact, evolved from placing almost exclusive (some might argue unidirectional) emphasis on inept parenting practices as the major determinant of childhood conduct problems (e.g., Patterson, DeBaryshe, & Ramsey, 1989) to an acknowledgment that child characteristics may also contribute to the development of maladaptive parent–child interactions (e.g., Dishion, French, & Patterson, 1995; Patterson, Reid, & Dishion, 1992). However, for a model of development to be considered transactional, it must explain how forces from each level of the environment, as well as characteristics of the individual child and parent, exert reciprocal influences on each other and shape the course of each other's development. That a coercive cycle requires two interaction partners does not, in and of itself, denote a transactional conceptualization. The social interactional model still places primary emphasis on parental characteristics—with a specific emphasis on inadequate parenting practices—rather than on reciprocal parent–child influences (Greene & Doyle, 1999). Moreover, it is not clear that most recent representations of this model posit child characteristics as a *necessary* consideration in the development of coercive adult–child interchanges, though it is quite clear that inept or inadequate parenting practices are viewed as essential to the development of such cycles (e.g., Dishion, French, & Patterson, 1995; Patterson, Reid, & Dishion, 1992; Snyder et al., 1994). Finally, the social interactional model appears to view the coercive cycle as the sole pathway to oppositional behaviour in children. From a transactional perspective, multiple potential pathways to oppositional behaviour in a child would be assumed, all viewed as distinct manifestations of parent–child incompatibility (Greene, Ablon, & Goring, 2003).

While poorly studied, we find (anecdotally) that parents (and teachers) of children with ODD are as heterogeneous as their children (and students). Indeed, we find that many of the characteristics of children that contribute to oppositional adult–child interchanges are also present in their adult caretakers. In other words, poor self-regulation (e.g., executive impairments) and affective modulation (e.g., depression and anxiety), language-processing impairments, and cognitive deficiencies and distortions are found in many of the adults who have "oppositional" interactions with children. If adult–child incompatibility is to be improved, it will certainly be necessary to take these adult characteristics into account in treatment planning.

For example, some adults have difficulty prioritizing (perhaps because of an obsessive-cognitive style) and deciding the relative importance of their parenting agenda. Thus, they may consider all components of their parenting agenda to be of equal and critical importance. Other adults may bring very rigid definitions regarding adult "authority" to parent–child interactions, leaving little room for discussion, processing, "meeting halfway", or inviting the child to participate in arriving at solutions to conflictual interactions. Other adults have a limited repertoire of options for pursuing the behavioural goals they have set for their children. Still other adults have difficulty envisioning and predicting the likely outcomes of their options. Some adults have abandoned most of their parenting agenda, often in order to avoid an aversive response from a child. Still others—often those with executive impairments—parent (and manage a household or classroom) in a manner that can be less organized and structured, leading to impulsive discipline decisions. Yet others experience irritability or depression, leaving little energy to devote to routine issues of parenting or teaching, and often over-react to child behaviours that might not fall outside of what would be considered developmentally appropriate. Again, it is important to remember that these adult characteristics alone do not account for the development of oppositional behaviour in a child. Rather, it is the degree to which these characteristics are poorly matched to the characteristics of a child that accounts for the variant of adult–child incompatibility called ODD.

In sum, children's emotional regulation, frustration tolerance, adaptation, and problem-solving skills do not develop independently of the manner by which important adults teach and model these skills (Kochanska, 1993). Nor do children's capacities for complying with adult directives develop independently of the manner by which caregivers impose expectations for compliance and respond to deviations from these expectations. Indeed, adult–child transactions are thought to exert influence on a child's evolving cognitive skills quite early in development, and may be especially crucial at the point at which oppositional behaviour emerges (Greene, Ablon, & Goring, 2003). As noted earlier, it is at this point in development where two important forces—a child's capacity for compliance and adults' expectations for compliance—are thought to intersect. The method by which caregivers interpret and respond to deviations from expectations for compliance can serve to increase or decrease frustration and arousal in child and adult (e.g., Hoffman, 1983; Kochanska & Askan, 1995; Kopp, 1989) and to alter or fuel emerging response biases in child and adult.

ASSESSMENT

There are myriad combinations of parent–child incompatibility that might contribute to the development of oppositional behaviour in a child, and myriad factors that might contribute to such incompatibility. Assessment can be defined as the identification and understanding of, and factors contributing to, compatibility and incompatibility between a given individual and given aspects of his or her environment. Assessment can be expected to play a critical role as researchers and clinicians endeavour to achieve better outcomes for children with oppositional behaviour and prevent the development of more severe behaviours. Indeed, as argued elsewhere, assessment should contribute directly to the effectiveness of treatment (e.g., Hayes, Nelson, & Jerrett, 1987).

A variety of assessment components are considered to be extremely useful. First and foremost, we believe a *situational analysis* provides indispensable information about the child, adult, and environmental characteristics contributing to oppositional transactions and the incompatibility that gives rise to such transactions. In other words, with whom (mother, father, peer, soccer coach) is the child interacting when oppositional episodes occur, and how are the combined characteristics of interaction partners related to incompatibility? What cognitive tasks precipitate oppositional episodes, and how is this understood in terms of incompatibility? Where do oppositional episodes occur, and how is this understood in terms of incompatibility?

The following assessment components may apply to *both* the child and his or her adult interaction partners: *developmental history* (e.g., early temperament, trauma history, attachment history, family history); *school history* (e.g., the degree to which the child's oppositional behaviours are cross-situational); *treatment history* (i.e.,

previously implemented medical and non-medical interventions and their effectiveness). Given the prior discussion regarding factors contributing to the development of oppositional behaviour, formal and/or informal assessment is also
considered to be invaluable (in both child and adult interaction partners) in the following domains: *general cognitive skills* (provides a backdrop for general level of
expectations and a basis for judging relative strengths and limitations); *executive
functions* and *language-processing skills*; *social skills*, and *problem-solving skills*.

TREATMENT

As stated above, intervention options are most potent when they are well matched
to the needs of those persons for whom intervention is being designed. In other
words, "*What* treatment, by *whom*, is most effective for *this* individual with *that*
specific problem, and in *which* set of circumstances?" (Kiesler, 1966). Diverse
psychosocial treatment approaches have been applied to children's ODD-related
behaviours. Models known alternatively as "parent training" (PT) and "behavioural
family therapy", while differing slightly in their relative emphases on specific aspects
of social learning theory, have focused primarily on altering patterns of parental discipline that contribute to the development of oppositional behaviour and problematic parent–child exchanges (McMahon & Wells, 1998). Skills typically taught to
parents in such models include positive attending; use of appropriate commands;
contingent attention and reinforcement; and use of a time-out procedure (see
McMahon & Wells, 1998). In general, research has documented the efficacy of these
procedures (see Brestan & Eyberg, 1998, for a comprehensive review), and several
intervention programs emanating from these models have been identified as either
"well-established" (the *Living with Children* program [Patterson & Gullion, 1968]
and videotape modelling parent training [Webster-Stratton, 1984, 1990, 1994]) or as
"probably efficacious" (including parent–child interaction therapy [e.g., Eyberg,
Boggs, & Algina, 1995]).

However, this same body of research has also documented various limitations of
PT. First, a substantial number of parents who receive PT do not fully comply with
implementation or dropout of treatment altogether (e.g., Prinz & Miller, 1994), suggesting that this form of intervention may, in fact, not be well matched to the needs
and characteristics of many of those responsible for implementation (Greene &
Ablon, 2004; Greene, Ablon, & Goring, 2003). Most studies examining the efficacy
of PT have presented data only for those who remained in treatment rather than
those who began treatment. Among those who remain in treatment, PT has been
shown to produce statistically significant changes in oppositional behaviour, but
very few studies have reported clinically significant changes (Kazdin, 1997). Indeed,
30 to 40% of those children remaining in treatment continue to evidence behaviour
problems in the clinical range at follow-up (e.g., Kazdin, 1993; Webster-Stratton,
1990). Data have shown that a significant percentage of children—perhaps higher
than 50%—are not functioning within the normal range when such treatment is
completed (Dishion & Patterson, 1992). Finally, the vast majority of studies examining the efficacy of PT has not included clinically referred youth (Kazdin, 1997;
Patterson & Chamberlain, 1994), and has typically failed to examine long-term
treatment effects (Kazdin, 1993, 1997), although noteworthy exceptions to the latter

issue exist (e.g., Ialongo et al., 1993). In view of these limitations, it is reasonable to conclude the following about PT: (a) a meaningful percentage of children and parents do not derive substantial benefit from PT; and therefore (b) alternative treatments that more adequately address the needs of these children and parents must be developed and studied (Greene & Ablon, 2004).

Alternative models of intervention have placed relatively greater emphasis on *cognitive* factors underlying ODD rather than on behaviour *per se* (see Coie & Dodge, 1998; Crick & Dodge, 1996; Kendall, 1985, 1991; Kendall & MacDonald, 1993). Such models emanate from research highlighting the frustration and emotional arousal that often accompany externally imposed demands for compliance (e.g., Amsel, 1990; Hoffman, 1975; Kochanska, 1993; Kopp, 1989; Stifter, Spinrad, & Braungart-Rieker, 1999). As described above, a variety of factors may compromise a child's skills in these domains, and these alternative models of intervention have focused on addressing the cognitive deficiencies and distortions of oppositional or aggressive children. Several such intervention models have been identified as "probably efficacious", including problem-solving training (e.g., Kazdin et al., 1987; Kazdin, Siegel, & Bass, 1992), anger management programs (e.g., Feindler, 1990, 1991, 1995; Lochman, 1992; Lochman et al., 1984, 1987), and multisystemic therapy (e.g., Henggeler, Melton, & Smith, 1992).

It can be argued that, in its exclusive focus on addressing the cognitive distortions and deficiencies of oppositional children, the cognitive model of intervention is no more focused on improving adult–child compatibility than models aimed at altering patterns of parental discipline. As noted earlier, conceptualizing oppositional behaviour as the byproduct of *incompatibility* between characteristics of youth compromised in the domains of emotion regulation, frustration tolerance, problem-solving, and adaptability and characteristics of their adult caretakers (Greene & Ablon, 2004; Greene & Doyle, 1999) has important implications for the process and goals of treatment (reiterated from above). First, interventions aimed at reducing children's oppositional behaviour must take into account the transactional processes (incompatibilities between child and adult characteristics) giving rise to such behaviour. Second, effective treatment requires the active involvement of child *and* adult. Third, the primary goal of treatment is to address and resolve issues related to adult–child incompatibility.

These intervention components have been incorporated into a cognitive-behavioural model of intervention known as the Collaborative Problem Solving (CPS) approach (Greene, 2001; Greene & Ablon, 2004; Greene, Ablon, & Goring, 2003). The specific goals of the CPS approach are to help adults (1) to understand the specific adult and child characteristics contributing to the development of a child's oppositional behaviour; (2) to become cognizant of three basic strategies for handling unmet expectations, including (a) imposition of adult will, (b) collaborative problem-solving, and (c) removing the expectation; (3) to recognize the impact of each of these three approaches on parent–child interactions; and (4) to become proficient, along with their children, at collaborative problem-solving as a means of resolving disagreements and defusing potentially conflictual situations in order to reduce oppositional episodes and improve parent–child compatibility.

The first goal highlights the need for a comprehensive assessment and understanding of the specific factors (reviewed earlier) underlying each child's oppositional behaviour. In the CPS model, adults are helped to conceptualize oppositional behaviour as the byproduct of a "learning disability" in the domains of emotion regulation, frustration tolerance, problem-solving, and/or flexibility. Such a conceptualization helps adults to respond to oppositional behaviour in a less personalized, less reactive, and more empathic manner, and is crucial to helping adults to understand the necessity for a specialized approach to intervention emphasizing remediation of these cognitive issues. The role of *adult* characteristics as a contributing factor to a given child's oppositional behaviour is typically not a major emphasis early in treatment (thereby facilitating adult participation in treatment), but increases in importance as treatment progresses. Indeed, the second goal speaks to the need to help adults to understand that the manner by which they pursue unmet expectations with the child is a major factor influencing the frequency and intensity of oppositional outbursts. Adults are taught that imposing adult will (in the parlance of CPS, this approach to unmet expectations is referred to as "Basket A") is the most common precipitant of oppositional outbursts; that removing the expectation (known as "Basket C") is effective at reducing tension between child and adult and decreasing explosive outbursts, but not effective at helping adults to pursue unmet expectations; and that collaborative problem-solving ("Basket B") is an effective way to pursue expectations without increasing the likelihood of oppositional outbursts while simultaneously training and practicing emotion regulation, frustration tolerance, problem-solving, and adaptability.

Adults are viewed as the "facilitators" of collaborative problem-solving. In fact, adults are often told that their role is to serve as the child's "surrogate frontal lobe" so as to (a) reduce the likelihood of oppositional outbursts in the moment and (b) train lacking thinking skills over the longer term. Adults are trained to proactively focus on antecedent events that precipitate oppositional outbursts rather than reactively focus on consequences. In other words, adults are strongly encouraged to adopt a "crisis prevention" mentality instead of a "crisis management" mentality. As part of this mentality, adults are also helped to focus on situational factors that may be associated with oppositional outbursts, and are taught that the majority of such outbursts are, in fact, quite predictable.

The CPS approach is thought to differ from other anger management and problem-solving training programs in its emphasis on helping adults and children to develop the skills to resolve issues of disagreement *collaboratively*. It has been argued that the equivocal effects of many interventions aimed at training cognitive skills to children have likely been due, at least in part, to the manner in which such interventions were delivered (e.g., Greene & Barkley, 1996; Hinshaw, 1992). For example, in a majority of studies cognitive skills have been trained *outside* the settings where skills were actually to be performed. It has been suggested that training cognitive skills proximally to the setting(s) where behaviour is to be performed might greatly enhance the maintenance and generalization of trained skills (e.g., Greene & Ablon, 2004; Greene & Doyle, 1999), and would be more congruent with a transactional perspective. As has been observed in children with ADHD, the more distant in time and space a treatment is from the situations in which trained skills are to be performed, the less beneficial the treatment is likely to be (e.g., Bloomquist et al., 1997; Greene & Barkley, 1996; Ingersoll & Goldstein, 1993); presumably, the same notion applies to children with ODD. Training cognitive skills proximally to where such skills are to be performed requires, by necessity, considerably greater involvement from and training of interaction partners (e.g., parents, teachers, class-mates) present in the environments where oppositional behaviour is most likely to occur (Greene & Doyle, 1999).

CPS is a manualized treatment program, but session content is not circumscribed. Rather, therapists choose to focus on any combination of five treatment modules based on their assessment of the needs of each child and family. This feature of the CPS approach is thought to enhance the ecological validity of the model. The modules represent important components of CPS (as described above), as follows: (1) educating adults about characteristics (of child, adult, and environment) that may contribute to the incompatibilities giving rise to non-compliant behaviour; (2) use of the "baskets" framework; (3) medication education (helping adults to under-stand that some pathways may be more effectively treated pharmacologically); (4) family communication (identifying and altering communication patterns [e.g., sarcasm] that may fuel oppositional outbursts; and (5) cognitive skills training (remediating additional cognitive issues that are not specifically being addressed in Basket B).

Empirical evaluation of CPS has provided evidence of its effectiveness (Greene et al., 2002a). An initial study of CPS (funded by the Stanley Foundation) involved 50 clinically referred youth (boys and girls between the ages of 4 and 13 years) with ODD. In addition to ODD, all children receiving treatment also had at least subthreshold symptoms of either bipolar disorder or severe major depression. The 50 children were randomly assigned (using a 3:2 randomization scheme) to either CPS or PT; and 47 children completed treatment (CPS $n = 28$, PT $n = 19$).

Parents receiving PT were treated using Barkley's (1997b) program for defiant youth. All participants in this condition received 10 weeks of treatment (nine consecutive weeks and a one-month follow-up). The length of treatment for par-ticipants in the CPS condition was variable, and ranged from 7 weeks to 16 weeks, depending on clinicians' assessment of the needs of each child and family. The average length of treatment in the CPS condition was 11 weeks.

A variety of instruments were used to assess treatment response at the beginning and end of treatment and at four-month follow-up, including clinical global im-pression (CGI) ratings by therapists and parents; parent ratings of the frequency and severity of their children's oppositional behaviour; parenting stress; and parent–child relationship. Comprehensive results from this study are presented else-where (Greene et al., 2002a) but summarized here. Briefly, the two groups did not differ significantly at baseline on any measures of treatment outcome. As noted above, duration of treatment was constant in the PT condition but variable in the CPS condition. To protect against the potential confounds this presented, we assessed the degree to which treatment duration was a significant predictor of outcome for all outcome variables; it was not.

The CPS condition produced significant improvement in parents' ratings of their children's oppositional behaviour from baseline to post-treatment and from base-line to four-month follow-up. No significant differences were found between the two treatment groups at either point in time, nor were time by group interactions sig-nificant from pre-treatment to post-treatment or from pre-treatment to four-month follow-up. Large effect sizes were found for both CPS (1.19) and PT (0.80) from baseline to post-treatment; from baseline to four-month follow-up, a large effect size was found for CPS (1.19) and a moderate effect size for PT (0.48).

The CPS condition produced borderline significant improvement from baseline to post-treatment in global parenting stress. No significant differences were found between the two treatment groups, nor was the time by group interaction significant. The CPS condition produced significant improvement in a variety of domains of parenting stress, including child adaptability and parent competence. The time by group interaction was not significant on any subscale. As regards parent–child relationship, the CPS condition produced significant improvements in limit-setting and in parent–child communication. There was a significant time by group interaction on the child autonomy subscale, with children in the PT condition evidencing deterioration, and children in the CPS condition evidencing improvement, in this domain from pre-treatment to post-treatment.

We next examined ratings of the two treatment conditions on the therapist-completed (at post-treatment) and parent-completed (at four-month follow-up) clinical global impression (CGI) instrument, entering treatment group as a predictor in regression models. At post-treatment, treatment group emerged as a significant predictor, with the behaviour of children in the CPS condition rated as having improved to a significantly greater degree as compared to children in the PT condition. Treatment group also emerged as a significant predictor on parent ratings on the CGI at four-month follow-up, with children in the CPS condition rated as having improved to a significantly greater degree as compared with children in the PT condition.

We identified children who evidenced an "excellent response to treatment" as those whose behaviour was, at post-treatment (rated by therapists) and at four-month follow-up (rated by mothers) as "very much improved" or "much improved" on the CGI. Treatment group was not a significant predictor of excellent response to treatment at post-treatment, although 71% of children in the CPS condition evidenced an excellent response to treatment at post-treatment, compared with 47% of those in the PT condition. At four-month follow-up, treatment group was a significant predictor of excellent response to treatment; 80% of children in the CPS condition evidenced an excellent response to treatment at this data point, compared with 44% of those in the PT condition.

Clinical significance was defined as an improvement of 30% or greater in ODD-related behaviours (as measured by the ODDRS) between baseline and post-treatment and between baseline and four-month follow-up (using methods for defining clinical significance articulated by Jacobson & Truax, 1991). No significant differences were found between the two groups in rates of children evidencing clinically significant change. At post-treatment 52% of children in the CPS condition were rated as having evidenced clinically significant improvement, compared with 32% of those in the PT condition. At four-month follow-up, 46% of children in the CPS condition were rated as having evidenced clinically significant improvement, compared with 32% of those in the PT condition.

While these data require confirmation in larger samples and by different investigators, they are promising as regards the effectiveness of CPS. Thus, CPS may offer significant promise to families of children with ODD who may not derive significant benefit from other approaches aimed at reducing oppositional behaviour. Naturally, this hypothesis awaits scientific evaluation. Researchers have yet to examine characteristics of children with ODD and their adult caretakers that might guide treatment selection. However, it has been suggested that children whose oppositional behaviour is proactive—in other words, aimed at securing rewards—may be more responsive to contingency management procedures, as such children are thought to be sensitive to environmental reinforcers and able to adjust their behaviour in response to extrinsic contingencies (e.g., Vitiello & Stoff, 1997). By contrast, it has been suggested that children whose oppositional behaviour is reactive—in other words, whose oppositional behaviour stems from poor affective modulation, poor self-regulation, or cognitive deficits—should be considered less capable of self-control and less able to adjust behaviour in response to environmental contingencies, and may therefore be more likely to respond to interventions aimed at decreasing hostility, impulsivity, and arousal (e.g., Coie & Koeppl, 1990; Crick & Dodge, 1996; Vitiello & Stoff, 1997). Such a paradigm, of course, is as yet untested.

SUMMARY AND FUTURE DIRECTIONS

While understudied, we now know that ODD—irrespective of the presence of CD—is a highly comorbid condition with the potential for highly adverse outcomes in children and adolescents who are so diagnosed. In this chapter, we reviewed the theoretical "lenses" through which ODD can be viewed, with particular emphasis on transactional models of development. Such models suggest that oppositional behaviour is one of many possible byproducts of "incompatibility" between characteristics of children and their adult caretakers. These characteristics were also reviewed, emphasizing cognitive skills related to emotion regulation, frustration tolerance, adaptation, and problem-solving, and suggesting mechanisms by which deficits in these domains may contribute to the form of adult–child incompatibility called ODD. Finally, we reviewed various models of psychosocial intervention that have been applied to ODD, with particular emphasis on the Collaborative Problem Solving (CPS) approach. CPS represents an attempt to integrate cognitive-behavioural, family systems, and transactional paradigms, and initial findings regarding the effectiveness of this approach have been promising.

However, given the relative neglect of ODD in the research literature, much remains unknown about this disorder and its treatment. As discussed above, it is rare for ODD to occur outside the context of other psychiatric disorders. While this has caused some to question the validity of ODD as a distinct diagnostic entity (it should be noted that CD, too, rarely occurs outside the context of other psychiatric disorders), others have argued that the unique profile of each child and adolescent with ODD has important implications for treatment selection and may have equally important ramifications for clinical severity and long-term prognosis.

It seems clear that, while ODD is defined by circumscribed diagnostic criteria, children and adolescents with ODD are a heterogeneous lot. Researchers have previously shown that different ADHD subtypes have unique patterns of comorbidity and differ in their risk for adverse long-term outcomes; the same may well be true in ODD. For example, emerging data suggest that ODD youth with mood disorders (referred to as a "dysphoric" or "irritable" subtype) evidence significantly greater social impairment and are at far greater risk for the development of CD as compared with youth whose ODD is of an "impulsive" subtype (i.e., those with ADHD) (Greene et al., 2003).

It also seems clear that there is no "one-size-fits-all" approach to the treatment of ODD. The treatment for a child whose oppositional behaviour is fuelled by executive deficits (as might be a sign in ADHD) should differ in meaningful ways from the treatment for a child whose oppositional behaviour is fuelled by irritability or obsessiveness, and should differ in still other ways from the treatment for a child whose oppositional behaviour is fuelled by language-processing issues. Thus, an important future direction for researchers is to study more aggressively the question (posed earlier) "*What* treatment, by *whom*, is most effective for *this* individual (with ODD) with *that* specific problem, and under *which* set of circumstances?" (Kiesler, 1966), and to develop algorithms for helping clinicians make sound treatment decisions based on data gathered through such study.

REFERENCES

Abikoff, H., & Klein, R.G. (1992). Attention-deficit hyperactivity disorder and conduct disorder: Comorbidity and implications for treatment. *Journal of Consulting and Clinical Psychology*, **60**, 881–892.

Akhtar, N., & Bradley, E.J. (1991). Social information processing deficits of aggressive children: Present findings and implications for social skills training. *Clinical Psychology Review*, **11**, 621–644.

American Psychiatric Association (1994). *Diagnostic and statistical manual of mental disorders* (4th edn). Washington, DC: Author.

Amsel, A. (1990). Arousal, suppression, and persistence: Frustration theory, attention, and its disorders. *Cognition and Emotion*, **4** (3), 239–268.

Anastopoulos, A.D., Guevremont, D.C., Shelton, T.L., & DuPaul, G.J. (1992). Parenting stress among families of children with attention deficit hyperactivity disorder. *Journal of Abnormal Child Psychology*, **20**, 503–520.

Anderson, K.E., Lytton, H., & Romney, D.M. (1986). Mothers' interactions with normal and conduct-disordered boys: Who affects whom? *Developmental Psychology*, **22**, 604–609.

Angold, A., & Costello, E.J. (1993). Depressive comorbidity in children and adolescents: Empirical, theoretical, and methodological issues. *American Journal of Psychiatry*, **150**, 1779–1791.

Arnold, E.H., & O'Leary, S.G. (1995). The effect of child negative affect on maternal discipline behavior. *Journal of Abnormal Child Psychology*, **23** (5), 585–595.

Barkley, R.A. (1997a). Behavioral inhibition, sustained attention, and executive functions: Constructing a unifying theory of ADHD. *Psychological Bulletin*, **121** (1), 65–94.

Barkley, R.A. (1997b). *Defiant children: A clinician's manual for assessment and parent training* (2nd edn). New York: Guilford Press.

Barkley, R.A., Anastopoulos, A.D., Guevremont, D.G., & Fletcher, K.F. (1992). Adolescents with attention-deficit hyperactivity disorder: Mother–adolescent interactions, family beliefs and conflicts, and maternal psychopathology. *Journal of Abnormal Child Psychology*, **20**, 263–288.

Bell, R. (1968). A reinterpretation of the direction of effects in socialization. *Psychological Review*, **75**, 81–95.

Belsky, J. (1984). The determinants of parenting: A process model. *Child Development*, **55**, 83–96.

Biederman, J., Faraone, S.V., Mick, E., Wozniak, J., Chen, L., Ouellette, C., Marrs, A., Moore, P., Garcia, J., Mennin, D., & Lelon, E. (1996a). Attention-deficit hyperactivity disorder and juvenile mania: An overlooked comorbidity? *Journal of the American Academy of Child and Adolescent Psychiatry*, **35** (8), 997–1008.

Biederman, J., Faraone, S.V., Milberger, S., Garcia, J., Chen, L., Mick, E., Greene, R.W., & Russell, R. (1996b). Is childhood oppositional defiant disorder a precursor to adolescent conduct disorder? Findings from a four-year follow-up study of children with ADHD. *Journal of the American Academy of Child and Adolescent Psychiatry*, **35** (9), 1193–1204.

Bloomquist, M.L., August, G.J., Cohen, C., Doyle, A., & Everhart, K. (1997). Social problem solving in hyperactive-aggressive children: How and what they think in conditions of controlled processing. *Journal of Clinical Child Psychology*, **26**, 172–180.

Borkowski, J.G., & Burke, J.E. (1996). Theories, models, and measurements of executive functioning: An information processing perspective. In G.R. Lyon & N.A. Krasnegor (Eds), *Attention, memory, and executive function* (pp. 235–262). Baltimore: Paul H. Brookes Publishing.

Brestan, E.V., & Eyberg, S.M. (1998). Effective psychosocial treatment of conduct-disordered children and adolescents: 29 years, 82 studies, and 5,272 kids. *Journal of Clinical Child Psychology*, **27** (2), 180–189.

Bretherton, I., Fritz, J., Zahn-Waxler, C., & Ridgeway, D. (1986). Learning to talk about emotions: A functionalist perspective. *Child Development*, **57**, 529–548.

Budman, C.L., Bruun, R.D., Park., K.S., & Olson, M.E. (1998). Rage attacks in children and adolescents with Tourette's disorder: A pilot study. *Journal of Clinical Psychiatry*, **59** (11), 576–580.

Budman, C.L., Brunn, R.D., Park, K.S., Lesser, M., & Olson, M. (2000). Explosive outbursts in children with Tourette's disorder. *Journal of the American Academy of Child and Adolescent Psychiatry*, **39**, 1270–1276.

Chamberlain, P., & Patterson, G.R. (1995). Discipline and child compliance in parenting. In M.H. Bornstein (Ed.), *Handbook of parenting (Vol. 4): Applied and practical parenting*. Mahwah, NJ: Lawrence Erlbaum Associates.

Chess, S., & Thomas, A. (1984). *Origins and evolution of behavior disorders: From infancy to early adult life*. New York: Brunner/Mazel.

Cicchetti, D. (1990). An historical perspective on the discipline of developmental psychopathology. In J. Rolf, A. Masten, D. Cicchetti, K. Neuchterlein, & S. Weintraub (Eds), *Risk and protective factors in the development of psychopathology*. New York: Cambridge University Press.

Cicchetti, D., & Lynch, M. (1993). Toward an ecological/transactional model of community violence and child maltreatment. *Psychiatry*, **56**, 96–118.

Cicchetti, D., & Lynch, M. (1995). Failures in the expectable environment and their impact on individual development: The case of child maltreatment. In D. Cicchetti & D.J. Cohen (Eds), *Developmental psychopathology: Vol. 2: Risk, disorder, and adaptation* (pp. 32–71). New York: John Wiley & Sons.

Coie, J.D., & Dodge, K.A. (1998). Aggression and anti-social behavior. In W. Damon (Ed.), *Handbook of child psychology* (5th edn). Vol. 3: *Social, emotional, and personality development* (pp. 779–862). New York: John Wiley & Sons.

Coie, J.D., & Koeppl, G.K. (1990). Adapting intervention to the problems of aggressive and disruptive aggressive children. In S.R. Asher & J.D. Coie (Eds), *Peer rejection in childhood*. Cambridge University Press.

Crick, N.R., & Dodge, K.A. (1996). Social information-processing mechanisms in reactive and proactive aggression. *Child Development*, **67**, 993–1002.

Crockenberg, S., & Litman, C. (1990). Autonomy as competence in two-year olds: Maternal correlates of child defiance, compliance, and self-assertion. *Developmental Psychology*, **26**, 961–971.

Danforth, J.S., Barkley, R.A., & Stokes, T.F. (1991). Observations of parent–child interactions with hyperactive children: Research and clinical implications. *Clinical Psychology Review*, **11**, 703–727.

Denckla, M.B. (1996). A theory and model of executive function: A neuropsychological perspective. In G.R. Lyon & N.A. Krasnegor (Eds), *Attention, memory, and executive function* (pp. 263–278). Baltimore: Paul H. Brookes Publishing.

Dishion, T.J., & Patterson, G.R. (1992). Age affects in parent training outcomes. *Behavior Therapy*, **23**, 719–729.

Dishion, T.J., French, D.C., & Patterson, G.R. (1995). The development and ecology of antisocial behavior. In D. Cicchetti & D.J. Cohen (Eds), *Developmental psychopathology: Vol. 2: Risk, disorder, and adaptation* (pp. 421–471). New York: John Wiley & Sons.

Dodge, K.A. (1980). Social cognition and children's aggressive behavior. *Child Development*, **51**, 162–170.

Dodge, K.A. (1993). The future of research on the treatment of conduct disorder. *Development and Psychopathology*, **5**, 311–319.

Dodge, K.A., & Coie, J.D. (1987). Social information processing factors in reactive and proactive aggression in children's peer groups. *Journal of Personality and Social Psychology*, **53**, 1146–1158.

Dodge, K.A., Pettit, G.S., McClaskey, C., & Brown, M. (1986). Social competence in children. *Monographs of the Society for Research in Child Development*, **58**, 213–251.

Dodge, K.A., Price, J.N., Bachorowski, J., & Newman, J.P. (1990). Hostile attributional biases in severely aggressive adolescents. *Journal of Abnormal Psychology*, **99**, 385–392.

Douglas, V.I. (1980). High level mental processes in hyperactive children: Implications for training. In R.M. Knights & D.J. Baker (Eds), *Treatment of hyperactive and learning disordered children: Current research* (pp. 65–92). Baltimore: University Park Press.

Dumas, J.E., & LaFreniere, P.J. (1993). Mother–child relationships as sources of support or stress: A comparison of competent, average, aggressive, and anxious dyads. *Child Development*, **64**, 1732–1754.

Dumas, J.E., LaFreniere, P.J., & Serketich, W.J. (1995). "Balance of power": A transactional analysis of control in mother–child dyads involving socially competent, aggressive, and anxious children. *Journal of Abnormal Psychology*, **104**, 104–113.

Eslinger, P.J. (1996). Conceptualizing, describing, and measuring components of executive function. In G.R. Lyon & N.A. Krasnegor (Eds), *Attention, memory, and executive function* (pp. 367–395). Baltimore: Paul H. Brookes Publishing.

Eyberg, S.M., Boggs, S.R., & Algina, J. (1995). Parent–child interaction therapy: A psychosocial model for the treatment of young children with conduct problem behavior and their families. *Psychopharmacology Bulletin*, **31**, 83–91.

Feindler, E.L. (1990). Adolescent anger control: Review and critique. In M. Hersen, R.M. Eisler, & P.M. Miller (Eds), *Progress in behavior modification* (vol. 26; pp. 11–59). Newbury Park, CA: Sage.

Feindler, E.L. (1991). Cognitive strategies in anger control interventions for children and adolescents. In P.C. Kendall (Ed.), *Child and adolescent therapy: Cognitive-behavioural procedures* (pp. 66–97). New York: Guilford Press.

Feindler, E.L. (1995). An ideal treatment package for children and adolescents with anger disorders. In H. Kassinove (Ed.), *Anger disorders: Definition, diagnosis, and treatment* (pp. 173–195). Washington, DC: Taylor & Francis.

Frick, P.J., Kamphaus, R.W., Lahey, B.B., Loeber, R., Christ, M.A.G., Hart, E.L., & Tannenbaum, L.E. (1991). Academic underachievement and the disruptive behavior disorders. *Journal of Consulting and Clinical Psychology*, **59**, 289–294.

Fuster, J.M. (1989). *The prefrontal cortex*. New York: Raven Press.

Fuster, J.M. (1995). Memory and planning: Two temporal perspectives of frontal lobe function. In H.H. Jasper, S. Riggio, & P.S. Goldman-Rakic (Eds), *Epilepsy and the functional autonomy of the frontal lobe* (pp. 9–18). New York: Raven Press.

Garland, E.J., & Weiss, M. (1996). Case study: Obsessive difficult temperament and its response to serotonergic medication. *Journal of the American Academy of Child and Adolescent Psychiatry*, **35** (7), 916–920.

Geller, B., & Luby, J. (1997). Child and adolescent bipolar disorder: Review of the past 10 years. *Journal of the American Academy of Child and Adolescent Psychiatry*, **36** (9), 1–9.

Gottlieb, G. (1992). *Individual development and evolution: The genesis of novel behavior*. New York: Oxford University Press.

Gottman, J. (1986). The world of coordinated play: Same and cross-sex friendship in children. In J.M. Gottman & J.G. Parker (Eds), *Conversations of friends: Speculations on affective development* (pp. 139–191). Cambridge, England: Cambridge University Press.

Greene, R.W. (2001). *The explosive child: Understanding and parenting easily frustrated, "chronically inflexible" children*. New York: HarperCollins.

Greene, R.W., & Ablon, J.S. (2004). *The Collaborative Problem-Solving approach: Cognitive-behavioural treatment of oppositional defiant disorder*. New York: Guilford Press (in press).

Greene, R.W., & Barkley, R.A. (1996). Attention Deficit/Hyperactivity Disorder: Diagnostic, developmental, and conceptual issues. In M. Breen & C. Fiedler (Eds), *Behavioral approach to assessment of youth with emotional/behavioral disorders: A handbook for school-based practitioners* (pp. 413–449). Austin, TX: Pro-Ed.

Greene, R.W., & Doyle, A.E. (1999). Toward a transactional conceptualisation of oppositional defiant disorder: Implications for assessment and treatment. *Clinical and Family Psychology Review*, **2** (3), 129–147.

Greene, R.W., & Ollendick, T.H. (1999). Behavioral assessment of children. In G. Goldstein & M. Hersen (Eds), *Handbook of psychological assessment* (3rd edn). New York: Elsevier.

Greene, R.W., Ablon, J.S., & Goring, J.C. (2003). A transactional model of oppositional behavior: Underpinnings of the Collaborative Problem Solving approach. *Journal of Psychosomatic Research*, **55**, 67–75.

Greene, R.W., Ablon, J.S., Monuteaux, M., Goring, J., Henin, A., Raezer, L., Edwards, G., Markey, J., & Biederman, J. (2002a). Effectiveness of Collaborative Problem Solving in affectively dysregulated youth with oppositional defiant disorder: Initial findings. (Under review.)

Greene, R.W., Beszterczey, S.K., Katzenstein T., Park, K., & Goring, J.C. (2002b). Are students with ADHD more stressful to teach? Predictors of teacher stress in an elementary-age sample. *Journal of Emotional and Behavioral Disorders*, **10**, 79–89.

Greene, R.W., Biederman, J., Faraone, S.V., Sienna, M., & Garcia-Jetton, J. (1997). Adolescent outcome of boys with attention deficit/hyperactivity disorder and social disability: Results from a 4-year longitudinal follow-up study. *Journal of Consulting and Clinical Psychology*, **65** (5), 758–767.

Greene, R.W., Biederman, J., Monuteaux, M., Goring, J., Faraone, S.V. (2002c). Family transmission of oppositional defiant disorder: Findings from relatives of probands with and without ADHD and conduct disorder. *American Journal of Psychiatry* (under review).

Greene, R.W., Biederman, J., Monuteaux, M., Morse, L., & Faraone, S. (2003). Dysphoric and impulsive subtypes of oppositional defiant disorder: Comorbidity, family dysfunction, social impairment, and adaptive functioning (under review).

Greene, R.W., Biederman, J., Zerwas, S., Monuteaux, M., Goring, J.C., & Faraone, S.V. (2002d). Psychiatric comorbidity, family dysfunction, and social impairment in referred youth with oppositional defiant disorder. *American Journal of Psychiatry* (in press).

Harter, S. (1983). Developmental perspectives on the self-system. In P.H. Mussen (Ed.), *Handbook of child psychology* (vol. 4). New York: John Wiley & Sons.

Hayes, S.C., Gifford, E.V., & Ruckstuhl, L.E. (1996). Relational frame theory and executive function: A behavioral analysis. In G.R. Lyon & N.A. Krasnegor (Eds), *Attention, memory, and executive function* (pp. 279–306). Baltimore: Paul H. Brookes Publishing.

Hayes, S.C., Nelson, R.O., & Jerrett, B.B. (1987). The treatment utility of assessment: A functional approach to evaluating assessment quality. *American Psychologist*, **42**, 963–974.

Henggeler, S.W., Melton, G.B., & Smith, L.A. (1992). Family preservation using multisystemic therapy: An effective alternative to incarcerating serious juvenile offenders. *Journal of Consulting and Clinical Psychology*, **60**, 953–961.

Hinshaw, S.P. (1992). Intervention for social competence and social skill. *Child and Adolescent Psychiatric Clinics of North America*, **1** (2), 539–552.

Hinshaw, S.P. (1994). Conduct disorder in childhood: Conceptualisation, diagnosis, comorbidity, and risk status for antisocial functioning in adulthood. In D.C. Fowles, P. Sutker, & S.H. Goodman (Eds), *Experimental personality and psychopathology research 1994* (pp. 3–44). New York: Springer.

Hinshaw, S.P., & Erhardt, D. (1991). Attention-deficit hyperactivity disorder. In P.C. Kendall (Ed.), *Child and adolescent therapy: Cognitive-behavioral procedures* (pp. 98–128). New York: Guilford Press.

Hinshaw, S.P., Lahey, B.B., & Hart, E.L. (1993). Issues of taxonomy and comorbidity in the development of conduct disorder. *Development and Psychopathology*, **5**, 31–49.

Hoffman, M.L. (1975). Moral internalization, parental power, and the nature of parent–child interaction. *Developmental Psychology*, **11**, 228–239.

Hoffman, M.L. (1983). Affective and cognitive processes in moral internalization. In E.T. Higgins, D. Ruble, & W. Hartup (Eds), *Social cognition and social development: A sociocultural perspective* (pp. 236–274). New York: Cambridge University Press.

Huizinga, D. (1995). Developmental sequences in delinquency. In L. Crockette & N. Crowder (Eds), *Pathways through adolescence: Individual development in context*. Mahwah, NJ: Lawrence Earlbaum Associates.

Ialongo, N.S., Horn, W.F., Pascoe, J.M., Greenberg, G., Packard, T., Lopez, M., Wagner, A., & Puttler, L. (1993). The effects of a multimodal intervention with attention-deficit hyperactivity disorder children: A 9-month follow-up. *Journal of the American Academy of Child and Adolescent Psychiatry*, **32**, 182–189.

Ingersoll, B., & Goldstein, S. (1993). *Attention-deficit disorder and learning disabilities*. New York: Doubleday.

Jacobson, N.S., & Truax, P. (1991). Clinical significance: A statistical approach to defining meaningful change in psychotherapy research. *Journal of Consulting and Clinical Psychology*, **59**, 12–19.

Kazdin, A.E. (1993). Treatment of conduct disorder: Progress and directions in psychotherapy research. *Development and Psychopathology*, **5**, 277–310

Kazdin, A.E. (1997). Parent management training: Evidence, outcomes, and issues. *Journal of the American Academy of Child and Adolescent Psychiatry*, **36** (10), 1349–1356.

Kazdin, A.E., Siegel, T.C., & Bass, D. (1992). Cognitive problem-solving skills training and parent management training in the treatment of antisocial behavior in children. *Journal of Consulting and Clinical Psychology*, **60** (5), 733–747.

Kazdin, A.E., Esveldt-Dawson, K., French, N.H., & Unis, A.S. (1987). Problem-solving skills training and relationship therapy in the treatment of antisocial child behavior. *Journal of Consulting and Clinical Psychology*, **55**, 76–85.

Kendall, P.C. (1985). Toward a cognitive-behavioral model of child psychopathology and a critique of related interventions. *Journal of Abnormal Psychology*, **13**, 357–372.

Kendall, P.C. (1991). Guiding theory for therapy with children and adolescents. In P.C. Kendall (Ed.), *Child and adolescent therapy: Cognitive-behavioral procedures* (pp. 3–22). New York: Guilford Press.

Kendall, P.C. (1993). Cognitive-behavioral therapies with youth: Guiding theory, current status, and emerging developments. *Journal of Consulting and Clinical Psychology*, **61** (2), 235–247.

Kendall, P.C., & MacDonald, J.P. (1993). Cognition in the psychopathology of youth and implications for treatment. In K.S. Dobson & P.C. Kendall (Eds), *Psychopathology and cognition* (pp. 387–426). San Diego, CA: Academic Press.

Kendall, P.C., Ronan, K.R., & Epps, J. (1991). Aggression in children/adolescents: Cognitive-behavioral treatment perspective. In D.J. Pepler & K.H. Rubin (Eds), *The development and treatment of childhood aggression* (pp. 341–360). Hillsdale, NJ: Erlbaum.

Kiesler, D.J. (1966). Some myths of psychotherapy research and the search for a paradigm. *Psychological Bulletin*, **65**, 110–136.

Kochanska, G. (1993). Toward a synthesis of parental socialization and child temperament in early development of conscience. *Child Development*, **64**, 325–347.

Kochanska, G. (1995). Children's temperament, mothers' discipline, and security of attachment: Multiple pathways to emerging internalization. *Child Development*, **66**, 597–615.

Kochanska, G., & Askan, N. (1995). Mother–child mutually positive affect, the quality of child compliance to requests and prohibitions, and maternal control as correlates of early internalization. *Child Development*, **66**, 236–254.

Kopp, C.B. (1982). Antecedents of self-regulation: A developmental perspective. *Developmental Psychology*, **18** (2), 199–214.

Kopp, C.B. (1989). Regulation of distress and negative emotions: A developmental view. *Developmental Psychology*, **25** (3), 343–354.

Kuhne, M., Schachar, R., & Tannock, R. (1997). Impact of comorbid oppositional or conduct problems on attention-deficit hyperactivity disorder. *Journal of the American Academy of Child and Adolescent Psychiatry*, **36**, 1715–1725.

Lahey, B.B., & Loeber, R. (1994). Framework for a developmental model of oppositional defiant disorder and conduct disorder. In D.K. Routh (Ed.), *Disruptive behavior disorders in childhood*. New York: Plenum.

Lahey, B.B., Loeber, R., Quay, H.C., Frick, P.J., & Grimm, S. (1992). Oppositional defiant and conduct disorders: Issues to be resolved for the DSM-IV. *Journal of the American Academy of Child and Adolescent Psychiatry*, **31**, 539–546.

Langbehn, D.R., Cadoret, R.J., Yates, W.R., Troughton, E.P., & Stewart, M.A. (1998). Distinct contributions of conduct and oppositional defiant symptoms to adult antisocial behavior. *Archives of General Psychiatry*, **55**, 821–829.

Little, S.S. (1993). Nonverbal learning disabilities and socioemotional functioning: A review of recent literature. *Journal of Learning Disabilities*, **26** (10), 653–665.

Lochman, J.E. (1992). Cognitive-behavioral interventions with aggressive boys. *Child Psychiatry and Human Development*, **16**, 45–56.

Lochman, J.E., White, K.J., & Wayland, K.K. (1991). Cognitive-behavioral assessment and treatment with aggressive children. In P.C. Kendall (Ed.), *Child and adolescent therapy: Cognitive-behavioral procedures* (pp. 25–65). New York: Guilford Press.

Lochman, J.E., Burch, P.R., Curry, J.F., & Lampron, L.B. (1984). Treatment and generalization effects of cognitive-behavioral and goal-setting interventions with aggressive boys. *Journal of Consulting and Clinical Psychology*, **52**, 915–916.

Lochman, J.E., Lampron, L.B., Gemmer, T.C., & Harris, S.R. (1987). Anger coping intervention with aggressive children: A guide to implementation in school settings. In P.A. Keller & S.R. Heyman (Eds), *Innovations in clinical practice: A source book* (vol. 6; pp. 339–356). Sarasota, FL: Professional Resource Exchange.

Loeber, R. (1990). Development and risk factors of juvenile antisocial behavior and delinquency. *Clinical Psychology Review*, **10**, 1–41.

Loeber, R., & Keenan, K. (1994). Interaction between conduct disorder and its comorbid conditions: Effects of age and gender. *Clinical Psychology Review*, **14** (6), 497–523.

Loeber, R., Green, S.M., Lahey, B.B., Christ, M.A.G., & Frick, P.J. (1992). Developmental sequences in the age of onset of disruptive child behaviors. *Journal of Child and Family Studies*, **1**, 21–41.

Lynam, D.R. (1996). Early identification of chronic offenders: Who is the fledgling psychopath? *Psychological Bulletin*, **120** (2), 209–234.

Lyon, G.R. (1996). The need for conceptual and theoretical clarity in the study of attention, memory, and executive function. In G.R. Lyon & N.A. Krasnegor (Eds), *Attention, memory and executive function*. Baltimore: Paul H. Brookes Publishing.

Maccoby, E.E. (1980). *Social development*. New York: Harcourt, Brace, Jovanovich.

Matthys, W., Cuperus, J.M., & Van Egeland, H. (1999). Deficient social problem-solving in boys with ODD/CD, with ADHD, and with both disorders. *Journal of the American Academy of Child and Adolescent Psychiatry*, **38** (3), 311–321.

McMahon, R.J., & Wells, K.C. (1998). Conduct problems. In E.J. Mash & R.A. Barkley (Eds), *Treatment of childhood disorders* (2nd edn; pp. 111–210). New York: Guilford.

Milich, R., & Dodge, K.A. (1984). Social information processing in child psychiatric populations. *Journal of Abnormal Child Psychology*, **12**, 471–490.

Milner, B. (1995). Aspects of human frontal lobe function. In H.H. Jasper, S. Riggio, & P.S. Goldman-Rakic (Eds), *Epilepsy and the functional autonomy of the frontal lobe* (pp. 67–81). New York: Raven Press.

Mischel, W. (1983). Delay of gratification as process and as person variable in development. In D. Magnusson & V.P. Allen (Eds), *Interactions in human development* (pp. 149–165). New York: Academic Press.

Moore, L.A., Hughes, J.N., & Robinson, M. (1992). A comparison of the social information-processing abilities of rejected and accepted hyperactive children. *Journal of Clinical Child Psychology*, **21** (2), 123–131.

Newcorn, J.H., & Halperin, J.M. (1994). Comorbidity among disruptive behavior disorders: Impact on severity, impairment, and response to treatment. *Child and Adolescent Psychiatric Clinics of North America*, **3** (2), 227–252.

Patterson, G.R., & Chamberlain, P. (1994). A functional analysis of resistance during parent training therapy. *Clinical Psychology: Science and Practice*, **1** (1), 53–70.

Patterson, G.R., & Gullion, M.E. (1968). *Living with children: New methods for parents and teachers*. Champaign, IL: Research Press.

Patterson, G.R., DeBaryshe, B.D., & Ramsey, E. (1989). A developmental perspective on anti-social behavior. *American Psychologist*, **44**, 329–335.

Patterson, G.R., Reid, J.B., & Dishion, T.J. (1992). *Antisocial boys*. Patterson, OR: Castalia Publishing.

Pennington, B.F. (1994). The working memory function of the prefrontal cortices: Implications for developmental and individual differences in cognition. In M.M. Haith, J. Benson, R. Roberts, & B.F. Pennington (Eds), *The development of future oriented processes* (pp. 243–289). Chicago: University of Chicago Press.

Pennington, B.F., & Ozonoff, S. (1996). Executive functions and developmental psychopathology. *Journal of Child Psychology and Psychiatry*, **37**, 51–87.

Perry, D.G., & Perry, L.C. (1983). Social learning, causal attribution, and moral internalization. In J. Bisanz, G.L. Bisanz, & R. Kail (Eds), C.J. Brainerd (Series Ed.), *Learning in children: Progress in cognitive development research* (pp. 105–136). New York: Springer-Verlag.

Prinz, R.J., & Miller, G.E. (1994). Family-based treatment for childhood antisocial behavior: Experimental influences on dropout and engagement. *Journal of Consulting and Clinical Psychology*, **62**, 645–650.

Quiggle, N.L., Garber, J., Panak, W.F., & Dodge, K.A. (1992). Social information processing in aggressive and depressed children. *Child Development*, **63**, 1305–1320.

Richard, B., & Dodge, K.A. (1982). Social maladjustment and problem solving in school-aged children. *Journal of Consulting and Clinical Psychology*, **50**, 226–233.

Rothbart, M.K., & Derryberry, D. (1981). Development of individual differences in temperament. In M.E. Lamb & A.L. Brown (Eds), *Advances in developmental psychology* (vol. 1; pp. 37–86). Hillsdale, NJ: Erlbaum.

Rourke, B.P. (1989). *Nonverbal learning disabilities: The syndrome and the model*. New York: Guilford.

Rourke, B.P., & Fuerst, D.R. (1995). Cognitive processing, academic achievement, and psychosocial functioning: A neurodevelopmental perspective. In D. Cicchetti & D.J. Cohen (Eds), *Developmental psychopathology (Vol. 1): Theory and methods* (pp. 391–423). New York: John Wiley & Sons.

Sameroff, A. (1975). Early influences on development: Fact or fancy? *Merrill-Palmer Quarterly*, **21**, 263–294.

Sameroff, A. (1995). General systems theory and developmental psychopathology. In D. Cicchetti & D.J. Cohen (Eds), *Developmental psychopathology (Vol. 1): Theory and methods* (pp. 659–695). New York: John Wiley & Sons.

Schachar, R.J., & Wachsmuth, R. (1990). Oppositional disorder in children: A validation study comparing conduct disorder, oppositional disorder, and normal control children. *Journal of Child Psychology and Psychiatry*, **31**, 1089–1102.

Semrud-Clikeman, M., & Hynd, G.W. (1990). Right-hemisphere dysfunction in nonverbal learning disabilities: Social, academic, and adaptive functioning in adults and children. *Psychological Bulletin*, **107** (2), 196–209.

Snyder, J., Edwards, P., McGraw, K., Kilgore, K., & Holton, A. (1994). Escalation and reinforcement in mother–child conflict: Social processes associated with the development of physical aggression. *Development and Psychopathology*, **6**, 305–321.

Speltz, M.L., McClellan, J., DeKlyen, M., & Jones, K. (1999). Preschool boys with oppositional defiant disorder: Clinical presentation and diagnostic change. *Journal of the American Academy of Child and Adolescent Psychiatry*, **38**, 838–845.

Stifter, C.A., Spinrad, T.L., & Braungart-Rieker, J.M. (1999). Toward a developmental model of child compliance: The role of emotion regulation in infancy. *Child Development*, **70** (1), 21–32.

Stormschak, E., Speltz, M., DeKlyen, M., & Greenberg, M. (1997). Family interactions during clinical intake: A comparison of families of normal or disruptive boys. *Journal of Abnormal Child Psychology*, **25**, 345–357.

Taylor, T.K., & Biglan, A. (1998). Behavioral family interventions for improving child rearing: A review of the literature for clinicians and policy makers. *Clinical Child and Family Psychology Review*, **1** (1), 41–60.

Vitiello, B., & Stoff, D.M. (1997). Subtypes of aggression and their relevance to child psychiatry. *Journal of the American Academy of Child and Adolescent Psychiatry*, **36** (3), 307–315.

Webster-Stratton, C. (1984). Randomized trail of two parent-training programs for families with conduct-disordered children. *Journal of Consulting and Clinical Psychology*, **52**, 666–678.

Webster-Stratton, C. (1990). Enhancing the effectiveness of self-administered videotape parent training for families with conduct-problem children. *Journal of Abnormal Child Psychology*, **18**, 479–492.

Webster-Stratton, C. (1994). Advancing videotape parent training: A comparison study. *Journal of Consulting and Clinical Psychology*, **62**, 583–593.

Whalen, C.K. (1989). Attention-deficit hyperactivity disorder. In T.H. Ollendick & M. Hersen (Eds), *Handbook of child psychopathology* (2nd edn; pp. 131–169). New York: Plenum.

Wozniak, J., & Biederman, J. (1996). A pharmacological approach to the quagmire of comorbidity in juvenile mania. *Journal of Child and Adolescent Psychiatry*, **35** (6), 826–828.

Wozniak, J., Biederman, J., Kiely, K., Ablon, S., Faraone, S.V., Mundy, E., & Mennin, D. (1995). Mania-like symptoms suggestion of childhood-onset bipolar disorder in clinically referred children. *Journal of the American Academy of Child and Adolescent Psychiatry*, **34** (7), 867–876.

Zillman, D. (1988). Cognition-excitation interdependencies in aggressive behavior. *Aggressive Behavior*, **14**, 51–64.

CHAPTER 17

Treatment of Conduct Problems in Children and Adolescents

Robert J. McMahon

and

Julie S. Kotler

University of Washington, USA

INTRODUCTION

Phenomenology

Conduct problems in children constitute a broad range of "acting-out" behaviours, ranging from annoying but relatively minor oppositional behaviours, such as yelling and temper tantrums, to more serious forms of antisocial behaviour including aggression, physical destructiveness, and stealing. Typically, these behaviours do not occur in isolation but as a complex or syndrome, and there is strong evidence to suggest that oppositional behaviours (e.g., noncompliance) are developmental precursors to antisocial behaviours. When displayed as a cluster, these behaviours have been referred to as "oppositional", "antisocial", and "conduct-disordered" (see Hinshaw & Lee, 2002, for a discussion of terminology). In this chapter, we use the term *conduct problems* (CP) to refer to this constellation of behaviours. However, we will concentrate on treatment-focused interventions for the more severe portion of the CP spectrum that is most commonly associated with a diagnosis of Conduct Disorder (CD). (See Greene, this volume, for a discussion of interventions for the less severe end of the CP spectrum.)

There are a number of current approaches to the description and classification of severe CP. In the *Diagnostic and statistical manual of mental disorders* (4th edn—

Correspondence to Robert J. McMahon, Department of Psychology, University of Washington, Box 351525, Seattle, WA 98195; email: mcmahon@u.washington.edu

Handbook of Interventions that Work with Children and Adolescents: Prevention and Treatment.
Edited by P.M. Barrett and T.H. Ollendick. © 2004 John Wiley & Sons, Ltd. ISBN 0-470-84453-1.

text revision) (DSM-IV-TR; APA, 2000), CP are classified in the category of Disruptive Behavior Disorders and severe CP may warrant a diagnosis of CD (see Angold & Costello, 2001, for a consideration of nosological issues related to CD). The essential feature of CD is a "repetitive and persistent pattern of behavior in which the basic rights of others or major age-appropriate societal norms or rules are violated" (APA, 2000, p. 98). At least 3 of the 15 behaviours listed below must have been present in the past 12 months, with at least one of the behaviours present in the past six months. The behaviours are categorized into four groups: aggressiveness to people and animals (bullying, fighting, using a weapon, physical cruelty to people, physical cruelty to animals, stealing with confrontation of victim, forced sexual activity); property destruction (fire setting, other destruction of property); deceptiveness or theft (breaking and entering, lying for personal gain, stealing without confronting victim); and serious rule violations (staying out at night [before age 13], running away from home, being truant [before age 13]). It is important to note that Oppositional Defiant Disorder (ODD) includes behaviours (e.g., noncompliance) that are also included in CD. However, ODD does not involve the more serious behaviours that represent violations of either the basic rights of others or age-appropriate societal norms or rules. Thus, if a child meets the diagnostic criteria for both disorders, only the diagnosis of CD is made.

Two subtypes of CD are described in the DSM-IV-TR (2000); these are differentiated on the basis of the child's age at the appearance of the first symptom of CD. The Childhood-Onset Type is defined by the onset of at least one of the 15 behaviours prior to 10 years of age, whereas CD behaviour does not appear until age 10 or older in the Adolescent-Onset Type. The validity of these subtypes has also been supported in that children with the Childhood-Onset Type were more likely to display more aggressive symptoms, to be boys, to have a family history of antisocial behaviour, to experience neurocognitive and temperamental difficulties, and to have additional psychiatric diagnoses, whereas Adolescent-Onset Type CD is more highly related to ethnic minority status and exposure to deviant peers (e.g., Lahey et al., 1998; McCabe et al., 2001; Moffitt & Caspi, 2001; Waldman & Lahey, 1994).

In addition to subtypes based on age of onset, several other subtypes of CP are salient when considering the diagnosis and treatment of CD. First, Loeber and Schmaling (1985a) proposed a bipolar, one-dimensional typology of "overt" and "covert" CP behaviours. Overt CP behaviours typically involve direct confrontation with or disruption of the environment (e.g., aggression, temper tantrums, argumentativeness), whereas covert CP behaviours usually occur without the awareness of adult caretakers (e.g., lying, stealing, fire setting). More recent studies (e.g., Tiet et al., 2001; Tolan, Gorman-Smith, & Loeber, 2000; Willoughby, Kupersmidt, & Bryant, 2001) have provided additional validation for this typology. For example, the earlier phase of the developmental trajectory of Childhood-Onset Type CD consists primarily of overt CP, followed by a rapid increase in covert CP (Patterson & Yoerger, 2002).

Focusing specifically on aggressive behaviour, Dodge (Dodge, 1991; Dodge & Coie, 1987) has distinguished between "reactive" and "proactive" forms of aggression. The former is a response to perceived provocation, whereas the latter occurs as a means of obtaining some self-serving outcome. This reactive/proactive subtype has been found to have good criterion validity, to differ in terms of antecedent characteristics (e.g., difficult temperament and inattention are more related to reactive aggression), and to differentially predict maladaptive outcomes (e.g., proactive aggression tends to predict more delinquency and disruptive behaviour) (e.g., Vitaro, Brendgen, & Tremblay, 2002; Vitaro et al., 1998; Waschbusch, Willoughby, & Pelham, 1998). There is also a subgroup of children who are both proactively and reactively aggressive and who have more difficulties than their non-aggressive and proactively aggressive peers, but fewer difficulties than reactively aggressive children in terms of social information-processing deficits (Dodge & Coie, 1987) and on dimensions of reactivity, attention, and depression (Vitaro, Brendgen, & Tremblay, 2002).

In contrast to proactive and reactive forms of aggression, both of which are overt in nature, Crick and colleagues have identified a form of indirect aggression, called relational aggression, that involves strategies such as social isolation and exclusion and behaviours including slandering, rumour spreading, and friendship manipulation (e.g., Crick & Grotpeter, 1995; Crick & Werner, 1998). It occurs more frequently in girls.

In a third approach to the identification of CP subtypes, Frick and colleagues have suggested that youth with CP may be distinguished on the basis of their affective and interpersonal style (Frick & Ellis, 1999). They suggest that, within the group of children with childhood-onset CP, two groups can be identified that differ, based on the presence or absence of callous and unemotional (CU) traits (e.g., lack of guilt and empathy, callous use of others; Christian et al., 1997). Christian et al. (1997) found that children diagnosed with CD who also have high scores on the dimension of CU traits tend to have more diverse and serious CP, an increased likelihood of parental Antisocial Personality Disorder, and an increased likelihood of police contacts. These children also showed higher levels of behavioural dysregulation and lower levels of behavioural inhibition compared to children with CP who are low on CU traits (Frick et al., 2003).

Epidemiology

Prevalence

Prevalence rates generally range from 2% to 9% for CD in various non-clinic samples (e.g., Lahey et al., 1999). Prevalence rates have been shown to vary as a function of age and sex of the child, as well as the type of CP behaviour. For example, younger children are more likely to engage in oppositional, overt behaviours, whereas older children and adolescents are more likely to engage in more covert CP behaviour (e.g., stealing) (Patterson & Yoerger, 2002). In general, boys are more likely to begin engaging in overt CP behaviours earlier and at higher rates than girls throughout the developmental period. In fact, gender is the most consistently documented risk factor for CP (Robins, 1991). Perhaps due to the lower rates of antisocial behaviour in girls, much of the research on CP has focused exclusively on boys or, when girls have been included, has failed to consider possible gender effects. Many questions about the onset and development of antisocial behaviour in girls remain unanswered. However, some evidence does suggest that, compared to boys, girls' antisocial behaviour tends to be less chronic, more experimental, and more likely to desist. During adolescence, gender differences in prevalence decrease dramatically; this seems to be largely accounted for by an increase in the number of girls engaging in covert CP behaviours. For a comprehensive discussion of CP in girls, the reader is referred to Eme and Kavanaugh (1995), Keenan, Loeber, and Green (1999), Silverthorn and Frick (1999), Zahn-Waxler (1993), and Zoccolillo (1993).

There is a high degree of continuity in CP behaviours from infancy to early childhood (e.g., Keenan et al., 1998), from early childhood to later childhood (e.g., Campbell, 1995), from childhood to adolescence (e.g., Lahey et al., 2002; Offord et al., 1992), and from adolescence to adulthood (e.g., Farrington, 2003; Rutter et al., 1994). There is also evidence for cross-generational consistency (e.g., Huesmann et al., 1984; Loeber et al., 2003). Stability also appears comparable for boys and girls (e.g., Coie & Dodge, 1998; Stanger, Achenbach, & Verhulst, 1997). Both boys and girls with CP are at increased risk as adults for engaging in criminal activity (e.g., Kratzer & Hodgins, 1997; Pajer, 1998); girls also seem to be more at risk for a broad array of other adverse outcomes, including various internalizing disorders (e.g., Bardone et al., 1996; Pajer, 1998).

Comorbidity

Children with CP are also at increased risk for manifesting a variety of other behaviour disorders and adjustment problems. In their review of the relationship of CP to various comorbid conditions, Loeber and Keenan (1994) have stressed the importance of considering the temporal ordering of comorbid conditions, as well as the different patterns and influences of these comorbid disorders for boys versus girls. For example, although girls are less likely to display CP than are boys, when girls do display CP, they may be more likely than boys to develop one or more of these comorbid disorders.

ADHD is the comorbid condition most commonly associated with CP, and is thought to precede the development of CP in the majority of cases. In fact, some investigators consider ADHD (or, more specifically, the impulsivity or hyperactivity components of ADHD) to be the "motor" that drives the development of early-onset CP, especially for boys (e.g., Burns & Walsh, 2002; Coie & Dodge, 1998; Loeber et al., 1998; White et al., 1994). Coexisting ADHD also predicts a more negative life outcome than does CP alone (see Abikoff & Klein, 1992, and Taylor et al., 1996, for reviews).

Internalizing disorders, such as the depressive and anxiety disorders and Somatization Disorder, also co-occur with CP at rates higher than expected by chance (Zoccolillo, 1992). In most cases, CP precedes the onset of depressive symptoms (Loeber & Keenan, 1994), although in some cases depression may precipitate CP behaviour (e.g., Kovacs et al., 1988). Risk for suicidality has also been shown to increase as a function of pre-existing CP (e.g., Capaldi, 1991, 1992a/b), and this risk appears to be higher for girls than for boys (Loeber & Keenan, 1994). Additionally, Loeber and Keenan (1994) indicate that the co-occurrence of anxiety disorders with CP is also especially likely for girls. In some studies, boys with CP and a comorbid anxiety disorder are less seriously impaired than are children with CP alone (e.g., Walker et al., 1991); in other studies, the presence of a comorbid anxiety disorder has not been shown to have a differential effect (e.g., Campbell & Ewing, 1990). It is notable that, although the base rate of Somatization Disorder alone is much higher in girls than in boys, its comorbid occurrence with CP may actually be higher in boys (Lilienfeld, 1992; Offord, Alder, & Boyle, 1986).

Both longitudinal and cross-sectional studies have documented that pre-existing CP constitutes a significant risk factor for substance use (e.g., Angold, Costello, & Erkanli, 1999; Hawkins, Catalano, & Miller, 1992). This may be particularly true for girls (Loeber & Keenan, 1994). In addition, concurrent substance use may increase the risk of more serious delinquent behaviour (Angold, Costello, & Erkanli, 1999).

An association between CP and academic underachievement has long been noted. In a comprehensive review, Hinshaw (1992) concluded that during pre-adolescence, this relationship is actually a function of comorbid ADHD, rather than of CP *per se*. In adolescence, the relationship is more complex, with pre-existing ADHD (and perhaps other neuropsychological deficits), a history of academic difficulty and failure, and long-standing socialization difficulties with family and peers all playing interacting roles.

AETIOLOGY

Developmental Progressions

The preceding description of CP and various comorbid conditions fails to convey three different but related considerations that must guide assessment and intervention procedures for children with CP: the developmental, contextual, and transactional aspects of CP (McMahon & Estes, 1997). With respect to developmental considerations, it is clear that the behavioural manifestation of CP changes over time. With respect to context, the development and maintenance of CP are influenced by genetic/constitutional characteristics of the child, family, peers, and broader ecologies. Ethnicity and cultural considerations may also apply to these contexts (e.g., Prinz & Miller, 1991). By "transactional", we mean that these developmental and contextual processes unfold over time and continuously influence one another. Space considerations preclude an extensive description of the roles these various developmental, contextual, and transactional influences play in the development and maintenance of CP. Instead, we present summary descriptions of two developmental progressions of CP as a means of illustrating many of these influences. The reader is referred to several recent excellent reviews for more extensive treatment of these issues (Coie & Dodge, 1998; Lahey, Waldman, & McBurnett, 1999; Patterson & Yoerger, 2002; Raine, 2002).

Early-Starter Pathway

The most thoroughly delineated pathway, and the one that seems to have the most negative long-term prognosis, has been variously referred to as the "early-starter"

(Patterson, Capaldi, & Bank, 1991), "childhood-onset" (Hinshaw, Lahey, & Hart, 1993), or "life-course-persistent" (Moffitt, 1993) pathway. The Childhood-Onset Type of CD in DSM-IV-TR (APA, 2000) would seem to be a likely diagnostic outcome of this pathway. The early-starter pathway is characterized by the onset of CP in the pre-school and early school-age years, and by a high degree of continuity throughout childhood and into adolescence and adulthood. It is thought that these children progress from relatively less serious to more serious CP behaviours over time; that overt behaviours appear earlier than covert behaviours; and that later CP behaviours expand the children's behavioural repertoire rather than replacing earlier behaviours (Edelbrock, 1985; Loeber & Farrington, 2000; Patterson et al., 1998; Patterson & Yoerger, 2002). Furthermore, there is an expansion of the settings in which the CP behaviours occur over time, from the home to other settings such as the school and the broader community.

There is a growing body of evidence concerning the many individual, familial, and broader contextual factors that may increase the likelihood of a child's entering and progressing along the early-starter pathway (see Loeber & Farrington, 2000, and Patterson et al., 1998, for reviews). Child factors that may increase risk for entering the early-starter pathway include hyperactivity (e.g., Loeber & Keenan, 1994; Moffitt, 1993) and a difficult temperament (Moffitt, 1993). The development of the child's social-cognitive skills may also be affected by these neuropsychological deficits (e.g., Coie & Dodge, 1998; Crick & Dodge, 1994).[1] These child characteristics may then predispose the child to both the development of an insecure attachment to the parent (DeKlyen & Speltz, 2001; Greenburg, 1999) and a coercive style of parent–child interaction (Patterson, Reid, & Dishion, 1992). Both of these interaction patterns have been implicated in the development of CP. Various other risk factors that may have an impact on the family and serve to precipitate or maintain child CP have been identified. These include familial factors such as parental social cognitions, parental personal and marital adjustment, other familial stressors, and certain extrafamilial factors (e.g., Capaldi et al., 2002; Coie & Jacobs, 1993; Keenan & Wakschlag, 2000), such as low SES, neighbourhood risk, and parental insularity/low social support.

Late-Starter Pathway

A second major pathway for the development of CP has been proposed, but there has been less consistency in how it has been described. In general, this second pathway begins in adolescence rather than early childhood; it is also thought to result in less serious forms of CP (e.g., property offences rather than violent offences) and to have a higher rate of desistance. However, more children are involved in this pathway than in the early-starter pathway (e.g., 24% vs 7%, respectively, in the Dunedin Multidisciplinary Health Study; Moffitt et al., 1996). It has

---

[1] It should be noted that some recent research has brought the neuropsychological risk hypothesis into question, finding that neuropsychological deficits may not develop until late childhood or adolescence, sometime after entry onto the early-starter pathway (Aguilar et al., 2000).

been referred to as the "late-starter" (Patterson, Capaldi, & Bank, 1991), "adolescent-onset" (Hinshaw, Lahey, & Hart, 1993), or "adolescence-limited" (Moffitt, 1993) pathway. The Adolescent-Onset Type of CD in DSM-IV-TR (APA, 2000) would seem to be a likely diagnostic outcome of this pathway. Patterson and colleagues (e.g., Patterson & Yoerger, 2002) have hypothesized that the process leading to the late-starter pathway begins in families that have marginally effective family management skills. Inadequate parental supervision in middle and high school increase the likelihood of significant involvement in a deviant peer group. However, because these adolescents have a higher level of social skills and a longer learning history of employing such skills successfully than do early starters, they are far less likely to continue to engage in CP behaviours than are early starters. Nonetheless, some evidence suggests that adolescents who develop CP through the late-starter pathway may still be at substantial risk for future maladjustment. For example, Hämäläinen and Pulkkinen (1996) found that late starters constituted nearly one-third of their group of young adult (age 27) criminal offenders.

ASSESSMENT

The delineation of different developmental pathways of CP has a number of important implications for the assessment of children with CP (McMahon & Estes, 1997). First, the assessment must be developmentally sensitive, not only with respect to the child's age and sex, but also in terms of the child's status and progression on a particular developmental pathway of CP. The possibility of comorbid conditions should also be investigated. The assessment must also be contextually sensitive, and provide not only for the assessment of child CP behaviour and other behaviour problems, but also assess other child characteristics, and familial and peer influences. Furthermore, this assessment must examine the broader ecologies of home, school, neighbourhood, and community to the extent that each is warranted. Cultural sensitivity in the development, administration, and interpretation of assessment instruments also requires increased attention (Prinz & Miller, 1991). Finally, the clinician needs to recognize the transactional nature of these developmental and contextual processes, and conduct the assessment accordingly. In addition to focusing on each of these issues, a proper assessment of the child with CP must make use of multiple methods completed by multiple informants concerning the child's behaviour in multiple settings, and the familial and extrafamilial context in which the child functions must also be assessed (McMahon & Estes, 1997).

Child Behaviour *Per Se* and in an Interactional Context

In order to obtain an accurate representation of the referred child's CP behaviour, particularly with regard to its interactional aspects, the therapist must rely on multiple assessment methods, including interviews with the parents, child, and other relevant parties (e.g., teachers); behavioural rating scales; and behavioural observations in the clinic, home, and/or school settings.

Interviews

Interviews conducted with children with CP and their families, and other important adults, can be divided into two general categories: clinical interviews and structured diagnostic interviews. Because parent–child interactions are an important aetiological factor in CP, the clinical interview with the parent is of major importance. An individual interview with the child may or may not provide useful content-oriented information, depending upon the age and/or developmental level of the child and the nature of the specific child behaviours. When assessing overt types of CP, Loeber and Schmaling (1985b) have suggested that maternal and teacher reports may be preferable to child reports, since children often underestimate their own aggressive behaviour. However, when assessing covert types of CP, more valid reports are likely to be obtained from the child.[2] When the presenting problems include classroom behaviour or academic underachievement, an interview with the child's teacher or teachers is also appropriate.

Structured interviews have been used in efforts to improve the reliability and validity of diagnostic (using DSM criteria) interviewing. They can be employed with multiple informants. Two structured diagnostic interviews that are frequently employed in the diagnosis of children with CP are the Diagnostic Interview Schedule for Children (DISC; e.g., Shaffer et al., 2000) and the Diagnostic Interview for Children and Adolescents (DICA; e.g., Reich, 2000). For recent reviews of these and other structured diagnostic interviews see Kamphaus and Frick (2001) and McClellan and Werry (2000).

Behavioural Rating Scales

Behavioural rating scales, completed by adults or the child in reference to the child's behaviour or characteristics, are very useful as screening devices, both for covering a broad range of CP behaviours and for assessing the presence of other child behaviour disorders. Although there are many behavioural rating scales, several have been recommended as most appropriate for clinical and research use with children with CP (McMahon & Estes, 1997). There are a number of instruments in the Achenbach System of Empirically Based Assessment (ASEBA) designed for use with children between the ages of 6 and 18 (Achenbach & Rescorla, 2001). There are parallel forms of the Child Behavior Checklist (CBCL) for parents (CBCL/6–18), teachers (Teacher's Report Form; TRF/6–18), youth (Youth Self-Report; YSR/11–18), and observers (Direct Observation Form; DOF/5–14). They are designed to be self-administered, and each can usually be completed in 15–20 minutes. The instruments include sections concerning competence and problem items (the DOF includes only problem items).

Various other behavioural rating scales, completed by parents, teachers, or children, focus on specific aspects of CP. An example of a child self-report measure that focuses specifically on CP is the Self-Report Delinquency Scale (SRD; Elliott, Huizinga, & Ageton, 1985). The SRD consists of 47 items that are derived from

---

[2] However, given the strong positive correlations between stealing and lying, children who steal may not be veridical in their self-reports.

offences listed in the Uniform Crime Reports and covers index offences (e.g., stole motor vehicle, aggravated assault), other delinquent behaviours (e.g., hit parent, panhandled), and drug use.

Behavioural Observation

A variety of coding systems, developed for use in both natural and structured observational settings, are currently available. For example, the Interpersonal Process Code (IPC; Rusby, Estes, & Dishion, 1991) has been developed by the Oregon Social Learning Center (OSLC), which has been at the forefront in the development of observational coding systems. The IPC, used in a variety of interactional contexts (e.g., playground, home, laboratory), consists of three behavioural dimensions: activity (e.g., on-task, off-task), content (i.e., verbal, non-verbal, physical), and affect (e.g., happy, aversive, sad). Alternatively, structured clinical observational paradigms have been developed for the direct assessment of parent–child communication and problem-solving (see Foster & Robin, 1997, for a review). When behavioural observations in the school setting are indicated, the DOF/5–14 (Achenbach & Rescorla, 2001) may be used as part of a multimodal assessment with the other versions of the CBCL described above. Additionally, Dishion has developed a structured observational paradigm for assessing adolescent peer interactions (e.g., Dishion et al., 1996).

An alternative to observations by independent observers in the natural setting is to train significant adults in the child's environment to observe and record certain types of child behaviour. The most widely used procedure of this type is the Parent Daily Report (PDR; Chamberlain & Reid, 1987), a parent observation measure that is typically administered during brief telephone interviews. Parents are asked which of a number of overt and covert behaviours have occurred in the past 24 hours.

Associated Child Characteristics

A brief developmental and medical history of the child should be obtained in order to determine whether any medical factors might be associated with the development or maintenance of the child's CP behaviours and whether the child's early temperament may have contributed to the development of a coercive style of parent–child interaction. Because children with CP may also present with a variety of other behaviour disorders, behavioural rating scales that provide information about a wide range of narrow-band behaviour disorders (e.g., the ASEBA family of instruments; e.g., Achenbach & Rescorla, 2001) can serve as useful screening devices in addition to more open-ended interview techniques. The Antisocial Process Screening Device (Frick & Hare, 2002), which is a behavioural rating scale completed by parents and teachers, can be used to identify children with CP who also exhibit CU traits (Christian et al., 1997; Frick, Bodin, & Barry, 2000; Frick et al., 1994).

In addition to having comorbid behaviour disorders, children with CP frequently have problems with peer interactions and classroom behaviour. Bierman and Welsh (1997) provide a comprehensive review of assessment tools commonly used to evaluate children's social skills. If the presenting problem concerns classroom behaviour, a functional analysis of the problem behaviours should also include an assessment of the child's academic behaviour. Although interviews, observations, and rating scales can provide information concerning the child's academic behaviour, additional evaluation in the form of intelligence and achievement tests is necessary to determine whether the child may have learning difficulties in addition to CP.

Familial and Extrafamilial Factors

McMahon and Estes (1997) delineated six areas that are relevant to the assessment of children with CP. *Parenting practices* are typically assessed via direct observation of parent–child interaction. However, questionnaire measures (e.g., Alabama Parenting Questionnaire; Frick, 1991) may often be more appropriate with parents of older children and in instances when parental behaviours occur infrequently or otherwise difficult to observe. *Parents' (and teachers') perceptions of the child and social cognitions* are a second important area to be assessed. Perceptions of the child may be best assessed through the behaviour rating scales described above. Measures of parental self-esteem (e.g., Parenting Sense of Competence Scale, adapted by Johnston & Mash, 1989) may also be appropriate. The third area involves the assessment of the role that *parents' personal and marital adjustment problems* may be playing in the child's presenting behaviour problems. Measures of maternal depression (e.g., Beck Depression Inventory; Beck et al., 1979), parental antisocial behaviour (e.g., Antisocial Behavior Checklist; Zucker & Fitzgerald, 1992), parental substance use (e.g., Drug Abuse Screening Test (DAST); Skinner, 1982), marital discord (e.g., Dyadic Adjustment Scale; Spanier, 1976), marital conflict (e.g., Conflict Tactics Scale-Partner (CTS-Partner); Straus, 1979, 1990), and parenting-related conflict (e.g., Parenting Alliance Inventory; Abidin, 1988) are some of the most widely used instruments with parents of children with CP. The fourth area is *parenting stress*, which includes general measures of stress (e.g., Family Events List; Patterson, 1982) and specific measures of parenting-related stress (e.g., Parenting Stress Index; Abidin, 1995). With respect to *extrafamilial functioning*, the Community Interaction Checklist (CIC; Wahler, Leske, & Rogers, 1979), which is a brief interview designed to assess maternal insularity, has been extensively employed in research with children with CP and their families. Finally, it is important to assess *parental satisfaction with treatment*, which may be assessed in terms of satisfaction with the outcome of treatment, therapists, treatment procedures, and teaching format (McMahon & Forehand, 1983). At present, no single consumer satisfaction measure is appropriate for use with all types of interventions for children with CP and their families.

TREATMENT

As demonstrated in the preceding material, CP is multifaceted in the diversity of specific behaviours that are manifested, the ages of the children who engage in those behaviours, and the settings in which the behaviours occur. Not surprisingly, a plethora of interventions have been developed to deal with the various manifestations of CP (e.g., Frick, 1998; Hill & Maughan, 2001). In order to impose some structure in our discussion of this array of interventions, we will describe three broad categories of psychosocial interventions: (a) family-based interventions; (b) multi-component interventions; and (c) community-based programs.[3]

Because available interventions vary widely in the extent to which they have been empirically validated, we have selected interventions that are generally considered to meet currently accepted criteria for determining whether an intervention is considered efficacious (see Part I of this volume for a discussion of the selection of empirically supported treatments; see Brestan and Eyberg (1998) for a discussion of this issue specifically related to CP). We also limited our review to interventions that: (a) focus on school-aged children and adolescents; (b) are intended for children and youth with more serious CP (e.g., a CD diagnosis); (c) are treatment-focused, rather than preventive in nature; and (d) focus on interventions for overt CP. Chapters in this volume by Prinz and Dumas and by Sanders address preventive interventions, and the chapter by Greene addresses treatment of ODD. Although covert CP behaviours (e.g., lying, stealing, fire setting) are key components of later developmental manifestations of CD, most interventions primarily targeting covert CP do not qualify as empirically supported treatments (see McMahon & Wells, 1998, for a review of these interventions).

PSYCHOSOCIAL INTERVENTIONS FOR CONDUCT PROBLEMS

Family-Based Interventions

Because of the primary role of the family in the development and maintenance of CP (e.g., Loeber & Stouthamer-Loeber, 1986; Patterson, Reid, & Dishion, 1992), we focus first on interventions directed at the child with CP in the context of the family.

OSLC Parent Training Program

The work of Gerald Patterson and his associates at OSLC with children with CP and their families has been seminal in the development of the theoretical and empirical knowledge base concerning CP. Patterson's efforts over the past 30 years have also been extremely influential with respect to the development and evaluation of family-based intervention strategies for children with CP. Here, we briefly review

---

[3] Some evidence suggests that a number of psychopharmacologic treatments may also be helpful for children and adolescents with CP. These drug therapies have been of primary benefit in treating the aggressive symptoms associated with CP, and although no specific anti-aggressive drug is currently available, some drugs have been evaluated in controlled research for their secondary anti-aggressive properties (Vitiello & Stoff, 1997). The drugs most commonly used to treat CP, which also have some empirical support for their use, include methylphenidate, lithium (primarily for explosive aggression), and in a few specialized cases, antipsychotics. We recommend several useful reviews, which detail the available literature in this area (Conner, 2002; Waslick, Werry, & Greenhill, 1998).

Patterson's parent training program for pre-adolescent children (3–12 years of age) who engage in overt CP.

The parent training program for pre-adolescent aggressive children is delineated in the treatment manual by Patterson et al. (1975) and has been summarized by Forgatch (1991). Prior to beginning treatment, parents are given a copy of either *Living with Children* (Patterson, 1976) or *Families* (Patterson, 1975) to provide a conceptual background for the specific skills training in the treatment sessions and to facilitate generalization and maintenance. After completion of the reading assignment, the next step is to teach the parents to pinpoint the problem behaviours of concern and to then track the child's behaviour. Once the parents are pinpointing and tracking child behaviour appropriately, they are assisted in establishing a positive reinforcement system, using points, backup reinforcers such as privileges or treats, and social reinforcement (i.e., praise). Over time, the tangible reinforcers are faded. After the point system is well established, the parents are taught to use a 5-minute time-out procedure for noncompliance or aggressive behaviour. Response cost (e.g., loss of privileges) and work chores are also sometimes used with older children. As treatment progresses, parents become increasingly responsible for designing and implementing behaviour management programs for various child behaviours. Parents are also taught to monitor or supervise their children, even when they are away from home. Problem-solving and negotiation strategies are taught to the parents at this point in treatment. Patterson and Chamberlain (1988) estimate that approximately 30% of treatment time is devoted to dealing with problems such as marital difficulties, parental personal adjustment problems, and family crises.

This parent training program has been extensively evaluated at OSLC and in community settings. Patterson, Cobb, and Ray (1973) treated 13 consecutive referrals of boys with CP and their families. Behavioural observation data indicated that 9 of the 13 families demonstrated improvements equal to or greater than a 30% reduction from baseline levels of observed deviant behaviour. In subsequent replication studies, similar effects were obtained (Patterson, 1974; Patterson & Reid, 1973). Improvements in maternal perceptions of the child's adjustment have also been reported, and there is evidence for generalization across settings, time (up to two years post-treatment), behaviour, and siblings (e.g., Arnold, Levine, & Patterson, 1975; Horne & Van Dyke, 1983; Patterson, 1974; Patterson & Fleischman, 1979; Patterson & Forgatch, 1995). The program has been shown to have comparable effects for families with older (6.5 to 12.5 years old) and younger (2.5 to 6.5 years old) children, although families with older children were more likely to drop out of treatment (Dishion & Patterson, 1992).

Comparable findings to those reported by Patterson (1974) have been obtained in a mixed sample of children who stole or were socially aggressive (Fleischman, 1981), and for a subset of children who were socially aggressive (Weinrott, Bauske, & Patterson, 1979). These families were treated by clinicians who, although affiliated with Patterson, had not participated in the 1974 investigation and were not supervised by the OSLC staff during the course of the studies. Not only were positive treatment effects maintained at a one-year follow-up, but standardization of treatment procedures and use of a group format in the replication studies reduced treatment time per family from 31 hours to 13–16 hours. Fleischman and Szykula (1981) conducted another replication study in a community setting with 50 families, and reported comparable improvements at post-treatment and at one-year follow-up.

The OSLC group has also conducted a number of comparison studies. Early investigations comparing the parent training program with attention-placebo (Walter & Gilmore, 1973) and wait-list control (Wiltz & Patterson, 1974) conditions reported significant reductions in targeted deviant child behaviours, whereas there were no significant changes for the comparison groups. A later study (Patterson, Chamberlain, & Reid, 1982) randomly assigned 19 families to parent training or wait-list control conditions. The control condition actually became a comparison treatment condition by default, since eight of nine families obtained treatment from various clinicians in the community. Treatment ranged from "eclectic" to behavioural in orientation. Observational data in the home indicated significant reductions in child deviant behaviour for the parent training program only. However, both groups demonstrated significant improvements on the PDR with respect to frequency of parent-reported problem behaviours.

Findings from a large-scale comparative study at OSLC were reported by Patterson and Chamberlain (1988) and Reid (1987). Seventy families with children with CP (aged 6 to 12 years) were randomly assigned to parent training ($n = 50$) or to a community agency employing eclectic family therapy ($n = 20$). Preliminary findings based on the first 34 families in the study indicate significant reductions in child CP behaviour for families in the parent-training condition, but no significant reduction for children in the family therapy condition (Reid, 1987). Only mothers in the parent-training condition demonstrated significant reductions in self-reported levels of depression.

Patterson and his colleagues also modified their parent-training intervention for use with adolescents with CP (Bank et al., 1991; Forgatch & Patterson, 1989; Patterson & Forgatch, 1987). Modifications for delinquent adolescents include: (a) targeting any behaviours that put the adolescent at risk for further delinquency; (b) emphasizing parental monitoring/supervision; (c) revising punishment procedures to include work details, point loss, restriction of free time, and restitution of stolen/damaged property; (d) encouraging parents to report legal offences to juvenile authorities and then to act as advocates for the adolescent in court; and (e) promoting greater involvement of the adolescent in treatment sessions (Bank et al., 1991). A study of the efficacy of this modification (Bank et al., 1991) revealed that, although adolescents in the parent-training condition did have fewer offences during the treatment year compared to the control condition (i.e., community treatment as usual), by the first year after treatment offence rates for the two conditions were comparable, and remained so throughout the three-year follow-up. Despite these somewhat positive findings, Bank et al. are pessimistic as to the feasibility of this approach on a larger scale, given the extreme distress of the families and the high likelihood of therapist burnout. Instead they argue for intervention with these families at an earlier stage, before the problems have increased to such severity and duration.

Functional Family Therapy

Another family-based intervention for adolescents engaging in CP behaviours has been developed and evaluated by James Alexander and his colleagues. Functional

Family Therapy (FFT; Alexander & Parsons, 1982; Barton & Alexander, 1981) represents a unique integration and extension of family systems and behavioural perspectives. The model has also incorporated cognitive and affective perspectives (Alexander et al., 1996).

FFT consists of three main components (e.g., Alexander & Sexton, 2002; Sexton & Alexander, 2002). The *engagement/motivation* phase is concerned with family members' expectations prior to therapy and in the initial sessions. Factors that enhance the perception that positive change is possible are maximized, while factors that might lessen this perception are minimized. During this phase, the clinician identifies the behavioural, cognitive, and emotional expectations of each family member and the family processes in need of change (e.g., interpersonal functions such as closeness and distance). In addition, the clinician takes steps to modify the inappropriate attributions and expectations of family members. Various cognitive therapy techniques, especially relabelling of "negative" behaviour as more positive or benign, are employed. This re-attribution process among family members is seen as necessary, but not sufficient, for successful treatment. Actual behaviour change must follow. In the *behaviour change phase*, a variety of behavioural techniques are employed, including communication skills training, behavioural contracting, and contingency management. In the *generalization phase*, the therapist's job is to facilitate maintenance of therapeutic gains while also fostering the family's independence from the therapy context through gradual disengagement. It is also during this phase that relevant extrafamilial factors (e.g., school, the legal system) are dealt with as necessary.

Much of the empirical research on the efficacy of FFT was conducted in the 1970s, prior to the inclusion of the cognitive and affective components described above. A series of three studies was conducted using a single sample of 86 status delinquents and their families (Alexander & Parsons, 1973; Klein, Alexander, & Parsons, 1977; Parsons & Alexander, 1973). At the conclusion of treatment, families in the FFT condition performed better than families in the comparison conditions on a number of communication variables assessed in a 20-minute family discussion. An examination of juvenile court records 6–18 months after treatment indicated that adolescents in the FFT condition had a significantly lower recidivism rate (26%) compared to adolescents in comparison conditions (Alexander & Parsons, 1973). Within the FFT condition, a poorer outcome on the behavioural family interaction measures was associated with an increased likelihood of recidivism, thus lending direct support to the relationship between the two measures.

These earlier investigations focused on the families of adolescent delinquents with relatively minor status offences. The current version of FFT, in conjunction with supportive adjuncts such as remedial education and job training, has been shown to be effective with multiply offending, previously incarcerated delinquents (Barton et al., 1985). In this investigation, adolescents who participated in FFT were less likely to be charged with committing an offence in the 15-month follow-up period than were adolescents placed in group homes (60% vs 93%, respectively). FFT participants who did commit additional offences committed significantly fewer offences than adolescents in the group home condition.

Gordon, Arbuthnot, and their colleagues (Gordon et al., 1988; Gordon, Graves, & Arbuthnot, 1995) successfully employed a slightly modified version of FFT (longer treatment, treatment in the home as opposed to clinic, and longer training and supervision of therapists) with a sample of 27 disadvantaged, rural families with a delinquent adolescent, many of whom were multiple offenders. Recidivism rates for the FFT and comparison (probation-only) groups at a 2.5-year follow-up were 11% and 67%, respectively. In a subsequent follow-up when the subjects were 20 to 22 years old, Gordon, Graves, and Arbuthnot (1995) reported recidivism rates of 9% vs 41% for the FFT and comparison groups, respectively.

A cross-cultural replication of FFT with juvenile delinquents was completed recently in Sweden by Hansson, Cederblad, and Alexander (2002). In this study, 49 youth received FFT while 40 comparison subjects received treatment as usual (e.g., counselling, case management, referral to other treatment resources). At a one-year follow-up, only 33% of the FFT group had relapsed compared to 65% of the comparison group. This pattern was maintained at the two-year follow-up with a 41% relapse rate in the FFT group compared to an 83% relapse rate in the group of youth that received treatment as usual.

When analysed as part of a cost–benefit study conducted by the Washington State Institute of Public Policy (Aos et al., 1999), FFT was shown to save taxpayers between approximately $14 000 (includes taxpayer benefits only) and $59 000 (includes taxpayer and crime victim benefits) per participant in the program, compared to the cost of one offence (including the crime itself, associated law enforcement costs, adjudication, and punishment/rehabilitation).

Multicomponent Interventions

While the family unit has clearly been a successful focus of interventions for CD, children with CP and their families commonly present with a range of problems that are demonstrated in multiple settings. Thus, it is often the case that no single treatment modality will be sufficient. We present two examples of multicomponent treatments designed to address the complex set of problems often found in children with CD.

Kazdin's Problem Solving Skills Training + Parent Management Training

Kazdin and colleagues have combined skills-based training influenced by the cognitive-behavioural model (Problem Solving Skills Training; PSST) with a behavioural parent-training approach (Parent Management Training; PMT)(see Kazdin, 1996, for a review) to treat pre-adolescent children with CD. PSST emphasizes teaching skills related to the latter stages of the information-processing model (skills for problem identification, solution generation and evaluation, solution selection, and enactment) and utilizes skills training and *in-vivo* practice techniques. PSST is administered individually over 20 sessions, each of which lasts approximately 45–50 minutes. PMT is a traditional behavioural parent-training approach, focusing on the parent as the agent of change, clearly defining child target behaviours, and using role-play of parent behaviour, homework, monitoring, and reinforcement techniques. PMT is administered individually over approximately 15 sessions, with each session lasting 1.5 to 2 hours. When combining these two protocols, procedures are individualized to address a particular family's structure and needs (e.g., single- or dual-parent status, number of children in the home, parents' work schedule).

In an initial study, the combined effect of PSST and PMT was compared to non-directive relationship therapy (Kazdin et al., 1987) in an inpatient sample of children aged 7–12. At post-treatment and one-year follow-up, children in the combined condition showed significantly less aggression and externalizing behaviour at home and school as well as demonstrating improved prosocial behaviour and improvements in overall adjustment.

Kazdin, Siegel, and Bass (1992) evaluated the unique and combined effects of PSST and parent training. At one-year follow-up, the combined treatment was more effective than either one alone. Children in the combined group fell within the normative range of CP behaviour according to parent report; all treatment groups were rated in the normative range by teacher report. In a further analysis of the data from this study, Kazdin and Wassell (2000) found that, in addition to improvements in child functioning, family functioning improved in terms of quality of family relationships, functioning of the family as a system, and perceived social support. Parent functioning also improved (i.e., decreases in depression, overall symptoms, and stress).

Multisystemic Therapy

Multisystemic Therapy (MST) is a multicomponent intervention that has been extensively tested with adolescents with CP and serious, multi-problem, juvenile offenders. The MST approach to treating adolescents with CP emphasizes both the interactional nature of adolescent psychopathology and the role of multiple systems in which the adolescent is embedded, such as the family, school, and peer group (Henggeler & Borduin, 1990; Henggeler et al., 1998). The family is viewed as a core focus of the intervention. Assessment and treatment are concerned with the adolescent as an individual, his or her role in the various systems, and the interrelationships among those systems. Therapists intervene at one or more levels as required, and employ a variety of therapy approaches, such as family therapy, school consultation, peer intervention strategies, marital therapy, or individual therapy. Treatment techniques are similarly wide-ranging, and may include traditional family therapy procedures (e.g., paradoxical intent) as well as behavioural and cognitive-behavioural techniques (e.g., reinforcement, contingency contracting, self-instructions) (Schoenwald et al., 1996). Clinicians are guided by a set of nine treatment principles (e.g., focus on systemic strengths, promote responsible behaviour and decrease irresponsible behaviour among family members, interventions should be developmentally appropriate) (Henggeler et al., 1998; Schoenwald, Brown, & Henggeler, 2000).

MST has been evaluated in multiple studies across problems, therapists, and settings (Henggeler et al., 1998; Schoenwald, Brown, & Henggeler, 2000). Most of the evaluations of MST have been conducted with samples of juvenile offenders (often chronic and/or violent offenders), although the effectiveness of MST with adolescent sexual offenders, juvenile offenders who met criteria for substance abuse or dependence, and youth presenting with psychiatric emergencies has also been investigated. In an initial examination of MST efficacy, Henggeler et al. (1986) conducted an evaluation of MST with inner-city adolescent delinquents, most of whom were repeat offenders, and their families ($n = 57$). At the conclusion of treatment, parents in the MST condition reported fewer behaviour problems, whereas parents of adolescents in an alternative mental health services condition ($n = 23$) and in the normal control condition ($n = 44$) reported no change. Families in the MST condition had also improved at post-treatment on several observational measures of family interaction, whereas the families in the alternative treatment condition either did not change or deteriorated on those measures from pre-treatment to post-treatment.

Henggeler, Melton, and Smith (1992) assessed the effects of MST with a sample of 84 violent, chronic juvenile offenders (mean age = 15.2 years). The offenders were randomly assigned to receive either MST or "usual services" through the Department of Youth Services. One year following referral, youth whose families had participated in MST reported fewer CP behaviours and were less likely to have been arrested or incarcerated than youth in the comparison group. Families who received MST also reported greater cohesion and less peer aggression than families in the comparison group. In a follow-up study conducted 2.4 years post-referral (Henggeler et al., 1993), survival analyses indicated that MST continued to be the superior treatment—39% of the MST group had not been rearrested, compared to 20% of the comparison group.

In an application of MST to a sample of juvenile offenders with substance abuse or dependence, youth were randomly assigned to MST or usual community services (Henggeler, Pickrel, & Brondino, 1999). Compared to the youth receiving community services as usual, the youth receiving MST had higher treatment completion (Henggeler et al., 1996) and increased mainstream school attendance (Brown et al., 1999). Treatment with MST also resulted in cost savings compared to treatment with community services as usual (Schoenwald et al., 1996). Although significant treatment effects for substance abuse were reported at post-treatment, they were not maintained at six-month follow-up (Henggeler, Pickrel, & Brondino, 1999). A four-year follow-up revealed significant reductions in aggressive criminal behaviour (Henggeler et al., 2002). Findings in terms of long-term reductions in illicit drug use were mixed. Although biological indices of drug use (i.e., urine and head hair samples) indicated the superiority of MST, self-report measures did not distinguish MST from community treatment as usual.

The Aos et al. (1999) cost–benefit analysis suggested that MST saved taxpayers between approximately $32 000 (includes taxpayer benefits only) and $132 000 (includes taxpayer and crime victim benefits) per participant in the program.

Community-Based Programs

The systematic development and evaluation of community-based residential programs for aggressive and delinquent adolescents began over 35 years ago, arising from several national directives (e.g., The Presidential Commission on Law Enforcement and the Administration of Justice, 1967) that highlighted the inhumane, expensive, and ineffective nature of traditional institutional programs. Since that time, numerous programs have been developed to address the challenges presented by juvenile offenders who also often display other emotional or behavioural conditions.

Achievement Place/Teaching Family Model

The Achievement Place model (currently known as the Teaching Family Model [TEM]) was originally developed in 1967 and has become the prototypical community-based residential program for aggressive and delinquent adolescents. Each TFM group home is run by a young married couple, referred to as "teaching parents", who undergo a rigorous one-year training program. While living in the group home, the adolescents, most of whom are adjudicated delinquents, attend local schools and are involved in community activities. The primary treatment components of TFM include a multilevel point system, self-government procedures, social skills training, academic tutoring, and a home-based reinforcement system for monitoring school behaviour. The average stay for a participant in the program is about 1 year (Kirigin, 1996).

In terms of effectiveness, the TFM approach appears to be more effective than comparison programs while the adolescents are active participants. Specifically, the developers of TFM compared TFM to other community-based programs (nearly all of which were group homes) and found that, during treatment, a lower percentage of TFM participants engaged in offences and fewer offences were recorded (Kirigin et al., 1982). Independent evaluators (Weinrott, Jones, & Howard, 1982) found that participants in TFM showed slightly more academic improvement compared to participants in community-based comparison programs. However, once the adolescents complete treatment and leave the group home setting, these differences have generally been found to disappear (Kirigin, 1996). It is notable that results from a recent evaluation of TFM at Girls and Boys Town (Larzelere et al., 2001) suggest that some improvements in youth functioning are maintained at a 10-month follow-up. However, as this study did not include a control group, it is difficult to compare these results to those of youth in other types of treatment settings. With respect to cost-effectiveness, TFM is cheaper than alternative group homes. However, both approaches are very expensive; only 45% of the adolescents complete treatment; and by two to three years later, there are few meaningful differences between treatment completers and dropouts (Weinrott, Jones, & Howard, 1982).

Multidimensional Treatment Foster Care

Treatment foster care models are seeing a proliferation in use and evaluation. In a meta-analytic review, Reddy and Pfeiffer (1997) analysed 40 published studies encompassing 12 282 subjects that employed some kind of treatment foster care model for a variety of child and adolescent populations. There were large positive effects on increasing placement permanency of difficult-to-place and difficult-to-maintain youth and on social skills, and medium positive effects on reducing behaviour problems, improving psychological adjustment, and reducing restrictiveness of post-discharge placement.

Over the past 10 years, Chamberlain and her colleagues at OSLC have developed and systematically evaluated a multicomponent intervention for youth with CP that is called the Multidimensional Treatment Foster Care (MTFC) model (e.g., Chamberlain, 1994; Chamberlain & Moore, 1998; Chamberlain & Reid, 1994, 1998; Eddy & Chamberlain, 2000). This model is based on previous intervention work at OSLC and was also influenced by the work of Hawkins and colleagues (Hawkins, 1989; Hawkins et al., 1985), who were the first to use treatment foster care in community-based settings. The key components of MTFC include: (a) recruitment and up to 20 hours of pre-service training for foster parents in a social learning-based parent-training model; (b) ongoing case management consisting of individualized consultation to foster parents, weekly group foster parent meetings, and 24-hour on-call services for crisis management and support to foster parents; (c) daily structure and telephone contact support; (d) school consultation consisting of teaching foster parents school advocacy skills and setting up a home–school daily report card for the adolescent; (e) family therapy with biological parents (or relatives) to coordinate gradual transfer of care from the MTFC parents to the home, if possible; and (f) individual therapy for skills training in problem-solving, anger management, educational issues, and other individual issues. A hallmark of the program is the provision of some adjunctive services that are individualized to meet the needs of youth and their families, similar to MST.

The MTFC program has been evaluated in a number of experimental trials. In an early pilot study of the program, Chamberlain and Reid (1991) randomly assigned 19 adolescents with CP discharged from the state hospital to post-discharge MTFC treatment or control treatment consisting of traditional community placements (e.g., group homes, training school). There were significantly greater reductions in PDR ratings of behaviour problems at three months for MTFC compared to control subjects and a trend for differences at seven months. There was a significantly shorter time from referral to placement for MTFC subjects with associated cost savings. However, social competency and problem-solving skills did not improve for either group.

Another study was conducted with a sample of regular foster parents and the children placed in their care (Chamberlain, Moreland, & Reid, 1992). This study compared one group of foster parents who received the MTFC model of training and support plus a small increase in their monthly stipend to a control group of foster parents who received only the increased stipend. The enhanced MTFC group had increased foster parent retention rates, increased ability to manage child behaviour problems, decreased reports of child behaviour problems, and a decreased number of disrupted placements over the two-year study period.

In more recent work, Chamberlain and Reid (1998) randomly assigned 79 boys referred for out-of-home care due to chronic delinquency to either MTFC or one of 11 group care (GC) placements. During the one-year follow-up, significant differences were found in length of time in placement, runaway rates, arrest rates, days incarcerated, and self-reported delinquency, all in favour of MTFC. Four-year follow-up data showed that boys in MTFC continue to have significantly fewer arrests (Chamberlain, Fisher, & Moore, 2002). Family management skills and peer associations mediated the effect of MFTC on antisocial behaviour and delinquency, accounting for approximately one-third of the variance in boys' subsequent anti-social behaviour (Eddy & Chamberlain, 2000).

The Aos et al. (1999) cost–benefit analysis estimated that the MTFC model saved taxpayers between approximately $22000 (includes taxpayer benefits only) and $88000 (includes both taxpayer and crime victim benefits) per participant in the program.

These studies indicate that MTFC is an efficacious and cost-effective intervention for seriously delinquent and aggressive youth requiring out-of-home placement. The program is multicomponent and staff- and time-intensive; however, it still results in greater cost savings than traditional group home and residential placements.

SUMMARY AND FUTURE DIRECTIONS

Over the past 15 years, there have been significant advances in the application and evaluation of a variety of intervention approaches for children and adolescents who are engaging in severe CP, often including serious and chronic delinquent offend-ing. The OSLC parent training program is a model for treatment-evaluation research; this well-established intervention has been systematically and extensively evaluated by its developers (e.g., Patterson, 1974; Patterson & Chamberlain, 1988; Patterson & Forgatch, 1995) and their work has been replicated and extended by outside researchers (e.g., Fleischman & Szykula, 1981). Also in the area of family interventions, Gordon and colleagues' (1988, 1995) adaptation of FFT suggests that FFT is effective not only with status offenders treated in the earlier outcome studies, but with more serious offenders as well, thus providing a good example of efforts to modify an efficacious program for use with a broader population—an important step in the development effective treatments. Additionally, the cross-cultural replication of FFT in Sweden (Hansson, Cederblad, & Alexander, 2002) provides further evidence of the wide-ranging applicability of this intervention.

With respect to multicomponent interventions, Kazdin and colleagues have com-bined two efficacious intervention programs (PSST and PMT; e.g., Kazdin et al., 1987; Kazdin, Siegel, & Bass, 1992) to establish a program that can address the often complex and diverse CP presented by older children and adolescents. Perhaps most significant in terms of advances in treatment has been the series of large-scale studies by Henggeler and his colleagues (e.g., Henggeler, Melton, & Smith, 1992; Henggeler et al., 1993, 1998) that have demonstrated the effectiveness and gen-eralization of MST with chronic and severe offenders. Their emphases on focusing on multiple risk factors in multiple social contexts using carefully selected, devel-opmentally appropriate interventions represent a state-of-the-art approach for treating youth with severe CP.

Community-based residential programs for adolescents with severe CP have pro-gressed dramatically in the last 35 years. However, widely used community-based residential programs, such as TFM, with its rigorous standards for staff training, quality control, and multilevel evaluation, have yet to demonstrate their superior-ity to multicomponent interventions such as MST in terms of reducing recidivism once adolescents have left the treatment setting (e.g., Kirigin, 1996). These findings have prompted calls for an emphasis on a continuum of intervention services for youth with severe CP (Fagan, 1991; Wolf et al., 1995). A growing body of evidence suggests that other out-of-home systems of care, such as the MTFC model developed and evaluated by Chamberlain and her colleagues (e.g., Chamberlain, 1994; Chamberlain & Moore, 1998), appear both efficacious and cost-effective. In addition to representing an important component in the continuum of available interventions, in some cases, MTFC may also represent an alternative to residential placements.

The discussion of these six psychosocial treatments, all with substantial evidence for efficacy, naturally leads to a number of follow-up questions that require additional attention. The first of these issues has to do with questions of effectiveness. While each of the treatments presented has shown documented improvements under controlled and ideal conditions (i.e., efficacy), it is essential to know whether effects can be maintained when interventions are transitioned to real-world settings (i.e., effectiveness). Some of the treatments presented in this chapter (e.g., MST, FFT, MTFC, and the OSLC Parent Training Program) have studies to support effectiveness and process research has been conducted to examine factors that may impact treatment success once it is implemented outside the relatively controlled environment of efficacy trials. However, in most cases, adequate effectiveness trials have yet to be conducted.

A second issue concerns the cost-effectiveness of various programs. Although there is growing documentation of the cost-effectiveness of some of these interventions (e.g., MST, FFT, MTFC), few studies have compared the cost-effectiveness of multiple validated treatments. Further, little evidence is available to determine what treatment may be most cost-effective for a given population of children with serious CP.

This issue of matching treatment to child leads to a third area requiring additional attention. At this point, we have limited ability to determine what intervention will be most effective for a particular child or adolescent (e.g., Kazdin, 2001). Obtaining this kind of understanding will require conducting studies that (a) include considerations of the various developmental trajectories that can lead to a presentation of serious CP (e.g., early- and late-starter pathways, the presence of CU traits); (b) compare multiple validated treatments; and (c) examine treatment efficacy with subpopulations of children with CP (e.g., children of a given gender or ethnicity, children with comorbid conditions, children presenting primarily with covert CP).

Significant advances have been made in the early identification of children at risk for serious CP. As the boundaries between prevention and treatment become increasingly blurred, a fourth issue to consider involves the need for an increased focus on developing coherent continua of service and transitioning from prevention efforts to treatment efforts when appropriate (see Prinz & Dumas, this volume).

Finally, as groups of services continue to develop that address CP at a variety of ages and developmental stages, researchers will also need to dedicate increasing time and attention to the issue of possible iatrogenic effects as a function of intervention. For example, Dishion, McCord, and Poulin (1999) reviewed evidence suggesting that the placement of high-risk adolescents in peer-group interventions may result in increases in both CP behaviour and negative life outcomes compared to control youth. These findings have led to the development and promotion of treatments that minimize the influence of groups of high-risk adolescent peers and involve the youngsters in conventional peer activities (e.g., sports teams, school clubs) with low-risk peers.

In conclusion, substantial progress has been made in the development and evaluation of efficacious interventions for CP in children and adolescents. In home and community settings, a variety of empirically validated approaches are currently available. However, a number of factors, including the cost and the availability of these treatments, prevent many youth from receiving the help they need. Additionally, even the well-validated treatments presented in this chapter seldom result in the elimination of CP behaviours. Thus, the continued development, evaluation, and dissemination of effective interventions that are sensitive to our growing knowledge about early starter models and the developmental course of CP and are designed to address the wide array of CP behaviours should be primary goals for researchers and clinicians in our field.

REFERENCES

Abidin, R.R. (1988). *Parenting Alliance Inventory.* Unpublished scale, University of Virginia, Charlottesville.

Abidin, R.R. (1995). *Parenting Stress Index—professional manual* (3rd edn). Odessa, FL: Psychological Assessment Resources.

Abikoff, H., & Klein, R.G. (1992). Attention-deficit hyperactivity and Conduct Disorder: Comorbidity and implications for treatment. *Journal of Consulting and Clinical Psychology*, **60**, 881–892.

Achenbach, T.M., & Rescorla, L.A. (2001). *Manual for ASEBA School-Age Forms and Profiles.* Burlington, VT: University of Vermont, Research Center for Children, Youth, & Families.

Aguilar, B., Sroufe, A., Egeland, B., & Carlson, E. (2000). Distinguishing the early-onset/persistent and adolescence-onset antisocial behavior types: From birth to 16 years. *Development and Psychopathology*, **12**, 109–132.

Alexander, J.F., & Parsons, B.V. (1973). Short-term behavioral intervention with delinquent families: Impact on family process and recidivism. *Journal of Abnormal Psychology*, **81**, 219–225.

Alexander, J.F., & Parsons, B. (1982). *Functional Family Therapy.* Monterey, CA: Brooks/Cole.

Alexander, J.F., & Sexton, T.L. (2002). Functional Family Therapy (FFT) as an integrative, mature clinical model for treating high risk, acting out youth. In F. Kaslow (Ed.), *Comprehensive handbook of psychotherapy: Vol. 4. Integrative/eclectic* (pp. 111–132). New York: John Wiley & Sons.

Alexander, J.F., Jameson, P.B., Newell, R.M., & Gunderson, D. (1996). Changing cognitive schemas: A necessary antecedent to changing behaviors in dysfunctional families? In K.S. Dobson & K.D. Craig (Eds), *Advances in cognitive-behavioral therapy* (pp. 174–191). Thousand Oaks, CA: Sage.

American Psychiatric Association. (2000). *Diagnostic and statistical manual of mental disorders* (4th edn—text rev.). Washington, DC: Author.

Angold, A., & Costello, E.J. (2001). The epidemiology of disorders of conduct: Nosological issues and comorbidity. In J. Hill & B. Maughan (Eds), *Conduct disorders in childhood and adolescence* (pp. 126–168). Cambridge, UK: Cambridge University Press.

Angold, A., Costello, E.J., & Erkanli, A. (1999). Comorbidity. *Journal of Child Psychology and Psychiatry and Allied Disciplines*, **40**, 57–87.

Arnold, J.E., Levine, A.G., & Patterson, G.R. (1975). Changes in sibling behavior following family intervention. *Journal of Consulting and Clinical Psychology*, **43**, 683–688.

Aos, S., Phipps, P., Barnoski, R., & Lieb, R. (1999). *The comparative costs and benefits of programs to reduce crime: A review of national research findings with implications for Washington State*. Olympia: Washington State Institute for Public Policy.

Bank, L., Marlowe, J.H., Reid, J.B., Patterson, G.R., & Weinrott, M.R. (1991). A comparative evaluation of parent training interventions for families of chronic delinquents. *Journal of Abnormal Child Psychology*, **19**, 15–33.

Bardone, A.M., Moffit, T.E., Caspi, A., Dickson, N., & Silva, P.A. (1996). Adult mental health and social outcomes of adolescent girls with depression and Conduct Disorder. *Development and Psychopathology*, **8**, 811–829.

Barton, C., & Alexander, J.F. (1981). Functional Family Therapy. In A.S. Gurman & D.P. Kniskern (Eds), *Handbook of family therapy* (pp. 403–443). New York: Brunner/Mazel.

Barton, C., Alexander, J.F., Waldron, H., Turner, C.W., & Warburton, J. (1985). Generalizing treatment effects of Functional Family Therapy: Three replications. *American Journal of Family Therapy*, **13**, 16–26.

Beck, A.T., Rush, A.J., Shaw, B.F., & Emery, G. (1979). *Cognitive therapy for depression*. New York: Guilford Press.

Bierman, K.L., & Welsh, J.A. (1997). Social relationship deficits. In E.J. Mash & L.G. Terdal (Eds), *Assessment of childhood disorders* (3rd edn; pp. 328–365). New York: Guilford Press.

Brestan, E V., & Eyberg, S.M. (1998). Effective psychosocial treatments of conduct-disordered children and adolescents: 29 years, 82 studies, and 5,272 kids. *Journal of Clinical Child Psychology*, **27**, 180–189.

Brown, T.L., Henggeler, S.W., Schoenwald, S.K., Brondino, M.J., & Pickrel, S.G. (1999). Multisystemic treatment of substance abusing and dependent juvenile delinquents: Effects on school attendance at posttreatment and 6-month follow-up. *Children's Services Social Policy Research and Practice*, **2**, 81–93.

Burns, L.G., & Walsh, J.A. (2002). The influence of ADHD-hyperactivity/impulsivity symptoms on the development of Oppositional Defiant Disorder symptoms in a 2-year longitudinal study. *Journal of Abnormal Child Psychology*, **30**, 245–256.

Campbell, S.B. (1995). Behavior problems in preschool children: A review of recent research. *Journal of Child Psychology and Psychiatry and Allied Disciplines*, **36**, 113–149.

Campbell, S.B., & Ewing, L.J. (1990). Follow up of hard to manage preschoolers: Adjustment at age 9 and predictors of continuing symptoms. *Journal of Child Psychology and Psychiatry and Allied Disciplines*, **31**, 871–889.

Capaldi, D.M. (1992a). Co-occurrence of conduct problems and depressive symptoms in early adolescent boys: I. Familial factors and general adjustment at age 6. *Development and Psychopathology*, **3**, 277–300.

Capaldi, D.M. (1992b). Co-occurrence of conduct problems and depressive symptoms in early adolescent boys: II. A 2-year follow-up at grade 8. *Development and Psychopathology*, **4**, 125–144.

Capaldi, D., DeGarmo, D., Patterson, G.R., & Forgatch, M. (2002). Contextual risk across the early life span and association with antisocial behavior. In J.B. Reid, G.R. Patterson, & J. Snyder (Eds), *Antisocial behavior in children and adolescents: A developmental analysis and model for intervention* (pp. 123–146). Washington, DC: American Psychological Association.

Chamberlain, P. (1994). *Family connections*. Eugene, OR: Castalia.

Chamberlain, P., & Moore, K.J. (1998). Models of community treatment for serious juvenile offenders. In J. Crane (Ed.), *Social programs that really work* (pp. 258–276). New York: Russell Sage.

Chamberlain, P., & Reid, J.B. (1987). Parent observation and report of child symptoms. *Behavioral Assessment*, **9**, 97–109.

Chamberlain, P., & Reid, J.B. (1991). Using a specialized foster care community treatment model for children and adolescents leaving the state mental health hospital. *Journal of Community Psychology*, **19**, 266–276.

Chamberlain, P., & Reid, J.B. (1994). Differences in risk factors and adjustment for male and female delinquents in treatment foster care. *Journal of Child and Family Studies*, **3**, 23–39.

Chamberlain, P., & Reid, J.B. (1998). Comparison of two community alternatives to incarceration for chronic juvenile offenders. *Journal of Consulting and Clinical Psychology*, **66**, 624–633.

Chamberlain, P., Fisher, P.A., & Moore, K. (2002). Multidimensional Treatment Foster Care: Application of the OSLC intervention model to high-risk youth and their families. In J.B. Reid, G.R. Patterson, & J. Snyder (Eds), *Antisocial behavior in children and adolescents: A developmental analysis and model for intervention* (pp. 203–218). Washington, DC: American Psychological Association.

Chamberlain, P., Moreland, S., & Reid, K. (1992). Enhanced services and stipends for foster parents: Effects on retention rates and outcomes of children. *Child Welfare*, **71**, 387–401.

Christian, R.E., Frick, P.J., Hill, N.L., Tyler, L., & Frazer, D.R. (1997). Psychopathy and conduct problems in children: II. Implications for subtyping children with conduct problems. *Journal of the American Academy of Child and Adolescent Psychiatry*, **36**, 233–241.

Coie, J.D., & Dodge, K.A. (1998). Aggression and antisocial behavior. In W. Damon (Series Ed.) & N. Eisenberg (Vol. Ed.), *Handbook of child psychology: Vol. 3. Social, emotional, and personality development* (5th edn; pp. 779–862). New York: John Wiley & Sons.

Coie, J.D., & Jacobs, M.R. (1993). The role of social context in the prevention of Conduct Disorder. *Development and Psychopathology*, **5**, 263–275.

Conner, D.F. (2002). *Aggression and antisocial behavior in children and adolescents: Research and treatment*. New York: Guilford Press.

Crick, N.R., & Dodge, K.A. (1994). A review and reformulation of social information-processing mechanisms in children's social adjustment. *Psychological Bulletin*, **115**, 74–101.

Crick, N.R., & Grotpeter, J.K. (1995). Relational aggression, gender, and social-psychological adjustment. *Child Development*, **66**, 710–722.

Crick, N.R., & Werner, N.E. (1998). Response decision processes in relational and overt aggression. *Child Development*, **69**, 1630–1639.

DeKlyen, M., & Speltz, M.L. (2001). Attachment and Conduct Disorder. In J. Hill & B. Maughan (Eds), *Conduct disorders in childhood and adolescence* (pp. 320–345). Cambridge, UK: Cambridge University Press.

Dishion, T.J., & Patterson, G.R. (1992). Age effects in parent training outcome. *Behavior Therapy*, **23**, 719–729.

Dishion, T.J., McCord, J., & Poulin, F. (1999). When interventions harm: Peer groups and problem behavior. *American Psychologist*, **54**, 755–764.

Dishion, T.J., Spracklen, K.M., Andrews, D.W., & Patterson, G.R. (1996). Deviancy training in male adolescents' friendships. *Behavior Therapy*, **27**, 373–390.

Dodge, K.A. (1991). The structure and function of reactive and proactive aggression. In D.J. Pepler & K.H. Rubin (Eds), *The development and treatment of childhood aggression* (pp. 201–218). Hillsdale, NJ: Erlbaum.

Dodge, K.A., & Coie, J.D. (1987). Social-information processing factors in reactive and proactive aggression in children's peer groups. *Journal of Personality and Social Psychology*, **53**, 1146–1158.

Eddy, J.M., & Chamberlain, P. (2000). Family management and deviant peer association as mediators of the impact of treatment condition on youth antisocial behavior. *Journal of Consulting and Clinical Psychology*, **68**, 857–863.

Edelbrock, C. (1985). *Conduct problems in childhood and adolescence: Developmental patterns and progressions*. Unpublished manuscript.

Elliott, D.S., Huizinga, D., & Ageton, S.S. (1985). *Explaining delinquency and drug use*. Beverly Hills, CA: Sage.

Eme, R.F., & Kavanaugh, L. (1995). Sex differences in Conduct Disorder. *Journal of Clinical Child Psychology*, **24**, 406–426.

Fagan, J. (1991). Community-based treatment for mentally disordered juvenile offenders. *Journal of Clinical Child Psychology*, **20**, 42–50.

Farrington, D.P. (2003). Key results from the first forty years of the Cambridge study in delinquent development. In T.P. Thornberry & M.D. Krohn (Eds), *Taking stock of deliquency: An overview of findings from contemporary longitudinal studies* (pp. 137–183). New York: Kluwer Academic/Plenum Press.

Fleischman, M.J. (1981). A replication of Patterson's "Intervention for boys with conduct problems." *Journal of Consulting and Clinical Psychology*, **49**, 342–351.

Fleischman, M.J., & Szykula, S.A. (1981). A community setting replication of a social learning treatment for aggressive children. *Behavior Therapy*, **12**, 115–122.

Forgatch, M.S. (1991). The clinical science vortex: Developing a theory for antisocial behavior. In D. Pepler & K.H. Rubin (Eds), *The development and treatment of childhood aggression* (pp. 291–315). Hillsdale, NJ: Erlbaum.

Forgatch, M., & Patterson, G.R. (1989). *Parents and adolescents living together. Part 2: Family problem solving.* Eugene, OR: Castalia.

Foster, S.L., & Robin, A.L. (1997). Family conflict and communication in adolescence. In E.J. Mash & L.G. Terdal (Eds), *Assessment of childhood disorders* (3rd edn; pp. 627–682). New York: Guilford Press.

Frick, P.J. (1991). *The Alabama Parenting Questionnaire.* Unpublished rating scale. University of Alabama.

Frick, P.J. (1998). *Conduct disorders and severe antisocial behavior.* New York: Plenum Press.

Frick, P.J., & Ellis, M. (1999). Callous-unemotional traits and subtypes of Conduct Disorder. *Clinical Child and Family Psychology Review*, **2**, 149–168.

Frick, P.J., & Hare, R.D. (2002). *Antisocial Process Screening Device.* Toronto: Multi-Health Systems.

Frick, P.J., Bodin, S.D., & Barry, C.T. (2000). Psychopathic traits and conduct problems in community and clinic-referred samples of children: Further development of the Psychopathy Screening Device. *Psychological Assessment*, **12**, 382–393.

Frick, P.J., Cornell, A.H., Bodin, S.D., Dane, H.E., & Barry, C.T. (2003). Callous-unemotional traits and developmental pathways to severe conduct problems. *Developmental Psychology*, **39**, 246–260.

Frick, P.J., O'Brien, B.S., Wootton, J.M., & McBurnett, K. (1994). Psychopathy and conduct problems in children. *Journal of Abnormal Psychology*, **103**, 700–707.

Gordon, D.A., Graves, K., & Arbuthnot, J. (1995). The effect of Functional Family Therapy for delinquents on adult criminal behavior. *Criminal Justice and Behavior*, **22**, 60–73.

Gordon, D.A., Arbuthnot, J., Gustafson, K.E., & McGreen, P. (1988). Home-based behavioral-systems family therapy with disadvantaged juvenile delinquents. *American Journal of Family Therapy*, **16**, 243–255.

Greenburg, M.T. (1999). Attachment and psychopathology in childhood. In J. Cassidy & P. Shaver (Eds), *Handbook of attachment: Theory, research, and clinical applications* (pp. 469–496). New York: Guilford Press.

Hämäläinen, M., & Pulkkinen, L. (1996). Problem behavior as a precursor of male criminality. *Development and Psychopathology*, **8**, 443–455.

Hansson, K., Cederblad, M., & Alexander, J.F. (2002). *A method for treating juvenile delinquents—a cross-cultural comparison.* Manuscript submitted for publication.

Hawkins, J.D., Catalano, R.F., & Miler, J.Y. (1992). Risk and protective factors for alcohol and other drug problems in adolescence and early adulthood: Implications for substance abuse prevention. *Psychological Bulletin*, **112**, 64–105.

Hawkins, R.P. (1989). The nature and potential of therapeutic foster family care programs. In R.P. Hawkins & J. Breiling (Eds), *Therapeutic foster care: Critical issues* (pp. 17–36). Washington, DC: Child Welfare League of America.

Hawkins, R.P., Meadowcroft, P., Trout, B.A., & Luster, W.C. (1985). Foster family-based treatment. *Journal of Clinical Child Psychology*, **14**, 220–228.

Henggeler, S.W., & Borduin, C.M. (1990). *Family therapy and beyond: A multisystemic approach to treating the behavior problems of children and adolescents.* Pacific Grove, CA: Brooks/Cole.

Henggeler, S.W., Pickrel, S.G., & Brondino, M.J. (1999). Multisystemic treatment of substance abusing and dependent delinquents: Outcomes, treatment fidelity, and transportability. *Mental Health Services Research*, **1**, 171–184.

Henggeler, S.W., Clingempeel, G.W., Brondino, M.J., & Pickrel, S.G. (2002). Four-year follow-up of Multisystemic Therapy with substance-abusing and substance-dependent juvenile offenders. *Journal of the American Academy of Child and Adolescent Psychiatry*, **41**, 868–874.

Henggeler, S.W., Melton, G.B., & Smith, L.A. (1992). Family preservation using Multisystemic Therapy: An effective alternative to incarcerating serious juvenile offenders. *Journal of Consulting and Clinical Psychology*, **60**, 953–961.

Henggeler, S.W., Melton, G.B., Smith, L.A., Schoenwald, S.K., & Hanley, J.H. (1993). Family preservation using multisystemic treatment: Long-term follow-up to a clinical trial with serious juvenile offenders. *Journal of Child and Family Studies*, **4**, 283–293.

Henggeler, S.W., Pickrel, S.G., Brondino, M.J., & Crouch, J.L. (1996). Eliminating (almost) treatment dropout of substance abusing or dependent delinquents through home-based Multisystemic Therapy. *American Journal of Psychiatry*, **153**, 427–428.

Henggeler, S.W., Rodick, J.D., Borduin, C.M., Hanson, C.L., Watson, S.M., & Urey, J.R. (1986). Multisystemic treatment of juvenile offenders: Effects on adolescent behavior and family interaction. *Developmental Psychology*, **22**, 132–141.

Henggeler, S.W., Schoenwald, S.K., Borduin, C.M., Rowland, M.D., & Cunningham, P.B. (1998). *Multisystemic treatment of antisocial behavior in youth.* New York: Guilford Press.

Hill, J., & Maughan, B. (2001). *Conduct disorders in childhood and adolescence.* Cambridge, UK: Cambridge University Press.

Hinshaw, S.P. (1992). Externalizing behavior problems and academic underachievement in childhood and adolescence: Causal relationships and underlying mechanisms. *Psychological Bulletin*, **111**, 127–155.

Hinshaw, S.P., & Lee, S.S. (2002). Conduct and oppositional defiant disorders. In E.J. Mash & R.A. Barkley (Eds), *Child psychopathology* (2nd edn; pp. 144–198). New York: Guilford Press.

Hinshaw, S.P., Lahey, B.B., & Hart, E.L. (1993). Issues of taxonomy and comorbidity in the development of Conduct Disorder. *Development and Psychopathology*, **5**, 31–49.

Horne, A.M., & Van Dyke, B. (1983). Treatment and maintenance of social learning family therapy. *Behavior Therapy*, **14**, 606–613.

Huesmann, L.R., Eron, L.D., Lefkowitz, M.M., & Walder, L.O. (1984). Stability of aggression over time and generations. *Developmental Psychology*, **20**, 1120–1134.

Johnston, C., & Mash, E.J. (1989). A measure of parenting satisfaction and efficacy. *Journal of Clinical Child Psychology*, **18**, 167–175.

Kamphaus, R.W., & Frick, P.J. (2001). *Clinical assessment of child and adolescent personality and behavior* (2nd edn). Boston: Allyn & Bacon.

Kazdin, A.E. (1996). Problem solving and parent management in treating aggressive and antisocial behavior. In E.S. Hibbs & P.S. Jensen (Eds), *Psychosocial treatments for child and adolescent disorders: Empirically-based strategies for clinical practice* (pp. 377–408). Washington, DC: American Psychological Association.

Kazdin, A.E. (2001). Treatment of Conduct Disorder. In J. Hill & B. Maughan (Eds), *Conduct disorders in childhood and adolescence* (pp. 408–448). Cambridge, UK: Cambridge University Press.

Kazdin, A.E., & Wassell, G. (2000). Therapeutic changes in children, parents, and families resulting from treatment of children with conduct problems. *Journal of the American Academy of Child and Adolescent Psychiatry*, **39**, 414–420.

Kazdin, A.E., Siegel, T.C., & Bass, D. (1992). Cognitive problem-solving skills training and parent management training in the treatment of antisocial behavior in children. *Journal of Consulting and Clinical Psychology*, **60**, 733–747.

Kazdin, A.E., Esveldt-Dawson, K., French, N.H., & Unis, A.S. (1987). Effects of parent management training and problem-solving skills training combined in the treatment of antisocial child behavior. *Journal of the American Academy of Child and Adolescent Psychiatry*, **26**, 416–424.

Keenan, K., & Wakschlag, L.S. (2000). More than the terrible twos: The nature and severity of behavior problems in clinic-referred preschool children. *Journal of Abnormal Child Psychology*, **28**, 33–46.

Keenan, K., Loeber, R., & Green, S. (1999). Conduct Disorder in girls: A review of the literature. *Clinical Child and Family Psychology Review*, **2**, 3–19.

Keenan, K., Shaw, D., Delliquadri, E., Giovannelli, J., & Walsh, B. (1998). Evidence for the continuity of early problem behaviors: Application of a developmental model. *Journal of Abnormal Child Psychology*, **26**, 441–454.

Kirigin, K.A. (1996). Teaching-Family Model of group home treatment of children with severe behavior problems. In M.C. Roberts (Ed.), *Model programs in child and family mental health* (pp. 231–247). Mahwah, NJ: Erlbaum.

Kirigin, K.A., Braukmann, C.J., Atwater, J.D., & Wolf, M.M. (1982). An evaluation of Teaching-Family (Achievement Place) group homes for juvenile offenders. *Journal of Applied Behavior Analysis*, **15**, 1–16.

Klein, N.C., Alexander, J.F., & Parsons, B.V. (1977). Impact of family systems intervention on recidivism and sibling delinquency: A model of primary prevention and program evaluation. *Journal of Consulting and Clinical Psychology*, **45**, 469–474.

Kovacs, M., Paulauskas, S., Gatsonis, C., & Richards, C. (1988). Depressive disorders in childhood. *Journal of Affective Disorders*, **15**, 205–217.

Kratzer, L., & Hodgins, S. (1997). Adult outcomes of child conduct problems: A cohort study. *Journal of Abnormal Child Psychology*, **25**, 65–81.

Lahey, B.B., Waldman, I.D., & McBurnett, K. (1999). Annotation: The development of antisocial behavior: An integrative causal model. *Journal of Child Psychology and Psychiatry and Allied Disciplines*, **40**, 669–682.

Lahey, B.B., Loeber, R., Burke, J., & Rathouz, P.J. (2002). Adolescent outcomes of childhood Conduct Disorder among clinic-referred boys: Predictors of improvement. *Journal of Abnormal Child Psychology*, **30**, 333–348.

Lahey, B.B, Loeber, R., Quay, H.C., Applegate, B., Shaffer, D., Waldman, I., Hart, E., McBurnett, K., Frick, P.J., Jensen, P.S., Dulcan, M.K., Canino, G., & Bird, H.R. (1998). Validity of the DSM-IV subtypes of Conduct Disorder based on age of onset. *Journal of the American Academy of Child and Adolescent Psychiatry*, **37**, 435–442.

Lahey, B.B., Miller, T.L., Gordon, R.A., & Riley, A.W. (1999). Developmental epidemiology of the Disruptive Behavior Disorders. In H.C. Quay & A.E. Hogan (Eds), *Handbook of disruptive behavior disorders* (pp. 23–48). New York: Kluwer/Plenum Press.

Larzelere, R.E., Dinges, K., Schmidt, M.D., Spellman, D.F., Criste, T.R., & Connell, P. (2001). Outcomes of residential treatment: A study of the adolescent clients of Girls and Boys Town. *Child and Youth Care Forum*, **30**, 175–185.

Lilienfeld, S.O. (1992). The association between Antisocial Personality and Somatization Disorders: A review and integration of theoretical models. *Clinical Psychology Review*, **12**, 641–662.

Loeber, R., & Farrington, D.P. (2000). Young children who commit crime: Epidemiology, developmental origins, risk factors, early interventions, and policy implications. *Development and Psychopathology*, **12**, 737–762.

Loeber, R., & Keenan, K. (1994). Interaction between Conduct Disorder and its comorbid conditions: Effects of age and gender. *Clinical Psychology Review*, **14**, 497–523.

Loeber, R., & Schmaling, K.B. (1985a). Empirical evidence for overt and covert patterns of antisocial conduct problems: A meta-analysis. *Journal of Abnormal Child Psychology*, **13**, 337–352.

Loeber, R., & Schmaling, K.B. (1985b). The utility of differentiating between mixed and pure forms of antisocial child behavior. *Journal of Abnormal Child Psychology*, **13**, 315–336.

Loeber, R., & Stouthamer-Loeber, M. (1986). Family factors as correlates and predictors of juvenile conduct problems and delinquency. In M. Tonry & N. Morris (Eds), *Crime and justice* (vol. 7; pp. 29–149). Chicago: University of Chicago Press.

Loeber, R., Farrington, D.P., Stouthamer-Loeber, M., Moffitt, T.E., Caspi, A., White, H.R., Wei, E.H., & Beyers, J.M. (2003). The development of male offending: Key findings from fourteen years of the Pittsburg Youth Study. In T.P. Thornberry & M.D. Krohn (Eds), *Taking stock of delinquency: An overview of findings from contemporary longitudinal studies* (pp. 93–136). New York: Kluwer Academic/Plenum Press.

Loeber, R., Farrington, D.P., Stouthamer-Loeber, M., & Van Kammen, W.B. (1998). Multiple risk factors for multiproblem boys: Co-occurrence of delinquency, substance use, attention deficit, conduct problems, physical aggression, covert behavior, depressed mood, and shy/withdrawn behavior. In R. Jessor (Ed.), *New perspectives on adolescent risk behavior* (pp. 90–149). Cambridge, UK: Cambridge University Press.

McCabe, K.M., Hough, R., Wood, P.A., & Yeh, M. (2001). Childhood and adolescent onset Conduct Disorder: A test of the developmental taxonomy. *Journal of Abnormal Child Psychology*, **29**, 305–316.

McClellan, J.M., & Werry, J.S. (2000). Introduction. *Journal of the American Academy of Child and Adolescent Psychiatry*, **39**, 19–27.

McMahon, R.J., & Estes, A.M. (1997). Conduct problems. In E.J. Mash & L.G. Terdal (Eds), *Assessment of childhood disorders* (3rd edn; pp. 130–193). New York: Guilford Press.

McMahon, R.J., & Forehand, R. (1983). Consumer satisfaction in behavioral treatment of children: Types issues, and recommendations. *Behavior Therapy*, **14**, 209–225.

McMahon, R.J., & Wells, K.C. (1998). Conduct problems. In E.J. Mash & R.A. Barkley (Eds), *Treatment of childhood disorders* (2nd edn; pp. 111–207). New York: Guilford Press.

Moffitt, T.E. (1993). "Adolescence-limited" and "life-course-persistent" antisocial behavior: A developmental taxonomy. *Psychological Review*, **100**, 674–701.

Moffitt, T.E., & Caspi, A. (2001). Childhood predictors differentiate life-course persistent and adolescence-limited antisocial pathways among males and females. *Development and Psychopathology*, **13**, 355–375.

Moffitt, T.E., Caspi, A., Dickson, N., Silva, P., & Stanton, W. (1996). Childhood-onset versus adolescent-onset antisocial conduct problems in males: Natural history from ages 3 to 18 years. *Development and Psychopathology*, **8**, 399–424.

Offord, D.R., Alder, R.J., & Boyle, M.H. (1986). Prevalence and sociodemographic correlates of Conduct Disorder. *American Journal of Social Psychiatry*, **6**, 272–278.

Offord, D.R., Boyle, M.H., Racine, Y.A., Fleming, J.E., Cadman, D.T., Blum, H.M., Byrne, C., Links, P.S., Lipman, E.L., MacMillan, H.L., Grant, N.I.R., Sanford, M.N., Szatmari, P., Thomas, H., & Woodward, C.A. (1992). Outcome, prognosis, and risk in a longitudinal follow-up study. *Journal of the American Academy of Child and Adolescent Psychiatry*, **31**, 916–923.

Pajer, K.A. (1998). What happens to "bad" girls? A review of the adult outcomes of anti-social adolescent girls. *American Journal of Psychiatry*, **155**, 862–870.

Parsons, B.V., & Alexander, J.F. (1973). Short-term family intervention: A therapy outcome study. *Journal of Consulting and Clinical Psychology*, **41**, 195–201.

Patterson, G.R. (1974). Interventions for boys with conduct problems: Multiple settings, treatments, and criteria. *Journal of Consulting and Clinical Psychology*, **42**, 471–481.

Patterson, G.R. (1975). *Families: Applications of social learning to family life* (rev. edn). Champaign, IL: Research Press.

Patterson, G.R. (1976). *Living with children: New methods for parents and teachers* (rev. edn). Champaign, IL: Research Press.

Patterson, G.R. (1982). *Coercive family process.* Eugene, OR: Castalia.

Patterson, G.R., & Chamberlain, P. (1988). Treatment process: A problem at three levels. In L.C. Wynne (Ed.), *The state of the art in family therapy research: Controversies and recommendations* (pp. 189–223). New York: Family Process Press.

Patterson, G.R., & Fleischman, M.J. (1979). Maintenance of treatment effects: Some considerations concerning family systems and follow-up data. *Behavior Therapy*, **10**, 168–185.

Patterson, G.R., & Forgatch, M. (1987). *Parents and adolescents living together. Part 1: The basics.* Eugene, OR: Castalia.

Patterson, G.R., & Forgatch, M.S. (1995). Predicting future clinical adjustment from treatment outcome and process variables. *Psychological Assessment*, **7**, 275–285.

Patterson, G.R., & Reid, J.B. (1973). Intervention for families of aggressive boys: A replication study. *Behaviour Research and Therapy*, **11**, 383–394.

Patterson, G.R., & Yoerger, K. (2002). A developmental model for early and late onset delinquency. In J.B. Reid, G.R. Patterson, & J. Snyder (Eds), *Antisocial behavior in children and adolescents: A developmental analysis and model for intervention* (pp. 147–172). Washington, DC: American Psychological Association.

Patterson, G.R., Capaldi, D., & Bank, L. (1991). An early starter model for predicting delinquency. In D.J. Pepler & K.H. Rubin (Eds), *The development and treatment of childhood aggression* (pp. 139–168). Hillsdale, NJ: Erlbaum.

Patterson, G.R., Chamberlain, P., & Reid, J.B. (1982). A comparative evaluation of a parent training program. *Behavior Therapy*, **13**, 638–650.

Patterson, G.R., Cobb, J.A., & Ray, R.S. (1973). A social engineering technology for retraining the families of aggressive boys. In H.E. Adams & I.P. Unikel (Eds), *Issues and trends in behavior therapy* (pp. 139–210). Springfield, IL: Charles C Thomas.

Patterson, G.R., Reid, J.B., & Dishion, T.J. (1992). *Antisocial boys*. Eugene, OR: Castalia.

Patterson, G.R., Forgatch, M.S., Yoerger, K.L., & Stoolmiller, M. (1998). Variables that initiate and maintain an early-onset trajectory for juvenile offending. *Development and Psychopathology*, **10**, 531–547.

Patterson, G.R., Reid, J.B., Jones, R.R., & Conger, R.E. (1975). *A social learning approach to family intervention: Vol. 1. Families with aggressive children*. Eugene, OR: Castalia.

Presidential Commission on Law Enforcement and the Administration of Justice (1967). *Task force report: Juvenile delinquency and youth crime*. Washington, DC: US Government Printing Office.

Prinz, R.J., & Miller, G.E. (1991). Issues in understanding and treating childhood conduct problems in disadvantaged populations. *Journal of Clinical Child Psychology*, **20**, 379–385.

Raine, A. (2002). Biosocial studies of antisocial and violent behavior in child and adults: A review. *Journal of Abnormal Child Psychology*, **30**, 311–326.

Reddy, L.A., & Pfeiffer, S.I. (1997). Effectiveness of treatment foster care with children and adolescents: A review of outcome studies. *Journal of the American Academy of Child and Adolescent Psychiatry*, **36**, 581–588.

Reich, W. (2000). Diagnostic Interview for Children and Adolescents (DICA). *Journal of the American Academy of Child and Adolescent Psychiatry*, **39**, 59–66.

Reid, J.B. (1987, March). *Therapeutic interventions in the families of aggressive children and adolescents*. Paper presented at the meeting of the Organizzato dalle Cattedre di Psicologia Clinica e delle Teorie di Personalita dell'Universita di Roma, Rome.

Robins, L.N. (1991). Conduct Disorder. *Journal of Child Psychology and Psychiatry*, **32**, 193–209.

Rusby, J.C., Estes, A., & Dishion, T. (1991). *The Interpersonal Process Code (IPC)*. Unpublished manuscript. Oregon Social Learning Center, Eugene.

Rutter, R., Harrington, R., Quinton, D., & Pickles, A. (1994). Adult outcome of Conduct Disorder in childhood: Implications for concepts and definitions of patterns of psychopathology. In R.D. Ketterlinus & M.E. Lamb (Eds), *Adolescent problem behaviors: Issues and research* (pp. 57–80). Hillsdale, NJ: Erlbaum.

Schoenwald, S.K., Brown, T.L., & Henggeler, S.W. (2000). Inside Multisystemic Therapy: Therapist, supervisory, and program practices. *Journal of Emotional and Behavioral Disorders*, **8**, 113–127.

Schoenwald, S.K., Henggeler, S.W., Pickrel, S.G., & Cunningham, P.B. (1996). Treating seriously troubled youths and families in their contexts: Multisystemic Therapy. In M.C. Roberts (Ed.), *Model programs in child and family mental health* (pp. 317–332). Mahwah, NJ: Erlbaum.

Schoenwald, S.K., Ward, D.M, Henggeler, S.W., Pickrel, S.G., & Patel, H. (1996). MST treatment of substance abusing or dependent adolescent offenders: Costs of reducing incarceration, inpatient, and residential placement. *Journal of Child and Family Studies*, **5**, 431–444.

Sexton, T.L., & Alexander, J.F. (2002). Functional Family Therapy: An empirically supported, family-based intervention model for at-risk adolescents and their families. In T. Patterson (Ed.), *Comprehensive handbook of psychotherapy. Volume 2: Cognitive-behavioral approaches* (pp. 117–140). New York: John Wiley & Sons.

Shaffer, D., Fisher, P., Lucas, C.P., Dulcan, M.K., & Schwab-Stone, M.E. (2000). NIMH Diagnostic Interview Schedule for Children—Version IV (NIMH DISC-IV): Description, differences from previous versions, and reliability of some common diagnoses. *Journal of the American Academy of Child and Adolescent Psychiatry*, **39**, 28–38.

Silverthorn, P., & Frick, P.J. (1999). Developmental pathways to antisocial behavior: The delayed onset pathway in girls. *Development and Psychopathology*, **11**, 101–126.

Skinner, H.A. (1982). The Drug Abuse Screening Test. *Addictive Behaviors*, **7**, 363–371.

Spanier, G.B. (1976). Measuring dyadic adjustment: New scales for assessing the quality of marriage and similar dyads. *Journal of Marriage and the Family*, **38**, 15–28.

Stanger, C., Achenbach, T.M., & Verhulst, F.C. (1997). Accelerated longitudinal comparisons of aggressive versus delinquent syndromes. *Development and Psychopathology*, **9**, 43–58.

Straus, M.A. (1979). Measuring intrafamily conflict and violence: The Conflict Tactics (CT) Scales. *Journal of Marriage and the Family*, **41**, 75–88.

Straus, M.A. (1990). The Conflict Tactics Scales and its critics: An evaluation and new data on validity and reliability. In M.A. Straus & R.J. Gelles (Eds), *Physical violence in American families: Risk factors and adaptations to violence in 8,145 families* (pp. 49–73). New Brunswick, NJ: Transaction Publishers.

Taylor, E., Chadwick, O., Heptinstall, E., & Danckaerts, M. (1996). Hyperactivity and conduct problems as risk factors for adolescent development. *Journal of the American Academy of Child and Adolescent Psychiatry*, **35**, 1213–1226.

Tiet, Q.Q., Wasserman, G.A., Loeber, R., Larken, S.M., & Miller, L.S. (2001). Developmental and sex differences in types of conduct problems. *Journal of Child and Family Studies*, **10**, 181–197.

Tolan, P.H., Gorman-Smith, D., & Loeber, R. (2000). Developmental timing of onsets of disruptive behaviors and later delinquency of inner-city youth. *Journal of Child and Family Studies*, **9**, 203–220.

Vitaro, F., Brendgen, M., & Tremblay, R.E. (2002). Reactively and proactively aggressive children: Antecedent and subsequent characteristics. *Journal of Child Psychology and Psychiatry and Allied Disciplines*, **43**, 495–505

Vitaro, F., Gendreau, P.L., Tremblay, R.E., & Oligny, P. (1998). Reactive and proactive aggression differentially predict later conduct problems. *Journal of Child Psychology and Psychiatry*, **39**, 377–385.

Vitiello, B., & Stoff, D.M. (1997). Subtypes of aggression and their relevance to child psychiatry. *Journal of the American Academy of Child and Adolescent Psychiatry*, **36**, 307–315.

Wahler, R.G., Leske, G., & Rogers, E.S. (1979). The insular family: A deviance support system for oppositional children. In L.A. Hamerlynck (Ed.), *Behavioral systems for the developmentally disabled: Vol. 1. School and family environments* (pp. 102–127). New York: Brunner/Mazel.

Waldman, I.D., & Lahey, B.B. (1994). Design of the DSM-IV Disruptive Behavior Disorder field trials. *Child and Adolescent Psychiatric Clinics of North America*, **3**, 195–208.

Walker, J.L., Lahey, B.B., Russo, M.F., Frick, P.J., Christ, M.A., McBurnett, K., Loeber, R., Stouthamer-Loeber, M., & Green, S.M. (1991). Anxiety, inhibition, and Conduct Disorder in children: I. Relations to social impairment. *Journal of the American Academy of Child and Adolescent Psychiatry*, **30**, 187–191.

Walter, H.I., & Gilmore, S.K. (1973). Placebo versus social learning effects in parent training procedures designed to alter the behavior of aggressive boys. *Behavior Therapy*, **4**, 361–377.

Waschbusch, D.A., Willoughby, M.T., & Pelham, W.E. (1998). Criterion validity and the utility of reactive and proactive aggression: Comparisons to Attention Deficit Hyperactivity Disorder, Oppositional Defiant Disorder, Conduct Disorder, and other measures of functioning. *Journal of Clinical Child Psychology*, **27**, 396–405.

Waslick, B., Werry, J.S., & Greenhill, L.L. (1998). Pharmacology and toxicology of Oppositional Defiant Disorder and Conduct Disorder. In H.C. Quay & A.E. Hogan (Eds), *Handbook of disruptive behavior disorders* (pp. 455–474). New York: Kluwer Academic/Plenum Press.

Weinrott, M.R., Bauske, B.W., & Patterson, G.R. (1979). Systematic replication of a social learning approach to parent training. In P.O. Sjoden (Ed.), *Trends in behavior therapy* (pp. 331–351). New York: Academic Press.

Weinrott, M.R., Jones, R.R., & Howard, J.R. (1982). Cost-effectiveness of teaching family programs for delinquents: Results of a national evaluation. *Evaluation Review*, **6**, 173–201.

White, J.L., Moffitt, T.E., Caspi, A., Bartusch, D.J., Needles, D., & Stouthamer-Loeber, M. (1994). Measuring impulsivity and examining its relationship to delinquency. *Journal of Abnormal Psychology*, **103**, 1922–1205.

Willoughby, M., Kupersmidt, J., & Bryant, D. (2001). Overt and covert dimensions of anti-social behavior in early childhood. *Journal of Abnormal Child Psychology*, **29**, 177–187.

Wiltz, N.A., & Patterson, G.R. (1974). An evaluation of parent training procedures designed to alter inappropriate aggressive behavior of boys. *Behavior Therapy*, **5**, 215, 221.

Wolf, M.M., Kirigin, K.A., Fixsen, D.L., Blase, K.A., & Braukmann, C.J. (1995). The Teaching Family Model: A case study in data-based program development and refinement (and dragon wrestling). *Journal of Organizational Behavior Management*, **15**, 11–68.

Zahn-Waxler, C. (1993). Warriors and worriers: Gender and psychopathology. *Development and Psychopathology*, **5**, 79–89.

Zoccolillo, M. (1992). Co-occurrence of Conduct Disorder and its adult outcomes with depressive and anxiety disorders: A review. *Journal of the American Academy of Child and Adolescent Psychiatry*, **31**, 547–556.

Zoccolillo, M. (1993). Gender and the development of Conduct Disorder. *Development and Psychopathology*, **5**, 65–78.

Zucker, R.A., & Fitzgerald, H.E. (1992). *The Antisocial Behavior Checklist*. Michigan State University Family Study, Department of Psychology, E. Lansing MI 48824-1117.

PART III

Prevention Initiatives for Specific Emotional and Behavioural Disorders

CHAPTER 18

Prevention of Childhood Anxiety and Depression

Paula M. Barrett

and

Cynthia M. Turner

Griffith University, Australia

INTRODUCTION

Anxiety disorders and depression account for a large proportion of the burden of disease in Western countries (Murray & Lopez, 1996), and by 2020 it is predicted that depression will be the second leading cause of death and disability across the world (Murray & Lopez, 1996). Recent evidence suggests that anxiety in childhood may play a causal role in the development of depression in young people (Cole et al., 1998; Seligman & Ollendick, 1998). At the very least, an anxiety disorder in childhood or adolescence is associated with a two- to three-fold increase in risk for anxiety and depressive disorders nine years later (Pine et al., 1998). Clearly there is a strong rationale for pursuing prevention of anxiety and depression in children and youth, and one needs to look no further than the available epidemiological data to be persuaded.

In childhood, 2–10% of children under 12 years of age experience a clinical anxiety or depression, with these rates increasing to between 15 and 20% in adolescence (e.g., Angold & Rutter, 1992; Bird, 1996; Harrington, Rutter, & Fombonne, 1996; Kashani & Orvaschel, 1990; Zubrick et al., 1995). The prevalence of subclinical symptomatology is even higher, with evidence suggesting that between 21 and 40% of children and youth experience a distressing level of anxious or depressive symptomatology (Kashani & Orvaschel, 1990; Petersen et al., 1993). Although significant advances have been made in the development of effective treatment approaches (e.g., Barrett, Dadds, & Rapee, 1996; Barrett, 1998; Kendall, 1994;

Correspondence to Paula M. Barrett, Griffith University—Mt Gravatt Campus, School of Applied Psychology, Mt Gravatt, QLD, 4111; email: p.barrett@griffith.edu.au

Handbook of Interventions that Work with Children and Adolescents: Prevention and Treatment.
Edited by P.M. Barrett and T.H. Ollendick. © 2004 John Wiley & Sons, Ltd. ISBN 0-470-84453-1.

Silverman & Kurtines, 1999), the majority of children with mental health problems do not attend any agency for treatment (Hirschfeld et al., 1997; Tuma, 1989; Zubrick et al., 1997). For those who do seek professional help, treatment remains ineffective for between 12 and 40% (e.g., Barrett, Dadds, & Rapee, 1996; Kendall, 1994). Combining this with information that shows anxiety and depression persist if left untreated (e.g., Dadds et al., 1999; Harrington et al., 1990), the rationale for pursuing prevention is clear, and it is not surprising that prevention of mental health problems has become a priority for Governments, both in terms of funding research initiatives and in practice.

The United States Institute of Medicine produced a definitive review of the evidence for prevention in mental health (Mrazek & Haggerty, 1994), and specific prevention programs have now been established in the United States by government mandate (US Department of Health and Human Services, 1999). There have also been major initiatives in Europe and Australia, including the formation of the European Network on Mental Health Promotion, and the Australian National Action Plan for Promotion, Prevention and Early Intervention for Mental Health (Commonwealth Department of Health and Aged Care, 2000). In addition, the World Health Organization has contributed to the field, producing the document Primary Prevention of Mental, Neurological and Psychosocial Disorders (WHO, 1998). There are now several international journals specifically focused on mental health promotion and prevention, and the US Surgeon General has emphasized the role of promotion and prevention, particularly in relation to a growing understanding of the factors that are risks to, or protective of, mental health (US Department of Health and Human Services, 1999).

However, to ensure continued funding for prevention initiatives, governments and other funding agencies need to be assured that their investments are worth while. Although the evidence base pointing to the need for prevention is vast, the evidence base supporting the efficacy of prevention is not. The goal of this chapter is to review the existing evidence base for the prevention of anxiety and depression in children and youth. We will review some of our own initiatives in the area of anxiety prevention, and examine the evidence base behind this work. We will argue that the research to date suggests that preventive interventions hold promise, however there is a long way to go before prevention can be shown to have a significant impact upon the prevalence or incidence of childhood anxiety and depressive disorders. We also examine some of the common characteristics of successful prevention programs, and make recommendations for future research into anxiety and depression prevention programs. Our ultimate goal in writing this chapter is to place prevention of childhood anxiety and depression firmly on the mental health agenda, both at a policy and a practical level, and to motivate clinicians to implement prevention and early intervention initiatives within their workplace.

PREREQUISITES TO PREVENTION

The increased attention given to prevention of mental health problems has led to the identification of a number of prerequisites to effective prevention (Spence, 1994, 1996). These include a framework for applying prevention in practice, effective methods for reducing risk, and knowledge and identification of risk and protective factors associated with childhood anxiety and depression. We look briefly at each these prerequisites before proceeding to a review of preventive interventions.

A Framework for Prevention

Prevention approaches, aiming to reduce the incidence of a targeted disorder within the general population, or to prevent the further development of early symptoms of the disorder, are not new (e.g., Caplan, 1964; Gordon, 1987). However, the Institute of Medicine (see Mrazek & Haggerty, 1994) has provided an updated framework for prevention, which has allowed for a clearer understanding of the goals for preventive interventions and approaches to evaluation. This framework is based on the presence and extent of risk factors related to the development of a disorder, and recognizes that most forms of psychopathology lie on a continuum from few or mild symptoms, to more severe and/or numerous symptoms.

Universal prevention is targeted toward whole populations, regardless of their risk status, and aim to reduce risk for a targeted disorder or problem within the population as a whole. For example, an intervention seeking to prevent anxiety might provide all sixth grade students in a school with a program to enhance coping skills. In some instances, universal preventive interventions are designed to enhance general mental health or to build resiliency, whereas others are targeted toward specific outcomes. Selective prevention is applied to those individuals or subgroups of the population who, although not displaying symptoms of the problems or disorder, are considered to be at risk for particular problems or disorders because of certain predisposing risk factors. For example, parental depression is a risk factor for childhood depression, and a selective intervention might target children whose parents have a depressive disorder. Finally, indicated prevention are those interventions applied to individuals or groups who display mild symptoms of the condition or disorder, thereby identifying them as being at extremely high risk for the future development and/or reoccurrence of severe mental health disorders. For example, young people who report a high level of depressive symptomatology are considered to be at high risk for the development of a diagnosable depression, and therefore may be targeted in an indicated intervention. This review will discuss programs in terms of universal, selective, and indicated interventions, as this is currently the most widely accepted model.

Effective Techniques for Reducing Risk

Previous chapters in this volume have highlighted clinical interventions that have proven to be effective in treating diagnosed anxiety and depression. These trials have allowed for the establishment of a knowledge base regarding what works for anxious and/or depressed children and youth. For example, we know that anxious children tend to avoid their feared situation/object. Helping them to overcome anxiety typically involves graduated exposure to the fearful stimuli, combined with relaxation strategies to help them to manage physiological arousal and cognitive strategies to help them to develop mastery over the situation. Similarly, in treating depression we have learned that it is essential to target pessimistic attribution patterns and cognitive errors, and assist young people to test the reality of overly negative self-perceptions. Providing positive social skills, friendship skills and social problem-solving skills, and building social support networks also assists depressed young people to feel more confident and less isolated. This knowledge, drawn directly from clinical interventions, has been utilized in many of the preventive interventions that will be reviewed in this chapter. Although a review of treatment trials is beyond the scope of the present chapter, we have summarised empirically supported treatment and prevention interventions for childhood depression in Table 18.1 and for childhood anxiety in Table 18.2.

The Role of Risk and Protective Factors

Risk factors may be biological, psychological, or environmental in nature, and refer to variables that increase the likelihood that a disorder will develop, or variables that exacerbate the burden of an existing disorder (Coie et al., 1993). Risk factors may (a) be non-specific and applicable to several mental health problems, (b) impact upon anxiety or depressive disorders in general, or (c) be specific to a particular anxiety or depressive disorder. Risk factors may or may not be causal, and they may have a cumulative or a dosage effect so that the stronger or more numerous the risk factor(s), the more severe the disorder (Coie et al., 1993; Dekovic, 1999). Furthermore, risk factors may appear and disappear over time, emerge differently at different times, and may vary in importance at different developmental stages (Coie et al., 1993; Mrazek & Haggerty, 1994).

However, not all children who are exposed to risk factors for a particular disorder proceed to develop the disorder. This had led researchers to explore the possibility of protective factors, which give people resilience in the face of adversity, and moderate the impact of stress and transient symptoms on social and emotional well-being, thereby reducing the likelihood of disorders (Coie et al., 1993). Protective factors can be truly protective (that is, reducing a child's exposure to risk), or they may be compensatory, by reducing the effect of risk factors (Rutter, 1985). Protective factors may be either intrinsic to the child or be part of their environment (Coie et al., 1993; Cowen, 1985; Rutter, 1985). The presence of more protective factors, regardless of the number of risk factors, has been shown to lower the level of risk (Resnick et al., 1997).

Risk and protective factors specific to childhood anxiety and depression are reviewed below, and general risk and protective factors potentially influencing the development of psychopathology are presented in Tables 18.3 and 18.4.

Risk and Protective Factors for Childhood Anxiety

A number of risk factors for childhood anxiety are evident from a very young age. Included among these are childhood temperament (Kagan, Reznick, & Gibbons, 1989; Kagan & Snidman, 1991), a pattern of anxious/resistant attachment (Warren

Table 18.1 Empirically supported treatment and prevention interventions for childhood depression

Trial	Reference	Sample	Intervention or program	Outcome	Follow-up
Treatment	Butler et al. (1980)	n = 56 5th–6th grades	1. Behavioural CBT (Role Play) 2. Cognitive CBT (Cognitive restructuring) 3. Attention placebo 4. Wait-list	Both CBT interventions more effective than wait-list; behavioural CBT the most effective	N/A
	Reynolds & Coats (1986)	n = 30 9th–12th grades	1. CBT 2. Relaxation 3. Wait-list	Both interventions associated with greater reduction in depressive symptoms than the wait-list; no significant differences between interventions	5 weeks: Results maintained
	Stark, Reynolds & Kaslow (1987)	n = 29 9–12 years Self-reported moderate to severe depression	1. Behavioural CBT 2. Cognitive CBT 3. Wait-list 12 Sessions over 5 weeks	Both interventions associated with significantly reduced depressive symptoms in comparison to wait-list	8 weeks: Results maintained
	Kahn et al. (1990)	n = 68 6th–8th grades	1. CBT 2. Relaxation 3. Self-modelling 4. Wait-list 6–8 weeks, bi-weekly	All interventions associated with significant reductions in depressive symptoms in comparison to wait-list	1 month: Results maintained

continues overleaf

Table 18.1 (continued)

Trial	Reference	Sample	Intervention or program	Outcome	Follow-up
	Lewinsohn et al. (1990)	n = 59 14–18 years Diagnosis of MDD or DD.	Coping with Depression Program (CWD-A) and CWD plus parent groups (CWD-A+P). 1. CWD-A 2. CWD-A+P 3. Wait-list 14 bi-weekly adolescent group sessions. Seven weekly parent sessions.	Interventions associated with significant reductions in self-reported depression in comparison to wait-list Parental depression improved in CWD-A+P condition Strong trend favouring the CD-A+P over the CWD-A	2 years: Results maintained.
	Liddle & Spence (1990)	n = 31 3rd–6th grades Self-reported and clinician-rated depression.	1. Behavioural CBT (social competence training) 2. Attention placebo 3. No treatment 8 weekly sessions.	Decline in symptoms across all three conditions, with no significant differences	2 months: Results maintained
	Fine et al. (1991)	n = 66 13–17 years Diagnosis of MDD or DD	1. Behavioural Group CBT (social skills) 2. Supportive group therapy Duration unclear (short term)	Supportive therapy more effective than CBT in reducing depressive symptoms	9 months: Differences no longer evident. Supportive group maintained improvements, and CBT group caught up.

Study	Sample	Intervention	Results	Follow-up
Stark et al. (1991)	n = 24, 4th–7th grades, Self-report and clinician-rated depression	1. CBT + parent 2. School counselling + parent, 24–26 sessions, 14 weeks, + monthly parent groups	Reduced depressive symptoms in both interventions, with CBT significantly more effective than counselling	N/A
Mufson et al. (1994), Mufson & Fairbanks (1996)	n = 14, Mean age = 14.75 years, Participants diagnosed with MDD or DD	Manualized interpersonal psychotherapy for adolescents (IPT-A; Mufson et al., 1993), 12 weekly sessions	Significant decreases in depressive symptomatology, significant improvement in social adjustment and overall functioning, and decrease in all other physical and psychological symptoms of distress	12 months: Improvements maintained
Vostanis et al. (1996a), Vostanis et al. (1996b)	n = 57, 8–17 years, Diagnosed with MDD and DD	1. CBT 2. Non-focused control intervention (NFI), 6 sessions in 14 weeks	Both groups improved significantly on depressive and anxiety symptoms, self-esteem and social functioning, with the majority of children (87% of CBT subjects and 75% of controls) no longer being clinically depressed; No significant differences between groups	9 months: Significant improvement maintained in both groups, with no significant differential treatment effects

continues overleaf

Table 18.1 (continued)

Trial	Reference	Sample	Intervention or program	Outcome	Follow-up
	Wood et al. (1996)	n = 48 9–17 years Diagnosed with MDD and DD	1. CBT 2. relaxation	CBT more effective than relaxation in reducing depressive symptomatology, with 54% remission in CBT group, compared with 21% of relaxation participants No significant differences between treatments on comorbid anxiety and conduct symptoms	6 months: Differences between the groups reduced due to high relapse rate in the CBT group, and continued recovery in the relaxation group
	Brent et al. (1997) Birmaher et al. (2000)	n = 107 13–18 years Diagnosed with MDD	1. CT (Cognitive Therapy) 2. Systematic Behaviour Family Therapy (SBFT) 3. Non-directive supportive therapy (NST) 12 to 16 weekly sessions	CT lead to greater percentage of participants recovered than SBFT and NST	2 years: No significant differences in outcome among each intervention group, with 80% of all intervention participants recovered
	Weisz et al. (1997)	n = 48 3rd–6th grades Depressive symptoms based on self-report and structured interview	CBT (Primary and Secondary Control Enhancement Training program) 8 weekly sessions	Significantly better outcome following CBT, with 50% of children in CBT group in normal range, compared with 16% of controls	9 months: Results maintained
	Clarke et al. (1999)	n = 123 14–18 years	Coping with Depression Program (CWD-A) and CWD-A+P (CWD-A incorporating parent groups).	Significantly better outcomes following two intervention groups, compared with waitlist. No significant	2 years: Booster did not reduce rate of recurrence in follow-up period, but seemed to

Study	Sample	Intervention	Results	Follow-up
	MDD and DD diagnosis	1. CWD-A 2. CWD-A+P 3. Wait-list Eight weeks of treatment, with adolescent group meeting biweekly, and parent group meeting weekly Adolescents in active interventions also randomly assigned to 1. Booster sessions and assessments every 4 months 2. Assessments every 4 months 3. Annual assessments	differences in recovery rates from two groups.	accelerate recovery in those who were still depressed at the end of the acute treatment phase
Mufson et al. (1999)	n = 48 12–18 years Diagnosed with MDD	Interpersonal Psychotherapy for Depressed Adolescents (IPT-A) 12 weekly sessions 1. IPT-A 2. Clinical monitoring	IPT-A group reported significantly fewer depressive symptoms, had a significantly greater proportion meeting recovery criteria, and were clinician-rated to be significantly less depressed, and more improved, than control group. IPT-A significantly better social functioning and social problem-solving than controls	N/A
Rossello & Bernal (1999)	n = 71 13–18 years Diagnosed MDD	1. CBT 2. IPT 3. Wait-list	CBT and IPT superior to wait-list in reduction of depressive symptoms	3 months: Results maintained, and additional improvements in self-

continues overleaf

Table 18.1 (continued)

Trial	Reference	Sample	Intervention or program	Outcome	Follow-up
	Santor & Kusumakar (2001)	n = 25 12–19 years Diagnosed with MDD	IPT (based on guidelines by Mufson et al., 1993)	Improvement in self-concept, and social adaptation in IPT group. 96% diagnosis-free at post-treatment	concept, and social adaptation for the CBT group. N/A
Indicated prevention	Clarke et al. (1995)	n = 150 Mean age = 15.3 years Elevated self-report depressive symptomatology	Coping with Stress Program (CBT) 15 weekly sessions		12 months: Significantly fewer diagnoses of depression or dysthymia in the intervention group, compared with usual care controls
	Jaycox et al. (1994)	n = 217 10–13 years At risk on basis of current depressive symptoms and parental conflict	1. The Penn Prevention Program (PPP), later renamed the Penn Optimism Program (POP) 2. Control	Intervention children reported significantly fewer depressive symptoms than controls	6 months: Significantly fewer depressive symptoms reported by intervention group compared with controls
	Gillham et al. (1995)				12, 18, and 24 months: Intervention children reported fewer depressive symptoms than controls, and significantly less symptoms in the moderate to severe range. Initially symptomatic children reported fewer symptoms than controls

Study	Sample	Intervention	Results	Follow-up
Eggert et al. (1995)	n = 105 9th–12th Grades At risk for high-school dropout and suicide potential	School-based program called "Personal Growth Class" offered as a high school elective	Reductions in suicide-risk behaviours, depression, hopelessness, stress, and anger. Increased personal control, self-esteem, and social support resources	5 months: Effects maintained
Hannon et al. (2000)	n = 21 10–12 years Mean age = 10.9 years (SD = 0.6) High scorers on measures of depressive symptoms	Adolescents Coping with Emotions (ACE) Group CBT program	Significant reductions in self-reported depression and anxiety, and in parent-reported externalizing behaviour; parent-reported internalizing behaviour showed reductions but did not reach significance	6 months: Continued decrease from post-treatment on all measures, although differences from post-treatment to follow-up not significant
Clarke et al. (2001)	n = 94 13–18 years Children of depressed parents, and with subclinical symptoms	1. Group CBT -Adolescent Coping with Depression (n = 45) 2. Control (n = 49)	Intervention group associated with significant reductions in self-reported, but not parent-reported depression symptoms	18 months: Reductions in depressive symptoms maintained, and showed small continued improvement 24 months: Results maintained and small reductions continued
Randell et al. (2001)	n = 341 9th–12th Grades "At risk" for high school dropout and suicide potential	1. C-CARE: brief counselling intervention and social support facilitation 2. CAST: C-CARE plus 12-session group skills training program	Adolescents in all three conditions reported significant reductions in depression, suicide risk behaviours, anger control problems, and family distress	N/A

continues overleaf

Table 18.1 (continued)

Trial	Reference	Sample	Intervention or program	Outcome	Follow-up
			3. Control: brief interview plus social support facilitation	C-CARE and CAST conditions associated with a significant reduction in depression, and increases in personal control, problem-solving coping, self-esteem, and perceived family support	
	Asarnow et al. (2002)	n = 23 High scores on depression self-report measure	Stress-busters	Significant reductions in depressive symptoms, negative cognitions, and internalizing coping, compared with wait-list	N/A
Selective prevention	Beardslee et al. (1997b)	n = 37 8–15 years Parent with a recent MDD or DD	1. Clinician-facilitated psychoeducational intervention (6–10 sessions) 2. Lecture intervention (two one-hour presentations)	Both interventions resulted in positive change in children and their parents. Significantly greater benefits associated with the clinician-facilitated group. Greater benefit reported by parents was associated with more positive change in children	N/A
Universal prevention	Clarke et al. (1993)	n = 361 Mean age = 15.4 years	3-session and 5-session interventions	No effect on depressive symptoms Authors concluded program too brief	

Study	Sample	Intervention	Results	Follow-up
Rice et al. (1993)	n = 151 Adolescents	16 bi-weekly group sessions Psychoeducational intervention program	Significant improvements in coping skills, perceived control over problems, and interpersonal relationships in comparison to control condition. Fewer negative life events in intervention participants in comparison to controls	N/A
Cunningham et al. (1999)	n = 58 9–12 years	Bright Ideas: Skills for Positive Thinking (Brandon et al., 1999) 6 weekly sessions in school class groups	Significantly improved scores concerning attributional style, and perceived control, with significantly reduced use of non-productive coping strategies	N/A
Pattison & Lynd-Stevenson (2001)	n = 66 Mean age = 10.44 years	Penn Prevention Program 1. Intervention 2. Attention-placebo control 3. No-intervention control	No effect on symptoms of depression and anxiety, social skills, or cognitive style	8 months: No effects at follow-up
Quayle et al. (2001)	n = 47 Grade 7 girls	Aussie Optimism Program, adapted from the Penn Prevention Program (Jaycox et al., 1994) 8 weekly sessions at school	Intervention group less pessimistic about negative events than controls, although not statistically significant No significant difference between intervention and control group in level of depressive symptoms and self-worth	6 months: Intervention group had significantly fewer depressive symptoms, and higher self-worth, compared with control. Reduction in number of "at risk" participants in intervention, compared with increase in control.

continues overleaf

Table 18.1 (continued)

Trial	Reference	Sample	Intervention or program	Outcome	Follow-up
	Shochet et al. (2001)	n = 260 Grade 9 students	Resourceful Adolescent Program (RAP), based on CBT and IPT 11 sessions 1. RAP 2. RAP plus parent program	Lower levels of hopelessness and depressive symptoms (on one of two measures) in intervention group compared with controls	10 months: Continued preventive effect.
	Spence et al. (in press)	n = 1500 Adolescents	Problem-Solving for Life Program (PSL), based on CBT 1. PSL 2. Control	High-risk participants in intervention reported significantly reduced depressive symptoms and improved problem-solving. Low-risk participants in intervention reported small reduction in depressive symptoms. Participants in control condition reported increased depressive symptoms	12 months: Effects not maintained.

Note: CBT = Cognitive Behavioural Therapy; IPT = Interpersonal Therapy; MDD = Major Depressive Disorder; DD = Dysthymic Disorder; N/A = Not Available.

Table 18.2 Empirically supported treatment and prevention interventions for childhood anxiety

Trial	Reference	Sample	Intervention or program	Outcome	Follow-up
Treatment	Kendall (1994)	$n = 47$ 9–13 years Diagnosis of OAD, SAD, or AD	Coping Cat Program (Kendall, 1990) 16–20 weekly sessions	64% of intervention participants diagnosis-free, in comparison to 5% of wait-list participants diagnosis-free	1 year: Treatment gains maintained 2–5 year follow-up: Treatment gains maintained
	Kendall & Southam-Gerow (1996)				
	Barrett et al. (1996)	$n = 79$ 7–14 years Diagnosis of SAD, OAD, or SP	1. Coping Koala Program (CK), later renamed Friends Program 2. Coping Koala Program + Family Involvement (CK + FAM)	57% of participants in CK condition were diagnosis-free; 84% of participants in CK + FAM condition were diagnosis-free	6 months: CK condition 71% diagnosis-free CK + FAM condition 84% diagnosis-free 1 year: CK condition 70% diagnosis-free CK + FAM condition 95% diagnosis-free
	Barrett et al. (2001a)		10 sessions		6 years: 85.7% diagnosis-free No significant differences between groups
	Kendall et al. (1997)	$n = 94$ 9–13 years Primary diagnosis of OAD, SAD, & AD	1. Coping Cat 2. Wait-list 16 weekly sessions	Significant improvement in intervention condition	1 year: Treatment gains maintained

continues overleaf

Table 18.2 (continued)

Trial Reference	Sample	Intervention or program	Outcome	Follow-up
Barrett (1998)	n = 60 7–14 years Diagnosed with OAD, SP, SAD, or AD	1. Coping Koala (CK) Group format 2. CK + FAM Group Format	CK Group condition 55.9% diagnosis-free; CK + FAM Group condition 70.7% diagnosis-free Differences between groups not significant	12 months: CK Group condition 64.5% diagnosis-free; CK + FAM Group condition 84.8% diagnosis-free Differences between groups not significant
Cobham et al. (1998)	n = 67 7–14 years Diagnosis of SAD, OAD, GAD, SP, SoP	CBT treatment based on the Coping Koala Program (Barrett et al., 1991) 1. CBT + parental anxiety management (PAM) 2. CBT only 10 weekly sessions over 14 weeks	CBT only condition 60% of participants diagnosis-free; CBT + PAM condition 78% participants diagnosis-free No significant differences between groups	6 months: CBT only condition 65% diagnosis-free; CBT + PAM condition 75% diagnosis-free. No significant differences between groups 1 year: CBT only condition 67% diagnosis-free; CBT + PAM condition 75% diagnosis-free. No significant differences between groups
King et al. (1998)	n = 34 5–15 years School refusers	1. CBT (including parent training) 2. Wait-list condition Six individual child sessions, and five parent sessions, over 4 weeks	CBT intervention associated with significantly greater level of school attendance, significant improvements on measures of fear, anxiety, depression, and self-efficacy, and significant improvements on caregiver and clinician reports	12 weeks: Treatment gains maintained

Study	Sample	Intervention	Results	Follow-up
Last et al. (1998)	n = 56 Diagnosis of an anxiety disorder, and anxiety-based school refusal	1. CBT 2. Educational-support therapy (ES) 12 weekly sessions	Anxiety and depressive symptoms were significantly reduced, and school attendance was significantly improved in both intervention groups. No significant differences between interventions.	1 month: Treatment gains maintained in both interventions
Muris et al. (1998)	n = 26 8–17 years Diagnosis of specific phobia (Spiders)	1. Eye movement desensitization and reprocessing (EMDR) 2. Exposure *in vivo* 3. Computerized exposure Duration of each condition was 2.5 hours, followed by 1.5 hours of exposure *in vivo*	EMDR: Significant improvement on self-reported fear of spiders only. Did not enhance the efficacy of subsequent exposure *in vivo* Exposure *in vivo*: Significant improvement on all outcome measures (self-reported fear, behavioural avoidance test, ratings of treatment effectiveness). Computerized exposure: No significant improvement	N/A
Mendlowitz et al. (1999)	n = 62 7–12 years Diagnosis of Axis 1 anxiety disorder	"The Coping Bear" (Scapillato & Mendlowitz, unpublished) and "Keys to Parenting your Anxious Child" (Manassis, 1996) 1. Parent and child intervention 2. Child only intervention 3. Parent only intervention 12 weekly sessions	Children in all three groups reported less frequent use of avoidant and distraction coping strategies, and decreases in anxious and depressed symptoms. More active coping strategies used by participants in parent and child intervention than in the other two groups, and significantly greater improvement in children's emotional well-being reported by parents in this group	N/A

continues overleaf

Table 18.2 *(continued)*

Trial	Reference	Sample	Intervention or program	Outcome	Follow-up
	Silverman et al. (1999)	$n = 56$ 6–16 years Primary diagnosis of SoP, OAD, or GAD	1. Group CBT (GCBT) 2. Wait-list 12 weekly sessions	64% of GCBT condition participants were diagnosis-free, compared to 13% of wait-list participants diagnosis-free	3 months: 77% of GCBT participants diagnosis-free 6 months: 79% of GCBT participants diagnosis-free 12 months: 76% of GCBT participants diagnosis-free
	Beidel et al. (2000)	$n = 67$ 8–12 years Primary diagnosis of social phobia	1. Social Effectiveness Therapy for Children (SET-C) 2. Active, nonspecific treatment (Testbusters) 24 bi-weekly sessions	67% of participants in SET-C condition diagnosis-free; 5% of participants in Testbusters condition diagnosis-free	6-months: 85% of participants in SET-C condition diagnosis-free
	Flannery-Schroeder & Kendall (2000)	$n = 37$ 8–14 years Primary diagnosis of GAD, SAD, or SoP	1. Individual CBT (ICBT) 2. Group CBT (GCBT) Both conditions received Coping Cat Program (Kendall, 1990) 3. Wait-list 18 weekly sessions	73% of ICBT condition diagnosis-free, 50% of GCBT condition diagnosis-free, 8% of wait-list condition diagnosis-free	3 months: 79% of ICBT condition diagnosis-free; 53% of GCBT condition diagnosis-free

	Study	Sample	Intervention/conditions	Results	Follow-up
	Toren et al. (2000)	n = 24 6–13 years SAD, OAD, or both	1. Group CBT family-based (Toren et al., 1998) 2. Wait-list 10 weekly sessions	70% of GCBT condition diagnosis-free, compared with 0% of wait-list condition	3 year: 91% of GCBT condition diagnosis-free
	Shortt et al. (2001)	n = 91 6.5–14 years Primary diagnosis of SAD, GAD, or SoP	Friends Program (formerly Coping Koala Program) (Barrett et al., 2000) 10 weekly sessions, plus two booster sessions	69% of intervention participants diagnosis-free, compared with 6% of wait-list participants diagnosis-free	12 months: 68% of intervention participants diagnosis-free
	Oest et al. (2001)	n = 60 7–17 years Primary diagnosis of SP	1. One session exposure: Child alone 2. One session exposure: With parent	Both treatment conditions significantly improved No significant differences between conditions	N/A
Indicated Prevention	LaFreniere & Capuano (1997)	n = 43 2.5–6 years Identified by pre-school teacher as being anxious-withdrawn	Intensive 20-session home-based intervention	Reductions in maternal stress and over-controlling behaviour, and increased maternal warmth and support. Children showed increased social competence, as rated by teachers	N/A
Selective Prevention	Rapee (2002)	n = 120 Families with children 3.5–4.5 years	Macquarie University Preschool Intervention 6 sessions	N/A	12 months: Significant reduction in diagnostic status of intervention participants

continues overleaf

Table 18.2 (continued)

Trial	Reference	Sample	Intervention or program	Outcome	Follow-up
		Parent-reported inhibited temperament			
	Dadds et al. (1997)	n = 128 7–14 years	Coping Koala Program (later re-named Friends Program)	90% of intervention participants diagnosis-free	6 months: 84% of intervention participants diagnosis-free; 46% of control participants diagnosis-free
			Monitoring Control Condition		
	Dadds et al. (1999)				1 year: 63% of intervention participants diagnosis-free; 58% of control participants diagnosis-free
					2 years: 80% of intervention participants diagnosis-free; 61% of control participants diagnosis-free
	Barrett et al. (2000)	n = 20 females, 14–19 years Former-Yugoslavian refugees	Friends Program 10 weekly sessions	Intervention participants reported significantly fewer internalizing symptoms than wait-list participants	N/A
	Muris & Mayer (2000)	n = 36 Grades 5–8	Coping Koala Program (later re-named Friends Program)	Clinically significant treatment effects in 75% of children	N/A

Study	Sample	Intervention/Control	Findings	
Barrett et al. (2001)	n = 204 former-Yugoslavian, Chinese, and mixed-ethnic children; 7–19 years	Friends Program	Intervention participants reported significantly increased self-esteem, significant reductions in internalizing symptoms, trauma symptoms, and hopelessness in comparison to wait-list. Wait-list participants reported significant decreases in self-esteem, but no change in internalizing symptoms.	N/A
Cooley-Quille et al. (in press)	n = 10 children exposed to high levels of community violence; Grade 5 students	Friends Program	Participants reported significant decreases in general anxiety and manifestations of anxiety that were contextually relevant to the community violence exposed youth	N/A
Universal Prevention — Lowry-Webster et al. (2001)	n = 594; 10–13 years	Friends Program; Monitoring control	Intervention participants reported significant reductions in anxiety scores, regardless of risk status, and significant reductions in depression scores for (pre-intervention) students with high anxiety	N/A
Barrett & Turner (2001)	n = 489; 10–12 years	Teacher-led (TI) condition or Psychologist-led (PI) condition or Monitoring Control	Both groups of intervention participants reported fewer anxiety symptoms at post-intervention than those in the monitoring control condition. No significant differences in effects of PI & TI.	N/A
Essau et al. (2001)	n = 124 German 8–12 years	Friends Program	Intervention participants reported significant reductions in anxiety scores and increased social skills	N/A

Note: OAD = Overanxious Disorder; SAD = Separation Anxiety Disorder; AD = Avoidant Disorder; SP = Simple Phobia/Specific Phobia; GAD = Generalised Anxiety Disorder; SoP = Social Phobia; N/A = Not Available.

Table 18.3 Risk factors potentially influencing the development of psychopathology in children and youth

Individual factors
- complications in pregnancy
- prenatal brain damage
- neurochemical imbalance
- premature birth
- birth injury
- low birth weight
- birth complication
- physical or intellectual disability
- learning disability
- physical health problems
- insecure attachment to caregiver
- low intelligence
- difficult temperament
- chronic illness
- poor social skills
- low self-esteem
- peer rejection
- impulsivity
- attentional deficits

Family/Social factors
- teenage mother
- single parent
- absent father in childhood
- large family size
- antisocial role models in family
- exposure to family or community violence
- marital discord or conflict
- poor supervision and monitoring of child, harsh or inconsistent discipline
- parental abuse or neglect
- long-term parental unemployment
- criminality in family
- parental substance use/abuse
- parental mental illness

School context
- bullying
- peer rejection
- no connection to school
- inadequate behaviour management
- deviant peer group
- school failure

Life events and situations
- physical, sexual or verbal abuse
- frequent school changes
- family divorce or separation
- death of family member
- severe physical illness or injury to self or family member
- parental unemployment
- homelessness
- parental imprisonment
- poverty
- war or natural disasters
- witnessing trauma
- migration

Community and cultural factors
- socioeconomic disadvantage
- social or cultural discrimination isolation
- exposure to community violence or crime
- high-density living
- poor housing conditions
- isolated from support services including transport, shopping, recreational facilities

et al., 1997), emotional arousal (Rapee, 2002), and an avoidant coping style (Barrett et al., 1996; Prior et al., 2000). Temperament is widely considered to be shaped by a combination of both genetic and environmental factors (Robinson et al., 1992), and temperaments labelled as inhibited or withdrawn are those most closely linked with the later expression of anxiety and anxiety disorders (Rapee, 2002). Children described as inhibited at 3 years of age have been found to be significantly more at risk for depression and suicide and alcohol problems at 21 years (Caspi et al., 1998).

In addition to these individual risk factors, a number of family and environmental factors have been shown to increase risk for later anxiety. Parental anxiety and/or a family history of anxiety are associated with a greater risk for the development of childhood anxiety (Beidel & Turner, 1997; Last et al., 1987). The mechanisms for this association are unclear. In addition to a genetic link, the transmission of anxiety

Table 18.4 Protective factors potentially influencing the development of psychopathology in children and youth

Individual factors
- easy temperament
- adequate nutrition
- positive attachment to family
- above-average intelligence
- school achievement
- problem-solving skills
- internal locus of control
- social competence
- social skills
- adequate coping skills
- proactive coping style
- optimism
- positive self-esteem

Family/Social factors
- supportive caring parents
- family harmony
- small family size
- more than two years between siblings
- responsibility within the family
- supportive relationship with another adult (aside from parents)
- strong family norms and prosocial values

School context
- sense of belonging
- positive school climate
- prosocial peer group
- required responsibility and helpfulness
- opportunities for some success and recognition of achievement
- school norms against violence
- positive school–home relations
- quality schools

Life events and situations
- involvement with significant other person (e.g., mentor)
- availability of opportunities at critical turning points or major life transitions
- economic security

Community and cultural factors
- attachment to networks within the community
- participation in church or other community groups
- strong cultural identity and ethnic pride
- access to support services
- community/cultural norms against violence

is thought to result from both parenting practices, such as overcontrol or over-protective parenting (Krohne & Hock, 1991; Hudson & Rapee, 2001; Rapee, 1997) and modelling of anxious behaviour (Gerull & Rapee, 2002). Exposure to traumatic, negative, and stressful life events also represent risk factors for childhood anxiety (e.g., Goodyer & Altham, 1991; Yule & Williams, 1990), and exposure to deviant peer groups represents a risk for general internalizing pathology in adolescence (Dekovic, 1999). Investigation of protective factors for childhood anxiety has been largely restricted to the areas of social support (e.g., Compas, 1987) and child coping skills (e.g., Folkman & Lazarus, 1985).

Risk and Protective Factors for Childhood Depression

Risk for depression can be similarly categorized into individual, family and environmental factors. Individual child risk characteristics include genetic vulnerability (Thapar & McGuffin, 1994), the presence of other disorders (Angold & Costello, 1993; Bird, 1996), previous depressive episodes (Ge et al., 1996; Lewinsohn et al., 1994b), previous anxiety disorder (Pine et al., 1998); and chronic illness (Lewinsohn et al., 1996). Additional individual risk characteristics include cognitive factors such as attributional style, cognitive errors, and negative self-perception (Cole & Turner, 1993), and personal competencies such as social skills, social problem-solving, and peer acceptance (Cole, 1990; Cole, Martin, & Powers, 1997; Hammen, 1992; Kennedy, Spence, & Hensley, 1989).

Family factors are also highly relevant. Children of depressed parents are six times more likely to become depressed than children of non-depressed parents (Beardslee et al., 1993; Downey & Coyne, 1990; Goodyer et al., 1993). Again, the mechanisms for this association are not limited to genetic transmission (Thapar & McGuffin, 1994). Other variables of interest include parental interaction patterns and parenting practices (Dadds & Barrett, 1996). Depressed parents tend to reward their children less, display less reciprocity than controls, and are more emotionally restricted, slower to respond, and less consistent in their responses (Downey & Coyne, 1990). General family functioning serves as a risk factor for depression (Kaslow et al., 1990; Stark et al., 1990, 1993), as does marital conflict (Emery, 1992; Nolen-Hoeksema, Girgus, & Seligman, 1992; Puig-Antich et al., 1993), and exposure to a deviant peer group (Dekovic, 1999).

Negative life events and chronic daily stressors have been implicated as environmental risk factors for both anxious and depressive disorders (Hammen, Adrian, & Hiroto, 1988; Hammen, Burge, & Adrian, 1991; Reinherz et al., 1989; Lewinsohn et al., 1994b). A number of studies have found that stressful daily hassles predict depressive symptoms, even after controlling for the effect of initial depression symptoms (e.g., Dixon & Ahrens, 1992). Goodyer and Altham (1991) found significantly more stressful life events in the histories of children with anxiety or depression compared to normal controls, however they did not find a greater probability of becoming depressed than anxious (Goodyer, Wright, & Altham, 1990).

As with anxiety, the search for protective factors in childhood depression has lagged behind its risk factor counterpart. The research that has been done has emphasized the role of social support (e.g., Petersen et al., 1993; Toth & Cicchetti, 1996) and positive self-perceptions (e.g., Downey & Walker, 1992). For example, Reinherz et al. (1989) found that parent and peer social support, family cohesiveness, and positive self-perceptions mediated the development of depressive symptoms in adolescence.

The risk and protective factors associated with a particular disorder are important considerations when devising and/or implementing a preventive intervention. As noted above, the current framework for prevention relies upon identifying and using risk factors to try to alter the trajectory of childhood development toward greater health and well-being. Children and youth cannot be protected from aversive life events and experiences, however they can be provided with skills that will help them to cope with these events, and that is a primary goal of many of the programs reviewed below.

PREVENTION OF CHILDHOOD AND ADOLESCENT DEPRESSION

Indicated Preventive Interventions

Demonstrating the use of knowledge developed in clinical treatment trials, Clarke et al. (1995) adapted their successful depression treatment program (Lewinsohn et al., 1990) for use as an indicated group-based cognitive-behavioural intervention. After screening 1652 adolescents, a final sample of 150 (mean age = 15.3 years) were selected for inclusion in the Coping With Stress program based on an elevated level of depressive symptomatology. Participants were provided with an educational and cognitive-behavioural intervention, which sought to provide them with skills that would reduce their vulnerability to the development of a depressive disorder. The intervention was offered over a period of 15 weeks, and was implemented after school by trained school psychologists and counsellors. The sample was criticized for being self-selected in that fewer than 50% of those initially identified agreed to participate in the program. However, the study used diagnostic status as the primary outcome measure, and therefore represents the first published report of prevention of a mental health disorder in a child and youth population. The results were positive, with significantly fewer cases of diagnosed depression or dysthymia at 12-month follow-up in the intervention participants (14.5% diagnosed) than in the no-intervention control group (25.7%).

Another successful depression prevention program, called the Penn Prevention Program (later renamed the Penn Optimism Program; POP), was developed by Jaycox et al. (1994). This program combined an indicated intervention with selective prevention because they recruited 93 children (10–13 years) considered to be at risk because of an elevated level of depressive symptomatology (indicated prevention) and/or high levels of child-reported marital conflict (selective prevention). Four different intervention conditions were tested: a cognitive intervention, a social problem-solving intervention, a combined group (receiving both cognitive and social problem-solving components), and a no-intervention comparison wait-list. All programs were conducted in small groups after school hours. No significant differences between the active treatment modalities were found and results therefore combined the three treatment groups into a single comparison with wait-list children. Results indicated that depressive symptoms significantly reduced and classroom behaviour improved, with benefits observable through to a two-year follow-up (Jaycox et al., 1994; Gillham et al., 1995). The authors also found preliminary evidence for the mediational effect of pessimistic attributional style in the relief and prevention of depression symptoms. The study has been criticized for low initial participation rates (13–19% of identified children) and high attrition rates (30%), with concerns being raised that only a self-selection of highly motivated participants remained in the study through to the two-year follow-up. Regardless, no difference in level of depressive symptoms between intervention and control participants was observed at a three-year follow-up (Gillham & Reivich, 1999).

Two studies have used modified versions of the POP as indicated depression prevention programs (Hannon, Rapee, & Hudson; 2000; Roberts et al., in press). Hannon, Rapee, and Hudson (2000) piloted the Adolescents Coping with Emotions (ACE) program with 20 children (mean age = 10.9 years), selected for participation on the basis of elevated CDI scores (7 or greater). Self-report and parent-report measures revealed mean reductions in scores from pre- to post-assessment. The design of the pilot study (small sample, no control condition, examination of mean scores only) limited the conclusions that could be drawn; however, the results provided enough promise for the researchers to undertake a larger evaluation trial, the results of which are still pending.

Roberts et al. (in press) made modifications to the language of the POP and to the process of delivery (i.e., 12×90-minute sessions adapted to fit into 8×80-minute sessions implemented by school personnel), and after achieving a small reduction in level of depressive symptoms in a pilot study (Quayle et al., 2001), implemented a controlled trial with 7th grade rural school children. Of those families approached, 51% ($n = 369$) consented to participate in a screening phase, and a final sample of 189 (mean age = 11.89 years) with elevated CDI scores were allocated to either an intervention (Aussie Optimism Program) or control condition. Contrary to the results from the pilot study, the intervention was not associated with a lower level of depressive symptoms, although results indicated a short-term reduction in both self- and parent-reported anxiety symptoms. No significant differences in explanatory style or social skills were found and the reductions in anxiety symptoms did not persist beyond the six-month follow-up. The authors speculated that as the program was implemented within an existing service delivery model (i.e., facilitated by school staff within school hours), the sample size may have been insufficient to detect small program effects. This may be the case, as participants reported a high level of satisfaction with the intervention. However, in terms of prevention of depressive symptoms in school children, the study failed to replicate the findings of Jaycox et al. (1994).

Selective Preventive Interventions

Beardslee and colleagues (Beardslee et al., 1993, 1996, 1997a, 1997b, 1997c; Gladstone & Beardslee, 2000) have dominated the area of selective prevention for adolescent depression. Parental depression was the risk factor used for identifying eligible participants by these researchers. Families with a child aged between 8 and 15 years were engaged into the program, and were randomly assigned to either a clinician-facilitated intervention or a lecture condition. The content offered within each condition was similar, and sought to strengthen the ability of parents to provide support and assistance to their children by seeking long-term change in family functioning through the modification of marital and parental risk factors. The interventions also sought to enhance the target child's understanding of the parental illness, and encourage the child to develop supportive networks outside of the home; however, children did not actively participate in the lecture condition. Families who received the intervention in the clinician-facilitated condition reported a more positive outcome and more sustained effects (Beardslee et al., 1993, 1996). Overall, however, results indicated that both conditions were associated with improved communication about the parental depression, a reduced level of parental guilt, and an increased understanding of parental illness within the target child (Beardslee et al., 1997a, 1997b, 1997c). Children whose parents reported a positive response to the intervention correspondingly reported better outcomes, in terms of both depressive symptoms and overall functioning (Beardslee et al., 1997b).

Gladstone and Beardslee (2000) report that these positive results will be further developed through the implementation of a skills-based program for adolescent children with depressed parents; however, no results from this investigation were available at the time of writing.

Universal Preventive Interventions

Clarke et al. (1993) reported on two of the earliest trials of universal depression prevention for adolescents. In their first trial, 361 youths (mean age 15.4 years) were randomly allocated to either an intervention or a control condition. The three-session intervention was offered during school hours as part of the Health curriculum, and was largely education-based, with session content covering the various symptoms, causes, and treatment of adolescent depression. Participants were also advised of the benefits of pleasant events scheduling and encouraged to seek further intervention if they felt it was required. School teachers implemented the curriculum after receiving two hours of training from the program authors. Students allocated to the control condition received no variation to the standard Health curriculum. The intervention failed to produce any appreciable effect on depression symptoms, resulting in the development of an expanded five-session program that included problem-solving skills training. The expanded intervention also failed to produce changes in depressive symptoms across conditions, or across time, and the authors speculated that the intervention may still have been too brief, and/or that a cognitive component may have been necessary. As noted above, Clarke et al.'s (1995) evaluation of an indicated cognitive-behavioural intervention found a clear prevention effect.

Australian researchers appear to have dominated the field of universal depression prevention. A number of Australian-based studies have utilized the Penn Program as a universal intervention with differing levels of success (Cunningham, Brandon & Frydenberg, 1999; Pattison & Lynd-Stevenson, 2001; Quayle et al., 2001). As noted above, Quayle et al. (2001) piloted their modified Penn Program (Aussie Optimism Program) as a universal intervention, and reported a reduction in depression symptoms, which maintained through to a six-month follow-up. Similarly, Cunningham et al. (1999) found that participants reported gains in optimism and self-efficacy from pre- to post-test, and reductions in the use of emotion-focused coping strategies. However, these were time effects only and a control condition was not included.

In contrast, Pattison and Lynd-Stevenson (2001) failed to replicate the results reported by Jaycox et al. (1994) when they implemented the Penn Program (unmodified) universally with a group of 5th and 6th grade ($n = 66$) Australian children (age mean = 10.44 years). Of the 100 families invited to participate, 44% ($n = 66$) consented and students were randomly assigned to the Penn Program, an attention-placebo control, or a no-intervention control. The authors failed to find evidence that the program had any impact upon depressive symptoms, anxiety symptoms, social skills, or cognitive style, either at post-intervention or at eight-month follow-up. Pattison and Lynd-Stevenson (2001) speculated that the lack of significant results may be a function of the different implementation process (i.e., universal prevention versus indicated intervention), where the majority of participants were initially healthy and therefore had little room for improvement (i.e., a floor effect). To test this hypothesis, analyses were repeated on a group of high-risk participants who were identified as such on the basis of pre-intervention depression scores. Again, however, no significant effects were found.

Other Australian studies have reported on preventive interventions that are loosely based on the Penn Program, although there is more of an emphasis on independent content. Shochet et al. (2001) implemented the Resourceful Adolescent Program (RAP) with a sample of 9th grade adolescents. RAP combined elements of cognitive-behavioural therapy with interpersonal therapy to provide participants with 11 skill-building sessions focused on cognitive restructuring, problem-solving, seeking social support, and conflict management. A parallel parent program focused upon enhancing parent–adolescent relationships and reducing family conflict. The program was evaluated in a multiple cohort design within the same school, with the first cohort of 9th grade students serving as a no-intervention control, and the second cohort receiving the intervention. Two treatment conditions were evaluated, one involving just the adolescent program, and the second combining the adolescent and parent program. Although a large proportion of adolescents consented to participate in the intervention (88%), parent involvement was poor, with only 10% of parents attending all three workshops in the program, and intervention results were therefore combined for the treatment conditions. Overall, adolescents reported lower levels of depressive symptoms on one of two depression measures at post-intervention and 10-month follow-up, and also lower levels of hopelessness. An additional positive effect was that at follow-up, 1.2% of initially healthy adolescents in the intervention group compared with 10.1% of adolescents in the comparison group had moved into the subclinical category.

Trained psychologists implemented the intervention in the Shochet et al. (2001) study, although a second universal trial was undertaken using school personnel (teachers, guidance counsellors, school nurses) as the group facilitators (Shochet, 2002). Results of this intervention were less favourable, with an initial post-intervention effect being maintained at follow-up for girls only. However, there appeared to be no difference in the effects of the program for teachers compared with facilitators drawn from health professionals (guidance counsellors, school nurses), thus suggesting that prevention programs can be effectively implemented by school staff.

Further evidence for the use of school staff in the delivery of universal depression prevention comes from a recent study reported by Spence, Sheffield, and Donovan (in press). An eight-session intervention (Problem-Solving for Life Program: PSL) was evaluated with a large sample of adolescents ($n = 1500$), who were randomly assigned to either an intervention or control condition. Active intervention components were cognitive restructuring and problem-solving skills training. The intervention was evaluated for participants stratified into high- and low-risk samples. From pre- to post-intervention, high-risk participants evidenced significantly greater reductions in depressive symptoms compared to control participants. Similarly, low-risk participants showed a slight reduction in depressive symptoms, while their control group counterparts evidenced a slight increase. Improvements in problem-solving orientation were also noted, with high-risk participants showing a greater reduction in negative problem-solving orientation from pre- to post-intervention. However the benefits of program participation were not maintained over a 12-month follow-up period, at which time there were no differences between groups on measures of depression, social functioning, attributional style, and parent-reported internalizing or externalizing problems. The only significant difference between groups over the follow-up period related to significant reductions in avoidant problem-solving strategies and negative problem-solving orientation among the high-risk intervention versus control participants.

Rice and colleagues (Rice, Herman, & Petersen, 1993; Rice & Meyer, 1994) implemented a classroom-based 16-session universal prevention program for 7th grade students. Results indicated significant increases in perceived coping skills, perceived control over interpersonal and school problems, improved relationships with peers and family members when compared to a control group. Participants also reported a decrease in negative life events, while the control group reported an increase in aversive life events.

PREVENTION OF CHILDHOOD AND ADOLESCENT ANXIETY

In comparison to the literature pertaining to prevention of depression, there has been limited research into the prevention of childhood anxiety. The little work that has been done has typically focused on preventing anxiety in specific-situational or medical contexts such as dental phobia, school transitions, and surgery (see Spence, 2001, for a review). As these programs are well reviewed by Spence (2001) and are beyond the scope of the current chapter, they are not included here. Rather, it is our intent to review programs that seek to prevent broad-based anxiety in a child and adolescent population. Our own work in this area is presented in addition to two published studies that have satisfactorily addressed the question of anxiety prevention in children and/or adolescents.

Indicated Preventive Intervention

LaFreniere and Capuano (1997) reported on a preventive intervention for preschool children (aged 2.5–5.5 years) identified by teachers as exhibiting anxious-withdrawn behaviour. Of the 137 children identified, 43 mothers (31.4%) consented to participate, and families were randomly assigned to either an intervention or a monitoring control condition. The intensive 20-session home-based intervention sought to provide mothers with education about children's developmental needs, promote parenting competence through parent skills training techniques, and alleviate maternal stress through the provision of social support. As predicted, levels of maternal stress reduced, and parent–child interactions showed an increase in maternal warmth and support and a decrease in levels of intrusive, over-controlling behaviour. Teachers rated children as more socially competent, and although positive changes in anxious-withdrawn behaviour were also noted, these changes fell short of reaching significance. Parental over-control is a specific risk factor for childhood anxiety because it tends to interfere with children's acquisition of effective problem-solving, resulting in a failure to learn to deal successfully with stressful life situations, and undermining children's belief in their ability to succeed (Krohne & Hock, 1991). Therefore, reducing levels of parental over-control theoretically should impact positively on child anxiety. Unfortunately, however, the study did not include a follow-up assessment to ascertain whether positive changes in child anxious-withdrawn behaviour persisted.

Selective Preventive Intervention

A second study has looked at altering parenting practices in an attempt to avert the trajectory toward anxiety in childhood. Rapee (2002) recently reported the preliminary results from this trial, termed the Macquarie University Preschool Intervention. The intervention was a short-term (six-session) education program for parents of pre-school children (3.5–4.5 years of age). Inhibited temperament was the risk factor used for entry into the program, and children were identified through parent-report measures of childhood temperament, with elevated scores, indicating inhibition, being the criterion for program entry. The child's inhibited style was then confirmed with a laboratory observation. Children and their mothers were randomly allocated to an intervention or monitoring condition, and the intervention was offered in a small group format to parents only. Intervention components included education about child development, childhood anxiety and anxiety management, parent promotion of non-anxious behaviour, and parent-assisted exposure.

To-date, 120 families have participated in the study, with data available on 78 families through to a 12-month follow-up. Outcome variables were child temperament (questionnaire assessment), social play (laboratory observation), and presence of anxiety disorder, as assessed by a structured clinical interview with the child's mother. Positive changes in child temperament were observed over the 12 months of the study, although positive changes were also noted in the monitoring condition. Most significantly, the intervention was associated with a significant reduction in diagnostic status for participants over the 12-month follow-up period. Results and effect sizes were not strong; however, this project remains at an early stage of evaluation and, as noted above, prevention effects require a long-term follow-up. Nonetheless, the project is promising because of the suggestion that inhibited temperament can be modified through early intervention with parents, and temperament is one of the greatest risk factors for childhood anxiety.

Childhood Anxiety Prevention Using the FRIENDS Program

Aside from these two studies, the majority of available literature examining prevention of child and youth anxiety comes from our own research group, and others, using the FRIENDS program. The theoretical bases and structure of the program, and evaluations of the effectiveness of the program to-date will be discussed, along with some important issues around future directions.

The FRIENDS program (Barrett, Lowry-Webster, & Turner, 2000a, 2000b, 2000c, 2000d) is a 10-session intervention designed to meet the different developmental needs of children (FRIENDS for Children 7–11 years) and youth (FRIENDS for Youth 12–16 years). The program is uniquely designed to permit easy implementation at all levels of the prevention continuum, and through to early intervention and treatment. The program is usually implemented in weekly sessions of 60–70 minutes' duration, with one or two facilitators depending upon group size. The program is very cost-efficient, involving a professionally published and reasonably priced group leader's manual and participant workbooks for each student/participant. After attending an accredited training workshop, the program can be implemented by school personnel (e.g., by teachers, school counsellors or nurses, youth workers, etc.) within the classroom as a universal preventive intervention. Alternatively it can be offered as a selected or indicated prevention program by more specialized staff (e.g., school counsellor or school psychologist, mental health worker), or as an early intervention and treatment program by specialist mental health teams (clinical nurses, social workers, psychologists, etc.).

The FRIENDS program is very positively focused, with the content designed to enhance and develop skills and competencies in children and youth. The program integrates key elements from a cognitive-behavioural perspective and combines those with useful strategies from both family therapy and interpersonal approaches. The CBT components include recognizing the link between thoughts and feelings, identifying feelings, relaxation strategies, cognitive restructuring, attention training, problem-solving, self-reward, and relapse prevention. The family and interpersonal components include the establishment and utilization of a social support network, conflict management, and helping others. The content and process of each session is specified in a Group Leader Manual (Barrett, Lowry-Webster, & Turner, 2000a, 2000c), supported by participant workbooks (Barrett, Lowry-Webster, & Turner, 2000b, 2000d). The common thread that runs through the program is the enhancement and/or development of skills and competencies which can be utilized in facing difficult situations, whether they be fears and worries, daily hassles (e.g., difficult homework assignments) or aversive and stressful life events (e.g., transition to a new school). The program is developed around the acronym FRIENDS (see Table 18.5), which helps participants to remember and utilize the skills taught. Each letter of the word stands for a different skill, and each skill builds upon the skills previously presented.

The program also incorporates four parent sessions, which can be implemented as a series of brief (2.5 hour) workshops or as a companion program to the child program (10 × 1-hour sessions). The parent program is designed to educate parents (on childhood development, the development and transition of normal fears and worries, and the known risk and protective factors for childhood anxiety), and also seeks to help parents to manage their anxious child, and recognize and modify any negatively reinforcing parenting practices. Despite the evidence for the importance of family factors in the development and maintenance of childhood anxiety and depression, few programs incorporate such knowledge into the program content. Evidence suggests that the inclusion of parents can have a positive impact upon

Table 18.5 The FRIENDS acronym

F	=	Feelings
R	=	Relax and feel good
I	=	Inner helpful thoughts
E	=	Explore plans
N	=	Nice work, reward yourself
D	=	Don't forget to practice
S	=	Stay calm

treatment efficacy for anxious children (Barrett, Dadds, & Rapee, 1996), although contrary evidence is available for adolescent depression (Lewinsohn et al., 1990).

How Effective is the FRIENDS Program?

Evaluation of the efficacy of the FRIENDS program has been a priority for our research team, and has had positive consequences for the dissemination and uptake of the program. An initial controlled clinical trial was conducted in 1994 and 1995 to evaluate the program as a clinical intervention for children and youth diagnosed with DSM-IV anxiety disorders (Barrett, Dadds, & Rapee, 1996). The 14-session program (formerly known as the Coping Koala Program) was offered as individual treatment to anxious children, and parents attended concurrent sessions. The intervention was successful and, at post-treatment, 80% of those treated were free from an anxiety disorder, and have remained so for up to six years following the intervention (Barrett et al., 2001a). The intervention was later tested in a group format, with equal success (Barrett, 1999; Shortt, Barrett, & Fox, 2001).

Indicated Prevention Trials

Following on from the successful results achieved in treating anxious children, the program was trialled as a school-based early intervention (Dadds et al., 1997). This study represented a combination of indicated prevention and early intervention because it targeted children who were disorder-free but exhibited anxious symptomatology (indicated prevention), as well as children who met the criteria for an anxiety disorder but were in the less severe range (early intervention). Children were selected for participation following a four-stage screening process that incorporated both children's, teachers' and parents' report. Screening resulted in an initial cohort of 1786 children being reduced to a final sample of 128 children aged 7–14 years, who were invited to participate in the program. Students were assigned to either the intervention or the monitoring condition on the basis of the school they attended, and all participating schools were matched for size and sociodemographic variables. A clinically trained psychologist, assisted by a graduate student, facilitated all sessions. Diagnostic status was the primary outcome measure. As a group, children who received the intervention emerged with lower rates of anxiety disorder at six-month follow-up, compared to those who were identified but monitored only. Of those who had features of, but no full disorder at pre-intervention, 54% progressed to a diagnosable disorder at the six-month follow-up in the monitoring group, compared with only 16% in the intervention group. These results indicate that the intervention was successful in reducing rates of disorder in children with mild to moderate anxiety disorders, as well as preventing the onset of anxiety disorder in children with early features of a disorder. The intervention effect remained through to a two-year follow-up (Dadds et al., 1999).

This study was later replicated with an independent research group in The Netherlands (Muris & Mayer, 2000; Muris et al., 2001). Children ($n = 425$) from grades 5–8 across four schools ($n = 425$) completed childhood anxiety questionnaires during regular classes. Of the 42 children who were invited to participate in the intervention on the basis of elevated scores, 36 (85.7%) consented. The intervention successfully prevented 75% of children from developing an anxiety disorder.

Selective Prevention Trials

Selective prevention requires identification of risk factors, and it is widely known that cultural change and migration serves as a significant risk for the development of anxiety in children and youth (Barrett & Turner, 2000). This risk factor was the basis for piloting the FRIENDS program as a selective preventive intervention with 20 young adolescents from the former-Yugoslavia (Barrett, Moore, & Sonderegger, 2000). In spite of the small sample size, post-assessment indicated that participants receiving the intervention reported significantly less internalizing symptoms than wait-list, and social validity data indicated that participants were highly satisfied with the intervention. The promise of these pilot results served as the basis for implementing a larger selective intervention for migrant children and youth from diverse cultural backgrounds (Barrett, Sonderegger, & Sonderegger, 2001). In this study, 106 primary school and 98 secondary school students, differentiated by cultural origin (former-Yugoslavian, Chinese, and mixed-ethnic origin), completed standardized measures of internalizing symptoms and were allocated to either an intervention ($n = 121$) or a wait-list ($n = 83$) condition. Consistent with the pilot results, participants receiving the FRIENDS intervention reported lower anxiety and a more positive future outlook than wait-list participants, and also reporting high levels of satisfaction with the intervention.

An independent research group in America (Cooley-Quille, Boyd, & Grados, in press) recently piloted the FRIENDS intervention with a group of inner-city African Americans (aged 10–11) who were exposed to community violence, and experienced moderate anxiety problems. Pre- and post-intervention analyses revealed significant decreases in general anxiety and anxiety contextually relevant to the community violence (i.e., worry regarding safety and environmental stressors). A larger controlled trial is currently underway.

Universal Prevention Trials

Universal prevention strategies have the potential to be of enormous benefit in terms of reducing the prevalence of childhood anxiety, as these disorders are one of the most prevalent forms of psychopathology in children and youth. Furthermore, given that all children are targeted, those who do need assistance to overcome anxiety problems but who may never come to the attention of a mental health professional are nonetheless engaged in a program of change (Greenberg, Domitrovich, & Bumbarger, 2001; Shure, 2001). For these reasons, our research team has recently explored the use of the FRIENDS program as a universal school-based intervention. Preliminary results indicated that intervention participants reported fewer symptoms of anxiety at post-intervention, compared with monitoring participants (Barrett & Turner, 2001; Lowry-Webster, Barrett, & Dadds, 2001).

These intervention effects were demonstrated equally across psychologist-led and teacher-led interventions, suggesting that the FRIENDS program can be successfully implemented by lay-providers (i.e., school teachers) within existing systems. Most encouraging, however, were the positive effects shown for children who displayed high levels of anxious symptomatology at pre-intervention. In comparison to the monitoring condition, the intervention condition resulted in a significant reduction in the number of children who reported clinical levels of anxious symptomatology at post-intervention.

We are currently in the process of replicating these findings in a large-scale controlled trial, with both primary and secondary school students (Barrett, Johnson, & Turner, in press). Schools were randomly assigned to either an intervention or control condition, and all participants within the intervention schools received FRIENDS as part of the class curriculum in the subject areas of health and social development. Preliminary results indicate that the intervention is associated with reductions in anxiety symptoms, and these effects have been maintained through to a 12-month follow-up. We will also evaluate the effectiveness of the intervention in terms of its ability to enhance participant self-esteem, and to promote more positive, proactive coping strategies. However, the preliminary results lend support to the utility of a universal strategy, and give further evidence for the efficacy of the FRIENDS program as an intervention that is applicable to all stages of the prevention continuum.

Replication trials utilizing a universal implementation strategy for the FRIENDS interventions are currently underway in Seychelles (Hawton, 2002) and Germany (Essau et al., 2001), with preliminary results from the German study already showing reductions in anxiety and improvements in social skills (Essau et al., 2001).

Social Validation of the FRIENDS Intervention

It is important to establish not only whether an intervention works, but also whether the participants consider the program beneficial and worth while. Barrett et al. (2001b) conducted the first evaluation of social validity for the FRIENDS program. Parents, children, and adolescents were surveyed over time on their global satisfaction with the program, the acceptability of treatment components, and the completion of homework tasks. Results indicated a high level of satisfaction with the FRIENDS program and a high completion rate of homework tasks.

Sustainability of a Prevention Program

We will conclude this review of our own work in the area of anxiety prevention with a brief look at some of the initiatives we have recently undertaken to enhance the sustainability of the FRIENDS program. As researchers are often dependent upon funding received from government agencies, the first step taken toward sustainability was the establishment of a partnership with an independent publisher. This partnership ensures the availability of the FRIENDS program and program resources, independent of research finding. Thus, schools, mental health clinics, and community agencies that seek to implement the program have ongoing and ready access to resources whenever they are required. Second, given the positive results achieved with universal implementation strategies, we are currently seeking to have the program more fully integrated into existing school systems, utilizing existing resources. To achieve this, we are developing a tool for teachers, which will link the FRIENDS program into the existing health curriculum, thus ensuring that the program can be run each year as part of the standard classroom syllabus. Finally, to support schools and agencies in their ongoing use of the program, we are seeking sponsorship from corporations within local communities. Sponsorship assists parents and schools with the purchase of student workbooks, and promotes the benefits of mental health prevention within the local community.

Commonalities to Successful Interventions

With the exception of Beardslee and colleagues (e.g., Beardslee et al., 1993, 1996) in the area of depression prevention, and Rapee (2001) and LaFreniere and Capuano (1997) in the areas of anxiety prevention, programs have historically targeted children and youth with elevated levels of anxious/depressive symptomatology. Active intervention components are typically cognitive-behavioural with a focus on emotional regulation, the cognitive deficits and distortions associated with the disorders, and the acquisition of coping skills. These interventions have usually taken place in schools and are offered to students who have been screened and selected from the general population. Only two of these school-based studies have demonstrated a prevention effect with respect to future development of the targeted disorder (Clarke et al., 1995; Dadds et al., 1997; 1999). Although many other studies can boast a reduction in depressive or anxious symptoms, the mechanisms leading to this symptom reduction are unclear, as few studies have found replicable changes in risk factors (e.g., attributional style, which is considered to be a key factor in a cognitive-behavioural conceptualization of depression).

More recently, researchers have expanded these selective/indicated interventions to evaluate their implementation universally, again with interventions based on cognitive-behavioural strategies. Many universal programs report that a primary goal is to facilitate the child's ability to cope effectively with situations that are an inevitable and essential part of normal development. From the point of view of engagement, recruitment, attrition, and de-stigmatization, universal interventions have produced encouraging results. Universal programs have typically been integrated into the existing school system and curriculum, and sustainability is likely to be higher. However, from the point of view of effectiveness, evidence for universal interventions lag behind selected or indicated counterparts.

Clearly, this review offers evidence that important and meaningful progress has been made in the prevention of child and youth anxiety and depression, and much of the value of the reviewed research lies in the promise of future possibilities. Prevention of anxiety and depressive disorders is a possibility. There is little doubt that further work is needed to strengthen these initial effects, and it is likely that a combined approach to prevention is required. However, there is evidence to show that changes in parenting practices are possible (e.g., LaFreniere & Capuano, 1997), changes in early childhood temperament are possible (e.g., Rapee, 2002), changes in cognitive style are possible (e.g., Jaycox et al., 1994), symptom reduction is possible, and prevention of disorders is possible (e.g., Clarke et al., 1995; Dadds et al., 1999). There is also evidence to suggest that participants are satisfied with the interventions they receive (e.g., Barrett et al., 2001b), and that program facilitators find such interventions relatively easy to implement within their settings (e.g., Barrett & Turner, 2001). Given this perspective, clinicians are encouraged to implement existing and well-validated prevention programs (e.g., FRIENDS, POP) within their workplace, and contribute to the development of sustainable practice in mental health prevention and promotion.

FUTURE DIRECTIONS IN PREVENTION RESEARCH

It is easy to locate and critique methodological flaws in existing research, but substantially more difficult to overcome such limitations within the context of one's own research. We are fully cognizant of the difficulties inherent in mounting large-scale prevention programs, and these recommendations, based on those of Greenberg et al. (2001), are therefore made with the awareness that methodological compromises are often required. Nonetheless, given the need for effective research in this field, the following are suggestions for improving upon the research that has been conducted to-date.

- Given the ease with which researchers can reliably and validly assess symptoms, the majority of programs use symptom presence as a selection criterion for program entry. However, use of other risk factors as variables for both recruitment and evaluation of program outcome is recommended because of the potential for risk factor research to contribute to our understanding of the aetiology and course of disorders, as well as the potential for such programs to target multiple disorders. Multiple informants reporting on each variable of interest would also be best practice.
- Where possible, researchers need to obtain large sample sizes in order to accurately assess the incidence of the targeted disorder in the general population, and to subsequently determine whether the prevention program can impact upon disorder incidence.
- As a number of programs have shown (e.g., Dadds et al., 1999; Gillham, Shatté, & Reivich, 2001), stronger prevention impacts are observed at follow-up than at post-test. Reliance on post-intervention assessment and short-term follow-up is likely to underestimate program effects, and provides no indication of the duration of program effects. This information is required in order to determine whether improvements can be made in the process of prevention (e.g., including regular booster sessions to renew participants use of the strategies taught in the intervention).
- Many of the reviewed programs have reduced symptoms of psychological disorder, however there is still a need for diagnostic outcome, as it is necessary to determine whether prevention of symptoms will result in prevention of disorder over

time. Although the use of symptom-level data is often appropriate for initial evaluations, and can be used to approximate diagnosis, it is difficult to establish whether overall reduction in mean symptoms is prevention (Gillham, Shatté & Reivich, 2001).

- Cost-effectiveness is a difficult thing to establish in preventive interventions; however, if governments and funding agents are to be convinced of their investment decisions, it would seem important to demonstrate that prevention is a cost-effective approach to mental health disorders. This would also serve to enhance the utility and widespread acceptability of prevention programs.

- The importance of intervention providers is attracting more interest (e.g., Barrett & Turner, 2001; Lowry-Webster, Barrett, & Dadds, 2001; Spence, Sheffield, & Donovan, in press; Shochet et al., 2001).

- Future studies should evaluate intervention integrity and the relationship of such compliance to outcome. Where interventions can be successfully delivered within existing systems and resources (e.g., by school teachers within the classroom), their cost-effectiveness is improved and sustainability is enhanced.

- There remains a need to assess the mediators and moderators of intervention effectiveness. Few studies have attempted to ascertain whether changes in risk/protective factors are responsible for intervention outcomes. Even fewer have evaluated the impact of moderating variables, for example, age, gender, current symptom level, academic ability, ethnicity. Knowledge of moderating variables provides important information about the limits of interventions. The FRIENDS program has been trialled with different cultural and ethnic groups, and effectiveness of the program has been demonstrated in pilot studies with NESB children and youth, and youth in Germany, Seychelles, and The Netherlands. Sample-specific feedback has been used in each of these studies to make modifications to the program in order to develop the most powerful intervention possible. There is also some evidence that the POP has established validity with ethnic subgroups, including minority American children and Chinese nationals (Gillham & Reivich, 1999).

- There is a need to expand the range of outcome measures used in prevention research. Given the high levels of comorbidity observed in childhood psychopathology, many programs provide participants with skills that could theoretically impact upon a number of emotional and behavioural domains. Therefore, the breadth of intervention effects needs to be established via broader outcome assessment.

CONCLUSIONS

An increasing body of evidence shows that interventions seeking to prevent childhood depression and anxiety have significant potential to improve the lives and wellbeing of both participants and their families. However, mental health prevention and promotion are relevant to the whole community, regardless of mental health status. Governments across the world are to be applauded for placing mental health prevention firmly on the agenda. It is now up to clinicians and researchers to move the field of prevention forward. What can you do to ensure that prevention and early intervention initiatives are undertaken in your workplace?

REFERENCES

Angold, A., & Costello, E.J. (1993). Depressive comorbidity in children and adolescents: Empirical, theoretical and methodological issues. *American Journal of Psychiatry*, **150**, 1779–1791.

Angold, A., & Rutter, M. (1992). Effects of age and pubertal status on depression in a large clinical sample. *Development and Psychopathology*, **4**, 5–28.

Asarnow, J.R., Scott, C.V., & Mintz, J. (2002). A combined cognitive-behavioural family education intervention for depression in children: A treatment development study. *Cognitive Therapy and Research*, **26** (2), 221–229.

Barrett, P.M. (1998). Evaluation of cognitive-behavioural group treatments for childhood anxiety disorders. *Journal of Clinical Child Psychology*, **27**, 459–468.

Barrett, P.M. (1999). Interventions for child and youth anxiety disorders: Involving parents, teachers, and peers. *Australian Educational and Developmental Psychologist*, **16**, 5–24.

Barrett, P.M., & Turner, C.M. (2000). Childhood anxiety in ethnic families: Current status and future directions. *Behaviour Change*, **17**, 113–123.

Barrett, P.M., & Turner, C.M. (2001). Prevention of anxiety symptoms in primary school children: Preliminary results from a universal school-based trial. *British Journal of Clinical Psychology*, **40**, 399–410.

Barrett, P.M., Dadds, M.R., & Rapee, R.M. (1991) *Coping koala workbook*. Unpublished manuscript. School of Applied Psychology, Griffith University, Nathan, Australia.

Barrett, P.M., Dadds, M.R., & Rapee, R. (1996). Family treatment of childhood anxiety: A controlled trial. *Journal of Consulting and Clinical Psychology*, **64**, 333–342.

Barrett, P.M., Johnson, S., & Turner, C.M. (in press). Examination of developmental differences in school-based prevention of anxiety and depressive symptoms and disorders. *Clinical Child Psychology and Psychiatry*.

Barrett, P.M., Lowry-Webster, H., & Turner, C.M. (2000a). *Friends for Children Group Leader Manual*. Brisbane, Australia: Australian Academic Press.

Barrett, P.M., Lowry-Webster, H., & Turner, C.M. (2000b). *Friends for Children Participant Workbook*. Brisbane, Australia: Australian Academic Press.

Barrett, P.M., Lowry-Webster, H., & Turner, C.M. (2000c). *Friends for Youth Group Leader Manual*. Brisbane, Australia: Australian Academic Press.

Barrett, P.M., Lowry-Webster, H., & Turner, C.M. (2000d). *Friends for Youth Participant Workbook*. Brisbane, Australia: Australian Academic Press.

Barrett, P.M., Moore, A.F., & Sonderegger, R. (2000). The FRIENDS program for young former-Yugoslavian refugees in Australia: A pilot study. *Behaviour Change*, **17** (3), 124–133.

Barrett, P.M, Sonderegger, R., & Sonderegger, N.L. (2001). Evaluation of an anxiety-prevention and positive-coping program (FRIENDS) for children and adolescents of non-English speaking background. *Behaviour Change*, **18**, 78–91.

Barrett, P.M., Duffy, A., Dadds, M.R., & Rapee, R. (2001a). Cognitive-behavioural treatment of anxiety disorders in children: Long term (6 year) follow-up. *Journal of Consulting and Clinical Psychology*, **69** (1), 135–141.

Barrett, P.M., Rapee, R., Dadds, M.R., & Ryan, S. (1996). Family enhancement of cognitive style in anxious and aggressive children. *Journal of Abnormal Child Psychology*, **24**, 187–203.

Barrett, P.M., Shortt, A.L., Fox, T.L., & Wescombe, K. (2001b). Examining the social validity of the FRIENDS treatment program for anxious children. *Behaviour Change*, **18**, 63–77.

Beardslee, W.R., Keller, M.B., Lavori, P.W., Staley, J.W., & Sacks, N. (1993). The impact of parental affective disorder on depression in offspring: A longitudinal follow-up in a non-referred sample. *Journal of the American Academy of Child and Adolescent Psychiatry*, **32**, 723–730.

Beardslee, W.R., Salt, P., Versage, E.M., Gladstone, T.R.G., Wright, E.J., & Rothberg, P.C. (1997a). Sustained change in parents receiving preventive interventions for families with depression. *American Journal of Psychiatry*, **154** (4), 510–515.

Beardslee, W.R., Versage, E.M., Wright, E., Salt, P., Rothberg, P.C., Drezner, K., & Gladstone, T.G. (1997b). Examination of preventive interventions for families with depression: Evidence of change. *Developmental Psychopathology*, **9**, 109–130.

Beardslee, W.R., Wright, E., Rothberg, P.C., Salt, P., & Versage, E.M. (1996). Response of families to two preventive intervention strategies: Long-term differences in behaviour and attitude change. *Journal of the American Academy of Child and Adolescent Psychiatry*, **35**, 774–782.

Beardslee, W.R., Wright, E., Salt, P., Drezner, K., Gladstone, T.G., Versage, E.M., & Rothberg, P.C. (1997c). Examination of children's responses to two preventive intervention strategies over time. *Journal of the American Academy of Child and Adolescent Psychiatry*, **36**, 196–204.

Beidel, D.C., & Turner, S.M. (1997). At risk for anxiety: I: Psychopathology in the offspring of anxious parents. *Journal of the American Academy of Child and Adolescent Psychiatry*, **36**, 918–924.

Beidel, D.C., Turner, S.M., & Morris, T.L. (2000). Behavioral treatment of childhood social phobia. *Journal of Consulting and Clinical Psychology*, **68** (6), 1072–1080.

Bird, H. (1996). Epidemiology of childhood disorders in a cross cultural context. *Journal of Child Psychology and Psychiatry*, **37**, 35–49.

Birmaher, B., Brent, D.A., Kolko, D., Baugher, M., Bridge, J., Holder, D., Iyengar, S., & Ulloa, R.E. (2000). Clinical outcome after short-term psychotherapy for adolescents with major depressive disorder. *Archives of General Psychiatry*, **57** (1), 29–36.

Brent, D.A., Holder, D., Kolko, D., Birmaher, B., Baugher, M., Roth, C., Iyengar, S., & Johnson, B.A. (1997). A clinical psychotherapy trial for adolescent depression comparing cognitive, family, and supportive therapy. *Archives of General Psychiatry*, **54** (9), 877–885.

Butler, L., Mietzitis, S., Friedman, R., & Cole, E. (1980). The effect of two school-based intervention programs on depressive symptoms in preadolescents. *American Educational Research Journal*, **17** (1), 111–119.

Caplan, G. (1964). *Principles of preventive psychiatry*. New York: Basic Books.

Caspi, A., Moffitt, T.E., Newman, D.L., & Silva, P.A. (1998). Behavioral observations at age 3 years predict adult psychiatric disorders: Longitudinal evidence from a birth cohort. In M.E. Hertzig & E.A. Farber (Eds), *Annual progress in child psychiatry and child development: 1997* (pp. 319–331). Philadelphia, PA: Brunner/Mazel, Inc.

Clarke, G.N., Hawkins, W., Murphy, M., & Sheeber, L. (1993). School-based primary prevention of depressive symptomatology in adolescents: Findings from two studies. *Journal of Adolescent Research*, **8**, 183–204.

Clarke, G.N., Hawkins, W., Murphy, M., Sheeber, L.B., Lewinsohn, P.M., & Seeley, J.R. (1995). Targeted prevention of unipolar depressive disorder in an at-risk sample of high school adolescents: A randomized trial of a group cognitive intervention. *Journal of the American Academy of Child and Adolescent Psychiatry*, **34**, 312–321.

Clarke, G.N., Hornbrook, M., Lynch, F., Polen, M., Gale, J., Beardslee, W.R., O'Connor, E., & Seeley, J.R. (2001). A randomized trial of a group cognitive intervention for preventing depression in adolescent offspring of depressed parents. *Archives of General Psychiatry*, **58**, 1127–1134.

Clarke, G.N., Rohde, P., Lewinsohn, P.M., Hops, H., & Seeley, J.R. (1999). Cognitive-behavioral treatment of adolescent depression: Efficacy of acute group treatment and booster sessions. *Journal of the American Academy of Child and Adolescent Psychiatry*, **38** (3), 272–279.

Cobham, V.E., Dadds, M.R., & Spence, S.H. (1998). The role of parental anxiety in the treatment of childhood anxiety. *Journal of Consulting and Clinical Psychology*, **66** (6), 893–905.

Coie, J.D., Watt, N.F., West, S.G., Hawkins, J.D., Asarnow, J.R., Markman, H.J., Ramey, S.L., Shure, M.B., & Long, B. (1993). The science of prevention: A conceptual framework and some directions for a national research program. *American Psychologist*, **48**, 1013–1022.

Cole, D.A. (1990). The relation of social and academic competence to depressive symptoms in childhood. *Journal of Abnormal Psychology*, **99**, 422–429.

Cole, D.A., & Turner, J.E. (1993). Models of cognitive mediation and moderation in child depression. *Journal of Abnormal Psychology*, **102**, 271–281.

Cole, D.A., Martin, J.M., & Powers, B. (1997). A competency-based model of child depression: A longitudinal study of peer, parent, teacher, and self-evaluations. *Journal of Child Psychology and Psychiatry*, **38**, 505–514.

Cole, D.A., Peeke, L.G., Martin, J.M., Truglio, R., & Seroczynski, A.D. (1998). A longitudinal look at the relation between depression and anxiety in children and adolescents. *Journal of Consulting and Clinical Psychology*, **66**, 451–460.

Commonwealth Department of Health and Aged Care (2000). *National Action Plan for Promotion, Prevention and Early Intervention for Mental Health*. Mental Health and Special Programs Branch, Commonwealth Department of Health and Aged Care: Canberra.

Compas, B. (1987). Coping with stress during childhood and adolescence. *Psychological Bulletin*, **101**, 393–403.

Cooley-Quille, M., Boyd, R.C., & Grados, J.J. (in press). Feasibility of an anxiety prevention intervention for community violence exposed children. *Journal of Primary Prevention*.

Cowen, E.L. (1985). Person-centered approaches to primary prevention in mental health: Situation focussed and competence enhancement. *American Journal of Community Psychology*, **13**, 31–49.

Cunningham, E.G., Brandon, C.M., & Frydenberg, E. (1999). Building resilience in early adolescence through a universal school-based prevention program. *Australian Journal of Guidance and Counselling*, **9**, 15–23.

Dadds, M.R., & Barrett, P.M. (1996). Family processes in child and adolescent anxiety and depression. *Behaviour Change*, **13** (4), 231–239.

Dadds, M.R., Holland, D.E., Laurens, K.R., Mullins, M., Barrett, P.M., & Spence, S.H. (1999). Early intervention and prevention of anxiety disorders in children: Results at 2-year follow-up. *Journal of Consulting and Clinical Psychology*, **67** (1), 145–150.

Dadds, M.R., Spence, S.H., Holland, D., Barrett, P.M., & Laurens, K. (1997). Prevention and early intervention for anxiety disorders: A controlled trial. *Journal of Consulting and Clinical Psychology*, **65**, 627–635.

Dekovic, M. (1999). Risk and protective factors in the development of problem behaviour during adolescence. *Journal of Youth and Adolescence*, **28**, 667–685.

Dixon, J.F., & Ahrens, A.H. (1992). Stress and attributional style as predictors of self-reported depression in children. *Cognitive Therapy and Research*, **16**, 623–634.

Donovan, C.L., & Spence, S.H. (2000). Prevention of childhood anxiety disorders. *Clinical Psychology Review*, **20**, 509–531.

Downey, G., & Coyne, J.C. (1990). Children of depressed parents: An integrative review. *Psychological Bulletin*, **108**, 50–76.

Downey, G., & Walker, E. (1992). Distinguishing family level and child-level influences on the development of depression and aggression in children at risk. *Development and Psychopathology*, **4**, 81–95.

Eggert, L.L., Thompson, E.A., Herting, J.R., & Nicholas, L.J. (1995). Reducing suicide potential among high-risk youth: Tests of a school-based prevention program. *Suicide and Life Threatening Behavior*, **25** (2), 276–296.

Emery, R.E. (1992). Inter-parental conflict and the children of discord and divorce. *Psychological Bulletin*, **9**, 310–330.

Essau, C.A., Conradt, J., Kuhle, R., & Low, R. (2001). *Feasibility and efficacy of the FRIENDS program for the prevention of anxiety in children*. Submitted for publication.

Fine, S., Forth, A., Gilbert, M., & Haley, G. (1991). Group therapy for adolescent depressive disorder: A comparison of social skills and therapeutic support. *Journal of the American Academy of Child and Adolescent Psychiatry*, **30** (1), 79–85.

Flannery-Schroeder, E.C., & Kendall, P.C. (2000). Group and individual cognitive-behavioral treatments for youth with anxiety disorders: A randomized clinical trial. *Cognitive Therapy and Research*, **24** (3), 251–278.

Folkman, S., & Lazarus, R.S. (1985). If it changes it must be a process: A study of emotion and coping during three stages of a college examination. *Journal of Personality and Social Psychology*, **48**, 150–170.

Ge, X., Best, K.M., Conger, R.D., & Simons, R.L. (1996). Parenting behaviours and the occurrence and co-occurrence of adolescent depressive symptoms and conduct problems. *Developmental Psychology*, **32**, 717–731.

Gerull, F.C., & Rapee, R.M. (2002). Mother knows best: Effects of maternal modelling on the acquisition of fear and avoidance behaviour in toddlers. *Behaviour Research and Therapy*, **40** (3), 279–287.

Gillham, J.E., & Reivich, K.J. (1999). Prevention of depressive symptoms in school children: A research update. *Psychological Science*, **10**, 461–462.

Gillham, J.E., Shatté, A.J., & Reivich, K. (2001). Needed for prevention research: Long-term follow-up and the evaluation of mediators, moderators, and lay providers. *Prevention and Treatment*, **4**.

Gillham, J.E., Reivich, K.J., Jaycox, L.H., & Seligman, M. (1995). Preventing depressive symptoms in school children: Two-year follow-up. *Psychological Science*, **6**, 343–351.

Gladstone, T.G., & Beardslee, W.R. (2000). The prevention of depression in at-risk adolescents: Current status and future directions. *Journal of Cognitive Psychotherapy: An International Quarterly*, **14**, 9–23.

Goodyer, I.M., & Altham, P.M. (1991). Lifetime exit events and recent social and family adversities in anxious and depressed school-aged children. *Journal of Affective Disorders*, **21**, 219–228.

Goodyer, I.M., Wright, C., & Altham, P.M. (1990). Recent achievements and adversities in anxious and depressed school age children. *Journal of Child Psychology and Psychiatry*, **31**, 1063–1077.

Goodyer, I.M., Cooper, P.J., Vise, C.M., & Ashley, L. (1993). Depression in 11–16 year girls: The role of past psychopathology and exposure to recent life events. *Journal of Child Psychology and Psychiatry*, **34**, 1103–1105.

Gordon, R. (1987). An operational classification of disease prevention. In J.A. Steinberg & M.M. Silverman (Eds), *Preventing mental disorders* (pp. 20–26). Rockville, MD: Department of Health and human Services.

Greenberg, M.A., Domitrovich, C., & Bumbarger, B. (2001). The prevention of mental disorders in school-aged children: Current state of the field. *Prevention and Treatment*, **4**.

Hammen, C. (1992). Cognitive, life stress, and interpersonal approaches to a developmental psychopathology model of depression. *Development and Psychopathology*, **2**, 189–206.

Hammen, C., Adrian, C., & Hiroto, D. (1988). A longitudinal study of the attributional vulnerability model in children at risk of depression. *British Journal of Clinical Psychology*, **27**, 37–46.

Hammen, C., Burge, D., & Adrian, C. (1991). Timing of mothers and child depression in a longitudinal study of children at risk. *Journal of Consulting and Clinical Psychology*, **59**, 341–345.

Hannon, A.P., Rapee, R.M., & Hudson, J.L. (2000). The prevention of depression in children: A pilot study. *Behaviour Change*, **17**, 78–83.

Harrington, R., Rutter, M., & Fombonne, E. (1996). Developmental pathways in depression: Multiple meanings, antecedents, and endpoints. *Development and Psychopathology*, **8**, 601–616.

Harrington, R., Fudge, H., Rutter, M., Pickles, A., & Hill, J. (1990). Adult outcomes of childhood and adolescent depression. *Archives of General Psychiatry*, **47**, 465–473.

Hawton, M. (2002). Personal communication. The National Council for Children, funded by the Australian High Commission Direct Aid Project.

Hirschfeld, R., Keller, M., Panico, S., Arons, B., Barlow, D., Davidoff, F., Endicott, J., Froom, J., Goldstein, M., Gorman, J., Guthrie, D., Marek, R., Mauren, T., Meyer, R., Philips, K., Ross, J., Schwenk, T., Sharfstein, S., Thase, M., & Wyatt, R. (1997). The National Depressive and Manic-Depressive Association consensus statement on the undertreatment of depression. *Journal of the American Medical Association*, **277**, 333–340.

Hudson, J.L., & Rapee, R.M. (2001). Parent–child interactions and anxiety disorders: An observational study. *Behaviour Research and Therapy*, **39**, 1411–1427.

Jaycox, L.H., Reivich, K.J., Gillham, J., & Seligman, M. (1994). Preventing depressive symptoms in school children. *Behaviour Research and Therapy*, **32**, 801–816.

Kagan, J., & Snidman, N. (1991). Infant predictors of inhibited and uninhibited profiles. *Psychological Science*, **2**, 40–43.

Kagan, J., Reznick, J.S., & Gibbons, J. (1989). Inhibited and uninhibited types of children. *Child Development*, **60**, 838–845.

Kahn, J.S., Kehle, T.J., Jenson, W.R., & Clark, E. (1990). Comparison of cognitive-behavioral, relaxation, and self-modeling interventions for depression among middle-school students. *School Psychology Review*, **19** (2), 196–211.

Kashani, J.H., & Orvaschel, H. (1990). A community study of anxiety in children and adolescents. *American Journal of Psychiatry*, **147**, 313–318.

Kaslow, N.J., Rehm, L.P., Pollack, S.L., & Siegal, A.W. (1990). Depression and perception of family functioning in children and their parents. *American Journal of Family Therapy*, **18**, 227–235.

Kendall, P.C. (1990). *Coping cat workbook*. Ardmore, PA: Workbook Publishing.

Kendall, P.C. (1994). Treatment of anxiety disorders in children: A randomized clinical trial. *Journal of Consulting and Clinical Psychology*, **62**, 100–110.

Kendall, P.C., & Southam-Gerow, M.A. (1996). Long-term follow-up of a cognitive-behavioral therapy for anxiety-disordered youth. *Journal of Consulting and Clinical Psychology*, **64** (4), 724–730.

Kendall, P.C., Flannery-Schroeder, E., Panichelli-Mindel, S.M., Southam-Gerow, M., Henin, A., & Warman, M. (1997). Therapy for youths with anxiety disorders: A second randomized clinical trial. *Journal of Consulting and Clinical Psychology*, **65** (3), 366–380.

Kennedy, E., Spence, S.H., & Hensley, R. (1989). An examination of the relationship between childhood depression and social competence amongst primary school children. *Journal of Child Psychology, Psychiatry and Allied Disciplines*, **30**, 561–573.

King, N.J., Tonge, B.J., Heyne, D., Pritchard, M., Rollings, S., Young, D., Myerson, N., & Ollendick, T.H. (1998). Cognitive-behavioral treatment of school-refusing children: A controlled evaluation. *Journal of the American Academy of Child and Adolescent Psychiatry*, **37** (4), 395–403.

Krohne, H.W., & Hock, M. (1991). Relationships between restrictive mother–child interactions and anxiety of the child. *Anxiety Research*, **4**, 109–124.

LaFreniere, P.J., & Capuano, F. (1997). Preventive intervention as a means of clarifying direction of effects in socialization: Anxious-withdrawn preschoolers case. *Development and Psychopathology*, **9**, 551–564.

Last, C.G., Hansen, C., & Franco, N. (1998). Cognitive-behavioral treatment of school phobia. *Journal of the American Academy of Child and Adolescent Psychiatry*, **37** (4), 404–411.

Last, C.G., Hersen, M., Kazdin, A.E., Francis, G., & Grubb, H.J. (1987). Psychiatric illness in the mothers of anxious children. *American Journal of Psychiatry*, **144**, 1580–1583.

Lewinsohn, P.M., Clarke, G.N., Hops, H., & Andrews, J. (1990). Cognitive behavioural treatment for depressed adolescents. *Behavior Therapy*, **21**, 285–401.

Lewinsohn, P.M., Clarke, G.N., Seeley, J.R., & Rohde, P. (1994a). Major depression in community adolescents: Age at onset, episode duration, and time to recurrence. *Journal of the Academy of Child and Adolescent Psychiatry*, **33**, 809–818.

Lewinsohn, P.M., Roberts, R.E., Seeley, J.R., Rohde, P., Gotlib, I.H., & Hops, H. (1994b). Adolescent psychopathology: II. Psychosocial risk factors for depression. *Journal of Abnormal Psychology*, **103** (2), 302–315.

Lewinsohn, P.M., Seeley, J.R., Hubbard, J., Rohde, P., & Sack, W.H. (1996). Cross-sectional and prospective relationships between physical morbidity and depression in older adolescents. *Journal of the American Academy of Child and Adolescent Psychiatry*, **33**, 714–722.

Liddle, B., & Spence, S.H. (1990). Cognitive-behaviour therapy with depressed primary school children: A cautionary note. *Behavioural Psychotherapy*, **18** (2), 85–102.

Lowry-Webster, H., Barrett, P.M., & Dadds, M.R. (2001). A universal prevention trial of anxiety and depressive symptomatology in childhood: Preliminary data from an Australian study. *Behaviour Change*, **18**, 36–50.

Manassis, K. (1996). *Keys to parenting your anxious child*. Hauppauge, NY: Barron's Educational Series.

Mendlowitz, S.L., Manassis, K., Bradley, S., Scapillato, D., Miezitis, S., & Shaw, B.F. (1999). Cognitive-behavioral group treatments in childhood anxiety disorders: The role of parental involvement. *Journal of the American Academy of Child and Adolescent Psychiatry*, **38** (10), 1223–1229.

Mrazek, P.J., & Haggerty, R.J. (1994). *Reducing risks for mental disorders: Frontiers for preventive intervention research.* Washington, DC: National Academy Press.

Mufson, L., & Fairbanks, J. (1996). Interpersonal psychotherapy for depressed adolescents: A one-year naturalistic follow-up study. *Journal of the American Academy of Child and Adolescent Psychiatry,* **35** (9), 1145–1155.

Mufson, L., Moreau, D., Weissman, M.M., Klerman, G.L. (1993). *Interpersonal Psychotherapy for Depressed Adolescents.* New York: Guilford Press.

Mufson, L., Moreau, D., Weissman, M.M., Wickamartne, P., Martin, J., & Samoilov, A. (1994). Modification of interpersonal psychotherapy with depressed adolescents (IPT-A): Phase I and II studies. *Journal of the American Academy of Child and Adolescent Psychiatry,* **33** (5), 695–705.

Mufson, L., Weissman, M.M., Moreau, D., & Garfinkel, R. (1999). Efficacy of interpersonal psychotherapy for depressed adolescents. *Archives of General Psychiatry,* **56** (6), 573–579.

Muris, P., & Mayer, B. (2000). Vroegtijdige behandeling van angststoornissen bij kinderen (Early treatment of anxiety disorders in children). *Gedrag-and-Gezondheid: Tijdschrift voor Psychologie and Gezondheid,* **28**, 235–242.

Muris, P., Mayer, B., Bartelds, E., Tierney, S., & Bogie, N. (2001). The revised version of the Screen for Child Anxiety Related Emotional Disorders (SCARED-R): Treatment sensitivity in an early intervention trial for childhood anxiety disorders. *British Journal of Clinical Psychology,* **40**, 323–336.

Muris, P., Merckelbach, H., Holdrinet, I., & Siksenaar, M. (1998). Treating phobic children: Effects of EMDR versus exposure. *Journal of Consulting and Clinical Psychology,* **66** (1), 193–198.

Murray, C.J.C., & Lopez, A.D. (1996). *The global burden of disease.* Harvard: WHO, World Bank, and Harvard School of Public Health.

Nolen-Hoeksema, S., Girgus, J.S., & Seligman, M.E.P. (1992). Predictors and consequences of childhood depressive symptoms: A five-year longitudinal study. *Journal of Abnormal Psychology,* **101**, 405–422.

Oest, L.G., Svensson, L., Hellstroem, K., & Lindwall, R. (2001). One-session treatment of specific phobias in youths: A randomized clinical trial. *Journal of Consulting and Clinical Psychology,* **69** (5), 814–824.

Pattison, C., & Lynd-Stevenson, R.M. (2001). The prevention of depressive symptoms in children: The immediate and long-term outcomes of a school-based program. *Behaviour Change,* **18**, 92–102.

Petersen, A.C., Compas, B.E., Brooks-Gunn, J., Stemmler, M., Ey, S., & Grant, K.E. (1993). Depression in adolescence. *American Psychologist,* **48** (2), 155–168.

Pine, D.S., Cohen, P., Gurley, D., Brook, J., & Ma, Y. (1998). The risk for early adulthood anxiety and depressive disorders in adolescents with anxiety and depressive disorders. *Archives of General Psychiatry,* **55**, 56–64.

Prior, M., Smart, D., Sanson, A., & Oberklaid, F. (2000). Does shy-inhibited temperament in childhood lead to anxiety problems in adolescence? *Journal of the American Academy of Child and Adolescent Psychiatry,* **39**, 461–468.

Puig-Antich, J., Kaufman, J., Ryan, D., Williamson, D.E., Dahl, R.E., Lukens, E., Todak, G., Ambrosini, P., Rabinovich, H., & Nelson, B. (1993). The psychosocial functioning and family environment of depressed adolescents. *Journal of the American Academy of Child and Adolescent Psychiatry,* **32**, 244–253.

Quayle, D., Dziurawiec, S., Roberts, C., Kane, R., & Ebsworthy, G. (2001). The effect of an optimism and lifeskills program on depressive symptoms in preadolescence. *Behaviour Change,* **18**, 1–10.

Randell, B.P., Eggert, L.L., & Pike, K.C. (2001). Immediate post intervention effects of two brief youth suicide prevention interventions. *Suicide and Life Threatening Behavior,* **31** (1), 41–61.

Rapee, R.M. (1997). Potential role of childrearing practices in the development of anxiety and depression. *Clinical Psychology Review,* **17**, 47–67.

Rapee, R.M. (2001). The development of generalised anxiety. In M.W. Vasey & M.R. Dadds (Eds), *The developmental psychopathology of anxiety* (pp. 481–504). New York: Oxford University Press.

Rapee, R.M. (2002). The development and modification of temperamental risk for anxiety disorders: Prevention of a lifetime of anxiety? *Biological Psychiatry*. (Manuscript submitted.)

Reinherz, H.Z., Stewart-Berghauer, G., Pakiz, B., Frost, A.K., Moeykens, B.A., & Holmes, W.M. (1989). The relationship of early risk and current mediators to depressive symptomatology in adolescents. *Journal of the American Academy of Child and Adolescent Psychiatry*, **32**, 244–253.

Resnick, M.D., Bearman, P.S., Blum, R.W., Bauman, K.E., Harris, K.M., Jones, J., Tabor, J., Beuhring, T., Sieving, R.E., Shew, M., Ireland, M., Bearinger, L.H., & Udry, J.R. (1997). Protecting adolescents from harm: Findings from the National Longitudinal Study of Adolescent Health. *Journal of the American Medical Association*, **278**, 823–832.

Reynolds, W.M., & Coats, K.I. (1986). A comparison of cognitive-behavioral therapy and relaxation training for the treatment of depression in adolescents. *Journal of Consulting and Clinical Psychology*, **54** (5), 653–660.

Rice, K.G., & Meyer, A.L. (1994). Preventing depression among young adolescents: Preliminary process results of a psycho-educational intervention program. *Journal of Counselling and Development*, **73**, 145–156.

Rice, K.G., Herman, M.A., & Petersen, A.C. (1993). Coping with challenge in adolescence: A conceptual model and psycho-educational intervention. *Journal of Adolescence*, **16**, 235–251.

Roberts, C.M. (1999). The prevention of depression in children and adolescents. *Australian Psychologist*, **34**, 49–57.

Roberts, C.M., Kane, R., Thomson, H., Bishop, B., & Hart, B. (in press). The prevention of depressive symptoms in rural school children: A randomised controlled trial. *Journal of Consulting and Clinical Psychology*.

Robinson, J.L., Kagan, J., Reznick, J.S., & Corley, R. (1992). The heritability of inhibited and uninhibited behavior: A twin study. *Developmental Psychology*, **28**, 1030–1037.

Rossello, J., & Bernal, G. (1999). The efficacy of cognitive-behavioral and interpersonal treatments for depression in Puerto Rican adolescents. *Journal of Consulting and Clinical Psychology*, **67** (5), 734–745.

Rutter, M. (1985). Resilience in the face of adversity: Protective factors and resistance to psychiatric disorders. *British Journal of Psychiatry*, **147**, 598–611.

Santor, D.A., & Kusumakar, V. (2001). Open trial of interpersonal therapy in adolescents with moderate to severe major depression: Effectiveness of novice IPT therapists. *Journal of the American Academy of Child and Adolescent Psychiatry*, **40** (2), 236–240.

Seligman, L.D., & Ollendick, T.H. (1998). Comorbidity of anxiety and depression in children and adolescents: An integrative review. *Clinical Child and Family Psychology Review*, **1**, 125–144.

Shochet, I.M. (2002). The Resourceful Adolescent Program (RAP): Building resilience and preventing depression in adolescents through universal school-based interventions. In L. Rowling, G. Martin, & L. Walker (Eds), *Mental health promotion and young people: Concepts and practice* (pp. 172–184). Sydney: McGraw-Hill.

Shochet, I.M., Dadds, M.R., Holland, D., Whitefield, K., Harnett, P., & Osgarby, S.M. (2001). The efficacy of a universal school-based program to prevent adolescent depression. *Journal of Clinical Psychology*, **30**, 303–315.

Shortt, A., Barrett, P.M., & Fox, T. (2001). Evaluating the FRIENDS program: A cognitive-behavioural group treatment of childhood anxiety disorders: An evaluation of the Friends Program. *Journal of Clinical Child Psychology*, **30** (4), 525–535.

Shure, M.B. (2001). What's right with prevention? Commentary on "Prevention of mental disorders in school-aged children: Current state of the Field". *Prevention and Treatment*, **4**.

Silverman, W.K., & Kurtines, W.M. (1999). Short-term treatment for children with phobic and anxiety problems: A pragmatic view. *Crisis Intervention and Time Limited Treatment*, **5**, 119–131.

Silverman, W.K., Kurtines, W.M., Ginsburg, G.S., Weems, C.F., Lumpkin, P.W., & Carmichael, D.H. (1999). Treating anxiety disorders in children with group cognitive-behavioral therapy: A randomized clinical trial. *Journal of Consulting and Clinical Psychology*, **67** (6), 995–1003.

Spence, S.H. (1994). Prevention. In T.H. Ollendick, N. King, & W. Yule (Eds), *International handbook of phobic and anxiety disorders in children and adolescents* (pp. 453–474). New York: Plenum Press.

Spence, S.H. (1996). A case for prevention. In P. Cotton & H. Jackson (Eds), *Early intervention and prevention in mental health* (pp. 87–107). Melbourne, Australia: The Australian Psychological Society.

Spence, S.H. (2001). Prevention strategies. In M.W. Vasey & M.R. Dadds (Eds), *The developmental psychopathology of anxiety* (pp. 325–351). New York: Oxford University Press.

Spence, S.H., Sheffield, J.K., & Donovan, C.L. (in press). Preventing adolescent depression: An evaluation of the Problem Solving for Life Program. *Journal of Consulting and Clinical Psychology*.

Stark, K.D., Reynolds, W.R., & Kaslow, N.J. (1987). A comparison of the relative efficacy of self-control therapy and a behavioral problem-solving therapy for depression in children. *Journal of Abnormal Child Psychology*, **15**, 91–113.

Stark, K.D., Rouse, L., & Livingston, R. (1991). Treatment of depression during childhood and adolescence: Cognitive-behavioral procedures for the individual and family. In P. Kendall (Ed.), *Child and adolescent therapy* (pp. 165–206). New York: Guilford Press.

Stark, K.D., Humphrey, L.L., Crook, K., & Lewis, K. (1990). Perceived family environments of depressed and anxious children: Child's and maternal figure's perspectives. *Journal of Abnormal Child Psychology*, **18**, 527–547.

Stark, K.D., Humphrey, L.L., Laurent, J., Livingston, R., & Christopher, J. (1993). Cognitive, behavioural, and family factors in the differentiation of depressive and anxious disorders during childhood. *Journal of Consulting and Clinical Psychology*, **61**, 878–886.

Thapar, A., & McGuffin, P. (1994). A twin study of depressive symptoms in childhood. *British Journal of Psychiatry*, **65**, 259–265.

Toren, P., Rosental, B., Wolmer, L. et al. (1998). Cognitive-behavioral parent–child group psychotherapy for childhood anxiety disorders: A new manual-based treatment. The 14th International Congress of the International Association for Child and Adolescent Psychiatry and Allied Professions (IACAPAP), Stockholm.

Toren, P., Wolmer, L., Rosental, B., Eldar, S., Koren, S., Lask, M., Weizman, R., & Laor, N. (2000). Case series: Brief parent–child group therapy for childhood anxiety disorders using a manual-based cognitive-behavioral technique. *Journal of the American Academy of Child and Adolescent Psychiatry*, **39** (10), 1309–1312.

Toth, S.L., & Cicchetti, D. (1996). Patterns of relatedness, depressive symptomatology, and perceived competence in maltreated children. *Journal of Consulting and Clinical Psychology*, **64**, 32–41.

Tuma, J.M. (1989). Mental health services for children: The state of the art. *American Psychologist*, **44**, 188–199.

US Department of Health and Human Services (1999). *Mental Health: A report of the Surgeon General*. US Department of Health and Human Services, Substance Abuse and Mental Health Services Administration, Centre for Mental Health Services, National Institute of Mental Health: Rockville, MD.

Vostanis, P., Feehan, C., Grattan, E., & Bickerton, W.L. (1996a). Treatment for children and adolescents with depression: Lessons from a controlled trial. *Clinical Child Psychology and Psychiatry*, **1**, 199–212.

Vostanis, P., Feehan, C., Grattan, E., & Bickerton, W.L. (1996b). A randomised controlled outpatient trial of cognitive-behavioural treatment for children and adolescents with depression: 9-month follow-up. *Journal of Affective Disorders*, **40**, 105–116.

Warren, S.L., Huston, L., Egeland, B., & Sroufe, L.A. (1997). Child and adolescent anxiety disorders and early attachment. *Journal of the American Academy of Child and Adolescent Psychiatry*, **36**, 637–644.

Weisz, J.R., Thurber, C.A., Sweeney, L., Proffitt, V.D., & LeGagnoux, G.L. (1997). Brief treatment of mild-to-moderate child depression using primary and secondary control enhancement training. *Journal of Consulting and Clinical Psychology*, **65** (4), 703–707.

WHO. (1998). *Primary prevention of mental, neurological and psychosocial disorders.* World Health Organization: Geneva.

Wood, A., Harrington, R., & Moore, A. (1996). Controlled trial of a brief cognitive-behavioural intervention in adolescent patients with depressive disorders. *Journal of Child Psychology and Psychiatry and Allied Disciplines, 372* (6), 737–746.

Yule, W., & Williams, R. (1990). Post-traumatic stress reactions in children. *Journal of Traumatic Stress, 3,* 279–295.

Zubrick, S.R., Silburn, S.R., Garton, A., Burton, P., Dalby, R., Shepherd, C., & Lawrence, D. (1995). *Western Australian Child Health Survey: Developing health and wellbeing in the nineties.* Perth, Australia: Australian Bureau of Statistics.

Zubrick, S.R., Silburn, S.R., Teoh, H.J., Carlton, J., Shepherd, C., & Lawrence, D. (1997). *Western Australian Child Health Survey: Education, health and competency.* Perth, Australia: Australian Bureau of Statistics.

CHAPTER 19

Prevention of Oppositional Defiant Disorder and Conduct Disorder in Children and Adolescents

Ronald J. Prinz

University of South Carolina, USA

and

Jean E. Dumas

Purdue University, USA

INTRODUCTION

Interest in the prevention of youth violence and delinquency in general, and ODD and CD in particular, is not new. The Greek philosopher Plato discussed the issue some 25 centuries ago, as have countless authors ever since (Tremblay, LeMarquand, & Vitaro, 1999). This interest remains high today, fuelled by strong social pressures to reduce incidents of school and neighbourhood violence, as well as other acts of aggression on the part of young people (Ollendick, 1996).

Preventive interventions are generally distinguishable from clinical treatment of ODD and CD, although the two modalities share some approaches and procedures in common. Prevention involves intervention before the disorder has fully emerged, and preventive interventions are typically (though not always) initiated by others in contrast to the situation in which parents seek, or are referred for, treatment for their child.

Contrary to the widespread belief that antisocial behaviour is difficult to prevent, there is strong evidence to show that preventive interventions can succeed in this area. For example, Durlak and Wells (1997) conducted a comprehensive meta-analysis of 177 controlled outcome studies of programs designed to prevent a variety

Correspondence to Ron Prinz, Department of Psychology, University of South Carolina, Columbia, SC 29208; email: prinz@sc.edu

Handbook of Interventions that Work with Children and Adolescents: Prevention and Treatment.
Edited by P.M. Barrett and T.H. Ollendick. © 2004 John Wiley & Sons, Ltd. ISBN 0-470-84453-1.

of behavioural and social problems in youth. The study found not only that many programs significantly reduced problems, but also that they significantly increased coping-competence across social, affective, and academic domains. A similar conclusion comes from a more recent meta-analysis of 165 school-based prevention programs. Although that study found considerable heterogeneity in the nature and effectiveness of the interventions reviewed, it reported consistently positive effects for programs based on behavioural or cognitive-behavioural principles (Wilson, Gottfredson, & Najaka, 2001).

In this review, we focus on interventions that have been carefully evaluated through randomized or quasi-experimental designs and have been shown to have positive effects on antisocial behaviour directly, or on some of its known antecedents (e.g., interventions designed to promote academic learning to reduce the risk of school failure). Programs focused on prevention of ODD or CD have a wide range of intervention targets: some are designed to modify child behaviour directly, whereas others focus on parents, teachers, peers, or even entire communities. Prevention programs also vary in scope: some offer a single, stand-alone intervention, whereas others combine interventions into complex, multicomponent programs. Note that, given the current state of knowledge, our focus cannot be exclusively on the prevention of a diagnosis of ODD or CD, as too few studies have used these diagnostic categories as outcomes to be prevented (Tremblay, LeMarquand, & Vitaro, 1999).

FAMILY-BASED INTERVENTIONS

Family-based interventions aimed at preventing childhood and adolescent conduct problems divide roughly into two categories based on targeted age groups. For pre-adolescents including pre-school and elementary school ages, evidence-based family treatments concentrate on parenting and the parent/caregiver role as a socialization agent. For the adolescent age group, the evidence-based family interventions focus on parenting, parent–adolescent communication, and also how to address broader socioecological factors (such as managing peer influences and activities outside the home). Although there are some subtle differences in application, conduct-problem prevention programs for pre-school children are quite similar to those used with elementary school children. The focus for both age groups is on parenting, parent–child interaction, enhancement of family relations, and skill acquisition.

Illustrative Family-Based Interventions for Pre-School and Elementary-School Aged Children

The Incredible Years (BASIC) program developed by Webster-Stratton and colleagues has been well supported in a series of studies employed randomization and controls, primarily involving 4–8-year-old children with CD or ODD. The parenting program produced reductions in aggressive and destructive behaviour in several outcome studies (Webster-Stratton, 1981, 1982a, 1982b, 1984; Webster-Stratton, Hollinsworth, & Kolpacoff, 1989; Webster-Stratton, Kolpacoff, & Hollinsworth,

1988). Other researchers have replicated this work and also found positive impact of the program (Scott et al., 2001; Spaccarelli, Cotler, & Penman, 1992; Taylor et al., 1998).

Among the various SPFIs, of particular note is a set of programs developed by Sanders and colleagues called Triple P—Positive Parenting Program (Sanders, 1999; Sanders & Markie-Dadds, 1996; see Chapter 20). Triple P is actually a coordinated set or system of parenting programs combining universal and indicated intervention levels. Triple P uses a tiered system of intervention of increasing strength, ranging from media and information-based strategies, to two levels of moderate-intensity intervention using a brief consultation format, to a more intensive level of parent training, and finally to behavioural family intervention simultaneously targeting parenting skills and other family adversity factors such as marital conflict, depression and high levels of parenting stress. Elements of the core Triple P program include: observational skills (monitoring child and own behaviour), cognitive skills (challenging non-productive parental beliefs and explanations for child behaviour), parent–child relationship enhancement skills (spending quality time, talking with children, showing affection), encouraging desirable behaviour (using descriptive praise, giving non-verbal attention, providing engaging activities), teaching new skills and behaviours (setting developmentally appropriate goals, setting positive examples, using incidental teaching, using "Ask, Say, Do"), managing misbehaviour (establishing ground rules, using directed discussion, using planned ignoring, giving clear and calm instructions, using logical consequences, quiet time and time-out), preventing problems in high-risk situations (planning and preparing in advance, discussing ground rules for specific situations, selecting engaging activities, providing incentives, providing consequences, holding follow-up discussions), self-regulation skills (setting practice tasks, self-evaluation of strengths and weaknesses, setting personal goals for change), and maintenance skills (phasing out program materials, planning for high-risk situations, regularly reviewing family's progress, experimenting with new strategies).

The Triple P work is distinctive for several reasons. The programs have been well supported by an impressive collection of efficacy and effectiveness trials (Connell, Sanders, & Markie-Dadds, 1997; Dadds, Schwartz, & Sanders, 1987; Lawton & Sanders, 1994; Markie-Dadds & Sanders, in preparation; Markie-Dadds, Sanders, & Smith, 1997; Nicholson & Sanders, in press; Sanders, 1992, 1996, 1998, 1999; Sanders, Bor, & Dadds, 1984; Sanders & Christensen, 1985; Sanders & Dadds, 1982, 1993; Sanders & Duncan, 1995; Sanders & Glynn, 1981; Sanders & Markie-Dadds, 1992, 1996, 1997; Sanders et al., 2000; Sanders & McFarland, in press; Sanders & Plant, 1989a, 1989b; Williams et al., 1997). The programs are well resourced in terms of parent-friendly materials. Triple P has several different delivery formats and intensity levels, including some aimed at the general population.

Illustrative Family-Based Preventive Interventions for Adolescents

Most of the evidence-based interventions focusing on conduct problems during adolescence, such as Multi-Systemic Therapy (Henggeler, 1998; Henggeler et al., 2000) or Functional Family Therapy (Alexander et al., 2000), fall more in the realm of treatment than prevention. One exception is an emerging preventive approach called the Adolescent Transitions Program (ATP; Dishion & Kavanagh, 2000). The ATP approach employs a three-level blended prevention model that incorporates universal, selected, and indicated strategies and matches intervention intensity to family and youth need. Initial data on the ATP suggest that the program can significantly contribute to the reduction of adolescent problem behaviour and substance use (Dishion & Kavanagh, 2000).

PEER AND SCHOOL INTERVENTIONS

Children with ODD and CD are regularly in conflict with teachers and peers for the same reasons they have trouble at home: they are demanding, coercive, and aggressive, unable to effectively regulate their emotions, and slow to recognize and accept responsibility for the impact of their behaviour on others (Coie et al., 1995; Trachenberg & Viken, 1994). Consequently, many of the proximal risk factors that are targeted in preventive peer and school interventions overlap with those that are the focus of family interventions (Reid & Eddy, 1997).

Although their features overlap, peer and school intervention programs can be distinguished in terms of their intended impact: some are designed to reduce and prevent aggression and violence directly; others seek more broadly to develop social, affective, and/or academic competence in order to reduce risk; and still others focus on changing the school ecology rather than on modifying the behaviour of individual youth directly (Greenberg, Domitrovich, & Bumbarger, 2001). We will review key programs along these dimensions and, within each section, discuss universal interventions before indicated ones.

Illustrative Interventions Directly Targeting Aggression and Violence

Only a handful of universal prevention programs targeting aggression and violence directly have been evaluated. As Greenberg, Domitrovich, and Bumbarger (2001) recently concluded, evidence in this area is generally mixed. For example, Second Step is an anger-management training program designed to prevent youth violence through teaching emotion regulation and empathy in elementary school (Grossman et al., 1997). By the end of the program and at a six-month follow-up, observers found that participants displayed increases in prosocial behaviour and decreases in aggression. However, these positive changes were not confirmed by parent or teacher ratings of the children's adjustment. Similarly, Responding in Peaceful and Positive Ways (RIPP) is a skills training program seeking to prevent violence in middle school through teaching effective communication and conflict resolution with peers (Farrell, Meyer, & White, 2001). The program resulted in significant increases in knowledge and use of conflict resolution skills with peers, as well as in reductions in weapon carrying (at post-test) and in-school suspensions (at post-test and six-month follow-up). However, the program did not result in improvements in self-report measures of adjustment or reductions in school fighting and out-of-school suspensions.

Evidence is also mixed when it comes to indicated programs targeting aggression and violence directly. For example, Lochman and colleagues developed the Anger Coping Program, an anger management intervention for aggressive boys of elementary and middle school age (Lochman, 1985, 1992; Lochman & Lampron, 1988). The program teaches emotion regulation, problem-solving, and goal-setting through role-playing and practice in small peer groups. The program has been found to improve on-task behaviour and reduce disruptiveness and aggression in the classroom at post-test. However, reductions in disruptiveness and aggression were not maintained at seven-month and three-year follow-ups. More positive findings have been reported by Hammond and Yung (Hammond & Yung, 1993; Yung & Hammond, 1998) in a controlled evaluation of an anger management and conflict resolution program for aggressive adolescents. The program targeted inner-city, African American youth attending middle school. Results showed that at a three-year follow-up participants were significantly less likely than control youth to have appeared in juvenile court or to have been charged with a violent offence.

Illustrative Interventions Targeting Social and Affective Competence

A number of cognitive problem-solving programs have been developed to build children's social and affective competence as a universal means of preventing adverse behavioural outcomes, including aggression and violence. One of the best known and most carefully evaluated is Promoting Alternative Thinking Strategies (PATHS; Greenberg & Kusche, 1998; Greenberg et al., 1995). PATHS is a curriculum-based program promoting emotion recognition and regulation in elementary school children. A randomized-controlled evaluation has shown that the program leads to significant improvements in participating youth on self- and teacher-reported measures of adaptive functioning, as well as on measures of emotional and cognitive understanding of social situations requiring effective problem-solving. Most importantly, these gains have been maintained at one- and two-year follow-ups (Greenberg, Domitrovich, & Bumbarger, 2001).

Programs promoting social and affective competence have also been used successfully with indicated samples of at risk children. For example, two programs have sought to promote effective coping skills with peers as a means of reducing risk for later maladjustment in children already showing high levels of aggression in elementary school. The Social Relations Program developed by Lochman and colleagues (1993) was designed to teach at-risk youth prosocial skills to interact with peers, solve problems in social situations, and effectively regulate their negative emotions. The program, which is administered individually and in small groups of peers, has been found to improve peer acceptance and reduce aggression in a sample of African American children aged 9 to 11, this at post-test and at a one-year follow-up. Comparable results have been reported by Prinz, Blechman, and Dumas (1994) in a controlled evaluation of Peer Coping Skills (PCS) training. This program, which targets students with high levels of aggression in early elementary school, is delivered in small groups consisting of equal numbers of at risk and well-functioning peers. The program teaches prosocial communication skills through role-plays and group activities and requires participants to master the skills taught before the group can advance to more complex skill building and practice. Post-test and six-month follow-up results showed that PCS resulted in significant improvements in prosocial skills in program participants, as well as in significant reductions in teacher-rated aggression.

Illustrative Interventions Targeting the School Environment

Kellam and colleagues have conducted several large-scale prevention trials to test the impact of two classroom interventions: the Good Behaviour Game (GBG) and Mastery Learning (ML) (Kellam et al., 1994, 1998). The GBG is a classroom management program promoting positive social relationships and adherence to classroom rules by dividing the class into teams that compete for rewards they receive for meeting clearly set behavioural goals. ML is an educational program requiring a majority of students in the class to master specific reading and math skills before being introduced to more complex skills in the same areas. Both programs have been found to be effective when implemented for one or two years in early elementary school. For example, the GBG has been shown to reduce aggressive behaviour, and ML to improve basic learning skills, during childhood and early adolescence in boys and girls, thereby positively affecting key precursors of CD and related adverse outcomes (Dolan et al., 1993; Kellam et al., 1998). Importantly, and contrary to the common belief that prevention mostly helps those who need it least, a four-year follow-up found that long-term positive effects were most evident for boys who had very high levels of aggression in 1st grade. The same was not found for girls, although this may simply reflect the fact that girls were not particularly aggressive in 1st grade (Kellam et al., 1994). Combination of the GBG and ML has also yielded immediate and long-term (end of 6th grade) positive effects. Particularly impressive are findings that in early adolescence youth who participated in the combined program were less likely than control youth to meet diagnostic criteria for CD, to have received mental health services, and to have been suspended from school (Ialongo et al., 1999).

The program developed by Olweus for reducing school bullying provides another example of an effective school-based intervention (Olweus, 1993). This program, which began on a national scale in Norway in the 1980s, is designed to reduce bullying and peer victimization in elementary and middle school. It is a comprehensive intervention targeting change at the school level (through policy and other initiatives to implement the program throughout the school); at the classroom level (through the establishment of rules to reduce bullying and victimization, and of opportunities to discuss alternatives to antisocial behaviour); and at the individual and family level (by promoting communication between home and school, and discussing incidents of bullying with perpetrators, victims, and their families). Quasi-experimental evaluations have shown that the program reduces incidents of bullying by half or more in elementary and middle school students. Furthermore, the program has been found to improve student satisfaction with school and to reduce antisocial conduct in general, including fighting, stealing, vandalism, and truancy (Olweus, 1994, 1996).

Finally, Felner and colleagues conducted a series of studies aimed at modifying the school ecology at the time of transition from elementary to middle school, or middle to high school (Felner et al., 1993, 2001; Felner, Ginter, & Primavera, 1982). Specifically, the School Transitional Environment Project (STEP) is designed to facilitate transition to a new school environment for students at risk of failing academically and dropping out. STEP assigns new students to homerooms in which they interact with the same peers and participate in core academic activities for a significant part of the day. Classes are held in a particular section of the school each day and homeroom teachers take on an expanded role of academic adviser and counsellor. In particular, teachers help students to adjust to their new school environment, facilitate communication between home and school, and monitor students' social adjustment and academic progress throughout the year. STEP has been found to result in immediate and long-term positive changes. One year after transition to their new school, STEP students evidenced lower levels of stress and anxiety, and better social and academic adjustment than comparison students. More importantly, over a four-year follow-up period, STEP participants continued to be better adjusted socially and academically, and had much lower dropout rates than non-participants (43% vs 24%) (Felner et al., 1993).

MULTICOMPONENT INTERVENTIONS

Some of the interventions for prevention of conduct problems are actually combinations of interventions. Several of these multicomponent interventions have been deployed in clinical trials. These interventions have in common that programming takes in more than one setting (typically the school and the family) capitalizing on more than one social influence or change agent (e.g., teachers, parents and other caregivers, peers, academic tutors). In the conduct-problem prevention area, it is now the norm that preventive interventions tackle multiple behavioural domains in multiple settings to achieve greater impact.

Illustrative Multicomponent Interventions

Several multicomponent interventions are summarized here as illustrations of what the field has currently achieved. All of the chosen examples are based on controlled outcome studies.

The Montreal Longitudinal-Experimental Study is a first-generation multicomponent prevention trial that included parent training and child social skills training components with an indicated sample of boys beginning at age 7 (Tremblay et al., 1992). The parent program, based on the Oregon Social Learning Center model (Patterson, 1982; Patterson et al., 1975), involved two years of programming delivered in families' homes with an emphasis on encouragement of reading, monitoring of child behaviour, positive reinforcement for prosocial behaviour, effective punishment without abusiveness, management of family crises, and promotion of generalization. The social skills training component focused first on how the children could develop positive peer relations and then on cognitive-based skills aimed at invoking self-control. Although initial effects of intervention were not demonstrable, the Montreal Longitudinal-Experimental Study intervention yielded significant effects at five-year follow-up in terms of less delinquent involvement and better academic performance (McCord et al., 1994).

The Seattle Social Development Project (SSDP), also a first-generation multi-component prevention trial, involved teacher training, child skills training, and parent training during the early years of elementary school (Hawkins et al., 1992). Construction of the intervention components was guided conceptually by the social development model, which is an amalgamation of social control and social learning theories (Hawkins & Lam, 1987; Hawkins & Weis, 1985). The SSDP has yielded positive results in terms of lower rates of delinquency and to some extent substance abuse (O'Donnell et al., 1995).

Of the second-generation multicomponent trials, by far the largest and most extensive is the Fast Track project (Conduct Problems Prevention Research Group, 1992, 2002b). Fast Track is a customized hybrid of intervention components including the universally delivered PATHS classroom curriculum (Kusche & Greenberg, 1994), the indicated components focused on child social skills (groups), parent training (groups), and parent–child relationship enhancement, and individualized components which involved academic tutoring, pairing of children with prosocial peers, and family support via home visiting. Delivered in four diverse communities throughout the USA, Fast Track began with a large sample of kindergarten children who showed behavioural indications of risk for conduct disorder, and conducted the overall intervention program from 1st through 10th Grades with the participating children and families. This long-term intervention trial has a number of noteworthy features such as theoretically driven intervention components; rigorous implementation of interventions, fidelity assessment, and measurement procedures; integrity in the presentation and interpretation of results; and attention to issues of community engagement, sustainability, and replicability (Prinz, 2002). Published results of Fast Track, to date, have indicated that the intervention package after three years of programming produced significant though modest prevention or reduction of conduct problems and associated difficulties based on multiple sources of data (Conduct Problems Prevention Research Group, 2002a). In the next few years, the field will have a better idea of the long-term impact of Fast Track as outcome data for early adolescence are reported.

Two other emerging multicomponent interventions are noteworthy. The LIFT program (Linking Interests of Families and Teachers), developed by Reid and colleagues (1999), is a universally delivered package aimed at elementary school children. LIFT includes parent training, a classroom-based social skills program, a playground program, and enhancement of communication between teachers and parents. Results with LIFT indicate that the intervention is effective in reducing rates of aggressive behaviour in the general sample but particularly with higher-risk children (Reid et al., 1999; Stoolmiller, Eddy, & Reid, 2000).

A second emerging intervention of note is Early Alliance (Dumas et al., 1999a; Prinz et al., 2000). Early Alliance is a multicomponent intervention that includes a universal classroom program (Classroom Coping Skills), and three indicated components: a peer program (Peer Coping Skills), a family-based program that is home-delivered, and an after-school reading enhancement program. Although too recent for outcome data to be published, one of the distinctive features of Early Alliance is that all of the intervention components and their delivery processes are driven by a unifying conceptual model, coping-competence, which is also being tested as a primary mediator in the prevention trial.

CONCLUSIONS

Overall, evidence is strong that prevention is quite powerful in this area. This is true even when one works only in one setting, and when interventions are targeted to older children and adolescents. Furthermore, evidence is accumulating to suggest that preventive programs may have some of their greatest impact on children who are most at risk (Kellam et al., 1998; Stoolmiller et al., 2000).

However, this encouraging conclusion must be tempered in light of other observations:

1. Interventions may not have lasting effects in situations in which children and adolescents are exposed to multiple, chronic risks factors in their environment (such as poverty, community violence, and discrimination). This is true of interventions that focus on a single group of antecedents such as parenting and may also be true of multicomponent interventions.
2. Much remains to be learned about the effectiveness of preventive interventions with minority youth, particularly those who are disproportionately exposed to multiple, chronic risk factors in their environment. A review of the literature suggests that, overall, evidence in this area is mixed and that minority youth do not always benefit fully from well-established prevention programs (Guerra, Attar, & Weissberg, 1997). This may be so because some programs may not be culturally sensitive, may be too brief to have lasting effects, or may be difficult to implement with high levels of fidelity in environments characterized by high social and economic stress (Dumas et al., 1999b; Guerra, Attar, & Weissberg, 1997).
3. Some interventions have been found to have iatrogenic effects (Dishion & Burraston, 2001; Dishion, McCord, & Poulin, 1999).

In general, the prevention of ODD and CD is making progress because interventions with known fidelity are being tested using theoretical models of mediation in randomized trials with carefully selected samples tracked longitudinally and assessed in multiple domains through multiple data sources. With this trend of methodological rigor and theoretical direction, the field is likely to continue to improve our understanding of what kinds of interventions succeed under which conditions with which youth and families.

REFERENCES

Alexander, J., Pugh, C., Parsons, B., & Sexton, T. (2000). *Functional Family Therapy*. Boulder, CO: Center for the Study and Prevention of Violence.

Coie, J.D., Terry, R., Lenox, K., Lochman, J., & Hyman, C. (1995). Childhood peer rejection and aggression as predictors of stable patterns of adolescent disorder. *Development and Psychopathology*, **7**, 697–713.

Conduct Problems Prevention Research Group (1992). A developmental and clinical model for the prevention of conduct disorder: The FAST Track Program. *Development and Psychopathology*, **4**, 509–527.

Conduct Problems Prevention Research Group (2002a). Evaluation of the first three years of the Fast Track Prevention Trial with children at high risk for adolescent conduct problems. *Journal of Abnormal Child Psychology*, **30**, 19–36.

Conduct Problems Prevention Research Group (2002b). The implementation of the Fast Track Program: An example of a large-scale prevention science efficacy trial. *Journal of Abnormal Child Psychology*, **30**, 1–17.

Connell, S., Sanders, M.R., & Markie-Dadds, C. (1997). Self-directed behavioural family intervention for parents of oppositional children in rural and remote areas. *Behavior Modification*, **21**, 379–408.

Dadds, M.R., Schwartz, S., & Sanders, M.R. (1987). Marital discord and treatment outcome in the treatment of childhood conduct disorders. *Journal of Consulting and Clinical Psychology*, **55**, 396–403.

Dishion, T.J., & Burraston, B. (2001). Three-year iatrogenic effects associated with aggregating high-risk adolescents in cognitive-behavioral preventive interventions. *Applied Developmental Science*, **5**, 214–224.

Dishion, T.J., & Kavanagh, K. (2000). A multilevel approach to family-centered prevention in schools: Process and outcome. *Addictive Behaviors*, **25**, 899–911.

Dishion, T.J., McCord, J., & Poulin, F. (1999). When interventions harm: Peer groups and problem behavior. *American Psychologist*, **54**, 755–764.

Dolan, L.J., Kellam, S.G., Brown, C.H., Wethamer-Larsson, L., Rebok, G.W., Mayer, L.S. et al. (1993). The short-term impact of two classroom-based preventive interventions on aggressive and shy behaviors and poor achievement. *Journal of Applied Developmental Psychology*, **14**, 317–345.

Dumas, J.E., Prinz, R.J., Smith, E.P., & Laughlin, J. (1999a). The EARLY ALLIANCE Prevention Trial: An integrated set of interventions to promote competence and reduce risk for conduct disorder, substance abuse, and school failure. *Clinical Child and Family Psychology Review*, **2**, 37–52.

Dumas, J.E., Rollock, D., Prinz, R.J., Hops, H., & Blechman, E.A. (1999b). Cultural sensitivity: Problems and solutions in applied and preventive intervention. *Applied and Preventive Psychology*, **8**, 175–196.

Durlak, J.A., & Wells, A.M. (1997). Primary prevention mental health programs for children and adolescents: A meta-analytic review. *American Journal of Community Psychology*, **25**, 115–151.

Farrell, A.D., Meyer, A.L., & White, K.S. (2001). Evaluation of Responding in Peaceful and Positive Ways (RIPP): A school-based prevention program for reducing violence among urban adolescents. *Journal of Community Psychology*, **30**, 451–463.

Felner, R.D., Ginter, M., & Primavera, J. (1982). Primary prevention during school transitions: Social support and environmental structure. *American Journal of Community Psychology*, **10**, 277–290.

Felner, R.D., Brand, S., Adan, A.M., Muhall, P.F., Flowers, N., Sartain, B. (1993). Restructuring the ecology of the school as an approach to prevention during school transitions: Longitudinal follow-ups and extensions of the School Transitional Environmental Project (STEP). *Prevention in Human Services*, **10**, 103–136.

Felner, R.D., Favazza, A., Shim, M., Brand, S., Gu, K., & Noonan, N. (2001). Whole school improvement and restructuring as prevention and promotion: Lessons from STEP and the Project on High Performance Learning Communities. *Journal of School Psychology*, **39**, 177–202.

Greenberg, M.T., & Kusche, C.A. (1998). Preventive interventions for school-age deaf children: The PATHS curriculum. *Journal of Deaf Studies and Deaf Education*, **3**, 49–63.

Greenberg, M.T., Domitrovich, C.E., & Bumbarger, B. (2001). The prevention of mental disorders in school-aged children: Current state of the field. *Prevention and Treatment*, **4**.

Greenberg, M.T., Kusche, C.A., Cook, E.T., & Quamma, J.P. (1995). Promoting emotional competence in school-aged children: The effects of the PATHS curriculum. *Development and Pslychopathology*, **7**, 117–136.

Grossman, D.C., Neckerman, H.J., Koepsell, T.D., Liu, P., Asher, K.N., Beland, K., et al. (1997). Effectiveness of a violence prevention curriculum among children in elementary school. *Journal of the American Medical Association*, **277**, 1605–1611.

Guerra, N.G., Attar, B., & Weissberg, R.P. (1997). Prevention of aggression and violence among inner-city youths. In D.M. Stoff & J. Breiling (Eds), *Handbook of antisocial behavior* (pp. 375–383). New York: Plenum.

Hammond, W.R., & Yung, B. (1993). Psychology's role in the public health response to assaultive violence among young African American men. *American Psychologist*, **48**, 142–154.

Hawkins, J.D., & Lam, T. (1987). Teacher practices, social development and delinquency. In J.D. Burchard & S.N. Burchard (Eds), *Prevention of delinquent behavior* (pp. 241–274). Beverly Hills, CA: Sage.

Hawkins, J.D., & Weis, J.G. (1985). The social development model: An integrated approach to delinquency prevention. *Journal of Primary Prevention*, **6**, 73–97.

Hawkins, J.D., Catalano, R.F., Morrison, D.M., O'Donnell, J., Abbott, R.D., & Day, L.E. (1992). The Seattle Social Development Project: Effects of the first four years on protective factors and problem behaviors. In J. McCord & R.E. Tremblay (Eds), *Preventing antisocial behavior: Interventions from birth through adolescence* (pp. 139–161). New York: Guilford.

Henggeler, S.W. (1998). *Multisystemic Therapy*. Boulder, CO: Center for the Study and Prevention of Violence.

Henggeler, S.W., Schoenwald, S.K., Borduin, C.M., Rowland, M.D., & Cunningham, P.B. (2000). *Multisystemic treatment of antisocial behavior in youth*. New York: Guilford.

Ialongo, N.S., Werthamer, L., Kellam, S.G., Brown, C.H., Wang, S., & Lin, Y. (1999). Proximal impact of two first-grade preventive interventions on the early risk behaviors for later substance abuse, depression, and antisocial behavior. *American Journal of Community Psychology*, **27**, 599–641.

Kellam, S.G., Ling, X., Merisca, R., Brown, C.H., & Ialongo, N. (1998). The effect of the level of aggression in the first grade classroom on the course and malleability of aggressive behavior into middle school. *Development and Psychopathology*, **10**, 165–186.

Kellam, S.G., Rebok, G.W., Ialongo, N., & Mayer, L.S. (1994). The course and malleability of aggressive behavior from early first grade into middle school: Results of a developmental epidemiology-based preventive trial. *Journal of Child Psychology and Psychiatry and Allied Disciplines*, **35**, 259–281.

Kusche, C.A., & Greenberg, M.T. (1994). *The PATHS Curriculum*. Seattle, WA: Developmental Research and Programs.

Lawton, J.M., & Sanders, M.R. (1994). Designing effective behavioural family interventions for stepfamilies. *Clinical Psychology Review*, **14**, 463–496.

Lochman, J.E. (1985). Effects of different treatment lengths in cognitive-behavioral interventions with aggressive boys. *Child Psychiatry and Human Development*, **16**, 45–56.

Lochman, J.E. (1992). Cognitive-behavioral intervention with aggressive boys: Three-year follow-up and preventive efforts. *Journal of Consulting and Clinical Psychology*, **60**, 426–432.

Lochman, J.E., & Lampron, L.B. (1988). Cognitive behavioral interventions for aggressive boys: Seven months follow-up effects. *Journal of Child and Adolescent Psychotherapy*, **5**, 15–23.

Lochman, J.E., Coie, J.D., Underwood, M.K., & Terry, R. (1993). Effectiveness of a social relations intervention program for aggressive and nonaggressive, rejected children. *Journal of Consulting and Clinical Psychology*, **61**, 1053–1058.

Markie-Dadds, C., & Sanders, M.R. (in preparation). Effectiveness of a self-directed program for parents of children at high and low risk of developing conduct disorder.

Markie-Dadds, C., Sanders, M.R., & Smith, J.I. (1997). *Self-directed behavioural family intervention for parents of oppositional children in rural and remote areas.* Paper presented at the 20th National Conference of the Australian Association for Cognitive and Behavior Therapy, Brisbane, Qld.

McCord, J., Tremblay, R.E., Vitaro, F., & Desmarais-Gervais, L. (1994). Boys' disruptive behavior, school adjustment, and delinquency: The Montreal prevention experiment. *International Journal of Behavioral Development,* **17,** 739–752.

Nicholson, J.M., & Sanders, M.R. (in press). Behavioural family intervention with children living in step families. *Journal of Marriage and Divorce.*

O'Donnell, J., Hawkins, J.D., Catalano, R.F., Abbott, R.D., & Day, L.E. (1995). Preventing school failure, drug use, and delinquency among low-income children: Long-term intervention in elementary schools. *American Journal of Orthopsychiatry,* **65,** 87–100.

Ollendick, T.H. (1996). Violence in society: Where do we go from here? *Behavior Therapy,* **27,** 485–514.

Olweus, D. (1993). *Bullying at school: What we know and what we can do.* Oxford, England: Blackwell.

Olweus, D. (1994). Bullying at school: Basic facts and effects of a school-based intervention program. *Journal of Child Psychology and Psychiatry,* **33,** 1171–1190.

Olweus, D. (1996). Bullying at school: Knowledge base and an effective intervention program. In C.F. Ferris & T. Grisso (Eds), *Understanding aggressive behavior in children* (vol. 794; pp. 265–276). New York: New York Academy of Sciences.

Patterson, G.R. (1982). *Coercive family process.* Eugene, OR: Castalia.

Patterson, G.R., Reid, J.B., Jones, R.R., & Conger, R.E. (1975). *A social learning approach to family intervention: Vol. 1. Families with aggressive children.* Eugene, OR: Castalia.

Prinz, R.J. (2002). The Fast Track Project: A seminal intervention efficacy trial. *Journal of Abnormal Child Psychology,* **30,** 61–64.

Prinz, R.J., Blechman, E.A., & Dumas, J.E. (1994). An evaluation of peer coping-skills training for childhood aggression. *Journal of Clinical Child Psychology,* **23,** 193–203.

Prinz, R.J., Dumas, J.E., Smith, E.P., & Laughlin, J. (2000). The EARLY ALLIANCE prevention trial: A dual design to test reduction of risk for conduct problems, substance abuse, and school failure in childhood. *Controlled Clinical Trials,* **21,** 286–302.

Reid, J.B., & Eddy, J.M. (1997). The prevention of antisocial behavior: Some considerations in the search for effective interventions. In D.M. Stoff, J. Breiling, & J.D. Maser (Eds), *The handbook of antisocial behavior* (pp. 343–356). New York: John Wiley & Sons

Reid, J.B., Eddy, J.M., Fetrow, R.A., & Stoolmiller, M. (1999). Description and immediate impacts of a preventive intervention for conduct problems. *American Journal of Community Psychology,* **27,** 483–517.

Sanders, M.R. (1992). Enhancing the impact of behavioural family intervention with children: Emerging perspectives. *Behaviour Change,* **9,** 115–119.

Sanders, M.R. (1996). New directions in behavioral family intervention with children. In T.H. Ollendick & R.J. Prinz (Eds), *Advances in clinical child psychology.* (vol. 18; pp. 283–330). New York: Plenum.

Sanders, M.R. (1998). The empirical status of psychological interventions with families of children and adolescents. In L. L'Abate (Ed.), *Family psychopathology: The relational roots of dysfunctional behavior.* New York: Guildford Press.

Sanders, M.R. (1999). Triple P—Positive Parenting Program: Towards an empirically validated multilevel parenting and family support strategy for the prevention of behavior and emotional problems in children. *Clinical Child and Family Psychology Review,* **2,** 71–90.

Sanders, M.R., & Christensen, A.P. (1985). A comparison of the effects of child management and planned activities training across five parenting environments. *Journal of Abnormal Child Psychology,* **13,** 101–117.

Sanders, M.R., & Dadds, M.R. (1982). The effects of planned activities and child-management training: An analysis of setting generality. *Behaviour Therapy,* **13,** 1–11.

Sanders, M.R., & Dadds, M.R. (1993). *Behavioral family intervention.* Boston: Allyn & Bacon, Inc.

Sanders, M.R., & Duncan, S.B. (1995). Empowering families: Policy, training, and research issues in promoting family mental health in Australia. *Behaviour Change*, **12**, 109–121.

Sanders, M.R., & Glynn, T. (1981). Training parents in behavioural self-management: An analysis of generalisation and maintenance. *Journal of Applied Behaviour Analysis*, **14**, 223–237.

Sanders, M.R., & Markie-Dadds, C. (1992). Toward a technology of prevention of disruptive behaviour disorders: The role of behavioural family intervention. *Behaviour Change*, **9**, 186–200.

Sanders, M.R., & Markie-Dadds, C. (1996). Triple P: A multilevel family intervention program for children with disruptive behavior disorders. In P. Cotton & H. Jackson (Eds), *Early intervention and prevention in mental health* (pp. 59–85). Melbourne: Australian Psychological Society.

Sanders, M.R., & Markie-Dadds, C. (1997). Managing common child behaviour problems. In M.R. Sanders, C. Mitchell, & G.J.A. Byrne (Eds), *Medical consultation skills: Behavioural and interpersonal dimensions of health care*. Melbourne, Australia: Addison-Wesley-Longman.

Sanders, M.R., & McFarland, M.L. (in press). The treatment of depressed mothers with disruptive children: A controlled evaluation of cognitive behavioural family intervention. *Behavior Therapy*.

Sanders, M.R., & Plant, K. (1989a). Generalization effects of behavioural parent training to high and low risk parenting environments. *Behavior Modification*, **13**, 283–305.

Sanders, M.R., & Plant, K. (1989b). Programming for generalisation to high and low risk parenting situations in families with oppositional developmentally disabled preschoolers. *Behaviour Modification*, **13**, 283–305.

Sanders, M.R., Bor, B., & Dadds, M.R. (1984). Modifying bedtime disruptions in children using stimulus control and contingency management procedures. *Behavioural Psychotherapy*, **12**, 130–141.

Sanders, M.R., Markie-Dadds, C., Tully, L., & Bor, B. (2000). The Triple P—Positive Parenting Program: A comparison of enhanced, standard and self-directed behavioral family intervention for parents of children with early onset conduct problems. *Journal of Consulting and Clinical Psychology*, **68**, 624–640.

Scott, S., Spender, Q., Doolan, M., Jacobs, B., & Aspland, H. (2001). Multicentre controlled trial of parenting groups for childhood antisocial behaviour in clinical practice. *British Medical Journal*, **323**, 1–6.

Spaccarelli, S., Cotler, S., & Penman, D. (1992). Problem-solving skills training as a supplement to behavioral parent training. *Cognitive Therapy and Research*, **16**, 1–18.

Stoolmiller, M., Eddy, J.M., & Reid, J.B. (2000). Detecting and describing preventive intervention effects in a universal school-based randomized trial targeting delinquent and violent behavior. *Journal of Consulting and Clinical Psychology*, **68**, 296–306.

Taylor, T.K., Schmidt, S., Pepler, D., & Hodgins, H. (1998). A comparison of eclectic treatment with Webster-Stratton's Parents and Children Series in a children's mental health center: A randomized control trial. *Behavior Therapy*, **29**, 221–240.

Trachenberg, S., & Viken, R.J. (1994). Aggressive boys in the classroom: Biased attributions or shared perceptions? *Child Development*, **65**, 829–835.

Tremblay, R.E., LeMarquand, D., & Vitaro, F. (1999). The prevention of oppositional defiant disorder and conduct disorder. In H.C. Quay & A.E. Hogan (Eds), *Handbook of disruptive behavior disorders* (pp. 525–558). New York: Kluwer Academic.

Tremblay, R.E., Vitaro, F., Bertrand, L., LeBlanc, M., Beauchesne, H., Boileau, H., et al. (1992). Parent and child training to prevent early onset of delinquency: The Montreal Longitudinal-Experimental Study. In J. McCord & R.E. Tremblay (Eds), *Preventing antisocial behavior: Interventions from birth through adolescence* (pp. 117–138). New York: Guilford.

Webster-Stratton, C. (1981). Modification of mothers' behaviors and attitudes through videotape modeling group discussion program. *Behavior Therapy*, **12**, 634–642.

Webster-Stratton, C. (1982a). The long-term effects of a videotape modeling parent training program: Comparison of immediate and one-year followup results. *Behavior Therapy*, **13**, 702–714.

Webster-Stratton, C. (1982b). Teaching mothers through videotape modeling to change their children's behaviors. *Journal of Pediatric Psychology*, **7**, 279–294.

Webster-Stratton, C. (1984). Randomized trial of two parent-training programs for families with conduct-disordered children. *Journal of Consulting and Clinical Psychology*, **52**, 666–678.

Webster-Stratton, C., Hollinsworth, T., & Kolpacoff, M. (1989). The long-term effectiveness and clinical significance of three cost-effectiveness training programs for families with conduct-problem children. *Journal of Consulting and Clinical Psychology*, **57**, 550–553.

Webster-Stratton, C., Kolpacoff, M., & Hollinsworth, T. (1988). Self-administered videotape therapy for families with conduct-problem children: Comparison with two cost-effective treatments and a control group. *Journal of Consulting and Clinical Psychology*, **56**, 558–566.

Williams, A., Zubrick, S., Silburn, S., & Sanders, M. (1997). *A population based intervention to prevent childhood conduct disorder: The Perth Positive Parenting Program demonstration project*. Paper presented at the 9th National Health Promotion Conference, Darwin, Northern Territory, Australia.

Wilson, D.B., Gottfredson, D.C., & Najaka, S.S. (2001). School-based prevention of problem behaviors: A meta-analysis. *Journal of Quantitative Criminology*, **17**, 247–272.

Yung, B.R., & Hammond, W.R. (1998). Breaking the cycle: A culturally sensitive violence prevention program for African American children and adolescents. In J.R. Lutzker (Ed.), *Handbook of child abuse research and treatment. Issues in clinical child psychology* (pp. 319–340). New York: Plenum.

CHAPTER 20

Using the Triple P System of Intervention to Prevent Behavioural Problems in Children and Adolescents

Matthew R. Sanders

Carol Markie-Dadds

Karen M.T. Turner

and

Alan Ralph

The University of Queensland, Australia

INTRODUCTION

The increasing recognition that inadequate or dysfunctional parenting practices are risk factors associated with the development of a range of mental health, educational, and social problems in children and adolescents has led to calls for the widespread implementation of evidence-based parenting interventions as part of a strategy to prevent serious mental health problems in children and adolescents. This chapter outlines a comprehensive, multilevel system of parenting and family support that can be implemented as a population level strategy to support parents in the complex and demanding task of raising their children.

Correspondence to Matthew R. Sanders, Parenting and Family Support Centre, School of Psychology, The University of Queensland, Brisbane, Qld, 4072; email: m.sanders@psy.uq.edu.au

Handbook of Interventions that Work with Children and Adolescents: Prevention and Treatment.
Edited by P.M. Barrett and T.H. Ollendick. © 2004 John Wiley & Sons, Ltd. ISBN 0-470-84453-1.

What is the Triple P-Positive Parenting Program?

The Triple P-Positive Parenting Program is a multilevel, preventively oriented parenting and family support strategy developed by the first author and his colleagues at the University of Queensland in Brisbane, Australia. The program aims to prevent severe behavioural, emotional, and developmental problems in children by enhancing the knowledge, skills, and confidence of parents. It incorporates five levels of intervention on a tiered continuum of increasing strength (see Table 20.1) for parents of children and adolescents from birth to age 16 years. Level 1, a universal parent information strategy, provides all interested parents with access to useful information about parenting through a coordinated media and promotional campaign using print and electronic media, as well as user-friendly parenting tip sheets and videotapes which demonstrate specific parenting strategies and professional seminars. This level of intervention aims to increase community awareness of parenting resources and receptivity of parents to participation in programs; it also aims to create a sense of optimism by depicting solutions to common behavioural and developmental concerns. Level 2 is a brief primary health care intervention providing early anticipatory developmental guidance to parents of children with mild behavioural difficulties. Level 3 targets children with mild to moderate behavioural difficulties and includes an individually tailored parenting plan to manage a specific behavioural or developmental concern. It typically involves active skills training for parents. Level 4 is an intensive broad-focused parent-training program for children with more severe behavioural difficulties and Level 5 is an enhanced behavioural family intervention program for families where parenting difficulties are complicated by other sources of family distress (e.g., marital conflict, parental depression, or high levels of stress).

The rationale for this tiered multilevel strategy is that there are differing levels of dysfunction and behavioural disturbance in children and adolescents, and parents have differing needs and preferences regarding the type, intensity and mode of assistance they may require. The multilevel strategy is designed to maximize efficiency, contain costs, avoid waste and over-servicing and ensure wide reach of parenting and family support services in the community. Also the multidisciplinary nature of the program involves the better utilization of the existing professional workforce in the task of promoting competent parenting.

The Triple P system targets five developmental periods from infancy to adolescence. Within each developmental period the reach of the intervention can vary from being broad (targeting an entire population) to narrow (targeting only high-risk children). This flexibility enables practitioners to determine the scope of the intervention given their own service priorities and funding limitations.

THEORETICAL BASIS OF TRIPLE P

Triple P is a form of behavioural family intervention based on social learning principles (e.g., Patterson, 1982). This approach to the treatment and prevention of childhood disorders has the strongest empirical support of any intervention with children, particularly those with conduct problems (see Kazdin, 1987; Sanders, 1996; Taylor & Biglan, 1998; Webster-Stratton & Hammond, 1997). Triple P aims to

Table 20.1 The Triple P model of parenting and family support

Level of intervention	Target population	Intervention methods	Program resources	Possible target areas
1. *Universal Triple P* Media-based parenting information campaign	All parents interested in information about parenting and promoting their child's development	A coordinated information campaign using print and electronic media and other health promotion strategies to promote awareness of parenting issues and normalize participation in parenting programs such as Triple P. May include some contact with professional staff (e.g., telephone information line)	• *Guide to Triple P* • Triple P media and promotions kit (including promotional poster, brochure, radio announcements, newspaper columns)	General parenting issues; Common every day behavioural and developmental issues
2. *Selected Triple P* Information and advice for a specific parenting concern	Parents with specific concerns about their child's behaviour or development	Provision of specific advice on how to solve common child developmental issues and minor child behaviour problems. May involve face-to-face or telephone contact with a practitioner (about 20 minutes over two sessions) or (60–90 minute) seminars	• *Guide to Triple P* • *Positive Parenting* booklet • *Positive Parenting for Parents with Teenagers* booklet • *Triple P Tip Sheet Series* • *Every Parent Video Series* • Developmental wall charts	Common behavioural difficulties or developmental transitions, such as toilet training, bedtime or sleep problems, diet and nutrition, puberty
3. *Primary Care Triple P* Narrow focus parenting skills training	Parents with specific concerns about their child's behaviour or development who require consultations or active skills training	A brief program (about 80 minutes over four sessions) combining advice with rehearsal and self-evaluation as required to teach parents to manage discrete child problem behaviour. May involve face-to-face or telephone contact with a practitioner	• Level 2 materials • *Practitioner's Manual for Primary Care Triple P* • *Practitioner's Manual for Primary Care Teen Triple P* • Consultation flip charts	Discrete child behavioural problems, such as tantrums, whining, fighting with siblings; aggressive or oppositional behaviour; home-school problems

continues overleaf

Table 20.1 (continued)

Level of intervention	Target population	Intervention methods	Program resources	Possible target areas
4. *Standard Triple P* *Group Triple P* *Self-Directed Triple P* Broad focus parenting skills training	Parents wanting intensive training in positive parenting skills. Typically targets parents of children with more severe behavioural problems	A broad focus program (up to 12 one-hour sessions) for parents requiring intensive training in positive parenting skills and generalization enhancement strategies. Application of parenting skills to a broad range of target behaviours, settings and children. Program variants include individual, group or self-directed (with or without telephone assistance) options	• Level 2 and 3 materials • *Every Parent* • *Practitioner's Manual for Standard Triple P* and *Every Parent's Family Workbook* • *Facilitator's Manual for Group Triple P* and *Every Parent's Group Workbook* • *Facilitator's Manual for Group Teen Triple P* and *Teen Triple P Group Workbook* • *Every Parent's Self-Help Workbook* • *Teen Triple P Self-Help Workbook*	Multiple child behavioural problems, such as persistent conduct problems, opposition/defiance; learning difficulties; alcohol, tobacco, or other drug use; family conflict
5. *Enhanced Triple P* Behavioural family intervention	Parents of children with concurrent child behavioural problems and family dysfunction	An intensive individually tailored program (up to 11 one-hour sessions) for families with child behavioural problems and family dysfunction. Program modules include home visits to enhance parenting skills, mood management strategies and stress coping skills, and partner support skills	• Level 2 to 4 materials • *Practitioner's Manual for Enhanced Triple P* and *Every Parent's Supplementary Workbook*	Concurrent child behavioural problems and parent problems such as relationship conflict, depression, stress, family violence

Note: Adapted with permission from Sanders, M.R., Markie-Dadds, C., & Turner, K.M.T. (2001). *Practitioner's Manual for Standard Triple P*. Brisbane, Australia: Families International Publishing (p. 4).

enhance family protective factors and to reduce risk factors associated with severe behavioural and emotional problems in pre-adolescent children. Specifically the program aims to: (1) enhance the knowledge, skills, confidence, self-sufficiency and resourcefulness of parents of pre-adolescent children; (2) promote nurturing, safe, engaging, non-violent, and low conflict environments for children; and (3) promote children's social, emotional, language, intellectual, and behavioural competencies through positive parenting practices.

The program content draws on several theoretical perspectives including:

1. Social learning models of parent–child interaction that highlight the reciprocal and bidirectional nature of parent–child interactions (e.g., Patterson, 1982).
2. Research in child and family behaviour therapy and applied behaviour analysis which has developed many useful behaviour change strategies, particularly research which focuses on rearranging antecedents of problem behaviour through designing more positive engaging environments for children (Risley, Clark, & Cataldo, 1976; Sanders, 1992, 1996).
3. Developmental research on parenting in everyday contexts. The program targets children's competencies in naturally occurring everyday contexts, drawing heavily on work which traces the origins of social and intellectual competence to early parent–child relationships (e.g., Hart & Risley, 1995; White, 1990).
4. Social information-processing models which highlight the important role of parental cognitions such as attributions, expectancies, and beliefs as factors which contribute to parental self-efficacy, decision-making, and behavioural intentions (e.g., Bandura, 1977, 1995).
5. Research from the field of developmental psychopathology has identified specific risk and protective factors which are linked to adverse developmental outcomes in children (e.g., Emery, 1982; Grych & Fincham, 1990; Hart & Risley, 1995; Rutter, 1985). Specifically the risk factors of poor parent management practices, marital family conflict and parental distress are targeted risk factors.
6. A public health perspective to family intervention involves the explicit recognition of the role of the broader ecological context for human development (e.g., Biglan, 1995; Mrazek & Haggerty, 1994; National Institute of Mental Health, 1998). As pointed out by Biglan (1995), the reduction of antisocial behaviour in children requires the community context for parenting to change.

TOWARD A MODEL OF PARENTAL COMPETENCE

The educative approach to promoting parental competence in Triple P views the development of a parent's capacity for self-regulation as the central skill. This involves teaching parents skills that enable them to become independent problem-solvers. Karoly (1993, p. 25) defined self-regulation as follows:

> Self-regulation refers to those processes, internal and or transactional, that enable an individual to guide his/her goal directed activities over time and across changing circumstances (contexts). Regulation implies modulation of thought, affect, behaviour, and attention via deliberate or automated use of specific mechanisms and supportive metaskills. The processes of self-regulation are initiated

when routinised activity is impeded or when goal directedness is otherwise made salient (e.g., the appearance of a challenge, the failure of habitual patterns; etc.)

This definition emphasizes that self-regulatory processes are embedded in a social context that not only provides opportunities and limitations for individual self-directedness, but implies a dynamic reciprocal interchange between the internal and external determinants of human motivation. From a therapeutic perspective self-regulation is a process whereby individuals are taught skills to modify their own behaviour. These skills include how to select developmentally appropriate goals, monitor a child's or a parent's own behaviour, choose an appropriate method of intervention for a particular problem, implement the solution, self-monitor their implementation of solutions via checklists relating to the areas of concern; and identify strengths or limitations in their performance and set future goals for action.

This self-regulatory framework is operationalized to include:

1. *Self-sufficiency:* As a parenting program is time limited, parents need to become independent problem-solvers to enable them to trust their own judgment and become less reliant on others in carrying out basic parenting responsibilities.
2. *Parental self-efficacy:* This refers to a parents' belief that they can overcome or solve a parenting or child management problem.
3. *Self-management:* As parents are responsible for the way they choose to raise their children, parents select which aspects of their own and their child's behaviour they wish to work on, to set goals for themselves, to choose specific parenting and child management techniques they wish to implement, and to self-evaluate their success with their chosen goals against self-determined criteria. Triple P aims to help parents to make informed decisions by sharing knowledge and skills derived from contemporary research into effective child-rearing practices.
4. *Personal agency:* Here the parent increasingly attributes changes or improvements in their situation to their own or their child's efforts rather than to chance, age, maturational factors or other uncontrollable events (e.g., spouses' bad parenting or genes).

Encouraging parents to become self-sufficient means that parents become more connected to social support networks such as partners, extended family, friends and childcare supports. However, the broader ecological context (e.g., poverty, dangerous neighbourhoods, community, ethnicity, and culture) within which a family lives cannot be ignored. It is hypothesized that the more self-sufficient parents become, the more likely they will be to seek appropriate support when they need it, advocate for children, become involved in their child's schooling, and protect children from harm (e.g., by managing conflict with partners, and creating a secure low-conflict environment).

EFFECTIVENESS OF TRIPLE P

The evaluation of the Triple P system is a continuous process. Although there is considerable existing evidence demonstrating the benefits of various levels of intervention and modes of delivery, Triple P as a population level approach is subject to ongoing evaluation. Research into the system of behavioural family intervention that has eventually become known as Triple P began in 1977 with the first findings published in the early 1980s (e.g., Sanders & Glynn, 1981). Since that time the intervention methods used in Triple P have been subjected to a series of controlled evaluations using both intrasubject replication designs and traditional randomized-controlled group designs (see Sanders, 1999, for a review).

Early studies (Sanders & Christensen, 1985; Sanders & Dadds, 1982; Sanders & Glynn, 1981) demonstrated that parents could be taught to implement behavioural change and positive parenting strategies in the home and many parents applied these strategies in other situations. However, not all parents generalized their skills to high-risk situations after initial active skills training. These high-risk situations are often characterized by competing demands, time constraints, and social evaluation or scrutiny by others (e.g., shopping). For these parents, the addition of self-management skills such as planning ahead, goal-setting, self-monitoring, and planning engaging activities to keep children busy was effective in teaching parents to generalize their skills (Sanders & Dadds, 1982; Sanders & Glynn, 1981). This research established the core program as a 10-session individual parent-training intervention, now known as Level 4 Standard Triple P.

Since this time, over 20 years of experimental clinical research has established the efficacy and effectiveness of the Triple P intervention strategies for reducing children's behavioural problems in a variety of populations including children from maritally discordant homes (Dadds, Schwartz, & Sanders, 1987), children of depressed parents (Sanders & McFarland, 2000), children in step-families (Nicholson & Sanders, 1999), children with persistent feeding difficulties (Turner, Sanders, & Wall, 1994), children in socially disadvantaged areas (Sanders et al., 2000; Zubrick et al., 2002) and children with developmental disabilities (Sanders & Plant, 1989). These parenting skills training methods also have been evaluated independently in other groups with mildly and moderately intellectually disabled children (e.g., Harrold et al., 1992).

The major research findings from group trials in the Triple P system to date are detailed in Table 20.2. In summary, this research shows that when parents change problematic parenting practices, children experience fewer problems, are more cooperative, get on better with other children, and are better behaved at school. Parents have greater confidence in their parenting ability, have more positive attitudes toward their children, are less reliant on potentially abusive parenting practices, and are less depressed and stressed by their parenting role. The interested reader is referred to Sanders (1999) for a thorough review of the empirical basis of Triple P.

Inspection of Table 20.2 shows that the sample sizes used in various trials are quite varied ($N = 1$ to $N = 1615$). These studies represent the progression of the evidence base from case studies and efficacy trials to effectiveness trials and, finally, to studies examining the dissemination of the program. The approach to evaluation to date has been to evaluate each level of intervention and different delivery modalities within levels. These outcome studies have included both efficacy trials conducted within a University clinical research setting (e.g., Sanders & McFarland, 2000) and effectiveness trials conducted within regular health services in the community (e.g., Zubrick et al., 2002). Evaluation of the program for parents of teenagers is currently focused on the effectiveness of parenting groups aimed at reducing difficulties

Table 20.2 Behavioural family intervention outcomes from group design studies in the Triple P research series

Authors	Method/Population	Sample size (attrition at post)	Age range (yrs)	Measures	Outcomes
Markie-Dadds & Sanders (in prep.)	RCT comparing Self-Directed Triple P and a wait-list control. Parents of children with clinically elevated disruptive behaviour	63 (SD 28%) (WL 23%)	2–5	Child disruptive behaviour, parenting style and confidence, parental adjustment, and parenting conflict	Self-Directed Triple P was associated with significantly lower levels of disruptive child behaviour and dysfunctional parenting strategies, and significantly higher parenting confidence in comparison to WL controls. No differences were found on parent adjustment measures. Intervention results were maintained at six-month follow-up, with the exception of parenting confidence, which had decreased significantly from post
Markie-Dadds & Sanders (in prep.)	RCT comparing Self-Directed Triple P, Self-Directed Triple P with telephone sessions, and a wait-list control. Parents of children with clinically elevated disruptive behaviour living in a rural area	41 (SD nil) (SD + T 7%) (WL nil)	2–6	Child disruptive behaviour, parenting style and confidence, parental adjustment, and parenting conflict	Both interventions were associated with significantly lower levels of mother-reported disruptive child behaviour in comparison to WL controls, with the telephone-assisted group significantly more improved than the standard group. Significantly less dysfunctional parenting (laxness) and higher parental confidence were evident in the telephone-assisted group in comparison to SD and WL. No differences were found on measures of parent adjustment or parenting conflict. Results for the telephone-assisted condition were generally maintained at six-month follow-up, while some catch up was seen for families in the standard condition relating to disruptive child behaviour and dysfunctional parenting (over-reactivity)

Study	Design	N	Age	Measures	Results
Sultana et al. (in prep.)	RCT comparing Selected Triple P, Primary Care Triple P and a wait-list control. Parents with concerns about discrete child behavioural problems	50 (SE nil) (PC nil) (WL 38%)	1–5	Child disruptive behaviour, parenting style, and parental adjustment	Parents in the Primary Care Triple P condition reported significantly fewer child behavioural problems and dysfunctional parenting strategies than the WL controls. Moderate positive changes in child and parent behaviour were found for Selected Triple P, however these did not differ significantly from controls. No differences were found on parent adjustment measures. Results for the intervention groups were maintained at four-month follow-up
Sanders, Turner, & Wall (in prep.)	RCT comparing Behavioural Parent Training, Nutrition Education and a wait-list control. Parents of children with persistent feeding problems	56 (BPT 16%) (NE 4%) (WL nil)	1–7	Child dietary intake, anthropometrics, mealtime behaviour, disruptive behaviour, and parent–child mealtime interaction, and parental perception of the child's eating problem	Children in the Behavioural Parent Training group showed significant increases in weight for age and height for age in comparison to the Nutrition Education and wait-list conditions. They also showed decreases in some observed problem mealtime behaviours in comparison to others. Children in both intervention conditions showed a significant increase in the variety of foods eaten and significant decreases in mothers' ratings of the severity of the child's eating problem. All children increased their energy intake over time. No changes were found for mothers' mealtime behaviour or child general adjustment. At six-month follow-up, children in the BPT condition maintained their significant increase in weight for age, and mothers reported significant decreases in disruptive mealtime behaviour at home

continues overleaf

Table 20.2 (continued)

Authors	Method/Population	Sample size (attrition at post)	Age range (yrs)	Measures	Outcomes
Ralph & Sanders (in prep.)	Non-random matched sample design comparing Group Teen Triple P in one high school with a wait-list control school. Parents of first-year high school children	67 (GR 30%) (WL nil)	12–13	Child behavioural strengths and difficulties, parent-teenager conflict, parenting style, parenting conflict and relationship satisfaction, and parental adjustment	Analyses of parent self-report data collected before and after the groups revealed significant improvements in parenting efficacy and style, reductions in conflict between parent and teenager, and reductions in parental anxiety, depression and stress. Parents in the group intervention condition reported significantly more positive experiences and fewer problem behaviours at 12-month follow-up relative to matched parents in the wait-list condition
Zubrick et al. (in prep.)	Non-random two-group concurrent prospective observation design evaluating Group Triple P in one high-risk health region with a comparable region as control. All parents of children in the age-range	1615 (GR 11%) (CON 4%)	3–4	Child disruptive behaviour, parenting style, parental adjustment, parenting conflict and relationship satisfaction	Parents in the intervention group had significantly higher pre-intervention levels of dysfunctional parenting strategies, which decreased significantly following intervention and although slightly increased, remained lower at 12- and 24-month follow-up than control parents who showed a gradual decline in dysfunctional parenting over time. Children in the intervention group showed significant decreases in parent-reported disruptive child behaviour following intervention, which maintained at 12- and 24-month follow-up. Two years following universal intervention, there was a 37% decrease in prevalence of child behavioural

Reference	Design/Sample	N (%)	Age	Measures	Results
Bor, Sanders, & Markie-Dadds (2002)	RCT comparing Standard Triple P, Enhanced Triple P and a wait-list control. Parents of children with comorbid significantly elevated disruptive behavioural and attention problems	87 (ST 28%) (EN 42%) (WL 16%)	3	Child disruptive behaviour, parent–child interaction, parenting style and confidence, parental adjustment, parenting conflict and relationship satisfaction	problems in the intervention region. Although poorer than controls at pre, parental adjustment (depression, anxiety, and stress) and marital adjustment also improved significantly for intervention families. This was maintained at 12- but not 24-month follow-up. The same pattern was found for parenting conflict, however this did not maintain at follow-up assessments. Both intervention programs were associated with significantly lower parent-reported child behavioural problems and dysfunctional parenting and significantly greater parenting confidence than the WL condition. Enhanced Triple P was also associated with significantly less observed disruptive child behaviour than the WL condition. Results were maintained at one-year follow-up. Both interventions produced significant reductions in children's comorbid disruptive behavioural and attention problems
Ireland, Sanders, & Markie-Dadds (2003)	RCT comparing Group Triple P and Group Triple P with a partner support module. Couples with concerns about disruptive child behaviour and concurrent clinically elevated marital conflict	44 (GR 14%) (GR + PS 22%)	2–5	Child disruptive behaviour, parenting style, parental adjustment, parenting conflict, relationship satisfaction, and communication	Both interventions were associated with significant improvements in parent-reported disruptive child behaviour, dysfunctional parenting strategies, parenting conflict, relationship satisfaction and communication. Treatment effects were generally maintained at three-month follow-up. For some measures, Group Triple P effects were achieved by follow-up rather than post-assessment. No differences were found on parent adjustment measures

continues overleaf

Table 20.2 (continued)

Authors	Method/Population	Sample size (attrition at post)	Age range (yrs)	Measures	Outcomes
Sanders et al. (2000)	RCT comparing Standard Triple P, Self-Directed Triple P, Enhanced Triple P and a wait-list control. Parents of children with clinically elevated disruptive behaviour, and at least one family adversity factor (e.g., low income, maternal depression, relationship conflict, single parent)	305 (ST 17%) (SD 19%) (EN 24%) (WL 8%)	3	Child disruptive behaviour, parent–child interaction, parenting style and confidence, parental adjustment, parenting conflict and relationship satisfaction	Children in the three intervention conditions showed greater improvement on mother-reported disruptive behaviour than the WL control, however only those in the Enhanced Triple P and Standard Triple P conditions showed significant improvement on observed disruptive child behaviour and father reports. Parents in the two practitioner assisted programs also showed significant reduction in dysfunctional parenting strategies (self-report) for both parents. No intervention effects were found for observed mother negative behaviour toward the child or for parent adjustment, conflict or relationship satisfaction. Mothers in all three intervention conditions reported greater parenting confidence than controls. At one-year follow-up, children receiving Self-Directed Triple P had made further improvements on observed disruptive behaviour and all intervention groups were comparable on measures of child behaviour and parenting style

Sanders & McFarland (2000)	RCT comparing Standard Triple P and Enhanced Triple P. Parents of children with oppositional defiant disorder or conduct disorder, and mothers with major depression	47 (ST 21%) (EN 13%)	3–9	Child disruptive behaviour, parent–child interaction, parenting confidence and parental adjustment	Both interventions were effective in reducing observed and parent reported disruptive child behaviour, as well as mothers' and fathers' depression. Both interventions also significantly increased parental confidence. Intervention results were maintained at six-month follow-up, with more mothers in the Enhanced Triple P intervention experiencing concurrent clinically reliable reductions in disruptive child behaviour and maternal depression
Sanders, Montgomery, & Brechman-Toussaint (2000)	RCT comparing Triple P television segments (12 episodes) and a wait-list control. Parents reporting concerns about disruptive child behaviour	56 (Int nil) (WL nil)	2–8	Child disruptive behaviour, parenting style and confidence, parental adjustment and parenting conflict	Mothers in the television intervention condition reported significantly lower levels of disruptive child behaviour and higher levels of parenting confidence than controls following intervention. No changes were found on parenting strategies, conflict or parental adjustment. Results for the intervention group were maintained at six-month follow-up
Nicholson & Sanders (1999)	RCT comparing Enhanced Triple P (for step-families), Enhanced Self-Directed Triple P (for step-families) and a wait-list control. Parents and step-parents of children with oppositional defiant disorder or conduct disorder in step-families	60 (EN 36%) (SD 43%) (WL 6%)	7–12	Child disruptive behaviour and adjustment (depression, anxiety, self-esteem), and parenting conflict	No differences were found between the therapist-directed and self-directed programs. Children in the intervention groups showed significant reductions in parent reported disruptive child behaviour (with smaller changes for the waitlist group on one measure only). Significant reductions in parenting conflict were reported by parents and step-parents in the intervention conditions only. All children showed reductions in anxiety and increases in self-esteem

continues overleaf

Table 20.2 (continued)

Authors	Method/Population	Sample size (attrition at post)	Age range (yrs)	Measures	Outcomes
Connell, Sanders, & Markie-Dadds (1997)	RCT comparing Self-Directed Triple P with telephone sessions and a wait-list control. Parents of children with clinically elevated disruptive behaviour living in a rural area	24 (SD nil) (WL 8%)	2–6	Child disruptive behaviour, parenting style and confidence, and parental adjustment	Only children in the intervention group showed significant reductions in parent reported disruptive child behaviour. Significant reductions in dysfunctional parenting styles, increases in parenting confidence, and decreases in depression and stress were reported by mothers (but not fathers) in the intervention group. Results for the intervention group were maintained at four-month follow-up
Sanders et al. (1994)	RCT comparing Cognitive-Behavioural Family Intervention and Standard Pediatric Care. Children with recurrent abdominal pain and their parents	44 (Int 11%)	7–14	Child pain intensity, adjustment, and parent observations of pain behaviour	Both intervention conditions resulted in significant improvements on measures of pain intensity and pain behaviour, which maintained at 6- and 12-month follow-up. Children receiving BFI had higher rates of complete elimination of pain, lower levels of relapse at follow-up assessments and lower levels of interference with usual activities due to pain. Significant improvements on measures of child adjustment were found for both conditions, which maintained at both follow-up assessments
Turner, Sanders, & Wall (1994)	RCT comparing Behavioural Parent Training and Standard	21 (BPT nil) (SDE 11%)	1–5	Child dietary intake, anthropometrics, mealtime behaviour,	Children in both intervention conditions showed significant improvements on observed and home mealtime behaviour.

	Design	Age	N	Measures	Results
	Dietary Education. Parents of children with persistent feeding problems			disruptive behaviour, parent–child mealtime interaction, parenting confidence, and parental adjustment	There was a significant increase in observed mother positive mother–child interaction at mealtimes in the Behavioural Parent Training group only. Results are maintained at three-month follow-up. At follow-up, children in both conditions also showed a significant increase in the variety of foods eaten. No changes were observed on measures of children's weight or height for age, or measures of child or parent adjustment
Sanders et al. (1989)	RCT comparing Cognitive-Behavioural Family Intervention and a wait-list control. Children with recurrent abdominal pain and their parents	6–12	16 (Int nil) (WL nil)	Child pain intensity, adjustment, parent–child interaction, and parent and teacher observations of pain behaviour	The intervention group reduced their self-reported levels of pain and mother observed pain behaviour quickly, with significant decreases occurring in phase 2 if the intervention (working directly with the child on coping strategies). Both groups had improved significantly on pain measures by three-month follow-up. However, intervention group effects also generalized to the school setting, and a significantly larger proportion were completely pain free by follow-up. Both groups also showed decreases in parent-reported disruptive behaviour, which maintained at follow-up. No effects were found for observed mother or child behaviour, although baseline levels of observed disruptive child behaviour approximated those of a normal comparison group
Dadds, Schwartz, & Sanders (1987)	Group design with crossed factors of marital type and intervention type, evaluating Standard Triple P and Standard Triple P with a partner support module. Parents of children with	2–5	24 (Int nil)	Child disruptive behaviour, parent–child interaction, and relationship satisfaction	All groups showed a significant improvement on observed and parent-reported disruptive child behaviour, and observed mother implementation of targeted strategies and aversive parenting. However, a relapse effect was found for parents with relationship discord who received only the standard program without partner support

continues overleaf

Table 20.2 (continued)

Authors	Method/Population	Sample size (attrition at post)	Age range (yrs)	Measures	Outcomes
	oppositional defiant disorder or conduct disorder (split according to relationship discord)				training. The partner support training added little to the maintenance of change for parents without relationship distress, however it produced gains over Standard Triple P for the discordant group. There was an increase in marital satisfaction for all parents following intervention, although by follow-up this had relapsed for mothers and fathers in the distressed group who did not receive partner support training
Christensen & Sanders (1987)	RCT comparing Habit Reversal, Differential Reinforcement of Other Behaviour and a wait-list control. Children with thumb-sucking behaviour and their parents	30 (HR nil) (DRO nil) (WL nil)	4–9	Child thumb-sucking and disruptive behaviour	Both interventions effectively reduced thumb-sucking in a training setting and two generalization settings, and intervention effects were maintained at three-month follow-up. No changes were observed in the WL controls. However, both interventions were associated with some temporary increases in disruptive child behaviour and elimination rates were low
Sanders & Christensen (1985)	RCT comparing Child Management Training (without Planned Activities Training) and Standard Triple P. Parents of children with oppositional behaviour	20 (CMT nil) (ST nil)	2–7	Child disruptive behaviour and parent–child interaction	Both interventions were associated with significant reductions in observed child disruptive behaviour and mother aversive behaviour and increased use of targeted parenting strategies in all observation settings. Results were maintained at three-month follow-up. At follow-up, rates of disruptive child behaviour were not significantly different from a group of non-problem controls

encountered at the transition to high school. An effectiveness trial evaluating the full implementation of the multilevel system with tracking of population level outcomes will be the ultimate test of the benefits of the population approach advocated. Such an evaluation trial is being planned at time of writing. Our current research activity also includes studies evaluating the efficacy of our approach to the dissemination of Triple P into regular clinical services.

Intervention Methods

The core features of the Triple P system involve creating supportive environments for parents where parents can readily learn the skills they need to get on well with their children. This involves creating easily accessible learning environments for parents that facilitate skills acquisition. Hence, Triple P uses the media, primary care services, schools, telephone counselling services, and the workplace as contexts which enable parents to access program support.

Five core positive parenting principles form the basis of the program. These principles address specific risk and protective factors known to predict positive developmental and mental health outcomes in children and include:

1. *Ensuring a safe and engaging environment.* Children of all ages need a safe, supervised and therefore protective environment that provides opportunities for them to explore, experiment, play, and interact with others.
2. *Creating a positive learning environment.* This involves educating parents in their role as their child's first teacher. The program specifically targets how parents can respond positively and constructively to child-initiated interactions (e.g., requests for help, information, advice, attention) to assist children to learn to solve problems for themselves.
3. *Using assertive discipline.* Specific child management strategies are taught that are alternatives to coercive and ineffective discipline practices (such as shouting, threatening, or using physical punishment).
4. *Having realistic expectations.* This involves exploring with parents their expectations, assumptions, and beliefs about the causes of children's behaviour and choosing goals that are developmentally appropriate for the child and realistic for the parent.
5. *Taking care of oneself as a parent.* Parenting is affected by a range of factors that impact on a parent's self-esteem and sense of well-being. Parents are encouraged to view parenting as part of a larger context of personal self-care, resourcefulness and well-being.

These core positive parenting principles translate into a range of specific parenting skills, which are outlined in Table 20.3. Triple P teaches parents strategies to encourage their child's social and language skills, emotional self-regulation, independence, and problem-solving ability. It is hypothesized that attainment of these skills promotes family harmony, reduces parent–child conflict, fosters successful peer relationships and prepares children to be successful at school. To achieve these child outcomes, parents are taught a variety of child management skills. Parents learn to apply these skills to a wide range of target behaviours. The strategies fall

Table 20.3 Core parenting skills

Observation skills	Parent–child relationship enhancement skills	Encouraging desirable behaviour	Teaching new skills and behaviours	Managing misbehaviour	Preventing problems in high risk situations	Self-regulation skills	Mood management and coping skills	Partner support and communication skills
Monitoring children's behaviour	Spending quality time	Giving descriptive praise	Setting developmentally appropriate goals	Establishing ground rules	Planning and advanced preparation	Setting practice tasks	Catching unhelpful thoughts	Improving personal communication habits
Monitoring own behaviour	Talking with children	Giving non-verbal attention	Setting a good example	Using directed discussion	Discussing ground rules for specific situations	Self-evaluation of strengths and weaknesses	Relaxation and stress management	Giving and receiving constructive feedback
	Showing affection	Providing engaging activities	Using incidental teaching	Using planned ignoring	Selecting engaging activities/risk reduction strategies	Setting personal goals for change	Developing personal coping statements	Having casual conversations
			Using Ask, Say, Do	Giving clear, calm instructions				Supporting each other when problem behaviour occurs
			Coaching problem solving	Using logical consequences	Providing incentives		Challenging unhelpful thoughts	
			Using behaviour charts/contracts	Using quiet time	Providing consequences		Developing coping plans for high risk situations	Problem-solving
			Holding family meetings	Using time-out	Holding follow up discussions			Improving relationship happiness
				Dealing with emotional behaviour				
				Using behaviour contracts				

into four main categories: (1) skills to strengthen parent-child relationships; (2) skills to encourage desirable behaviour; (3) skills for teaching children new behaviours and skills; and (4) skills for managing misbehaviour. Parents learn to apply these skills both at home and in the community. Specific strategies such as planned activities training are used to promote the generalization and maintenance of parenting skills across settings and over time.

DELIVERY FORMATS

Level 1: Universal Triple P (Media and Promotional Strategy)

A universal prevention strategy targets an entire population of parents (e.g., national, local community, neighbourhood, or school) with a program aimed at preventing inadequate or dysfunctional parenting (Mrazek & Haggerty, 1994). Several authors have noted that the media have been underutilized by family intervention researchers (e.g., Biglan, 1992). Evidence from the public health field shows that media strategies can be effective in increasing community awareness of health issues and has been instrumental in modifying potentially harmful behaviour such as cigarette smoking, lack of exercise, and poor diet (Biglan, 1995; Sorenson et al., 1998).

Universal Triple P aims to use health promotion and social marketing strategies to: (1) promote the use of positive parenting practices in the community; (2) increase the receptivity of parents toward participating in the program; (3) increase favourable community attitudes toward Triple P and parenting in general; (4) destigmatize and normalize the process of seeking help for children with behavioural problems; (5) increase the visibility and reach of parenting and family support services; and (6) counter alarmist, sensationalized, or parent-blaming messages in the media.

The universal delivery of Triple P information consists of a range of elements including: (1) 30-second television commercial promoting the program for broadcast as a community service announcement (CSA); (2) 30-second radio commercial announcing the program; (3) a series of 40 60-second audio sound capsules on positive parenting for use as CSAs; (4) more than 50 newspaper columns on Triple P dealing with common parenting issues and topics of general interest to parents; (5) self-directed information resources in the form of positive parenting tip sheets and a range of videos for parents that depict how to apply behaviour management advice to common behaviour and developmental problems; (6) an overview of a 90-minute Introductory Positive Parenting Seminar and overhead transparencies for practitioners; (7) printed advertising materials (posters, brochures, business cards, coffee mugs, positive parenting tee shirts, fridge magnets); and (8) a series of press releases, and sample letters to editors of local television, radio, newspapers, and community leaders requesting their support and involvement with the program.

A carefully planned media campaign has the potential to reach a broad cross-section of the population and to mobilize community support for the initiative. For some families, a brief universal exposure to parenting and family support messages is all the participation they will have in the system. This level of intervention may be particularly useful for parents who have sufficient personal resources such as motivation, literacy skills, commitment, time and support to implement suggested strategies with no additional support other than a parenting tip sheet on the topic. However, a universal strategy is unlikely to be effective on its own if the parent has a child with a severe behavioural disorder or where the parent is depressed, maritally distressed or suffering from major psychopathology. In these instances more intensive forms of intervention are likely to be needed.

Level 2: Selected Triple P

Level 2 is a selective intervention delivered through primary care services. These are services that typically have wide reach because a significant proportion of parents take their children to them and are therefore more readily accessible to parents than traditional mental health services. They may include child health services, general practitioners and family doctors, childcare centres, kindergartens, and schools. These services are well positioned to provide brief preventively oriented parenting programs because parents see primary care practitioners as credible sources of information about children and are not associated with the stigma often attached to seeking specialist mental health services.

Primary health practitioners can offer brief individual consultations with parents or brief topic-specific seminars to groups of parents. In its individual format, Selected Triple P is a brief (5–10 minute), one-session consultation for parents with specific concerns about their child's behaviour or development. A series of parenting tip sheets is used to provide basic information to parents on the prevention and management of common problems in each of five age groups (viz., infants, toddlers, pre-schoolers, primary school-aged children, and teenagers). Twelve videotape programs complement the tip sheets for use in brief primary care consultations. Brief (45–60 minute) topic-specific seminars provide a cost-effective mechanism for concurrently reaching a large number of parents. In these seminars, tip sheets and video segments provide the basis of the content for the seminar, while a practitioner is available to discuss strategies and respond to questions as needed.

This level of intervention is designed for the management of discrete child problem behaviours that are not complicated by other major behaviour management difficulties or family dysfunction. With Level 2 interventions, the emphasis is on the management of specific child behaviours rather than developing a broad range of child management skills. Key indicators for a Level 2 intervention include: (1) the parent is seeking information, hence the motivational context is good; (2) the problem behaviour is relatively discrete; (3) the problem behaviour is of mild to moderate severity: (4) the problem behaviour has a recent onset; (5) the parents and/or child are not suffering from major psychopathology; (6) the family situation is reasonably stable; and (7) the family has successfully completed other levels of intervention and is returning for a booster session.

Level 3: Primary Care Triple P

This is another selective prevention strategy targeting parents who have mild and relatively discrete concerns about their child's behaviour or development (e.g., toilet training, tantrums, sleep disturbance, anxiety, rudeness). Level 3 is brief information-based strategy that incorporates assessment of the presenting problem, identification of possible causes of the presenting problem, and the selective use of parenting tip sheets covering common developmental and behavioural problems of children and adolescents. It typically incorporates active skills training techniques to teach parents the appropriate positive parenting strategies and is conducted in one-on-one consultations, usually over three or four brief consultations. However, it may be adapted to involve fewer sessions, even to one 80-minute consultation where parents' access to services is constrained by remoteness or other factors. Regardless of delivery format, this level of intervention typically involves four distinct phases of intervention as described below.

The first phase clarifies the history and nature of the presenting problem (through interview and direct observation), negotiates goals for the intervention, and sets up a baseline monitoring system for tracking the occurrence of problem behaviours. Phase 2 discusses the baseline monitoring, including the parents' perceptions of the child's behaviour; shares conclusions with the parents about the nature of the problem (i.e., the diagnostic formulation) and its possible aetiology, and negotiates a parenting plan (using a tip sheet or designing a planned activities routine). This phase also involves identifying and countering any obstacles to implementation of the new routine by developing a personal coping plan with each parent. Each parent then implements the program. Phase 3 involves monitoring the family's progress and discussing any implementation problems; it may also involve introduction of additional parenting strategies. Phase 4 involves a progress review, troubleshooting for any difficulties the parents may be experiencing, positive feedback and encouragement, and termination of contact. Contact between the parents and practitioner for phases 3 and 4 may be via telephone and in many cases is brief—about 5 minutes. If positive results are not achieved, the family may be referred to a higher level of intervention.

As in Level 2, this level of intervention is appropriate for the management of discrete child problem behaviours that are not complicated by other major behaviour management difficulties or family dysfunction. The key difference is that provision of advice and information alone is supported by active skills training for those parents who require it to implement the recommended parenting strategies. Children would not generally meet full diagnostic criteria for a clinical disorder such as oppositional defiant disorder, conduct disorder or ADHD, but there may be significant subclinical levels of problem behaviour.

Level 4: Intensive parenting skills training

This indicated preventive intervention targets high-risk individuals who are identified as having detectable problems, but who do not yet meet diagnostic criteria for a behavioural disorder. It should be noted that this level of intervention can target individual children at risk or an entire population to identify individual children at risk. For example, a group version of the program may be offered universally in low-income areas, with the goal of identifying and engaging parents of children with severe disruptive and aggressive behaviour. Parents are taught the principles of positive parenting, strategies for promoting children's social competence and strategies for managing misbehaviour as well as planned activities routines for minimizing the likelihood of child behavioural problems in high-risk parenting situations. Parents are trained to apply these positive parenting skills both at home and in the community. As in Level 3, this level of intervention combines the provision of information with active skills training and support. In addition, Level 4 interventions teach parents to apply parenting skills to a broad range of target behaviours in both home and community settings with the target child and siblings. There are several different delivery formats available at this level of intervention.

Standard Triple P

In this version, parents typically attend ten 60-minute individual consultations with a practitioner. This program incorporates active skills training methods such as modelling, rehearsal, feedback, and homework tasks. Video segments may be used to demonstrate positive parenting skills. In addition, generalization enhancement strategies are incorporated (e.g., training with sufficient exemplars, training loosely by varying the stimulus condition for training) to promote the transfer of parenting skills across settings, siblings, and time. Practise sessions are also conducted in which parents self-select goals to practice, are observed interacting with their child and implementing parenting skills, and subsequently receive feedback from the practitioner. Parents of teenagers are encouraged to involve them in sessions to improve family communication and participation in family decision-making. Additional clinic sessions then cover how to identify high-risk situations for parents and/or teenagers and develop planned activity routines. Finally, maintenance and relapse issues are covered.

Group Triple P

Group Triple P is an eight-session program conducted in groups of 10–12 parents. It also employs an active skills training process to help parents to acquire new knowledge and skills. The program consists of four two-hour group sessions, which provide opportunities for parents to learn through observation, discussion, practice, and feedback. Video segments are also used to demonstrate positive parenting skills. These skills are then practised in small groups. Between sessions, parents complete homework tasks to consolidate their learning from the group sessions. Following the group sessions, three 15–30 minute follow-up telephone sessions are available to families requiring additional support as they put into practice what they have learned in the group sessions. The final session, Week 8, can be completed as either a telephone session or a group session.

Self-Directed Triple P

In the self-directed delivery mode, the parenting information is provided in a workbook which outlines a 10-week self-help program for parents. Each weekly session contains a series of set readings and suggested homework tasks for parents to complete. This format was originally designed as an information-only control group for clinical trials. However, positive reports from families have shown this program to be a powerful intervention in its own right with more than two-thirds of families completing this program reporting clinically reliable change on measures of disruptive child behaviour. However, the effectiveness of the intervention can be enhanced through the addition of weekly 15–30 minute telephone consultations. This consultation model aims to provide brief, minimal support to parents as a means of keeping them focused and motivated while they work through the program and assists in tailoring the program to the specific needs of the family. Rather than introducing new strategies, these consultations direct parents to those sections of the written materials, which may be appropriate to their current situation.

Overall, Level 4 intervention is indicated if the child has multiple behavioural problems in a variety of settings and there are clear deficits in parenting skills. Possible obstacles to consider include major family adversity and the presence of psychopathology in the parent/s or child. In these cases, a Level 4 intervention may be begun, with careful monitoring of the family's progress. A Level 5 intervention may be required following Level 4, and in some cases Level 5 components may be introduced concurrently.

Level 5: Enhanced Triple P (Family Intervention)

This indicated level of intervention is for families with additional risk factors that have not changed as a result of participation in a lower level of intervention. It extends the focus of intervention to include marital communication, mood management, and stress-coping skills for parents. Usually at this level of intervention children have severe behavioural problems in the context of additional family adversity factors.

The first session is a review and feedback session in which parents' progress is reviewed, goals are elicited and a treatment plan negotiated. Three enhanced individual therapy modules may then be offered to families individually or in combination: Practice Sessions, Coping Skills, and Partner Support. Each module is ideally conducted in a maximum of five sessions lasting up to 90 minutes each, with the exception of practice sessions which should last 40–60 minutes each. Within each additional module, the components to be covered with each family are determined on the basis of clinical judgment and needs identified by the family (i.e., certain exercises may be omitted if parents have demonstrated competency in the target area). All sessions employ an active skills training process to help parents to acquire new knowledge and skills. Parents are actively involved throughout the program with opportunities to learn through observation, discussion, practice, and feedback. Parents receive constructive feedback about their use of skills in an emotionally supportive context. Between sessions, parents complete homework tasks to consolidate their learning. Following completion of the individually tailored modules, a final session is conducted which aims to promote maintenance of treatment gains by enhancing parents' self-management skills and thus reduce parents' reliance on the practitioner.

Several additional Level 5 modules have recently been developed and trialed. These include specific modules for changing dysfunctional attributions, improving home safety, modifying disturbances in attachment relationships, and strategies to reduce the burden of care of parents of children with disabilities. When complete these additional modules will comprise a comprehensive range of additional resources for practitioners to allow tailoring to the specific risk factors that require additional intervention.

This level of Triple P is designed as an indicated prevention strategy. It is designed for families who are experiencing ongoing child behavioural difficulties after completing Level 4 Triple P, or who may have additional family adversity factors such as parental adjustment difficulties and partner support difficulties that do not resolve during Level 4 interventions.

ACCESSING TRIPLE P INTERVENTIONS

The Triple P model is not designed to involve sequential exposure of the parent to more intensive intervention since families can enter the Triple P system of intervention at any level. Some families may be referred immediately to Level 4 or 5 interventions and may then receive support to maintain intervention gains within the Level 2 or 3 brief consultation format as part of anticipatory well childcare with a general medical practitioner or other health professional, or through accessing further information resources (Level 1). Completion of one level of intervention does not preclude access to other services, and should in some cases be encouraged (e.g., completion of a Level 4 group program while on a wait-list for individual sessions may be cost-effective and reduce the number of individual sessions subsequently required). At all points of contact, families are encouraged to re-present if they are experiencing further difficulties.

At Levels 1 to 4 parents gain access to information about the principles of positive parenting, causes of child behavioural problems, strategies for promoting social competence and managing misbehaviour, and planned activities routines to promote the generalization and maintenance of parenting skills across behaviours, siblings, settings and over time. It is important to note that the parenting information contained in Levels 1 to 4 is identical. The key difference across these levels of intervention is the extent or intensity with which these concepts are discussed with parents. For example, one parent may only need to attend a Universal 90-minute seminar whereas another family may need intensive discussion, modelling, rehearsal, and practice of the information such as in a 10-hour Level 4 Standard Triple P intervention. Also when multiple delivery options are available within a level of intervention, it is important to note that families receive the same information. For example at Level 4 Triple P, the content and order of presentation of the parenting information is identical for Standard, Group and Self-Directed Triple P. The differing feature is simply the mode of delivery (i.e., one-on-one with a practitioner, group-based, or alone in a self-directed format).

The major differences between the Universal level of Triple P and the more intensive levels of intervention include the wider reach of the universal program, the lower "dosage" level of intervention available, the lower per parent cost of delivery of the intervention, the focus on shifting community attitudes and values about parenting, and increasing awareness of parents as to where they can access additional support. Exposure of the parent to the Universal level is viewed as helpful and facilitatory but non-essential for parents to benefit from other levels of intervention. The Universal level is seen as promoting a healthier ecological context for parenting. It supports all other levels of intervention in promoting program participation and in potentially providing after care for families who have already completed one or more of the more intensive levels of intervention.

Another key difference across the levels of intervention is the extent of assessment that occurs. For Levels 1 and 2, little if any assessment is conducted. For Level 3, the first phase of intervention involves an assessment of the individual family. This typically involves conducting a brief (10-minute) clinical interview and behavioural monitoring. It may also include an observation of parent–child interaction. However at Levels 4 and 5, assessment of participating families is more involved. For example, for Standard and Enhanced Triple P, the assessment phase typically constitutes two sessions and involves a clinical interview, observation of parent–child interaction, and the completion of behavioural monitoring and self-report questionnaires. For the Self-help and Group Triple P interventions, self-report questionnaires and behavioural monitoring tasks are completed.

ISSUES REGARDING SUCCESSFUL PROGRAM IMPLEMENTATION

Triple P has been successfully delivered by a variety of providers in several different delivery contexts including universal child health services, general medical practices, schools, mental health services, and in a range of non-government agencies providing family support services. In our experience an ecological perspective is needed to lay the foundations for the program properly so that it is embraced by staff. This process involves the initial orientation and engagement of staff, the provision of staff training, the provision of consultative support to an agency so they can properly support their staff to implement the program, the provision of supervision through a peer support network, the provision of periodic updates to staff to trouble-shoot any implementation problems, and the building in of an evaluation strategy from the beginning so that clinical outcomes with families can be defined. The adoption of an evidence-based program still requires ongoing evaluation to ensure that the program remains effective with the clientele for whom it is currently being used. Ongoing program evaluation continues to inform the further development and refinement of the system and has led to program adaptations to address the parenting needs of parents of children with disabilities, ADHD, obese and overweight children, and indigenous parents.

REFERENCES

Bandura, A. (1977). Self-efficacy: Toward a unifying theory of behavioral change. *Psychological Review*, **84** (2), 191–215.

Bandura, A. (1995). *Self-efficacy in changing societies.* New York: Cambridge University Press.

Biglan, A. (1992). Family practices and the larger social context. *New Zealand Journal of Psychology,* **21** (1), 37–43.

Biglan, A. (1995). Translating what we know about the context of antisocial behavior into a lower prevalence of such behavior. *Journal of Applied Behavior Analysis,* **28** (4), 479–492.

Bor, W., Sanders, M.R., & Markie-Dadds, C. (2002). The effects of Triple P-Positive Parenting Program on children with co-occurring disruptive behaviour and attentional/hyperactive difficulties. *Journal of Abnormal Child Psychology,* **30**, 571–587.

Christensen, A.P., & Sanders, M.R. (1987). Habit reversal and differential reinforcement of other behaviour in the treatment of thumb sucking: An analysis of generalization and side effects. *Journal of Child Psychology and Psychiatry and Allied Disciplines,* **28** (2), 281–295.

Connell, S., Sanders, M.R., & Markie-Dadds, C. (1997). Self-directed behavioural family intervention for parents of oppositional children in rural and remote areas. *Behaviour Modification,* **21** (4), 379–408.

Dadds, M.R., Schwartz, S., & Sanders, M.R. (1987). Marital discord and treatment outcome in the treatment of childhood conduct disorders. *Journal of Consulting & Clinical Psychology,* **55**, 396–403.

Emery, R.E. (1982). Interparental conflict and the children of discord and divorce. *Psychological Bulletin,* **92** (2), 310–330.

Grych, J.H., & Fincham, F.D. (1990). Marital conflict and children's adjustment: A cognitive-contextual framework. *Psychological Bulletin,* **108** (2), 267–290.

Harrold, M., Lutzker, J.R., Campbell, R.V., & Touchette, P.E. (1992). Improving parent–child interactions for families of children with developmental disabilities. *Journal of Behavior Therapy and Experimental Psychiatry,* **23** (2), 89–100.

Hart, B., & Risley, T.R. (1995). *Meaningful differences in the everyday experience of young American children.* Baltimore: Paul H. Brookes Publishing Co.

Ireland, J.L., Sanders, M.R., & Markie-Dadds, C. (2003). The impact of parent training on marital functioning: A comparison of two group versions of the Triple P-Positive Parenting Program for parents of children with early-onset conduct problems. *Behavioural and Cognitive Psychotherapy,* **31**, 127–142.

Karoly, P. (1993). Mechanisms of self-regulation: A systems view. *Annual Review of Psychology,* **44**, 23–52.

Kazdin, A.E. (1987). Treatment of antisocial behaviour in children: Current status and future directions. *Psychological Bulletin,* **102**, 187–203.

Markie-Dadds, C., & Sanders, M.R. (in preparation). Effectiveness of a self-directed program for parents of children at high and low risk of developing conduct disorder.

Markie-Dadds, C., Sanders, M.R., & Turner, K.M.T. (1999). *Every parent's self-help workbook.* Brisbane, Australia: Families International Publishing.

Mrazek, P., & Haggerty, R.J. (1994). *Reducing the risks for mental disorders.* Washington: National Academy Press.

National Institute of Mental Health (1998). *Priorities for prevention research at NIMH: A report by the national advisory mental health council workgroup on mental disorders prevention research* (NIH Publication No. 98–4321). Washington, DC: US Government Printing Office.

Nicholson, J.M., & Sanders, M.R. (1999). Randomised control trial of behavioural family intervention for the treatment of children child behaviour problems in stepfamilies. *Journal of Divorce and Remarriage,* **30**, 1–20.

Patterson, G.R. (1982). *Coercive family process.* Eugene, OR: Castalia Press.

Ralph, A., & Sanders, M.R. (in preparation). *Preliminary evaluation of the Group Teen Triple P program for parents of teenagers.*

Risley, T.R., Clark, H.B., & Cataldo, M.F. (1976). Behavioural technology for the normal middle class family. In E.J. Mash, L.A. Hamerlynck, & L.C. Handy (Eds), *Behavior modification and families* (pp. 34–60). New York: Brunner/Mazel.

Rutter, M. (1985). Family and school influences on behavioral development. *Journal of Child Psychology and Psychiatry,* **26**, 349–368.

Sanders, M.R. (1992). Enhancing the impact of behavioural family intervention with children: Emerging perspectives. *Behaviour Change*, **9** (3), 115–119.

Sanders, M.R. (1996). New directions in behavioral family intervention with children. In T.H. Ollendick & R.J. Prinz (Eds), *Advances in clinical child psychology* (vol. 18; pp. 283–330). New York: Plenum Press.

Sanders, M.R. (1999). The Triple P–positive parenting program: Towards an empirically validated multilevel parenting and family support strategy for the prevention and treatment of child behaviour and emotional problems. *Clinical Child and Family Psychology Review*, **2**, 71–90.

Sanders, M.R., & Christensen, A.P. (1985). A comparison of the effects of child management and planned activities training across five parenting environments. *Journal of Abnormal Child Psychology*, **13**, 101–117.

Sanders, M.R., & Dadds, M.R. (1982). The effects of planned activities and child management training: An analysis of setting generality. *Behaviour Therapy*, **13**, 1–11.

Sanders, M.R., & Glynn, E.L. (1981). Training parents in behavioural self-management: An analysis of generalization and maintenance effects. *Journal of Applied Behaviour Analysis*, **14**, 223–237.

Sanders, M.R., & McFarland, M.L. (2000). The treatment of depressed mothers with disruptive children: A controlled evaluation of cognitive behavioural family intervention. *Behavior Therapy*, **31**, 89–112.

Sanders, M.R., & Plant, K. (1989). Generalization effects of behavioural parent training to high and low risk parenting environments. *Behavior Modification*, **13**, 283–305.

Sanders, M.R., Markie-Dadds, C., & Turner, K.M.T. (2001). *Practitioner's manual for standard Triple P*. Brisbane, Australia: Families International Publishing.

Sanders, M.R., Montgomery, D.T., & Brechman-Toussaint, M.L. (2000). The mass media and child behaviour problems: The effect of a televisions series on child and parent outcomes. *Journal of Child Psychology and Psychiatry and Allied Disciplines*, **41** (7), 939–948.

Sanders, M.R., Turner, K.M.T., & Wall, C.R. (in preparation). The treatment of persistent childhood feeding difficulties: A comparison of behavioural family intervention and nutrition education for parents.

Sanders, M.R., Markie-Dadds, C., Tully, L., & Bor, B. (2000). The Triple P—Positive Parenting Program: A comparison of enhanced, standard and self-directed behavioural family intervention for parents of children with early onset conduct problems. *Journal of Consulting and Clinical Psychology*, **68**, 624–640.

Sanders, M.R., Rebgetz, M., Morrison, M., Gordon, M., Bor, W., Dadds, M., & Shepherd, R.W. (1989). Cognitive-behavioural treatment of recurrent nonspecific abdominal pain in children: An analysis of generalization, maintenance, and side effects. *Journal of Consulting an Clinical Psychology*, **57**, 294–300.

Sanders, M.R., Shepherd, R.W., Cleghorn, G., & Woolford, H. (1994). The treatment of recurrent abdominal pain in children: A controlled comparison of cognitive-behavioral family intervention and standard pediatric care. *Journal of Consulting and Clinical Psychology*, **62**, 306–314.

Sorensen, G., Emmons, K., Hunt, M., & Johnston, D. (1998). Implications of the results of community intervention trials. *Annual Review of Public Health*, **19**, 379–416.

Sultana, C.R., Matthews, J., De Bortoli, D., & Cann, W. (in preparation). *An evaluation of two levels of the Positive Parenting Program (Triple P) delivered by primary care practitioners.*

Taylor, T.K., & Biglan, A. (1998). Behavioral family interventions for improving child-rearing: A review of the literature for clinicians and policy makers. *Clinical Child and Family Psychology*, **1** (1), 41–60.

Turner, K.M.T., Sanders, M.R., & Wall, C.R. (1994). Behavioural parent training versus dietary education in the treatment of children with persistent feeding difficulties. *Behaviour Change*, **11** (4), 242–258.

Webster Stratton, C., & Hammond, M. (1997). Treating children with early-onset conduct problems: A comparison of child and parent training interventions. *Journal of Consulting and Clinical Psychology*, **65** (1), 93–109.

White, B.L. (1990). *The first three years of life*. New York: Prentice Hall Press.

Zubrick, S.R., Silburn, S.R., Burton, P., & Blair, E. (2002). Mental health disorders in children and young people: scope, cause and burden. *Australian and New Zealand Journal of Psychiatry*, **34**, 570–578.

Zubrick, S.R., Northey, K., Silburn, S.R., Williams, A.A., Blair, E., Robertson, D., & Sanders, M.R. (in preparation). *Prevention of child behaviour problems via universal implementation of a group behavioural family intervention*.

CHAPTER 21

Prevention of Substance Abuse in Children and Adolescents

Cecilia A. Essau

Universität Münster, Germany

INTRODUCTION

Children and adolescent substance use and abuse have attracted much research interest (Table 21.1). Findings from recent epidemiological studies have provided grounds for this interest (see review: Adams, Cantwell, & Matheis, 2002; Essau, Stigler, & Scheipl, 2002): (1) a high rate of substance use in children and adolescents; (2) a decrease in the age of onset of substance use disorders (SUD); (3) alcohol and other substances is one of the leading causes of adolescent morbidity and mortality as a result motor vehicle accidents, consensual sexual behaviour resulting in unwanted pregnancies or high risk of HIV infection; (4) SUD is associated with psychosocial impairment in various life domains such as decline in academic functioning, failing to fulfil major role obligations, and recurrent social or interpersonal problems; (5) early onset of SUD may increase a risk of developing other disorders in adulthood.

Both the frequency and the magnitude of problems related to substance use and abuse have led to the development of prevention programs for substance use. This chapter focuses on primary prevention of substance abuse in children and adolescents (the term *youth* will be used interchangeably to refer to both children and adolescents). Studies that select participants because they meet the criteria for substance abuse at the start of the study will be excluded. Before presenting the different types of prevention programs, recent findings on the epidemiology, comorbidity, course, and risk factors of substance use and abuse will be reviewed. The chapter concludes by giving some recommendations for future studies.

Correspondence to Cecilia A. Essau, Westfälische Wilhelms-Universität Münster, Psychologisches Institut I, Fliednerstr. 21, 48149 Münster; email: essau@uni-muenster.de

Handbook of Interventions that Work with Children and Adolescents: Prevention and Treatment.
Edited by P.M. Barrett and T.H. Ollendick. © 2004 John Wiley & Sons, Ltd. ISBN 0-470-84453-1.

Table 21.1　Examples of prevention programs for substance use and abuse

Name (Authors)	Theoretical background	Focus	Setting	Components/Content
Life Skills Training Program (Botvin & Dusenburg, 1987)	Cognitive-behavioural theory; Problem behaviour theory; social learning theory	Tobacco, alcohol, marijuana, and other illicit drugs	School	Enhance generic competence; Problem specific skills and knowledge related to smoking, drinking and drug use; Application of general assertiveness skills in situations of pressure; Decreasing social acceptability of use
STARS (Start Taking Alcohol Risks Seriously) (Johnson et al., 1990)	Multicomponent motivational stages; health belief model; social learning theory; behavioural self-control theory	Alcohol	School	Enhance awareness of preventive issues; alcohol avoidance and resistance skills-building
Project ALERT (Ellickson & Bell, 1990)	Social influence model; self-efficacy theory; health belief model	Tobacco, marijuana, alcohol use	School	Perceived consequences of substance use; Normative beliefs; Resistance self-efficacy; Expectations of future use
"Drug Abuse Resistance Education" (DARE) program (Ennett et al., 1994)	Social learning theory	Drug use	School	Information about drug effects; media awareness; normative education; peer resistance and decision-making skills; healthy alternatives.
Alcohol Misuse Prevention Study (AMPS; Dielman et al., 1986)	Social learning theory	Alcohol	School	Norm setting; Refusal skills; Decision making and problem solving skills
Midwestern Prevention Project (MPP; Pentz et al., 1989)	Social learning theory	Tobacco, alcohol, marijuana, cocaine	Community, school, family	Resistance skills to drug use; correction of beliefs about prevalence; recognition and counteraction of peer and media influences; assertiveness and problem-solving skills.
Project Northland (Perry et al., 1996)	Social cognitive theory	Alcohol	School, home, family, community	Parent involvement; education programs; peer participation and leadership; community task force initiatives.
Project Six Teen (Biglan et al., 2000)	Social cognitive theory	Tobacco	School, community	Effect of smoking; refusal skills training for dealing with pressure to use substance, or engage in antisocial behaviour.

Epidemiology of Substance Use and Abuse

The use of substance among children and adolescents is widespread world wide (see review: Adams, Cantwell, & Matheis, 2002; Essau, Stigler, & Scheipl, 2002). For example, data from the Monitoring the Future Survey (Johnston, O'Malley, & Bachman, 2000) indicated that over 80% have consumed alcohol, and about 54% of adolescents have tried an illicit drug by the time they finish high school. The most commonly used illicit drug was marijuana, with a lifetime prevalence of 20.3%, 40.3%, and 48.8% in the 8th, 10th, and 12th grades, respectively. These rates showed a steady but gradual decline since the 1996 survey among those in grade 8, with little change found in grades 10 and 12. However, the use of ecstacy or the so-called "club drug" has increased significantly. Other drugs such as inhalants (e.g., glue, solvents, butane, gasoline, aerosols), LSD, crystal methamphetamine and rohypnol decreased following their peak levels in the mid-1990s. The rates of alcohol use in many European countries are even higher (see Essau, Stigler, & Scheipl, 2002, for review). As many as 95% of youth had consumed alcohol in the past year, and 82.4% in the past month (e.g., Kokkevi & Stefanis, 1991). These findings indicate that some degree of experimentation with the so-called "gateway" substance of alcohol is common even before children and adolescents reach the legal age to consume alcohol, and in some countries, is even socially accepted.

Although a high proportion of children and adolescents may discontinue substance use after a period of experimentation, some of them may develop into a maladaptive behaviour. When substance use becomes abuse, it is a diagnosable psychiatric disorder. As defined in DSM-IV (American Psychiatric Association, 1994), substance abuse is recurrent use of one or more substances (e.g., alcohol, amphetamine, cannabis, cocaine, hallucinogens, inhalants, nicotine, phencyclidine, sedatives) resulting in a failure to fulfil major role obligations at work, school, or home; use of physically hazardous situations; use related to legal problems; or use causing or exacerbating persistent social or interpersonal problems.

According to recent epidemiological studies, between 3.5 and 32.4% of youth met the lifetime diagnosis of alcohol use disorders (Essau et al., 1998; Fergusson, Horwood, & Lynskeyl, 1993; Lewinsohn et al., 1993; Giaconia et al., 1994; see review: Essau, Stigler, & Scheipl, 2002). The lifetime rate for drug use disorders ranged from 0.1 to 9.8%. Within the illicit substances, cannabis use disorder was the most common (Essau et al., 1998).

Comorbidity

Substance abuse co-occurs frequently with a wide range of mental disorders (see review: Essau, Stigler, & Scheipl, 2002). As reported in the Bremen Adolescent Study (Essau et al., 1998), 37.1% of the adolescents who met the diagnosis of any substance use disorders (SUD) had one additional mental disorder and 12.7% had at least two others. Furthermore, about a third of those with any SUD had at least one other substance abuse/dependence, with alcohol use disorders being the most common comorbid disorder. In several studies, adolescents with SUD, compared to adolescents without SUD, have two to three times higher rates of anxiety, depressive, and eating disorders; disruptive disorders such as conduct and oppositional defiant disorders, and Attention-Deficit/Hyperactivity Disorder also co-occurred frequently with SUD (Fergusson, Horwood, & Lynskeyl, 1993; Kandel et al., 1997; Kilpatrick et al., 2000). Substance abuse has also been linked to several antisocial behaviours such as impulsivity, aggression, and violence (Matykiewiecz et al., 1997). The finding of the high comorbidity between SUD and other disorders (especially delinquent-type behaviour) was interpreted as being consistent with problem-behaviour theory (Jessor & Jessor, 1977), which postulates problem behaviour as a single syndrome associated with underlying construct of unconventionality.

The presence of comorbid disorders was associated with negative outcome of SUD, including chronic psychosocial impairment, suicidality, high use of mental health services, and poor treatment response (Rao et al., 1999; Rohde, Lewinsohn, & Seeley, 1996). In the 1996 study by Rohde and colleagues, comorbidity was associated with an early onset of SUD.

COURSE AND OUTCOME

Kandel's "gateway" theory (1982) postulates that there are distinct developmental stages in substance use. That is, early use of licit substance (e.g., beer, wine, tobacco) paves the way to the consumption of "softer" illicit drug (e.g., marijuana), and then followed by the use of "harder" illicit drugs such as heroin or cocaine. Despite its popularity in the 1980s, more recent studies have not been able to confirm the gateway theory. In some studies, marijuana use preceded alcohol use, and in certain cases, marijuana use was absent (Golub & Johnson, 1994).

The few studies on the natural course and outcome of SUD have shown adolescent substance abuse to be quite stable over time (Stice, Myers, & Brown, 1998; see review: Wagner & Tarolla, 2002), exerting negative development effects extending into young adulthood and beyond. Poor prognosis was related with poor school performance, aggression, and self-injurious behaviour (Doyle, Delaney, & Trobin, 1994).

Risk Factors

In designing prevention program for substance abuse, it is important to have a complete understanding of factors that are related to their development and maintenance. Knowledge about risk factors for substance abuse should enable the selection of optimum approaches for prevention (i.e., school, family, and community-based approach) and the identification of high-risk children and their families (Sullivan & Farrell, 2002). Aetiological and maintaining factors of substance abuse can be divided into those related to the individuals and to the social situations in which they live (Sullivan & Farrell, 2002). The individual's factors can further be divided into: demographic factors (e.g., age, gender, and social class), biological factors (e.g., temperament), and general psychopathology (e.g., the presence of comorbid disorders). Likewise, the social factors can be divided to: environmental factors (e.g., community disintegration and drug availability), school factors (e.g., school climate), family factors (e.g., family management practices, discipline, monitoring, parental drug use), mass media (e.g., tobacco and alcohol advertising), and peer influences (e.g., friend's drug use and prodrug attitudes).

The developmental stage "adolescence" has also been regarded as a risk factor for substance use. As a natural process for establishing identity, developing autonomy and independence, and for acquiring skills needed in adulthood, the experimentation with various types of behaviour and life styles is common among adolescents. For example, adolescents in the study by Hendry and colleagues (1998) associated drinking with relaxation, increased sociability, and the experience of sensory and cognitive changes that alcohol produces. Yet, there are some youths who perceive substance use as a way to obtain pleasure and social bonding, alleviate boredom, and as a means to cope with stress (Arnett, 1992). In this respect, substance use can be regarded as a functional behaviour. Substance use can also be symbolic, that is, being a symbol of grown-up or being "cool". Additionally, with increasing age, children are more socially oriented and more dependent on the peer group, and are more likely to conform to group norms (Arnett, 1992). The extent to which youths are susceptible to conformity pressure is dependent on their personality characteristics (e.g., dependent, anxious, low self-esteem, high social sensitivity) and gender (i.e., with girls being more conforming to peer group pressure than boys).

Table 21.2 shows a summary of risk factors for substance abuse. Much of the information summarized in this table has been taken from various sources (Bukstein, 2000; Hawkins, Catalano, & Miller, 1992; Hawkins et al., 1997; Sullivan & Farrell, 2002).

Although numerous factors have been identified as risk for the development of substance, there is a general consensus that no one factor is strong enough to account for this association (Sullivan & Farrell, 2002). In fact, multiple risk factors have been shown to contribute to the presence and continuation of substance use by adolescents. Bry, McKeon, and Pandina (1982) were among the first to have used a risk factor model to the study of drug use. Their model postulates that the probability of getting involved in substance use, abuse, and dependence is dependent on the number of available risk factors. As hypothesized, the risk for substance abuse increased with the number of risk factors; the types of risk factors covered in this study were poor grades, no religious affiliation, early initial use of alcohol, psychological distress, low self-esteem and low perceived parental love. That is, subjects with one risk factor were 1.4 times more likely to have substance abuse, compared to 4.5 times among those with four risk factors. Similar findings have been reported by Newcomb et al. (1987). Among adolescents who had at least seven risk factors, 56% had cigarette, 18% alcohol, 40% marijuana, and 7% cocaine abuse.

Studies have also been able to differentiate moderate substance use from abuse based on the presence of specific risk factors. In the study by Brook et al. (1992), the four risk factors that differentiated moderate alcohol use from abuse were aggression during childhood, acting out, low maternal attachment, and illegal drug use by peers. Slightly different types of risk factors differentiated moderate from heavy marijuana use. These included: low paternal attachment, illegal drug use by peers, and acting out. The findings that the combination of risk factors increase an

Table 21.2   Risk factors and prevention potentials

Domains	Examples of risk factors	Potential focus of prevention
Individual factors	• Poor social skills • Comorbid disorders • Academic difficulties • Low commitment to school • Difficult temperament • Interpersonal difficulties • Alienation • Low bond to teachers • Negative life events	• Social skill training • Assertive skill training • Problem-solving and decision-making skill training • Interpersonal skill • Skills to increase self-control and self-esteem • Enhance positive coping • Mental health services utilization • Academic assistance/cooperative learning • Improve school environment and teaching practice • Provide recreational non-drug related activities
Peer factors	• Affiliation with drug-using peers • Pressure to use substance • Peer attitude toward substance • Peer rejection	• Resistance skill teaching • Correcting misperception of social norms about substance • Promote awareness of social influence to use substance
Family factors	• Lack of parent discipline • Poor and inconsistent family management practices • Low level of monitoring • Dysfunction parent–child interaction • Parental substance use or abuse • Parental psychopathology • Marital dysfunction	• Parenting skill training • Parent management training • Social support services • Family therapy
Community factors	• Community attitudes/values • Lack of recreational/alternative activities • Economic deprivation • Low bond to neighbourhood	• Changes in policies/laws • Provide recreational non-drug related activities (e.g., sports, entertainment activities) • Encourage anti-substance use and norms • Health promotion
Laws and regulation	• Availability • Easy access to substance	• Increase legal drinking and smoking age • Restrict sales of alcohol and tobacco • Increase price of substance • Laws against minors in possession of substance

individuals likelihood to develop substance abuse indicate the complexity of this disorder.

In contrast to the number of studies on risk factors, very few have examined protective factors of substance abuse. Some examples of factors that tend to protect the youth against substance abuse include resilient temperament, high intelligence and skills, and having warmth, as well as supportive relationship and social bonding to adults (see Sullivan & Farrell, 2002, for a review).

PREVENTION PROGRAMS

Although much effort have been dedicated to the treatment of SUD in children and adolescents, there are many serious limits to such approaches (Ozechowski & Liddle, 2002). Only 25% of the adolescents with SUD received treatment for their substance problems (Essau et al., 1998), and treatment is effective in less than half of those who receive treatment. As reported by Williams (2002), the average drug usage at discharge decreased to about 50% of pre-treatment levels. An average sustained abstinence at six months is 38% and at 12 months 32% (Williams, 2002). Even if treatment is effective, two-thirds of adolescents relapse within the first three months after treatment (Brown, 1993).

Primary prevention is important, given the finding that the earlier children and adolescents start using substance, the more likely it is that they will abuse substance (Kandel & Yamaguchi, 1993). An early onset of any substance use is also associated with high involvement and frequency of use. Furthermore, an early onset of alcohol and tobacco use is a risk factor for progression to more serious types of drug use (Kandel & Yamaguchi, 1993). The ability to prevent the onset of substance abuse may help to reduce the personal suffering of children and their families, and the use of mental health services.

The main goals of primary prevention are to prevent the onset of substance use or progression to substance abuse and their consequences, to reduce factors that increase the chances of developing substance use (i.e., risk factors), and to increase factors that protect individual factors (i.e., protective factors).

Most prevention programs for substance use and abuse take place within the school settings (i.e., school-based). Schools offer the best setting for universal programs for children and adolescents because they guarantee access to the largest number of children who are at the age for the highest risk of initiating substance use. As a setting known for building competencies and preventing the development of unhealthy behaviour, prevention programs that take place in schools are generally accepted by the community.

A school-based substance abuse primary prevention program has undergone three phases: information-only model, affective-only model, and social influence model (Botvin, 2000; Table 21.3). There has also been a shift in the target groups from high school and college students to younger adolescents or children.

Information-Only Model

The first phase took place in the early 1960s and 1970s and was dominated by the information-only model (see Norman & Turner, 1993). This model is based on the assumption that adolescent substance abuse was caused by inadequate knowledge of the negative consequences of substance consumption, which enable the adolescents to make a rational decision to avoid drug use. It is argued that informing youth about the risks and negative (social and health) consequences of substance use will

Table 21.3 Prevention efforts at different developmental stages

Developmental stages	Examples of prevention efforts	Examples of prevention programs
Early childhood	• Provide parenting efficacy • Promote effective child-rearing behaviour • Provide a nurturing healthy environment • Reduce parenting stress	• Triple P approach (Sanders, 1999) • REACH for Resilience (Roth & Dadds, 1999)
Middle childhood	• Teach children to cope with anxiety • Reduce conduct problems • Reduce poor achievement and concentration problems	• Coping Cat (Kendall, 1994); • Coping Koala Prevention Program (Dadds et al., 1997); • FRIENDS (Barrett et al., 2000); • The Montreal Prevention Experiment (Tremblay et al., 1996)
Adolescence	• Resilience building • Enhance decision-making and assertive skills • Enhance coping skills • Reduce depressive symptoms	• The Pennsylvania Depression Programme (Jaycox et al., 1994) • The Resourceful Adolescent Program (Shochet, Holland, & Whitefield, 1997)

produce negative attitudes toward substance use and thereby reduce its use. Although this model significantly affected knowledge acquisition and awareness of the adverse effects of substance use, it failed to have a significant impact on actual substance use behaviour (Tobler, 1992). Providing information about the dangers and risks could even arouse curiosity among some adolescents. As shown by several studies (e.g., Hawkins, Lisher, & Catalano, 1985; Goodstadt, 1978), an increased knowledge about how to identify, where to get, and how to use substance was significantly associated with curiosity and experimentation of substance use. This approach has furthermore been criticized because it insufficiently addresses the role of psychosocial factors (e.g., peer pressure) which promote substance use and abuse (Tobler, 1992).

Affective-Only Model (Affective Education/ Social Competency Model)

The second phase of primary prevention (1970s–1980s) was dominated by the affective-only approach (Norman & Turner, 1993). The main assumption of this model is that children and adolescents who use substances do so because they lack psychosocial skills (i.e., low self-esteem, inadequate decision-making, problem-solving, or communication skills) to act appropriately in social interaction and to refuse social pressure to use substance. Therefore, in addition to teaching children and adolescents substance refusal or resistance skills, they are taught several generic skills such as self-concept building, stress management, rational decision-making, problem-solving training, and assertiveness and communication enhancement techniques. Very little focus is made on substance use *per se*.

The social competency model was first used by Evans (1976) in the area of smoking prevention. It was proposed that children and adolescents could be "inoculated" against social influence to smoke. That is, students are exposed to increasingly more intense pro-smoking influences and should be provided with counter-arguments to resist these pressures. Through a gradual exposure to pro-smoking influences to smoke, children and adolescents would build up resistance to the powerful pro-smoking messages. Most studies, however, showed no prevention effects on student substance use (Tobler, 1992).

Social Influence Model (Social Environmental Model)

The third phase (since early 1980s) has been dominated by the social influence model (Norman & Turner, 1993). This model assumes that children and adolescent substance use is the result of social influences from parents, peers, and the media to smoke or drink alcohol beverages, or to use illicit drugs. Specifically, social influences may take the form of modelling of drug use by parents and peers, media (i.e., persuasive advertising appeal), and direct offers by peers to use drugs. The social influence approach generally involves:

- Making adolescents aware of the social influences that promote the use of substance.
- Teach adolescents specific skills to resist social influence. The *Social Resistance Skills* approach involves teaching adolescents personal and social skills (i.e., decision-making, problem-solving, and assertiveness), and how to identify and respond to messages in advertisement and movies. Specifically, they are taught to identify advertising techniques, to analyse advertising messages, and to formulate counter-arguments to common advertising appeals. Another approach is to teach adolescents verbal and non-verbal skills for resisting (i.e., what to say and how to say it when being forced to engage in drug use) offers from their peers to smoke, drink, or use drugs. That is, children and adolescents are taught what to say in a peer pressure situation and on how to say it in the most effective way (e.g., eye contact, tone of voice, and facial expression). These techniques are taught through small-group discussions, role-playing, and demonstrations. Adolescents are also taught skills to recognize high-risk situations—i.e., situations in which they are likely to experience peer pressure to smoke, drink, or use illicit drugs (Botvin, 2000).
- Normative education, through which children and adolescent misperception about drug use is corrected. One of the methods used to modify or correct normative expectations is to provide adolescents with information about the prevalence of drug use from national or local surveys.
- Another method involves having adolescents conduct their own surveys of drug use.

Some examples of programs based on the social influence model are Life Skills Training (LST; Botvin & Dusenbury, 1987) and Drug Abuse Resistance Education (DARE; Ennett et al., 1994).

Life Skills Training (LST; Botvin & Dusenbury, 1987)

The LST program is both a substance abuse prevention program and a competency enhancement program, designed to facilitate the development of skills for coping with social influences to smoke, drink, or drug use. The program comprises five conceptual components, which are carried out in 16 sessions. The first two components focus on social factors that promote the use of substance. Youths are taught to increase awareness of social influences toward drug use (e.g., tactics used by advertisers to sell substance), correct the misperception about drugs, promote anti-drug norms, teach prevention-related information about drug abuse, and drug resistance skills. A third component focuses on skills for increasing independence, personal control, and a sense of self-mastery. This includes teaching general problem-solving and decision-making skills, skills for resisting peer and media influences, skills for increasing self-control and self-esteem (e.g., self-monitoring, self-reinforcement), and techniques to relieve stress and anxiety. The fourth component focuses on social and communication (verbal and non-verbal) skills. These skills are taught through instruction, demonstration, feedback, reinforcement, and behavioural rehearsal. The final component deals with the way to improve specific skill or behaviour. The program also includes booster sessions, which are conducted at one year (10 class sessions) and two years (5 class sessions) following the prevention in order to help to maintain program effects.

The effectiveness of the LST in the prevention of alcohol and marijuana use has been examined in numerous studies. Youths who participated in LST showed 59 to 75% lower levels (relative to controls) of tobacco, alcohol, and marijuana use (Botvin, 2000). Youths who participated in LST also showed improvement in their interpersonal and communication skills. Although most of the early studies on LST have focused on white populations, later studies by Botvin and colleagues (1992, 1995) have shown the LST approach to be as effective in reducing cigarette smoking (relative to controls), alcohol, and marijuana use in minority youth.

The long-term effects of LST have been examined in a large-scale, randomized field trial that involved about 6000 7th-grade students from 56 public schools in New York State (Botvin et al., 1995). The students in the prevention conditions received the LST program during the 7th grade, with booster sessions in the 8th and 9th grades. Treatment effects were maintained at six-year follow-up. That is, at the end of the 12th grade, the prevalence of cigarette smoking, alcohol, and marijuana use among students in the prevention condition was 44% lower than for controls, and the regular (weekly) use of multiple drug was 66% lower.

Project DARE (Drug Research Resistance Education; Ennett et al., 1994)

DARE focuses on teaching pupils the skills needed to recognize and resist social pressures to use drugs, providing information about drugs, teaching decision-making skills, building self-esteem, and choosing healthy alternatives to drug use. The DARE core curriculum consists of 17 lessons which are taught to children in the 5th grade by uniformed police officers. The DARE officers are required to undergo

80 training hours in classroom management, teaching strategies, communication skills, adolescent development, drug information, and curriculum instruction. DARE officers with classroom experience can also undergo further training to qualify as instructors/mentors. These officers monitor the integrity and consistency of the program's delivery through periodic classroom visits.

Most studies showed immediate effects of the DARE (e.g., Dukes, Ullman, & Stein, 1995; Ennett et al., 1994). That is, youths who participated in the DARE reported higher self-esteem, stronger anti-drug attitudes, and are more resistance to peer pressure compared to those who did not receive the program. These adolescents also reported less substance use. However, its effectiveness over a period of longer than one year has been inconsistent; most studies failed to find significant difference in substance use among youths who participated on the DARE and those in the control group (Ennett et al., 1994), or on self-esteem, resistance to peer pressure, and delay of experimentation with drugs (Dukes, Ullman, & Stein, 1996). Ennett and colleagues (1994) examined the magnitude of the DARE's effectiveness using meta-analysis of eight studies on the following outcome measures: knowledge about drug use, social skills, self-esteem, attitude toward police, and drug use. The largest mean effect size was for knowledge, followed by social skills. The lowest mean effect was found for drug behaviour.

OTHER APPROACHES

Family-Based Approaches

Given the role of family in the initiation of substance using behaviour, recent programs have included the family in their prevention systems. Parents can prevent substance use problems through their parental role by monitoring children's behaviour and by establishing a strong parent–child relationship. Parenting programs can support this role by teaching parents how to model healthy behaviours, communicate effectively with their children, develop problem-solving skills, and provide appropriate reinforcement. Parents are also given information on the various substances of abuse and their effects, to enable them to discuss drug use knowledgably with their children.

One example of a family-based program is the Seattle Social Development Project (Hawkins et al., 1992), a six-year intervention that comprises teacher/classroom, parent, and child components. The teacher/classroom component is intended to enhance attachment and commitment to school through active classroom management, interactive teaching strategies, and cooperative learning. Specifically, teachers are taught to establish classroom management by creating consistent patterns of expectations, minimizing interruption of learning, and encouraging and rewarding students for appropriate effort. Interactive teaching involves assigning children grades based on mastery of material and improvement over past performance. Through the use of cooperative learning, students with different abilities and backgrounds are encouraged to work together.

The parent component is designed to reward children's prosocial involvement in both school and family settings. Through such involvement, it is hoped that children will increase their bonds to school and family and commitment to the norm of not using drugs. Parents are also taught to support their children's progress at school by creating a positive learning environment in the home, and to positively reinforce desired behaviour and give negative consequences for inappropriate behaviour in a consistent manner. The child component is intended to develop skills related to problem-solving, communication, as well as decision-making, negotiation, and conflict resolution.

The Seattle Social Development Project has been tested for its efficacy with students in grades 4 to 6. Results showed positive outcomes for students in the experimental group in the following areas: reduction of antisocial behaviour, improved academic skills, increased commitment to school, reduced levels of alienation, and poor bonding to prosocial others and reduced school misbehaviour. Reduced incidents of getting high on drugs at school are also reported. The positive effects of prevention could be maintained six years after the end of the intervention (Hawkins et al., 1999). That is, students who participated in the program showed reductions in antisocial behaviour, improved academic skills, increased commitment to school, reduced levels of alienation and better bonding to prosocial others, and reduced school misbehaviour (e.g., cheating on test). There were also effects on heavy drinking, however, no significant effects were found for lifetime use of tobacco, alcohol, marijuana, or other substance use. These findings suggest the importance of starting early, and involving the whole school and parents.

Community-Based Approaches

Alternative Activities

One of the community-based approaches, popular in the 1970s, used to prevent substance use is to involve youth in physical and recreational activities (i.e., alternative activity). Participation in such activities is assumed to increase self-esteem, relieve boredom, and to provide a sense of responsibility. This in turn is intended to alleviate their need to use substance. Despite its popularity in the 1970s, alternative programs have not been effective in preventing substance use among children and adolescents (Moskowitz et al., 1983, 1984). A study by Swisher and Hsu (1983) showed that if substance users are present, socially related events (e.g., sports, entertainment) were associated with increased substance use.

Numerous community-based approaches have been introduced in recent years, such as the Project Northland (Perry et al., 1996) and the North Kavelia Project (Vartiainen et al., 1990).

Project Northland (Perry et al., 1996) is a community multilevel approach to alcohol prevention that involves parents, teachers, and community members (e.g., government officials, business representatives, health professionals). Prevention generally takes place when the children are at the 6th, 7th, and 8th grades. During the 6th grade, children learn skills to communicate with their parents about alcohol. During the 7th grade, they learn strategies to resist and counteract influences on children and adolescents to alcohol use, and in the 8th grade, they become involved with groups that influence adolescent alcohol use and availability. The program has been evaluated in 20 schools districts (Perry et al., 1996). Results showed significantly lower tendencies of students in the intervention districts to use alcohol, marijuana, and cigarette compared to those in the "reference condition" (i.e., district where standard alcohol and other drug education programs are employed). The strongest difference was found among non-users of alcohol at baseline. Children in the prevention condition also reported significantly greater self-efficacy to resist alcohol at a party or when offered by a boyfriend or girlfriend.

The *North Kavelia Project* (Vartiainen et al., 1990) is a community wide cardiovascular risk reductions program that has been carried out in Finland. In the context of that program, a classroom-based smoking prevention program was provided to youths in four schools (two schools with intensive curriculum; two schools with short curriculum) in North Kavelia. The prevalence of smoking among students in these four schools (i.e., intervention group) were compared with students at the two schools from another county who did not receive any interventions (i.e., control group). Students in the intervention group were taught about social pressures to smoke exerted by peers, adults, and mass media, and on how to deal with such pressures. Results showed prevention effects on smoking at immediate and at follow-up investigations. The effects of prevention could be maintained among students in the intensive intervention group (42%) at six-year follow-up; among those who received the short curriculum, a slight decay was observed. At 15-year follow-up, the mean lifetime cigarette consumption among those in the prevention group was 22% lower than those in the control group (Vartiainen et al., 1998).

The Midwestern Prevention Project (MPP; Pentz et al., 1989) is a multicomponent, community-based program designed to reduce the prevalence of substance use in adolescents. The program comprised five components: a school-based component (also called a project "Students Taught Awareness and Resistance"; STAR), a parent program, mass media advertising, community organization, and policy change. The school-based component includes curriculum that is incorporated into 10 classroom and homework sessions. The sessions focused on resistance skills training, psychosocial consequences of drug abuse, correction of misconceptions about the prevalence of drug use by teens, and problem-solving training. The school-based component also included a 5-session booster school programs and homework. The parent program included educating parents about substance use prevention, and on how to communicate prevention at home. These components were supported by a mass media campaign through television, radio, and print media promotions to increase community awareness of the substance-related problems and to introduce the strategies being implemented by the program. The community component involved the implementation of prevention and treatment services for the community, and planning changes in local policy. Policy changes took place during the fourth and fifth year of the project, which included the establishment of drug-free school zones, restriction of smoking in public places, the introduction of policies that require proof of age for alcohol purchases, and penalties for selling drugs to under-aged youth.

Results showed positive long-term effects; students who participated in the program used significantly less marijuana, cigarettes, and alcohol than children in schools that did not receive the program (Pentz et al., 1989). The program also had an impact on children's perceptions of the negative effects of substance use, and they were better able to communicate with their friends about substance use and other problems.

Mass Media

The findings that youth generally obtain information about substance from television stress the importance of using mass media campaigns in preventing substance use. Therefore, one way to counteract the influence of media is to train youth to analyse media content, its origins, and the difference levels of meaning, and to be critical and sceptical of advertising messages (Alverman & Hagwood, 2000). Mass media can also help to increase awareness and motivation of community members to participate in prevention programs at a community level.

The strongest evidence for the effectiveness of mass media as a supplement to a school-based prevention program has been provided by the work of Flynn and colleagues (Flynn et al., 1997; Worden, 1999). Their program focuses on the advantages of not smoking, disadvantages of smoking, techniques to refuse a cigarette and to understand the advertising techniques of the tobacco industry. These messages are delivered through cartoon, rock video, and testimonials. Principles of social learning are also followed by, for example, showing successful models, saying "I don't smoke and I feel great". The results showed the strong effects of media campaigns on smoking behaviour. After four years of intervention, fewer students who received both the school and media programs smoked compared to those who received only the school program (Flynn et al., 1992), and these effects were maintained at a two-year follow-up (Flynn et al., 1994). The program is especially effective among high-risk youths—that is, youths who are at risk to become smokers because they had previously tried smoking or because their parents, sibling, and friends were smokers.

Laws and Regulations

Availability and easy access to substance is an important factor which promotes substance use. In most countries, cigarettes can be obtained from grocery stores, supermarkets, or automatic machines. Furthermore, less than 50% of under-age youth who attempt to buy tobacco are requested to show their age identification cards (Hobbs et al., 1997). Unlike tobacco, the access of alcohol differs tremendously in different countries. In the USA and in Canada, for example, alcohol beverages are sold mostly in liquor stores, and the sale of alcohol to minors can lead to liquor licence suspension or revocation. In most European countries, alcohol is easily available in most supermarkets, grocery stores, and gas stations. As reported by Balding (1997), about 25% of the 15 year olds had purchased alcohol from a supermarket in the past week, and 10% in a pub.

Regulatory efforts which render the purchase or affordability of alcohol more difficult may influence adolescent normative beliefs about the desirability of use and may reinforce the message about non-use. Therefore, much effort has been made by the government in many countries to regulate alcohol outlets, to limit the legal blood alcohol for drinking and driving, to impose advertising restrictions, and to enforce laws regarding the legal drinking age. The next important step would be to make sure that these regulations are put into practice. A study by Klepp, Schmid, and Murray (1996) showed that an increase in legal drinking age significantly reduced drinking and driving rates and other alcohol-related problems. Numerous studies in North America have shown an increase in the price of alcohol and cigarettes to be associated with a significant decrease in drinking and smoking behaviour (Brown et al., 1996; Chaloupka, Saffer, & Grossman, 1993).

School Policies

School policies about substance use and school environment may be an important component of preventive strategy about substance use in youth. The former include policy in dealing with substance use and possession on school property, such as school suspension, detention, and suspension from curricular activities. The impact of school policies in the prevention of substance use has been inconsistent. In a study by Pentz et al. (1989), for example, the lower amount of smoking was related to school policies that were characterized by a ban on smoking on or near school grounds, limited opportunity for smoking off grounds, and a formal education. School policies that focus on prevention and cessation also had an effect on smoking behaviour. Those with a punitive focus showed no positive effect on smoking behaviour. Findings from the Monitoring the Future Study (Chaloupka & Grossman, 1996) also showed more restricted policies about smoking in schools being associated with a reduced number of cigarettes smoked. In contrast to these findings, Clarke and colleagues (Clarke et al., 1994) found no association between school policy and smoking behaviour.

Another preventive strategy involves changing teaching practices and the school environment. It has been argued that a school with a positive climate where students are involved and feel respected could lead to increased involvement and bonding. This is intended to deter youth from involving with antisocial peers, which in turn deters drug involvement (Kumpfer & Turner, 1990).

The way in which teachers interact with students may improve students' engagement with the school and teachers—school bonding; such behaviour may lead to a lower level of substance use, which in turn may lead to improved behaviour and school performance. For example, Kellam and Anthony (1998; Kellam et al., 1994) examined the extent to which two interventions, designed to reduce aggressive and disruptive behaviour, could improve children's academic achievement and reduce the incidence of smoking initiation. The two interventions were the so-called "good behaviour game", designed to help teachers to reduce aggressive and disruptive classroom behaviour, and "mastery learning", designed to raise reading achievement scores. Results showed that boys in both interventions were less likely to have initiated tobacco smoking seven years after participating in the program, in comparison to their control counterparts.

PREVENTION OF SUBSTANCE ABUSE THROUGH OTHER MENTAL HEALTH PREVENTION PROGRAMS

In addition to the existing programs and approaches specifically designed to prevent substance use and abuse, programs developed to prevent other disorders may be useful (Dadds & McAloon, 2002). As mentioned earlier, there are high comorbidity rates between substance abuse and other disorders. Among those with comorbid disorders, there seems to be a specific sequence of disorders. For example, in a study of adults by Wittchen, Hand, and Hecht (1989), substance abuse is generally preceded by anxiety and depressive disorders. Conduct and anxiety are also two disorders which commonly preceded the onset of SUD (Rohde, Lewinsohn, & Seeley, 1996). In other studies, the presence of one disorder seems to act as a risk factor for the development of other disorders. As shown by Miller-Johnson et al. (1998), children and adolescents who displayed high levels of conduct problems during early adolescence were at risk for increased levels of substance use from the 6th through the 10th grades. These findings suggest that it is important to prevent the development of a disorder that may put the child at risk for other disorders. Prevention should disrupt the transition from one disorder to the next.

Substance abuse and a range of psychiatric disorders (e.g., anxiety and depression) in children and adolescents seemed to have the same risk factors (see Essau et al., 1998; and Sullivan & Farrell, 2002, for a review). Dadds and McAloon (2002) recently argued that some of the developmental pathways to SUD may exist through internalizing and externalizing disorders. Greenberg, Domitrovich, and Bumbarger (1999) similarly argued that alternative developmental pathways may be interweaving and may represent diverse developmental trajectories. On this theoretical basis and on the findings showing the comorbidity and temporal sequence of SUD with other disorders, interventions which are aimed at reducing other disorders (e.g., anxiety and depression) may also reduce the prevalence of SUD if conducted at an appropriate developmental stages (see Table 21.4, modified from Dadds & McAloon, 2002). Some support for this hypothesis has been shown by Tremblay et al. (1996). In that study, children with high aggressive and disruptive behaviour who participated in a two-year intervention program compared to those in the placebo control condition were less likely to engage in various forms of antisocial behaviour (e.g., stealing, delinquent activity) and substance use when interviewed at early adolescence.

Methodological Issues

Although several studies have shown strong prevention effects, they have been criticized due to methodological problems (e.g., Botvin, 2000; Williams, 2002). First, most of these critics are related to the validity of self-report data. Due to the illegal status of substance use, social desirability may influence the reporting of substance use and associated problems. Thus, youth who perceive substance use as undesirable would under-report substance use, and those who perceive such behaviour as desirable would over-report the use of substance. Therefore, it may be useful to employ an objective method to assess substance use such as the use of blood or

Table 21.4 Facts about substance use and abuse

Areas	Summary of research findings/contents
Classification systems	• Diagnostic and Statistical Manual of Mental Disorders • International Classification of Mental and Behavioural Disorders
Assessment of substance abuse (see review: Ridenour et al., 2002)	• Diagnostic Interview for Children and Adolescents (DICA) • Diagnostic Interview Survey for Children (DISC) • Adolescent Diagnostic Interview (ADI) • Children's Interview for Psychiatric Syndromes (ChIPS) • Pictorial Instrument for Children and Adolescents (PICA-III-R) • Assessment of Liability and Exposure to Substance Use and Antisocial Behavior (ALEXSA)
Epidemiology	• Widespread use of substance: up to 95% of the youths have consumed alcohol and up to 54% had tried an illicit drug at some time in their lives • Higher rates in males than females • The rates increase with age
Comorbidity	• SUD co-occur frequently with other psychiatric disorders • Other disorders (depression, anxiety and disruptive disorders) generally preceded the onset of SUD • Associated with negative outcome
Risk factors	• Individual factors (e.g., poor social skills, academic difficulties) • Peer factors (e.g., affiliation with drug-using peers) • Family factors (e.g., poor family management practices, parental substance use or abuse) • Community factors (e.g., community values, lack of recreational activities) • Laws and regulation (e.g., availability)
Course and outcome	• Stable over time
Prevention programs	• Information-only model • Affective-only model • Social influence model • Family-based approaches • Community-based approaches • Prevention of substance abuse through other mental health prevention programs
Specific components of prevention programs	• Information about substance use and abuse • Social resistance skills • Problem-solving and decision-making skills • Adaptive coping strategies • Skills for increasing self-control and self-esteem

urine sample. Another issue is related to the lack of guidelines for measuring prevention effects. Most early studies used knowledge and attitudes toward substance use, and in more recent studies, the major focus has been on substance use behaviour. It would be most useful in the future to measure improvement in specific life domains or life satisfaction, or to measure improvement of skills that have been taught to the children.

Second, despite many advantages of school-based prevention programs, their implementation in schools is not unproblematic. By conducting prevention program in schools, children and adolescents who drop out of school or those who are chronically truant will not be able to participate in such programs. These children are generally those with a high risk of developing substance abuse and other psychiatric disorders, but who would not have access to school-based programs. Furthermore, social learning does not only occur in schools, but in other environment as well. School-based prevention programs also need to be compatible with both the time and personnel commitments of the schools.

Third, program trainers play an important role for the successful implementation of the prevention programs. This means that the program trainers need to be well trained about all aspects of the programs (i.e., theoretical background, the content, and administration techniques), and should be properly monitored to make sure that the material is being covered as intended. As argued by Weissberg, Caplan, and Harwood (1991, p. 837):

> Regardless of a program's quality, its potential for positive effects is diminished when program implementers are poorly trained, have inadequate organizational support for program delivery or lack the necessary skills to provide effective training.

To what extent and the manner in which monitoring (e.g., using trainers self-report, video- or audio-taping of sessions, and random visits of a program supervisor) is done has rarely been reported.

Fourth, although evaluation studies have generally shown the effectiveness of such approaches, little is known about the factors or mechanism that are associated with prevention efficacy. Furthermore, since many recent prevention programs have different components, we have little knowledge of the combination of strategies that are most effective.

CONCLUSION

Prevention programs have historically moved from information to affective approaches to social influence. With an accumulative amount of knowledge on the aetiology of substance abuse, prevention approaches have been broad and developmentally focused, with the integration of a classroom-based curriculum and intervention components that include parent involvement, mass media, and the community. With this advance, most evaluation studies have shown prevention effects at post-test and follow-up. The most effective prevention programs seem to be those that focus on changing adolescent norms and enhancing social and resistance skills.

To ensure prevention success, the following points need to be considered:

• How motivated are children and adolescents in participating in the prevention program? The degree to which the youth are motivated to participate and comply with the program curriculum is important. Therefore, special efforts need to be cultivated to increase youth's motivation, such as counselling or special incentives, and by involving them in the prevention planning.

- Are any other problems or psychiatric disorders present? Since substance use and abuse may be a part of larger behavioural and emotional disorders, it is important that the youth be assessed systematically using age-appropriate instruments. Such an effort should enable us to differentiate those youth who may benefit from individualized or specific interventions.
- Are the prevention goals clearly defined? The goals to be achieved should be clearly defined, and some forms of reward may be important for the achievement of these goals.
- How are prevention outcomes evaluated? Systematic evaluation of the prevention outcome serve to evaluate an improvement and identification of remaining problems. Outcome measures should not be limited to substance-using behaviour, but should also contain a detailed assessment of youth's functioning in various life domains (e.g., academic and family functioning).
- What strategies are available to maintain the prevention effect? Most studies reviewed in this chapter showed prevention effects at post-treatment. Prevention effects may be made possible through booster sessions, or through continued contact with the youth after completion of the training. Continued contact enables problems and the emergence of any new symptoms, such as depression, to be assessed.

This review suggests that while great advances have been achieved in recent years, there is much more to be done in the future.

REFERENCES

Adams, G., Cantwell, A.M., & Matheis, S. (2002). Substance use and Adolescence. In C.A. Essau (Ed.), *Substance abuse and dependence in adolescence*. London: Brunner-Routledge.

Alverman, D.E., & Hagwood, M.C. (2000). Critical media literacy: Research, theory and practice in new times. *Journal of Educational Research*, **93**, 193–205.

American Psychiatric Association (1994). *Diagnosticu and statistical manual of mental disorders* (4th edn). Washington, DC: Author.

Arnett, J. (1992). Review: Reckless behavior in adolesence: A developmental perspective. *Developmental Review*, **12**, 339–373.

Balding, J. (1992). *Young people in 1991*. Exeter: Schools Health Education. Unit.

Balding, J. (1997). *Young people in 1996. Schools Health Education Unit*. Exeter: University of Exeter.

Barrett, P.M., Lowry-Webster, H.M., & Turner, C. (2000). *The FRIENDS program*. Bowen Hills, Queensland: Australian Academic Press.

Biglan, A., Ary, D., Smolkowski, T.D., & Black, C. (2000). A randomized controlled trial of a community intervention to prevent adolescent tobacco use. *Tobacco Control*, **9**, 24–32.

Botvin, G.J. (2000). Preventing drug abuse in schools: Social and competence enhancement approaches targeting individual-level etiological factors. *Addictive Behaviors*, **25**, 887–897.

Botvin, G.J., & Dusenbury, L. (1987). Substance abuse prevention and the promotion of competence. In L. Bond & B. Compas (Eds), *Primary prevention promotion in the schools* (pp. 146–178). Newbury Park, CA: Saga Publications.

Botvin, G.J., Dusenbury, L., Baker, E., James-Ortuz, S., Botvin, E.M., & Kerner, J. (1992). Smoking prevention among urban minority youth: Assessing effects on outcome and mediating variables. *Health Psychology*, **11**, 290–299.

Botvin, G.J., Schinke, S.P., Epstein, J.A., & Diaz, T. (1994). Effectiveness of culturally-focused and generic skills training approaches to alcohol and drug abuse prevention among minority adolescents. *Psychology of Addictive Behaviors*, **8**, 116–127.

Botvin, G.J., Schinke, S.P., Epstein, J.A., Diaz, T., & Botvin, E.M. (1995). Effectiveness of culturally-focused and generic skills training approaches to alcohol and drug abuse prevention among minority adolescents: Two-year follow-up results. *Psychology of Addictive Behaviors*, **9**, 183–194.

Brook, J.S., Cohen, P., Whiteman, M., & Gordon, A.S. (1992). Psychosocial risk factors in the transition from moderate to heavy use or abuse of drugs. In M.D. Glantz & R. Pickens (Eds), *Vulnerability to drug abuse* (pp. 359–388). Washington, DC: American Psychological Association.

Brown, S.A. (1993). Recovery patterns in adolescent substance abuse. In J.S. Baer, G.A. Marlatt, & R.J. McMahon (Eds), *Addictive behaviours across the lifespan: Prevention, treatment and policy issues* (pp. 161–183). Newbury Park, CA: Sage Publications.

Brown, K.S., Taylor, T.E., Madill, C.L., & Cameron, R. (1996). *The relationship between the tobacco tax decrease and smoking among youth: Results of a survey in south-western Ontario*. Toronto: Ontario Tobacco Research Unit.

Bry, B.H., McKeon, P., & Pandina, R.S. (1982). Extent of drug use as a function of number of risk factors. *Journal of Abnormal Psychology*, **91**, 273–279.

Bukstein, O.G. (2000). Disruptive behavior disorders and substance use disorders in adolescents. *Journal of Psychoactive Drugs*, **32**, 67–70.

Chaloupka, F.J., & Grossman, M. (1996). *Price, tobacco control policies and youth smoking*. National Bureau of Economic Research Working Paper No. 5740.

Chaloupka, F.J., Saffer, H., & Grossman, M. (1993). Alcohol-control policies and motor-vehicle fatalities. *Journal of Legal Studies*, **22**, 161–186.

Clarke, V., White, V., Hill, D., & Borland, R. (1994). School structural and policy variables associated with student smoking. *Tobacco Control*, **3**, 339–346.

Dadds, M.R., & McAloon, J. (2002). Prevention. In C.A. Essau (Ed.), *Substance abuse and dependence in adolescence*. London: Brunner-Routledge.

Dadds, M.R., Spence, S.H., Holland, D.E., Barrett, P.M., & Laurens, K.R. (1997). Prevention and early intervention for anxiety disorders: A controlled trial. *Journal of Consulting and Clinical Psychology*, **65**, 627–635.

Dielman, T.E., Shope, J.T., Butchart, A.T., & Campanelli, P.C. (1986). Prevention of adolescent alcohol misuse: An elementary school program. *Journal of Pediatric Psychology*, **11**, 259–282.

Doyle, H., Delaney, W., & Trobin, J. (1994). Follow-up study of young attendees at an alcohol unit. *Addiction*, **89**, 183–189.

Dukes, R.L., Ullman, J.B., & Stein, J.A. (1995). An evaluation of DARE (Drug Abuse Resistance Education) using a Solomon four group design with latent variables. *Evaluation Review*, **19**, 409–435.

Dukes, R.L., Ullman, J.B., & Stein, J.A. (1996). Three-year follow-up of Drug Abuse Resistance Education (DARE). *Evaluation Review*, **20**, 49–66.

Ellickson, P., & Bell, R. (1990). Drug prevention in junior high: A multi-site longitudinal test. *Science*, **247**, 1299–1305.

Ennett, S.T., Tobler, N.S., Ringwalt, C.L., & Flewelling, R.L. (1994). How effective is Drug Abuse Resistance Education? A meta-analysis of project DARE outcome evaluations. *American Journal of Public Health* **84** (9), 1394–1401.

Essau, C.A., Stigler, H., & Scheipl, J. (2002). Epidemiology and comorbidity. In C.A. Essau (Ed.), *Substance abuse and dependence in adolescence*. London: Brunner-Routledge.

Essau, C.A., Karpinski, N.A., Petermann, F., & Conradt, J. (1998). Häufigkeit und Komorbidität von Störungen durch Substanzkonsum (Frequency and comorbidity of substance use disorders). *Zeitschrift Kindheit und Entwicklung*, **7**, 199–207.

Evans, R.I. (1976). Smoking children: Developing a social psychological strategy of deterrence. *Preventive Medicine*, **5**, 122–127.

Fergusson, D.M., Horwood, L.J., & Lynskeyl, M.T. (1993). Prevalence and comorbidity of DSM-III-R diagnoses in a birth cohort of 15 year olds. *Journal of the American Academy of Child and Adolescent Psychiatry*, **32**, 1127–1134.

Flynn, B.S., Worden, J.K., Secker-Walker, R.H., Badger, G.J., Geller, B.M., & Costanza, M.C. (1992). Prevention of cigarette smoking through mass media intervention and school programs. *American Journal of Public Health*, **82**, 827–834.

Flynn, B.S., Worden, J.K., Secker-Walker, R.H., Pirie, P.L., Badger, G.J., Carpenter, J.H., & Geller, B.M. (1994). Mass media and school interventions for cigarette smoking prevention: Effects 2 years after completion. *American Journal of Public Health*, **84**, 1148–1150.

Flynn, B.S., Worden, J.K., Secker-Walker, R.H., Pirie, P.L., Badger, G.J., & Carpenter, J.H. (1997). Long-term responses of higher and lower risk youths to smoking prevention interventions. *Preventive Medicine*, **26**, 389–394.

Giaconia, R., Reinherz, H.Z., Silverman, A.B., Pakiz, B., Frost, A.K., & Cohen, E. (1994). Ages of onset of psychiatric disorders in a community population of older adolescents. *Journal of the American Academy of Child and Adolescent Psychiatry*, **33**, 706–717.

Golub, A., & Johnson, B.D. (1994). The shifting importance of alcohol and marijuana as gateway substances among serious drug abusers. *Journal of Studies on Alcohol*, **55**, 607–614.

Goodstadt, M.S. (1978). Alcohol and drug education: Models and outcomes. *Health Education Monographs*, **6**, 263–279.

Greenberg, M.T., Domitrovich, C., & Bumbarger, B. (1999). *Preventing mental disorders in school-aged children: A review of the effectiveness of prevention programs*. Rockville, MD: US Department of Health and Human Services, Public Health Service.

Hawkins, J.D., Catalano, R.F., & Miller, J.Y. (1992). Risk and protective factors for alcohol and other drug problems in adolescence and early adulthood: Implications for substance abuse prevention. *Psychological Bulletin*, **112**, 64–105.

Hawkins, J.D., Lisher, D., & Catalano, R.F. (1985). Childhood predictors and the prevention of adolescent substance abuse. In C.L. Jones & R.J. Battjes (Eds), *Etiology of drug abuse: Implications for prevention* (pp. 75–126). Rockville, MD: Department of Health and Human Services. National Institute on Drug Abuse.

Hawkins, J.D., Catalano, R.F., Morrison, D.M., O'Donnell, J., Abbott, R.D., & Day, L.E. (1992). The Seattle Social Development Project: Effects of the first four years on protective factors and problem behaviors. In J. McCord & R.E. Tremblay (Eds), *Preventing antisocial behavior: Interventions from birth through adolescence* (pp. 139–161). New York: Guilford Press.

Hawkins, J.D., Kosterman, R., Maguin, E., Catalano, R.F., & Arthur, M.W. (1997). Substance use and abuse. In R.T. Ammerman & M. Hersen (Eds), *Handbook of prevention and treatment with children and adolescents*. New York: John Wiley & Sons.

Hawkins, J.D., Catalano, R.F., Kosterman, R., Abbott, R., & Hill, K.G. (1999). Preventing adolescent health-risk behaviors by strengthening protection during childhood. *Archives of Pediatrics and Adolescent Medicine*, **153**, 226–234.

Hendry, L., Glendinning, A., Reid, M., & Wood, S. (1998). *Lifestyles, health and health concerns of rural youth: 1996–1998*. Report to Department of Health, Scottish Office: Edinburgh.

Hobbs, F., Pickett, W., Brown, S.K., Madill, C., & Ferrence, R. (1997). *Monitoring the Ontario Tobacco Strategy. Youth and tobacco in Ontario: A cause for concern*. Toronto: Ontario Tobacco Research Unit.

Jaycox, L.H., Reivich, K.J., Gillham, J., & Seligman, M.E.P. (1994). Prevention of depressive symptoms in school children. *Behaviour Research Therapy*, **32**, 801–816.

Jessor, R., & Jessor, S.L. (1977). *Problem behavior and psychosocial development: A longitudinal study of youth*. New York: Academic Press.

Johnston, L.D., O'Malley, P.M., & Bachman, J.G. (2000). *The monitoring the future national results on adolescent drug use: Overview of key findings, 1999*. Bathesda, MA: National Institute on Drug Abuse.

Johnson, C.A., Pentz, M.A., Weber, M.D., Dwyer, J.H., Baer, N., MacKinnon, D.P., Hansen, W.B., & Flay, B.R. (1990). Relative effectiveness of comprehensive community programming for drug abuse prevention with high-risk and low-risk adolescents. *Journal of Consulting and Clinical Psychology*, **58**, 447–456.

Kandel, D.B. (1982). Stages in adolescent involvement in drug use. *Science*, **190**, 912–914.

Kandel, D.B., & Yamaguchi, K. (1993). From beer to crack: Developmental patterns of drug involvement. *American Journal of Public Health*, **83**, 851–855.

Kandel, D.B., Johnson, J.G., Bird, H.R., Canino, G., Goodman, S.H., Lahey, B.B., Regier, D.A., & Schwab-Stone, M. (1997). Psychiatric disorders associated with substance use among children and adolescents: Findings from the Methods for the Epidemiology of Child and Adolescent Mental Disorders (MECA) Study. *Journal of Abnormal Child Psychology*, **25**, 121–132.

Kellam, S.G., & Anthony, J.C. (1998). Targeting early antecedents to prevent tobacco smoking: Findings from an epidemiologically based randomized field trial. *American Journal of Public Health*, **88**, 1490–1495.

Kellam, S.G., Rebok, G.W., Ialongo, N., & Mayer, L.S. (1994). The course and malleability of aggressive behavior from early first grade into middle school: Results of a developmental epidemiologically-based preventive trial. *Journal of Child Psychology and Psychiatry and Allied Disciplines*, **35**, 259–281.

Kendall, P.C. (1994). Treating anxiety disorders in children: Results of a randomized clinical trial. *Journal of Consulting and Clinical Psychology*, **62**, 100–110.

Kilpatrick, D.G., Acierno, R., Schnurr, P.P., Saunders, B., Resnick, H.S., & Best, C.L. (2000). Risk factors for adolescent substance abuse and dependence: Data from a national sample. *Journal of Consulting and Clinical Psychology*, **68**, 19–30.

Klepp, K.I., Schmid, L.A., & Murray, D.M. (1996). Effects of the increased minimum drinking age law on drinking and driving behavior among adolescents. *Addiction Research*, **43**, 237–244.

Kokkevi, A., & Stefanis, C. (1991). The epidemiology of licit and illicit substance use among high school students in Greece. *American Journal of Public Health*, **81**, 48–52.

Kumpfer, K., & Turner, C. (1990). The social ecology model of adolescent substance abuse: Implications for prevention. *The International Journal of Addictions*, **25**, 435–463.

Lewinsohn, P.M., Hops, H., Roberts, R.E., Seeley, J.R., & Andrews, J.A. (1993). Adolescent psychopathology: I. Prevalence and incidence of depression and other DSM-III-R disorders in high school students. *Journal of Abnormal Psychology*, **102**, 133–144.

Matykiewiecz, L., La Grange, L., Reyes, E., Vance, P., & Wang, M. (1997). Adolescent males, impulsive/aggressive behaviour, and alcohol abuse: Biological correlates. *Journal of Child and Adolescent Substance Abuse*, **6**, 27–37.

Miller-Johnson, S., Lochman, J., Coie, J., Terry, R., & Hyman, C. (1998). Comorbidity of conduct and depressive problems at sixth grade: Substance use outcomes across adolescence. *Journal of Abnormal Child Psychology*, **26**, 221–232.

Moskowitz, J., Malvin, J., Schaeffer, G., & Schaps, E. (1983). Evaluation of a junior high school primary prevention program. *Addictive Behaviors*, **8**, 393–401.

Moskowitz, J., Malvin, J., Schaeffer, G., & Schaps, E. (1984). The effects of drug education at follow-up. *Journal of Drug Education*, **14**, 45–49.

Newcomb, M.D., Maddahian, E., Skager, R., & Bentler, P.M. (1987). Substance abuse and psychosocial risk factors among teenagers: Associations with sex, age, ethnicity, and type of school. *American Journal of Drug and Alcohol Abuse*, **13**, 413–433.

Norman, E., & Turner, S. (1993). Adolescent substance abuse prevention programs: Theories, models, and research in the encouraging 80s. *Journal of Primary Prevention*, **14**, 3–20.

Ozechowski, T., & Liddle, H.A. (2002). Family-based therapy. In C.A. Essau (Ed.), *Substance abuse and dependence in adolescence*. London: Brunner-Routledge.

Pentz, M.A., MacKinnon, D.P., Flay, B.R., Hansen, W.B., Johnson, C.A., & Dwyer, J.H. (1989). Primary prevention of chronic diseases in adolescence: Effects of Midwestern Prevention Project on tobacco use. *American Journal of Epidemiology*, **130**, 713–724.

Perry, C.L., Williams, C.L., Veblen-Mortenson, S., Toomey, T.L., Komro, K.A., Anstine, P.S., McGovern, P.G., Finnegan, J.R., Forster, J.L., Wagenaar, A.C., & Wolfson, M. (1996). Project Northland: Outcomes of a community-wide alcohol use prevention program during adolescence. *American Journal of Public Health*, **86**, 956–965.

Rao, U., Ryan, N.D., Dahl, R.E., Birmaher, B., Roa, R., Williamson, D.E., & Perel, J.M. (1999). Factors associated with the development of substance use disorder in depressed adolescents. *Journal of the American Academy of Child and Adolescent Psychiatry*, **38**, 1109–1117.

Ridenour, T.A., Fazzone, P., & Cottler, L.B. (2002). Classification and assessment. In C.A. Essau (Ed.), *Substance abuse and dependence in adolescence* (pp. 21–62). London: Brunner-Routledge.

Rohde, P., Lewinsohn, P.M., & Seeley, J.R. (1996). Psychiatric comorbidity with problematic alcohol use in high school students. *Journal of the American Academy of Child and Adolescent Psychiatry*, **35**, 101–109.

Roth, J., & Dadds, M.R. (1999). Reach for resilience: Evaluation of a universal program for the prevention of internalizing problems in young children. *Griffith Early Intervention Project*. School of Applied Psychology, Griffith University.

Sanders, M.R. (1999). Triple P—Positive Parenting Program: Towards an empirically validated multilevel parenting and family support strategy for the prevention of behavior and emotional problems in children. *Clinical Child and Family Psychology Review*, **2**, 71–90.

Shochet, I., Holland, D., & Whitefield, K. (1997). *The Griffith Early Intervention Depression Project: Group Leader's Manual*. Brisbane: Griffith Early Intervention Project.

Stice, E., Myers, M.G., & Brown, S.A. (1998). A longitudinal grouping analysis of adolescent substance use escalation and de-escalation. *Psychology of Addictive Behaviors*, **1**, 12–27.

Sullivan, T., & Farrell, A.D. (2002). Risk factors. In C.A. Essau (Ed.), *Substance abuse and dependence in adolescence*. London: Brunner-Routledge.

Swisher, J.D., & Hsu, T.W. (1983). Alternatives to drug abuse: Some are and some are not. In T.J. Glynn, C.G. Luekefeld, & J.P. Ludford (Eds), *Preventing adolescent drug abuse: Intervention strategies* (NIDA Research Monograph No. 47, pp. 141–153). Washington, DC: US Government Printing Office.

Taylor, T.K., & Biglan, A. (1998). Behavioral family interventions for improving child-rearing: A review of the literature for clinicians and policy makers. *Clinical Child and Family Psychology Review*, **1**, 41–59.

Tobler, N. (1992). Drug prevention programs can work: Research findings. *Journal of Addictive Diseases*, **11**, 1–28.

Tremblay, R.E., Vitaro, F., Bertrand, L., LeBlanc, M., Beauchesne, H., & David, L. (1996). Parent and child training to prevent early onset of delinquency: The Montreal longitudinal-experimental study. In J. McCord & R.E. Tremblay (Eds), *Preventing antisocial behavior: Interventions from birth through adolescence* (pp. 117–138). New York: Guilford.

Vartiainen, E., Pallonen, U., McAlister, A.L., & Puska, P. (1990). Eight year follow-up results of an adolescent smoking prevention programs: The North Karelia Youth Project. *American Journal of Public Health*, **80**, 78–79.

Vartiainen, E., Paavola, M., McAlister, A., & Puska, P. (1998). Fifteen-year follow-up of smoking prevention effects in the North Karelia Youth Project. *American Journal of Public Health*, **88**, 81–85.

Wagner, E.F., & Tarolla, S.M. (2002). Course and outcome. In C.A. Essau (Ed.), *Substance abuse and dependence in adolescence*. London: Brunner-Routledge.

Weissberg, R.P., Caplan, M., & Harwood, R.L. (1991). Promoting competent young people in competence-enhancing environments: A systems-based prospective on primary prevention. *Journal of Consulting and Clinical Psychology*, **59**, 830–841.

Williams, R. (2002). Psychological intervention. In C.A. Essau (Ed.), *Substance abuse and dependence in adolescence*. London: Brunner-Routledge.

Wittchen, H.-U., Hand, I., & Hecht, H. (1989). Prävalenz, Komorbidität und Schweregrad von Angststörungen: Ergebnisse der Münchner Follow-up Studie (MFS). *Zeitschrift für Klinische Psychologie*, **18**, 117–133.

Worden, J.K. (1999). Research in using mass media to prevent smoking. *Nicotine and Tobacco Research*, **1**, S117–S121.

Index